THE ROUTLEDGE COMPANION
TO THE CRUSADES

The Routledge Companion to the Crusades is an essential reference guide to a crucial and formative period in European history. Spanning over seven hundred years, from the earliest Christian pilgrimages to the Holy Land to the height of the crusading movement during the Middle Ages and its culmination at the fall of Malta in 1798, this handbook provides a comprehensive compendium of information across a range of subjects, including:

- chronologies of military campaigns and battles and introductory guides to significant Crusades, including the First Crusade, the Children's Crusade and the Crusades against Bosnian heretics
- maps detailing the main kingdoms and empires, and genealogical tables showing key dynasties across Europe and the Middle East
- biographies of figures central to the crusading movement
- a thorough analysis of the historiography, from the first analytical history in 1184 to the present day, including biographies of major historians of the crusades
- an extensive and completely up-to-date bibliography of both primary and secondary sources
- essential FAQs including what is a crusade? What methods were used? How were soldiers recruited? What was women's involvement? How much was known about Islam in the West? When did the Crusades end?

An invaluable resource for students and scholars alike, this essential reference tool offers a user-friendly guide to the Holy Wars and the relationship between Europe and the Islamic world – an association that remains of vast significance in the twenty-first century.

Peter Lock is Professor of History at York St John University College. He is a fellow of both the Royal Historical Society and the Society of Antiquaries. He is co-author of *The Archaeology of Medieval Greece* (1996) and author of *The Franks in the Aegean, 1204–1500* (1995).

Routledge Companions to History

Series Advisors: Chris Cook and John Stevenson

Routledge Companions to History offer perfect reference guides to key historical events and eras, providing everything that the student or general reader needs to know. These comprehensive guides include essential apparatus for navigating through specific topics in a clear and straightforward manner – including introductory articles, biographies and chronologies – to provide accessible and indispensable surveys crammed with vital information valuable for beginner and expert alike.

The Routledge Companion to World History since 1914
Chris Cook and John Stevenson

The Routledge Companion to European History since 1763
Chris Cook and John Stevenson

The Routledge Companion to Decolonization
Dietmar Rothermund

The Routledge Companion to Fascism and the Far Right
Peter Davies and Derek Lynch

The Routledge Companion to American Civil War Era
Hugh Tulloch

The Routledge Companion to Twentieth Century Britain
Harriet Jones and Mark Clapson

The Routledge Companion to Medieval Europe
Baerbel Brodt

The Routledge Companion to Historiography
Alun Munslow

The Routledge Companion to the Stuart Age, 1603–1714
John Wroughton

THE ROUTLEDGE COMPANION
TO THE CRUSADES

Peter Lock

Routledge
Taylor & Francis Group

LONDON AND NEW YORK

First published 2006
by Routledge
2 Park Square, Milton Park, Abingdon, Oxon OX14 4RN

Simultaneously published in the USA and Canada
by Routledge
270 Madison Avenue, New York, NY 10016

Routledge is an imprint of the Taylor & Francis Group

Typeset in Times by RefineCatch Ltd, Bungay, Suffolk
Printed and bound in Great Britain by Antony Rowe Ltd, Chippenham, Wiltshire

British Library Cataloguing in Publication Data
A catalogue record for this book is available from the British Library

Library of Congress Cataloging in Publication Data
Lock, Peter, 1949–
The Routledge companion to the crusades / Peter Lock.
    p.   cm. – (Routledge companions to history)
Includes bibliographical references and index.
    1. Crusades–Handbooks, manuals, etc.   I. Title.   II. Series.
D157.L64 2005
909.07–dc22   2005020923

ISBN10: 0–415–24732–2   ISBN13: 9–78–0–415–24732–0 (hbk)
ISBN10: 0–415–39312–4   ISBN13: 9–78–0–415–39312–6 (pbk)

CONTENTS

CONTENTS

PREFACE

Crusades and crusading is a huge topic. The range of reference is enormous. It is, however, a topic that continues to attract interest from a whole range of starting points. Perhaps more so now than ever before an understanding of the worlds of Islam and Christendom is vital for a positive outcome of the present turmoil in that troubled part of the world, the Middle East.

The reason for yet another work on the crusades is to make that work comprehensible and accessible to students in universities, in sixth forms and in adult education, a convenient work of reference and vade-mecum in a world of modularisation. The book was conceived with students in mind but it is hoped that their teachers and anyone interested in the subject will gain some benefit from reading and using it. The references are complete, as far as humanly possible, up to and including the year 2004. Older works are not ignored, some of which, like those of du Cange, Kügler, Röhricht, and Runciman to name but four, continue to be used and referred to after the passage of decades and even centuries. Clearly the old still continue to have their uses! The new, too, is incorporated, with a section on the Crusades on the Internet.

The book, then, is conceived as a reference work for students and anyone interested in the Crusades. Part I is designed to provide a quick reference to the events of each particular crusade and the sources. Bibliographies appear at the beginning of each specialist theme in Part VI, and at every crusade discussed in Part II and *in extenso* in the full bibliography in Part VII. They are intended as complete reference systems for the topics and events covered.

Each section is interdependent and is intended to be used as such. Part I is a very full chronology, giving not just details of the events and principal participants in the various crusades but a full background to pilgrimage, Armenia, Byzantium, Islam and the Gregorian reform movement. It should be used in conjunction with the narrative outlines in Part II, both as a factual supplement and background. Part V contains outline biographies of the principal crusade historians, now deceased. The choice for inclusion is, I hope, self-evident but ultimately it reflects my own enthusiasms. Of those still happily alive references to their works may be found, and indeed in the spirit of league tables, measured by column inches in the bibliography in Part IV. The Internet contains a wealth of information that should not be ignored as a quick and convenient starting point for further work. It is, however, just that, and must be used with care. There is no substitute for the reading of refereed and referenced books and articles. Part III contains brief biographies of the main crusading figures.

Neither the sections nor the themes are conceived as watertight units.

Convenience alone has dictated what is discussed where. The topics, themes, and events all interrelate as for example pilgrims, women, worship and art. The index should be used as a guide to these interrelated topics and events.

In the Levant the territories, which form the subject of this book, were old lands with biblical and classical pasts and a set of place-names that reflected that past. At the time of the Crusades they were variously inhabited by Greeks, Armenians, Turks and Arabs and usually have a triple or even quadruple toponymy. I have followed Frankish names, with the most common local equivalent given in parentheses and in the index. The problem is not so severe for the Iberian Peninsula, although the Baltic Lands usually have dual toponyms, German or Slav, Swedish or Finnish. I have used the modern version, with older forms in parentheses.

As might be expected in the production of such a work with a prodigious range of reference and expertise I have relied heavily, if not always entirely, upon the work of other scholars. I hope that I have reflected their work and opinions accurately and given due acknowledgement. The bibliographies attached to each section form the basis for that section and should provide a full and sound platform for further research, seminar discussions, essays, dissertations or, for that most important and best of reasons, just for interest, ideas and information.

This is very much the work of one author, who alone is responsible for any errors or shortcomings. The academic obligations that I have incurred are too numerous to list here, but they should all be given due acknowledgement in the appropriate places in the text. I would like to thank professors Malcolm Barber, Bernard Hamilton and Graham Loud for help and encouragement, and also my colleagues and students, both undergraduate and postgraduate, in the History Department at York St John and at the Centre for Medieval Studies at the University of Leeds, in particular Mirko Lezzi, Nicky Tsigourakis and Dr Gill Page; Sue Smith, the History Programme Administrator at York St John for much practical help; the librarians at Leeds University and York St John College; Ann Craig-Barker who taught me the necessary German; the History editors at Routledge, Vicky Peters and Philippa Grand; and, of course, my family, Joan, Sophie and Alexander, who have lived with the Crusades longer than some of the participants and provided help and support in innumerable ways. In particular I would like to thank my son Alexander who has chased up references, photocopied prodigiously, read and commented from an undergraduate perspective, and criticised where clarity has been lacking. He has been a real source of inspiration during the writing of this book. I hope that he likes the result, and it is to him that it is dedicated.

I
A CHRONOLOGICAL OUTLINE OF THE CRUSADES
Background, military expeditions, and crusader states

The letters 'BC' after an entry indicate an event or personage from the Baltic or Northern Crusades, whilst the letters 'SC' indicate the same for crusading in the Iberian Peninsula.

Not all dates are exact or agreed. Where there is dispute or uncertainty this has been indicated, and c. *for 'circa' has been used for an approximate or insecurely known date.*

160s

Melito of Sardis is the earliest known Christian pilgrim in the Holy Land, although certainly not the only one. Attempts to identify the topographical location of the scenes of Christ's life, death and Passion are made.

325

According to legend, Constantine's mother Helena makes a pilgrimage to the Holy Land at the time of the Council of Nicaea. She sponsors the building of the Church of the Holy Sepulchre and is said to have found the wood of the True Cross on the construction site.

325–431

The Byzantine emperors sponsor the construction of pilgrim churches on sites that are accepted as associated with Christ's life, passion and resurrection to provide foci for pilgrims.

610

Muhammad receives his vision of the angel Gabriel as a messenger of Allah.

622

Muhammad flees from Mecca to Medina (the *Hegira*). There he becomes a religious leader of a new faith known as Islam, the 'surrender' to Allah. His followers are known as *Muslimin* or Muslims, the 'surrendering ones'. The Muslim calendar dates from the year of the Hegira (AH = *anno Hegirae*).

630

Muhammad captures Mecca and makes the town his capital. The former pagan black stone is incorporated into the *Kaaba*, the religious centre of the holy city of Mecca from which all non-believers are banned.

632

Muhammad dies. Abu Bakr is elected the first caliph or 'Representative'. The Arabs of Syria appeal to him for help against Byzantine persecution and the period of the rapid expansion of Islam begins.

633

The revelations made to Muhammad by Gabriel are collected in the Qur'ān (henceforth, 'Koran').

634

Nov. 26: Persians annihilate an Arab army on the Euphrates at the battle of the bridge, near al-Hirah.

For the first time Greek chroniclers refer to the Muslims as *Sarakenoi* or Saracens.

636

Aug. 20: Rout of the Byzantine army under Heraklios by Arabs at the Battle of the Yarmuk (Jubeya-Yarmuk), followed by the collapse of the Byzantine position first in North Syria and then in Mesopotamia.

637

May 31 or June 1: Arabs defeat Persians at the Battle of al-Qadisiyah, near al-Hirah.

Dec.: Following another victory at Jalula they occupy all of Iraq west of the Tigris. Antioch captured by the Arabs (see 944).

638

Mar.: Jerusalem is surrendered to the Arabs after a long siege (see 1071, 1076, 1098).

Edessa is captured by the Arabs (see 944).

642

Egypt is captured.

643

Arabs occupy the Mukran and reach the borders of India.

644–56

The third caliph, Uthman ibn Affan, orders the collection and writing of a definitive version of the Koran (see 1143).

647

Arabs attack Cappadocia and capture Caesarea (Kayseri).
   Construction of an Arab fleet.

647–88

Arabs gain control of Cyprus.

653

Arabs complete the conquest of Persia by occupying the province of Khorasan.
The River Oxus forms their north-eastern boundary.
   Rhodes is captured and the remains of the Colossus of Rhodes are recycled.

661

The Ummayad clan take over the caliphate and make Damascus their capital,
employing Byzantine craftsmen to decorate its major buildings. The Muslim
Shia sect is formed.

667

Saracens conquer North Africa and reach the Atlantic.

670–1

Saracens make their first unsuccessful naval assault on Constantinople.

673–8

Saracens make yearly naval attacks on Constantinople.

685–91

Caliph Abd al-Malik sponsors the building of the Qubbat as-Salkiah or the
Dome of the Rock. It is also erroneously known as the Mosque of Omar. It is not
a mosque but a *mashhad* or pilgrim shrine. It is the oldest extant Muslim monument; by the eleventh century it was considered by both Christians and Muslims
to be the site of the Temple of Soloman (Templum Domini). Byzantine influence
and practice is evident in its many mosaics.

698

Arabs capture Carthage.

706–14

The great mosque of Damascus is built and the mosques in Mecca, Medina and Jerusalem are enlarged.

711–20

Saracens conquer Spain.

716

The Ummayad Caliph Abd al-Malik establishes the town of Ramla on the Damascus – Cairo road. It was the administrative centre for Palestine until 1099 and the only new town in Palestine founded by the Arabs.

717–18

The Saracens mount an all-out, but ultimately unsuccessful, siege of Constantinople.

720–59

Arabs capture Septimania in south-west France and use it as a base for raids. Their expulsion by the Franks has been claimed as the first war of reconquest (see 915).

732

Charles Martel defeats and kills Abd-er-Rahman at the battle of Poitiers (or Tours). The Saracen advance in Western Europe is stopped.

750

The Abbasid clan replace the Ummayids as caliphs. The take-over is a bloody one and many refugees flee to Spain.

751

Saracens reach the confines of China.

756

Saracens in Spain declare an independent caliphate, around Abd-er-Rahman I, a survivor from the massacres in Damascus. Cordova becomes the capital.

760

The Ismaili sect is founded, accepting Ismail as the last and true imam (or reincarnation).

762

Mansur, the Abbasid caliph, moves the capital of his caliphate to Baghdad, a completely new city. The Abbasid caliphs remain there until their extinction by the Mongols in 1258.

763

Ibu Hisham writes the *Life of Muhammad*.

824–8

Arabs from Spain capture Crete.

826–40

Arab pirates raid Balearic Islands, Corsica and Sardinia.

830–902

Arabs from North Africa take Sicily from the Byzantines.

840–60

Arab raids along the Italian coast, including the sacking of Benevento and St Peter's, Rome (841). An Arab fleet on its way to attack Rome is sunk in a storm off Ostia in 849.

840–975

Arab pirates make sporadic raids in southern Gaul, particularly in Provence. In 842 Marseilles, Nîmes and Arles are sacked, and in 869 Roland, archbishop of Arles, is captured and held to ransom.

860

First Russian naval attack on Constantinople; Michael III abandons a projected campaign against the Arabs to meet the threat (see 911).

902

Aug. 1: Arabs capture Taormina, the last Byzantine naval base in Sicily.

904

Summer: Arab fleet proceeds to attack Constantinople and its environs. It diverts to Thessalonika.

July 31: Arabs capture Thessalonika after a three-day siege, devastating the second city of the Byzantine Empire. A Greek renegade, Leo of Tripoli, leads the Arab fleet.

905

Oct. 6: Byzantine fleet under Himerios defeats an Arab squadron in the Aegean.

907

Oleg of Kiev attacks Constantinople by sea (see 860, 911, 914, 943, 1043).

909

The Fatimid caliphate is founded in Tunis.

911

Second naval attack by Oleg of Kiev on Constantinople; he signs a commercial treaty with Byzantium by which Russian merchants were granted a commercial quarter around the church of St Mamas and were exempted from customs dues (see 860, 914, 943, 944, 1043).

Unsuccessful Byzantine naval expedition to Crete led by Himerios the Logothete. The fleet contains many Russian sailors.

912

Byzantine fleet under Himerios returning from Crete is defeated off Chios by Arabs.

914

Russian fleet devastates Asiatic shore opposite Constantinople (see 860, 907, 911, 943, 1043).

915

Pope John X organises a Christian coalition, including Byzantine naval support, to drive Muslims from Campagna. Garigliano is captured. This was the first war of reconquest (see 720–59, 1015, 1059, 1061–91, 1085).

917

Aug.: Bulgarian khan Symeon (893–927) annihilates a Byzantine army at Anchialos in Thrace and extends control over most of the Balkans up to the walls of Constantinople.

929

Abd-ar-Raman III emphasises his role as Ummayad caliph in Spain and thus asserts independence from Baghdad. He begins the construction of the al-Zahru palace on the outskirts of Cordova.

930–51

The black stone is removed from Mecca by the Qarmatians (see also 630).

943

Russians, with Pechneg allies, raid along the Danube.

944

Byzantines defeat a Russian fleet on the Black Sea. The trading concessions of 911 are revoked.

Byzantines recover control of Antioch and Edessa. The *mandylion*[1] removed from Edessa to Constantinople for safe keeping.

961

Nikephoros Phokas captures Candia after a nine-month siege. Crete returns to Byzantine control, having been in Arab hands since 826.

---

[1] The *mandylion* or *sudarion* was a cloth said to have been miraculously imprinted with the face of Christ. Its reception in Constantinople was commemorated by a feast day. It became an important piece of evidence for the Iconodoules in the eighth century and was either lost subsequent to 1204 or was removed to the Sainte Chapelle in 1249 and subsequently lost during the French Revolution. It is not to be confused with the Holy Shroud of Turin.

965

Tarsus and Mopsuestia captured by Byzantines after a two-year siege.
   Byzantine fleet recaptures Cyprus.

969

Oct.: The Byzantines recover Antioch from the Arabs, who had occupied it since 637. It now serves as their main military base in Syria.
   The fourth Fatimid caliph, al-Mu'izz (953–75), through his general, Jawhar, conquers Egypt from his base at al-Mahdiyya in Tunis. He builds a new capital at Cairo (al-Qahira, 'the Victorious').

975

Saracens finally expelled from southern France by William, count of Arles.
   John I Tzimiskes campaigns in Syria as far as Caesarea and establishes the Byzantine frontier on the Yarmuk River. There was apparently never any intention to recover Jerusalem.

982

Otto II decisively defeated by Saracens at Capo Colonna, south of Cortone, on the east coast of Apulia.

983

Revolt of the Wends; Hamburg attacked and burned (BC).

992

First Byzantine commercial treaty with Venice; reduced customs duties are granted to Venetian merchants in return for the transport of Byzantine troops to Italy (see 911 and 1082).

998–1040

Seljuk Turks emigrating from central Asia settle in Khorasan under control of Mahmud the Ghaznavid (d. 1030).

1000–50

Byzantines absorb Armenia into the Empire, providing compensation in lands and titles in Cappadocia for those who cede their lands to the emperor.

1001

Nov. 27: Battle at Peshawar; Mahmud the Ghaznavid occupies the Punjab.

1002

Venetian fleet defeats Muslims besieging Bari.

1004

Pisa sacked by the Saracens.

1006

Saracen fleet defeated near Reggio by Pisans.

1009

Sept. 27: Church of the Holy Sepulchre at Jerusalem destroyed on the orders of the Egyptian caliph al-Hakim (996–1021). Pope Sergius IV responded with a call to arms of the faithful; this was the first such appeal that was to evolve into the crusade by the end of the century (see also 1064, 1074, 1095). He also commissioned frescoes of the lost sites associated with Christ's life over the entrance to San Paolo fuori le mura in Rome.

1011

Second sack of Pisa by Saracens.

1013

Saracens from Spain conquer Sardinia.

1015

Pisans and Genoese recapture Sardinia (see 915).

1016

Mahmud the Ghaznavid conquers Samarkand.

1018

First Seljuk raid into Armenia.

1021

Feb. 13: Murder of al-Hakim, caliph of Egypt; succeeded by his son al-Zahir (–1035).

Saracen pirates sack Narbonne.

Muslims from Azerbaijan (the Daylamites) invade Armenia.

Byzantines invade Georgia.

1027

Treaty between Byzantines and the Fatimids allowing for the rebuilding of the Holy Sepulchre in Jerusalem and the repair of the mosque in Constantinople (see 1063).

1029

First record of Turks raiding Byzantine and Armenian territory.

1030

Apr. 21: Death of Mahmud, emir of Ghazni; succeeded by his son Mas'ud I (–1040).

1032

Edessa captured by Byzantines under George Maniakes.

1033

Pechnegs (Patzinaks) raid in the Balkans.

Many pilgrimages made to Jerusalem on millennium of Christ's Passion.

1034

Genoese and Pisans take Bona (formerly Hippo Regius) in North Africa.

1036

Second Pechneg raid in the Balkans.

1037

Byzantines recapture Edessa from Arabs, who had ruled it since 639.

1040

Feb.: Seljuk Turks under Tughril Bey (1038–63) defeat Mas'ud at Taliqan and occupy Ghaznavid territory in Persia; Turks effectively free of Ghaznavid control.

1042–8

Constantine IX Monomachos sponsors rebuilding of the cupola and the tomb of Christ in the Church of the Holy Sepulchre, partly bringing together the sites of Christ's Passion and resurrection under one roof.

1043

Last Russian attack on Constantinople (see 860, 907, 911, 943).

1045

Regular Seljuk raids into Armenia begin.

1047

Seljuk raiders defeated by Byzantines near Erzerum.

Pechnegs (Patzinaks) cross the Danube and make devasting raids in the Balkan provinces of Byzantium. Their raiding is to pose a major threat to the security of Constantinople until 1091 (see also 1122).

1048

Seljuks sack Erzerum.

1050

Tughril Bey takes Ispahan and makes it his capital.

1053

Byzantine government forced to accept Pechneg settlement on imperial lands south of Danube

1054

Tughril raids into eastern Asia Minor, but Manzikert not taken.

1055

Dec. 18: Tughril enters Baghdad as protector (sultan) of the Abbasid caliph.

1057

Seljuks sack Malatya and massacre the inhabitants.

1059

Seljuks raid as far as Sebastaea.

Treaty of Melfi: Pope Nicholas II recognises Robert Guiscard as Duke of Apulia, and grants him the lordship of Sicily if he can recover it from the Muslims (see 915).

1061–91

Norman conquest of Sicily and Malta from the Muslims.

1063

Sept. 20: Death of Tughril Bey; succeeded by his nephew Alp Arslan as Grand Seljuk and sultan (–1072).

Norman mercenary Roussel of Bailleul abandons his Byzantine employer and sets up his own power base around Kayseri.

Constantine X Doukas (1059–67) arranges with the Fatimid caliph, al-Mustansir, to pay for the building of a wall around the patriarchal quarter in Jerusalem. The Byzantine emperor thus affirms his position as the protector of Christian holy places and of Christians under Muslim rule (see 1027).

1064

Alp Arslan conquers Ani and the Kingdom of Kars; beginning of Armenian migration to Cilicia.

Devastating Pechneg raid into Greece. Byzantines recruit Anglo-Norman mercenaries to confront the threat.

Aug.: An army of Aquitainians, Aragonese, Burgundians, Catalans and Normans capture the Muslim fort of Barbastro after a siege of forty days. Despite terms being granted to the defenders they are massacred and their women and children enslaved. Pope Alexander II issued a plenary indulgence that made this campaign a crusade in all but name (see also 1009, 1074) (SC).[2]

---

[2] It is possible that the so-called Barbastro indulgence was issued for an expedition in 1073. The international recruitment for Spanish campaigns went back to the ninth century, but papal interest and sponsorship was new and made the campaign very crusade-like.

Great German pilgrimage (7,000 pilgrims) led by Bishop Gunther of Bamberg to Jerusalem (–1065); the pilgrims ward off a three-day attack by the Bedouin at Ramla.

1065

Apr.: Al-Muqtadir of Zaragossa recaptures Barbastro (see 1100) (SC).
Alp Arslan invades Transoxiana; Seljuks invade Syria attacking Edessa.

1066

Wends rise against Gottschalk, their Christian ruler, killing him together with John, bishop of Mecklenburg, and the monks of Ratzeburg. The dioceses of Oldenburg and Mecklenburg are in abeyance until 1149 (BC).

1067

Seljuks sack Caesarea and defeat Byzantine armies at Malatya and Sebastaea; Greater Armenia is virtually controlled by the Seljuks.

1068

Seljuk raids on Neocaesarea and Amorion. Romanos IV Diogenes (1068–71) mounts first campaign to contain the threat.

1069

Seljuks attack Iconium; provokes the second campaign of Romanos IV.

1070

Seljuks attack Chonae near Aegean coast.

1071

Apr.: Robert Guiscard captures Bari, the last Byzantine base in Italy.

Aug. 21: Greek army destroyed at Manzikert (Malazgerd) and Romanos IV captured; Greater Armenia finally overrun and Syria conquered. Edessa passes from Byzantine to Armenian control. Seljuks dispute control of Cilicia with the Armenians. The Armenian diaspora gathers momentum, with many settling in Cilicia, Cappadocia and Georgia.
Atsiz ibn-Abak takes Jerusalem from Egyptians.

Oct. 24: Michael VII (–1078) proclaimed emperor and appeals to the West for help against the Turks.

1072

Dec. 15: Alp Aslan murdered on campaign in Transoxiana; succeeded by his son Malik Shah (–1092).

1073

Apr. 22: Hildebrand elected as Pope Gregory VII (–1085).
    Sulayman ibn-Qutlamish begins conquest of Asia Minor (–1077).

1074

Mar. 1: Gregory VII proposes military aid to the Byzantine Empire out of brotherly love; the appeal is to the *fideles sancti Petri* and there is no mention of indulgences. However, the biographer of Urban II attributed the idea of crusade to Gregory VII (see also 1009, 1064).
    Malik Shah captures Aleppo.

1075–1122

The Investiture Disputes, over the lay investiture of bishops and abbots with ring and pastoral staff by the ruling monarch, between the papacy and the German emperors Henry IV (1056–1106) and Henry V (1106–25). A formal settlement was reached at the Concordat of Worms in 1122; investiture with ring and crozier became a spiritual activity, but the consecrated bishop performed homage to the German king. The Second Lateran Council confirmed the agreement in 1123. In England the dispute was brief and was concerned essentially with the appointment of Anselm, archbishop of Canterbury (1093–1109). In France and Spain there was no open breach.

1076

Egyptians recover Jerusalem, but after a siege Atsiz regains the city.

1077

Sulayman ibn-Qutlamish establishes Seljuk sultanate of Rum with Nicaea as his capital (–1096, see also 1307).

1078

Mar.: Nikephoros III Botaneites uses Turkish troops to garrison Nicomedia, Kyzikos and Chalcedon in his successful bid for the Byzantine throne; Michael VII abdicates. Tutush, the brother of Malik Shah granted Syria and Palestine

1079

Oct.: Atsiz surrenders Damascus to Tutush; Artuk his lieutenant at Jerusalem; Atsiz murdered on orders of Tutush.

1080

Armenian leadership in Cappadocia liquidated by the Byzantines.
  Roupen establishes himself as leader of Armenian exiles in Cilicia (Lesser Armenia).
  Chaka begins to establish himself as emir of Smyrna (–1092) with control of Lesbos, Samos and Rhodes.

1081

Apr.: Accession of Alexios I Komnenos (–1118).

June: Treaty with Sulayman, sultan of Rum, in which Alexios cedes all Turkish conquests east of Dracon (10 miles south of Civetot).

June 17: Robert Guiscard captures Corfu and begins siege of Dyracchium.
  Alfonso VI of Leon begins the siege of Toledo (–1085) (SC).

1082

Feb. 21: Dyrrachium captured by Guiscard.

May: Byzantine–Venetian commercial treaty in return for Venetian naval support against the Normans. The Doge and his successors are granted the title of *Protosebastos* (usually reserved for members of the imperial family) in perpetuity, and Venetian merchants are granted exemption from the *Kommerkion*. Venice is set fair to monopolise the trade between Europe and the East (see 992, 1126).[3]

1083

Venetians disrupt Norman supply lines across the Adriatic.

---

[3] G. Tafel and G. Thomas, eds, *Urkunden zur Alreren Handels- und Staatsgeschichte der Republik Venedig*, I (Vienna 1856; reprinted Amsterdam, 1964), 43–55, 95–108.

Dyrrachium recovered by the Greeks.
Antioch lost to the Seljuks (see 944, 1098).

Dec. 1: Anna Komnene born (–1153/4).

1085

May 6: Toledo capitulates to Alfonso VI (see 1081). Muslims are allowed to keep their lives and property and to continue to use the Great Mosque. They may come and go without forfeiting their property, and should Alfonso capture Valencia he promised to restore it to Toledo (SC).

May 25: Triumphal entry of Alfonso VI into Toledo (SC).

May 25: Death of Pope Gregory VII at Salerno.

July 17: Death of Robert Guiscard on Cephalonia; Norman attack on Byzantium abandoned.
Byzantines recapture Ankara and Nicomedia from the Seljuks.
El Cid protects the Muslim taifa states of Zaragossa and Valencia against the Aragonese (–1099). This brings him into confrontation with Alfonso VI of Leon-Castile (1065–1109) and Peter I of Aragon (1094–1104), both of whom wish to seize Zaragossa and the Ebro valley (SC).

1086

Oct. 23: The Almoravid ruler of Morocco, Yusuf ibn-Tashfin, invited to Spain by al-Mu'tamid of Seville, defeats Alfonso of Castile and Leon at Sagrajas (Azagal/Zalaca) near Badajoz. Almoravid intervention bolsters Muslim resistance for the next half century (SC).
Sulayman, sultan of Rum, defeated and killed by Tutush while attempting to take Aleppo; succeeded by his son, Khilij Arslan I (–1107; known to crusaders as Soloman or Kerbogha).

1087

Aug. 6: Genoese and Pisans sack Mahdia in Tunisia. Pope Victor III grants a banner of St Peter and remission of all sins to the participants.
Pechnegs attempt to storm Constantinople.
Edessa lost to the Seljuks (see 944).

1088

Mar. 12: Cardinal Otto of Châtillon (Odo of Lagery) elected Pope Urban II (–1099).

1089

Sept.: Council of Melfi, negotiations regarding crusade against the Turks.
Fatamids recover Ascalon, Tyre and Acre from the Seljuks.
Urban II instructs Bernard, archbishop of Toledo, to restore former arch-
bishoprics still under Muslim control, like Seville and Tarragona (SC).

1090

Nov.: Yusuf ibn-Tashfin takes Granada and founds Almoravid dynasty in Spain
(–1147) (SC).
Al-Hasan ibn-al-Sabbah, founder of the Assassins, established at Alamut
(–1124).
Pechnegs raid up to the walls of Constantinople.

1091

Apr. 29: Alexios I, with Cuman allies, virtually annihilates the Pechnegs at
Mount Levunion on the Maritsa River, thus removing a substantial threat to
the hinterland of Constantinople (see 1122). The surviving Pechnegs were
incorporated into the Byzantine army as light cavalry.

1092

Nov.: Death of Malik Shah; succeeded by his son, Mahmud I, who fights his
brothers (–1094) while the Seljuk Empire disintegrates as independent rulers
emerge.
Khilij Arslan takes Nicaea and Smyrna from independent rulers.
Assassination of Nizam-al-Mulk, vizier of Malik Shah; first political victim of
the Assassins.
Pisan fleet collaborates first with forces from Aragon against Valencia and then
with those of Castile against Tortosa. Both attacks are unsuccessful (SC).

1094

Dec. 29: Death of al-Mustansir, caliph of Egypt; caliphate held by a series of
non-entities.
El Cid seizes Valencia on the assassination of al-Qadar, who held Valencia
under his protection. The Cid defeats the Almoravids at Cuert de Pueblo and
holds Valencia until his death in 1099 (SC).
Tutush seizes Aleppo.
Barkiyaruk succeeds Mahmud I as Seljuk sultan (–1105).
Peter the Hermit on pilgrimage to Jerusalem (–1095).

1095

Mar.: Synod at Piacenza, Greek delegates ask for western aid against the Turks.

Apr. 4: Shower of stars, which Gislebert of Lisieux subsequently linked to the crusade.

Nov. 18–28: Council at Clermont; on the 27th Urban proclaims the crusade to liberate Jerusalem, with indulgences for participants; Adhemar of Le Puy made papal legate to the proposed crusade.

Dec. 1: Raymond IV, count of Toulouse, is the first magnate to take the cross.

Dec.: Peter the Hermit begins preaching the crusade in Berry; threats to French Jews; Urban gives 15th August 1096 as date of departure and confirms Adhemar as his representative.

La Chanson de Roland

1096

Feb. 6–12: Urban II preaches crusade at Angers.

Feb. 10: Urban commissions Robert d'Arbrissel to preach crusade in Loire valley.

Feb. 11: Philip I meets with Hugh of Vermondois and other magnates in Paris to discuss the crusade.

Mar.: Departure of Walter Sans Avoir and Peter the Hermit in separate groups of around 10,000 to 15,000 each.

Mar. 16–22: Synod at Tours to consider and confirm progress.

Apr. (?): Departure of Hugh of Vermondois.

Apr.–June: Persecution of Jews at Metz, Spires (Speyer), Worms, Mayence (Mainz), Cologne, Andernach, Xanten, Moers, Kerpen, Ghelders, Treves, Ratisbon (Regensburg) and Prague.

Aug.–Sept.: German groups under Emicho, Gottschalk and Folkmar disperse in Hungary.

July 20: Walter Sans Avoir arrives in Constantinople.

Aug. 1: Peter the Hermit arrives in Constantinople.

Aug. 6–7: Crossing of Bosphoros and move via Nicomedia to Civetot.

Aug. 15: Departure of Adhemar (with Provençal army?); Godfrey departs, together with Baldwin of Boulogne and Baldwin Le Bourg.

Sept.: Robert of Normandy, Robert of Flanders and Stephen of Blois depart; in

Apulia Bohemond and Tancred leave Roger Borsa at the siege of Amalfi to join the crusade.

Oct.: Hugh of Vermondois crosses from Bari to Dyrrachium.

Oct. 21: People's crusade annihilated by Kilij Arslan at Civitot.

Oct. 26: Bohemond crosses from Bari to Avlona.

Nov.: Hugh of Vermondois arrives in Constantinople; arrival of Robert of Flanders and companions in Calabria where they winter with Roger Borsa.

Dec. 20: Raymond of Toulouse prepares to cross Dalmatia.

Dec. 23: Godfrey of Bouillon arrives at Constantinople.
    Peter I of Aragon captures Huesca (SC).

1097

Jan. 13–19: Rioting by Godfrey's army in Constantinople.

Feb. 20: Godfrey's army crosses to Bithynia.

Apr. 2: Bohemond leaves his army at Rusa (Roskoi) under the command of Tancred whilst he goes to Constantinople to meet Alexios.

Apr. 5 (Easter): Robert of Normandy and colleagues begin crossing from Brindisi to Dyrrachium; one large ship with 400 crusaders sinks.

Apr. 10: Bohemond meets Alexios.

Apr. 18: Raymond leaves Provençal army at Rodosto and goes to meet Alexios.

Apr. 22: Raymond meets Alexios.

Apr. 26: Bohemond's army under Tancred arrives at Constantinople and crosses immediately to Bithynia.

Apr. 27: Provençal army arrives at Constantinople.

May 6: Armies of Godfrey, Baldwin, Tancred and Robert of Flanders arrive at Nicaea.

May 14–28: Robert of Normandy and Stephen of Blois in Constantinople.

May 14: Formal siege of Nicaea begins.

May 16: Provençal army arrives; Kilij Arslan defeated outside Nicaea.

June 3: Stephen of Blois and Robert of Normandy arrive at Nicaea.

June 18: Attack on Nicaea by land and water.

June 19: Formal surrender of Nicaea to Boutoumites; Greeks enter city, crusaders kept out.

June 26: Normans leave Nicaea.

June 28: Provençal army leaves Nicaea.

July 1: Kilij Arslan defeated at Dorylaion (Karasu).

July 4: Army leaves Dorylaion.

July 31: Army arrives at Antioch in Pisidia.

Aug. 15: Capture of Iconium (Konya), Kilij Arslan's capital, after the loss of Nicaea.

Sept. 1: Crusaders capture Heraklea (Eregli).

Sept. 14: Army moves towards Caesarea in Cappadocia; Tancred and Baldwin Le Bourg leave army and head towards Tarsus.

Sept. 21: An abandoned Tarsus is occupied, but dispute breaks out as to whom it belongs – a dispute which has considerable ramifications on the later history of Antioch and Edessa.

Sept. 27: Main army arrives at Caesarea in Cappadocia.

Oct. 3: Army arrives at Plastenzia (Comana), which had been besieged by the Turks for three weeks; inhabitants hand over town that is granted to Pierre d'Aulps.

Oct. 13: Army arrives at Marasch.

Oct. 16: Jagi Sian expels Christian men from Antioch.

Oct. 17: Between Marasch and Antioch Baldwin of Boulogne leaves the army for Edessa (see 944, 1087).

Oct. 21: Siege of Antioch begins (see 944, 1084).

Nov. 17: Fleet of thirteen ships, which left Genoa on 15 July, arrives at Port St Simeon.

Dec. 31: Drawn battle at el-Bara with army from Damascus led by Dukak.

1098

Pisan fleet of 120 ships ready for crusade.

Feb. (beginning): Tatikios leaves crusading army, apparently granting Tarsus, Mamistra and Adana to Bohemond; Thoros invites Baldwin to Edessa to defend it against the Turks.

Feb. 9: Relieving force led by Ridwan of Aleppo defeated near the lake of Antioch, together with destruction of fort at Harenc (Harim).

Feb. 15: Jagi Sian sends for help to Kerbogha, the governor of Mosul.

Feb. 20: Baldwin arrives at Edessa.

Mar. 4: English ships arrive at Port St Simeon.[4]

Mar. 7: Revolt of the Edessenes against Thoros.

Mar. 9: Murder of Thoros; Baldwin takes control of Edessa.

May 4–25: Kerbogha on way to Antioch besieges Edessa for three weeks.

June 3: Capture of the town of Antioch.

June 4: Kerbogha's advance guard arrives at Antioch.

June 14: Finding of the Holy Lance.

June 20: Raymond ill; Bohemond given command of crusading army.

June 28: Defeat of Kerbogha and pillage of his camp.

July (beginning): Dispute over possession of Antioch; Hugh of Vermondois and Baldwin of Hainaut sent to Constantinople to announce its fall.

July 3: March to Jerusalem postponed to Nov. 1 because of the heat.

July 14: Bohemond grants a commercial quarter in Antioch to the Genoese around the church of St John, consisting of the church itself, a market and thirty houses.

July 14: Raymond Pilet, with volunteers, raids Saracen territory.

July 17: Pilet captures fort at Tellmanas.

July 25: Hugh of Vermondois arrives in Constantinople; Pilet fortifies Tellmanas.

July 27: Pilet defeated at Marra and withdraws to Tellmanas.

Aug. 1: Adhemar of Le Puys dies of plague at Antioch.

Aug. 26: Egyptian vizier al-Afdal captures Jerusalem from the Seljuks.

Sept. 11: Letter to Pope Urban inviting him to Antioch to occupy the Patriarchate of St Peter and to lead the crusade on to Jerusalem.

Sept. 25: Raymond of Toulouse captures Albara and installs a bishop. This is the first Latin bishop created by the crusade army.

Oct. 3–10: Council of Bari to discuss the crusade.

Nov. 5–18: Council at Antioch to decide its future; majority in favour of giving it to Bohemond.

Nov. 23: Raymond and Robert of Flanders leave Antioch to besiege Marra.

---

[4] It is sometimes erroneously claimed that Edgar the Atheling (1051–1125) commanded this fleet, but he was in Scotland at the time.

Dec. 12: Sack of Marra.

Dec. 29: Council at Marra to discuss the march to Jerusalem; Bohemond returns to Antioch.

1099

Jan. 5: Common people raze the walls of Marra.

Jan. 7: Bohemond drives the Provençals from Antioch.

Jan. 12: March towards Jerusalem begins.

Jan. 29: Krak occupied.

Feb. 14: Arrival at Arqah.

Apr. (beginning): Messengers from Alexios I ask crusaders not to advance beyond St Jean but to await his arrival.

Apr. 8: Test by fire of Peter Bartholomew (Pierre-Barthélemy).

Apr. 18: Attack from Arqah towards Tripoli.

Apr. 20: Death of Peter Bartholomew.

May 13: Crusaders leave Arqah for Tripoli.

May 16: Crusaders arrive at Bethelon (Batrun).

May 19: Arrive at Beirut.

May 24: Arrive by the river Belus near Acre.

May 26: Arrive at Caesarea.

June: Byzantines regain control of Trebizond from Danishmend.

June 3: Enter Rama; Robert of Rouen created bishop of Rama.

June 7: Crusaders arrive at Jerusalem.

June 13: First assault on Jerusalem (on advice of a hermit on the Mount of Olives).

June 15: Council decides to construct siege machines.

June 17: News of arrival of a Genoese fleet at Joppa (Jaffa).

July: Venetian fleet of 200 ships under Doge Vitale I Michiel (1096–1101) sets sail for Holy Land.

July (beginning): Council decides to elect a king of Jerusalem and to occupy Bethlehem.

July 10–13: Raid by Tancred and Eustace in the Nablus region.

July 13–14: General attack on Jerusalem.

July 15 (Friday): Jerusalem is captured.

July 16: Massacre of 300 Saracens under Tancred's protection on roof of the Temple of Soloman (Aqsa Mosque).

July 22: Godfrey of Bouillon elected Advocate of the Holy Sepulchre and Prince of the Holy City.

Aug. 1: Election of Arnulf of Chocques (also of Rohes) as patriarch of Jerusalem.

Aug. 12: Al-Afdal defeated at Ascalon by Godfrey and Tancred.

Aug. (end): Many crusaders leave Haifa for Europe.

Sept. (early): Daimbert, archbishop of Pisa, arrives at Laodicea with 120 ships and takes part in the siege.

Sept./Oct.: Many crusaders, estimated at 20,000, embark for the west at Laodicea.

Oct. 15–Dec. 15: Siege of Arsuf.

Oct. 28: Venetian fleet winters at Rhodes (until 27 May 1100).

Dec. 21: Bohemond, Baldwin of Edessa and Daimbert arrive in Jerusalem with a large number of pilgrims.

Dec. 25: Daimbert of Pisa is enthroned as patriarch in Jerusalem; Godfrey of Bouillon and Bohemond of Antioch do homage to him for their lands. Five Latin dioceses set up in the patriarchate of Antioch: Albara, Edessa and Bohemond's three creations at Tarsus, Mamistra and Artah.
   Order of St John of Jerusalem founded (militarised in the 1130s).

Castle built at Ramla, that attracts settlers from Lydda.

1100

Early: Byzantine army from Trebizond recovers coast of Cilicia from Bohemond.

May: Paschal II appoints Maurice, cardinal bishop of Porto, as his legate to the east, possibly in response to complaints about Daimbert from Godfrey.

June: Bernard of Valence, since Dec. 1099 bishop of Artah, is appointed patriarch of Antioch (–1135).

July–Aug.: Tancred besieges and takes Haifa.

July 18: Unexpected death of Godfrey of Bouillon.

Mid-Aug.: On his way to Melitene (Malatya), Bohemond is taken prisoner by Malik-Ghazi ibn-Danishmend of Sebastia.

Sept.: Maurice arrives with a Genoese fleet at Latakia.

Oct.: Baldwin, travelling from Edessa to Jerusalem via Antioch, hears of his brother's death and declines the regency, determining to become ruler of Jerusalem; Baldwin Le Bourg succeeds him as Baldwin II of Edessa.
   Tancred besieges Frankish garrison in Jaffa.

Nov. 9: Baldwin and his supporters enter Jerusalem, winning the support of Godfrey's knights and sealing off the city. Baldwin and his followers decide that kingship is the appropriate step for the next ruler of Jerusalem. Daimbert remains in the monastery of Mount Zion outside Jerusalem, a house that he had founded. He makes some sort of rapprochement with Baldwin but refuses to conduct a coronation in Jerusalem.

Dec. 25: Coronation of Baldwin of Edessa as Baldwin I of Jerusalem. Daimbert crowns him in the Church of the Nativity at Bethlehem. No homage paid to the Church, but soon after Baldwin was formally confirmed in his title by Paschal II.
   Peter I of Aragon captures Barbastro (see 1064, 1065) (SC).

Anon., *Gesta Francorum et aliorum Hierosolimitanorum* (chronicle of First Crusade, 1096–9).

1101

Early: Defeat of Baldwin Le Bourg of Edessa at Saruj by Sokman ibn-Artuk of Mardin.

Feb.: Peter I of Aragon, having taken the cross for Jerusalem, is persuaded by Paschal II to continue his fight against the Muslims in Spain. He begins the unsuccessful siege of Zaragossa bearing the banner of Christ, perhaps the first crusader to fight in Spain (SC).

Mar.: Tancred is regent of Antioch for Bohemond who is held prisoner at Neocaesarea by Danishmend Turks. He recovers the Cilician cities of Mamistra, Adana and Tarsus from the Byzantines.

Easter (?): Greek Orthodox monks allowed back into the Church of the Holy Sepulchre after the failure of the Paschal flame to ignite. It was assumed in 1099 that this church would be for Latins only.

May 9: Capture of Arsuf by Baldwin I with aid of a Genoese fleet.

May 31: Capture of Caesarea by the Genoese, who sack the port and bring away the green basin as a trophy for their cathedral church of San Lorenzo in Genoa.

June 23: Raymond of Toulouse captures Ankara with crusading armies advancing through Asia Minor.

Aug.–Sept.: Defeat of three crusading armies in Asia Minor at Mersivan and near Heraklea.

Sept. 4: Baldwin I defeats Egyptians at the first battle of Ramla with 250/300 knights.

Winter: Daimbert charged with treason by Baldwin; after judgment and deposition he sought shelter with Tancred at Antioch.

Nov. 15–Dec. 21: Baldwin campaigns towards Ascalon and then the Dead Sea.

1102

Feb.: Survivors of the crusade of 1101, including Stephen of Blois, Stephen of Burgundy, Raymond of Toulouse and Welf of Bavaria, arrive at Antioch. Joscelin of Courtenay, a cousin of Baldwin Le Bourg, is given the lordship of Tell Bashir on the border of Edessa with Antioch.

Mar.: With the assistance of a Genoese fleet they capture Tortosa and spend Easter in Jerusalem.

May 17: Many of these survivors fight with Baldwin at the second battle of Ramla (280 knights), where they are defeated by a superior Fatimid army. Baldwin escapes to Arsuf, but most – including Stephen of Blois – are killed.

May 28: Baldwin defeats Fatimid army at Jaffa.

In return for military support for Baldwin against the Fatimids, Tancred of Antioch enforces the return of Daimbert to the Patriarchate of Jerusalem. Daimbert is again charged with treason, again deposed, and again flees to Antioch.

First construction of the castle at Saphet.

Raymond of Aguilers, *Historia Francorum Qui Ceperunt Iherusalem* (chronicle of the First Crusade, 1096–9).

1103

Apr./May: Tancred captures Byzantine Latakia/Laodicea after 18-month siege.

May: Bernard of Valence arranges the ransoming of Bohemond from the Danishmend Turks against the wishes of Tancred the regent of Antioch.

Raymond of Toulouse fails to take Homs following the death of janah-ad-Daulah and settles down around Mount Pilgrim to besiege Tripoli and live off the land.

Autumn: Byzantines retake Cilician coast after renewing demands for return of Antioch.

1104

Early: Bohemond captures Germanicea from Alexios' few remaining Armenian allies.

Spring: Rulers of Mosul andArdin move against Edessa. Baldwin II summons help from Antioch. Bohemond, Tancred, Joscelin of Tell-Bashir and Baldwin II move on Hauran (ancient Carrhae).

May 7: Frankish army defeated in two sections at Hauran. Baldwin Le Bourg and Joscelin are captured, whilst Bohemond and Tancred escape to Edessa. Tancred becomes regent of Edessa.

May 26: Capture of Acre by Baldwin I, with aid of Genoese fleet (besieged since 1103).

Late May: Byzantine fleet recaptures Laodicea, al-Marqab and Jabala. Raymond of Toulouse, with Genoese help, seizes Jubail (ancient Byblos). Ridwan of Aleppo seizes border fortresses of the Principality of Antioch-al-Fu'ah, Sarmin, Ma'arrat-Misrin, Artah, Kafartab, Ma'arrat-an-Nu'man and Albara.

?: Danishmend dies.

June 14: Shams-al-Muluk Dukak, ruler of Damascus, dies;Tughtigin sets up independent rule at Damascus as atabeg for Dukak's infant son Tutush. Baldwin I supports a disappointed heir, Ertash (Bektash), and incurs hostility from Damascus.

Autumn: Bohemond, accompanied by Daimbert, sails for Italy – the former to raise a crusade against Alexios I, the latter to plead his case before Paschal II. Tancred resumes regency of Antioch, and Richard of Salerno becomes governor of Edessa.

Saewulf, a monk of Malmesbury, writes the earliest pilgrimage narrative of his journey to Jerusalem in 1102/3.

1105

Feb. 28: Raymond of Toulouse dies at the siege of Tripoli; command of the army taken on by his cousin William Jordan, count of Cerdagne.

Spring: Tancred recaptures Artah and defeats the army of Ridwan of Aleppo, possibly followed by a five-year truce. Chokurmish of Aleppo raids territory of Edessa.

Aug. 27: Baldwin I, with 500 knights, defeats coalition of Fatimid and Damascene troops at the third battle of Ramla.

Tughtigin destroys castle of Al, east of Lake Tiberias, built by Baldwin I.

The scholar Ibn al-Sulami wrote *Kitab al-jihad* (Book of the Holy War) in Damascus. He saw the First Crusade as part of a pattern of western expansion, and called for Muslim unity and religious purity. He seems to have been the first to call for a jihad which had not been called by those who had actually lost lands to the Franks in 1099 and who would therefore have been

quite within their rights to have done so. Its influence seems to have been negligible in political circles.

1106

May 26: Council at Poitiers; Bruno of Segni confirms summoning of a crusade under Bohemond's leadership.

Philip I gives Bohemond his daughter Constance in marriage and his illegitimate daughter Cecilia as a wife for Tancred.

Bohemond recruits a force of 34,000 men from Italy and France, ostensibly for an *Iter Hierosolymitanum* but with a direct attack on Byzantine territory on the way.

Tancred captures Apamea.

Kilij Arslan of Iconium raids Edessa.

Alexios I hires mercenaries from Kilij Arslan and recovers Trebizond, which had been lost by the rebellion of its governor in 1104.

Fulcher of Chartres, *Gesta Francorum Iherusalem Peregrinantium*, first version (see also 1108, 1118, 1127).

(–1107) Pilgrimage of the Russian abbot Daniel of Kiev – details difficulties encountered by pilgrims.

1107

Spring: Kilij Arslan again raids Edessa.

June 3: Kilij Arslan killed in battle at the Khabur, near Mosul, by the Seljuks of Iran.

Oct. 9: Bohemond lands in Epirus, captures Avlona and besieges Dyrrachium.

Alexius uses Venetian ships to supply Dyrrachium and deny supplies to Bohemond.

Crusade of the Norwegians under Sigurd 'Jorsalfar' (–1110).

Late: Tancred recaptures Mamistra from Byzantines.

Robert of Rheims/Robert of Marmoutier/Robert the Monk, *Historia Iherosolimnita*, places the crusade as a definnig moment in the history of Christendom. Robert had attended the Council of Clermont.

1108

Early: Tancred recaptures Latakia.

Summer: Baldwin of Edessa released from captivity in Mosul in return for military help. He demands the return of Edessa from Tancred, but is refused unless he holds it as a vassal of Tancred.

Sept.: Bohemond sues for peace and, by the Treaty of Devol (Deabolis), agrees to surrender the Cilician coast and Laodicea to Byzantium, to acknowledge Byzantine suzerainty over Antioch and to restore the Greek patriarch (John the Oxite).

Bohemond retires to Apulia. Leaving the treaty a dead letter. Parts of Bohemond's army made their way to Jerusalem by sea; one of them, Hugh le Puisset, was made Count of Jaffa by Baldwin I.

Sept. 18: Edessa restored to Baldwin II.

Late Sept.: Battle near Tell Bashir between Tancred and Ridwan of Aleppo on one side and Baldwin II and Chavli of Mosul on the other. Tancred prevails and besieges Baldwin in Dukak.

Oct.: Sharaf-ad-Din Maudud replaces Chavli in Mosul as official of the Seljuk sultan and leader of opposition to crusader states in north Syria.

Sigurd of Norway, on his way to Syria with sixty ships, attacks Muslim ports, including Cintra and Lisbon (SC).

Guibert, abbot of Nogent (b. 1053), *Historia quae dicitur Gesta Dei per Francos,* provides a history of the First Crusade up to 1101.

Bartulf of Nangis, *Gesta Francorum Hierusalem expugnantium,* a paraphrase of Fulcher of Chartres, with topographical additions especially of Constantinople, a city he visited in 1097. His work ends with Tancred's capture of Latakia.

1109

Mar.: Bertrand, son of Raymond of Toulouse, claims the area around Tripoli.
William Jordan turns to Tancred for assistance.

Apr.: Baldwin I summons Tancred in the name of the Church of Jerusalem to answer charges brought against him by Bertrand, Baldwin Le Bourg and Joscelin of Tell Bashir. Conciliation worked out whereby Tancred held Tiberias, Nazareth, Haifa and the Templum Domini as vassal of Baldwin; William Jordan to hold Tortosa and Arqah; Bertrand to hold Tripoli, when it fell; and Baldwin Le Bourg confirmed as ruler of Edessa. Great increase in Baldwin I's prestige.

July 12: Tripoli falls to Bertrand and the Genoese; Bertrand becomes count.

Tughtigin concedes castles of Moinetre and Gibelcar to counts of Tripoli, from which they strive to control the Beqah valley.

1110

Byzantines drive Turks from Lampe, which provokes a raid as far as Philadelphia.

Apr.–May: Maudud ravages Edessa and opens a brief siege of the city.

May 13: Capture of Beirut by Baldwin I with aid of Genoese squadron.

Early summer: Baldwin I, Bertrand, and later Tancred, with a force of 600 knights in Edessa, fortify the city and remove Armenian settlers from the countryside to places of safety.

Late summer: Maudud joins with Tughtigin of Aleppo to attack Armenian refugees and to further raid in Edessene territory.

Dec. 4: Capture of Sidon by Baldwin I, with aid of Venetian and Norwegian flotillas.

Arab castle at Krak des Chevaliers (Hisn al-Akrad) occupied by forces from County of Tripoli.

Baudri of Bourgueil/Baudri of Dol (1045–1130), Historia Hierosolymitana, is an underrated account of the First Crusade by one who had attended the Council of Clermont.

1111

Mar. 5 or 7: Death of Bohemund at Bari. He was buried next to the church of St Sabinus the Confessor in Canossa di Puglia.

Byzantines raise question of suzerainty over Antioch with Tancred and seek alliances against him with Baldwin and Bertrand and with the Seljuk sultan.

Byzantine trade treaty with Pisa in return for naval support against Tancred (?).

Maudud ravages Edessa.

Aug.: Maudud seeks to join with Ridwan of Aleppo; latter shuts gates on him and Maudud ravages territory of Aleppo.

Sept.: Maudud joins with Tughatin of Damascus in an unsuccessful attempt to recover Tripoli.

Peter Tudebode of Civray, Historia de Hierosolymitano itinere (chronicle of First Crusade, 1095–9).

1112

Feb. 3.: Bertrand dies; his son Pons succeeds as count of Tripoli.

Apr.–June: Maudud attacks Edessa.

Dec. 12: Tancred dies; succeeded by Roger of Salerno (son of Roger of Salerno who had governed Edessa from 1104 to 1108).

Sigebert of Gembloux, Chronographia (world history down to 1111, with material on the First Crusade and on the Second Crusade in its continuation to 1186).

1113

May–June: Maudud joins forces with Tughtigin to attack the Kingdom of Jerusalem via Tiberias.

June 28: Baldwin I defeated at Sinn al-Nabra near Tiberias, losing 1,200 infantry and thirty knights.

July–Aug.: Maudud raids the Kingdom up to Jaffa and Jerusalem.

Aug. (–May 1115): Combined naval operations of fleets from Pisa, Catalonia and southern France against the Balearic Islands to liberate Christian captives. Participants received crusade indulgences and a papal banner (see 1092) (SC).

Oct. 2: Maudud of Mosul killed by Assassins at Damascus. Tughtigin suspected of complicity and makes treaties with Frankish rulers to protect his own position.
     The sultan appoints Aksungur al-Bursuki to replace Maudud.

Nov.: Ridwan dies; Aleppo now under his son Alp Arslan and the regent Lu'lu.

Late: Baldwin I repudiates his Armenian queen, Arda, in order to marry Adelaide the mother of Roger II of Sicily.
     Malik Shah, sultan of Rum, raiding into Byzantine territory up to walls of Nicaea.
     Papal bull *Pie postulatio voluntatis* recognises Hospital of St John in Jerusalem.

1114

Augustinian canons are appointed to serve the Church of the Holy Sepulchre. This year witnesses the beginning of construction work on the Church of the Holy Sepulchre to bring all the sites associated with Christ's Passion and resurrection under one roof; tombs of the kings of the Kingdom of Jerusalem are placed close to Calvary (see 1042–8 and 1149).

May: Aksungur leads unsuccessful attack on Edessa.

Late: Aksungur is defeated by a local emir of Mardin and replaced by Bursuk ibn-Bursuk of Hammadan.

Nov.: Earthquakes cause severe damage in north Syria.

1115

Bursuk attacks Edessa unsuccessfully and then moves towards Aleppo to make it his base.

Summer: Rulers of Aleppo make an alliance with Damascus and the Franks of Antioch against Bursuk.

June: Roger and the Antiochene army at Apamea.

July: Bursuk advances to Shaizar on the borders of the Principality of Antioch.

July 7: Death of Peter the Hermit.

Autumn: Baldwin I begins construction of Montroyal in Galilee and Krak de Montreal (ash-Shaubak), south of the Dead Sea (control of Wadi Musa).

Sept. 14: Roger of Antioch's defeat of Bursuk at Tell Danith (between Aleppo and Apamea) brings considerable prestige and security to the crusader states.

Malik Shah maintains pressure on Byzantine frontier in Bithynia.

1116

Baldwin I leads expedition to Aqaba and visits Monastery of St Catherine in Sinai.

Building of castle at Aila/Eilat on the Red Sea.

Late: Baldwin I divorces Adelaide of Sicily in order to preserve his kingdom from the claims of Roger of Sicily and also because the legitimacy of his divorce of Arda is questioned. He has already spent Adelaide's dowry on the affairs of his kingdom.

Count of Tripoli captures castles at Rafaniyah (lost 1126) and Tuban to control plain of Homs.

Alexios I defeats Malik Shah near Philomelion and forces him to acknowledge Byzantine frontier.

1117

Malik Shah, the sultan of Rum, deposed and murdered by his brother Ma'sud, leaving a stalemate in the centre of Anatolia.

1118

Mar.: Baldwin I leads campaign to Pelusium and the Nile mouth.

Apr. 2: Baldwin I dies at al-Arish whilst returning from campaign in Egypt. The frontiers of the Kingdom of Jerusalem now remain substantially the same until 1187.

Apr. 14: The consecration of Baldwin Le Bourg, formerly Baldwin II of Edessa, as Baldwin II of Jerusalem. Baldwin was Baldwin I's cousin and had been unanimously elected king despite emissaries having been sent to Baldwin I's brother, Eustace, count of Boulogne, who returned to Boulogne from Apulia when he heard of Baldwin II's succession.

May–July: Tughtigin establishes himself at Tiberias and raids Kingdom of Jerusalem; al-Afdal advances from Egypt to Ascalon. Baldwin summons help from Antioch and Tripoli and covers the invaders.

Late summer: Frankish counter-raids against Damascus and Aleppo with Franks winning skirmishes involved.

Roger of Antioch, aided by Leon the Armenian, captures Azaz.

Aug. 15: Death of Alexios I Komnenos; succeeded by his son, John II Komnenos (–1143).

Dec. 15: Alfonso I of Aragon (1104–34) captures Saragossa after a seven-month siege (SC).

Ralph (Raoul) of Caen, *Gesta Tancredi*, a Norman version of the events of the First Crusade down to 1105, dedicated to the patriarch Arnulf (Arnoul). Ralph was in Tancred's service from 1107.

Second version of Fulcher of Chartres, *Historia Hierosolymitana* (see also 1106 and 1127).

1119

Hugh of Payns founds the Knights Templar. The patriarch of Jerusalem acknowledged their vows. There were very few of them, possibly only nine by 1129, and they were attached to the regular canons of the Holy Sepulchre.

June: Il-Ghazi moves towards Antioch via Edessa and awaits forces of Tughtigin at Buza'ah. Roger concentrates the Antiochene army at Artah.

June 28: Defeat and death of Roger of Antioch at Darb Sarmada (Ager Sanguinis), north of Antioch.

Baldwin secures Antioch and is invited to become bailli or regent (until the arrival of Bohemond II in 1126). Appeal to Pope Calixtus II (1119–24) for help.

Aug. 14: Baldwin defeats Il-Ghazi and Tughtigan at the second battle of Tell Danith (Hab).

Sept.: Joscelin II of Courtenay of Tiberias invested with county of Edessa.

Baldwin II builds castle at Habis Jadak (the Cave of Sueth) near site of Al destroyed in 1105.

1120

Jan.: Parlement/Council of Nablus: barons and prelates discuss how to obtain divine mercy. Of its twenty-five decrees, three gave the Church control of tithes; the rest dealt with sodomy, buggery, adultery, sexual relations with Muslims, and theft. The beginning of a law code for the Kingdom of Jerusalem, as distinct from sentences passed by judges based on their home experience.

Jan. 23: Embassy sent to the Pope and to Venice soliciting military help for the Kingdom of Jerusalem.

Fulk of Anjou and 100 knights arrive to spend one year fighting in the Holy Land (–1121).

May: Il-Ghazi and his nephew Belek launch two-pronged attacks on Edessa and Antioch. Edessa attack defeated by Joscelin, with high casualties for Belek.

June: Campaign towards Antioch (joined by Tughtigin) held in check by Baldwin. Il-Ghazi destroyed Zardana to prevent Frankish use. A one-year truce leaves Franks in possession of Albara, Ma'arrat-Misrin and Kafartab.

June 18: Alfonso I of Aragon defeats Almoravids at Cutanda, confirming his hold on territorial gains south of the Ebro valley (SC).

Albert of Aix, *Liber Christianae expeditionis pro ereptione, emundatione, restitutione sanctae Hierosolymitanae ecclesiae* (a history of the First Crusade and Latin kingdom down to 1120).

Gilon of Toucy's poem *De Via Hierosolymitana* gives the most detailed account of the capture of Jerusalem in 1099. He visited the Holy Land as papal legate in 1128.

1121

Jan.: Joscelin attacks Naqirah and Ahass.

Feb.: Joscelin attacks Buza'ah just north of Aleppo.

Apr.–June: Baldwin II raids area around Shaizar.

May: Joscelin attacks Al-Atharib and threatens Aleppo.

June: Tughtigin attacks towards Tiberias but is contained by Baldwin.

July: Baldwin captures Jarash and razes the fortress constructed by Tughtigin in 1120 to the ground.

Aug.–Oct.: Baldwin besieges and captures Zardana, Khunasirah, Burj Sibna, Naqirah and al-Ahass.

Nov.: Truce arranged.

Dec.: Al-Afdal, vizier of Egypt, assassinated, his successor al-Mamun to follow a forward policy in Syria.

1122

Early: Baldwin II tries to enforce his overlordship of Pons of Tripoli.

June/July: Il-Ghazi and Belek attack Zardana. Driven off by Joscelin and Baldwin.

Aug. 8: A venetian fleet of 120 ships, marked with the sign of the cross, carrying a papal banner and commanded by doge Domenico Michiel, sailed for the East.

Fleet winters at Corfu trying unsuccessfully to capture the island from the Byzantines.

Early Sept.: Belek attacks Edessa unsuccessfully.

Sept. 13: Joscelin ambushed and captured by Belek near Saruj.

Baldwin appoints Geoffrey the Monk, lord of Marash, as regent of Edessa (–1123).

Oct.: Baldwin raids into Aleppan territory and destroys the garrison of al-Bab.

Nov. 3: Il-Ghazi dies returning from Zardana to Aleppo.

Nov.: Baldwin resumes raids in the Buzaʿah valley, extracts tribute from al-Bab and captures Bir.

David III of Georgia captures Tiflis from the Muslims.

John II Komnenos crushes Pechneg raiders in Macedonia and Thrace and effectively ends their threat to Byzantium's northern frontier (see 1047, 1091).

Walter the Chancellor, *Bella Antiochena* (history of the principality of Antioch, 1114–15 and 1119–22).

1123

Mar. 18–Apr. 5: Calixtus II convokes First Lateran Council. Canon 10 of its twenty-two canons dealt with crusading vows, protection of crusaders' property and remission of sins for crusaders. It also imposed sanctions on defaulting crusaders.

Crusading privileges were definitely extended to those fighting the Moors in Spain (see 1118) (SC).

Apr. 2: Calixtus II sends letters to Venice, and probably to France and Germany, regarding a new crusade. He also promotes a crusade in Spain. Possibly this implies a general encyclical which does not survive (see 1145).

Apr. 9: Treaty with the Artukud ruler of Aleppo by which al-Atharib ceded to Franks.

Apr.: Baldwin moves against Belek who was besieging the castle of Gargar 40 miles north of Edessa.

Apr. 18: Baldwin ambushed and captured by Belek at Shenchrig. Imprisoned with Joscelin and Galeran at Kharput, 100 miles north-east of Edessa. William of Bures becomes regent in Jerusalem during Baldwin's captivity.

May: Egyptian naval and land forces from Ascalon attack Jaffa after Baldwin's capture.

May 29: Egyptian army defeated at Ibelin near Jaffa; the Egyptian fleet returns to Ascalon.

May: Venetian fleet arrives; intercepts and destroys Egyptian navy as it returns to Ascalon from Jaffa.

June: Belek captures Aleppo from his cousin Sulaiman for conceding al-Atharib to the Franks in April.

May–Sept. 16: Baldwin attempts to escape from captivity by seizing Kharput, where he is confined; Joscelin escapes and goes to Jerusalem to raise a rescue force. Hearing of this, Belek abandons the siege of Kafartab (Aug.), storms Kharput, and recaptures his prisoners and moves them to Hauran.

Dec.: Discussions with Venetians *re* assault on Ascalon or Tyre.

Pactum Warmundi grants commercial privileges to the Venetians in the Kingdom of Jerusalem. The grant was issued by Warmund (Gormond), patriarch of Jerusalem, in the absence of Baldwin.

1124

Feb. 16: Beginning of the siege of Tyre by land and sea.

Apr.: Belek attacks Manbij. The governor of the town, Hassan, approaches Joscelin for aid.

May 5: Frankish army defeated by Belek at Manbij.

May 6: Belek killed by an arrow at the siege of Manbij.

Late May: Edessan raiding force defeated in battle near Marj Aksas.

June: Timurtash transfers Baldwin and Galeran to Shaizar and agrees on Baldwin's release.

July 7: Tyre falls to the Franks.

Aug. 29: Baldwin released in return for hostages, a ransom of 80,000 gold pieces and the surrender of Azaz.

Sept. 6: Baldwin released from terms of oath to Timurtash by Bernard of Valence, patriarch of Antioch: Baldwin unable to concede Azaz which belonged to Bohemond II.

Oct. 6 (–Jan. 25, 1125): Baldwin besieges Aleppo. Timurtash, who was at Mardin, does not send aid to the citizens, who turn instead to Aksungur al-Bursuki, the Seljuk governor of Mosul.

Death of al-Hasan ibn-al-Sabah (*Pers.:* Hasan-I-Sabbab) founder and master of the Assassins and the conqueror of Alamut (1090).

1125

Jan. 18: Church council at Santiago de Compostela discussed the Spanish crusade, and spoke of Spanish crusaders as knights of Christ (*milites Christi*) in same terms as those fighting in the east. First mention of the idea of aiding the Holy Land by extending the Spanish crusade along the coast of North Africa (SC).

Jan. 25: Siege of Aleppo lifted.

Apr. 3: Baldwin enters Jerusalem for first time in three years.

May (end of): Baldwin I, leading the armies of Antioch, Edessa and Tripoli, defeats a Muslim coalition from Mosul, Damascus and Homs under al-Bursuki at Azaz (Hasart) in one of the bloodiest engagements in the history of the crusader states.

Sept.: Baldwin II pays his ransom to Aksungur: hostages Yvette and Joscelin II are released.

Oct.: Baldwin II builds castle at Mont Glavien, 6 miles south-east of Beirut, to prevent brigandage and secure tax returns.

Nov.: Baldwin leads expeditions into Damascene territory and towards Ascalon in response to closer relations between Egypt, Damascus and Aleppo.
   Death of David III of Georgia; succeeded by his son Demetrius I.

Raymond, archbishop of Toledo, begins the translation of the works of Aristotle into Latin.

Ekkehard of Aura, *Chronicon universale*.

William of Malmesbury, *Gesta Regum Anglorum*, uses Fulcher for his account of the First Crusade.

1126

Jan. 13: Baldwin leads expedition from Tiberias towards Damascus.

Jan. 25: Defeat of Tughtigin at Marj-as-Siffar in a close-fought battle. Two towers destroyed on return journey.

Mar. 31: Rafaniyah, 20 miles west of Homs, surrenders to Pons and Baldwin.

May: Pons and Baldwin ravage territory of Homs.

July 1: Aksungur sends Babek against al-Atharib.

July: Baldwin and Joscelin move to Artah, 30 miles west of Aleppo, and offer to surrender Rafaniyah in exchange for withdrawal of Aksungur's forces from al-Atharib. Truce not honoured by either side, but armies disperse in early August.

Aug.: John II Komnenos renews the commercial treaty of 1082 with the Venetians.

Oct.: Arrival of Bohemond II from Apulia; Antioch restored to him. Marries Alice, the second daughter of Baldwin II.

Nov.: Tughtigin grants castle at Banyas to the Assassins.

Nov. 26: Aksungur murdered by Assassins at Mosul. His son, Izz-ad-Din Masïd, and Tughtigin quarrel; the Artukids regain control of Aleppo and take revenge on those who had ousted them in 1123.

(?) Sometime during this year the first revolt of Romanus of Puy against Baldwin II. Romanus loses his castle of Montroyal; this is granted to Paganus, now of Montroyal and lord of Transjordan (see also 1115 and 1134). It is generally accepted that the *Etablissement du roi Baudoin* was promulgated to deal with the confiscation of lands from Romanus. It dealt with the building of ports and roads into the lands of the Saracens contrary to the royal prerogative.

1127

Apr.: Sultan confers control of a unified Syria on Imad-ad-Din Zengi; Zengi had to impose this unity before he could move against the Franks.

May: Sudden death of Tughtigin at siege of Rahba.

Summer: Joscelin and Bohemond dispute over Antioch. Whilst Bohemond is absent in Cilicia, Joscelin ravages the principality of Antioch, with Turkish troops to support him. Baldwin and the patriarch are eager to restore peace and a united front.

Sept.: Zengi enters Mosul as atabeg for the sultan's son, the malik Alp Arslan, and gains control of Nisibin, Sinjar and Hauran.

Oct.: Joscelin attacks Aleppo, but is bought off.

First Latin archbishop of Tyre appointed (William, prior of the Church of the Holy Sepulchre, an Englishman).

William Bures, constable of Jerusalem, sent to Anjou to offer the hand of Melisende, and the crown of Jerusalem in succession to Baldwin II, to Fulk V of Anjou. Issue of the lawful position of Baldwin discussed.

Stephen II of Hungary invades Byzantine territory and captures Belgrade and Sofia.

Final version of Fulcher of Chartres, *Historia Hierosolymitana,* a chronicle of the first Crusade and Kingdom of Jerusalem to 1127 (see also 1106, 1108 and 1118).

1128

Jan.: Zengi's forces occupy Aleppo.

Feb.: Death of Tughtigin of Damascus; succeeded by his son Bori.

June 18: Zengi enters Aleppo.

Late: Zengi appointed atabeg of Aleppo after many misgivings on sultan's part.

1129

Jan.: Council of Troyes approves Latin rule of the Templars.

May: Hugh of Payns returns to the East with considerable force, including Fulk of Anjou. This force is sufficient to encourage planning for the capture of Damascus. Fulk and Melisende are married.

June: Zengi occupies Manbij and Buzaʿah.

Sept.: Zengi occupies Hamah. Plot of vizier and Ismaïl, leader of the Assassins in Syria, to hand over Damascus to the Franks foiled, but Ismaïl offers to hand over Banyas in return for asylum.

Autumn: Homs successfully resists Zengi.

Nov.: Franks occupy Banyas and begin the siege of Damascus. This was abandoned in early December following defeat at Marj as-Suffar, which affected Frankish ability to interfere in Damascus for a number of years.

Castle at L'Assebebe/Qal'at Subeibe/Paneas built on hill above Banyas (–1132).

1130

Feb.: Bohemond II, on his way to attack Armenians, is killed fighting Danishmends on the Jihan in Cilicia. His widow, Alice, approaches Zengi to help maintain her in power. This scheme is scotched by Baldwin II, who confines Alice to the cities of Latakia and Jabala and assume the regency of Antioch for his granddaughter Constance.

Spring: Zengi raids territory of Antioch and besieges al-Atharib, defeating the Frankish relieving force under Baldwin.

Chanson des Chetifs (romance legend of the First Crusade).

Earliest pilgrim handbook to the Holy Land. Its author is unknown, but it is traditionally attributed to Fetellus/Fretellus, archdeacon of Antioch in 1200; however, it is certainly not by him (see 1170 and 1172).

1131

Aug. 21: Baldwin II dies. On his deathbed Baldwin reneges on the agreement made with Fulk in 1129: the succession is no longer to go solely to him but in addition to Melisende and the two-year-old Baldwin. This change was apparently to protect Melisende from feared repudiation by Fulk.

Leo I (1129–38) of the Roupenid dynasty of Lesser Armenia seizes Mamistra, Tarsus and Adana from the principality of Antioch.

Sept. 14: Coronation of Fulk and Melisende without formal election; apparently the wishes of Baldwin II were carried through without opposition from the baronage of the kingdom.

Sept.: Death of Joscelin I de Courtenay; succeeded by his son Joscelin II (b. 1113).

Mughith-ud-Din Mahmud II, the Seljuk sultan of western Iran and Iraq since 1118, dies. Zengi becomes entangled in Iraqi affairs until 1135, leaving his interests in Syria in the hands of Sawar, governor of Aleppo.

1132

Alice of Antioch reasserts claim to the regency of her daughter Constance, supported by Pons of Tripoli and Joscelin II of Edessa who do not acknowledge overlordship of the king of Jerusalem. Fulk defeats rebels at Chastel Rouge.

(?) Summer: Possible date for the rebellion of Hugh le Puiset, count of Jaffa, against Fulk, but more probably dated in 1134 (see p. 42).

June: Tughtigin's son Buri dies at Damascus as a result of wounds inflicted by Assassins; succeeded as atabeg by his son Ismail.

Dec. 11: Ismail recaptures Banyas.

The Assassins purchase al-Qadmus from the emir of Kahf and begin settlement in the Nusairi Mountains.

1133

Spring: Fulk rescues Pons of Tripoli, besieged in the castle of Montferrand. Pons' son Raymond marries Hodierna, the sister of Melisende. His daughter Agnes marries the son of Fulk's constable at Antioch, Reynald Mazoir of Marqab.

Spring: Sawar, with Turkoman recruits, attacks Turbessel and Antioch. Forced to retire by Fulk after a surprise attack at Qinnasrin.

Summer on: Withdrawal of Fulk; raids continue.

Aug.: Ismail of Damascus recaptures Hammah.

Construction of Chastel Hernaut/Castle Arnoldl (Bait Nuba) by patriarch of Jerusalem on Jaffa–Jerusalem road, east of Lydda, to protect pilgrims.

Fortified Cave de Tyron in the hills west of Jordan taken from an Arab sheik friendly to the Franks by the atabeg of Damascus.

1134

Franks campaign in the Hauran. Ismail counter-attacks towards Acre, Tiberias and Tyre; this movement forces a Frankish withdrawal in October.

Late: Rebellion of Hugh, count of Jaffa, possibly joined by Romanus of Puy (see 1132). The rebellion is put down. Count Hugh is exiled for life and dies sometime later in Apulia. Queen Melisende is for some reason very angry at her husband's proceedings in this matter and incensed at the death of Hugh. It is very possible that the revolt was caused by Fulk's attempts to reduce the power of Melisende, or was perhaps Fulk's reaction to a plot by Melisende and Hugh to sideline him.

1135

Feb. 1: Ismail, having offered to hand Damascus over to Zengi in return for protection, murdered in Damascus by his mother.

Mid-Feb.–7 Mar.: Zengi besieges Damascus unsuccessfully.

Apr.: Zengi attacks county of Edessa and captures the fortresses of Kafartab, Maarat, Zerdana and Athareb on the border of Antioch.

May: At the Council of Pisa, Innocent II decrees that those who fought against the Pope's enemies (the Normans of southern Italy) would enjoy the same indulgence as that granted by Urban II at the Council of Clermont.

Early summer: death of Bernard of Valence, patriarch of Antioch. Succeeded by Radulph of Domfront, the bishop of Mamistra, who was acclaimed by the people rather than canonically elected.

Aug.: Fulk in Antioch; accepts Radulph and allows Alice to return to Antioch.
    Envoy sent to England to offer Raymond of Poitiers the hand of Constance of Antioch, which is accepted.
    Alice sends to John Komnenos, urging the marriage of his son Manuel to Constance.
    Assassins purchase Kahf from the emir of Kahf.

1136

Apr.: Raymond of Poitiers arrives at Antioch. Sawar makes a destructive raid as far as Latakia. Marriage to Constance of Antioch.
    Raids into Cilicia.

Fortress of Bait Jibrin (Eleutheropolis) built to prevent raids from Ascalon.

1137

Mar.: Forces of Damascus invade Tripoli, defeating the small defence force led by Pons.

Mar. 25: Pons executed by his captors, having been handed over by the Christians of Mount Lebanon. Castle of Ibn-al-Ahmar captured.

Raymond II of Tripoli, Pons' successor, ravages Christian communities on Mount Lebanon as a reprisal.

June–July: Zengi fails to take Homs.

July 11: Zengi besieges Montferrand/Ba'rin. Initial relief force led by Raymond II and Fulk is defeated. Raymond is captured and Fulk besieged in Montferrand. Field army from Jerusalem, Antioch and Edessa comes to its relief, but a negotiated surrender is agreed before the army arrives. Montferrand is surrendered to Zengi and Raymond is released.

July–Aug.: John II Komnenos recaptures Cilician towns from Roupenids.

Aug. 29: Byzantine army begins the siege of Antioch.

Sept.: Raymond II, with Fulk's agreement, renders fealty to John and promises to hand over Antioch if the latter will capture Aleppo, Shaizar, Hamah and Homs and grant them to Raymond II.

Winter: John withdraws to Cilicia.

1138

Feb.: Arrest of Muslim merchants in Antioch.

Mar. 31: Franco-Greek expeditionary force sets out.

Apr. 9: Buza'ah is captured.

Apr. 14–20: Unsuccessful siege of Aleppo.

Apr. 21: Al-Atharib captured.

Late Apr.: Kafartab captured.

Apr. 28–May 21: Unsuccessful siege of Shaizar.

May 21: Zengi regains Kafartib as Graeco-Frank expedition withdraws.

May: Zengi successfully proposes a marriage alliance to Shihab al-Din Mahamud, the atabeg of Damascus: Zengi to marry the atabeg's mother, Zummurud Hatun, while Shihab al-Din will marry Zengi's daughter. Zengi would receive Homs as his dowry and hoped to rule Damascus through his wife as regent.

John Komnenos demands citadel of Antioch and access to military supplies. Popular protest leads to Byzantine withdrawal from the city.

Summer: Zengi captures 'Arqah.

Sept. 8: Marriages arranged in May take place and Zengi receives Homs. His plans for Damascus are unsuccessful and he abandons his new wife.

Sept. 27: Zengi captures Buza'ah.

Oct. 10: Zengi captures al-Atharib.

Oct. 20(–mid-1139): Earthquakes in northern Syria.

1139

June 23: Shihab-al-Din Mahamud assassinated. The governor of Damascus, Mu'in al-Din Unur, instals Shihab al-Din's brother as the new atabeg. Zummurud Hatun appeals to Zengi for help.

Dec.: Zengi makes a demonstration outside Damascus but does not besiege the city.
   Latter half of the year, Mu'in al-Din Unar approaches King Fulk for an alliance, offering Banyas to the Franks – although they must first capture it. This is the beginning of a Jerusalem–Damascus alliance that lasts until the spring of 1147.

First building of the castle at Belvoir in the mountains south of Lake Tiberias overlooking the Jordan valley (see 1168).

1140

Feb.: Fleet of seventy ships from the Low Countries and England on the way to the Holy Land is persuaded to attack Lisbon. This unsuccessful attack was a precursor of the attack of 1147.

Apr.: Zengi besieges Damascus.

May 4: Zengi lifts siege of Damascus and moves to the Hauran to fight the Franks advancing from Tiberias.
   Zengi withdraws to Baalbek; Franco-Damascene forces besiege Banyas.

June 12: Banyas surrenders.

June 22: Zengi withdraws to Iraq.
   Raid and counter-raids, Antioch against the Turkomans.

Ibn-al-Qalanisi, *Dhail ta'rikh Dimasbq* (Continuation of the History of Damascus), provides the earliest Muslim account of the First Crusade, but is essentially focused on Damascene affairs.

Aimery of Limoges, archdeacon of Antioch, *La Fazienda de ultra mare*, a pilgrim's guide written for Archbishop Raymond of Toledo (1124/5–52).

Cantore di mio Cid (Song of the Cid), a verse account of the life of Rodrigo de Vivar, known as the Cid (d. 1099).

1141

Antiochene raids into Damascus with sack of Sarmin and Kafartab.
  Raid and counter raids against Turkomans.

Castle of Ibelin (Yabna) built by Fulk and granted to Barisan, constable of Jaffa. About this time the castles at Château Maen (Beit – Dajan) and Château des Plains (Yazur), between Ramla and Jaffa, were completed.

Orderic Vitalis, *Historia Ecclesiastiica* (much material on the First Crusade).

1142

Apr.: Invasion of Antioch from Damascus.

Castle at Blanche Garde (Tell as-Safiyah) built 8 miles from Ascalon.

Castle of Kerak (Krak des Moabites) in Transjordan built by Pagan le Bouteiller.

Raymond II of Tripoli cedes castle of Krak des Chevaliers to the Hospitallers.

Sept.–Oct: Campaign of John II Komnenos in Edessa and Antioch. Winters in Cilicia.

Dec. 25: melisende, as queen mother, is crowned for the second time; her son, the thirteen-year-old Baldwin III, crowned and anointed for the first time (see also, 1131). They are to be joint rulers of Jerusalem (not a regency exercised by Melisende).

Matthew of Edessa (Urfa), *Chronicle* of Armenian history from 951 to 1136, continuation to 1162, has some observations on the First Crusade and the crusader states from an Armenian perspective.

William of Malmesbury, *Gesta Regum Anglorum,* has some material on the First Crusade and is one of the main sources for the Council of Clermont, 1095.

1143

Jan.: Retaliatory raids from Damascus into Antiochene territory.

Apr. 8: John Komnenos dies in Cilicia as result of a hunting accident; succeeded by his son Manuel I (–1180).

Nov. 10: Death of Fulk of Jerusalem.
  Peter the Venerable, abbot of Cluny, commissions the translation of the Koran into Latin in an attempt to refute the errors of Islam. The English scholar, Robert of Ketton, living in Toledo, undertakes the work.

1144

Spring (?): Baldwin III leads a military expedition to quell a revolt by the native inhabitants of Wadi Musa. Melisende apparently resents her son's success.

Nov. 24: Zengi begins siege of Edessa whilst Joscelin is away in the western part of his county. Melisende sidelines Baldwin III and arranges the sending of a relieving force commanded by her dependants (Manasses of Hierges; the constable, Philip of Nablus; and Elinard of Tiberias).

Dec. 24–26: First capture of Edessa, Latins massacred and their churches destroyed. The Frankish relieving force arrives too late. Raymond of Antioch is unable to give military assistance. Joscelin still holds the west of his county, in particular Turbessel and al-Bira, with every hope of regaining Edessa.

1145

Nov.: Embassies asking for military assistance sent from the rulers of the Latin East to Louis VII and the Pope; the most important was led by Hugh, bishop of Jabala.

Dec. 1: Encyclical letter *Quantum praedecessores* that enlarged and defined the indulgence granted by Urban II in 1095: remission of sins conceded, together with a moratoria on debts and protection of property of crusaders.

Christmas court at Bourges. Louis VII, apparently without knowledge of the encyclical, publicises his intention to aid the Christians of the East.

Building of the Great Mosque at Mosul begins.

1146

Early: Armenian plot to restore Edessa to Joscelin halts Zengi's proposed campaign against Damascus and leads to the complete destruction of the site of Edessa.

Mar. 1: The encyclical *Quantum praedecessores* reissued to encompass Louis VII's proposals and to authorise preaching of a crusade by Bernard of Clairvaux.

Mar. 31: Sermon at Vezelay; Louis VII fixes departure date for one year hence and sends out embassies to rulers through whose territory he must pass.

Spring/summer: Manuel I campaigns against Masud of Iconium (Konya) in an attempt to regain fortresses from Turkish control and limit raids into Byzantine territory. He is near Konya when the letters from Louis VII arrive.

Sept. 14: Zengi assassinated. Safadin succeeds in Mosul and Nur ed-Din becomes ruler of Aleppo after a brief power struggle with his brother.

Oct.: Bernard of Clairvaux at Mainz; Radulf's preaching brought to an end by confining to a monastery.

Oct.–Nov.: Joscelin briefly retakes the lower town of Edessa, besieging the Muslim garrison in the citadel. Nur ed-Din retakes the city for the second time and virtually razes it to the ground. Joscelin succeeds in escaping but his force is wiped out.

Dec. 24: Bernard of Clairvaux arrives at Speyer for the Christmas court of Conrad III. His moving sermon confirms Conrad in his resolve to go on crusade, and many take the cross.

Otto of Freising's *Chronica sive Historia de duabus civitatibus* contains brief notice of the First Crusade and the crusade of 1101. It is the first known western source to mention Prester John.

1147

Jan.–Mar.: Eugenius III makes progress from Viterbo to Paris, via Burgundy, preaching the crusade.

Jan.: Alfonso VII of Castile (1126–57) captures Calatrava (SC).

Feb. 16: French crusaders meet at Étampes to receive updates on recruitment in France and to hear from Bernard of Clairvaux the progress of crusade enrolment in Germany. Date for departure fixed for June; Roger II of Sicily withdraws from crusade.

Mid-Feb.: Diet at Regensburg. Papal bull read out by Adam, Cistercian abbot of Erbach, and recruitment continues to an already very large army.

Spring: Treaty of alliance between Nur ed-Din and Damascus: apparent change in Damascene foreign policy and end of the Jerusalem–Damascus alliance of 1140.

Mar. 13: Frankfurt Diet declares peace in the German Empire, accepts regency for Conrad's son, finalises arrangements with French army and sets departure date for mid-May. Saxons declare desire to crusade against the Wends and adopt the cross on orb as their badge; Bernard of Clairvaux accepts this idea.

Spring: The Muslim commander of the castles of Bosra and Salkhad in the Hauran offers to hand them over to the Kingdom of Jerusalem. This offer, if accepted would threaten the food supplies of Damascus and end the treaty of 1139 between Jerusalem and Damascus. The proposed campaign led to the calling up of every able-bodied man in the kingdom to serve in the army (the *arrière ban*).

Apr. 13: Eugenius III issues the bull *Divina dispensatione* that grants crusade indulgences to the Wendish crusaders and appoints Anselm of Havelburg as papal legate to the Wendish crusade.

Easter: Eugenius III at St Denis; appoints Theodwin of Porto as legate to the German army and Guido of Florence for the French army.

Apr. 27: Fleet of 50/60 ships leaves Cologne via Dartmouth for the Holy Land.

Mid-May: German army leaves Nuremberg for journey down the Danube to Constantinople.

June: The army of Jerusalem forced to withdraw from the Hauran by two armies from Damascus. Melisende uses this inglorious campaign to try to downgrade the standing of Baldwin III.

June: French army gathers at Metz and leaves for Constantinople.

June 16: Fleet arrives in Portugal and is persuaded to assist in the siege of Lisbon (SC).

June 26: The Wends sack Lübeck (BC).

July–Sept.: First Northern Crusade against the Wends. The Danish contingent is defeated by the Wends and the Saxons abandon their crusade (BC).

Mid-Aug.: Provençal contingent, led by Alfonso Jordan, take ship at the mouth of the Rhône for the Holy Land.

Sept.–Oct.: The fleet of Roger II of Sicily captures Corfu and Cephalonia and sacks Athens, Chalkis, Corinth and Thebes, taking silk workers from Thebes back to Sicily. The presence of the Normans in central Greece occupies the bulk of Manuel's military resources, making them unavailable to assist the crusade.

Sept. 10: German army arrives at Constantinople.

Oct. 4: Louis VII and the French army arrive at Constantinople to find that Conrad has crossed the Bosphorus without waiting for him.

Oct. 17: Alfonso VII of Castile captures Almeria after four-month siege by land and sea. He is assisted by a Genoese fleet in return for commercial privileges (SC).

Oct. 24: The Almohads in Lisbon surrender to Alfonso Henriques after the siege conducted by men from Frisia, Flanders, Cologne, Normandy and England. Fortresses at Cintra, Almada and Palmela are also captured, securing the Tagus estuary. The Englishman Gilbert of Hastings becomes Latin bishop of Lisbon (SC).

Nov.: German crusade defeated in the vicinity of Dorylaion and withdraws to Nicaea to await the arrival of the French. The remnant of the German army, and the French, moves forward to Ephesus.

Nov. 11: Army arrives at Ephesus; Conrad, in poor health, goes to Constantinople at the invitation of the Emperor Manuel to recuperate.

Dec. 24: Army leaves Ephesus and bests the Turks in a skirmish just east of the city.
First translation of the Koran into Latin, sponsored by Peter the Venerable at Cluny.

1148

Jan. 4: Crusaders force their way throught to Laodicea and Lycum.

Jan. 20: Army reaches Antalya, badly mauled, short of supplies and exhausted.

Feb. 1: Fleet leaves Lisbon to continue journey to the Holy Land.

Late Feb.: Louis VII and leading men of the crusade sail to Antioch in ships procured from the Byzantines, leaving the main army under the counts of Flanders and Bourbon to make its way by land to Antioch, an estimated march of forty days. The Turks destroy the bulk of this army, with just a remnant making it through to Antioch.

Spring: Emperor Manuel prepares a counter-attack against the Normans. First he signs a truce with the Seljuk ruler of Iconium and then a naval alliance with Venice. The Venetian fleet defeats the Sicilian fleet off Cape Malea.

Mar. 19: Louis VII arrives in Antioch and is exposed to plans by Raymond for an attack on Aleppo. Louis' army is depleted and he insists on going to Jerusalem to fulfil his vow.

Mid-Apr.: Conrad arrives in Acre and proceeds to Jerusalem.

June 24: Council at Acre made up of the crusade leadership and all the principal rulers of the crusader states, with the exception of the Raymond of Antioch, Raymond II of Tripoli and Joscelin of Edessa. Based upon expert knowledge, the decision is taken to attack Damascus.

July 23–27: Unsuccessful attack on Damascus. Abandoned in the face of Nur ed-Din's relieving army that was at Homs.

Sept.: Raymond II of Tripoli seeks assistance from Damascus and Nur ed-Din to dislodge the Provençal Bertram, son of Afonso Jordan and grandson of Raymond of Toulouse, from the citadel of al-Arimah.

Sept. 8: Conrad III leaves Acre by ship bound for Thessalonika on his way back to Germany.

Oct.: Conrad in Thessalonika as guest of Manuel on campaign against the Normans. Here he agrees an alliance against Roger II.

Nov.: Raymond of Antioch, supported by the Assassins of Masyaf, surprises and defeats Nur ed-Din at Yaghra (Famiya). Nur ed-Din's army was mounting diversionary raids on the Antiochene frontier to enable the sultan of Iconium (Konya) to attack Marash.

Nov.–Dec.: Nur ed-Din attempts to break up Shi'ite leadership in Aleppo.

Dec. 31: Ramon Berenguer IV of Catalonia (1131–62) captures Tortosa with the aid of a Genoese fleet. The Genoese receive a third of the port (SC).

Anna Komnene, *The Alexiad*, chronicles the reign of her father, the emperor Alexios I, from a Byzantine perspective, with much colourful material on the First Crusade and Bohemond.

Anon., *De Expugnatione Lyxbonensi*, an account of the siege and capture of Lisbon during the Second Crusade.

1149

Feb.: Conrad takes leave of Manuel and starts his return to Germany.

Spring: A Sicilian fleet raids Constantinople, burning the suburbs and vandalising the imperial gardens.
  Raiding and counter-raiding on the borders of the principality of Antioch; Nur ed-Din, using Kurdish Turkoman raiders, involved in this move. His aim is to gain possession of Antiochene territory east of the Orontes. Increasing use of Kurds in Muslim armies is noticeable from this time.

May: Conrad III back in Germany. Louis VII leaves Acre in Byzantine ships that defeat a Sicilian squadron in a naval battle. Louis seems to have transferred to the Sicilian fleet.

May: Truce between Damascus and both Raymond of Tripoli and Baldwin III of Jerusalem to free a Damascene contingent to raid with Nur ed-Din towards Apamea.
  Nur ed-Din brings pressure on Damascus to provide support for his attacks on the Franks and thus recognise his suzerainty.

June 29: Raymond of Antioch defeated and killed near Inab by the forces of Damascus and of Nur ed-Din. His skull is fashioned into a drinking cup for Nur ed-Din. This victory established Nur ed-Din as the leader of the counter-crusade against the Franks. For the next three years pressure is brought on Constance, the princess-regnant of Antioch, to remarry for the good of Antioch – preferably either a relative of Manuel I or a noble Frank.

July 15: Consecration of the Church of the Holy Sepulchre, a Latin Christian interpretation centre of the Passion and resurrection of Christ.

July: Apamea and Harim captured by Nur ed-Din and Antioch besieged.
  Louis VII is the guest of Roger II.

Mid-Sept.: Louis travels back to France through Italy, calling at Monte Casino and Rome.

Oct. 24: Ramon Berenguer IV expels last Muslim garrisons from Catalonia with the capture of Fraga and Lleida (SC).

Late Nov.: Louis VII back in the Ile de France.

Dec.–May 1150: Baldwin III rebuilds the castle at Gaza and gives it to the Templars.

1150

Early: Nur ed-Din besieges Damascus but is forced to withdraw due to Frankish troop movements.

Spring: Attacks on the rump of the county of Edessa; Samosata and Bira captured. Tell Bashir (Turbessel), where Joscelin's wife Beatrice still holds out, is besieged. Manuel bought the remaining fortresses of Edessa from Beatrice, and for a time the siege of Tell Bashir is lifted by Nur ed-Din.

May 4: Joscelin II of Edessa ambushed and captured by Turkomans on his way to Antioch. He was blinded and imprisoned in Aleppo until his death in 1159.

May–June: Supporters of Melisende amongst the vassals of the crown fail to answer the summons of Baldwin III. This is tantamount to treason, and the break-up of the kingdom might result. Baldwin's power base at this time seems confined to Acre. During the summer and autumn Baldwin is forced to do what he can for Antioch and Edessa with the forces at his disposal. He negotiates with Manuel I, and oversees the installation of a Greek garrison in Turbessel and the withdrawal of the Latin garrison to Antioch

Odo of Deuil, *De profectione Ludovici VII in orientem*, is the best account of the Second Crusade by an eyewitness.

1151

Spring: Nur ed-Din again besieges Damascus and is again forced to abandon his attack due to Baldwin III's manoeuvres in the Hauran. Nonetheless, Turkomans gain virtual control of the Hauran area from Damascus.

July: An Egyptian fleet of seventy vessels raids the coast around Jaffa, Acre, Sidon, Beirut and Tripoli. Baldwin concerned in resisting these depredations.

July 12: Tell Bashir surrenders, bringing the existence of the county of Edessa to an end – the first established and the first lost of the Frankish states in the east. With the intervention of Manuel I in the affairs of the rump of Edessa, Melisende is unable to blame the fall of the county on her son.

Late: Raymond II of Tripoli is killed by the Assassins; Baldwin III, who is present in Tripoli at the time, persuades the barons to swear allegiance to the twelve-year-old Raymond III and his mother, Countess Hodierna.

Dec.: Turkoman raiders attack the Frankish garrison at Banyas, inflicting heavy casualties. Frankish raids in the Biqa Valley as a form of reprisal.

During the year Melisende appoints her younger son, Amalric (Amaury), count of Jaffa.

1152

Easter: Coronation of Baldwin III as the sole ruler of Jerusalem. He must have gained the assurance of the patriarch that Melisende would not be crowned separately in her own right. He assigns Jerusalem and Nablus to Melisende and bases himself in Acre and Tyre.

Apr.: Civil war between Baldwin III and his mother Melisende. Baldwin III appoints Humphrey II of Toron constable of the kingdom. Besieges Manasses of Hierges in the castle of Mirabel and on his surrender forces him into exile. He is admitted to Jerusalem and besieges Melisende in the Tower of David. After some days of street-fighting, Melisende agrees to retire to Nablus and not to intervene in the politics of the kingdom again. Baldwin reconciles himself with the Church and the military orders. He re-establishes the royal chancery under the Englishman Ralph of Tyre, whom Melisende seems to have forced to step down in 1147.

Thoros II, the son of Leon I, reasserts his claim to Cilician Armenia.

Spring: Nur ed-Din captures Tortosa and Yahmur, whilst Damascenes regain control of the Hauran.

John of Salisbury, *Historia Pontificalis*.

1153

Jan.: Beginning of the siege of Ascalon by combined forces of the Latin states.

Spring: Nur ed-Din demands military support from Damascus for a campaign to relieve Ascalon from the Frankish siege.

Reynald of Châtillon, a knight who had stayed behind after the Second Crusade, marries Constance of Antioch. There is displeasure in the courts of Antioch, Jerusalem and Byzantium at this marriage

May: An Egyptian fleet drives of a squadron of fifteen ships commanded by Gerard of Sidon and succeeds in reprovisioning Ascalon.

June: Bernard de Tremolay, the master of the Temple, and forty men are trapped and killed storming a breach at Ascalon; despondency in crusader camp, but abandonment of siege rejected.

June: The allied army from Aleppo and Damascus breaks up after an unsuccessful attack on Banyas.

Aug. 20: Death of Bernard of Clairvaux (born 1090; canonised 1174).

Aug. 23: Garrison at Ascalon surrenders to the crusaders; the whole coastline of Syria now in Frankish hands.

Late: Nur ed-Din blockades Damascus by intercepting food supplies from his base at Homs.

1154

Early: Reynald takes Alexandretta from the Armenians as an ally of Manuel I against the Armenian ruler Thoros. He hands the port over to the Templars, who rebuild the *fortifications at Baghras and Gastun to cover the Syrian Gates.*

Apr. 25: Nur ed-Din enters Damascus. Muslim Syria virtually under Nur ed-Din's control, along with the former county of Edessa.
    The caliph confers the title *al-malik al-'adil* (the just king) on Nur ed-Din.

Henry of Huntingdon, *Historia Anglorum,* contains some pithy accounts on the First and Second Crusades. Henry accepts the idea of crusading in Spain and the Baltic, as well as in the Holy Land.

Al-Edrisi, *Al-kitab al-Rujari* (Roger's Book), gives elaborate descriptions, with maps of the world dedicated to Roger II of Sicily (d. 1154).

1155

June: Nur ed-Din negotiates one-year truce with the Kingdom of Jerusalem and captures Baalbek, the last Damascene stronghold to hold out against him.

Summer: Alfonso VII of Castile captures Andujar (SC).

1156

Reynald of Antioch defeated near Harim whilst raiding towards Aleppo.

Spring: Reynald, now allied with Thoros, attacks and pillages the Byzantine island of Cyprus, severely weakening its economic and military capabilities.

June: Nur ed-Din renews the truce with Jerusalem in return for a payment of 8,000 dinars.

1157

Apr.: An Hospitaller and Templar convoy bringing food to Banyas is ambushed and dispersed by the forces of Nur ed-Din.

May: Nur ed-Din attacks Banyas.

June 19: Frankish relieving army under Baldwin III ambushed and virtually destroyed at Jacob's Ford.

July: Combined forces of Antioch, Tripoli and Jerusalem force Nur ed-Din to abandon the siege of Banyas and withdraw to Shaizar, having attempted to renew the truce with Baldwin.

Sept.: Embassy sent from Jerusalem to Manuel I to seek a bride for Baldwin III.

Oct.: On the arrival of a crusading force under Thierry of Alsace, count of Flanders, at Antioch the combined Frankish armies advance on Shaizar, how earthquake damaged and possibly indefensible.

Aug. 1157–Nov. 1158: Severe earthquakes damage most towns and fortifications in the Near East.

1158

Jan./Feb.: Combined forces of Antioch, Tripoli and Jerusalem recapture Harim.

Spring: Peace between Manuel I and William I of Sicily (1154–66) brings to an end ten years of sporadic conflict in Greece, Italy and at sea.

Frankish forces ravage the territory of Damascus, whilst Egyptians troops raze southern Palestine. An Egyptian fleet makes raids on Cyprus.

May: Nur ed-Din attacks the castle of Habis Jaldak on the river Yarmuk.

July 15: Baldwin defeats Nur ed-Din at al-Batikal (Butaila), north of Lake Tiberias, and forces him to lift the siege.

Sept.: Baldwin III marries Theodora, niece of Manuel I, in Jerusalem.

Oct.: Manuel I campaigns in Cilicia with a huge army; Thoros II is forced to flee to the mountains and the area is restored to Byzantine control.

Late: Reynald of Châtillon abases himself before Manuel I at his headquarters at Mopsuestia in Cilicia, and in addition acknowledges Byzantine overlordship of Antioch (as in the Treaty of Devol, 1108, and John II Komnenos visits to the city in 1137/8 and 1142/3) and the right of Manuel to appoint a Greek patriarch for the city. Manuel does not exercise this right until 1165. He also obtains the pardon of Thoros, who becomes the Byzantine governor of Cilicia.

Otto of Freising, *Gesta Frederici imperatoris*, has some brief comments on the First Crusade and a much fuller account of the Second Crusade and St Bernard's role in it.

1159

Apr. 12: Manuel I makes a triumphal imperial entry into Antioch, making the point of Byzantine suzerainty and significance in north Syria. Eight days of celebrations and negotiations that confirm a Byzantine alliance with the Kingdom of Jerusalem for a joint expedition against Nur ed-Din.

May: Alarmed by events in Antioch and by the large expeditionary force now forming to attack Aleppo, Nur ed-Din concludes a truce by which he agrees to release various Frankish prisoners and forms an alliance with Manuel I against Kilij Arslan of Konya. Soon after this Manuel receives an urgent summons to return to Constantinople. Whatever the reason for his departure he thereby attracted much acrimony from Latin chroniclers for abandoning the crusade cause.

1160

Negotiations underway with Raymond III of Tripoli for the hand of his daughter Melisende as a wife for Manuel I; by July 1161 Melisende styles herself 'future empress of Constantinople'.

Throughout the 1160s Manuel I pays for the restoration of the Church of the Nativity at Bethlehem and may well have sent Byzantine mosaisists to work at the church.

June: Henry the Lion begins the conquest of the Wends (BC).

Nov.: Reynald, returning from a raid on Aintab, captured by the forces of Nur ed-Din. Reynald was to be kept in captivity for sixteen years, bringing some instability in Antiochene affairs.

Baldwin, then at Tripoli, came to Antioch as bailli and fortified the bridge over the Orontes. He appointed the patriarch Aimery de Valence (in voluntary exile in Jerusalem since 1153 due to a disagreement with Reynald) as regent.

Baldwin found Byzantine ambassadors in Antioch negotiating the marriage of Constance's daughter Maria with Manuel I. Despite the well-known negotiations with the ruling house of Tripoli, Baldwin gave his consent to this marriage proposal.

Two-year truce agreed between Baldwin III and Nur ed-Din.

1161

July: Baldwin III ensures his control of Nablus from his ailing mother Melisende.

Aug.: Raymond III of Tripoli insulted by Manuel's rejection of his daughter, Melisende, as a bride; sends twelve ships to raid the coast of Byzantine territories.

Sept. 11: Queen Melisende, the queen mother, dies and is buried in the nunnery at Josaphat.

Dec. 25: Manuel I and Maria of Antioch married in Constantinople.

Late: The murder of Stephen, a brother of Thoros, by Andronicus Euphorbenos, the Byzantine governor of Cilicia, at his residence in Tarsus, led to reprisal raids on Byzantine garrisons in Cilicia.

1162

July 6: Wends defeated at Demmin (BC).
  Marriage of Bohemond III and Theodora, the niece of Manuel I.

1163

Feb. 10: Baldwin III died at Beirut, aged 33, after a long illness first apparent at Antioch. He was buried in the Church of the Holy Sepulchre in Jerusalem. Friend and foe alike held him in high esteem. Out of respect for Baldwin III, Nur ed-Din, who had just returned from a pilgrimage to Mecca, forbade any attack on the crusader kingdom that sought to exploit the king's death. Baldwin died childless, and the succession passed to his brother Amalric, lord of Jaffa and Ascalon. At his election Amalric agreed to divorce his wife, Agnes of Courtenay, who had proved unacceptable to the barons and high clergy of Jerusalem. She was the daughter of Joscelin II of Edessa, and her power and family interests proved unacceptable to the notables of Jerusalem. They had married in 1157, and the legitimacy of their children, Baldwin and Sybilla, was accepted and guaranteed.

Feb. 18: Amalric I crowned king in Jerusalem.

Feb.: Barons of Antioch, with the aid of Thoros, expel Constance, the princess regnant, from the city and make Bohemond III sole ruler of Antioch. Amalric mediates the settlement.

Feb./Mar.: Manuel I ignores the appeal for help from Constance. He pardons Thoros and appoints Constantine Coloman as the new Byzantine governor in Cilicia. By now Manuel is very much the power-broker in north Syria.

Sept.: Amalric leads attack on Bilbais in Egypt.

1164

Early: Appeal for help sent by Amalric to Louis VII of France; the crusader states will either fall to the Greeks or the Turks without western aid.

Apr.: Nur ed-Din sends an expedition to Egypt led by the Kurd, Shirkuh, to restore a former vizier, Shivar, who had appealed to him for help.

May: Shivar restored to power in Cairo. Shirkuh occupies Bilbais in lieu of tribute due from Shivar, who appeals to Amalric for help.

Summer: Nur ed-Din besieges Artah (Harim) and raids into the area around Krak des Chevaliers.

Aug.-Oct.: Amalric's second siege of Bilbais; Bohemond III acts as regent in Jerusalem during his absence.

Aug.: Bohemond III of Antioch, Raymond of Tripoli and Constantine Coloman, the Byzantine governor of Armenia, defeated and captured at Artah as they attempt to relieve it.

Aug. 12: Artah surrenders to Nur ed-Din. The way to Antioch was now open, and perhaps only fear of Byzantine military intervention prevented Nur ed-Din from mounting a direct attack.

Sept.: Nur ed-Din besieges Banyas, which surrenders to him.

Oct.: Amalric returns to Jerusalem and takes steps to stabilise Antioch and Tripoli. He becomes regent of Tripoli for the ten years of Raymond's captivity.
    Muslims recapture Cordoba (SC).

1165

The Armenian Alexios Axuch sent as new governor to Cilicia to replace the captured Coloman and to take a firm line with them. He meets with limited success and is replaced in turn by Andronikos Komnenos.
    Manuel I agrees to pay the ransoms for the release of Bohemond III and Constantine Coloman, both of whom are set free. In return for this ransom payment Bohemond agrees to the appointment of a Greek patriarch in Antioch. Raymond of Tripoli, who did not enjoy friendly relations with Manuel (see 1161), remains in captivity for a further ten years. The significance of Byzantium in the survival of the crusader states is now apparent to all, but appeals for help continue to be sent to the West rather than to Constantinople.
    Bohemond III visits Constantinople after his release. On his return to Antioch he installs Athanasios as Greek patriarch. Aimery de Valence withdraws to the castle of Qusair and places Antioch under interdict. Pope Alexander III and the Jacobite Christians of north Syria oppose Athanasios, who remains in office until his death in his cathedral in an earthquake in 1170, when Aimery returns to Antioch, attributing the death of the Greek patriarch to the just judgment of God. The difficulties that Bohemond was prepared to tolerate in regard to this appointment – so controversial in Latin Christian circles – is a mark of the importance that he attaches to the alliance with Manuel I.

1166

Boleslav IV of Poland defeated by Prussians (BC).

Caffaro di Caschifellone (*c.* 1080–1166), *Liber de liberatione civitatum orientis,* looking back as a participant on Genoese involvement in the First Crusade, and the *Historia captionis Almariae et Tortuose,* an account of the

Genoese naval expedition to Spain (1147–8) in which he also took part. He also wrote the *Annali* of Genoa from 1097 to 1163.

1167

Jan.: Shirkuh campaigns in Egypt.

Jan. 30: Amalric leads third expedition to Egypt to prevent encirclement of crusader states by Nur ed-Din. His army camps near Fustat, and a treaty is made with Shivar by which the Franks will not leave Egypt until Shirkuh is either defeated or himself withdraws.

Mar. 18: Battle at al-Babain (Ashmun); crusaders left in control of the battlefield and Shirkuh withdraws to Alexandria.

Mar.-Aug.: Siege of Alexandria; siege lifted by a truce by which both forces agree to withdraw from Egypt, leaving Shivar in power but as a tributary of Amalric's.

Aug. 29: Marriage of Amalric and Maria Komnene, the daughter of the Protosebastos John, Manuel I's nephew. Negotiations begin for a joint Latin–Byzantine campaign to conquer and partition Egypt.

1168

Summer: Diplomatic exchanges between Jerusalem and Constantinople to finalise the Byzantine–Latin alliance.

Oct.: Without waiting for the outcome of the negotiations, Amalric leads an army into Egypt, possibly because Shivar was making approaches to Nur ed-Din.

Nov. 4: Bilbais captured and the inhabitants enslaved or put to the sword.

Nov. 12: Fustat burnt on the orders of Shivar to prevent it falling into Almaric's hands.

Nov. 13: Siege of Cairo begins.

Dec. 25: Amalric withdraws to Bilbais in an unsuccessful attempt to intercept a relieving force under Shirkuh and prevent him crossing the Nile.

Castle at Saphet granted to the Templars and Belvoir to the Hospitallers, both are refortified. Saphet is no longer visible; the Belvoir rebuild is the earliest dated concentric castle.

1169

Jan. 2: Almaric withdraws from Egypt.

Jan. 18: Shivar assassinated and Shirkuh becomes vizier in his place. Almaric's ambitions to enlarge the base of the crusader states by the conquest of Egypt are now effectively at an end, and those very same states are now surrounded by the forces of Nur ed-Din. From this year onwards, regular embassies are sent to Western Europe asking for military assistance.

Mar. 23: Shirkuh dies in Cairo. On hearing the news Amalric is said to have dismounted from his horse and given thanks to God.

Mar. 26: Saladin appointed vizier to the Fatimid caliph in place of his uncle.

Spring: An embassy led by Frederick de la Roche, archbishop of Tyre, is sent to the courts of Europe to ask for a new crusade and to offer the hand of Amalric's daughter Sybilla to Stephen of Sancerre, a man with considerable family crusading links.

Easter: Syrian Jacobites are granted the Chapel of St James in the Church of the Holy Sepulchre by the Latin patriarch Amalric.

Sept.: Byzantine ships, military equipment and troops under the command of Andronikos Komnenos arrive in Acre for the proposed joint expedition against Egypt.

Oct. 15: Combined Franco–Byzantine force advances from Ascalon to the Egyptian frontier town of Pelusium (al-Farama), whilst a Byzantine fleet sails to the mouth of the Nile.

Oct. 20(?): The siege of Damietta begins. Despite impressive Byzantine siege engines the city does not run short of food: Nile boatmen supply it.

Dec. 13: The siege is abandoned due to strained relations between Amalric and Andronikos.

Dec. 21: The expeditionary force arrives back in Ascalon having destroyed its siege engines and lost a proportion of the fleet.

1170

June: Severe earthquakes devastate the Near East.

Manuel I Komnenos donates a gold cover to the tomb of Christ in the Church of the Holy Sepulchre.

Amalric constructs fortress at Darum, south of Ascalon

Dec.: Saladin attacks Darum and Gaza. He withdraws on the approach of the field army of the Kingdom of Jerusalem.

John of Wurzburg, *Descriptio Terrae Sanctae*, a guidebook for pilgrims (see 1130 and 1172).

1171

Early: High court in Jerusalem discusses the military situation of the kingdom and decides to send another embassy to the West.

Mar. 12: Manuel I orders arrest of all Venetians in Byzantine territory, soon followed by Venetian retaliatory raids on Byzantine ports and islands.

Mar.–July: Amalric makes a visit to Constantinople to renew the alliance for an attack on Egypt.

Nur ed-Din orders Saladin to ensure that the name of the Abbassid caliph of Baghdad is substituted for that of the Fatimid caliph al-Adid in Friday prayers.

Sept. 13: Al-Adid dies and no Fatimid successor is named.

Oct.: Nur ed-Din campaigns towards Krak de Montreal (ash Shaubak). Saladin excuses himself from this campaign and arouses Nur ed-Din's suspicion.

Pope Alexander III declares a crusade against the heathens of the Baltic (BC).

Helmhold, priest of Bosau, *Cronica Slavorum,* gives material on the German crusades, both building upon and derivative of Adam of Bremen's *Gesta Hammaburgensis ecclesiae pontificum*; there is material on the Second Crusade.

1172

Theuderich/Theodoric, *Libellus de locis sanctis* – a detailed guidebook to the Holy Land for pilgrims (see 1130 and 1170).

1173

Embassy sent from crusader states to the West.

Spring: Nur ed-Din worried by the growing military strength of Saladin in Egypt and some talk of intervention there. Saladin campaigns against the Bedouin of Kerak to keep open communications with Syria; this seems to have assuaged suspicion of him amongst Nur ed-Din's advisers.

Saladin grants commercial concessions to the Pisans in Alexandria.

Late: Raymond III of Tripoli released from captivity; part of the ransom raised by Amalric.

Benjamin ben Jonah of Tudela, *Massoth Rabbi Binyamin,* an account in Hebrew of a thirteen-year journey from Castile to Baghdad noting Jewish communities.

1174

May 15: Nur ed-Din dies. There is trouble with Shiïtes in Aleppo and in Damascus *re* contention over the guardianship of his young son, al-Salih.

June 6: Saladin offers his condolences and protection to al-Salih in Damascus.

June: Amalric attacks Banyas, but agrees to a truce and returns in ill health. Saladin is unable to send help from Egypt since Manuel I, who also fears the presence of a Sicilian fleet in the east Mediterranean, has warned him of a proposed Sicilian attack.

July 11: Amalric I dies at Tiberias aged 38. His thirteen-year-old son Baldwin IV, 'the Leper King', succeeds him after three days of discussion as to his suitability – discussions of which Saladin was aware. There is no plan to appoint a regent; the seneschal Miles of Plancy carries on government.

July 15: Baldwin IV crowned in the Church of the Holy Sepulchre in Jerusalem.

July 25: Al-Salih leaves Damascus for Aleppo.

July–28 Aug. 1: Sicilian fleet sent by William II attacks Alexandria. The fleet is not supported by the field army of Jerusalem as planned due to the death of Amalric. Saladin forces their withdrawal, apparently badly impaired as an operational force.

Aug.: Dissatisfaction with Miles of Plancy as a result of his failure to liaise with the Sicilian fleet. Raymond III of Tripoli proposes himself as regent.

Oct: Miles of Plancy murdered in Acre, possibly a revenge killing for his failure to restore Beirut to the Brisbarre family.

Late Oct.: Raymond III of Tripoli becomes regent for Baldwin IV. He is thought by some to have murdered Miles of Plancy. He marries the greatest heiress in the kingdom – Eschiva II, princess of Galilee. Maria Komnene, Amalric's widow, retires to Nablus, leaving Agnes of Courtenay as the virtual queen mother of Jerusalem.

Oct. 28: Saladin occupies Damascus. His advance into Syria provokes a hostile reaction from many of Nur ed-Din's former advisers and from the Assassins. Al-Salih appeals to the Aleppans for aid against his would-be protector, Saladin.

Dec. 10: Saladin captures the lower town of Homs, halfway between Damascus and Aleppo. The citadel still holds out against him.

Dec. 28: Hama surrenders to Saladin.

Dec. 30: Saladin reaches Aleppo and camps outside it. Here Assassins in the employ of the Aleppans make an attempt on his life. Appeals for help are sent to Mosul, and overtures are made – either by the Aleppans or the garrison of Homs – to Raymond III of Tripoli to come to their assistance.

1175

Jan. 26: Saladin withdraws from Aleppo to Hama.

Feb. 2: Saladin draws up his troops to await Raymond III, who draws back from a fight.

Mar. 17: The citadel of Homs surrenders to Saladin.

Mar. 28: Baalbek surrenders without a fight, but the force from Mosul was approaching Hama. Negotiations ensue.

Apr. 2: Saladin agrees to withdraw from north Syria, keeping Damascus but handing back Homs, Hama and Baalbek to the Aleppans. Negotiations break down.

Apr. 13: Battle at the Horns of Hammah (Qurun Hamah) between Saladin and the forces of the Aleppo–Mosul alliance. Although 20,000 troops are committed on each side, Saladin gains an almost bloodless victory due to the timely arrival of reinforcements from Egypt.

May 6: Treaty between Aleppo and Saladin by which he gains control of most of north Syria except Aleppo. Thereafter he withdraws to Hama. Raymond III returns to Tripoli. Saladin had asked the caliph for a diploma of investiture covering not only Egypt, Yemen and the Maghrib but also all the former lands of Nur ed-Din. At Hama the caliph's envoys brought him robes of honour and a diploma for the lands that he held. The caliph thus adopted a neutral stance, but he did endorse Saladin's holy war against the Franks to recover Jerusalem.

June 8: The historian William of Tyre consecrated archbishop of Tyre, following the death of Archbishop Frederick on 30 October 1174.

July 22: A truce between Saladin and the Kingdom of Jerusalem that frees Saladin's hand for moves against Aleppo.

Autumn (?): A Sicilian fleet of forty galleys makes an abortive attack the port of Tinnis in Egypt; no support offered by the Kingdom of Jerusalem, now at peace with Saladin.

1176

Early: In view of his leprosy, which now seems to have been confirmed, Baldwin IV authorises embassies to be sent to William Longsword, the eldest son of William V, marquis of Montferrat, to offer him the hand of his sister Sybilla and hopefully secure the succession to the Kingdom of Jerusalem.

Apr. 22: Saladin defeats the combined forces of Aleppo and Mosul under Safadin at Tell al-Sultan; as in the previous year he does not set out to destroy his opponent's army.

May 1–June 21: Rather than besiege Aleppo Saladin seeks to weaken its economic and territorial base by capturing the ring of castles to the south and west: Buza'a, Manbij, Inal, A'zaz (Hazart) and Raban.

May (?): Bohemond III makes an alliance with the ruler of Aleppo in return for the release of Joscelin III of Courtenay (captured 1164) and Reynald of Châtillon (captured 1160).

May 22: Attempt on Saladin's life by the Assassins at A'zaz.

June 22–July 29: Saladin outside Aleppo.

July 15: Baldwin IV comes of age and Raymond III steps down as regent. The truce agreed with Saladin by Raymond is now at an end.

July 29: Peace agreed with Aleppo and Mosul by which Saladin gave up his claim to the guardianship of al-Salih and returned A'zaz to Aleppo.

Aug. 1–10: Saladin unsuccessfully besieges the Assassin stronghold at Masyaf in the Nusairi Mountains.

July–Aug.: Baldwin IV of Jerusalem and Raymond III of Tripoli raid into the Biqah valley nearly to the walls of Damascus.

Mid-Aug.: Baldwin and Raymond defeat an army from Damascus at 'Ain al-Jarr. This victory, which heartened the Franks, seems to have had little effect on Saladin's activities.

Aug. 25: Saladin at Damascus, where he marries Ismat al-Din Khatun, the widow of Nur ed-Din, a gesture of reconciling the past and the future. Little is known of Saladin's wives and concubines; apart from Ismat there is only the name of a certain Shamsi, who was the mother of three of his sons.

Late Aug.: Joscelin III of Courtenay appointed seneschal of the Kingdom of Jerusalem by Baldwin, who arranges his marriage with the heiress Agnes of Mily who brings Montfort and Chastiu dou Roy as her dowry.

Sept. 10: Saladin leaves Damascus for Egypt, where there is unrest due to a poor harvest and the heavy taxation to pay for his Syrian campaigns. His departure shows how secure he now felt in his Syrian possessions.

Sept. 17: Manuel I defeated by Kilij Arslan II at the battle of Myriokephalon. Losses to both sides were heavy and a truce was signed by which Manuel agreed to demolish certain fortifications, including that at Dorylaion. Apart from the loss of prestige the immediate effects of this defeat on the Byzantine frontier were not severe, but the Byzantine protectorate of the crusader states was effectively at an end.

Early Oct.: William Longsword arrives in Acre with a Genoese fleet.

Nov: The marriage of William and Sybilla. He is invested with the counties of Ascalon and Jaffa from the royal demesne.

Winter: Reynald of Châtillon sent to Constantinople to negotiate an alliance for an attack on Egypt with a fleet supplied by Manuel. The price is the restoration of the Orthodox patriarch to Jerusalem. The patriarch of Jerusalem had resided at Constantinople since 1099. Leontius, who was appointed in April 1176, arrived in the Holy Land in the summer of 1177 and died there in 1185. The marriage of Bohemond III of Antioch and the emperor's great-niece Theodora was also arranged. Manuel pays off Reynald's ransom of 120,000 dinars.

1177

Saladin prepares Egypt for attack by fortifying the major ports and cities, constructing a fleet based at Damietta and Alexandria and disposing his troops close to the frontier with the Kingdom of Jerusalem.

Spring: Reynald of Châtillon married to Stephanie of Mily, the widow of Miles of Plancy. He becomes lord of Kerak (Krak des Moabites) and Montreal (as-Shaubak). Baldwin also grants him the lordship of Hebron from the royal demesne.

June: Death of William Longsword, leaving his wife Sybilla pregnant (with the future Baldwin V). Reynald of Châtillon is appointed executive regent in his stead.

Aug. 1: Count Philip of Flanders arrives in Acre. His presence is resented by many of the local nobles. He causes difficulties over the regency, the command of the proposed expedition to Egypt, the remarriage of Sybilla, and the status of a conquered Egypt – a part of the Kingdom of Jerusalem, a Byzantine satellite or, as he hoped, an independent kingdom.

Aug.: Byzantine fleet of seventy galleys and transports under the command of Andronikos Angelos arrives in Acre for the joint campaign against Egypt. There is disinclination for this campaign, not only on the part of Philip of Flanders but on that of many of the leading men in the Kingdom.

Sept. (?): The Byzantine fleet returns to Constantinople. One of the best opportunities to inflict damage on Saladin is lost and Byzantine support for the crusader states is damaged. With the Egyptian expedition abandoned Saladin advances his troops deployed near the frontier to attack the kingdom from Egypt.

Nov.: Philip and Raymond III of Tripoli attack Hama, but break off their siege after six days to help Bohemond III capture Harim. Both campaigns are unsuccessful, although the siege goes on until the spring of 1178.

Nov. 23: Baldwin IV makes a surprise attack on Egyptian troops advancing on Gaza and Ascalon and routs them at Mont Gisard. Saladin just escapes with his life.

1178

Jan. (?): Sybilla gives birth to Baldwin, William of Montferrat's posthumous son.

Mar.: Saladin marches his army from Egypt to Damascus and relieves Harim.

Apr.: Reynald leads an unsuccessful attack on the fortress of Qalat Guinadi, a major watering place in the Sinai Peninsula and important point on Saladin's lines of communication between Egypt and Syria.

Late spring: A Sicilian fleet of forty ships sacks Tinnis.

Aug.: Franks mount an unsuccessful attack on Hamah.

Late summer: Humphrey II of Toron rebuilds the castle at Chastelneuf, abandoned in 1167.

Oct.: Baldwin IV begins construction of the castle of Le Chastellet at Jacob's Ford at the behest of the Templars. The field army of the kingdom remains in the area to protect the workforce.

1179

Mar. 5–19: Third Lateran Council meets in Rome; decrees against heretics and their patrons and denies Christian burial to those killed in tournaments.

Mar./Apr.: Hugh III, duke of Burgundy, accepts the proposal to go to Jerusalem and marry Sybilla. Baldwin IV hopes to abdicate in favour of Hugh when the marriage has taken place. Louis VII gives his consent. Hugh plans to leave for Jerusalem in the spring of 1180, and makes plans accordingly.

Apr.: The castle at Le Chastellet completed and handed over to the Templars.

Baldwin IV, cattle raiding near Banyas, is defeated by an army from Damascus near Belfort; the constable of the kingdom, Humphrey II of Toron, killed in the engagement.

Spring: Philip of Flanders returns home via Constantinople where he opens negotiations for a possible marriage between Manuel's son Alexios and a Capetian princess.

June 10: Defeat of Baldwin IV at Marj Uyan on the Litani River: 270 knights captured and the unhorsed Baldwin taken from the field of battle on the back of one of his knight's horses.

Aug. 24–29: Capture of Le Chastellet at Jacob's Ford; all the Templars and the archers are executed and some 700 prisoners taken. The castle is razed to the ground. The large numbers of mason's tools found at the site are now on display in the Israeli Museum, Jerusalem.

Seljuk army of Kilij Arslan II defeated near Raban, which it had been sent to recover from Saladin.

Oct.: The Egyptian fleet blockades Acre for two days and raids along the coast of the Kingdom of Jerusalem.

Nov.: Louis VII of France is incapacitated by a stroke (dies 18 Sept. 1180). Hugh of Burgundy feels unable to leave his duchy, as the Capetian monarchy appears weak.

1180

Early: Manuel I's only daughter Maria married Rainier, the youngest son of William V of Montferrat. This was a great honour for the family of Montferrat since this was the first time that a Byzantine emperor's daughter had married a non-royal husband. Rainier received a new name, 'John', the title of 'Caesar' and rights over the city of Thessalonika. It was to have some influence on the Fourth Crusade.

Mar. 11: Marriage of Manuel's ten-year-old son, the co-emperor Alexios II, with the eight-year-old Agnes, youngest daughter of Louis VII.

Apr. (Easter): With no Hugh of Burgundy on hand, Bohemond III and Raymond III attempt a coup by marching on Jerusalem, intending to marry Sybilla to Baldwin of Ibelin. Baldwin IV, who thought the Ibelin candidature unsuitable for the international standing of the kingdom, forestalls the coup by marrying his sister to Guy of Lusignan. Baldwin IV is now unable to abdicate in the short term. Pro-Ibelin and Lusignan factions begin to emerge, and tensions arise in the councils of the kingdom.

Spring: As a result of these difficulties Baldwin IV signs a two-year truce with Saladin. Raymond III of Tripoli refuses to sign the truce. As a result his territories are subjected to a series of raids by the Egyptian fleet, which captures the island of Ruad, just off Tortosa.

Baldwin IV sends Joscelin of Courtenay to Manuel I to explain events in the kingdom at Easter and the need for a truce with Saladin. Joscelin is to renew the alliance with Byzantium.

June: Saladin forms an alliance with Kilij Arslan II at a meeting on the Sanjar River. This meeting is followed by a joint campaign into Cilician Armenia against Roupen, who is accused of the harsh treatment of Turkomans.

June 29: Izz ad-Din secures power in Mosul on the death of his brother. There is reluctance in Mosul to support Saladin in his jihad against the Franks, and a dispute develops over lands secured by the rulers of Mosul on the death of Nur ed-Din that are now claimed by Saladin.

Sept. 24: Death of Manuel I Komnenos in Constantinople. His eleven-year-old son Alexios II (–1183), with his mother Mary of Antioch as regent, succeeds him. Mary renews the alliance.

1181

Jan. 16: Pope Alexander III, concerned by the leprosy and deteriorating health of Baldwin IV, calls for a new crusade in his encyclical *Cor nostrum*. There is little response to this appeal in Europe.

Jan.: Bohemond III of Antioch repudiates his Byzantine wife Theodora and marries Sibylla of Burcey. With Manuel I dead, and his own sister as regent in Constantinople, he fears no reprisals from the Byzantines. However, it leads Bohemond into disputes with the Church and his baronage. The patriarch Aimery of Limoges places the principality under interdict.

Spring(?): Aimery of Limoges brings about the union between the Maronite Church and the Latin Church. This first uniate Church would be endorsed by Innocent III in 1215.

Summer: Reynald of Châtillon attacks Tabuk and Taima in the northern Hejaz. Both towns are on the Damascus–Mecca pilgrim road, Taima being known as 'the gateway to Mecca'. On this raid he also attacks a caravan from Damascus to Mecca. Reynald is eventually forced to withdraw from Tabuk because of raids into Kerak by the army of Damascus.

Dec. 4: Al-Salih, Nur ed-Din's son and successor, dies at Aleppo after a short illness.

Izz ad-Din secures the treasury at Aleppo and installs a governor from Mosul. Treaty between Saladin and Byzantium may have been concluded.

1182

Apr.: Mary of Antioch is ousted as regent by Andronikos Komnenos who seizes power on a wave of anti-Latin feeling in Constantinople. All Pisans and Genoese in the city are killed and their property seized.

May 16: Andronikos has Alexios II crowned for a second time and himself recognised as regent. Over the next months all those significant figures at the Byzantine court with pro-Latin sympathies are liquidated. The policy of a Byzantine protectorate over the crusader states, in place since 1158, is abandoned.

May: Saladin marches from Egypt to Syria. His army is swollen by the presence of merchants and pilgrims seeking protection from Reynald.

July 13: Saladin besieges the castle of Bethsain in southern Galilee.

July 15: Baldwin IV and a Frankish relieving force defeat Saladin at the battle of Le Forbelet (Belvoir).

Aug.: Saladin, who has sworn to take Beirut, makes an unsuccessful attack on the city by land and sea. His failure damages his reputation. Saladin withdraws to

Baalbek and thence concentrates on occupying the former possessions of Nur ed-Din in northern Mesopotamia (al-Jazira), claimed since 1174 by Mosul.

Sept.: Baldwin IV raids as far as Bosra and recaptures the fort of Habis Jaldak.

Dec. 30: Sinjar surrenders, to Saladin who thus increases his pressure on Izz ad-Din of Mosul.

1183

Feb.: Reynald of Châtillon sends five galleys to attack Muslim shipping and pilgrim ports in the Red Sea. It had taken two years to build the ships at Kerak and camel transport to bring them to the launch site at Eilat where Reynald was besieging the town.

May: Saladin captures Amida (Diyarbakir) and thus ensures the support of the Artukids of Mardin.

Mid-May: On the march to Aleppo, the last of its perimeter forts at Tell Khalid and Aintab surrender to Saladin.

May 21–June 11: Saladin besieges Aleppo. After its surrender he is generous in his treatment of his former opponents.

June 22: The Aleppan garrison at Harim repudiates its commander and surrenders to Saladin.

Sept.: Andronikos I Komnenos crowned co-emperor (–1185) with Alexios II, who was murdered shortly afterwards.

Sept. 29: Saladin crosses the Jordan at Baisan, but fails to bring the field army of the Kingdom of Jerusalem to battle. The field army, numbering 1,300 knights and 15,000 foot soldiers, was perhaps the largest force ever assembled by the kingdom. Its presence forced Saladin to withdraw. Despite this success Guy had been unable to gain the support of the barons on campaign with him. Baldwin IV saw it as proof of the unfitness of Guy of Lusignan to be the next king of Jerusalem.

Nov.-Dec.: Saladin unsuccessfully besieges the castle of Kerak, crowded with guests for the wedding of Humphrey IV of Toron and the king's half-sister Isabel. A relieving army led by Baldwin IV forces Saladin to withdraw.

Nov.: Baldwin IV removes Guy from the executive regency, denies his rights of succession and tries to bring about a divorce with Sybilla on the grounds that he had forced her to marry Guy when she was in fact still betrothed to Hugh of Burgundy.

Nov. 20: Baldwin V, aged five, crowned and anointed co-king.

Dec: Guy goes to Ascalon and summons Sibylla to join him. From there he defies the king and his council.

Saladin orders the construction of the castle at Ajlun (Qalàat ar-Rabadh) to check crusader attacks from Belvoir castle just across the Jordan valley. It remains a rare surviving example of a wholly Islamic castle (see 1260, 1262).

Joannes Kinnamos, *Chronikai,* **details the reigns of John and Manuel Komnenos for the years 1118–76, with material on the Second Crusade and the Byzantine protectorate over the crusader states.**

1184

June: Heraclius, patriarch of Jerusalem, together with Arnold of Toroge and Roger of les Moulins, respectively master of the Templars and master of the Hospitallers, is sent to Europe to solicit help for the kingdom.

Aug. 23–Sept. 5: Second unsuccessful siege of Kerak; Saladin has brought together a large army composed of troops from all his new territories but is forced to withdraw by a relieving army, again with Baldwin IV present.

Sept. 7–10: As he withdraws to Damascus Saladin raids in Samaria. Maria Komnene defends Nablus; Sebaste buys immunity by releasing some Muslim prisoners; the Templar estates at Zarin are wrecked.

Sept.: Heraclius' mission arrives at Brindisi.

Oct.: Heraclius' mission meets with Pope Lucius III at Verona. The Templar Arnold of Toroge dies there.

Guy of Lusignan attacks the Bedouins of Darum. The Bedouins were under royal protection, and this attack was seen as further proof of his unsuitability to rule in the east.

Izz ad-Din approaches the atabeg of Persia for support against Saladin. He also allied with the atabeg of Azerbaijan for an attack on Irbil.

Four-year truce agreed with Raymond III of Tripoli.

Cyprus rebels against Byzantine rule.

George IV of Georgia dies; succeeded by his daughter Thamar.

Danish missionaries begin work in Latvia (BC).

William of Tyre, *Historia rerum in partibus transmarinis gestarum,* **an analytical history (with some shaky dating) of the crusades and the crusader states in the period 1095–1184, written in part by an insider.**

1185

Severe drought in Palestine limits military activity.

Jan.: Patriarch Heraclius' mission meets with Philip I in Paris.

Early.: As Baldwin IV is clearly dying, arrangements are made for the succession. Raymond III of Tripoli is appointed regent until Baldwin V comes of age in ten years. Joscelin of Courtenay is to be the guardian of the boy-king and all royal castles are to be placed in the hands of the military orders. Should Baldwin V die before then the Pope and the principal monarchs of Western Europe are to choose between Amalric's daughters Sibylla and Isabel. Raymond is granted Beirut to help defer his expenses.

Feb.: Heraclius' mission meets with Henry II at Reading.

Mar. 18: Heraclius speaks before a royal council at Clerkenwell, London, on the needs of the Holy Land. The discouraging response from this mission relayed to Jerusalem.

Apr./May (before May 16): Baldwin IV dies, aged 23, to be succeeded by his nephew Baldwin V.

Spring: Saladin arranges a four-year truce with the Kingdom of Jerusalem and Raymond III of Tripoli. Until May 1186 he campaigns in Iraq to complete the conquest of the lands of Nur ed-Din.

June: William II of Sicily captures Corfu and Dyrrachium (Durazzo) from the Byzantines.

Aug. 6-Mid–Nov.: Normans from Sicily attack, plunder and occupy Thessalonika, the second city of the Byzantine Empire.

Sept.: In Constantinople Andronikos I Komnenos replaced in a palace coup by Isaac II Angelos (–1195). The Normans are defeated at Mosynopolis.

Eustathios, archbishop of Thessalonika, *On the Capture of Thessalonika*, describes the depredations of the Normans in this year.

1186

Mar. 4: Izz ad-Din of Mosul acknowledges Saladin as his overlord and promises to supply military support when called upon to do so.

May 23: Saladin is in Damascus.

Late summer: Death of Baldwin V, aged nine, at Acre.

Sibylla and Guy, using their presence in Jerusalem for the young king's funeral, seize the crown in Jerusalem, outmanoeuvring a coup by Raymond III of Tripoli who had withdrawn to Nablus after the young king's death.

July 20/Aug./mid–Sept.: Coronation of Sibylla and Guy.

Oct.: Humphrey of Toron does homage to Guy, as king and thus prevents any attempts to proclaim his wife Isabel, Sibylla's half-sister, as counter-queen. Baldwin of Ibelin and Raymond of Tripoli refuse homage to Guy, who marches against Raymond's fief of Tiberias. Raymond admits Saladin's troops to Tiberias and Guy withdraws.

Bulgarians declare independence of Byzantine rule and raid in Thrace in alliance with the Cumans.

Hospitallers acquire the castle of Margat, which they rebuild on concentric lines.

1187

Early: Reynald of Châtillon captures a caravan going from Cairo to Damascus; despite the truce he refuses to return it. Legend is in error in placing Saladin's sister amongst the captives.

Mar. 14: Saladin bases himself at Bosra to protect caravans returning to Damascus. His troops raid the lands of Kerak and Montreal.

Apr. 26: Saladin attacks the lower town of Kerak for the third time, but lacks a siege train to attack the castle.

May 1: A force of 450 knights and sergeants, mainly Templars and Hospitallers, travelling from the Jezreel valley to Tiberias, annihilated as it attempts to intercept an Ayyubid war band of 7,000 at the springs of Cresson, east of Mount Tabor at Ain al-Jauza.

May 2: Raymond of Tripoli under censure from his barons, the Church and his wife for admitting a Muslim garrison to Tiberias. He agrees to expel the garrison and comes to terms with Guy of Lusignan in the interest of the safety of the kingdom. Garrisons throughout the kingdom are reduced to a minimum to form a field army to meet Saladin.

May 27: Muslim army begins to gather at Tell Ashtarah, whilst the army of the Kingdom of Jerusalem is ordered to muster at Sephorie.

June 26: Saladin invades the kingdom of Jerusalem with an army in excess of 20,000.

July 2: Saladin besieges Tiberias, which is defended by Raymond III's wife, Eshiva II of Galilee.

July 3: The field army of the kingdom leaves its well-watered and well-supplied camp at Sephorie (the Fountains of Saffuriyah) to relieve Tiberias. The march will take them through difficult and waterless terrain.

July 4: The field army of the Kingdom of Jerusalem is annihilated at the battle of (the Horns of) Hattin. Saladin orders the execution of captives from the international military orders and personally beheads Reynald of Châtillon. The relic of the True Cross was captured and never again came into Christian hands.

July 14: Conrad of Montferrat goes to Tyre, having nearly fallen into Muslim hands on his arrival in Acre. Unaware of the military disaster that had befallen the Christians in the East, his intention had been to escape murder charges in Constantinople by making a pilgrimage to Jerusalem.

July 5–Sept. 5.: With the destruction of the army of the Kingdom of Jerusalem all the towns and castles of the kingdom (Tiberias, Acre, Toron, Sidon, Ghibelet, Beirut, Nazareth, Caesarea, Nablus, Jaffa and Ascalon) surrender to Saladin or his generals. Unlike the other port cities Beirut was not dismantled (see 1197, 1212).

Sept. 20: Muslims begin the siege of Jerusalem.

Sept. 29: Northern wall of Jerusalem breached in almost the same spot as that made by the first crusaders in 1099.

Oct. 2: Jerusalem surrenders to Saladin.

Oct.: Joscius, archbishop of Tyre, is sent to the West by Conrad of Montferrat to ask for a new crusade.

Oct. 20: Pope Urban III dies, allegedly on hearing news of the fall of Jerusalem that was first brought to Italy by Genoese merchants.

Oct. 29: Pope Gregory VIII issues the encyclical *Audita tremendi* calling for a new crusade.

Nov. 13–Jan. 1: Saladin besieges Tyre, energetically defended by Conrad of Montferrat.

Late: Joscius tells William II of Sicily of the plight of the Holy Land. William sends a fleet in the short term and considers crusading to the East.

Late: The union of the County of Tripoli and the Principality of Antioch. Raymond III of Tripoli, who had escaped capture at Hattin, dies. With his death the Toulousain dynasty that had ruled Tripoli since 1102 ends. Raymond III bequeathed his county to his godson Raymond, heir to the principality of Antioch. Bohemond III of Antioch deputes his second son, Bohemond the One-Eyed, to become count of Tripoli.

Dec.: Diet of Strassburg: crusade preached.

1187–1260

Greek Orthodox, Jacobites, Copts and Armenians are granted chapels in the Church of the Holy Sepulchre in place of the expelled Latin clergy.

1188

Jan. 1: Saladin goes into winter quarters at Acre.

Mar. 27: The 'court of Christ' (*curia Christi*) at Mainz: continued preaching of crusade, and considerable response obtained.

Spring: Saladin returns to Damascus, leaving the isolated Frankish garrisons in the countryside to be starved into surrender. He directs his generals to capture the outlying fortifications of the principality of Antioch.

Saladin releases Guy of Lusignan from captivity on condition that Guy does not bear arms against him in the future. Guy rejoins his queen, Sibylla, at Tripoli.

July 22: Latakia captured and sacked. Antioch is now separated by land from Tripoli and Tyre.

July 29: Hospitaller castle at Sahyun captured.

Sept.: Templar castle at Baghras captured and later slighted (see 1191). Antioch surrounded.

Sept. 26: Bohemond III of Antioch agrees to an eight-month truce. In the principality of Antioch only the city itself and Marqab remain in Christian hands; in the county of Tripoli only the city of Tripoli and the Hospitaller castle at Krak des Chevaliers remain uncaptured.

Oct.: The Sicilian admiral Margarit of Brindisi, with a fleet sent by William II of Sicily, succours Tyre, Tripoli and Antioch.

Nov.: Garrison at Kerak surrenders.

Dec. 6: Garrison at Safad surrenders.

Dec.: Diet of Nuremberg, at which ambassadors from Serbia, Byzantium and the Seljuk Turks of Konya bring news of markets and facilities on the projected route of the German crusade.

Saladin sends samples of Chinese porcelain to Damascus; this is the first record of Chinese porcelain in the Middle East.

Meinhard, an Augustinian monk from Segeberg in Holstein, begins missionary work amongst the Liv. He travels eastward with a group of Lübeck merchants eager to open up contact with Russia along the valley of the Duna (BC).

Giraldus Cambrensis, *Itinerarium Cambriae*, gives details of the preaching of the Third Crusade by Baldwin, archbishop of Canterbury, in Wales and the response to it.

1189

Jan. 5: Belvoir surrenders.

Jan. 22: Joscius meets with Henry II, Philip I, and Philip, count of Flanders, at Gisors to discuss peace terms. All three take the cross.

Feb.: At Le Mans Henry II orders the levying of the 'Saladin Tithe' on income and movable goods to pay for his crusade.

Spring: A Danish and Frisian fleet on its way to the Holy Land calls at Lisbon and captures Alvor (SC).

Apr.: German crusade army gathers at Regensburg.

May 11: German army sets out to march to Constantinople.

May: Garrison at Krak de Montreal surrenders. Of the former Kingdom of Jerusalem only the port of Tyre and the castle at Belfort remain under European control

May 11: Frederick Barbarossa leaves Regensburg (Ratisbon) to march to the Holy Land.

Mid-June: German ambassadors in Constantinople notice the presence there of ambassadors from Saladin. Isaac I Angelos imprisons the German ambassadors and gives their horses and equipment as gifts to Saladin's ambassadors. Rumours of Isaac's hostility to the crusade are thereby confirmed.

July 6: Henry II dies at Chinon.

Aug.: Guy of Lusignan marches to Tyre with a small army, but is refused admission by Conrad of Montferrat who does not recognise his right to be king. He marches along the coast to Acre, covered by a Pisan fleet.

Aug. 26: Guy begins the siege of Acre.

Sept. 1: Sives surrenders to a fleet of thirty-seven ships from England and Germany that has campaigned in Portugal on its way to the Holy Land (see 1191)(SC).

Sept.: Fleets arrive from northern Europe and reinforce Guy.

Late Sept.: Conrad of Montferrat is forced by his barons to assist Guy at Acre. Their arrival forces Saladin into winter quarters some 10 miles off.

Nov. 18: Death of William II of Sicily, with no direct heirs. Henry VI declares that Sicily reverts to him by right of his wife Constance.

Nov. 22: Frederick Barbarrossa takes up winter quarters at Adrianople. Raiding takes place throughout Thrace because of the detention of Frederick's ambassadors.
    Frederick considers an attack on Constantinople.

Hugo Falcandus, *Historia de rebus gestis in Siciliae regno*, makes observations on the Second Crusade and relations with Byzantium in the period 1154–69.

1190

Jan.: An Egyptian fleet provisions and reinforces Acre from the sea.

Feb. 2: Isaac Angelos releases all Latin prisoners in Constantinople into Frederick's hands.

Mar. 18–24: German army crosses the Hellespont.

Mar. 28: German crusade begins its march across Asia Minor to Antioch.

Apr.: Fleet of 100 ships leaves England to meet up with Richard I at Marseilles at the end of July.

The Almohavid caliph, al-Mansur (1184–99), campaigns in Spain. He besieges Santarem, which is successfully defended by Sancho VI of Navarre (1150–94) and a force of English crusaders that had called at Lisbon on their way to the East (SC).

June 10: Frederick Barbarossa drowns in the Saleph River; German crusade breaks up. Saladin, who fears the designs of Queen Thamar of Georgia, sees Frederick's death as a great deliverance for Islam.

July 4: Richard I of England and Philip I of France set out on crusade from Vezelay.

July: Henry of Champagne arrives at Acre with the siege train of Philip I. Saladin is forced to withdraw from the vicinity of Acre.

July 29: Death of Queen Sibylla and her two surviving daughters from disease in the crusader camp at Acre. Since Guy of Lusignan was king by right of his wife, Conrad hopes to strengthen his position by marriage with Isabel, now the sole surviving heiress to the kingdom.

Aug. 7–9: Richard I sails from Marseilles to Genoa, where he hires more ships for his journey down the coast of Italy.

Sept. 14: Richard I arrives at Messina, where he has to gain custody of his sister Joan, the widow of William II, and secure her dowry of 20,000 ounces of gold.

Sept. 16: Philip I arrives at Messina.

Oct. 4: Messina captured and sacked. Richard gains his objectives from Tancred and quarrels with Philip I over the division of the spoils and the fate of Philip's sister Alice, betrothed to Richard since 1169.

Oct.: Remnant of German crusade led by Frederick of Swabia arrives in Acre with the bones of Frederick Barbarossa that they hope to bury in Jerusalem.

Nov.: Divorce of Isabel from Humphrey of Toron procured.

Nov. 24: Conrad of Montferrat married to Isabel, thus strengthening his claim to the crown of Jerusalem since Isabel was the only surviving child of Amalric I. Conrad was already married and the divorce was obtained on very dubious grounds.

1191

Baghras returned by Saladin to the Templars, but is occupied and rebuilt by the Armenians – much to the consternation of both Bohemond and Saladin since it controls the road from Antioch to Cilicia.

Jan. 20: Death of Frederick of Swabia; later buried in the church of the new German hospital in Acre.

Mar. 30: Philip I leaves Messina for Acre.

Apr. 10: Richard I leaves Messina with his sister Joan and his fiancée Berengaria of Navarre.

Apr. 17: Richard I in Crete.

Apr. 20: Philip I arrives at Acre and supports the claim of Conrad of Montferrat to the Kingdom of Jerusalem. Conrad now styles himself 'king-elect of Jerusalem'.

Apr. 22–May 1: Richard I at Rhodes.

May 6: Richard I arrives at Limassol.

May 11: Deputation of leading barons, led by Guy of Lusignan seeks Richard's support for his (Guy's) continued kingship of Jerusalem.

May 12: Richard I marries Berengaria of Navarre at Limassol and has her crowned queen of England.

Late May: Richard, assisted by Guy of Lusignan, conquers Cyprus from the Byzantine governor, Isaac Komnenos. Richard defeats Isaac at Tremetousha and occupies Nicosia and Kyrenia.

June 1: Philip of Flanders (see 1179) killed at the siege of Acre; his lands pass to the French crown.

June 5: Richard continues on his journey to Acre and leaves a small garrison in Cyprus.

June 6: Richard I arrives at Tyre, but Conrad refuses him entry to the city.

June 8: Richard I arrives at Acre, heralding his arrival by the capture of 'the great ship of Alexandria'.

July 1: Philip I attacks the walls of Acre.

July 3: A mine dug by Philip's engineers brings down part of the wall of Acre.

July 6: First assault by Richard I on Acre.

July 11: Another attack by the English and Pisans.

July 12: The Acre garrison surrenders on terms.

July 16: Christian churches of Acre purified by the papal legate.

July 24: Richard and Philip judge that Guy of Lusignan should remain king for the term of his life and then be succeeded by Conrad or his heirs.

July 31: Philip I sails home from Acre. Hugh III of Burgundy (see 1179–80) assumes leadership of the French army left behind.

July: The Almohad caliph, al-Mansur (1184–99), recaptures Silves (SC).

Aug.: Richard orders the massacre of 3,000 or so Muslim captives when there is a hitch in negotiations with Saladin for their ransom and the return of the True Cross.

Aug. 22: Richard I leaves Acre for Jaffa.

Sept. 5: Richard I defeats Saladin at the battle of Arsuf.

Sept. 8: Richard occupies Jaffa, the town had been evacuated and slighted by Saladin.

Sept./Oct.: Refortification of Jaffa and the fortresses in its immediate hinterland by Richard I.

Negotiations with Saladin.

Oct.: Saladin negotiates with Conrad of Montferrat to fight against Richard I.

Nov.: Leopold, duke of Austria, leaves Acre for home.

1192

Death of Kilij Arslan II, Seljuk sultan of Konya (Iconium), aged 77. His son Kai Kusraw I succeeds.

Jan.: Decision to capture Ascalon rather than Jerusalem. Hugh of Burgundy, who wished to besiege Jerusalem, withdraws to Acre. Richard I and Henry of Champagne march on Ascalon.

Jan. 20: Crusading army reaches Ascalon. It remains there until June refortifying the abandoned town.

Late Jan.: Hugh of Burgundy comes to Ascalon and quarrels with Richard I over funding for his troops.

Feb.: Hugh returns to Acre.

Apr. 16: Richard calls a council of his army. It is decided that Guy of Montferrat lacks the leadership qualities needed to be king of Jerusalem. He is to be divested of this position. Conrad of Montferrat should be crowned king of Jerusalem.

Apr. 28: Conrad of Montferrat murdered by the Assassins at Acre.

May: Guy of Lusignan gains Richard's permission to purchase Cyprus from the Templars, to whom he had sold the island. Guy leaves Acre for Cyprus, taking many dispossessed knights from the Kingdom of Jersualem with him.

May: Henry of Champagne elected king of Jerusalem and marries Conrad's widow Isabel. Henry was never crowned and does not seem to have used the title of 'king', although he remained fully in control of the kingdom until his death in 1197.

May 22: Richard captures Darum, south of Ascalon, and gives it to Henry of Champagne.

June 7–11: The march from Ascalon to Jerusalem. The army reaches Bait Nuba, 13 miles from Jerusalem.

June 21: Enrico Dandolo becomes doge of Venice.

Late June: The army withdraws to Ramla; Richard judges that his supply lines for a siege of Jerusalem would be overexposed to attack.

July 26: The army returns to Acre.

July 26–30: Saladin attacks Jaffa and captures the lower town.

July 30: Richard relieves Jaffa by sea and refortifies the town.

Aug.: Richard ill, but shows signs of recovery when he hears news that Hugh III of Burgundy has died at Acre.

Sept. 2: Three-year truce with Saladin; Ascalon is to be an open site, the Kingdom of Jerusalem is to extend from Tyre to Jaffa, and Christian pilgrims are to have access to Jerusalem and other holy sites under Muslim control. The crusader kingdom in the East is confined to a strip of land 90 miles long from north to south and 10 miles wide.

Sept. 29: Joan and Berengaria leave Acre for France.

Oct. 9: Richard I began his journey home by ship from Acre; the Third Crusade had ended.

Oct. 30: At Beirut, Bohemond III of Antioch signs a ten-year truce with Saladin covering the territories of both Antioch and Tripoli. Bohemond omitted his vassal Leon of Armenia because the Armenians had occupied the Templar castle of Baghras and refused to surrender it (see 1188 and 1191).

Dec. 21: Richard I arrested by Leopold, duke of Austria, near Vienna and kept at the castle of Durnstein on the Danube.

Richard of Devizes, *Chronicon de rebus gestis Ricardi Primi*, records the Third Crusade.

1193

Mar. 4: Death of Saladin at Damascus aged about 54. The family disputes that ensue effectively prevent the Ayyubids from taking major offensive action against the Kingdom of Jerusalem for the rest of the 1190s.

Mar.: Richard I handed over to Emperor Henry VI at Speyer. Richard is accused of betraying the Holy Land, complicity in the death of Conrad of Monterrat and breaking trust with the emperor. Richard agrees to pay a ransom of 100,000 marks and supply fifty galleys and 200 knights for one year for the emperor's service.
  Death of the Assassin leader Rashid ad-Din.

1194

Feb. 4: Richard I released from captivity into the custody of his mother Eleanor of Aquitaine at Mainz.

Early: Leon II captures Bohemond III of Antioch and his family at Baghras, having made false overtures for negotiations about the castle. He brings them to Sis, where he persuades Bohemond to surrender Antioch in return for his and his family's freedom. Roused by their clergy the Greeks and Latins in Antioch reject this accord, recognise Raymond as ruler pending his father's release, and send to Henry for help.

Spring: Henry goes to Sis and negotiates the release of Bohemond III: Leon's independence of Antioch is recognised, Baghras and its territory is conceded to him and a marriage between his niece Alice and Bohemond's son Raymond is arranged.
  Whilst returning from Antioch to Acre it is alleged by some fourteenth-century writers, like Marino Sanudo Torsello, that Henry of Champagne visited the Syrian Assassins at al-Kahf, where the Ismaili guards were said to throw themselves from the battlements at the orders of the dai Abu Mansur bin Muhammud.

May: Death of Guy of Lusignan in Cyprus. His younger brother Amalric (Amaury) is summoned from Jaffa to succeed him. Guy's death strengthens Henry of Champagne's position in that it removes a potential rival for the Kingdom of Jerusalem. Henry and Amalric arrange close ties based around the projected marriage of Amalric's three sons (Guy, John and Hugh) with the daughters of Queen Sybilla (Maria of Montfort, and Alice and Phillipa of Champagne).

1195

(? Date): Marriage of Raymond of Antioch and Alice of Armenia. Bohemond III hopes that any son of this marriage will inherit a unified and Latinised Antioch and Armenia.

Apr.: Henry VI takes the cross at Bari and summons his subjects to enrol for a crusade. Diplomatic missions sent to Constantinople demanding a Byzantine financial contribution to the proposed crusade.

Apr. 8: Isaac II Angelos deposed and blinded by his brother Alexios III Angelos (–1203).

July 19: Al-Mansur defeats Alfonso VIII of Castile at Alarcos. This catastrophic defeat opened the way for the possible Muslim reconquest of Toledo and the upper Tagus valley. Al-Mansur accepts a truce and withdraws to Seville (SC).

Aug. 1: Pope Celestine III issues an appeal for a new crusade aimed at Germany.

Oct.: Emissaries from Almaric of Cyprus arrive at the diet of Gelhausen asking Henry to crown him king in return for his acknowledgement of Henry's suzerainty. Henry agrees. A similar embassy arrives from Leon II of Cilician Armenia.

Dec.: Henry in Worms cathedral witnessing the taking of the cross by many of his subjects.

1196

Mar.: Diet of Wurzburg finalises arrangements for the German crusade.

Apr. 25: Death of Alfonso II of Aragon (SC).

July: Saladin's brother al-Adil takes control of Egypt.

Ambroise of Evreux, *L'Estoire de la guerre sainte*, a verse account in Old French of the Third Crusade.

Ephraim of Bonn, *Emek habacha*, details the persecution of the Jews in England, France and Germany in the second half of the twelfth century.

1197

Alexios III imposes the "Alamanikon", or German tax, to raise the crusade contribution demanded by Henry VI. Due to the latter's sudden death the money collected is never handed over.

(?) On the early death of his son Raymond of Antioch, Bohemond III sends his widow Alice and her son Raymond Roupen back to Leon II in Armenia.

Spring: Al-Mansur ravages the Tagus valley and negotiates a ten-year truce with the Christian kings of Spain, effectively accepting the Christian frontier on the line of the Tagus (SC).

Mar.–Sept.: German crusaders leave the ports of southern Italy for Acre.

Early Sept.: Jaffa captured by al-Adil. Its defender, Reynald Barlais, is charged with negligence.

Sept. 10: Henry of Champagne killed in an accidental fall from his window in Acre. The crown is offered to Amalric of Lusignan. Henry's county of Champagne passes to his younger brother Thibaut.

Sept.: The imperial chancellor, Bishop Conrad of Hildesheim, crowns Amalric of Lusignan king of Cyprus in Nicosia. Amalric acknowledges the suzerainty of the German emperor.

Mid-Sept. (?): Stephanie of Mily regains her castle of Jubail from its Muslim governor by bribery.

Sept. 22: German army musters at Acre.

Sept. 28: Henry VI, aged 31, dies at Messina leaving an infant son, the future Frederick II.

Sept.–Oct.: Germans, under Henry of Lorraine, capture Bostron, Sidon and Beirut. By 1200 John of Ibelin (d. 1236) has become lord of Beirut.
   Bohemond III reoccupies Latakia and Jabala (Jubail), both having been razed and indefensible.

Oct.: Almaric I, king of Cyprus, is elected king of Jerusalem. His wife Eschiva of Ibelin had recently died and so he is free to marry Henry's widow Isabel.

Nov. 28–Feb. 2: Siege of Toron.

1198

Early: Bohemond of Tripoli enters Antioch and seeks to be acclaimed as prince in the place of his aged father Bohemond III; an Armenian force led by Leon II effects Bohemond III's restoration.

Jan.: Almaric arrives in Acre, marries Isabel, and together they are crowned as king and queen of Jerusalem. He becomes Amalric II of Jerusalem and I of Cyprus. Although he spends much of his time in Acre he is clear that the resources of Cyprus should be kept distinct from those of his new kingdom.

Jan. 6: The imperial chancellor crowns Leon II, the first Roupenid king of Armenia, at Tarsus.The rulers of Cilician Armenia have thus declared their independence of the principality of Antioch (see 1193 and 1194) and also marked a distinction between Cilician and Greater Armenia, the former Armenian homeland in north-east Turkey.

Jan. 8: Election of Lothario dei Conti di Segni as Pope Innocent III.

Feb. 2: Siege at Toron abandoned when news of the death of Henry VI arrives.

July 1: German crusaders, now eager to return home, make a truce with the Muslims confirming the occupation of Sidon and Beirut; the whole coastline from Antioch to just south of Acre (but not Jaffa) is now in western hands.

Aug. 15: Innocent III proclaims a new (the Fourth) crusade.

Bishop Berthold of the Livs, the former Cistercian abbot of Loccum near Bremen, is killed in battle with the Livonians. Archbishop Hartwig II of Bremen appoints his nephew, Albert of Buxhövden, bishop in Berthold's place (BC).

1199

Apr. 6: death of Richard I, aged 42, at Chalus-Chabrol.

Oct. 5: Innocent III authorises the Livonian crusade to be preached in north Germany to defend the nascent Livonian church (BC).

Nov. 28: Thibaut of Champagne and Louis of Blois take the cross for the Fourth Crusade at the tournament at Ecry. They are followed in this by many of their vassals and others. Many of those taking the cross have impressive crusading antecedents: Thibaut's brother was Henry of Champagne.

Innocent III authorises a tax of one-fortieth for one year on clerical incomes to finance the crusade. This is the first tax of the clergy imposed by a pope and the first financial measure taken by the papacy to support crusading.

Michael the Syrian, Jacobite patriarch of Antioch. His Syriac *Chronicle from the Creation to 1196* contains some material on the First Crusade.

1200

Feb. 22: Baldwin of Flanders and his wife Marie, the sister of Henry and Thibaut, take the cross at Bruges.

Feb.: Saladin's brother al-Adil ('Saphet' to the crusaders) captures Cairo and proclaims himself sultan, thus restoring some unity in Muslim Egypt and Syria, this having been lost at Saladin's death.

Early spring: Albert of Buxhövden leads a fleet of twenty-three ships to the mouth of the Dvina River and begins the Baltic crusade preached in 1199 (BC).

Spring: Crusading leaders meet at Soissons.

June (?): Discussions at Compiègne; decided it is to go by sea to the East, to recapture Jerusalem by attacking Egypt as their secret target and to appoint six envoys to arrange shipping with the Venetians.

Aug. 4: The Abbasid caliph al-Nasir (1180–1225) confirms al-Adil in his title. The two surviving sons of Saladin occupy Aleppo and Samosata.

Albert of Buxhövden makes Riga the centre of his new Livonian diocese, building up the cult of 'Our Lady of Riga' and developing elaborate plans for the subjugation of the pagans to involve annual expeditions and a new military order (see 1202) (BC).

Anon., *Le Livre au Roi*, the earliest account of the laws and customs of the Kingdom of Jerusalem (see also 1257 and 1265).

Anon., *Les Assises D'Antioche*, surviving only in an Armenian translation (date approx.).

1201

Apr.: The treaty of Venice is agreed between the six envoys and the Venetians. The doge, Enrico Dandolo, plays a principal part in these negotiations. The Venetians will provide transports and supplies for 33,500 men in return for 85,000 marks. Venetians and crusaders will share any conquests equally. The army will assemble in Venice in April 1202.

Bohemond III of Antioch dies. The succession to the principality will be in dispute until 1219. His younger son, Bohemond of Tripoli, gains recognition as prince backed by the military orders.

Apr.–July: Leon II of Armenia besieges Antioch in the interests of the infant Raymond-Roupen. Bohemond asks support from the Aleppans, who invade Armenia and force Leon to lift the siege.

May 24: Death of Thibaut of Champagne at Troyes, aged 22.

June/July: Meeting at Soissons to discuss leadership of the projected crusade. It is decided to approach Boniface II, marquis of Montferrat, a ruler whose family has had long involvement in the crusader states and Byzantium (see 1180, 1187 and 1189–92).

Late Aug.: Boniface meets with crusade leadership at Soissons and agrees to take the leadership. He also takes the cross.

(?): At some point in 1201 Alexios (IV) the son of the deposed Isaac I Angelos, escapes to Italy and seeks refuge with his sister Irene and her husband Philip of Swabia at Hagenau. He begins to seek western backing for the restoration of his father to the Byzantine throne and the ousting of the usurper Alexios III.

1202

Spring: Leon II renews hostilities with Antioch. Some crusaders who had arrived early at Acre fight for Bohemond IV.

Renaud of Dampierre, Henry of Arzillières and Geoffrey of Villehardouin, the nephew of the chronicler, by-pass Venice and go to Apulia to take ship for the Holy Land. On arrival they take service with Bohemond IV on a raid into Aleppan territory. Renard is captured and remains a prisoner until late 1233.

July–Sept.: Some 12,000 of the projected 33,500 arrive in Venice; the proposal to move eastward as one crusading army is stillborn. Many go east from other ports, and the crusade is 34,000 marks short in the money owed to the Venetians. Dandolo proposes the attack on Zara as a means to postpone the payment of the debt, to keep the crusade together, and to save his own reputation. His proposal is accepted and Dandolo takes the cross. The papal legate Peter of Capuano is rejected as legate and sent back to Rome, where he tells Pope Innocent of the crusade's intentions.

Oct. 1: The fleet leaves Venice for Zara. Innocent III forbids the crusaders to attack any Christian city, and Zara in particular.

Nov. 11: Crusade army lands at Zara. Simon of Montfort and Guy of Vaux de Cernay, the Cistercian abbot, oppose the attack on Zara and withdraw from the camp. Simon makes his way to Syria via Hungary; six years later he will take a leading role in the Albigensian crusade.

Nov. 24: Zara surrenders to the Venetians and their crusade allies.

Mid-Dec.: Boniface of Montferrat joins the crusading forces in winter quarters at Zara. The bishops in the crusading army absolve all those who had incurred the ban of excommunication by attacking Zara despite the Pope's letter forbidding it, and Boniface writes to Innocent III asking for confirmation of this and excusing the action of the crusaders. The Pope concurs, but insists that the Venetians shall remain excommunicated because of their treatment of the legate Peter of Capuano. This latter decision is not announced in the crusader camp.

Late-Dec.: Envoys from Alexios (IV) arrive at Zara with the proposal to re-endow the crusade to the sum of 200,000 marks, provision the crusade for a year, and provide troops to crusade in the Holy Land and a garrison of 500 men for Jerusalem. Albert of Buxhövden establishes the order of the Livonian Sword Brothers at the centre of his Episcopal household. It is also known as the Brothers of the Militia of Christ. Their task is to conquer the heathen so that missionaries might do their work. Between 1202 and 1209 the Livs and the Letts are subjugated, and those who are Christianised join in expeditions against their erstwhile pagan neighbours (BC).

1203

Apr.: Crusading fleet leaves Zara for Constantinople, calling at Dyryachium and Corfu. Boniface and Dandolo await Alexios at Zara before rejoining the expedition at Corfu.

May: Dissension in the crusading army at Corfu regarding the diversion to Constantinople. Alexios succeeds in persuading those who wish to go direct to the Holy Land to remain with the army until September.

May 24: Fleet sails from Corfu, via Chalkis, to Constantinople.

June 24: Crusading army disembarks at Chalcedon and marches towards Constantinople via Scutari.

June: Innocent III writes to Boniface of Montferrat ordering him to make known the excommunication of the Venetians and banning any proposed attack on Constantinople; the crusading army has already left Zara.

July 6: The crusading army captures the water tower at Galata, securing one end of the huge chain that protected the harbour of the Golden Horn. The Venetian fleet forces an entry to the Golden Horn and thereby secures a safe anchorage.

July 17: First attack on Constantinople; the Venetians capture twenty-four towers on the sea wall but are forced to withdraw as the crusade army appears to be attacked. Alexios III withdraws without driving home his attack and during the night flees Constantinople. During the fighting the Venetians start a fire to defend themselves that gets out of control and burns 125 hectares of the city, making many homeless.

July 18: Isaac II Angelos (–1204) is restored and agrees to the terms made with the crusading army by his son Alexios.

July 19: Crusading army takes up quarters in the Jewish quarter of Estanor in Pera.

Aug. 1: Alexios IV Angelos (–1204) crowned co-emperor with his father at crusader insistence. He pays 100,000 marks to the crusaders. He and his patriarch, John X Kamateros, acknowledge Roman primacy in a letter to Innocent III.

Aug. 19: In an attempt to burn the Mitaton mosque crusaders start the second fire at Constantinople; it destroys over 182 hectares of buildings, including the mansion of the historian Niketas Choniates.

Late-Aug.: Letter from the crusade leadership to Pope Innocent III justifying their actions and announcing their plan to proceed to Egypt in the spring of 1204.

Summer: Hoping to settle matters before the anticipated arrival of the crusading army from the West, Amalric persuades both sides to put the question of the rulership of Antioch to arbitration by a committee chaired by the papal legate Soffredo. Delays ensue, with Bohemond IV unwilling to abide by the arbiters' decision.

Nov. 11: While Bohemond IV is absent in Tripoli dealing with a baronial revolt led by Renart of Nephin, Leon II enters Antioch; he is resisted by the inhabitants, strengthened by the Templars.

Dec.: Leon forced to withdraw by another Aleppan incursion into Armenia.

1204

Jan. 25: A meeting of nobles, civil servants and people in the Hagia Sophia declares the end of rule by the Angeloi and elects Nicholas Kanabos emperor.

Isaac II either dies of shock or is murdered. The inexperienced Kanabos spends his time in the Hagia Sophia supported by the lower classes.

Feb. 8: Kanabos imprisoned and Alexios IV murdered by the anti-Latin Alexios V. Dukas Murtzouphlos becomes emperor (–Dec. 1204).

Mar.: Pact between crusaders and Venetians aimed to maintain unity, acknowledging their desperate situation and for the first time agreeing to capture Constantinople.

Apr. 9: Second attack on Constantinople; crusaders repulsed.

Apr. 10–11: Expulsion of prostitutes from the crusader camp and period of repentence.

Apr. 12: Crusader army captures Constantinople. Alexios V flees, as does Constantine (XI) Laskaris, who sets up a new Greek empire around Nicaea.

Apr. 13–15: Crusaders sack Constantinople.

May 16: Baldwin, count of Flanders and Hainault, crowned as Latin emperor of Constantinople.

May: Alexios I Komnenos (–1222), grandson of Andronikos I, seizes Trebizond with the backing of Thamara of Georgia and sets up a new Greek empire.

With crusading forces present in Acre, Amalric raids Fuwah in the Nile delta.

Bohemond IV of Antioch pays homage to Mary of Flanders whose husband Baldwin has been elected Latin emperor of Constantinople. She has travelled by sea from Flanders to Acre expecting to meet her husband there.

June–Aug.: Baldwin I subdues Thrace as far as Adrianople and captures Thessalonika.

Aug.: Boniface of Montferrat sells Crete to the Venetians for 1,000 marks.

Sept.–Oct.: Committee of twenty-four partitions the Byzantine Empire along the lines agreed in March.

Sept.: Realisation that the crusade preached in 1198 will not bring substantial reinforcement to Acre. Almaric negotiates a six-year truce with al-Adil; Sidon and Lydda are conceded to the Franks and Jaffa returned to them.

Oct.?: Many crusaders – like Geoffrey of Villehardouin, the future prince of Achaea – return to Constantinople on hearing of the opportunities opened up by the capture of the city.

Nov.: Boniface of Montferrat conquers Boeotia and Attica.

Nov.: Thierry of Loos captures Alexios V.

Nov./Dec.: James of Avesnes conquers Euboea, whilst Boniface begins the sieges of Akrokorinth and Nauplia.

Dec.: Alexios V tried for treason and executed by being flung from the Column of Theodosios, Constantinople.

Late: Bohemond IV loses an eye in battle when Ralph of Nephin attacks Tripoli. Innocent III authorises any who had taken a crusading vow to go to Jerusalem, but could not afford it, to crusade in the Baltic instead (BC).

1205

Apr. 1: Death of Amalric II after an illness caused by eating too much white mullet. His infant son by Isabel had died on February 2. The Kingdom of Cyprus passed to Hugh I, his six-year-old son by Eschiva of Ibelin, whilst Queen Isabella ruled the Kingdom of Jerusalem.

Spring: Campaign to conquer the Morea led by William of Champlitte and Geoffrey of Villehardouin, the nephew, gets underway, leaving Boniface of Montferrat to continue his siege.

Apr.: Latins abandon conquests in Thrace and in Asia Minor in the face of fierce opposition by Kalojan of Bulgaria and Theodore Laskaris.

Apr. 14: Latin emperor Baldwin I defeated and captured by Kalojan near Adrianople.

May: Victory at the battle of Koundoura in Messenia virtually completes the Latin conquest of the Morea.

June 1: Death of Enrico Dandolo in Constantinople. He is buried in the Hagia Sophia.

Nov. 19: William of Champlitte first recorded as prince of Achaea.

Nov.: Peter II of Aragon (1196–1213) tries to impose a property tax, the *montaticum*, on his barons to pay for a crusade against the Muslims of Valencia. He meets substantial opposition and is unable to campaign for a further five years (SC).

Late (?): Isabel of Jerusalem dies, leaving five daughters by her three marriages: Maria of Montferrat, Alice and Philippa of Champagne, and Sybilla and Melisende of Lusignan. The eldest, Maria of Montferrat (aged 13), succeeded to the throne with John of Ibelin as regent.

Michael I Komnenos Doukas (d. 1215), a cousin of Isaac II Angelos and Alexios III, establishes the third Greek successor state to Byzantium at Arta in Epiros.

Gunther of Pairis, *Hystoria Constantinopolitana*, deals with the Fourth Crusade, and in particular with the relic hunting of Abbot Martin of Pairis to whose finds the book provides a sort of provenance.

1206

July: The death of the first Latin emperor of Constantinople, Baldwin of Flanders, in Bulgarian captivity, reported in Constantinople.

Aug. 20: Coronation of Baldwin's brother Henry of Flanders as Latin emperor.

Niketas Choniates, *Chronike diegesis,* **is the most important source for Greek–Latin relations in the period 1118–1206, with graphic details of the assault on Constantinople in 1203/4 and the setting up of the Latin Empire of Constantinople.**

1207

Spring: Marco Sanudo leads a coalition of Venetian nobles to conquer the Aegean islands. He sets himself up as Duke of Naxosand and agrees to hold the duchy as a vassal of the Latin emperor. Other members of the expedition hold their islands from Duke Marco.

May 29: Innocent III confirms the excommunication of Raymond VI of Toulouse.

Sept. 4: Boniface of Montferrat killed by Bulgarians near Mosynopolis. His infant son Demetrios becomes king of Thessalonika.

Oct. 8: Death of Kalojan, emperor of the Bulgarians.
   Kai Kusraw of Konya captures Alanya and secures a port for the Seljuks of Rum; potential area of dispute with the Kingdom of Cyprus.

Nov. 17: Innocent III urges Philip II to take military action against the heretics of the Languedoc.

1208

Jan. 15: Murder of the papal legate Peter of Castelnau on the banks of the Rhône, near Arles; this murder is seen in Rome as a direct challenge to papal authority on the part of the Cathars.

Apr.: Theodore I Laskaris crowned as Greek emperor at Nicaea.

Nov. 17: Innocent III appeals to the nobles of northern France to take military action against the Albigensian heretics. About the same time he taxes the French Church to support the military action against the Albigensians (see 1179).
   Florent, bishop of Acre, and Aymar, lord of Caesarea, sent to Philip I of France to ask him to nominate a husband for Maria.
   Hugh of Cyprus marries his stepsister Alice of Champagne, as arranged in 1194.

Dec.: Henry of Flanders marches to Thessalonika to enforce his overlordship and give support to Demetrios and his regent mother.

Saxo Grammaticus, *Historia Danorum*, with first mention of Hamlet (Amleth), Prince of Denmark.

1209

May 1–2: Parliament of Ravennika, near Lamia: Henry of Flanders is acknowledged as overlord of Greece. This is followed by a week-long progress to Thebes and Negroponte.

June 18: Raymond VI of Toulouse reconciled with the Church and takes the cross against the heretics in his lands.

July 22: Capture and sack of Beziers with great loss of life amongst the inhabitants.

Aug. 1–15: Siege and capture of Carcassone. Simon of Montfort, earl of Leicester, is elected leader of the crusade, although many knights now leave the army having completed their forty-days of military service.

Late: Thamar of Georgia captures Kars from the Turks.

Anon., *Gesta Innocentii Tertii*.

1210

Hugh I assumes kingship of Cyprus on reaching the age of 15.

Spring: Philip II of France nominates John of Brienne, a knight from Champagne, as husband for Maria of Montferrat. Both Philip II and Innocent III contribute 40,000 silver pounds to make him more acceptable to the barons of the Kingdom of Jerusalem.

May 2: Concordat of Ravennika attempts to settle the position of the Latin Church in the Latin empire of Constantinople

Summer: Peter II of Aragon extends his frontier south-west of Teruel by capturing Ademuz and Sertella (SC).

July: Negotiations to renew the truce between the kingdom and al-Adil stalled to await the arrival of the new king.

Sept. 13: John of Brienne arrives at Acre.

Sept. 14: John and Maria are married.

Oct. 3: Coronation of John and Maria at Tyre. Tyre now becomes the city for the coronations of the kings of Jerusalem.

Citadel at Tyre rebuilt.

Wolfram von Eschenbach, *Parzival*, is a free adaptation of Chrétien of Troyes' unfinished Grail legend. Much of the story takes place in Baldag

(Baghdad), with a positive view of Muslim values and an appeal to end the hatred between Christians and Muslims.

1211

Spring: Naval raid by the Templars and some knights from the kingdom on Damietta.

Oct. 15: Henry of Flanders/Constantinople defeats Theodore Laskaris on the Sangarios River and occupies Pergamon.

1212

All western merchants in Alexandria are arrested. They are said to number 3,000.

July: Five-year truce between the kingdom and al-Adil.

John sends emissaries to Innocent III to arrange a new crusade when the truce ends.

Queen Maria dies giving birth to Isabella ('Yolanda' in the western sources). John, who was king in right of his wife, now becomes regent for his daughter.

July 16: Alfonso VIII of Castille, Sancho VII of Navarre and Peter II of Aragon defeat the Muslims at Las Navas de Tolosa. In central Spain the Christian frontier is advanced to the Guadelquivar River, within striking distance of Cordoba and Granada. Almohad power in Spain is now on the decline. News of the victory occasioned great rejoicing in Rome where Innocent III linked it with successes against the schismatic Greeks and the heretic Cathars (SC).

Autumn: Simon of Montfort surrounds Toulouse.

Late: Death of Thamar the Great, queen of Georgia. Her son George IV (–1223) succeeds her.

John of Ibelin (d. 1236) completes the refortification of Beirut, apparently from his own resources.

Arnold of Lübeck's continuation of Helmhold's chronicle to 1209 (see 1171).

Wolfram von Eschenbach's, *Wilhelm* is another tale involving Saracens in which their bravery and chivalry are praised. It contains an appeal for peace and understanding between 'all men who speak the seventy-two languages'. This, like *Parzival*, reflects an awareness of a wider world that is not all Christian (see 1210).

1213

Apr. 19–29: Innocent III proclaims the Fifth Crusade in the encyclical *Quia maior*. The new crusade was linked to the forthcoming Church council. Crusading

90

vows might be be commuted and the crusade indulgence for Spain and Provence was suspended.

Sept. 12: Simon of Montfort defeats and kills Peter II of Aragon, attempting to relieve Toulouse, at the battle of Muret. Simon controls most of the county of Toulouse, but Innocent's proclamation seriously weakens his supply of recruits.

Geoffrey of Villehardouin, *De la Conquête de Constantinople*, is the prime source for the Fourth Crusade, 1198–1207, written by a participant and organiser.

Peter of Les Vaux-de-Cernay, *Historia Albigensis*.

1214

John de Brienne marries Leon II's daughter Rita (Stephanie).

1215

Jan. 8: Simon of Montfort elected lord of Languedoc by his supporters at Montpelier; this represents the height of Simon's power in southern France.

July 25: Frederick II crowned king of Germany by Siegfried, archbishop of Mainz, in Aachen cathedral. At the same time Frederick takes the cross. There will be repeated delays in the fulfilment of his vow, eventually leading to his excommunication in 1227.

Nov. 11–30: Fourth Lateran Council sets out the planning and logistics for the Fifth Crusade, imposes the first tithe on clerical incomes, and orders that Jews should wear distinctive clothing to be laid down by the communities in which they belong. The Fifth Crusade is set to depart on 1 June 1217, and a tax of 1/20 for three years is imposed on clerical incomes to support the crusade (see also 1199).

Dec.: Treaty between Henry of Flanders and Theodore Laskaris of Nicaea.
    Michael I Doukas of Epiros dies. He is succeeded by his half-brother Theodore, who assumes the title 'Despot of Epiros'. He captures parts of Macedonia from the Bulgarians, recaptures much of Thessaly from the Franks, and threatens the Kingdom of Thessalonika.

1216

June 11: Death of Henry of Flanders, Latin emperor of Constantinople, at Thessalonika.

July 16: Death of Pope Innocent III.

July 18: Electon of Cencio Savelli as Pope Honorius III.

Aug. 24: Raymond VI captures Beaucaire and inflicts the first reverse on the Albigensian crusaders.

Robert of Clari, *La Conquête de Constantinople*, gives an account of the Fourth Crusade up to April 1205 by an eyewitness and participant.

Henry of Valenciennes, *Histoire de l'Empereur Henri de Constantinople*, continues Villehardouin's history (see 1213) from 1207–16.

1217

Spring: Thoedore Doukas, despot of Epiros, captures Peter of Courtenay, the Latin emperor of Constantinople elect, on his way to Constantinople along the Via Egnatia. His wife Yolanda, acts as regent in Constantinople.

Sept.: Raymond VI occupies Toulouse.

Sept. 25: Afonso of Portugal defeats the Muslims at Alcazar do Sal. He is substantially assisted by the crews of 300 ships from Germany and Frisia on their way to the Holy Land (SC).

Nov.: First contingents of the Fifth Crusade led by Andrew, king of Hungary, and Leopold VI of Austria capture and sack Baisan.

Nov. 29–Dec. 7: Unsuccessful siege of the Muslim fortress at Mount Tabor.
   Honorius III authorises a crusade against the Prussians (BC).

1218

Jan.–May: Construction of fortresses at Caesarea and Château Pèlerin (Pilgrims' Castle); the latter was garrisoned by the Templars.

Jan. 10: Death of Hugh I, king of Cyprus, succeeded by his one-year-old son Henry (–1253).

May 27: Crusading army in Syria, together with contingents from the Kingdom of Jerusalem and Cyprus, leaves Acre for Damietta.

May 29: Main force of the Fifth Crusade lands at Damietta. A few days later they are joined by the contingent from the Holy Land. John of Brienne is elected leader.

June 25: Simon of Montfort killed at the siege of Toulouse.

Aug. 1: Honorius III proclaims a new Albigensian crusade.

Aug.: Al-Mu'azzam attacks Caesarea and Pilgrims' Castle unsuccessfully. Before marching to aid Egypt he orders the dismantling of the major Muslim fortresses at Mount Tabor, Toron and Jerusalem.

Aug. 31: Death of al-Adil; his son al-Kamil rules Egypt, and his other son al Mu'azzam rules Damascus.

Sept.: Cardinal Pelagius arrives at Damietta with reinforcements. He overrules John of Brienne.

Valdemar II of Denmark invades Estonia and founds Reval (BC).

1219

Spring: Raymond, son of Raymond VI, defeats Amaury of Montfort at Basiege.

May 2: Leon II of Armenia dies. He designates his infant daughter Isabel as his heiress. Her claim is disputed both by Raymond Roupen (see 1197) and by John of Brienne in right of his wife, Rita, Leon's eldest daughter. John uses this as a reason to withdraw from the crusading army. Rita's death later in the year ends the claim of John of Brienne to Armenia.

May: Leopold of Austria returns home.

Aug. 1: The dauphin, Louis, abandons his Albigensian crusade. He was not to lead another crusade into southern France until 1226.

Late Aug.: St Francis arrives at the crusader camp and preaches before al-Kamil.

Nov. 5: Damietta falls to the crusaders. John of Brienne claims it for the Kingdom of Jerusalem, Pelagius for the Church. John is placed in charge of the city pending the arrival of Frederick II.

1220

Feb.: Genghis Khan and the Mongols take Bokhara.

Spring: Bohemond IV of Antioch recaptures Antioch from Raymond Roupen of Armenia.

Summer: An Egyptian fleet destroys a crusader fleet at Limassol.

Nov. 22: Coronation of Frederick II and Queen Constance as Holy Roman Emperor and Empress at Rome by Honorius III. Frederick takes the cross a second time.

Oliver of Paderborn, scholasticus of Cologne's, *Gesta Obsidionis Damiate* is an account of the Fifth Crusade by a particpant and an ecclesiastic active in preaching the crusade.

1221

Feb.: Mongols gain control of Georgia.

Mar. 25: Robert of Courtenay, the second son of Peter and Yolanda, crowned Latin emperor of Constantinople since his father Peter is presumed dead after his capture in 1217.

Apr.: German crusaders who took the vow in Rome leave Taranto for Damietta under the leadership of Louis of Bavaria with instructions to await Frederick's arrival.

June: Frederick sends a fleet of forty ships to Damietta commanded by Henry of Malta and Walter of Pelaer, chancellor of Sicily.
   Arrival at Damietta of Louis of Bavaria with reinforcements.

July 6: John of Brienne returns to Damietta with an army from the Kingdom of Jerusalem.

July 12: A large crusade army advances towards Cairo and occupies Fariskur.

July 20: Sharimshah occupied.

Aug. 26: Crusade army trapped by the Nile flood and cut off from Damietta by al-Kamil's troops.

Aug. 28: Pelagius negotiates terms with al-Kamil; in return for the surrender of Damietta and the evacuation of Egypt and exchange of prisoners al-Kamil promises the return of the True Cross, together with an eight-year truce to be confirmed by Frederick II.

Sept. 1: Arrival of Henry of Malta's fleet at Damietta.

Sept. 8: The army of the Fifth Crusade leaves Damietta with the fleet of Henry of Malta.

Nov.: Demetrius of Thessalonika is in Montferrat seeking military assistance for his kingdom against the Epirote Greeks.

1216–21: seven letters written by James of Vitry to numerous addresses descibe daily life in the Holy Land.

1222

May 31: Mongols defeat the Russians at the Kalka River.

June: Death of the Empress Constance. She is buried at Palermo.

June: Mongols capture of Afghanistan is marked by the massacre of the inhabitants of Herat.

Aug.: Death of Raymond VI of Toulouse; his claims are inherited by his son Raymond VII.

1223

Mar.: Meeting at Ferrentino of Pope Honorius III, Frederick II, John de Brienne, Ralph, patriarch of Jerusalem, Cardinal Pelagius and the three grandmasters of the military orders to agree the marriage of John's daughter, Isabel of Brienne, to Frederick. Frederick renews his crusading vows and a date is set for departure in June 1225.

May 20: Honorius III taxes the French clergy to pay for the Albigensian crusade.

July 14: Death of Philip II Augustus.

Aug. 6: Coronation of Louis VIII.

1224

Feb.: Aimery of Montfort surrenders all conquests made during the Albigensian crusade to Louis VIII.

Mar.: William of Montferrat assembles troops at Brindisi for the relief of Thessalonika.

Spring: John of Brienne visits France, England, Spain and Germany to rouse support for the forthcoming crusade.

May: After pilgrimage to Compostella, John of Brienne marries Berenguella, the daughter of Ferdinand III of Castile-Leon (1217–52). The latter is encouraged to end his truce with the Moors (SC).

Honorius III takes steps to bolster crusade preaching in Germany, bring about peace between France and England, and win over Raymond VII of Toulouse to the crusade cause.

Dec.: The Latin garrison at Thessalonika under Guido Pallavicini surrenders to the Epirote Greeks.

Ralph of Coggeshall, *Chronicon Anglicanum*, contains much material on the Fourth Crusade.

1225

Feb. 15: Honorius III condemns Raymond VII of Toulouse as a heretic.

Mar.: Muslim governor of Valencia acknowledges the overlordship and protection of Ferdinand III of Castile, who raids deep into Al-Andalus to the walls of Granada. The campaign is celebrated for the liberation of many Christian captives. Ferdinand interferes in Moorish politics to impose Valencian rule over Seville and Cordoba (SC).

July 25: At a meeting in San Germano with Honorius III, Frederick renews his crusading vows, agrees a new crusade for August 1227 and undertakes to fight the

Saracens for two years. The poor response to the projected crusade for 1225 has made this step necessary. Frederick undertakes to provide ships and men and to deposit 100,000 ounces of gold in Acre for his war chest.

Aug.: Frederick II sends a fleet to Acre bearing James, bishop of Patti, as Frederick's proxy. The marriage with Isabel by proxy took place in Acre, and soon after Isabel was crowned queen of Jerusalem in her own right at Tyre. The fleet brings Isabel to Brindisi.

Oct.: Arrival of Isabel at Brindisi.

Nov. 1: Ferdinand III of Castile captures Andujar and Martos. The Muslims agree to a Castilian garrison in the citadel of Baeza (SC).

Nov. 9: Marriage of Frederick II and Queen Isabel in person.
   Frederick demands the crown of Jerusalem from John of Brienne; the Syrian Franks who had escorted Isabel to Italy acknowledge Frederick as their king.
   Frederick sends the bishop of Melfi east to receive homage from the barons of the kingdom on his behalf. John of Birenne is outraged by Frederick's behaviour and flees to Rome to seek the support of the Pope. With his personal interest in Jerusalem Frederick plans a crusade based on the crusader states rather than an attack on Egypt.

Nov.: John III Vatatzes defeats the Latins at Poimanenon and occupies all the territory of the Latin Empire in Asia Minor.

Snorri Sturluson, *Heimskringla*; the Norse sagas from 1030 to 1177 are useful for Scandinavian involvement in the Crusades to the East, especially the crusade of Sigurd, 1107–10.

1226

Jan. 30: Louis VIII takes control of the crusade against Raymond VII of Toulouse.

Spring: Ferdinand III of Castile captures Baeza and Capilla. The mosque at Capilla is turned into a Christian church with an elaborate ceremony of purification (SC).

July: Ferdinand's father, Alfonso IX of Leon (1188–1230), mounts a destructive raid in the Guadiana valley as far as Badajoz (SC).

Nov. 8: Death of Louis VIII, having captured Toulouse. His son Louis IX (–1270) succeeds him, with his mother, Blanche of Castile, as regent.
   Conrad of Mazovia grants Chlemno to the Teutonic Knights as a base of operations against the Prussians (BC).

James of Vitry, *Historia Orientalis et Occidentalis*, also known as *Historia Hierosolimitana,* gives accounts of the first three crusades and the Fifth Crusade to 1218.

1227

Mar. 18: Death of Pope Honorius III and the election of Ugolino of Ostia as Gregory IX.

Aug.: Crusading army from England, Germany and southern Italy assembles at Brindisi. Frederick sends Thomas of Acerra ahead as his bailli in the Kingdom of Jerusalem.

Aug. 24: Death of Genghis Khan; his empire is divided between his sons.

Sept. 8: The fleet sets sail with 800 knights and 10,000 infantry. Frederick is forced to return to Otranto due to ill health. The army is entrusted to Henry, duke of Limburg, and Gerald, patriarch of Jerusalem.

Sept. 29: Gregory IX excommunicates Frederick for refusal to fulfil his crusading vow, last renewed at San Germano.

Oct.: Crusading army arrives in Acre and busies itself with rebuilding the defences at Sidon, Jaffa and Caesarea. The fortifications at Montfort near Acre are repaired; this will soon be called Starkenberg and be the headquarters of the Teutonic Knights.

Many leave the crusading army frustrated by the delay.

Oct. 10: Excommunication of Frederick II published in full in a papal bull.

Nov. 11: Al-Kamil of Egypt occupies Jerusalem.

Henry of Latvia, *Chronicle of Livonia.*

1228

Apr. 25: Isabel gives birth to Conrad; Frederick is now regent of Jerusalem for his infant son.

May 5: Isabel dies at Andria.

June 28: Frederick sails from Brindisi for the East. Gregory IX repeats his excommunication.

July 21: Frederick arrives at Limassol where he is met by Thomas of Acerra and the chief nobles of the Kingdom of Jerusalem. The king of Cyprus was the infant Henry I, with his mother, Alice, as regent and John of Ibelin, lord of Beirut, as bailli. Frederick determines to assert his suzerainty over the island (see 1197).

Late July: Banquet at Limassol attended by Henry of Cyprus, Demetrius of Montferrat, the Latin claimant to the Kingdom of Thessalonika, and a gathering of Cypriot, German and Jerusalemite knights. Frederick attempts to arrest John of Ibelin to examine his record as bailli of Cyprus and to gain the surrender of Beirut from him.

Sept. 7: Frederick arrives at Acre to be well received by the people and the military orders.

Sept.: Frederick sends Henry of Malta and Marino Filangieri, archbishop of Bari, to Rome to seek his absolution and clear the way for the crusade. Gregory IX remains unmoved, and the loyalty of elements of the crusade is weakened.

Frederick sends Thomas of Acerra and Balian of Ibelin to al-Kamil to request that negotiations begun in 1226 be resumed, with the intended cession of Jerusalem to the Latins in return for military assistance in Syria.

Nov.: Frederick bases himself at Jaffa to bring some pressure on al-Kamil.

Revolt in Murcia in favour of the Abbasid caliphs in Baghdad, and against the claims of the Almohad caliphs, forces the latter to seek the protection of Ferdinand II of Castile (SC).

James I of Aragon (1213–76) begins the conquest of the Balearic Islands (–1235) (SC).

The Château de Mer, the island citadel of Sidon, built.

1229

Jan.: News arrives that John of Brienne, now procurator of the Patrimony of St Peter, is campaigning in southern Italy where he has captured San Germano and is threatening Capua. Frederick is now under pressure to conclude his involvement in Syria and return to defend his lands in Italy.

Feb. 18: Treaty of Jaffa between Frederick and al-Kamil. By this personal agreement Jerusalem, Lydda, Bethlehem, Sidon and Toron were restored to the emperor. Also, free access granted for Muslims to the sacred places, together with a separate court for Muslim subjects in the lands restored. In addition, the emperor pledged to maintain peace and not to assist in wars against al-Kamil, and apart from Jaffa, Montfort, Caesarea and possibly Jerusalem, no new fortifications were to be erected. And a general exchange of prisoners, including many captured at Damietta, took place. Tripoli, Antioch, Tortosa and the castles at Margat, Krak des Chevaliers and Safita were excluded from the treaty. This treaty accomplished more for the crusader states than any crusade since 1099, but it was denounced on all sides.

Mar. 17: Frederick enters Jerusalem.

Mar. 18: Frederick crowns himself king of Jerusalem in the Church of the Holy Sepulchre as regent for his infant son Conrad.

Mar. 25: Frederick returns to Acre.

Apr. 9: Conference at Perugia; John of Brienne agrees to become co-emperor of the Latin Empire of Constantinople with the twelve-year-old Baldwin II, who will become his son-in-law by marrying his daughter Marie of Brienne.

Apr. 11: Treaty of Paris ends the Albigensian crusade; Raymond VII submits to Louis IX, surrendering the duchy of Narbonne and the reversion of the county of Toulouse after his death. He agrees to go on crusade overseas and to fight there for five years (see 1249).

May 1: Frederick leaves Acre for Italy via Cyprus. He appoints Balian of Sidon and Werner the German (Garnier l'Aleman) as baillis for Jerusalem and leases the bailliage of Cyprus for three years to Amaury Barlais, Amaury of Bethsan, Gauvain of Chinchi, William of Revet and Hugh of Ghibelet (Jubail). He leaves a garrison in Acre to protect imperial interests and hands the castle of Montfort to the Teutonic Order.

June: John of Ibelin, lord of Beirut, goes to Cyprus and openly opposes the five baillis.

June 10: Frederick lands at Brindisi and begins the restoration of southern Italy, which he completes by October.

July 14: John of Ibelin defeats the baillis near Nicosia and drives them into the castles of Dieudamor, Kantara and Cerines which he then besieges. The siege of Dieudamor lasts until Easter 1230.

Summer: Bedouins attack Jeruslem and Jaffa, but are driven off.

Alice of Cyprus, the daughter of Isabel of Jerusalem and Henry of Champagne, advances her claim to the throne of Jerusalem if Conrad has not appeared to claim his rights within a year and a day. A deputation is sent to Frederick II to explain this.

Chronique de Ernoul provides a conspectus of the Kingdom of Jerusalem with much detail on the career of Godfrey of Bouillon, a description of Jerusalem and an account of its fall in 1187, together with a summary of crusading activity from 1190 to 1229 (see also 1231).

1230

Mar.: Alfonso IX captures Merida (SC).

Apr.: Alfonso IX defeats a Muslim relieving force at Alange. The Muslims are led by al-Hud (1228–38), the pro-Abbasid leader of the Murcian revolt and *de facto* ruler of Al-Andalus (SC).

Bulgarians defeat the Epirote Greeks at Klokotinitza and seem set to take Constantinople from the Latins. Theodore Doukas is captured and blinded.

Easter: The castle of Dieudamor (St Hilarion) is surrendered to John of Ibelin and with it the person of Henry I, king of Cyprus.

May: Deputation from the Kingdom of Jerusalem meets with Frederick at Foggia.

May 26: Badajoz surrenders to Alfonso IX. The Christian frontier is now on the Guadiana River (SC).

July 23: Treaty of San Germano between Frederick II and Gregory IX.

Sept. 1: At Agnani Frederick's excommunication is lifted and he is received once more into the Church. The patriarch of Jerusalem is ordered to acknowledge the Treaty of Jaffa, and over the next six months the Christian holy places are reoccupied by Christian clergy.

Sept. 23: Death of Alfonso IX of Leon. His son Ferdinand III of Castile succeeds him, thus uniting the two kingdoms (SC).

Oct.: Teutonic Knights occupy Chelmno and begin conquest of Prussia authorised by Pope Gregory IX (BC).

Late: Frederick sends an expedition of thirty-three ships under Richard Filangieri to re-establish his control in Cyprus and Syria. After an interview with Henry I, near Larnaka, the expedition fails to secure the exile of John of Ibelin and his supporters and is unable to land in Cyprus due to the presence of a strong Ibelin army. The expedition proceeds to besiege Beirut.

The Ayyubid governor, al-Aziz ʿUthman, builds the castle of Qalʿat al-Subayba (Nimrod's Castle) on Mount Hermon to block any attack from Acre on Damascus.

Estoire d'Oultremer et de la Naissance de Salahadin has much original material on Reynaud of Châtillon and Saladin's supposed descent from a noble French family.

Ibn Hammad, Akhbar Muluk Baniʾ Ubaid (History of Fatimid Egypt, 909–1171).

1231

Early: Richard Filangieri has his commission as imperial bailli for the Kingdom of Jerusalem and imperial legate in the Levant recognised by the High Court of Jerusalem meeting at Acre. The question of the siege of Beirut – that is, imperial confiscation versus the customs of the kingdom whereby no fief could be seized except with by the judgment of the High Court – remains a bone of contention.

Late July: John of Brienne arrives in Constantinople as emperor elect.

Nov./Oct.–Mar./Apr. 1232: Filangieri unsuccessfully besieges Beirut, the Ibelin power base.

Dec.: Gregory IX sends inquisitors against heresy to Germany with the strong support of the archbishop of Bremen in his dispute with the Stedinger.

John of Ibelin gathers an army at Famagusta to relieve the castle of Beirut.

Massacre of thirteen Orthodox monks on Cyprus for refusal to adopt the Latin rite; this unique act of violence demonstrates the lawlessness that civil war produced.

***Chronique de Bernard le Tresorier* is a virtually identical text with *Chronique de Ernoul* (see 1229), with an independent continuation to 1231.**

1232

Spring: Henry of Cyprus and John of Ibelin land at Puy du Constable in Tripoli and march south to Beirut. They camp outside the city and send aid to the garrison of the castle.

Apr.: John of Ibelin receives the oath of the commune of Acre, seizing the imperial fleet anchored there. He also sends representatives to gain the support of Bohemond IV of Tyre and Antioch.

Richard Filangieri sends a force to Cyprus that succeeds in subduing the island, apart from the castles of Dieudamor (St Hilarion) and Buffavento.

May 2: Richard Filangieri, Frederick's legate in Palestine, defeats John of Ibelin at Casal Imbert, near Tyre, seizing quantities of arms and horses. He now sends the bulk of his forces to Cyprus to complete the subjugation of the island.

May: Ibelin forces from Acre, Beirut and Tyre land at Famagusta to relieve the siege of Dieudamor.

June 15: John of Ibelin defeats Filangieri at Agridi in Cyprus. Dieudamor is saved from the Hohenstaufen.

1233

Apr.: John of Ibelin captures Kyrenia, expels Filangieri from Cyprus and restores Henry of Lusignan as king of Cyprus. Filangieri and the five baillies withdraw to Tyre. Filangieri vainly seeks allies in Armenia, then goes to Apulia to raise another imperial military expedition for the East.

Gregory IX sets up the Holy Office (Inquisition).

July 26: Gregory IX summons Gerold, patriarch of Jerusalem, and representatives of the Templars and Hospitallers to Rome. He replaces Gerold as papal legate by Albert, patriarch of Antioch, who is a supporter of Frederick II. Albert's brief is to restore peace in the Kingdom of Jerusalem. The years 1234 and 1235 saw many embassies and negotiations to establish peace and stability in the kingdom.

Ibn al-Athir, *Kitab al-Kamil fi-al-Tarikh* (Complete Book of Chronicles) offers an abridgement of al-Tabari's work down to 923 and continues Arab history up to 1231. It is perhaps the first Muslim history of the Crusades from 1095 onwards and places the Crusades at the centre of a perceived Christian–Muslim antagonism.

1234

Crusade against the men of Stedingen proclaimed by Gregory IX and organised to its brutal conclusion by the archbishop of Bremen

Sept./Nov.: Gregory IX proclaims a crusade to be ready for July 1239, when the ten-year truce agreed by Frederick II and al-Kamil expires. Preaching takes place in England and France. Those who took the cross but were unable to go might commute their vow for a cash payment and enjoy the crusade indulgence.

1235

June: Gregory IX declares a crusade tax of 1d. per week for all Christians who did not take the cross.

Sept.: Crusaders ordered not to depart from Syria until the truce has expired.

1236

John of Ibelin, lord of Beirut, dies. Richard Filangieri continues to 1241 as bailli in Tyre, and Eudes of Montbeliard is bailli in Acre. Neither recognises the other and both claim to be bailli for King Conrad.

Spring/summer: Frederick II begins campaign to recover Italy, his imperial heritage, whilst Gregory IX declares the whole earth as subject to the judgment of the Apostolic See according to the so-called Donation of Constantine. The bitter dispute undermines the planned crusade at the end of the 1229 truce with al-Kamil.

June 29: Ferdinand III of Castile and Leon takes Cordoba (SC).

Oct. 23: Gregory IX writes to Peter of Dreux, count of Brittany, in terms that suggest he had already agreed to lead a crusade to aid the Latin Empire of Constantinople.

Dec. 9: Gregory IX urges Thibaut IV (Theobald), king of Navarre and count of Champagne, who had already taken the cross, to aid the Latin Emperor in any way he could.
   Teutonic Knights complete conquest of Prussia (BC).
   Sword Brothers annihilated by the Lithuanians at Saule (BC).
   Richard of Cornwall takes the cross.

The eighteen-year-old Baldwin II of Constantinople comes to Europe to solicite aid for the Latin Empire.

Mongols occupy Armenia and Georgia, ending their links with the Mediterranean cultural world.

1237

Jan.: The Jews of England pay 3,000 marks as an aid for Richard of Cornwall's crusade.

Mar. 23: John of Brienne, co-emperor of the Latin Empire, dies at Constantinople.

May 27: Gregory IX acknowledges that two crusades are in preparation – one to Constantinople to depart in August 1238 and the other for Syria to depart in August 1239.

James I of Aragon captures Murcia (SC).

Gregory IX confirms the amalgamation of the Teutonic Knights and the rump of the Sword Brothers (BC).

1238

Mar. 9: Death of al-Kamil; his son al-Adil is secure in Egypt, but the succession to the lordship of Damascus is in dispute.

Sept.: James I of Aragon captures Valencia (SC).

1239

Mar. 20: Death of Hermann of Salza (BC). Gregory IX excommunicates Frederick II.

May 15: Louis IX knights Baldwin II at Melun.

July 5: Louis IX sent to enquire how many crusaders were going to Constantinople with Baldwin II; nothing more is known of this crusade.

Aug.: Crusading army led by Thibaut IV of Champagne, Hugh IV of Burgundy and Peter of Dreux leaves Aigues-Mortes and Marseilles.

Sept. 1: Thibaut arrives in Acre and the army assembles there throughout the month.

Nov.: Gregory IX tries to persuade Richard of Cornwall either to commute his crusading vow or to go to Constantinople. This suggestion is publicly rejected at Northampton.

Nov. 2: The army leaves Acre for Ascalon to rebuild the fortifications there.

Nov. 12: A dispute in the crusade army over Thibaut's leadership. Thibaut camps at Ascalon whilst Henry of Bar and the duke of Burgundy push on to Gaza.

Oath of Northampton: would-be English crusaders vow to serve in the Holy Land rather than in Italy or the Latin Empire of Constantinople.

Nov. 13: Advance guard of the crusade army under Henry of Bar defeated by the Egyptians near Gaza; 1,000 infantryman are slain and 600 captured. For reasons not clear the main army under Thibaut returns to Acre.

Dec. 7: The Muslim emir of Kerak occupies and slights the defences of Jerusalem.

1240

Apr. 9: Battle of Leignitz. The Mongols defeat the Poles and Teutonic Knights. They ravage Silesia and later winter on the Hungarian Plain (BC).

Apr. 11: Battle on the Sajo River. Another Mongol army, under Batu Khan, defeats the Hungarians and raids along the Danube.

June 10: Crusade of Richard of Cornwall leaves England.

Summer: Ismail of Damascus, fearing an attack from Egypt, proposes the return of Safed and Beaufort to the crusaders, with the return of Jerusalem if it is regained. In return the crusaders will guard the Egyptian frontier. The truce is unpopular with both Christians and Muslims. Thibaut moves to Ascalon. In the meantime Ayub of Egypt offers Ascalon in return for crusader neutrality.

Sept.: Thibaut, by now thoroughly unpopular, and Peter of Dreux return to France. It is unclear whether he had formalised the agreement with Ayub, but he had certainly laid the groundwork for the return of Ascalon and two important fortresses.

Oct. 11: Richard of Cornwall arrives in Acre with crusading forces from England.

Oct.: He hurries to Ascalon and confirms the truce with Ayub, asking in addition for the cession of Mount Tabor, Belvoir and Tiberias. This is agreed, and the prisoners taken at Gaza are returned.

Dec.: Death of Ögödai Great Khan of the Mongols at Karakorum. Budapest occupied by the Mongols.
   Swedes extend the Baltic crusades against the Russians and are defeated on the Neva River (BC).

Benedict of Alignan, bishop of Marseilles, rebuilds and extends the castle of Safed (Saphet), said to mark the tomb of Tobias. The cost was 100,000 bezants.

1241

May 3: Richard of Cornwall leaves Acre to return home.

Templars and Hospitallers disagree over the efficacy of alliances with Damascus or Egypt. The Templars besiege the house of the Hospitallers in Acre. Hospitallers side with Filangieri.

The Templars raid into Hebron. This provokes attacks on Christian pilgrims and merchants by Da'ud of Transjordan.

Mongols begin withdrawing from Eastern Europe on learning of Ögödai's death.

Hamburg and Lübeck lay foundations for the Hanseatic League. German colonisation in Poland encouraged, offsetting depopulation caused by Mongol inroads (BC).

1242

Apr. 5: Teutonic Knights defeated on Lake Peipus/Chud by Alexander Nevsky of Novgorod (BC).

July: Prussians rebel against the Teutonic Knights (BC).

Oct. 30: The Templars sack Nablus and burn the mosque. This provokes a military response from Egypt against the Templars.

Ibn al-ʿAdin (Kamal ad-Din), *Zubdat al-halab fi tàrikb Halab* (Chronicle of Aleppo).

1243

Apr. 25: King Conrad comes of age (15) thus ending the regency of Frederick II and the commissions of his agents such as Richard Filangieri. The claims of Alice of Cyprus to the regency until the arrival of Conrad are put forward.

June: Richard Filangieri is recalled for discussions to Italy. In his absence his brother Lothar commands Tyre. Alice of Cyprus demands the surrender of Tyre and Lothar is besieged in the citadel.

June 25: Sinbaldo dei Fieschi elected Pope Innocent IV.

June 26: Mongols defeat Kai Khusrau II at Kose Dagh near Erzinjan. The Seljuks of Rum acknowledge Mongol overlordship, as does Hethoum of Armenia.

July 10: Richard Filangieri returns to Tyre and is captured. Lothar surrenders the citadel to ensure Richard's safety. Imperial rule in the Kingdom of Jerusalem is virtually at an end. Imperial garrisons remain in Ascalon and Jerusalem until 1244. Richard Filangieri is recalled to Italy where he is disgraced and imprisoned. Thomas of Acerra becomes the new imperial bailli.

1244

June: Khwarizmian Turks ('Corasmins') ravage the lands of Damascus. Since the death of their leader Jelal ad-Din in 1231, these mounted warriors had operated as mercenaries and as freebooters on their own account, mainly in al-Jazira. Both Franks and Muslims hate them.

Aug. 23: The Khwarizmians sack Jerusalem, expelling the Franks and desecrating the tombs of the Latin kings of Jerusalem. They desolate the city and go to Gaza to sell their services to the Egyptian army there.

Oct. 17: Forces of Outremer, allied with Muslims from Damascus and Homs, annihilated at La Forbie near Gaza by the Egyptians and the Khwarizmian horsemen. The defeat is a catastrophe almost on the scale of Hattin in 1187. It negates the negotiated achievements of 1229 and 1241 and confines the Kingdom of Jerusalem to the coastal cities.

Oct.: Muslim attacks on Ascalon and Jaffa fail.

Dec.: Louis IX takes the cross, having recovered from malaria. The proposed start date seems to be the summer of 1247.
   Montsegur, the last Cathar stronghold, surrenders.

1245

Jan. 3: Innocent IV summons the Council of Lyons to discuss the Holy Land, the Latin Empire of Constantinople, and the Mongol threat to Hungary.

Jan. 23: Innocent IV invites Thibaut of Champagne to return to the Holy Land.

June 24–July 17: General Council at Lyons sends the Franciscan John of Piano Carpine to the court of the Great Khan at Karakorum. The preaching of a new crusade is agreed and Odo of Chateauroux is appointed legate to preach the crusade in Western Europe. Frederick II is formally deposed as emperor. Innocent IV prepared to extend crusade indulgences to those who supported William of Holland against Frederick II.

Apr.–Oct.: Ayub, sultan of Egypt, besieges and captures Damascus.

1246

Spring: Ismail, former ruler of Damascus, employs the Khwarizmians to recapture Damascus.

May: Ismail is defeated by a relieving force near Homs and the Khwarizmians virtually wiped out. The survivors move north to join the Mongols.
   Queen Alice of Cyprus/Champagne dies and the regency of Jerusalem passes to her son, Henry I of Cyprus.

1247

June 17: Ayub captures Tiberias.

Late June: Mount Tabor and Belvoir occupied by the Egyptians.

Aug. 22: Ferdinand III of Castile and Leon begins the siege of Seville (SC).

Oct. 15: Ascalon taken by storm and its defences slighted.

1248

Aug. 25: Louis IX embarks for the East at Aigues-Mortes.

Sept. 17: Louis IX arrives at Limassol. He stays in Cyprus for eight months, using it as a base to muster his forces and plan the crusade.

Dec.: The Dominican, Andrew of Longjumeau, returns from Tabriz and informs Louis IX of Christians amongst the Mongols. Genoese conquer Rhodes from the Byzantines.

Dec. 22: Ferdinand of Castile accepts the surrender of Seville. Principal Muslim families choose exile in Tunis. Acclaimed as a great triumph of Christian arms, Al-Andalus now confined to south of the Guadalquivar River (SC).

Rodrigo Ximenes de Rada, *Chronica Hispaniae,* **provides the first general history of the Iberian Peninsula dealing with both Muslim and Christian aspects.**

1248–75

Estoire/Livre/Roman d'Eracles are four Old French translations of the History of William of Tyre (see 1184), with continuations down to 1248, 1261, 1264 and 1275.

1249

May: Hugh IV, duke of Burgundy, arrives in Cyprus having wintered in Frankish Greece along with William of Villehardouin, prince of Achaea.

May 30: Louis IX and the crusade fleet leave Cyprus for Egypt.

June 5: Army lands in Egypt.

June 6: Crusade army occupy Damietta, abandoned by its defenders. The army stays there for five months, raiding and suffering counter-raids from Ayub, based at El Mansura.

Sept. 27: Raymond VII of Toulouse dies as he is about to fulfil his crusade vow taken in 1229. Blanche of Castile secures the Toulousain for the Capetians.

Oct. 24: Alphonse of Poitiers, the king's brother, arrives with reinforcements.

Nov. 20: The army begins its advance on Cairo down the right bank of the Nile.

Nov. 23: Sultan Ayub dies at El Mansura; his death is kept secret to allow for the arrival of his heir Turanshah from al-Jazira. There is, however, a loss of command in the Muslim army.

Dec. 19: Army drawn up opposite the fortress of El Mansura. It is placed on a defensive stance by the Nile flood.

Swedes begin the conquest of Finland (BC).

1250

Feb. 6: Robert of Artois, one of the king's brothers, leading the vanguard of the crusading army, seizes a Nile ford and successfully attacks the Egyptian camp outside El Mansura. He pushes on into the town where his force is annihilated in the narrow streets and he is killed. Louis, in the meantime, brings the main army over the ford but is unable to assist his brother.

Feb. 24: Turanshah arrives in El Mansura. The Egyptians intercept supply ships from Damietta and starvation threatens the crusade army.

Apr. 6: Louis IX begins the withdrawal from El Mansura. His army is surrounded at Fariskur and forced to surrender. Turanshah's behaviour alienates many of his Mameluke guards.

May 2: Turanshah, the last Ayyub sultan of Egypt, is murdered by his Mamaluke guards, who set up their commander, Izz ad-Din, as sultan and thus found the Mamaluke dynasty (–1517). The murder is witnessed by many of the captive crusaders, including John of Joinville. The conspirators, one of whom is Baybars, are eager to facilitate the departure of the captive crusade army.

May 6: Louis IX and the crusading army are released according to an agreement reached with Turanshah. A ransom of 800,000 bezants, the surrender of Damietta and a ten-year truce is agreed. With the help of the Templars half the ransom is raised in two days and Louis withdraws to Acre. Some 12,000 prisoners remain in Egypt to be released when the balance of the ransom is paid; some of them had been captured at Gaza and La Forbie (1239, 1244).

May 13: Louis IX arrives in Acre.

June: Groups of peasants, the Pastoreux, gather in northern France and Flanders to assist Louis; after attacks on Jews in Paris, Orleans and Bourges they are dispersed by force.

July 9: Damascus captured by the Aleppans.

Dec. 13: Frederick II dies. Conrad IV, king of the Romans, Sicily and nominal king of Jerusalem, succeeds him.

Winter: Suburbs of Acre protected by a wall.

(Approx.) Anon., *Le Livre des Assises de la Cour des Bourgeois* – a treatise on the burgess court and the law regarding the non-noble inhabitants of the Kingdom of Jerusalem.

1251

Mar. 29: Construction begins of a circuit wall around the town of Caesarea.

Alberic of Trois Fontaines, *Chronica*; a universal chronicle that contains valuable material on the crusades of the first half of the thirteenth century.

1252

Early: Alliance formed between Louis IX and the Mamelukes. In return for the release of prisoners and the restoration of the old Kingdom of Jerusalem, less Ascalon, Gaza and Hebron, the crusade army will fight against the Ayyubids of Syria.

Apr.: Mamelukes and Ayyubids come to an agreement – the Mameluke–crusade alliance allowed to lapse. Aleppans attack the suburbs of Acre.

May–June 1253: Crusade army at Jaffa waiting to join up with an Egyptian expedition against Damascus. Circuit wall around the town of Jaffa is built. Work begins on a circuit wall for Sidon.

Dec. 1: Blanche of Castile dies. Alphonse of Poitiers presides over the king's council.

Philip of Novare, *l'Estoire et le droit conte de la guerre qui fu entre l'empereur Frederic et messier Johan de Ybelin seigneur de Baruth.*

1253

Jan. 18: Death of Henry I of Cyprus. His son and successor is Hugh II, only a few months old. His mother Plaisance of Antioch (d. 1261) claims the regency of both Cyprus and Jerusalem. The former is agreed, but the latter only confirmed when she visits Acre in 1258.

May: Aleppans attack Sidon.

June: Part of the crusade army at Sidon and the other part at Jaffa mount an unsuccessful attack on the Ayyubs at Banyas.

Louis IX sends the Franciscans William of Rubruck and Bartholomew of Cremona to Karakorum to seek an alliance with the Great Khan against the Muslims.

Innocent IV forms the *Perigrinantes propter Christum* from Franciscans and Dominicans dedicated to missionary work.

Bull *athleta Christi* authorises the papal legate Eudes of Chateauroux to fill vacant sees amongst eastern Christians.

1254

Feb.: Two-year truce agreed with the Ayyubs of Aleppo and Damascus.

Mar. 6: Treaty of Toledo between Castile and England. Alfonso X (1252–84) concedes Castilian claims to Gascony, thus forestalling a proposed English attack, and agrees to the marriage of his daughter Eleanor with Prince Edward (SC).

Apr. 24: Louis IX leaves Acre for France.

May 21: Conrad IV dies at Lavello in Apulia aged 26. His two-year-old son Conrad V (Conradin) succeeds him as king of Sicily and of Jerusalem (Conrad II), but lives in Bavaria under the guardianship of Louis of Bavaria (see 1268).

July 3: Louis IX lands in France at Hyeres.

Sept. 7: Louis IX enters Paris and only then removes the sign of the cross.

Sept. 13: Cilician Armenia becomes a vassal kingdom of the Mongols.

Dec. 7: Pope Innocent IV dies at Naples.
Teutonic Knights begin the conquest of Samland (–1256) (BC).

1255

Sept.: Conradin recognised as king of Sicily, with his uncle Manfred as regent.

Hospitallers fortify the church and monastery on Mount Tabor.

1256

Jan. 28: William of Holland, king of the Romans, dies.

Dec.: Mongols take Alamut and execute the Grandmaster of the Assassins. Mongols move to destroy the Assassins in lands under their control.

1256–61: War of St Sabas in Acre between the Venetians and the Genoese supported by the Anconitans and the Pisans. Ostensibly the 'war' started over a dispute concerning some property of the Monastery of St Sabas. It reflects the deeper commercial and political rivalries of the two cities in the Levant and gradually involves most of the political and military groupings in the Kingdom of Jerusalem.

1257

May: Richard of Cornwall crowned king of the Romans in Aachen. Alfonso X of Castile (1252–84) is elected king of the Romans at this time by Hohenstaufen supporters amongst the Electors, but he never sets foot in Germany and his candidature remains a dead letter other than as a diplomatic embarrassment for Richard (SC).

Philip of Novare, *Livre a un sien ami en forme de plait*, a treatise on the usages of advocates in the High Courts of Cyprus and Jerusalem (see also 1265).

Ibn al-Jawzi, *Mir'at al-Zaman fi Tàrikh al-Ayyam*, a general Arab history down to 1256.

1258

Jan. 11: Mongols defeat the army of the Abbasid caliph at Anbar.

Feb. 10: Mongols take and destroy Baghdad.

Feb. 20: Execution of al-Mustaʾsim and his family, bringing an end to the Abbasid caliphate (see also 750).

Aug. 10: Following rumours that Conradin had died in Bavaria, Manfred is crowned king of Sicily in Palermo.

1259

Summer: The battle of Pelagonia in Macedonia; Michael VIII Palaiologos, emperor of Nicaea, defeats his rival Manuel II Doukas. Manuel's ally William of Villehardouin and many Frankish knights are captured.

Alexander IV preaches a crusade against the Greeks and urges Bela IV, king of Hungary, to attack them. Bela is, however, preoccupied with the Mongol threat.

Aug. 11: Death of the Great Khan Mongka in Karakorum.

Sept.: Mongols invade Syria. At the behest of his father-in-law, Hethoum, Bohemond IV of Antioch acknowledges the suzerainty of the Mongols in return for the restoration of Antiochene territory captured by the Mamelukes (see 1243).

Late: Mongols raid into Poland and Lithuania, but withdraw the next year on hearing news of the death of Mongka

Matthew Paris, *Chronica majora*, contains material on the Latin Empire of Constantinople.

1260

Mar. 1: Mongols capture Damascus and occupy Syria. Bohemond IV enters Damascus with the Mongols. Later the Mongols destroy the castle at Ajlun in the Jordan valley (see 1183, 1262).

May 25: Alexander IV preaches a crusade against the Tartars (Mongols) in Syria.

July 1: Lithuanians defeat the Sword Brothers at Durben; the survivors are incorporated within the Teutonic Knights (BC).

Sept. 3: Baybars, commanding the Mamaluke army, defeats the Mongols at 'Ain Jalut and occupies Syria.

Oct. 24: Baybars murders Saif ad-Din Qutuz who had seized the sultanate of Egypt in December 1259.

Nov. 27: Alexander IV summons a Church council for July 1261 to address the threats to Christendom in Syria, the Balkans and central Europe.
  Maffeo and Nicolo Polo set out for China.

Templars purchase and extend the castle of Beaufort/Belfort (see 1268).

Al-Juwaini, *Tàrikh-I-jahan gusha* (History of the World Conqueror) – a history in Persian of Genghis Khan and the Mongols, with much material on the Assassins.

1261

Mar. 13: Treaty of Nymphaion, by which the Genoese agree to assist Michael VIII to capture Constantinople from the Latins.

May 25: Pope Alexander IV dies.

July 4: Baybars becomes sultan of Egypt (–1277).

July 25: Michael VIII captures Constantinople; the end of the Latin Empire of Constantinople. Baldwin II flees to Greece and thence to the court of Manfred at Messina.

Aug. 15: Coronation of Michael VIII Palaiologos in the Hagia Sophia, Constantinople.

Aug. 29: James Pantaleon of Troyes elected Pope Urban IV. From April 1255 until his election as Pope he had been patriarch of Jerusalem.

Late summer: Release of William of Villehardouin (see 1259) in return for the cession of the fortresses of Maina, Mistra and Monemvasia to the Greeks.
  Baybars establishes a line of the Abbasid caliphs in Cairo that lasts until the Ottoman conquest in 1517. This move provides some legitimacy for the Mamelukes and gives a basis for Egyptian offensives against the Mongols and the Franks.
  Murcia rebels against Castilian rule (SC).

1262

Sept. 14: Alfonso X of Castile (1252–84) captures Cadiz (SC).
Baybars rebuilds the castle at Ajlun (see 1183, 1260).

1263

Mar.: Baybars moves his army to Galilee and destroys Nazareth and the Church of the Nativity. The fortified church and monastery on Mount Tabor are demolished (see 1255).

Apr. 4: Baybars attacks Acre and destroys its suburbs.
Alfonso of Castile captures Cartagena (SC).
Venetians defeat the Genoese in a large naval engagement at Settepozzi off the coast of northern Euboea.
In this and the following year the Greeks of Mistra attack the principality of Achaea, capturing territory and destroying Latin monasteries.

1264

Mar.: Gerard of Pinkney, castellan of Jaffa, captured as he raids towards Ramla.

*Apr.: **Baybars orders the construction of towers to protect the Damascus to Homs road and the rebuilding of the castle at the Cave of Toron and at Qal'at al-Subayba (Nimrod's Castle, see 1230).***

June: Hospitallers and Templars raid the territory around Ascalon. Baybars orders retaliatory raids on Caesarea and Chastel Pelerin. He demands the return of booty taken at Ascalon.

Sept.: Oliver of Termes and a small force of French knights land at Acre to relieve the garrison left by Louis IX under the command of Geoffrey of Sergines.

Oct. 2: Death of Pope Urban IV.

Nov.: Oliver of Termes raids Baisan.
Venetians defeat the Genoese in a naval engagement off Trapani.

1265

Jan.: Mongols attack the town and castle of al-Bira on the Euphrates. The siege is lifted as Baybars marches to its relief. Baybars believes that the Franks had encouraged the Mongols.

Feb. 5: Guy Folquoi elected Pope Clement IV.

Feb. 28–Mar. 5: Baybars besieges and captures Caesarea. It is razed to the ground. The castle at al-Malluha (Frankish name unknown) is demolished.

Mar. 16: Baybars attacks Chastel Pelerin (Athlit), capturing the lower town but not the citadel. Haifa is captured and razed to the ground.

Mar. 21–Apr. 30: Siege and capture of Arsuf (Apollonia) by Baybars. Arsuf is razed to the ground.

May 29: Baybars parades the prisoners from Arsuf in Cairo.

June 28: Treaty of Orvieto by which Clement IV grants Charles of Anjou the crown of Sicily, setting aside the rights of Conradin. Charles, as a champion of the Church, is to lead a crusade against Manfred.

Oct.: Odo of Nevers arrives in Acre with fifty knights.

John of Jaffa, *Le Livre des Assises* – a handbook on the High Court of Jerusalem and the law as it affected royal vassals (see also 1200 and 1257). In 1369 the High Court of Cyprus adopted it as the official work of reference.

1266

Jan.: Erhard of Valery and Erhard of Nanteuil bring a further trickle of reinforcements from Europe to Acre.

Jan. 6: Charles of Anjou crowned king of Sicily in Rome.

Feb. 26: Charles of Anjou defeats and kills Manfred at Benevento.

Summer: Baybars campaigns with two large Mamaluke armies in Syria, making demonstrations before Acre and Montfort (Starkenburg).

June 8–July 22: Baybars besieges and captures the Templar castle at Safed (Saphet) and gains control of Galilee.

Late Aug.: Mamaluke armies raid Cilician Armenia.
   Alfonso of Castile reconquers Murcia (SC).
   The papal legate Ottobuono ordered to preach the crusade in England.

1267

Mar. 27: Louis IX takes the cross for the second time.

May 24: Treaty of Viterbo I: William of Villehardouin becomes the vassal of Charles of Anjou and concedes that the succession to the principality of Achaea shall pass to the children of Charles's second son, Philip, and his future wife Isabelle of Villehardouin; should there be no offspring then direct rule would pass to the house of Anjou.

May 27: Treaty of Viterbo II: the Latin Emperor Baldwin II confirms the terms of the first treaty and assigns his interest in the Latin Empire to Charles of Anjou in return for a crusade to restore the Latin Empire. Baldwin agrees to a marriage between his son and heir Philip of Courtenay and Charles's daughter Beatrice. The marriage takes place later in the year. Pope Clement IV had brokered both these treaties to bolster the Latin position in the Aegean.

Dec.: Hugh II of Cyprus dies at the age of 14, bringing the direct Lusignan line from Guy (d. 1194) and Amalric (d. 1205) to an end. The regent Hugh of Antioch-Lusignan, the son of one of the sisters of Henry I (d. 1253) and actually present in Cyprus, is crowned Hugh III of Cyprus on Christmas Day. The disappointed claimant Hugh of Brienne, the son of the elder sister Maria, nurses a grudge and seeks service with Charles of Anjou.

1268

Mar. 7: After a siege of 12 hours Baybars captures Jaffa and demolishes the town.

Apr. 5: Michael VIII restores Venetian trading privileges within the Byzantine Empire as part of a peace settlement with Venice.

Apr. 5–15: Castle of Beaufort/Belfort near Sidon surrenders to Baybars.

May 14: St Simeon, the port of Antioch, captured; Antioch now cut off from the sea.

May 14–21: Baybars takes Antioch, massacres the inhabitants and destroys the city. His behaviour at Antioch shocks both Christian and Muslim commentators. Antioch becomes little more than a village, and the Templars abandon their castles at Baghras and La Roche de Russole.

June: Prince Edward, along with Edmund of Lancaster and Henry of Almain, takes the cross at Northampton. Henry III grants him 4,000 marks from the English Jewry for his expenses.

Aug. 23: Charles of Anjou defeats Conradin at Tagliacozzo.

Oct. 29: Conradin is beheaded at Naples, thus bringing to an end the house of Hohenstaufen and Conradin's reign as king of Jerusalem (see 1269 and 1277).

Sometime during 1268 Louis IX is persuaded by Charles of Anjou to attack the emir of Tunis, who had supported the Hohenstaufen cause in Sicily. No supplies are sent ahead to Cyprus, as in 1246, and it appears that a crusade to the East is removed from the agenda, unless Louis thought that Tunis was nearer to Egypt than is the case.

1269

Sept. 4: James I of Aragon (took the cross in 1267) sets sail on crusade from Barcelona. Scattered by severe storms, James gives up the idea of crusade.

His bastard sons Fernando Sanchez and Peter Fernandez start out again for Acre (SC).

Sept. 24: Hugh III of Cyprus is elected and crowned king of Jerusalem at Acre. His claim is based on descent from Queen Isabel and Henry of Champagne (d. 1197). The claim of Maria of Antioch as the granddaughter of Isabel from her fourth marriage to Amalric II of Lusignan is rejected (see 1274).

Late Oct.: Aragonese crusade arrives at Acre with much-needed food supplies and horses.

Nov.: Baybars virtually annihilates the Aragonese crusade outside Acre, but is prevented from any further move by fear of the arrival of Louis IX's crusade.

1270

Spring: Survivors from the Aragonese crusade return to Barcelona.

July 2: Louis IX and the French army embark at Aigues-Mortes.
   The crusade fleets rendezvous at Cagliari in southern Sardinia, where Tunis is announced as the destination of the crusade. Its wealth and weakness are used to overcome objections.

July 18: Crusade army lands near Tunis.

Aug. 20: Prince Edward and the English crusade army cross to France from Dover and march to Aigues-Mortes.

Aug. 25: Just as Charles of Anjou and the Sicilian fleet are arriving, Louis IX dies at Tunis. His eldest son Philip III (–1285), who is also on the crusade, succeeds Louis.

Early Sept.: News arrives in Cairo of the landing of Louis IX near Tunis. Baybars assured of no crusade for Syria and promises help to the emir of Tunis.

Sept. 25: English army arrives at Aigues-Mortes.

Nov. 1: Truce with the emir of Tunis who agrees to pay war indemnities, expel the Hohenstaufen supporters from his territory and open his lands to Sicilian merchants. Prince Edward arrives during this period of negotiations.

Nov. 11: The crusade army leaves Tunis for Sicily. Prince Edward winters there before going on to Acre.

1271

Jan. 24: Baybars leaves Cairo for campaign against the Franks in Syria.

Early Feb.: The Templar castle at Chastel Blanc surrenders without resistance to Baybars and the garrison withdraws to Tortosa.

116

Feb. 21–Apr. 8: Baybars besieges and captures Krak des Chevaliers from the Hospitallers. The survivors are given a safe conduct to Tripoli.

Apr. 29–May 12: The Hospitaller castle at Gibelacar (Akkar) near Tripoli is besieged and captured by Baybars.

May 9: Prince Edward of England arrives with an army in Acre having wintered in Sicily. With this new threat Baybars halts military action against Tripoli and agrees a ten-year truce with Bohemond VI of Tripoli.

Mar. 13: Revenge killing (for treatment of the body of Simon of Montfort after the battle of Evesham in 1265) of Henry of Almain, son of Richard of Cornwall, by Guy of Montfort during mass at Orvieto. Henry was returning from Prince Edward's crusade.

May 28: Marriage of Philip of Anjou and Isabelle of Villehardouin at Trani (see 1267, 1277, 1278).

May/June: Attempts by Edward to capture the small fortress of Qaqun on Mount Carmel are unsuccessful.

June 5–23: Baybars besieges and captures the headquarters of the Teutonic Knights at Montfort (Starkenburg); this is the last inland base available to the Kingdom of Jerusalem.

Sept. 1: Teobaldi Visconti, the archdeacon of Liege, on crusade with Prince Edward, is elected Pope Gregory X and returns to Italy.

Sept.: Small-scale Mongol raid across the Euphrates to Apamea withdraws on the approach of Baybars from Damascus. Prince Edward had negotiated this raid with the Mongol Il-khan.
  Marco Polo begins journey to China.

1272

May 12: Ten-year truce arranged between the Kingdom of Jerusalem and Baybars at Caesarea.

May: Edmund of Lancaster leaves Acre for England.

June 16: Attempted assassination of Prince Edward, possibly instigated by Baybars.

Late Sept.: Edward, now king, sails from Acre for England via Italy.

1273

July: The last Assassin stronghold in the Mountains of Lebanon, al-Kahf, surrenders to Baybars.

Teutonic Knights complete subjugation of pagan tribes in west Prussia (BC).

The Franciscan Raymond Lull (*c.* 1235–*c.* 1315) advocates missions to the Muslims and begins journey through North Africa and Asia to the confines of India (see 1276).

William of Tripoli, *Tractatus de statu Saracenorum* – a handbook for the Christian missionary on the history, law and beliefs of Islam.

1274

May 7-July 17: Second General Council at Lyons discusses crusade affairs and proposals to end the schism with the Greek Orthodox Church. A crusade is planned for 1283 and supportive taxation – a tenth of clerical incomes for six years and a poll tax of 1d. on everyone for six years – is decreed. The first public discussion of the amalgamation of the military orders takes place. The council is well attended, with 500 bishops, sixty abbots and some 1,000 clergy present.

Urged on by Pope Gregory X, Charles of Anjou begins negotiations to purchase the title to the Kingdom of Jerusalem from Mary of Antioch in the light of the unpopularity and poor record of Hugh III (see 1269).

Geoffrey of Beaulieu, *Vita Ludovici IX.*

1275

Mar.: Death of Bohemond VI of Tripoli; he is succeeded by his fourteen-year-old son Bohemond VII. Hugh III of Jerusalem claims the regency but custom assigns it to Sybilla, young Bohemond's mother, who sought the protection of her brother Leon III of Armenia. Hugh receives no support in his claim and continued to lose face.

Mar.: Baybars, marching to campaign against Armenia, demands the return of the Christian half of Latakia.

July 4: Hugh III negotiates a truce with Baybars that protects Latakia from attack in return for an annual tribute of 20,000 dinars.

Marco Polo arrives at the court of Kublai Khan.

1276

Oct.: Hugh III and the Templars quarrel over the sale of an estate called la Fauconnerie, without royal consent. Hugh gets little support and considers quitting Syria for Cyprus.

Raymond Lull founds the College of Miramar for the study of Arabic to further missionary work amongst the Muslims (see 1273).

1277

Jan.–Mar.: Death of Philip of Anjou without offspring. Title to the principality of Achaea reverts to his father Charles of Anjou (see 1267 and 1271).

Mar.: Baybars campaigns against the Mongols in Asia Minor, but withdraws fearing a Mongol attack on Syria.

Mar. 18: Charles of Anjou succeeds in purchasing the title of king of Jerusalem from Mary of Antioch for 1,000 bezants and an annuity of 4,000 livres tournois. The sale is conducted without reference to the High Court in Acre. Charles sends Roger of San Severino to Acre as his bailli. The latter is given entry to the citadel by Balian of Ibelin, Hugh III's bailli, and hoists the banner of the Angevins. He remains in the East until 1282.

July 1: Baybars, aged 57, dies at Damascus, possibly poisoned. His son Baraka succeeds him as sultan of Egypt and Syria.

Civil war in Tripoli between Bohemond VII and the Templars and the Embriaco family causes much damage to fortifications.

1278

Jan.: Coronation of Charles of Anjou as king of Jerusalem.

Barons in Acre do homage to Charles as the rightful king. Hugh III's brother Henry II will not regain control of Acre until 1286.

May 1: Death of William of Villehardouin, prince of Achaea; his lands revert to Charles of Anjou.

Trouble continues in Tripoli.

1279

Aug.: Qalawun becomes sultan of Egypt and Syria in a palace coup that deposes Baraka.

1280

Oct. 20: Mongols sack Aleppo.

1281

Apr. 10: Pope Martin IV excommunicates Michael VIII and renounces the Union of Churches agreed in 1274.

May: Qalawun renews truce with Kingdom of Jerusalem for ten years.

July: Bohemond VII of Tripoli follows suit.

July 3: Venice agrees to provide naval support for Charles of Anjou's proposed attack on Constantinople.

Sept.: Mongols invade Syria.

Oct. 30: Qalawun defeats a coalition army of Mongols, Armenians and Hospitallers near Homs.

Peter of Aragon and Michael VIII form an alliance against Charles of Anjou/ Sicily.

1282

Jan.: Bohemond VII captures and kills the Embriaco brothers. The Genoese open hostilities with Bohemond because of the fate of those they regard as compatriots.

Mar. 30: The massacres associated with the Sicilian Vespers in Palermo force Charles of Anjou to withdraw from Sicily, end his plans to capture Constantinople and force the recall of Roger of San Severino to Italy.

Aug. 30: Peter of Aragon lands in Sicily and assumes the crown as heir of Manfred.

Nov. 18: Pope Martin IV declares a crusade against Peter of Aragon.

Dec. 11: Michael VIII Palaiologos dies. He is succeeded by his son Andronikos II (–1328) who immediately repudiates the unpopular unionist Church policy of his father.

George Akroplites, *Chronike Syngraphe,* is the main Greek source for the period 1203–61.

1283

Prussian rebellion against the Teutonic Knights collapses (BC).

Burchard of Mount Sion, *Descriptio Terrae Sanctae,* is a tolerant and accurate account of travels in Syria, Egypt and Armenia by a Dominican who spent ten years, 1232–42, at the Monastery of Mount Sion, Jerusalem.

1284

Mar. 4: Hugh III dies at Tyre. His seventeen-year-old son John, who is recognised as king of Jerusalem only in Beirut and Tyre, succeeds him.

May 11: Coronation of John I as king of Cyprus at Nicosia.

Aug. 6: Pisa ruined as a commercial republic with the destruction of its fleet by the Genoese off the island of Meloria.

1285

Jan. 7: Death of Charles I of Anjou. The Kingdom of Sicily and the title to the Kingdom of Jerusalem pass to his son Charles II (–1309).

Apr. 25–May 24: Siege and capture of the Hospitaller castle of Margat (al-Marqab), near Tortosa, by Qalawun.

May 20: Death of John I of Cyprus and Jerusalem. His brother, Henry II (–1324), succeeds him.

June 27: Philip III of France invades Aragon in response to the crusade appeal of 1281.
    Teutonic Knights begin the conquest of Lithuania (BC).

1286

June 24: Henry II lands at Acre.

June 29: Eudes Poilechien, garrison commander for the Angevins, hands over the citadel to Henry, who now has the support of the three military orders.

Aug. 15: Henry is crowned king of Jerusalem at Tyre by Archbishop Bonacorso of Gloria, acting as vicar for the patriarch of Jerusalem. The kingdom has an undisputed ruler after two decades. The coronation festivities at Acre last for fifteen days.

1287

March: earthquakes affect Syria.

Apr. 20: Taking advantage of earthquake damage to Latakia, Qalawun receives the surrender of the harbour claiming it is excluded from the truce of 1281.

May 31: Genoese win naval engagment against Venice off Acre and blockade the city.

Oct. 19: Death of Bohemond VII of Tripoli, who is succeeded by his sister Lucy. She is the wife of Narjot of Toucy, a scion of a former noble family of the Latin Empire of Constantinople, and resident in Naples. Sybilla of Armenia is asked to take the regency once again.

1288

Lucy of Toucy arrives in Tripoli to claim the county. Sybilla retires to Armenia. Difficulties with Embriaco relatives and Venetian and Genoese rivalry cause disturbances.
    Last Mongol raid into Poland.

Pope Nicholas IV sends John of Monte Corvino to Persia and China.

1289

Mar. 27–Apr. 26: Siege and capture of Tripoli by Qalawun, followed by a general massacre of the inhabitants. Lucy of Toucy escapes to Cyprus on a Cypriote galley.

Early May: Botron and Nephin occupied by Qalawun. The sole survivor of the Latin county of Tripoli is Peter Embriaco, who is allowed to occupy his estates at Jubail.

1290

Aug.: Venetian and Aragonese crusaders arrive at Acre.

Late Aug.: Massacre of Muslim merchants in Acre in drunken rioting.

Nov. 10: Death of Qalawun. He is succeeded by his son al-Ashraf Khalil (–1293).
   Teutonic Knights complete conquest of Semigallia in Livonia (BC).

1291

Mar. 6: A massive Mameluke army, said to number 60,000 cavalry and 160,000 foot soldiers, leaves Cairo to attack Acre.

Apr. 5–May 28: Siege and capture of Acre, with attendant massacre. Henry II was present in the city all through May and then escaped to Cyprus. The Teutonic Knights move their headquarters to Venice. The Templars, Hospitallers and the Order of St Thomas of Acre transfer their headquarters to Cyprus.

May 19: Tyre abandoned without resistance.

July 14: Sidon surrenders.

July 31: The last effective crusader outpost, Beirut, surrenders.

Aug. 3: Templars abandon Tortosa.

Aug. 14: Templars abandon Chastel Pelerin (Athlit). They continue to occupy the waterless island of Ruad off Tortosa until 1302.

Aug.: Pope Nicholas IV issues the encyclical *Dirum amaritudinem calicem* for the recovery of the Holy Land. Its immediate effect was negligible, but it underpinned crusade proposals for the next half-century.
   Swedes found Viborg in Finland (BC).

Fidenzio of Padua, *Liber recuperationis terrae sanctae*, written before the fall of Acre, is the first of the recovery treatises that were to proliferate with Mongol invasions of Syria at the end of the decade.

1294

Genoese defeat the Venetians in a naval battle off Laiazzo in Cilicia.

1295

Ghazan, the Il-khan of Persia, adopts Islam and declares independence from the Great Khan. Kublai Khan had died the preceding year.

1297

Boniface VIII organises crusades against the Collona and against Frederick of Sicily.

1298

Sept.: Palaestrina captured and destroyed as part of the campaign against the Colonna.

1299

The Mongol Il-khan, Ghazan, approaches Henry II of Cyprus (1285–1324) and the military orders to participate in his planned invasion of Syria. The western interests took no action.

Dec.: Mongols defeat the Mamelukes at Homs.

1300

Jan.: Mongols occupy Damascus.

Feb.: Boniface VIII announces the first jubilee year in Rome. He uses the flock of visitors to promote a crusade and to capitalise on the Mongol successes.

Late: Mongols undertake a further campaign in Syria but fail to consolidate their conquests.

Swedes establish outpost at Landskrona on the Neva River (BC).

1301

July 27: First mention of the Ottoman Turks in western sources when Osman Ghazi defeats a Greek force at Bapheion near Nicaea.

1302

Sept. 24: The Treaty of Caltabellota ends the War of the Sicilian Vespers (see 1282).

The Catalan Grand Company negotiate service with the Byzantines against the Ottoman Turks, to whence they move in 1303.

1303

Apr.: Mamelukes defeat the Mongols near Damascus and reoccupy the city.

1304

The Genoese take Chios from the Greeks.
Ghazan dies, virtually ending the Mongol threat to Syria.
Osman occupies Nicaea (Iznik).

1305

Raymond Lull, *Liber de Fine*, argues for missionary work as well as military activity against the Muslims. Four monasteries should be dedicated to the teaching of Oriental languages. Crusades might be waged on all fronts, but especially in Spain.

1306

May: Hospitallers agree a project for the joint conquest of Rhodes with the Genoese Vignolo degli Vignoli.

June: Joint Hospitaller and Genoese expedition occupies the islands of Kos and Kastellorizo but fails to take the town of Rhodes from the Byzantines.

Oct. 13: All Templars in the kingdom of France arrested.

Nov. 22: Clement V orders the arrest of all Templars in Christendom.

Pierre Dubois, *De recuperatione Terre Sanctae*: proposals for the recovery of the Holy Land based upon the experiences of the last two centuries of crusading; he proposes the merger of the Templars and the Hospitallers.

1307

The Mongols annex the Seljuk sultanate of Rum and bring the dynasty to its end.

Sept. 5: Clement V confirms Hospitallers in the possession of Rhodes (yet to be conquered).

Marino Sanudo Torsello, first version of *Secreta fidelium crucis* (Secrets for True Crusaders), advocating a crusade against Egypt and the union of the Greek and Latin churches (see also 1313, 1321).

**Hethoum of Corycus, an Armenian prince and prior of the Premonstrat-
ensians near Poitiers,** *La Fleur des histoires de la terre d'Orient* – an account
of the rise of the Mongols, details of the military resources of the Mamelukes
and proposals for a crusade based in both Armenia and Cyprus.

1308

Aug. 12: In the bull *Regnans in coelis*, Clement V summons a general council to
meet at Vienne on 1 October 1310 (later postponed for one year).

    Forces from the Mongol khanate of Persia make an abortive invasion of Syria,
but reach Jerusalem.

    The Hospitallers take the city of Rhodes.

1309

Teutonic Knights move their headquarters from Venice to Marienburg; their
interests are now in the Baltic and Prussia rather than the Holy Land (BC).

Jean of Joinville, *Histoire de Chronique du tres chrétien roi saint Louis.*

Raymond Lull, *Liber de acquisitione terrae sanctae*, **proposed blockade,
land-based crusade via Constantinople and aid to Armenia, with a
simultaneous crusade in Spain.**

1311

Mar. 15: Catalan Grand Company annihilates the knights of Frankish Greece at
the battle of Halmyros (*not* Kephissos). Walter of Brienne, the duke of Athens, is
killed and the Company take over the Duchy of Athens.

Oct. 16–May 6, 1312: Council of Vienne suppresses the Templars and discusses
plans for a crusade, to be financed by a tax of a tenth on clerical incomes for six
years. All Templar estates are transferred to the Hospitallers.

    First general chapter of the Hospitallers held on Rhodes.

William Adam, *De modo Saracenos extirpandi*, **advocated a trade blockade
on Muslim lands and urged a new crusade to take the land route to
the East so that it could reconquer Constantinople and aid Armenia on
the way.**

1312

Early: Hospitallers defeat a Turkish fleet in the Cyclades; the news is reported to
the Council of Vienne.

Late: The last Mongol invasion of Syria is repulsed.

1313

Hospitallers try to attract settlers to Rhodes in return for military service. This attracts little response (see also 1335).

Pentecost: Philip IV of France, his three sons, and Edward II of England take the cross at Paris for a crusade planned to depart in the spring of 1319.

Marino Sanudo Torsello, second version of *Secreta fidelium crucis*, advocating economic warfare against Egypt, and in particular the substitution of Cypriot and Rhodian sugar imports to Europe rather than from Muslim lands. He included a short history of the Holy Land (see also 1307 and 1321).

1316

Early: Raymond Lull stoned to death on his third missionary journey to the Berbers at Bugia in Algeria.

1321

Marino Sanudo Torsello presents the final version of *Secreta fidelium crucis* to John XXII at Avignon. It contained a revised history of the Holy Land down to 1307 and a geographical discussion of the Latin Levant (see also 1307 and 1313).

1330

Ramon Muntaner, *Chronica, o descripcio del fets e hazanyes del inclyt rey Don Iaume primer rey Darago*; a chronicle in Catalan of the period 1204–1328 that has much information on the role of the Catalans in Sicily, the Byzantine Empire and Frankish Greece.

1332

Naval league formed by Venice, the Hospitallers and the Greeks to clear the Aegean of Turkish pirates.

1333

Marino Sanudo Torsello, *Istoria del regno di Romania*; a history of the Frankish principalities in Greece and the Aegean, especially useful for the last days of the Latin Empire.

1335

The Hospitaller chapter-general offers leases of land on Rhodes without the obligation of residence or the provision of military service, and open to both Latins and Greeks. This does much to fill the Rhodian countryside outside the town of Rhodes, but leaves the Order dependent on serving brethren and mercenaries for its military operations (see also 1313).

1341

French version of the Chronicle of the Morea, *Livre de la conqueste de la princee de l'Amoree*, written for Catherine de Valois-Courtenay (see also 1388 and 1393).

1342

Aug.: Alfonso XI of Castile (1312–50) begins the siege of Algeciras with contingents from all over Europe (SC).

1343

Aug. 31: A new naval league of the Pope, Venice, the Hospitallers and the Cypriots formed.

1344

Mar. 25: Algeciras surrenders to Alfonso XI. Only Gibraltar remains in Muslim hands (SC).

Oct. 24: The forces of the naval league capture Smyrna (Izmir). It is conceded to the West in 1348 and remains in Christian hands until 1404.

1346

Anon., *Les Assise de Romanie*, collected together the customs and usages of the Latin states in Greece as they had evolved since the early thirteenth century.

1347

Apr.: A Hospitaller fleet sinks 100 Turkish ships in a battle off Imbros.

1348–50

The Black Death causes demographic and economic catastrophe in Western Europe, seriously undermining the ability to mount a crusade.

1349

July: Alfonso XI begins the siege of Gibraltar.

1350

Mar. 27: Alfonso XI dies of the Black death; the siege of Gibraltar is lifted (SC).

1354

Pope Innocent VI threatens to remove the Hospitallers from Rhodes if they do not take a more active role against the infidel.

The Ottoman Turks capture Gallipoli and gain a foothold in mainland Europe.

1359

Oct. 10: Peter I succeeds his father Hugh IV as king of Cyprus.

Nikephoros Gregoras, *Rhomaike Historia*, is a major source for the Byzantine Empire in the period 1204–1359.

1360

Easter: Peter I of Cyprus crowned king of Jerusalem at Famagusta by the papal legate Peter Thomas.

1361

Aug. 24: Naval flotilla provided by the Hospitallers and the Cypriots captures Antalya (Satalia). The port remains in Cypriot hands until 1373.

Ottoman Turks capture Demotika and Adrianople.

1362

June: Peter I of Cyprus announces his attention to lead a crusade to recover the Holy Land.

Oct.: Peter I of Cyprus travels to the West to raise support for a crusade. He travels widely, visiting Avignon, Paris, Prague, Vienna, Germany, England and the Low Countries, until returning to Cyprus via Venice in early 1365. It has been suggested that Peter targeted Alexandria because it had displaced Famagusta commercially, and that his goal was either to destroy harbour facilities or hold on to Alexandria as a Cypriot possession.

1363

Mar. 31: Urban V proclaims a crusade.

1365

June 27: Peter II leaves Cyprus to attack Alexandria.

Aug.: Expedition musters at Rhodes where the fleet numbers 165 ships.

Oct. 10: Alexandria captured in one day. Massacres and huge destruction are caused, including the destruction of the library of Alexandria. Apart from a huge quantity of booty it is unclear what should be done with the city.

Oct. 16: Crusade withdraws to Cyprus.

1366

Aug.–Dec.: Crusade led by Amadeo VI of Savoy ('the Green Count') to Thrace; recovers Gallipoli from the Turks but is unable to hold on to it.

1368

Philip of Mézières, *Nova religio passionis*, a prospectus for a new religious order dedicated to the crusade and incorporating members from the existing orders, enlarged in 1385 and 1396.

1369

Jan. 17: Peter I of Cyprus murdered. His son Peter II succeeds him.

1371

Sept. 26: Ottoman Turks crush the Serbs at the battle of Chernomen.

Guillaume de Machaut, *La Prise d'Alixandre*, a sympathetic account of the reign of Peter I of Cyprus (1359–69).

1373–4

Genoese invade and devastate Cyprus.

1375

Mamelukes capture Sis (Kozan) and take Leon VI (1373–93) and the Armenian royal family as captives to Cairo. Cilician Armenia extinguished as an independent kingdom.

1377

June: Hospitallers lease the principality of Achaea for five years from Joanna I, queen of Naples. They abandon the project in 1381 following difficulties in Achaea and in Rhodes.

1378

Mar. 27: Death of Pope Gregory XI.

Apr. 8: Bartolomeo Prignano elected Pope Urban VIII (–1389).

Apr.–Aug.: Hospitallers campaign in Epiros where they are defeated; many, including Grandmaster Juan Fernandez de Heredia, are captured. Heredia is held captive until May 1379.

Sept. 20: Thirteen cardinals declare the election of Urban VIII invalid and elect Robert of Geneva as Pope Clement VII at Avignon. The papal schism begins and causes many problems within the crusading community. The Hospitallers recognise the Avignonese papacy.

1383

July 7: Death of James of Les Baux, the last titular Latin emperor of Constantinople.

1388

Greek version of the Chronicle of the Morea, *To Chronikon tou Moreos*, in existence in the castle at Thebes (see also 1341 and 1393).

1389

June 15: Ottoman Turks crush the Serbs at the battle of Kossovo.

Philip of Mézières, *Le Songe du vieil pèlerin*, advocates peace between England and France as a sure basis for a successful crusade.

1390

July–Sept.: The crusade of Louis of Bourbon attacks Mahdia, near Tunis.

1391

Widespread rioting leads to the forcible baptism of many Jews in Spain. The loyalty of these *conversos* was to remain suspect for the next century (SC).

1393

Aragonese/Castilian version of the Chronicle of the Morea, *Libro de los Fechos et Conquistas del principado de la Morea*, commissioned by Juan Fernandez de Heredia, completed (see also 1341 and 1388).

1396

Sept. 25: Franco-Burgundian and Hungarian crusade wiped out at Nicopolis (Nikopol) in Bulgaria.

1399

Charles VI sends John II Boucicaut, marshal of France, to Constantinople with 1,500 men. Within the year Boucicaut returns to France after some minor successes against the Ottomans.

1400–1

Timur (Tamerlane) invades Syria and sacks Aleppo and Damascus.

1402

July 28: Timur defeats the Ottomans at Ankara and captures Bayezid I. For almost a generation Ottoman military pressure is relieved on Constantinople and Greece.

Independent Anatolian emirates re-emerge with the apparent eclipse of the Ottomans.

Dec.: Timur captures Smyrna from the Hospitallers and slights its defences.

1405

Feb. 19: Timur dies at Samarkand.

1406

Florence occupies Pisa. Pisan commercial privileges in the Levant are transferred to the Florentines. During the fifteenth century Pisa ceases to be a viable galley port as the Arno silts up.

1410

Sept.: Prince Ferdinand, the regent of John II of Castile (1406–54), captures Antequara (SC).

1417

Nov. 11: The election of Odo of Colonna as Pope Martin V ends the Great Schism (see also 1378).

1420–2

The first three anti-Hussite crusades.

1425

Aug.: Mameluke fleet raids the coast of Cyprus and burns Limassol.

1426

July 7: Mamelukes defeat Cypriots at Khirokitia; the Lusignans become vassals of the Mamaluk sultan.

1427

July–Aug.: Fourth anti-Hussite crusade.

1431

June–Aug.: Fifth anti-Hussite crusade.

   John II of Castile routs the Granadan army at Hugueruela (La Higeura). He does not follow up his victory with an attack on Granada but contents himself with deposing Muhammud VIII in favour of Yusuf IV as king of Granada. *Reconquista* is slipping from the priorities of the Spanish monarchs, who leave campaigns against the Moors in the hands of Spanish marcher lords (SC).

1432

The end of the Frankish principality of Achaea with the death of Centurione I Zaccaria. The Peloponnese is ruled as part of the Byzantine Empire by Thomas Palaiologos, the despot of Mistra.

1439

July 6: The union of the Greek and Latin churches is declared at the Council of Florence.

1440

Summer: Mameluke fleet attacks Rhodes and devastates the island of Kos.

1444

Aug.–Sept.: Forty-day siege of Rhodes by the Mameluke fleet.

Nov. 10: Hungarian crusade annihilated at Varna in Bulgaria.

1452

Dec. 12: Union of the Greek and Latin churches proclaimed in Constantinople (see also 1439).

1453

May 29: Mehmed II takes Constantinople; the end of the Byzantine Empire and a new imperial capital for the Ottomans.

1456

June 4: Athens is captured by the Ottomans; the end of the Frankish Duchy of Athens and Thebes.

1460

Conquest of the Morea (Peloponnese) by the Turks; Venice retains control of Argos, Nauplia, Modon and Korone. A Venetian garrison occupies Monemvasia on behalf of the papacy.

1462

One of the Spanish marcher lords (see 1431), the duke of Medina-Sidonia, captures Gibraltar (SC).

1464

Sigismondo Malatesta campaigns in Messenia.

1470

July 12: Ottoman Turks capture Negroponte (Chalkis) and the island of Euboea from Venice.

1477

Ferdinand and Isabella set up the Inquisition in Spain, ostensibly to check on the loyalty of conversos and moriscos (SC).

1480

May 23–Aug. 17: First major siege of Rhodes by the Ottomans.

Aug. 18: Turks capture Otranto in southern Italy and occupy it until the summer of 1481.

1485–99

The first Arabic printing of the *Qur'ān*, (Koran) done in Venice by Alessandro di Pagannini.

1489

Feb. 26: Catherine Cornaro, the Venetian widow of James II of Lusignan (d. 1473), cedes Cyprus to the Venetians.

1490

Apr.: Forces of Ferdinand and Isabella invest Granada (SC).

1492

Jan. 2: Granada surrenders (SC).

Jan. 6: Ferdinand and Isabella make a triumphal entry into Granada (SC).
  Spanish Jews given the choice of baptism or exile (SC).

1500

Muslims of Granada offered the choice of baptism or exile. Half a million baptised Muslims (*moriscos*) remained in the Iberian Peninsula until their expulsion from 1606 to 1614 (SC).
  Turks capture Modon and Korone from the Venetians.

1517

Ottomans defeat the Mamelukes and end the Mameluke dynasty in Egypt, incorporating it into the Ottoman Empire.

1522

Dec. 18: Rhodes surrenders to the Ottomans after a six-month siege.

1523

Jan. 1: Hospitallers withdraw from Rhodes, Kos and Bodrum. In 1530 they occupy Malta as their new headquarters, granted to them by Charles V of Spain.

1526

Aug. 29: Louis II of Hungary defeated at the battle of Mohacs. The Turks occupy Buda, and Hungary becomes a battleground in the Habsburg–Ottoman conflict. In 1551 it was incorporated into the Ottoman Empire (–1688).

1529

Sept. 21–Oct. 14: The first Ottoman siege of Vienna attracts Protestant as well as Catholic troops to its relief.

1532

Summer: Charles V commissions the Genoese admiral Andrea Doria to ravage the coast of Greece. He recaptures Lepanto (Naupaktos) and Korone; they are lost again to the Ottomans in the following year.

1535

July: Charles V captures the port of Tunis, occupied by Barbarossa in 1533. The expedition was preached and financed as a crusade by Pius III.

1538

Feb.: Holy League of Charles V, Pope Pius III and Venice against the Turks operating in the Adriatic.

Sept. 27: Fleet of the Holy League defeated at Prevesa by Barbarossa.

1540

Turks capture Monemvasia and Nauplia.

1565

May–Sept. 12: Hospitallers withstand the Ottoman siege of Malta.

1566

Turks capture Chios from the Genoese.

1571

Oct. 7: The Spanish and Venetian fleets under John of Austria defeat the Ottomans at the battle of Lepanto (Naupaktos).

1645–69

The war for Candia (Crete) is fought between the Venetians and the Ottoman Turks. It centres on prolonged sieges of Heraklion. In September 1669 Crete passes under Ottoman control.

1649

First translation of the Koran into English*: The Alcoran of Mahomet, translated out of Arabique into French; by the Sieur Du Ryer . . . And newly Englished, for the satisfaction of all that desire to look into the Turkish Vanities* **(London).**

1683

July 14–Sept. 12: Last Turkish siege of Vienna.

1684–1715

The War of the Holy League of Austria, Poland and Venice with the Turks is fought.
   The Venetians reoccupy large parts of the Peloponnese.

1718

July 21: Peace of Passarowitz restores the Peloponnese and the Aegean to the Ottomans. Venice retains control of the Ionian Islands.

1798

June 17: The Grandmaster of the Hospitallers, Ferdinand von Hompesch, twelve knights and two sergeants-at-arms leave Malta for Trieste; the French occupy Malta. Many of the Order's treasures and relics were lost aboard the French fleet in the subsequent battle of Aboukir Bay. In September 1800 the British occupy Malta.

II
NARRATIVE OUTLINE OF
THE CRUSADES

These outlines deal with essentials; further information may be gained from the references cited in the footnotes. The list is compiled from a pluralist viewpoint and contains activities on a broad crusading front. The chronological table in Part I records the principal events associated with each crusade and should be consulted in conjunction with each listed crusade. Crusading was a continuous process and some of what have come to be called 'seasonal crusades' have been listed, especially if they bear some relationship to other larger crusading campaigns. The traditional numbering of the latter from one to eight has been retained. The Northern Crusades of the Teutonic Knights and the Reconquista in Spain are dealt with separately at the end of the narrative outlines (see p. 205). I have relied entirely on the work of other scholars as the basis for these summaries and have given references with each crusade, which should act as convenient starting point for further work.

THE FIRST CRUSADE, 1096–9[1]

In many ways the only crusade to accomplish its aims as outlined in Urban II's appeal at Clermont. Its help to the Byzantine Empire was solid, if questionable, and certainly contributed to Graecophobia amongst succeeding crusading expeditions; but it was focused on the capture of Jerusalem and this it achieved. Indeed it went beyond Urban's programme and established Latin states and a Latin diocesan organisation in the East. Its achievement was in great part due to lack of unity; both in its own ranks, which meant that Jerusalem was the only goal on which all could agree, and to political divisions amongst the Muslims of Syria which allowed the crusaders to ally with the rulers of coastal towns in Syria and with the Fatamid rulers of Jerusalem. The success of the expedition against all odds was surprising, and this was reflected in the accounts written about it in the decades after 1100 (see Part IV). Clearly the expedition fulfilled the will of God. The accounts of the First Crusade, and the events and procedures outlined in them, set the ground rules for the later crusading movement, certainly in terms of papal authorisation and preaching, the vow and the assumption of the mark of the cross, and the granting of indulgence. It is perhaps the most written about and studied of the various crusades.

Traditionally the crusade falls easily into two divisions: the crusade of the people and the crusade of the princes – and its progress may be seen in the march to Constantinople, the march to Antioch and the siege of Antioch, the crisis of leadership from 1098 to 1099 and the march on and capture of Jerusalem.

The crusading armies were to set out after harvest time in 1096 and to meet in Constantinople. Although Urban seems to have planned to keep monarchs out of the crusade he could not have anticipated the appeal that his speech would have amongst the common people of Europe. Some 100,000 people were inspired to leave their homes, although many turned back or died before they reached Constantinople or soon after at Xerigordon. Five contingents of paupers had gathered in April and May 1096. The first two contingents to leave, led by Peter the Hermit and Walter the Penniless (Gautier sans avoir), reached Constantinople in July. The remaining three, led by Fulcher of Orleans, Gottschalk, and William the Carpenter, were dispersed in Hungary between June and August having made

---

[1] This is the most studied of all the crusades and has a prime place in university undergraduate syllabuses. C. Erdmann, *The Origin of the Idea of Crusade* (1935; Princeton, 1977) is a fundamental study; S.Runciman, *A History of the Crusades*, I (Cambridge, 1951) provides the definitive if dated account; S.B. Edgington, *The First Crusade* (London, 1996); J. France, *Victory in the East: A Military History of the First Crusade* (Cambridge, 1994); M. Bull. J. Phillips and J. France in *History Today*, March–April 1997, 10–22, 37–42; J. Riley-Smith, *The First Crusade and the Idea of Crusading* (London, 1986); J. Phillips, ed., *The First Crusade: Origins and Impact* (Manchester, 1997); T. Asbridge, *The First Crusade, A New History* (London, 2004); C. Cahen, 'An Introduction to the First Crusade', *Past & Present*, 6 (1954), 6–31; H.E. Cowdrey, 'Pope Urban II's Preaching of the First Crusade', *History*, 55 (1970), 177–88; id., 'The Gregorian Papacy, Byzantium and the First Crusade', in J. Howard-Johnston, ed., *Byzantium and the West c.850–c.1200* (1988), 146–69.

themselves a thorough threat to settled life by plundering and by participating in Jewish pogroms in the Rhine valley. The two contingents began to threaten public order in Constantinople and were ferried across the Bosphorus in August to await the arrival of the main crusading armies. By late October they had been annihilated by Turkish forces in the area, largely as a response to the plundering activities of the People's Crusade. Their only memorial was their heaps of bleached bones noted by the main crusading army as it passed by in the spring of 1097.

The major armies were commanded by the great princes: Raymond, count of St Gilles of Toulouse, who had been the first to take the cross at Clermont; Godfrey of Bouillon; Robert, duke of Normandy; Robert, count of Flanders; Stephen of Blois; Hugh of Vermondois and Bohemond of Taranto. Of these men we know the most, since their rank and wealth attracted the attention of later chroniclers. Some even had such chroniclers travelling in their ranks. Thus we know more about Raymond and about Bohemond because their deeds were written up by Raymond of Aguilars, the count of St Gilles' chaplain, and the anonymous writer of the *Gesta Francorum*, a knight in the army of Bohemond. Yet we know relatively little about Hugh of Vermondois, the brother of Philip I of France, since no chronicler seems to have travelled with his men. On the other hand, Stephen of Blois was to be raised to the ranks of a European coward for his desertion of the army at Antioch. Apart from the great men who earned a place in the chronicles there were many other lords, each with his own contingent of men and each regarding himself as an independent commander. The problem was compounded by the polyglot nature of the army, many of whom could not understand or be understood by their fellows, and by regional animosities. There was then no overall leadership and the army had to proceed by consensus, in which it was helped by the presence of the papal legate, Adhemar of Le Puy, whose death at Antioch on 1 August 1098 was to lead to bickering in the councils of the crusaders, quarrels amongst the various national groups and a serious delay in the march from Antioch to Jerusalem.

In June 1097 the crusading armies came together for the first time at Nicaea (modern Iznik). It is estimated that it numbered some 60,000, including 6,000 to 7,000 knights. Nicaea was surrendered to the Greeks on 18 June after a siege of one month. Two weeks later, on 1 July, a Seljuk army under Kilij Arslan was defeated at Dorylaion, and the road lay open to Antioch. At the end of October the crusaders arrived at Antioch, which was held by Yaghi-Sihan. The siege of the city lasted from 21 October 1097 to June 3 1098. Divisions amongst the Muslims of Syria aided the crusaders; there was no co-ordination at attempts at relief, and two separate armies from Damascus and Aleppo were defeated piece-meal on 31 December 1097 and 9 February 1098 respectively. Having gained the lower city the crusaders had not only to continue the attack on the citadel still held by Yaghi-Siyan but also had to withstand a siege from a relieving force led by Kerbogha of Mosul. The twenty-five days that followed was the most stressful and testing period of the whole crusade. It was marked by heightened religious awareness, by a variety of miraculous phenomena, and the finding of the Holy Lance in the Church of St Peter. It was also marked by a series of desertions from the crusader army, including that of Stephen of Blois. Kerbogha was defeated on 28 June 1098 before the walls of Antioch and the citadel thereafter surrendered. Deciding to rest and recoup until November, there followed a considerable delay in the march on Jerusalem. Raymond and Bohemond squabbled over the future of Antioch: should it be restored to Alexios I or become an independent state belonging to either Bohemond or Raymond? It was not until January 1099 that Bohemond drove the last of Raymond's men from positions in the city. From November Raymond busied himself to the south of Antioch at Marra and Arqa setting up a base of operations – what was to become the county of Tripoli – to counter Bohemond in Antioch. During this period the poor suffered greatly as food shortages took hold, and it was also during this period that stories of crusader cannibalism began to circulate. In May 1099 Godfrey of Bouillon, speaking for the discontented crusaders, forced Raymond to abandon the siege of Arqa and, with the exception of Bohemond and his followers in Antioch, resumed the march to Jerusalem. Shortage of arms and the need to keep in contact with Europe made the coastal route preferable to an advance on Jerusalem via Damascus. The journey south was not opposed, and the crusading army encamped before Jerusalem on 7 June 1099.

According to Raymond of Aguilers war, disease and desertions had reduced the crusader army to some 13,000 combatants of which 1,200 were knights – that is, still mounted warriors. They did, however, have the advantage of surprise since the Fatimids of Egypt, who had formed an alliance with the crusaders and in August 1098 had taken advantage of Seljuk engagement with the crusaders to seize Jerusalem, were totally unprepared for a crusader attack. They had abandoned the cities of the coast to make their own terms with the crusading army and had slighted the defences of Jaffa, which they felt unable to defend. They now set about the impromptu defence of Jerusalem and relied on succour coming from Ascalon.

The city fell on 15 July 1099 amid massacres of the Jewish and Muslim defenders of the city. The massacres that took place were neither exceptional nor unusual in terms of European warfare of the day. However, the religious triumphalism and rejoicing that accompanied these events, as described by Raymond of Aguilers, who was present at the fall of Jerusalem, and later imaginatively engraved by Gustave Dore in 1870, have left a baleful legacy in East–West relations as laden with menace and suspicion as a Dore engraving. On 22 July Godfrey of Bouillon was elected advocate of the Holy Sepulchre, and on 12 August 1099 a relief force led by al-Afdai, the vizier of Egypt, was defeated at Ascalon. The conquest of Jerusalem was now secure for the immediate future. One of the disadvantages of linking military expedition and pilgrimage now became apparent. It was impossible to turn an army of conquest into an army of occupation since on the fulfilment of their crusader vows the forces of the First Crusade in large part returned home. On 29 July 1099 Pope Urban II died without knowing of the capture of Jerusalem by the forces of the crusade he had set in train nearly four years previously.

CRUSADE OF 1101[2]

If the First Crusade was envisaged as a one-off expedition in 1095, its very success seemed to justify such military campaigning. Encouraged by reports of the success of the First Crusade, the failure of this crusade – which was defeated piecemeal by the Turks in Anatolia in August and September 1101 – enhanced the reputation of the men who went on the First Crusade. For the first time it focused the attention of chroniclers on explaining the failure of an expedition sanctioned by God, and they explained it in terms of the necessity for right intent and for behaviour acceptable to God on the part of crusaders. In terms of the crusading movement this crusade is important because it provided the earliest evidence of the ceremony of taking the cross and of some indications of the personal motivation of individual crusaders and their families. It also contributed substantially to the developing Graecophobia in the West that was to be a feature of so many later crusades.

In December 1100 Pope Paschal II issued an encyclical letter to the clergy of France calling for a new crusade to aid the Christians in Palestine. He had previously continued the policy of Urban II and threatened excommunication on those who had not fulfilled their crusade vows for the First Crusade. The crusade was formerly known as the crusade of the faint-hearted because it contained so many of these defaulters. It included those who had deserted enroute, and most notoriously the so-called 'rope-dancers' who had left the army at Antioch. As news of the triumphs of the First Crusade spread in the West, coupled with the preaching of the new crusade, recruitment went well in Lombardy, Aquitaine, Burgundy and Germany; areas largely unrepresented on the crusade of 1096. According to Ekkehard of Aura, who accompanied the crusade, and Guibert of Nogent, recruitment was equal to that of 1096 but also included large numbers of non-combatants. The chroniclers themselves were unclear as to which contingents fitted into which army, and since Ekkehard chose to travel by sea from Constantinople to Syria there is no clear record of the routes that were taken once the armies left for the interior of Anatolia.

Three armies were to meet in Constantinople and proceed to Syria. Alexios I treated the crusaders much as he had done their predecessors; extracting oaths that captured territories would be restored to Byzantine control and giving a mixture of admonition, practical advice and support. He had hopes that the crusade would reopen the route across Anatolia to Antioch.

---

[2] Riley-Smith, *The First Crusade and the Idea of Crusading*, 120–34; J.L. Cate, 'The Crusade of 1101', in K. Setton, ed., *A History of the Crusades*, I (Madison, 1969), 343–67; Runciman, *A History of the Crusades*, II, 18–31; H. Mayer, *The Crusades* (2nd edn, Oxford, 1988), 38–57.

Lack of co-ordination seems to have bedevilled the crusade from the outset. The first army to leave was that of the Lombards on 13 September 1100, led by Anselm, archbishop of Milan, and Albert, count of Biandrate. It arrived in Constantinople in late February 1101. Their progress through Byzantine territory had been marked by pillage and disorder and this did not improve on their arrival outside Constantinople where they attacked the Blachernae palace. In April they crossed to Nicomedia (Izmit) to wait for the arrival of the other armies, of whose approach they now learned. William IX of Aquitaine (often designated of Poitou) left for the East between 12 and 19 March 1101, and Welf IV of Bavaria on 1 April. Both arrived in Constantinople in early June 1101, and spent nearly six weeks there. In June the Lombard army, together with some German and French contingents, including Stephen of Blois, decided not to wait for the other crusaders as Alexios had advised and left Nicomedia heading for Ankara. Alexios I had provided some military support and had also persuaded Raymond of St Gilles, who had been in Constantinople since September 1100, to return east with this army as an adviser. The third army under William of Nevers had left in early February 1101 and arrived in Constantinople on 14 June. Ten days later he pushed on to overtake the Lombard army, not waiting for William and Welf.

The Franco-Lombard-German army rejected the advice of the disgraced but experienced Stephen of Blois and did not follow the route of 1097.[3] Instead they made for Ankara. After capturing the city, which they dutifully restored to the Byzantines, they seem to have decided to liberate Bohemond of Antioch who had been captured by the Danishmend Turks in August 1100 and was held captive at Niksar. They thus headed north-east to Gangra and thence east. In early August their army was destroyed by a coalition of Turkish princes near Merzifon. The survivors, including Stephen of Blois and Raymond, fled to the coast. The Turkish coalition was made up of Malik-Ghazi of Sebastea, Ridvan of Aleppo and Karaja of Hauran; the divisions between the Seljuk rulers, which had made possible the success of the First Crusade, were clearly being healed.

William of Nevers gave up his pursuit of the Lombard army at Ankara and headed south to Konya to regain the route of the First Crusaders. The Turks harassed him all the way. He failed to capture Konya and was forced to occupy a waterless position at Heraklea (Ereghli) where the Turks destroyed his army. Meanwhile William and Welf crossed into Anatolia in the middle of July and chose to follow the route of the First Crusaders. Supply problems dogged this army despite their weeks spent in Constantinople laying in provisions. It too was annihilated near Heraklea. Its leaders escaped to Tarsus where Hugh of Vermondois died of his wounds. The Turks captured a number of significant persons who later become the stuff of European legend: Ida the dowager

---

[3] Interestingly, despite his reputation, Stephen did not lack for the companionship of other French knights when he set out on crusade for the second time in the spring of 1101.

margravine of Austria as the reputed mother of Zengi, and Thiemo, bishop of Salzburg, for his martyrdom.

By the end of February 1102 survivors from the various armies gathered in Antioch. These included Stephen of Blois, William of Aquitaine, Welf and Raymond of St Gilles. Mutual recriminations were rife, and both Alexios I and Raymond were blamed for betraying the crusade to the Turks; these accusations had more to do with Antiochene politics than any basis in fact. On the march south to Jerusalem the town of Tortosa was captured and given to Raymond. It was to form the base for operations that were to lead to the establishment of the county of Tripoli. This was to prove the one solid achievement of the crusade. Many of the survivors who went to Jerusalem, including Stephen of Blois, were killed at the battle of Ramla on 17 May 1102; another military defeat which marked the end of this crusade.

CRUSADE OF SIGURD OF NORWAY, 1107–10[4]

King Sigurd 'Jorlsalfar' (1103–30) was the first crowned head to visit the Kingdom of Jerusalem and was treated with all due honour by Baldwin I. The expedition was as much a pilgrimage as a military expedition. It had taken one year to prepare and three years to make the journey by sea from Bergen fighting Moors. With the help of Sigurd's fleet Sidon was captured in December 1110. As the epithet 'Jorlsalfar' implies, Sigurd gained a great reputation in his homeland for his pilgrimage, Snorri Sturluson collected many anecdotes, of which many were still circulating in the thirteenth century. This was the first crusading campaign in which a European king participated.

BOHEMOND'S CRUSADE, 1107–8[5]

When Bohemond sailed for Italy in January 1105 to promote a crusade against Byzantium, and to restage the Norman campaign in the Balkans in which he had taken part in 1081–5, he was impoverished by the ransom payment for his release from captivity in 1103, defeated along with the forces of Edessa at Hauran by a coalition of the emirs of Mosul and Mardin on 7 May 1104, and losing territory in Cilicia and along the Latakia littoral to Byzantine forces.

As a leader of the First Crusade he was feted in France and Italy. Bolstered with the *Gesta Francorum*, which took a prejudiced view of the dealings of

[4] Runciman, *A History of the Crusades*, II, 92–3; Setton, ed., *A History of the Crusades*, I, 386–7; Snorri Sturluson, *Heimskringla*.

[5] Runciman, *A History of the Crusades*, II, 46–55; Setton, ed., *A History of the Crusades*, I, 390–2; R.W. Yewdale, *Bohemond I, Prince of Antioch* (Princeton, 1924), 107–37; T. Asbridge, *The Creation of the Principality of Antioch, 1098–1130* (Woodbridge, 2000), 94–103, 131–2, 136; *Oxford Dictionary of Byzantium* (henceforth *ODB*), under *sub* 'Bohemond' and 'Devol'.

Alexios I with the First Crusaders, and which he seems to have commissioned for the purpose, Bohemond seems to have had little difficulty in persuading Pope Paschal II to appoint a legate, Bruno of Segni, to preach a new crusade which was formally launched at the Council of Poitiers in 1106. Bohemond, as prince of Antioch, initiated the crusade, with papal approval coming later. The crusade was publicised as aimed at securing the way to Jerusalem, although there seems to have been some shared idea that this way would be at the expense of the Byzantine Empire. This idea of an attack on the Byzantine Empire seems to have enjoyed some currency with the papacy since the time of Gregory VII, but coming at this juncture it ensured that relations between eastern and western Christians would be strained. Indeed, Paschal never denounced Bohemond's attack on Byzantium, and according to Yewdale this was the first political crusade. In the autumn of 1107 Bohemond sailed for Avlona with a force of 34,000 men. He took the port and proceeded to invest Dyrrachium (Durazzo), where he was in turn invested by Alexios I and forced to submit in September 1108. By the Treaty of Devol he agreed to withdraw to Italy and to acknowledge Byzantine overlordship of Antioch. He died in Apulia in 1111, to be buried in a splendid mausoleum at Canossa di Puglia redolent of Christian and Islamic styles.

CRUSADE OF POPE CALIXTUS II, *c.* 1120/THE VENETIAN CRUSADE, 1122–4[6]

Following the defeat and death of Roger of Salerno, the regent of Antioch, together with the field army of the principality of Antioch at Darb Sarmada, dubbed appropriately in the West as the Battle of the Field of Blood (*ager sanguinis*) on 28 June 1119, the northern principality was left leaderless and defenceless. Antioch passed under the protection of Baldwin II of Jerusalem who appealed to the Pope for help.

Calixtus II supported the appeal and seems to have planned a crusade on a large scale. The outcome was the Venetian crusade that set sail with over a hundred ships on 8 August 1122. It wintered in Corfu and sought unsuccessfully to wrest the island from Byzantine control. It left the island in April 1123 on hearing news of the capture of Baldwin II near Raban. The Venetians arrived at Acre the following month and destroyed an Egyptian fleet off Ascalon. From February to July 1124 they participated in the successful siege of Tyre, for which they were rewarded with important commercial concessions in that town. In July the fleet returned to Venice.

---

[6] Runciman, *A History of the Crusades*, II, 150–1, 166–71; Riley-Smith, *The First Crusade and the Idea of Crusading*, 132; J. Riley-Smith, 'The Venetian Crusade of 1122–24' in G. Airaldi and B. Kedar, eds, *I communi italiani nel regno crociato di Gerusalemme* (Genoa 1986), 342–6.

CRUSADE/PILGRIMAGE OF FULK V OF ANJOU, 1120[7]

Fulk visited the Kingdom of Jerusalem for a year, leaving Anjou in May 1120 and returning by January 1122. Although he maintained 100 knights for the defence of the kingdom, and was well regarded by the nobles that he met there, he did not seem to have engaged in any military campaign.

CRUSADE OF CONRAD III, 1124[8]

The chronicler Ekkehard of Aura noted this small expedition to serve God and defend His patrimony. It does seem to have been a crusade, but no other details are known.

THE DAMASCUS CRUSADE, 1129[9]

From the mid-1120s Baldwin II of Jerusalem took a forward policy to his Muslim neighbours with attacks on Aleppo (1124) and on Damascus (1125 and 1126). Eager to secure a larger army for a third Damascus campaign and at the same time to secure the succession for his kingdom in 1127/8, he sent three embassies to the West. One, to Fulk V, count of Anjou and Maine, offered the hand of Baldwin's daughter Melisende and with it the succession to the throne of Jerusalem; in conjunction with this another embassy went to Pope Honorius II to gain his approval for the marriage. Fulk was 36 years old, a widower and a wealthy and vigorous warrior with some experience of the Kingdom of Jerusalem. Hugh de Payns headed the third mission in order to raise men for an extended attack on Damascus and to obtain papal approval for the order of the Temple. Like Bohemond's visit to the West in 1105, the initiative for this crusade came from the Latins in the East. However, unlike his appeal there seems to have been no papal endorsement for this crusade, which perhaps points to a lack of clarity in how crusades should be started. Clearly papal backing and initiation of preaching a crusade might promote greater take-up in Western Europe.

Fulk accepted the proposals for his marriage to Melisende and in May 1128 took the cross for the Damascus campaign at Le Mans. In May 1129 he arrived in the East with a substantial crusading force estimated at 60,000 men, in part raised by Hugh and in part by followers of Fulk. He was married to Melisende and in November took part in the attack on Damascus that was a military failure. However, two substantial results emerged: one was the capture of Banyas as part of the Damascus campaign; the other was the new rule for

---

[7] J. Phillips, *Defenders of the Holy Land: Relations between the Latin East and the West, 1119–1187* (Oxford, 1996), 29 and notes 71–2.

[8] Ekkehard of Aura,'Chronicon Universale', *MGH*.SS6, 262, cited by J. Phillips in J. Phillips and M. Hoch, eds, *The Second Crusade: Scope and Consequences* (Manchester, 2001), 17.

[9] Phillips, *Defenders of the Holy Land*, 19–43.

the Order of the Templars, approved by the Pope at the Council of Troyes in January 1129.

THE FIRST POLITICAL CRUSADE (?), 1135[10]

The papal hold over the patrimony of St Peter had been threatened during the 1130s by the ambitions of Roger II of Sicily who had sought to strengthen his position by supporting the antipope Anaclitus II. At a council at Pisa in May 1135 Pope Innocent II decreed that those who fought against the Pope's enemies for the liberation of the Church should enjoy the same indulgence as those granted by Urban II for the First Crusade. Housley and Riley-Smith have seen this as the harbinger of the political crusades of the thirteenth century. However, it is unclear whether any military expedition actually took place as a result of this pronouncement, whether anyone actually took the cross and a crusade vow, or indeed whether there was a plenary indulgence for those who survived the crusade as was the case with the Holy Land crusades. The debate continues and once formed a central issue in the discussions over the broad and narrow view of crusading (see The 'crusade against Markward of Anweiler', p. 155).

THE SECOND CRUSADE, 1145–9[11]

Although this crusade was of considerable importance in crusading ideology it is the least studied of the major military expeditions to the East, perhaps because it ended in failure. It is notable because of the crusade encyclical *Quantum praedecessores* issued by Pope Eugenius III on 1 December 1145 that confirmed and established the crusader indulgence of Pope Urban II and extended the privileges of crusaders to include the protection of crusader families and property, a moratorium on interest payments for debts, and eased the means of raising funding for crusading. It also clarified and confirmed that papal involvement and endorsement were essential for a crusade and ushered in a new period for crusading, with ruling monarchs taking a significant role; this period was to end with the twelfth century.

On 24 December 1144 Zengi, the Muslim ruler of Aleppo and Mosul, captured Edessa and by April 1145 had secured his conquest by controlling all Edessan territory to the east of the Euphrates. The first established crusader state

[10] N. Housley, 'Crusades Against Christians: Their Origins and Early Developments, c.1000–1216', in P. Edbury, ed., *Crusade and Settlement* (Cardiff, 1985), 17–37; Mayer, *The Crusades*, 312 note 108; J. Riley-Smith, *The Crusades: A Short History* (London, 1987), 93.

[11] B. Kugler, *Studien zur Geschichte des Zweiten Kreuzzugs* (Stuttgart, 1866), remains the only monograph on this crusade; Setton, ed., *A History of the Crusades*, I, 463–512; Runciman, *A History of the Crusades*, II, 247–90; Mayer, *The Crusades*, 93–106 Phillips, *Defenders of the Holy Land* 73–99; M. Gervers, ed., *The Second Crusade and the Cistercians* (New York, 1992); Phillips and Hoch, eds, *The Second Crusade: Scope and Consequences*; G. Constable, 'The Second Crusade as Seen by Contemporaries', *Traditio*, 9 (1953), 213–79.

had become the first to be lost, and with it the security of the Latin states to the west. The principality of Antioch was directly threatened, and should that fall then the county of Tripoli and the Kingdom of Jerusalem might not long survive it. Raymond, prince of Antioch, sent an embassy to Louis VII of France hoping for military support. Louis was not only married to Raymond's niece Eleanor of Aquitaine but, as king of the Franks, might be expected to have a special relationship with the Frankish states in the East. Meanwhile Queen Melisende sent emissaries to the West. Apart from the name of the most distinguished of them, Hugh, bishop of Jabala, the names of the others are unknown. On 1 December 1144 the Pope issued the bull calling for a new crusade, but the bull had not reached the French king who, at his Christmas court at Bourges, proposed an expedition to bring aid to the Latins in the East. It seems to have been a military proposal, only with no reference to indulgences or privileges. Its reception at the French court was cool and any decision was postponed to Easter 1145 after Bernard, abbot of Clairvaux, had been consulted. Clearly neither the Pope nor the king had co-ordinated their response. It is noteworthy that whereas the rulers of the crusader states considered papal authorisation desirable if not essential, Louis VII was not so clear and was prepared to crusade on his own authority. His reaction shows the extent to which clarity was required in the crusading movement by the mid-twelfth century if papal authority over it was to be maintained.

Bernard brought about the necessary co-ordination, bolstered the papal initiative and soothed a potentially damaging situation. On 1 March 1145 Pope Eugenius III reissued the crusading bull, sent King Louis a crusading cross, and authorised Bernard to preach the crusade in France. Bernard began his preaching at Vezelay on 31 March 1146 and thereafter followed this up with further sermons and a prolific correspondence. At first it seems that the recruitment to the crusade was focused on France, but word had spread to Germany where an unauthorized preacher, a Cistercian monk called Radulf (Ralph), was not only preaching the crusade enthusiasm but was stirring up anti-Semitism and leading a life in Mainz not in keeping with his calling. Bernard silenced Radulf, preached against any anti-Semitic violence, and continued to preach the crusade in Germany and Switzerland culminating in his moving sermon before Conrad III at the Christmas court at Speyer where Conrad and many others took the cross.

The chronicler Otto of Freising, himself a participant in the crusade, noted the large numbers involved in the crusade in Europe and the change in atmosphere as a result of Bernard's preaching. There was an emphasis upon peace in Europe so that the crusade could go forward. In part this accounts for the presence of two eminent rulers like Conrad III and Louis VII. Crusaders were coming from France, Germany, Italy and England. Eugenius and Bernard seem to have gone with the flow of crusading enthusiasm and for the first time explicitly linked expeditions against the Muslims in Spain and the pagan Wends in north-east Germany to the crusade movement. From the time of the First Crusade little distinction had been made between liberating Christians in the East and in the Iberian Peninsula; now it was official they were both crusades with the same crusading indulgences and privileges, as defined by Eugenius in his encyclical letter of December 1145. Many German lords like Henry the Lion were eager to continue expeditions against the Wends, and these were clearly accommodated. Those intending to fulfil their crusading vows by fighting against the Wends adopted a distinctive badge, a cross on an orb. On 13 April 1147, in the encyclical letter *Divina dispensatione*, the huge scale of the crusade was revealed with reference to crusades in the East, in Spain and against the Wends in north-east Europe. Here was planning on a scale that may have been envisaged by Calixtus II in 1120.

Two armies converged on the East: those of Conrad III and Louis VII; in the latter's army marched substantial contingents led by Amadeus of Savoy and Alfonso Jordan of Toulouse. In addition an Anglo-Flemish naval expedition was to sail direct to the Holy Land; on the way it made a significant contribution to the capture of Lisbon (1147) and of Tortosa (1148), one of the few territorial acquisitions made during this vast crusade. Four armies operated against the Wends, including an army led by Henry the Lion of Saxony, and four campaigns were mounted in the Iberian Peninsula. Helmold, priest of Bossau, who wrote about all three campaigns, was in no doubt that all these separate campaigns formed part of one great crusade endeavour; it was the most numerous and most ambitious crusade ever mounted.

Between February and June 1147 the route and logistics were worked out between the participants in the crusade to the East. Conrad's army left Nuremberg on 15 June and in September crossed into Anatolia. The army was routed by the Turks near Dorylaion and the survivors gathered in Nicaea to await the arrival of Louis. Louis VII, accompanied by his wife, left Paris on 11 June and arrived in Constantinople in October. The Byzantine emperor, Manuel I Komnenos, attempted to deal with the crusade leadership, much as had his grandfather Alexios I. However, he was occupied with Norman attacks on central Greece in which Corinth and Thebes were sacked and therefore particularly suspicious of the French contingent. The crusaders paid homage to Manuel and agreed not to capture any Byzantine-held territory, but they refused to agree to hand back any territories captured that might once have belonged to the Byzantines since this included Edessa and might also compromise their relationship with Raymond of Antioch.

The armies suffered from food shortages and from Turkish attacks on the march across Anatolia. The large numbers of non-combatants made progress slower and exacerbated the shortages and the casualties. Conrad was forced to retire to Constantinople at one stage due to ill health, and Louis took ship from Atalya to Antioch.

All the crusade leadership and the remainder of their armies came together at Acre on 24 June 1148. The crusade army was now too small to mount an attack to recover Edessa. Instead it was decided to attack Damascus, a city of undoubted strategic value but one not actually opposed to the Latin states at that time. Grousset, Runciman and Mayer have seen this decision as ridiculous, but the military importance of Damascus had been realised as early as 1099 when the First Crusaders had to abandon any thought of a march to Jerusalem via Damascus for logistical reasons; the city had also figured as a target in the forward policy of Baldwin II from 1125–9. The city, which became the head-quarters of Nur ed-Din from 1154, would have made a strategically desirable possession between the coast and the desert, and to some extent its occupation might have offset the loss of Edessa. The attack failed utterly and the citizens of Damascus were propelled from a neutral position to one in favour of Nur ed-Din. Conrad III returned to Germany via Constantinople in September 1149 and Louis VII began his journey home in June 1150.

The collapse and failure of so great an expedition led to despondency in the West. Just how could a divinely endorsed enterprise fail in such a way? Chroniclers sought an explanation in the will of God or in the lack of right intent amongst the crusaders, and their comments reflected badly on all participants: the two most exalted rulers in Western Europe, Bernard of Clairvaux and the whole Cistercian Order, the Knights Templars, and the Byzantines. For the first time a crusade was assessed in terms of its achievements and measured by suc-cess or failure in fulfilling its declared aims. It encouraged Nur ed-Din in his counter-crusade; in 1150 he publicly declared his intention of waging the jihad to protect the Hirwan from the Franks. The city of Damascus was forcibly captured by Nur ed-Din on 25 April 1154; it seems that the crusade had not adversely affected the stance of the citizens to seek the protection of the Kingdom of Jerusalem. Equally, despite despondency in the West, the crusader kingdoms more than held their own in the East, with the years 1176 to 1186 witnessing a new forward policy in Transjordan and a policy of *détente* with the Byzantine Empire. However, from the point of view of the crusading movement in Western Europe there was no will to respond to appeals for military assistance from the East subsequent upon the Second Crusade. It took the wind out of crusading for some four decades until a new overwhelming military catastrophe in the East necessitated substantial military assistance from Europe.

THE CRUSADING PROJECT OF 1149–50[12]

Generally seen as a minor episode at the end of the Second Crusade, and possibly exploiting anti-Greek feeling, to mount an attack on Byzantium led by Roger of Sicily and Louis VII. In the last decade research has indicated that anti-Greek feeling was not as prevalent in the West as the writings of Odo of Deuil and Peter

---

[12] Mayer, *The Crusades*, 104; Phillips, *Defenders and of the Holy Land*, 100–39; T. Reuter, 'The Non-Crusade of 1150', in Phillips and Hoch, eds, *The Second Crusade: Scope and Consequence* 150–63; G. Constable, 'The Crusade Project of 1150' in B. Kedar *et al.*, eds, *Montjoie: Studies in Crusade History in Honour of Hans Eberhard Mayer* (Aldershot, 1997), 67–75.

the Venerable might suggest, and that the crusade discussions in France in mid-1150 were the result of the deteriorating military situation in the East following not just the collapse of the Second Crusade but the subsequent death in battle of Raymond of Antioch on 29 June 1149. Rather than being a prefiguration of the Fourth Crusade, this crusade that never was anticipated the Third Crusade.

THE 'CRUSADE'/PILGRIMAGE OF HENRY THE LION, 1172[13]

Henry the Lion, duke of Saxony and Bavaria (1131–89), had taken a substantial part in the Wendish crusade of 1147. He became a legendary figure amongst German medieval rulers: married to Matilda, the daughter of Henry II of England in 1168, her dowry made his pilgrimage possible, whilst his military prowess had subdued Saxony by 1171. In 1180 he was outlawed for treason against the emperor, Frederick Barbarossa, and spent some years in exile in England. At the height of his power in 1172 he made a visit to the Holy Land. A large retinue of knights accompanied him. Although these saw service in repulsing two Serb attacks during the passage through the Balkans, they were there as a mark of his rank and status rather than as crusaders. He left Saxony in January 1172, spent Easter in Constantinople, June–July in the Holy Land and was back in Bavaria in December 1172. This expedition is sometimes dubbed a crusade, but this is misleading since it was very much a pilgrimage and an opportunity to visit fellow rulers in Austria, Hungary and Constantinople. Henry was at pains not to offer any military assistance to the Latin states and contented himself with visiting religious sites, making bequests, and collecting relics that he later passed on to churches in Saxony. He was one of the most important visitors to the Holy Land in the twelfth century and was duly feted by Amalric I in Jerusalem and by Bohemond III in Antioch.

THE THIRD CRUSADE, 1187–92[14]

The destruction of the field army of the Kingdom of Jerusalem at Hattin, northwest of Tiberias, on 4 July 1187 left the kingdom defenceless and at the mercy of

[13] K. Jordan, *Henry the Lion: A Biography* (Oxford, 1986), 150–6; E. Joranson, 'The Palestine Pilgrimage of Henry the Lion', in J. Cate and E. Anderson, eds, *Medieval and Historigraphical Essays in Honor of James Westfall Thompson* (Chicago, 1938), 190–202; Runciman, *A History of the Crusades*, II, 393.

[14] Perhaps the best-known crusade to English-speaking audiences, in part due to the stirring tales associated with it and in part to films about Robin Hood starring Errol Flynn (1948) and Kevin Costner (1991). See K. Biddick, *The Shock of Medievalism* (Durham, N.C., 1998), 71–80. It still lacks a monograph, and the best studies are in the lives of the individual crusading monarchs. P. Munz, *Frederick Barbarossa* (London, 1969), 370–96; J. Gillingham, *Richard I* (London, 1999), 123–53; J. Bradbury, *Philip Augustus* (London, 1998), 72–105; Runciman, *A History of the Crusades*, III, 3–106: Mayer, *The Crusades*, 137–51; Setton, ed., *A History of the Crusades*, II, 45–122; J. Riley-Smith, *The Crusades: A Short History*, 109–117.

Saladin's victorious troops. With the exception of Tyre, ably defended by Conrad of Montferrat, the whole kingdom was now occupied by Saladin who entered Jerusalem on 2 October 1187 and immediately set about restoring the sacred sites of Islam and removing all trace of the Latin presence. Genoese merchants brought the news to Rome in mid-October. It came as a profound shock, both because of the extent and nature of the disaster and of its unexpectedness. This latter point has been emphasised, yet there had been an embassy from the East in 1184–5 asking for help and reporting on the parlous condition in the Kingdom of Jerusalem. Nonetheless, it is said that the elderly Pope Urban III died of grief on 20 October, but within nine days his successor Gregory VIII had issued the encyclical *Audita tremendi* calling for a crusade to liberate Jerusalem, at the same time emphasising the need for right intention and sincere repentance and amendment of their sins on the part of the intending crusaders. It appeared that the lessons of the last eighty-five years focused attention on Christian outlook, attitudes, and the behaviour of all Christians; there was a shift from peace and unity in Christendom to the lives of each and every Christian. This was an important development in crusading ideology.

In mid-October 1188 Archbishop Joscius of Tyre was in Rome bringing news of the current state of the Latin Holy Land, and in particular of the brave defence of Tyre. He was appointed to preach the crusade, along with the Cardinal Legate Henry of Albano. Joscius had visited William II of Sicily at Palermo on his way to Rome, and it was William who was the first western ruler to respond. He sent his admiral, Margarit of Brindisi, to Tyre with a fleet of fifty ships. These saved Tripoli from capture and kept the supply lines open for it and for Tyre and Antioch, making a considerable contribution in keeping at least three ports in Latin hands. On 18 November 1189 William II died and Margarit was recalled to Sicily; whatever plans William may have had for participation in a crusade died with him.

Preaching of the crusade went on apace. From the pen of Gerald of Wales there survives an account of the preaching of the crusade in Wales by Baldwin, archbishop of Canterbury, whom he accompanied. Here for the first time there is evidence of the way such campaigns were organised and delivered, together with some indication of the response to the preacher's exhortations. It is clear that penitence and right intent were to the fore in the preacher's message for this crusade. On 22 January 1188 Archbishop Joscius preached the crusade to Henry II of England, Philip II of France and Philip, count of Flanders, assembled at Gisors to discuss a truce. All took the cross, and at this meeting it was agreed that the date for departure would be Easter 1189 and that each grouping would wear distinctive crosses: the English white, the French red and the Flemish green. Was this following the trend in fashion set by the Wendish crusade in 1147 – and what colour did the German crusaders wear? Henry of Albano preached the cross in Germany. On 27 March 1188 Frederick I Barbarossa summoned a special court, a *curia Jesu Christi*, at which he and many German nobles took the cross; the date of departure was set for 23 April 1189.

Disputes between Henry II and Richard, and between the Plantagenets and the Capetians, delayed matters, as did the death of Henry II on 6 July 1189 and the subsequent coronation of Richard I. Eventually it was agreed that Richard and Philip would depart on crusade on 1 July 1190. Meanwhile, the German crusade had left Regensburg on 11 May 1189. After a difficult passage through Byzantine territory relations between Frederick and Manuel became so strained that Frederick seriously contemplated an attack on Constantinople itself. The Dardanelles were crossed in late March 1190 and, though harassed by Turkish light cavalry as they marched across Anatolia, they reached Cilician Armenia in good order in early June. It was here that disaster struck when the septuagarian emperor was drowned in the Saleph River (Goksu). The crusade fractured, some returning home, others going on to Antioch by either sea or land. What was left of one of the largest crusading armies ever to leave the German Empire gathered before Acre in October 1190. During the previous month a variety of flotillas arrived at Acre, some from Cologne, some from London and some from Messina, bringing much-needed reinforcements to Guy and alarming Saladin into renewed efforts to relieve Acre.

On his release from captivity after the battle of Hattin, King Guy of Jerusalem had gone to Tyre but had been refused entry into the city by Conrad of Montferrat who questioned his right to the Kingdom of Jerusalem. Guy had marched south and begun the siege of Acre, whence he had attracted many of his former knights from Tyre and where he had been involved for eighteen months prior to the arrival of the German crusaders.

Philip reached Acre on 20 April 1191; Richard, having spent one month in taking Cyprus, arrived on 8 June. On 12 July Acre was surrendered. Philip and Richard divided the city between them as they had agreed. On 28 July they also delivered their judgment on the claims of Conrad and Guy to the Kingdom of Jerusalem, since as two prominent European monarchs they were asked to adjudicate in the case that had become even more involved since Conrad's rejection of Guy at Tyre two years previously. Guy was king of Jerusalem in right of his wife Sibylla who, together with the two daughters she had borne Guy, had died in September 1190. The succession passed to Sibylla's half-sister Isabel who at the time was married to Humphrey of Tibnine, yet Guy was still the anointed king of Jerusalem. A baronial party at odds with the Lusignans and conscious of the many qualities of Conrad sought to set Guy aside in favour of Conrad by marrying him to Isabel. Accordingly, the necessary divorce was procured and the marriage celebrated despite the fact that Conrad was already married. It was this tangled situation that the kings were asked to adjudge. It was agreed that Guy of Lusignan was to remain king of Jerusalem for the remainder of his life but that on his death the succession would pass to Conrad and his new bride. In the meantime Conrad was to receive a lordship based around Tyre that he had so ably defended in 1187 and 1188. Philip of France returned home on 31 July leaving a substantial force of French crusaders behind under the command of Hugh, duke of Burgundy, and gifting his half of Acre to Conrad of Montferrat, revealing with whom his sympathies lay in the dispute over the kingship. It was during this period at Acre that negotiations between Richard and Saladin for the exchange of prisoners, payment of ransom and the return of the True Cross broke down and led to the massacre of the Muslim garrison of Acre that had previously surrendered.

On 22 August the crusade army, under its various commanders, set out to march to Jaffa where they arrived on 9 September having repulsed an attack by Saladin at Arsuf on 7 September. This battle, although celebrated as a victory, left a large Muslim force intact and its presence was to dictate just what the crusading force could achieve. Having twice marched on Jerusalem the crusaders drew back from besieging the city because they could not secure their supply lines to the coast nor invest the city in security with an undefeated Muslim army in their vicinity. Instead, the value of the coastal towns in Latin hands was preferred to the goal of Jerusalem. Having restored the defences of both Jaffa and Ascalon the army retired to Acre on 26 July 1192. In Acre itself, in early 1192 whilst this campaign was underway, anti-Lusignan elements dissatisfied with the judgment of the two monarchs in July 1191 had sought to overthrow King Guy and had been negotiating with Saladin to this end. In mid-April Richard heeded advice that Conrad should be king and granted the lordship of Cyprus to Guy, who had to buy it from the Templars to whom Richard had sold the island. All did not go as planned, since on 28 April 1192, before his coronation could take place, Conrad of Montferrat was murdered by members of the sect of Assassins. Some supporters of Conrad thought Richard responsible, but the case remains open. On 9 October Richard left Acre to begin his journey home. The crusade had achieved a great deal, leaving the Latin kingdom that consisted of just Tyre on its arrival now in possession of the coast from Tyre to Acre and with Ascalon as a demilitarised town. It had failed to restore Jerusalem, but strategy rather than emotion had prevailed and the Latin kingdom, with the coastal cities in its hands, was to last for another century; it remained the Kingdom of Jerusalem, but Jerusalem was no longer within its borders. The continuance of a Latin political and military presence in the East was the outcome of this crusade.

It is often seen as a peculiarly English crusade. This erroneous impression is due to the preponderance of Anglo-Norman sources in providing the detailed accounts of the crusade, in the larger-than-life figure of Richard within those sources, and to the work of Hollywood film studios in the twentieth century. It completely ignores the large contingent of German crusaders that enthusiasm for crusading had caused to set out in one of the largest crusade contingents ever, and many of whom, like Duke Frederick of Swabia, were to die at Acre. Philip II of France's contribution too was not insignificant during his six-week stay in the Holy Land. It was the first crusade in which naval transport and naval forces were used extensively, and in this it set a trend for future crusading expeditions. Ships were used in conjunction with land forces in the advance on Jaffa, whilst travelling to the East by sea reduced the number of camp followers and non-combatants substantially and eased the problem of supply en route.

THE GERMAN CRUSADE, 1197[15]

The initiative for this crusade came from the emperor Henry VI who took the cross at Bari in Holy Week 1195 and summoned his subjects to follow suit. The core of the new crusading army was to be composed of 3,000 mercenaries paid for by Henry and officered by imperial officials. The new crusade was in part to complete the work of his father Frederick Barbarossa, who had died on crusade before reaching the Holy Land, and to advertise the international prestige of the German emperor who seemed set on adding the former Norman Kingdom of Sicily to his possessions and thus becoming a player on the Mediterranean scene in his own right. In 1147, and again in 1189, a large crusading contingent had set out from German lands, and there was every prospect that the new army would match the previous expeditions in size and eminence.

On 1 August Pope Celestine III proclaimed a new crusade and instructed the German clergy to preach it. Henry planned and finalised the logistics for the crusade at the diet of Wurzburg in March 1196. It was to be a seaborne operation, and the crusaders departed from Bari and other ports in southern Italy in the following spring, arriving in Acre on 22 September 1197. Henry was unable to lead the crusade in person since poor health and rebellions amongst his new subjects in southern Italy necessitated his presence there. Overall command was entrusted to Conrad of Wittelsbach, the archbishop of Mainz.

The crusade achieved the linking of Tyre with the county of Tripoli by capturing the coastal towns of Sidon, Beirut, Jubail and Botron. However, news of the death of Henry VI at Messina on 28 September 1197 resulted in the abandonment of the crusade by the summer of 1198, as the leadership sought to return home to protect their interests. The prestige and renown of the German emperors had also been secured by the crowning of the king of Cyprus and the king of Cilician Armenia by the archbishop of Mainz. Whether all this would be lost now that Henry's infant son Frederick II was king remained to be seen.

THE CRUSADE AGAINST MARKWARD OF ANWEILER, 1198[16]

In November 1199 Innocent III declared a crusade against Markward of Anweiler who since 1198 had opposed papal claims to the regency of Sicily. This

---

[15] W. Leonhardt, *Der Kreuzzugsplan Kaiser Heinrich VI* (Leipzig, 1913); Runciman, *A History of the Crusades*, III, 91–7; Setton, ed., *A History of the Crusades*, 116–22; H.E. Mayer, *The Crusades*, 150–1; Riley-Smith, *The Crusades: A Short History*, 118–19.

[16] N. Housley, *The Italian Crusades* (Oxford, 1982), 1, 64, 66, 70; E. Kennan, 'Innocent III and the First Political Crusade', *Traditio*, 27 (1971), 231–49; T. van Cleve, *Markward of Anweiler and the Sicilian Regency* (Princeton, 1937); J. M. Powell, *The Deeds of Pope Innocent III by an Anonymous Author* (Washington, DC, 2004), 23–47; Riley-Smith, *The Crusades: A Short History*, 132–3.

is often seen as the first political crusade, despite the precedent set by Innocent II's declaration at Pisa in May 1135 (see p. 147), since there is substantial documentary evidence for it and it did result in limited military action.

Henry VI, who had gained the Kingdom of Sicily by marrying its heiress Constance in 1185, died in September 1197. His widow committed her infant son Frederick and the Kingdom of Sicily to the care of Innocent III. Markward, for his part, claimed to have been appointed regent of Sicily in the testament of Henry VI. Just prior to Constance's death in November 1198 he had threatened to invade the kingdom in the Hohenstaufen interest. Markward was an able and devoted *ministerialis* of the Hohenstaufen and in 1184 was appointed steward to Frederick Barbarossa. He was a prominent member of Frederick's crusade and served with his son Frederick of Swabia until the latter's death at Acre in 1191. Thereafter he was seneschal at the court of Henry VI and active in Italy. He is castigated in the *Gesta Innocenti* as 'another Saladin' and 'worse than the infidels'. All who fought against him received the same indulgences as crusaders to the East. Only a few took up the challenge, most notably Walter, count of Brienne, who had married the heiress of the late King Tancred of Sicily and who was eager to secure his claim to the county of Lecce and the principality of Taranto. The need for the crusade ended with the death of Markward in 1202. Interestingly, Innocent had written in 1199 that if Markward held Sicily transport and supplies to a crusade to the East would be adversely affected; a crusade against Markweiler was seen as a precondition for the recovery of the Holy Land.

THE FOURTH CRUSADE, 1198–1204[17]

Listed as the first of the misguided crusades by Runciman and as the unholy crusade by Godfrey, the Fourth Crusade has enjoyed a bad press. Yet from a crusading perspective it was innovative in many ways, and not just by its diversion to Constantinople and the subsequent conquest of parts of the Byzantine Empire. Its avowed aim was the liberation of Jerusalem by an attack on Egypt – the first time that such a strategy had been adopted. It was recognised that this strategy would not be popular during recruitment, and the idea was down-played at this stage; but at Zara in December 1202, when the crusading leadership was discussing the proposal of Alexios that it should go to Constantinople to restore him and thus to re-endow the crusade from his beneficence, it was clearly stated by

[17] D. Queller and T. Madden, *The Fourth Crusade: The Conquest of Constantinople* (2nd edn, Philadelphia, 1997); M. Angold, *The Fourth Crusade: Event and Context* (London, 2003); J. Phillips, *The Fourth Crusade and the Sack of Constantinople* (London, 2004); J. Godfrey, *1204: The Unholy Crusade* (Oxford, 1980); A. Andrea, *Contemporary Sources for the Fourth Crusade* (Leiden, 2000); Riley-Smith, *The Crusades: A Short History*, 121–30; Mayer, *The Crusades*, 196–213; Runciman, *A History of the Crusades*, III, 107–31; Setton, ed., *A History of the Crusades*, II, 153–276; K. Setton, *The Papacy and the Levant*, I (Philadelphia, 1976), 1–26; P. Lock, *The Franks in the Aegean* (London, 1995).

those in favour that 'We must insist that only by way of Egypt and Greece [Constantinople] can we hope to recover the land overseas [Outremer], if that ever happens at all. If we reject this agreement it will be to our everlasting disgrace.'

It was planned as a sea borne crusade, the first time that such a tactic had been tried on a crusade that contained no wealthy ruling monarchs and indicated that trends emerging in the crusades of the 1190s were becoming the norm. Such was the expense of sea transport that it virtually eliminated the presence of non-combatants and made for a much more professional crusading cadre. It also created the huge debt of 85,000 marks that was owed to the Venetians and that gave them a considerable influence in crusade counsels leading initially to the attack on the Christian city of Zara, itself acknowledging the lordship of a king who had recently taken the cross.

After a period, 1147–97, in which monarchs dominated the crusading cam-paigns, here was a crusade with predominately French and Flemish noblemen, many of whom came from families with a considerable crusading tradition and experience. It was not that Pope Innocent III had planned a crusade without reigning monarchs but that these were just not available in 1199; Richard I and Philip II of France were at war. Germany too was in turmoil. Frederick II was an infant. His uncle Philip of Swabia (1178–1208) was elected German king in March 1198, and the son of Henry the Lion, Otto of Brunswick (c. 1175–1218), was elected counter-king by the Welf interest in June of the same year. On 6 April 1199 Richard I died of wounds that he received besieging the castle of Chalus-Chabrol near Limoges; his successor, John, needed to establish himself in power and continue the defence of Angevin possessions in France. Leadership of the proposed crusade would have to be taken up by the nobility. This had worked during the First Crusade. The wrangling that the monarchical presence seemed always to entail would be obviated and papal control of the crusading movement would be reasserted. Yet the absence of monarchs also meant the absence of deep pockets, and papal control did not work in practice – either at the stage of the preaching of this crusade nor during the decision-making process actually on crusade.

Despite the emotive appeal of Jerusalem it had been put to one side in the crusades of the 1190s in favour of strategic assessment by the crusade leadership. Strategic assessment was to the fore in the planning and execution of this crusade. Equally it was not the first crusade in which an attack on Constantinople had been contemplated; indeed, some such scheme may be discerned in the correspondence of Pope Gregory VII in the mid-1070s, and every Byzantine emperor who had to deal with the crusader host in transit was concerned for the safety of Constantinople. Usually, however, it had been frustrations in dealing with the Byzantine emperors in the environs of the city that had led to such thoughts on the part of crusading monarchs. In September 1147 the advisers of Conrad III had urged an attack on the city in conjunction with the fleet of Roger II of Sicily, then present in the Aegean whilst his forces campaigned in Greece, and in November 1189 Frederick Barbarossa had written to his son Henry to arrange with the Italian maritime republics to send a fleet to Constantinople for March 1190 to besiege the city. In both cases crusading zeal had saved Constantinople and the armies had passed on their way to the East. During the late twelfth century the actions of the Greeks against Italian merchants in the city, and the news of diplomatic agreements with Saladin, possibly to delay and break up crusading armies, served to increase anti-Greek feeling in the West and in crusading terms to make Byzantium a dubious partner in the enterprise. An attack on Constantinople did not just come out of the blue. It had been contemplated for the last fifty years at least, and by 1200 a Constantinople in reliable western hands might be deemed as much of an asset for the liberation of Jerusalem as the conquest of Alexandria. From 1202 the presence of the refugee Alexios (IV), the son of the deposed emperor Isaac Angelos, in the west seeking military support for the restoration of his father and himself, and liberal with his promises of financial aid to the crusade, served to mollify any scruples that the crusading army might harbour about an attack on a Christian city. All this, though, had to wait until the position of the crusaders at Constantinople turned desperate with the murder of Alexios IV on 8 February 1204.

On 15 August 1198, probably following an appeal from the Latins in the East, Innocent III issued a crusade encyclical, *Post miserabile*, to all Christian people to be ready to set out for the East by March 1199 for a campaign anticipated to last two years. He appointed two legates to preach the crusade: Cardinal-priest Soffredo, who concentrated on Italy and Venice in particular, and Cardinal-deacon Peter Capuano, who worked north of the Alps. The crusade indulgence promised, on God's behalf, the remission of sins for which penitence had been expressed and a share in eternal salvation. This was a development of the theme of repentance, and, as the chronicler Villehardouin recorded, it was well received in France. The indulgence was also extended to those who provided funding for a crusader.

At the tournament at Ecry in late November 1199 Count Thibaut of Champagne and his cousin Count Louis of Blois, both grandsons of Louis VII of France and both from families with a formidable crusade tradition, took the cross and thereby set in train recruitment for the new crusade throughout France and Flanders. Regular meetings were held between the principal leaders; at one of these meetings at Compiègne in 1200 (most probably June, although the date is uncertain) it was agreed that envoys should be sent to Venice to negotiate the provision of sea transport for the expedition. The chronicler Villehardouin, who was one of the envoys, records that six envoys were appointed with full powers to conclude an agreement and armed with charters confirming this; two envoys each were selected by Thibaut, Louis of Blois and Baldwin of Hainault and Flanders, who had taken the cross on 23 February 1200. Venice was chosen as the possible carrier, both because of the mission of Cardinal Soffredo in November 1198 and because experience of Genoese transports during the Third Crusade prompted another supplier.

In April 1201, the so-called Treaty of Venice was agreed by which the

Venetians undertook to build transports for 4,500 horses and 9,000 squires and other ships to accommodate 4,500 knights and 20,000 foot soldier. Nine months' rations for the men and fodder for the horses was also to be supplied. The fleet to be ready by April 1202 with a sailing date set for 29 June. The Venetians would man and sail the flotilla for one year after its departure from Venice. The cost asked by the Venetians was 4 marks per horse and 2 marks per man – a total of 85,000 marks. A secret treaty stated that the destination of the expedition was Egypt. This was a tremendous undertaking for the Venetians and one that would involve the interruption of normal commercial trading activities for a year.

Between June and August 1202 the crusading army slowly gathered at Venice to be housed on the island of St Nicholas, now better known as the Lido. There had been no papal instruction for crusaders to take ship from Venice and indeed no obligation that they should do so. It seems that only 12,000 of the expected 33,500 were present. There was a shortage of some 34,000 marks in the sum due to the Venetians, and no immediate prospect of repaying it. The crusade might well have broken up at this point. The Venetian economy and the reputation of its doge, Dandolo, who had negotiated the treaty of 1201, seemed to be on the brink of very difficult times. Dandolo suggested that the debt payment might be deferred and the debt eventually cleared from future gains (plunder) made by the crusading army if it could be used to bring the city of Zara, a former Venetian colony in Dalmatia, back under Venetian suzerainty. This would have the benefit of removing the crusading army from the environs of Venice itself and – from the point of view of the crusade leadership, including the papal legate Peter of Capuano – of keeping up the crusading momentum. In early October the fleet eventually left Venice and arrived at Zara on 11 November 1202. Zara had changed its allegiance from Venice to the Hungarian monarchy in 1181. King Emico of Hungary had taken the cross, and the inhabitants of Zara were keenly aware of the siege of their and his city by a crusading host; they displayed banners with a cross on them from their walls. Despite misgivings of some crusaders like Simon of Montfort and Guy, abbot of Vaux-Cernay, the citizens of Zara surrendered on 24 November. Innocent III was furious and saddened by this action of the crusaders, apparently endorsed by the papal legate. He excommunicated the crusaders and the Venetians, an action that was kept a secret from the bulk of the crusading army since excommunication also meant the abrogation of their crusading indulgence. The army wintered at Zara, during which time a deputation was sent to Rome to placate the Pope and to point out the need for compromise if this under-funded crusading army was to be kept in being. During the same period there were numerous desertions and some more official withdrawals to take ship direct to Syria. In December 1202 envoys from Alexios, son of Isaac Angelos, and from Alexios' brother-in-law Philip of Swabia, arrived at Zara with a tempting proposal for the indigent crusaders. In return for restoring Alexios and his father to the Byzantine throne, the difficulties of which were minimised at this stage, the crusade would be substantially re-endowed. For the onward progress of the crusade Alexios promised a cash payment of 200,000 marks, a Byzantine contingent of 10,000 men for one year, and thereafter, for the term of his life, a garrison of 500 men to bolster the defence of the Kingdom of Jerusalem. In addition he would acknowledge the papal overlordship of the Orthodox Church and ensure that that Church was brought into canonical obedience to Rome. Despite the generosity of these terms there was dissension about such a use for the Christian army, but the group that prevailed were those who stressed the need to keep the crusade in being and the importance of the new strategy that would involve Egypt and Constantinople. Two months after the diversion to restore Alexios was agreed upon, letters from Innocent III arrived at Zara lifting the excommunication of the crusading army in return for penance and absolution by the papal legate and an undertaking that the crusade army would not be used to attack Christians in the future. The Venetians still remained excommunicated.

In April 1203 the fleet left Zara and was joined by Alexios in person. In early May there was trouble in the crusading ranks on Corfu as to the wisdom of going to Constantinople. Perhaps this was the crisis moment for the leadership since it was still possible to sail to Syria or Alexandria. After many tears and dramatic protestations the leadership prevailed and the expedition left Corfu on 24 May to sail via Chalkis to Constantinople, where it arrived on 24 June 1203.

The display of Alexios to his subjects did not result in mass acclaim and an invitation to resume the throne with his father. The crusade leadership seemed both surprised and distressed by this outcome. Instead, some resistance was offered that was overcome by 18 July when Alexios III fled from his capital. Palace officials freed the aged and blind Isaac Angelos from confinement and restored him to the throne. The crusader leaders sought and obtained guarantees from Isaac that he would honour the undertakings made by his son Alexios, who was then reunited with his father. A fortnight later, on 1 August, Alexios was crowned joint emperor with his father as Alexios IV. It was now time for the crusaders to collect their reward and continue on their way. It was a time of recuperation and expectation; Franco-Greek relations seem to have been amicable enough, and many guided tours of Constantinople were organised by the hosts. Even Innocent III seems to have hoped that all would come right at this stage since he ruled that it was in order for the crusaders to proceed on their crusade in Venetian ships even though the Venetians were still under ban of excommunication.

By November no payments had been received and Alexios IV was formally defied by the crusader leadership to honour his obligations by March 1204 or face the consequences. Alexios meanwhile followed the slippery path of encouraging anti-Latin feeling amongst his subjects whilst at the same time appeasing the crusading army that kept him in power. Conditions in Constantinople were clearly deteriorating for the numerous western residents in the city. On 28 January 1204 a hard-line anti-Latin leader deposed and imprisoned Alexios IV and assumed the purple as Alexios V Murtzouphlos. Conveniently

Isaac Angelos died or was murdered about the same time. The crusaders were given notice to quit Byzantine territory; the defences of Constantinople were strengthened against possible crusader assault and a series of attacks on foraging crusader groups were mounted. The last interview between Murtzouphlos and the crusaders was on 7 February when they demanded the release and reinstatement of Alexios IV and, once again, the honouring of the pledges that he had given on Zara. By 8 February the crusaders learned that Alexios IV had been murdered by Murtzouphlos' own hand. They had now lost the one link that had justified their presence outside of Constantinople and their one hope of gaining substantial support for the crusade. About this time many Latin residents escaped from Constantinople to seek safety in the crusader camp. By March 1204 the crusading army was desperate, with no supplies and no money and the distinct possibility of annihilation at Greek hands. The result was the so-called Pact of March 1204 that sought to establish unity, agreement and resolve into the Veneto-crusader force. It later became one of the bases of the Latin Empire of Constantinople, but at the time it was drawn up it was very much a document of desperation and not a considered attempt to lay the foundations of a new crusader state in the Levant. It was now that there was agreement to attack and capture Constantinople in order to save themselves and to guarantee the safety of the Latin residents. With a force numbering only 20,000 at most, the task of besieging the largest city in Christendom with an estimated population of 300,000 to 400,000 inhabitants seemed almost cartainly doomed to failure.

During Lent preparations were in hand for an assault on the city. The seemed attack by land and sea took place on Friday, 9 April, and was vigorously repulsed by the Greeks. Greatly disheartened, the crusaders spent the weekend in repairing their equipment, recuperating their strength and purging their souls – in part by the expulsion of prostitutes from their camp, perhaps in imitation of a similar practice during the siege of Jerusalem during the First Crusade. The attack on Monday, 12 April, was in part successful, with the capture of a part of the walls overlooking the Golden Horn and a foothold gained within the walls. During the night Murtzouphlos fled the city, and on 13 April the crusaders found no one to oppose them. Constantinople was now in their hands and subject to three days of plunder and rapine that was ended on the 15 April by the crusader leadership, with summary punishment following. On 9 May Baldwin of Flanders was elected the first Latin emperor of Constantinople and crowned seven days later in the Hagia Sophia. The crusade had effectively come to an end; a new Latin state had been set up and over the next five years expansion from Constantinople into Thrace, Asia Minor and mainland Greece and the islands was to take place with varying degrees of success. Within one year most of the crusading army had returned home, although Innocent III continued to address letters to the 'peregrini' until well into 1207, and to write in terms of the continuance of the crusade – but the crusade had effectively ended on 15 April 1204.

REQUEST FOR A CRUSADE AGAINST THE BULGARS, 1205[18]

Following the Fourth Crusade, Renier of Trit had been created duke of Philippopolis and set about the conquest of Thrace. For the Latin settlers in Constantinople seeking to expand northwards into Thrace their great enemy was Kalojan, the khan of the Bulgars. His kingdom had been recognised in 1203 by the provision of a papal crown and a papal banner, and by the provision of a papal legate in Trnovovo the following year. He had offered to co-operate with the crusaders in Constantinople in the spring of 1204 but had received a haughty reply. One year later the local population oppressed by Renier had appealed to Kalojan for help. He had seized the initiative from the Latins and seemed likely to take Constantinople itself. The violence of the Bulgarians was greatly feared by the Latins. The Latins in Constantinople urged Innocent to declare a crusade against the Bulgars because they allied themselves with the pagan Cumans and other enemies of the Cross of Christ, presumably Bogomils and Paulicians. Nothing came of this request. However, it is interesting to note that some French crusaders returning from Constantinople were thought to bring the Cathar heresy with them.

THE ALBIGENSIAN CRUSADE, 1208–29[19]

This crusade is often treated from the point of view of an aspect of the great heresy of the Middle Ages or from the point of view of the expansion of the Capetian kingdom of France. It is often, though mistakenly, described as the first crusade ostensibly preached against a Christian ruler, Raymond VI, count of Toulouse. It did offer another perspective on the crusading experience: the use of crusade against the enemies of the Church or those like heretics who might be considered in rebellion against the Church and its teachings; and it did have a very wide appeal amongst all levels of society.

The adherents of Catharism or Christian dualism might claim to represent the true Christian tradition – unlike the Catholic Church, which they saw as the work of an evil god designed to frustrate the work of Christ on earth. They explained the presence of evil and suffering in the world by reference to an evil god

---

[18] D. Obolensky, *The Bogomils* (Cambridge, 1948), 230-5; Lock, *The Franks in the Aegean*, 51–4; M.R.B. Shaw, trans., *Joinville and Villehardouin: Chronicles of the Crusades* (Harmondsworth, 1963), 115–41.

[19] B. Hamilton, *The Albigensian Crusade* (London, 1974); J. Strayer, *The Albigensian Crusades* (Ann Arbor, 1971); W. Wakefield, *Heresy, Crusade and Inquisition in Southern France 1100–1250* (London, 1974); M. Roquebert, *L'Epopée Cathare 1198–1212: L'Invasion* (Paris, 1970); J. Sumption, *The Albigensian Crusade* (London, 1978); M. Costen, *The Cathars and the Albigensian Crusade* (Manchester, 1997); B. Kienzle, *Cistercians, Heresy and Crusade in Occitania 1145–1229* (Woodbridge, 2001); Setton, ed., *A History of the Crusades*, II, 277–324; Riley-Smith, *The Crusades: A Short History*, 133–8. On Catharism, see S. Runciman, *The Medieval Manichee* (Cambridge, 1947); M. Lambert, *The Cathars* (Oxford, 1998); and Y. Stoyanov, *The Other God* (New Haven, 2000).

co-eternal with the good God and who had created the material world from nothing; the Pentateuch and the historical books of the Old Testament were rejected as the record and work of the evil god. Christ and the Holy Spirit were accepted but not regarded as equal and consubstantial with the good God. Church membership was open to both men and women who had received the *consolamentum* and who thereby became *perfecti/perfectae*. These men and women prayed on behalf of the community of Cathar believers. They lived in single-sex communities, and the bishop of the Cathar diocese in which they were located directed their activities. They renounced all worldly possessions and all family and sexual relationships. They followed a vegetarian diet, abstaining from all foods that might be the product of procreation, although they were allowed fish for these were deemed not to have a sex life. They believed that all procreated life was sacred and abstained from taking life, including that of animals, hence the later test devised by the Inquisition of inviting suspects to kill a cockerel. There were many superficial similarities between the ideals, practices and language of the Cathars and the Catholic Church, but the former propagated a new religion that denied the existence of one God, the creator of all things visible and invisible, and were bitterly hostile to the Catholic Church. Because the movement possessed no church buildings or assembly rooms, and because believers did not belong to a church as such and might well attend Catholic services, it was very difficult to distinguish convinced heretics from tolerant sympathisers or from anti-clerical but otherwise orthodox Catholics. Because of this it is impossible to ascertain the number of the Cathars in Languedoc and Lombardy.

Catharism seems to have struck roots in southern France in the early decades of the twelfth century; at the Church Council of Tours in 1163 it was compared to a cancer in its spread. St Bernard had certainly encountered dualists in the Ariani of the Toulouse area in 1145, and it is possible that some Cathar practices came to the West from the Balkan Bogomils in the baggage of the Second Crusade.[20] Be that as it may, dualism seems to have thrived in the wealthy, cosmopolitan and politically fragmented Languedoc. It was not just the multicultural climate that favoured the survival of Catharism. In addition there was tolerance, and indeed protection, on the part of the ruling nobility who, according to the Church, should have been to the fore in rooting out enemies of the Church and in setting an example of Christian orthodoxy. Added to this the poverty of the Church in the area, and the resulting low level of social and educational standards amongst the parish clergy, made the day-to-day combat of heresy a dispiriting task, especially as the Cathar *perfecti/perfectae* were

---

[20] Lambert, *The Cathars*, p. 69, traced the origin of the practice of describing Cathars as Albigensians to Geoffrey of Auxerre, companion to St Bernard on his preaching tour of 1145, who described Albi as a town contaminated above all others in the region. Perhaps more convincingly, Hamilton attributes this literary usage to the setting up of the first Cathar diocese in Albi some time before 1172.

generally reckoned to have an outstanding reputation for honest dealing and upstanding behaviour.

The bishops of the numerous small dioceses in the area made a concerted effort to stamp out the heresy – difficult at any time but, without the support of the nobility, impossible. Apart from a number of Church councils that condemned heresy and sought to establish local peace movements, and three legatine missions to the area to encourage the nobility to subscribe to these movements and to take a stand against the heretics, little was done or achieved either to extirpate or limit the spread of Catharism in the region.

On 15 January 1208 a retainer of Raymond VI of Toulouse, with or without the count's knowledge, murdered Peter of Castelnau, leader of the legatine mission in Languedoc. The previous month Peter had excommunicated Raymond for refusing to join a peace league. Innocent III's response to this provocation was to order the preaching of a crusade against Raymond and the Toulousain. The use of force against heretics was no new device, but to declare a crusade to do so was new. In the face of the complacency and reluctance of the nobility of Languedoc Innocent hoped to entice the nobility of France to fulfil the duties of every Christian magnate by offering them the indulgence of crusaders.

There was no lack of recruits from northern France. Languedoc was much nearer than Jerusalem. There was no expensive and arduous journey to undertake and the indulgence came as a result of the normal forty days' military service for which vows were now taken. Despite the essentially domestic nature of this crusade the participants dubbed themselves pilgrims and were not long in making their preparations. Indeed, some minor military activity broke out around Quercy in May 1208. Raymond VI was quick to recognise the danger that threatened him. On 18 June 1209 he submitted to the Church and he took the cross to combat the heretics.

The main crusade army, now joined by Raymond VI, was diverted to attack the lands of Raymond Roger of Trencaval, lord of Beziers and Carcassone. On 22 July 1209 Beziers was captured and all the inhabitants of whatever religious persuasion were massacred. Two weeks later Carcassone fell. Simon of Montfort, who had served on the Fourth Crusade and had raised so much trouble for the Crusade leadership at Zara in 1202, was elected leader of the crusade. He spent the years 1210–15 subduing the south and attempting to gain control of Toulouse. The forces at his disposal fluctuated wildly as forty-day periods of service expired. He also incurred the opposition of Peter II of Aragon, who feared the arrival of an able and courageous ruler on his borders. Peter was able to induce Pope Innocent to declare the end of crusading privileges in 1213, but on 12 September 1213 he was defeated and killed by Simon of Montfort at the battle of Muret as he attempted to relieve the siege of Toulouse. Whether those in Simon of Montfort's army at this point were technically crusaders is doubtful, but it is ironic that his army should have been responsible for the death of the victor of the battle of Las Navas de Tolosa against the Almohads in the previous year.

The Church now administered Toulouse. The Lateran Council of 1215 declared Simon of Montfort the new count of Toulouse. Whilst he was in Paris obtaining investiture from Philip II, the Toulousain revolted in favour of Raymond VI who once again gained possession of Toulouse. Simon hurried south but was unable to retake the city. Innocent's successor, Honorius III, had a new crusade preached for the capture of Toulouse. Operations were resumed in April 1218 and Simon of Montfort was himself killed during its siege on 25 June 1218. The following spring Prince Louis of France took up the siege of Toulouse, but to no effect. His withdrawal in August 1219 served to discourage many, whilst the recruitment for the Damietta crusade effectively brought the Albigensian crusade to an end. Raymond VI recovered all his lands by the time of his death in 1222, and his son Raymond VII succeeded him. In 1224 Amaury Simon of Montfort ceded his claims to the Languedoc to Louis VIII who had become king of France in 1223.

The crusade was resumed in 1226 when Honorius preached a new crusade. Louis led a royal army south but made slow progress, despite receiving the submission of most southern lords. His death on 8 November 1226 ushered in the regency of Blanche of Castile for the infant Louis IX. Hostilities were resumed in 1228 by Humbert of Beaujeu, the regent for the Capetians of the Trenceval lands, and were formally ended by the Treaty of Paris in April 1229. By the terms of this treaty all lands confiscated from southern lords since 1209 should be returned to them, provided they had not been found to be heretics; Raymond VII, now a widower, remained in possession of his county, agreed to pay indemnities of 20,000 marks and to do penance for five years by fighting the infidel. He also agreed that his daughter and heiress, Jeanne, should marry Alphonse of Poitiers, one of the king's brothers, and that they and their heirs should have sole rights to the succession of the county of Toulouse. Should they have no issue then the county would revert to the French crown. The exigencies of life meant that the Capetians were the winners of the Albigensian crusade: in 1249 on the death of Raymond VII Toulouse passed to the French crown. Heresy had not been extirpated by the crusade; simply it had been driven underground. New means were to be devised for tackling it.

THE CHILDREN'S CRUSADE, 1212[21]

Fanciful descriptions of this movement – the first of a number of such hysterical manifestations amongst peasant children in thirteenth-century Germany –

---

[21] P. Raedts, 'The Children's Crusade of 1212', *J. Medieval History*, 3 (1977), 279–323; D. Munro, 'The Children's Crusade', *American Historical Review*, 19 (1913–14), 516–24; J. Hansberry, 'The Children's Crusade', *Catholic Historical Review*, 24(1938), 30–8; P. Alphandery and A. Dupront, *La Chrétienté et L'Idée de Croisade* (2 vols, Paris, 1959), 115–48; Setton, ed., *A History of the Crusades*, II, 325–42; S. Shahar, *childhood in the Middle Ages* (London, 1990), 250–1; Runciman, *A History of the Crusades*, III, 39–44; Mayer, *The Crusades*, 215–16; Riley-Smith, *The Crusades: a Short History*, 141.

abound both in the Middle Ages and today. It was not a crusade in the formal sense but rather the hysterical response of a number of charismatic peasant boys to the preaching of the Albigensian crusade by Jacques de Vitry and William of Paris in northern France in the winter of 1211–12. It shows the enthusiasm for crusading amongst shepherds and peasants – it was not just, nor had ever been, an affair for knights – and the criticism of the achievements of noble crusaders on the part of common people. It also shows that children too had an understanding of what their parents and their neighbours talked about.

In the spring of 1212 in Cologne, Trier, Liège, Jumièges and Vendôme numbers of children left their homes to follow charismatic shepherd boys Stephen of Cloyes and Nicholas of Cologne, both of whom had experienced visions of Christ. Stephen's following, alleged to have numbered 30,000, contented itself with religious processions and prayer meetings aimed at seeking God. Later chroniclers linked this group with the child crusaders of Nicholas whose aim was to restore the True Cross and liberate the Holy Land. Relying on their innocence and purity the seas would part allowing them to go dry-shod to their goal. When this failed to happen it is noteworthy that this impromptu crusade was to go by sea. Both bands were seen at best as misguided, especially by the Church, and at worst as an issue of public order. Wherever opportunity presented, the Church authorities strove to dissuade and turn back the children. Nonetheless the child pilgrims received food and support on their journey to the Mediterranean ports from many, including country priests. The numbers of Nicholas's followers is unknown, but their progress southwards is recorded. Their numbers dwindled through death and desertion as they passed southwards. Some reached Genoa and there the crusade broke up. Two shiploads were reported to have left Pisa while another seven shiploads embarked at Marseilles were thought by Aubrey of Trois-Fontaines to have been sold into slavery. Another group, including Nicholas, were reported to have reached Rome and to have had an audience with Innocent III who relieved them of their vows or persuaded them to postpone them. He is also said to have remarked: 'These children put us to shame. They rush to recover the Holy Land while we sleep.' Nicholas is thought to have gone to Damietta with the Fifth Crusade. Unlike the later children's movements in Germany there is no record of parents dissuading their children or searching for them. Indeed, Nicholas's father was either hanged in Cologne for encouraging his son or committed suicide through a guilty conscience because he had sold children into slavery, implying that he journeyed with his son. Although Pope Gregory IX sponsored the building of the Church of the New Innocents in their memory on the island of San Petro, off Sardinia, most churchmen dwelt not upon the innocence of the would-be crusaders but upon the diabolic inspiration of such a crusade on the part of those of insufficient years and social status.

In 1237 a thousand children danced from Erfurt to Arnstadt, but their parents brought them back. In practice the Pied Piper incident in Hamelin on 26 June 1284 may have been a story about the departure of German colonists for eastern

Europe, but in legend it certainly recalled the Children's Crusade of 1212. In this story the parents, demented with grief, searched everywhere for their children, but to no avail.

A POLITICAL CRUSADE IN ENGLAND?, c. 1215–17[22]

Dr Lloyd has argued persuasively that two political crusades were declared on behalf of Henry III of England (1215–72) in dealing with his rebellious subjects; one from 1215–17 and another from 1263–5. In October 1216 the knight Savaric de Mauleon was described by Pope Honorius III as 'crucesignatus pro defensione Regni Anglie'. In terms of dress (the royalist wore red crosses), in terms of language (Henry's opponents were worse than Saracens; see 'Markward of Anweiler', pp. 147–8) and in terms of prerequisites for the Fifth Crusade there is every indication that the military actions of 1215–17 were seen as a crusade. Between 1263 and 1265 two papal legates came to England, both with the power to declare a crusade against Henry's enemies. The death of Simon of Montfort (the fourth son of the Simon of Montfort of the Fourth Crusade and the Albigensian crusade) at Evesham on 1265 obviated this step.

THE FIFTH CRUSADE, 1217–21[23]

Perhaps in the light of the Fourth Crusade Innocent III reasserted the role of the Pope at the centre of crusading and to this end declared a new crusade for 1217, along with a summons to the Fourth Lateran Council for 1215. On paper this appeared the best planned of all the crusades. It seemed to benefit from a century of crusade experience with a four-year lead-time, a team of first-rate preachers from the higher echelons of the Church and the imposition of papal taxation of the clergy, instituted again after its experimental introduction in 1199 but this time with mechanisms to transmit the funds raised direct to the Holy Land for use by the crusaders once they had arrived. Never before had the resources of the Church been committed to the Crusades on such a grand scale. Crusade privileges for the Spanish and Albigensian crusades were suspended to boost recruitment for the crusade to the East. For the first time all those who wished to take the crusading vow were allowed to do so regardless of their physical suitability. It was assumed that they would later commute their vow and that the money so raised would be applied to the financing of the crusade. As in previous crusades there was a strong emphasis on the moral preparation of Christendom by penance and the promulgation of peace in Christendom.

[22] S. Lloyd, 'Political Crusades in England, c.1215–17 and c.1263–5', in P. Edbury, ed., *Crusade and Settlement* (Cardiff, 1985), 113–20.

[23] J. Powell, *The Anatomy of a Crusade, 1213–1221* (Philadelphia, 1986); Setton, ed., *A History of the Crusades*, II, 377–428; Runciman, *A History of the Crusades*, III, 132–70; Mayer, *The Crusades*, 217–28; Riley-Smith, *The Crusades: A Short History*, 143–9.

It is now generally agreed that there was no papal agenda to exclude the monarchs of Europe from the crusade. Frederick II's assumption of the cross in 1215 was apparently welcomed, although it was understood that his need to establish his position in Germany and southern Italy would mean the postponement of the fulfilment of his vows. Likewise, attempts to enlist King John of England were called off since it was recognised that he was engaged in a struggle for survival against his barons, supported by the military intervention of the Dauphin Louis (see p. 167). In France royal participation was prevented by involvement in English affairs and by the disturbed nature of southern France. Rather, recruitment was aimed to extract commitments from the lay and spiritual leaders of society from the communes of north Italy to bishops and princes of Christendom, using their networks of lordship, patronage and kinship, together with family traditions of crusading, that after a century of the movement were now well entrenched. The bulk of the crusading forces on the crusade came from Germany, Frisia and Flanders, with Andrew II of Hungary leading a substantial Hungarian contingent on the first part of the crusade.

The first contingents of the crusade to arrive in Acre were the armies led by Andrew II of Hungary (who was at last fulfilling his crusade vow, taken in 1196 but postponed on a number of occasions due to political instability in his kingdom) and by Leopold VI, duke of Austria, a seasoned crusader. The armies left Spalato (Split) in late August 1217 and arrived in Acre in early October. The force was considerable in size, but in part due to famine in Syria and in part to the ill health of King Andrew, only limited raids were undertaken into Damascene territory – especially against the Muslim fort on Mount Tabor. All these campaigns were of limited success, and in January 1218 Andrew returned overland to Hungary, using his journey to cement diplomatic and marriage contracts in Tripoli, Armenia, Nicaea and Bulgaria. He took a considerable number of Hungarian crusaders with him, including many siege weapons.

Duke Leopold, now awaiting the second contingent from the West, which it was rumoured that the emperor Frederick II would lead, busied his army with reconstructing the defences of Caesarea and extending the Templar castle of Chateau Pelerin (Atlit). By early April 1218 German and Italian crusaders were arriving in Acre and on 27 May they disembarked for Damietta on the Nile delta, taking the Muslim authorities there entirely by surprise two days later. John of Brienne, king of Jerusalem, was elected leader of the expedition. The Egyptian campaign was to last until 1221. It was a major weakness of this expedition that the leadership of John of Brienne was challenged, first with the arrival of the papal legate Pelagius in September 1218 and then with the departure of Leopold of Austria in 1219. The various reinforcements arriving in Egypt during these years were neither acclimatised nor vigorous in their prosecution of the war, and the crusade leadership seemed unable to work together effectively.

Two offers of terms very advantageous to the crusading army were turned down amidst delays of nearly a year in prosecuting any advance. In the spring of 1221 Frederick II was expected to arrive with a German army; instead, only the latter arrived. In July 1221 an advance into the interior was begun, but only after John of Brienne had been ordered to return to the army by Pope Honorius III. In August the army was surrounded and isolated near El Mansura, and on 28 August agreed to withdraw from Egypt in return for an eight-year truce, to be confirmed by the emperor Frederick II, and for the return of the True Cross, captured at Hattin in 1187. This was never given back. The crusaders embarked for Acre on the imperial fleet commanded by Henry of Malta on 8 September. The Fifth Crusade was over. It firmly focused attention on the strategy of capturing the resources of Egypt and, with these in their control, proceeding to recapture Jerusalem and the Holy Land at leisure.

THE SIXTH CRUSADE, 1228–9[24]

Intimately linked with the career and personality of the Staufen emperor Frederick II, this crusade, perhaps the most successful after the capture of Jerusalem by the First Crusade in 1099, has inevitably attracted much attention and comment. The crusade was to fall foul of the dispute between empire and papacy as to who should direct and order the crusade movement; this hinged in particular on the character of Pope Gregory IX who was insistent on the centrality of the papacy in the direction of the movement and felt that in the frequent postponements that the emperor had called he had a weapon to stress the papal role.

Frederick had taken the cross at his coronation in Aachen on 25 July 1215. He had subsequently postponed going on Crusade in 1218, 1221 and 1225 but had renewed his vows on each occasion. His intention was sincere, but he was bitterly criticised for the failure of the Fifth Crusade, whose participants expected his arrival. His marriage to Isabel (Yolanda) of Brienne on 9 November 1225, and his assumption of the kingship of Jerusalem in her right, focused his attention on Jerusalem rather than on Egypt, although during the Fifth Crusade he had had no problems with providing military and naval support for the crusade campaign there.

In October 1226 preparations were well in hand for the departure of the crusade from Brindisi. Frederick had commissioned vessels to transport the crusaders, hired 1,000 mercenaries and declared himself ready to fund those crusaders who could not support themselves – all of this paid for from the revenues of the Kingdom of Sicily.

In early September 1227 the fleet sailed under the command of Duke Henry

---

[24] R. Röhricht, *Die Kreuzfahrt Kaiser Friedrichs des Zweiten* (Innsbruck, 1872); W. Sturner, *Friedrich II. Der Kaiser 1220–1250* (Darmstadt, 2002), 85–170; D. Abulafia, *Frederick II, A Medieval Emperor* (London, 1988), 164–201; T. van Cleve, *The Emperor Frederick II of Hohenstaufen* (Oxford, 1972), 179–236; Setton, ed., *A History of the Crusades*, II, 429–64; R. Grousset, *Histoire des croisades et du royaume de Jérusalem*, III (Paris, 1936), 271–347; Runciman, *A History of the Crusades*, III, 171–204; Mayer, *The Crusades* 228–38; Riley-Smith, *The Crusades: A Short History*, 149–51.

of Limburg. Frederick himself had fallen ill with the plague that had killed many of the crusaders mustering in the Brindisi region and had retired to Pozzuoli near Naples to recover, with the declared intention of joining up with his crusade in the following May.

On 29 September 1227 Gregory IX excommunicated Frederick, and in an encyclical letter of 10 October he summarised the history of Frederick and his crusading intentions, emphasising that Frederick himself had invited excommunication each time he had renewed his vow to go on crusade. He even accused Frederick of choosing Brindisi as the port of muster because it was a known plague-ridden area, in it is completely ignoring the fact that his great crusading predecessor Innocent III had designated this port for the Fifth Crusade. The Pope's ungenerous action was to cause much difficulty for Frederick, not only in the Holy Land but also in southern Italy where as an excommunicate his possessions would not come under the protection afforded a legitimate crusader. Frederick appealed to Christendom about the inequity of his treatment, and then on 28 June 1228, still excommunicated, he left to rejoin the Duke Henry of Limburg and the crusading forces at Acre where he arrived on 7 September.

Whilst waiting for the arrival of Frederick, Henry of Limburg had busied those troops that did not return home with extending the fortifications at Caesarea, Jaffa and Montfort (Starkenburg). Frederick was short in troops and short on time. Gerold, patriarch of Jerusalem, and the international military orders were bitterly opposed to the excommunicate, and he was well aware of the threat to his Kingdom of Sicily from Gregory IX whilst he was absent in the East. He resorted to negotiations with the sultan of Egypt, al-Kamil. These negotiations had originated with diplomatic exchanges in 1226 when al-Kamil was seeking Frederick's support against his brother al Mu'azzam, the governor of Damascus. The death of al-Mu'azzam in November 1227 might have removed many of al-Kamil's concerns, but the presence of Frederick, at al-Kamil's invitation, was an embarrassment as he sought to consolidate his hold over Damascus.

On 18 February 1229 an agreement was reached whereby Jerusalem was surrendered to the Christians except for the Dome of the Rock and the Temple of Solomon (Qubbat as-Sakhrah). There was to be mutual access for Christians and Muslims. It was agreed that the Kingdom of Jerusalem would run along the coast from just north of Beirut to just south of Jaffa, including within it the inland enclaves of Jerusalem, Bethlehem, Nazareth, Belfort, Montfort and Toron (Tibnin). Only Frederick and his German and South Italian crusaders supported the treaty; in the eyes of everyone else he was damned. Just what more could be expected to have been achieved it is difficult to say. On 1 May he left Acre to counter John of Brienne's invasion of Apulia. This was the last crusade to the East in which substantial German contingents participated. It was a successful crusade, but one carried out by an excommunicate and an enemy of the Church. Frederick's knowledge of Arabic and the sciences, and his attitude to the Christian religion, fascinated the Arabs with whom he negotiated and added richly to his later reputation as the 'stupor mundi'.

JOHN OF BRIENNE'S CRUSADE IN APULIA, 1229[25]

Although John of Brienne was thought by many to be creating lordships for himself and for his nephew Walter II of Brienne in southern Italy, he was fighting against Frederick II at the behest of Gregory IX, under a papal banner, funded by the papacy, and with Cardinal John Colonna as legate. It was a footnote to the crusade of Frederick II; certainly it was John's actions that threatened the loss of Apulia to Frederick and precipitated his urgent departure from the East.

John (born c. 1170) had been king of Jerusalem (1210–25) in right of his wife, Maria of Montferrat (d. 1212), and then for his daughter Isabel (Yolanda). He had served prominently on the Fifth Crusade and enjoyed a reputation as a warrior. He lost the Kingdom of Jerusalem to Frederick II on the latter's marriage to Isabel in November 1225. His treatment at Frederick's hands made him an enemy of his son-in-law. In the spring of 1226 he was invited to take command of the forces of the Lombard League against Frederick, but despite negotiations he refused the offer, probably to protect the interests of his daughter. She died on 5 May 1228 soon after the birth of her son Conrad. Frederick had sailed from Brindisi on 28 June.

In late 1228 John's army cleared the March of Ancona of imperial troops and in January 1229 entered the Kingdom of Sicily, capturing the towns of Monte Cassino, San Germano and Rocca Janula. John hoped to secure all the major ports to facilitate the capture of Frederick on his return, and besieged the imperial forces in Capua, threatening the loss of the whole of Apulia.

Frederick's unexpected return to Brindisi on 10 June 1229 seriously weakened the appeal of the papal army to many who had believed the emperor dead. The siege of Capua was raised and John driven back into papal territory by the end of October 1229. Frederick did not proceed into papal territory; instead seeking peace and to have his excommunication lifted. This was duly achieved on 1 September 1230. This regrettable political crusade had cast a shadow over the achievements of Frederick in Syria and had resulted in nothing more than the exacerbation of feelings between John and Frederick that were to result in Frederick's support for the enemies of the Latin Empire of Constantinople.

In the meantime (ratified at Perugia in April 1229), John of Brienne was negotiating his move to the Latin Empire of Constantinople as co-emperor and father-in-law of the twelve-year-old Baldwin II. Here he remained until his death in 1237, mounting a creditable defence of Constantinople.

---

[25] See references in note 24, especially Van Cleve, *The Emperor Frederich II of Hohenstaufch*, 183, 211–13 and 228–33; J. Buckley, 'The Problematical Octogenaianism of John of Brienne', *Speculum*, 32 (1957), 315–22; A. Kazhdan, ed., *The Oxford Dictionary of Byzantium* (3 vols, New York, 1991), 1062–3.

THE CRUSADE AGAINST THE STEDINGER 1234[26]

Stedingerland (Stedingen) is bounded by the Ochte, Weser and Hunte rivers between Bremen and Oldenburg. The land belonged to the archbishop of Bremen. In the atmosphere of the anti-heretical inquisitorial proceedings instituted by Gregory IX (1227–41), peasant protest was translated by the archbishop into heresy. He declared the peasants of the area heretics for their refusal to pay tithes. The archbishop Gebhard II zur Lippe (1219–58) obtained the support of Gregory IX, who imposed an interdict (1232) and then, two years later, declared a crusade. Recruitment was from the princes and knights of northern Germany from Brabant to Oldenburg, who annihilated the peasants at the battle of Altenesch on 27 May 1234. The event showed just how the idea of crusade might be twisted, turning popular protest into a peasant war. It became the subject of many historical novels in the nineteenth century, when the peasant resistance entered folk myth.

CRUSADES AGAINST BOSNIAN HERETICS, 1234 AND 1241[27]

During the 1220s, linked to the suppression of Catharism in the Languedoc, rumours spread of the existence of a Cathar antipope, Nicetas, living in the Bosnian banate. It was unclear then and remains unclear today whether there ever was a Cathar antipope. The rumours were inflamed by the Hungarians, eager to reassert their authority over Bosnia. It did, however, provoke such concern that in 1221 Honorius III called for a crusade against the heretics of Bosnia.

Two crusades were mounted by the Hungarians, eager to expand their territory; but they achieved little in the face of stubborn resistance and never reached the centres of power in the banate. The Mongol invasion of Hungary in 1241 brought the second Hungarian crusade to an abrupt end. Bosnia was transferred from the archdiocese of Dubrovnik to the Hungarian archdiocese of Bosnia. The official Catholic Hungarian archbishop was driven from Bosnia and forced to reside in Djakovo in Croatia.

The Bosnian Church developed as an independent church in schism with Rome. Although it remained Catholic in its theology it was widely regarded as a dualist or Bogomil church. The Franciscans established themselves in 1342 to combat the so-called heresy, but their influence was limited and they were to remain the only Catholic clergy in Bosnia until 1878. In Rome Bosnia was

---

[26] R. Kieckhefer, *Repression of Heresy in Medieval Germany* (Liverpool, 1979), 14; L. Förg, *Die Ketzerverfolgung in Deutschland unter Gregor IX* (Berlin, 1932), 62–4; J. Freed, *The Friars and German Society in the Thirteenth Century* (Cambridge, Mass., 1977), 142–7.

[27] Stoyanov, *The Other God*, 220–8; B. Hamilton, 'Catholic Perceptions of East European Dualism in the Twelfth and Thirteenth Centuries', reprinted as chapter XIV in his *Crusaders, Cathars and the Holy Places* (Aldershot, 1999); J.A. Fine, *The Late Medieval Balkans* (Ann Arbor, 1987), 143–9; J.A. Fine, *The Bosnian Church* (New York, 1975); R. Donia J. Fine, *Bosnia and Hercegovina: A Tradition Betrayed* (London, 1994), 6–34, for a convenient outline history.

regarded as a cesspool of heresy, and it was dubbed as such by Pope Urban IV (1362–70). Bosnia became an independent kingdom in 1377 when Ban Tvrtko I (1353–91) assumed the title of king, and thus it was to remain with its independent church until the Ottoman conquest in 1465.

CRUSADE OF THIBAUT OF NAVARRE TO ACRE 1239–40[28]

This crusade vies with that of Frederick II as achieving the most for the Holy Land since its conquest in 1099. Between September and November 1234 Gregory IX announced preparations for a new crusade to take place in July 1239 when the truce agreed by Frederick II and al-Kamil (d. 1238) on 18 February 1229 expired. The Dominicans were charged with preaching the crusade, which was to be financed by a tax of 1d. per week to be paid by all Christians who had not taken the cross and by a series of taxes levied on clerical incomes ranging from one-tenth to one-twentieth. Potential participants were urged not to depart until the truce had expired.

Thibaut IV, count of Champagne, and since 1234 also Thibaut I of Navarre where he had succeeded his uncle Sancho VII, came from an illustrious crusading family with close connections to the Kingdom of Jerusalem, where his uncle Henry of Champagne had been king until his accidental death at Acre in 1197. By late 1237 another set of plans for a crusade to Constantinople to assist the Latin Empire had emerged. Gregory IX urged both Thibaut and Peter of Dreux – the latter seeming to have made some commitment to the Constantinople crusade – to assist the Latin emperor Baldwin II who was then in the West raising an army to reinforce the Latin position in Constantinople. In the event neither joined Baldwin, who left for Romania in the summer of 1239. However, the inception of a second crusade for Constantinople, together with the disputes between Gregory and Frederick II, served only to make the organisation of the original crusade to Syria more difficult to co-ordinate.

The crusade army that mustered at Lyons in July 1239 was mainly a French affair. Apart from Thibaut and Peter of Dreux, there was Hugh, duke of Burgundy, and Amalric of Montfort, the constable of France, and several distinguished counts. The army left Marseilles and Aignes-Mortes in August, deliberately ignoring any previous negotiations with Frederick II to leave from the ports of southern Italy, and arrived in Acre in September. There they came up against the anti-Staufen stance of most of the Latin barons and the confused chain of command amongst the imperial representatives of the young king, Conrad. It was decided to march to Ascalon and repair the defences there and march thence to attack Damascus.

---

[28] R. Röhricht, 'Die Kreuzzuge des Grafen Theobald von Navarra und Richard von Cornwallis nach dem heiligen Lande', *Forschungen zur deutschen Geschichte*, 36 (1886), 67–81; Setton, ed., *A History of the Crusades*, II, 463–85; Grousset, *Histoire des Croisades*, III, 372–96; Runciman, *A History of the Crusades*, III, 211–19; Riley-Smith, *The Crusades: A Short History*, 154–7.

On 2 November 1239 the expedition left Acre. On 12 November, at Jaffa, Hugh of Burgundy and others defied Thibaut's leadership and instead of marching direct to Ascalon set off to attack the Egyptian army recently moved up to Gaza to shadow the movements of the crusaders. In this they were worsted, suffering many casualties both killed and captured. Their return to the main force at Ascalon provoked its withdrawal to Tripoli with nothing achieved. Just why this withdrawal took place is not understood.

Thibaut now opened negotiations with the ruler of Damascus. In return for guarding the frontier with Egypt the Christians would receive back the fortresses at Safed and Beaufort, and in addition the return of the territories granted to Frederick II when they were recovered from the Egyptians. Compliance with this agreement was a problem for both sides. As Thibaut moved to a rendezvous with the forces of Damascus somewhere between Jaffa and Ascalon the Hospitallers negotiated a treaty with the sultan of Egypt, Ayub. This provided more territory, including possession of Ascalon, than the previous agreement and included the release of prisoners taken in the battle at Gaza the previous year. Thibaut opted for the second treaty and abandoned his previous Damascene allies. At the end of September 1240 Thibaut returned to France, having discountenanced the nobility of the kingdom, many of his followers and his erstwhile Muslim allies. It was unclear whether Thibaut had bothered to ratify the treaty that had returned so much territory to the Christians. Hugh of Burgundy and the count of Nevers remained behind to fortify Ascalon. Inglorious as this expedition clearly was it demonstrated that even the small and divided Latin presence was still able to exert influence amongst its disunited Muslim neighbours.

GREGORY IX PROCLAIMS A CRUSADE AGAINST FREDERICK II, 1240[29]

The Treaty of San Germano of July 1230 had temporarily reconciled Frederick II and Pope Gregory IX. However, Frederick's successful military actions against the Lombard League during the 1230s and his brilliant victory over their troops at Cortennuova on 27 November 1237 seemed to secure Frederick's position in Italy and to ensure the union of the Kingdom of Sicily and the German Empire. Gregory IX had urged Frederick during his war with Lombards to make peace and to expend his resources on crusade. On 20 March 1239 Frederick was excommunicated for the second time; his impeding of aid to the Holy Land and to the Latin Empire of Constantinople (Romania) was one of the complaints cited against him. A wordy and virulent pamphlet war now ensued that encompassed most of the crown heads of Europe. Gregory sought to replace Frederick as German emperor whilst Frederick sought to elevate the position of the cardinals over the Pope and to appeal to a General Council to regulate the

---

[29] Van Cleve, *The Emperor Frederick II of Hohenstaufen*, 427–50; Housley, *The Italian Crusades*, 46–51.

affairs of Christendom. On 22 February 1240 Frederick entered the Tiber valley intent on entering Rome. On the same day Gregory IX, in a dramatic appeal to the Roman people, preached a crusade against Frederick and memorably had his own vestments torn up to make crosses for the Roman people. Frederick withdrew to the Kingdom of Sicily. Despite cogent papal justifications for the calling of crusades against the enemies of the Church there was a feeling that the interests of Christendom and those of the papacy did not always coincide, and this view was voiced during the 1240s as the papacy diverted subsidies intended for the Holy Land crusade to fight against Frederick II in Italy.

GENOESE CRUSADE AGAINST SAVONA AND ALBENGA, 1240[30]

A minor crusade summoned locally within Genoa to suppress the supporters of Frederick in the towns of Savona and Albenga eager to gain their independence from Genoa. Savona was the second city of Liguria after Genoa and therefore important for Genoese control. Genoa was divided between Guelf and Ghibelline interests, approximating to the self-interest of the parties and families concerned. Attacks on the cities continued until 1247 when both submitted to Genoese overlordship.

CRUSADE OF RICHARD OF CORNWALL AND SIMON OF MONTFORT TO JAFFA, 1240[31]

Richard of Cornwall, the younger brother of Henry III, had taken the cross in 1236. As the heir apparent it was in the interest of political stability in England that he remain in England. He resisted pressure from both Henry and Gregory IX to commute his vow and send the money to support Constantinople. The birth of Prince Edward in May 1239 removed any likelihood of Richard obtaining the throne of England and freed him to be absent from the kingdom. On 12 November 1239 the crusading barons swore at Northampton to go to Syria and not be diverted to crusade in Italy or Constantinople.

Richard left England on 10 June 1240 and landed at Acre on 11 October, some thirteen days after the departure of Thibaut of Champagne for France. Simon of Montfort travelled out separately. Richard assisted the duke of Burgundy in refortifying Ascalon and entered immediately into negotiations to ratify the treaty agreed between Thibaut and the sultan Ayub. The ratification was signed on 23 April 1241. It gained the release of Amalric of Montfort and greatly boosted Richard's reputation. Richard left Acre on 3 May 1241 and returned to England via Italy, where he spent four months at the court of Frederick II. He arrived in Dover on 7 January 1242 with his reputation on the European stage much enhanced.

---

[30] S. Epstein, *Genoa and the Genoese, 958–1528* (Chapel Hill, 1996), 124–7.
[31] See references in note 32; N. Denholm-Young, *Richard of Cornwall* (Oxford, 1947), 38–44.

CRUSADE AGAINST THE MONGOLS, 1241[32]

News of the Mongol advance into northern and western Russia was known in the West by the end of 1239 when Bela IV of Hungary allowed the nomadic Cumans, who were fleeing from the Mongols, to settle in his kingdom; the Mongol armies had captured Kiev in December 1240, and entered Poland and Hungary in February/March 1241. On 16 June 1241 Gregory IX offered crusading privileges to Bela IV of Hungary and those of his subjects who fought against the Mongols, and three days later extended the preaching of a crusade against the Mongols to Germany and Austria.

The response was good, and on 1 July an army left Nuremberg for Hungary under Frederick II's son, King Conrad. It was inteneded that the crusade would last until November or December. On 16 July the crusading army had reached Weiden, but thereafter it seems to have broken up. No more is heard of it, and by 11 September Conrad was back in Swabia. In the spring of 1242 the Mongol armies left Europe to return to Karakorum to elect a successor to the Great Khan Ogodai (d. 11 December 1241).

POPE INNOCENT IV PREACHES A CRUSADE AGAINST FREDERICK II, 1248[33]

Stemming from peace negotiations between Frederick and the Lombard League, Innocent IV decided to flee Italy rather than meet with Frederick at the head of an imperial army that might once again threaten Rome as in 1241. In July 1244 Innocent had set up residence in Lyons, and in January 1245, just one month after Louis IX had taken the cross, he summoned a Church council to assemble in the summer of 1245. Here he deposed Frederick as emperor. Frederick threatened to march on Lyons. Louis IX did all he could to bring the parties to agreement prior to his own departure for the East. Innocent was deaf to these approaches and in the summer of 1248 authorised the preaching of a crusade against Frederick in Italy and Germany, aimed primarily at the conquest of the Kingdom of Sicily. Complex and indeterminate as this crusade was, it served to complicate the preparations of Louis IX for his own crusade and forced him to rely upon the resources of France.

---

[32] P. Jackson, 'The Crisis in the Holy Land in 1260', *English Historical Review*, 95 (1980), 480–513; P. Jackson, 'The Crusade Against the Mongols (1241)', *Journal of Ecclesiastical History*, 42 (1991), 1–18; J. Richard, 'The Mongols and the Franks', *Journal of Asian History*, 3 (1969), 45–57, J. Richard, *The Crusades c.1071–c.1291* (Cambridge, 1999), 408–41.

[33] Van Cleve, *The Emperor Frederick II of Hohenstaufen*, 474–517, esp. 516; Riley-Smith, *The Crusades: A Short History*, 158.

SEVENTH CRUSADE, OR LOUIS IX's FIRST CRUSADE, 1248–54[34]

Following the capture of Jerusalem by the Khwarizmian Turks in late August 1244 Louis IX of France took the cross in December, a full month before the preaching of a new crusade had begun in France. Despite opposition from his mother, Blanche of Castile, Louis persisted in his vow that was taken after his recovery from a life-threatening illness. He came from a long line of crusading kings, and indeed his great-grandfather Louis VII had pre-empted the papal summons to the Second Crusade in 1145. It was this tradition, the prestige of the French monarch in the Latin East and Louis' own piety, that prompted an early response to the loss of Jerusalem rather than the need to exert his own authority and the need for personal space, as have been suggested.

This smacks too much of post-Freudianism. There were many compelling reasons for a king of France to undertake the onerous responsibilities of a crusade. The task was not made easier by the bitter dispute between Innocent IV and Frederick II. Louis spent much time trying to reconcile the parties and, indeed, broke his journey to Aigues-Mortes in the summer of 1248 to try to bring peace to Christendom.

The resources of the French monarchy were devoted to the crusade. Many commentators see it as the last grand crusade in the medieval tradition of such expeditions. It was certainly the best-resourced and the best-planned crusade to travel to the East.

Financial and logistical preparations began early in 1245. The French clergy voluntarily increased a papal grant of one-twentieth to one-tenth of their incomes for three years, and extraordinary funds were raised from the confiscated lands of heretics and from the Jews of France. The crusade cost some 1.5 million livres tournois; most of this was raised from sources other than the crown lands and the traditional dues of the French crown.

Louis, with his three brothers and their wives, embarked at Aigues-Mortes on 25 August 1248, arriving in Cyprus on 17 September. Cyprus was to be the crusade's marshalling area for crusaders coming independently from France, the principality of Achaea and Syria. It was here that strategies were planned and Egypt, rather than Asia Minor or Palestine, agreed upon as the target of the campaign. Amphibious landings were practised, and these were to pay off later. It was also here that information regarding the Mongols and the Christians in their midst was received in December 1248 when the Dominican, Andrew of Longjumeau, returned from Tabriz. The delay in Cyprus had impoverished many

---

[34]   J. Richard, *Saint Louis, Crusader King of France* (1983; English edn, Cambridge, 1992); W.C. Jordan, *Louis IX and the Challenge of the Crusade* (Princeton, 1979); Grousset, *Histoire des Croisades*, III, 426–531; Setton, ed., *A History of the Crusades*, II, 487–518; Runciman, *A History of the Crusades*, III, 255–94 Riley-Smith, *The Crusades: A Short-History*, 157–61; Mayer, *The Crusades*, 260–71; B.Z. Kedar, 'The Passenger List of a Crusader Ship, 1250: towards the History of the Popular Element on the Seventh Crusade', *Studi medievale*, 3rd series, 13 (1972), 278–9.

crusaders. Louis helped where he could with cash and by taking many of the indigent into his service.

The fleet sailed from Cyprus in late May 1249 and successfully completed an opposed landing at Damietta on 5 June. In sharp contrast to the Fifth Crusade, the town was occupied the next day having been abandoned by its garrison. Delay now set in as the army waited for the king's brother Alphonse of Poitiers to arrive with reinforcements. It was decided to attack Cairo rather than Alexandria. However, it was not until November 20 that an advance on Cairo was begun. It took over a month to advance along through the Nile delta to a crossing of the main Nile River near El Mansura. The Nile flood delayed any crossing. This was not finally achieved until 6 February 1250 when one of the king's brothers, Robert of Artois, was killed in a reckless charge into El Mansura. Muslim resistance now became organised, dysentery ravaged the crusading army, and it became surrounded and cut off from its base at Damietta. The retreat to Damietta was slow and heavily contested. Supplies were intercepted and on 6 April Louis was forced to surrender. On 6 May a ten-year truce was agreed, and an immediate cash payment of half the ransom of 800,000 bezants was raised with the help of the Templars. Louis then left for Acre, where he arrived on 13 May. Some 12,000 captives remained in Egypt to be released when the balance of the ransom was paid.

Although the bulk of the crusading army returned to France Louis stayed in Syria until the end of April 1254, repairing and extending the fortifications at Acre, Caesarea, Jaffa and Sidon. Louis seems to have spent time in getting to know the lesser players on the Levantine scene and trying to integrate them into the wider crusader picture. He met with ambassadors from the Komnenoi of Trebizond and urged support for the Latin Empire of Constantinople. When he met with representatives from the Assassins of Alamut he suggested co-operation with the military orders.

He was possibly the first crusade leader to attempt to penetrate the position of the minority Christian groups in the East. He also received reports from those Franciscans sent to the Mongol court during his stay on Cyprus, very much following the agenda of the Council of Lyons. He visited the major shrines except that of Jerusalem, lest he acknowledge Muslim suzerainty over the city. On his departure Louis paid 4,000 livres per year for a garrison of 100 knights to remain in Acre under Geoffrey of Sargines (d. 1269), who took a prominent role in restoring order in the city during the so-called war of St Sabas. His successor, Philip III, maintained the force in Acre until his death in 1285. The failure of this crusade focused his attention on his own unworthiness as an instrument of God and the need to atone for the sins that he considered had caused the crusade to founder.

'CRUSADE OF THE *PASTOREAUX*' (SHEPHERDS), 1251[35]

A movement amongst the poor of northern France roused by a charismatic leader, the master of Hungary, who claimed to have a letter from the Virgin Mary urging the shepherds, who had first visited Christ at his birth, to liberate the Holy Land, which the proud nobles and ecclesiastics of France had failed to do. The movement showed the appeal of crusading at all levels of society, and especially its continuing appeal in the mid-thirteenth century when it was once opined that all zeal for crusade was on the wane. At first seen as a pious reaction to the capture of Louis IX, the countrymen were well received in Paris by Blanche of Castile. Thereafter the group splintered, became disorderly and violent, and was forcibly dispersed.

CRUSADE AGAINST CONRAD IV, 1250[36]

The crusade that had been called against Frederick II in June 1246 was automatically transferred to one against his son Conrad IV on Frederick's death. Preaching for the crusade coincided with the captivity of Louis IX and provoked a strong reaction in France, where Blanche of Castile threatened to outlaw anyone who agreed to serve on this crusade.

CRUSADE AGAINST MANFRED OF SICILY, 1255–66[37]

The first crusade preached against Manfred, the illegitmate son of Frederick II, and after 1258 king of Sicly, was preached at Naples in 1255. Indulgences for participation in the war against him continued to be issued down to his defeat and death at the hands of Charles of Anjou at the battle of Benevento in 1266, after which the Kingdom of Sicily passed to Angevin control.

CRUSADE AGAINST EZZELINO II DA ROMANO, 1256[38]

Crusade preached in Venice against the pro-imperial (Ghibelline) brothers, Ezzelino II (1194–1259) and Alberico da Romano, who had built up extensive lordships and influence around Padua and Verona in the service of Frederick II. They were successfully removed from power. The reaction in Venice to the

[35] M. Barber, 'The Crusade of the Shepherds, in 1251', in J. Sweets, ed., *Proceedings of the Tenth Annual Meeting for the Western Society for French History* (Lawrence, Kans., 1984), 1–23; G. Dickson, 'The Advent of the Pastors (1251)', *Revue belge de philologie et d'histoire*, 66 (1988), 249–67; J. Richard, *St. Louis*, 143–4; Riley-Smith, *The Crusades: A Short History*, 172; S. Cohn, *Popular Protest in Late Medieval Europe* (Manchester, 2004), 19.
[36] Housley, *The Italian Crusades*, 16, 71–2, 82, 252–3.
[37] Housley, *The Italian Crusades*, 15–19, 82–3, 129–30, 137–9.
[38] Housley, *The Italian Crusades*, 17, 54–5, 167–8; J. Law, *The Lords of Renaissance Italy* (London, 1981), 6; Dante, *Inferno*, XII, 109–10.

preaching of this crusade leaves no doubt that crusades against imperial or Italian enemies of the Church were seen as genuine crusades, just as much as were those to Palestine. Ezzelino achieved lasting notoriety as a 'son of perdition' in Dante's *Inferno*.

CRUSADE PREACHED AGAINST THE MONGOLS IN SYRIA, 1260[39]

In February 1258 the Mongols sacked Baghdad and brought the Abassid caliphate to an end. This caused consternation in the Mameluke world. In January 1260 the Mongols moved on to sack Aleppo and on 1 March received the submission of Damascus. They were now in direct contact with the Franks of Outremer. Amongst the Franks, opinion was divided about how to treat with the Mongols: were they the long-awaited ally from the East or a direct threat to their existence? The Armenians had accepted Mongol suzerainty in 1243. Hethoum I of Armenia (1226–69) persuaded his son-in-law, Bohemond VI of Antioch, to accept Mongol overlordship. This he had done, receiving as a reward the return of certain towns and castles in the eastern part of his principality that had been lost to the Mamelukes. Both Christian rulers had participated in the capture of Damascus. However, the Franks in Acre, particularly the military orders, saw the Mongols as a threat to their existence.

Calls for help were sent to both Pope Alexander IV and Charles of Anjou. On 25 May 1260 Alexander issued the bull *Audiat orbis*, calling for a crusade against the Tartars (Mongols) and, at the same time, excommunicated Bohemond for his collaboration with the Mongols. The bishop of Marseilles, Benedict of Alignan, proceeded to Syria with the brief of organising the crusade. He was an old Levant hand who had sponsored the rebuilding of the castle of Saphet in 1240. He preached the crusade in Acre, but nothing seems to have come of it.

The defeat of the Mongols by the Mamelukes at 'Ain Jalut on 3 September 1260 removed the immediate Mongol threat, but considerably increased that to the rump crusader states from the Mamelukes who, for the first time since 1193, controlled both Egypt and Syria.

CRUSADE AGAINST CONRADIN, 1268[40]

During the attempt by Conrad IV's son Conradin (1252–68) to regain the Kingdom of Sicily in April 1268, a crusade was preached against him in Perugia. He was defeated at Tagliacozzo by Charles of Anjou on 23 August 1268 and executed in Naples on 29 October in the same year. Charles's ruthless treatment of the young prince provoked revulsion amongst many of the ruling families of Europe.

---

[39] Richard, 'The Mongols and the Franks', 45–57, summarised in Richard, *The Crusades, c.1071–c.1291*, 411–13; Jackson, 'The Crisis in the Holy Land in 1260', 488, 509–10.

[40] Housley, *The Italian Crusades*, 19, 63, 229–30.

CRUSADE AGAINST THE MUSLIMS OF LUCERA, 1268[41]

This crusade was preached locally in southern Italy in April 1268 against the Muslims of Lucera, who refused to submit to Charles of Anjou. They were starved into surrender in August 1269 and brought to an end a period of thirty years when crusades had been preached against the Staufen and their allies in defence of the temporal interest of the papacy. In all cases those who fought the Staufen were promised the same remission of sins as those who went on crusade to the Holy Land.

ANTI-BYZANTINE CRUSADES, 1261–1320[42]

The establishment of the Frankish states in Constantinople and Greece in the three years following the Fourth Crusade had never been part of Innocent III's crusade plan, but was accepted by 1207 as part of God's judgment on the schismatic Greeks. By the 1240s the existence of these states was threatened by the resurgent Greek successor states to the Byzantine Empire in Epiros and Nicaea. By 1261 Constantinople was lost to the Latins, and Greek garrisons in Mistra and Monemvasia threatened the principality of Achaea, the most viable of the Frankish states. With the destabilisation of the region the Popes sanctioned the preaching of crusades for the defence and recovery of Latin Romania.

The Latin emperor Baldwin II visited the West from 1236–9 and from 1244–8 to raise financial and military support for his threatened empire. Sometime before October 1236 Peter of Dreux was planning a crusade to Constantinople. Nothing came of his expedition, and he went to Acre with Thibaut of Champagne (see pp. 173–4). However, whatever troops that Baldwin took back to Constantinople with him in the summer of 1239 provided much-needed succour to the defenders of the city. At the same time Greek attacks on the Latin position in central Greece, especially Thebes, prompted Gregory IX to levy a tax of one-third of their movable goods and incomes on the clergy of the Morea in 1238 and again in 1239. This was difficult to collect, despite the imminent threat that Gregory emphasised to the Episcopal recipients of his letters. In 1239 Gregory had approached both Thibaut of Champagne and Richard of Cornwall to aid the Latin Empire. Richard and his followers were adamant that they would not be so diverted; Constantinople did not have the appeal of Jerusalem, but papal concern for its loss was clear.

On 25 July 1261 Greek troops entered Constantinople, and on 15 August

---

[41] Housley, *The Italian Crusades*, 19.

[42] Mayer, *The Crusades*, 196–213; N. Housley, *The Later Crusades* (Oxford, 1992), 49–79; Setton, *The Papacy and the Levant*, I; Lock, *The Franks in the Aegean*; S. Runciman, *The Sicilian Vespers* (Cambridge, 1958); R.I. Burns, 'The Catalan Company and the European Powers, 1305–1311', *Speculum*, 29 (1954), 751–71; Jean Dunbabin, *Charles I of Anjou* (London, 1998), who makes the interesting observation that the inclusive approach to crusading in the 1980s has not led to a revision of Charles's role as a crusader.

Michael VIII Palaiologos entered his capital and was crowned in the Hagia Sophia. Baldwin II had escaped to Negroponte, and thence to Italy where he became a papal pensioner. As titular emperor of Constantinople, he spent the 1260s trying a number of schemes to recapture his city, eventually assigning the interests of himself and his son to Charles of Anjou and his family at Viterbo in May 1267. The loss of Constantinople happened during a papal inter-regnum, and it was not until 29 August that Urban IV was elected Pope. In June 1262 he authorised the preaching of a crusade in France for the recovery of Constantinople, citing the willingness of the Venetians and the Frankish lords of Achaea to participate. Fund raising in England, France and Spain was disappointing. The papacy was fully occupied with its wars with the Staufen in Italy, and the prince of Achaea was unable to resource an attack on Constantinople, occupied as he was with defending his own principality from Greek attack. Nothing came of this crusade apart from the great naval action at Settepozzi in 1263 where the Venetians defeated a Genoese squadron in the waters off Negroponte; more ships were committed in this engagement than at the battle of Trafalgar in 1805.

On 13 May 1264, following a year of Greek razzias (plundering raids) into the principality of Achaea, Urban renewed the preaching of a crusade against the Greeks – this time for the succour of the Morea. Again nothing came of this appeal, and in May 1267 William of Villehardouin turned to Charles of Anjou for aid, like Baldwin signing away the rights of his family in the Morea. Angevin subsidies and military assistance undoubtedly prolonged the life of the principal-ity. Charles of Anjou was hampered in any military move that he might wish to make against Constantinople by negotiations between Michael VIII and Pope Clement IV for union between the Greek and Latin churches. These restraints were removed with Clement's death in November 1268, but Charles then became involved in his brother Louis IX's plans for a second crusade. The unionist proposals at the Council of Lyons brought further delay to any projected operation against Constantinople (see pp. 374–5).

On 3 July 1281 at Orvieto, Charles of Anjou, his son-in-law Philip of Courtenay (since Baldwin's death in 1273, the titular Latin emperor of Constantinople) and the Venetians signed an agreement for a military expedition or 'passage into Romania' for the recapture of Constantinople. The expedition was to assemble at Brindisi in April 1283. In November 1281 Pope Martin V excommunicated Michael VIII and gave the go-ahead for the proposed expedition, now a crusade. The expedition was thwarted by the revolt of the Sicilian Vespers on 30 March 1282, and the Angevins had their hands full for the next two decades in resisting attacks from the Aragonese for the throne of Sicily.

The final anti-Byzantine crusade is associated with the presence of the Catalan Grand Company in the Aegean. These mercenaries, thrown out of work by the Peace of Caltabellota that ended the war of the Sicilian Vespers in 1302, gained service with the Byzantine emperor Andronikos II who used them to fight against the Turks. From early in 1305 the Catalans fell out with their employer and raided Byzantine territory in the north Aegean. From August 1307 to some time in 1310 the Company was subsidised by Charles of Valois, the brother of the French king Philip IV and, since 1301, the husband of Catherine of Courtenay the titular Latin empress of Constantinople. Charles hoped to use the Catalans in an attack on Constantinople. To this end he sent the Picard knight Thibaut of Cepoy to liaise with them. Certainly they flew the standard of St Peter in their attacks on Byzantine settlements and monasteries, but Thibaut found them far to unbiddable to organise to his master's plan and nothing came of this final crusade against the Greeks. In 1311 the Company was to occupy a central position in the political and military life of fourteenth-century Frankish Greece, and at the same time to gain papal displeasure and excommunication.

THE EIGHTH CRUSADE, OR CRUSADE OF LOUIS IX TO TUNIS, 1270[43]

Louis IX is said to have died with the word 'Jerusalem' on his lips, so the choice of Tunis as the target for this crusade has raised many questions amongst historians. From the days of Sternfeld's monograph debate has centred on the role of Charles of Anjou in deciding the initial objective. Charles had many links with Tunis, political commercial and diplomatic, that would have made a military expedition there attractive. He was not keen to go on crusade at this particular time, but obligations to his elder brother and family traditions made a refusal out of the question. On Louis' behalf it is generally agreed that he saw the crusade in two parts. The first part an attack on Tunis that would satisfy Charles, followed by an advance along the coast to Egypt. The contracts for the hire of shipping would fit well with this interpretation, although it also required a hazy knowledge of the geography of North Africa. Louis left Aigues-Mortes on 2 July 1270, one month later than originally planned. The fleets rendezvoused at Cagliari in Sardinia, and then the objective of Tunis was announced. The fleet arrived at Tunis on 18 July. On 24 July Carthage was captured and made the base for operations. There was much illness in the army and within a fortnight Louis was laid low with dysentery. On 25 August he died, just as the Sicilian fleet led by Charles of Anjou entered harbour. With Louis' death the crusade was abandoned. Charles of Anjou negotiated a treaty with the sultan of Tunis and on 11 November the crusaders embarked for Sicily. Prince Edward of England arrived in the crusader camp on 10 November in time to join the embarkation for Sicily. Some saw a storm at Trapani that scattered the returning fleet as God's judgment on this inglorious crusade.

[43] See note 34; also R. Sternfeld, *Ludwigs des Heiligen Kreuzzug nach Tunis und die Politik Karls I von Sizilien* (Berlin, 1896) and F. Delaborde's critique in the *Revue del'Orient latin* (1896), 423–8; M. Mollat, 'Le passage de Saint Louis a Tunis. Sa place dans l'histoire des croisades', *Revue d'histoire economique et sociale*, 50 (1972); J. Richard, 'La croisade de 1270. premier "passage general" ', *Comptes rendus de l'Academie des Inscriptions* (1989).

CRUSADE OF PRINCE EDWARD TO PALESTINE, 1268–72[44]

Prince Edward, along with his brother Edmund, his cousin Henry of Almain and members of his household, took the cross at the parliament held at Nottingham in midsummer 1268. His wife, Eleanor of Castile, also took the cross and he seems to have been content that she accompanied him on crusade. That apart, recruitment in England was poor. Despite a grant of a twentieth of lay incomes by parliament in 1270, the financing of the crusade proved a problem that was only alleviated by a loan of 70,000 livres tournois from Louis IX, whom Edward visited in the summer of 1269. Edward agreed to be at Aigues-Mortes by 15 August 1270.

Edward's departure from England was delayed until 20 August, and his arrival in Carthage on 10 November was in time to join the withdrawal of the crusading army to Sicily. Edward stayed on in Sicily, determined to fulfil his crusading vow. He despatched Henry of Almain to England to oversee the government during the illness of Henry III. Even his shocking murder at Viterbo by the sons of Simon of Montfort did not divert Edward from his crusade goal.

In early May he sailed from Trapani and arrived in Acre on 9 May 1271 with a very small force incapable of undertaking major military operations. Edward opened negotiations with the Mongols regarding joint operations in Syria, and in June and November led raids to the east and south of Acre. In May 1272 King Hugh of Cyprus and Jerusalem agreed a ten-year truce with Baybars at Caesarea. This angered Edward, who still hoped for a Mongol alliance. The best-known event of the crusade was the assassination attempt on Edward, probably carried through about the time of the signing of the truce. Certainly the need to recover from the wound accounts for Edward not leaving Acre until 24 September 1272. Wintering in Trapani, Edward learned, in December, of the death of his father on 16 November 1272. Edward did not hurry back to England; it was not until August 1274 that he returned and was crowned.

Although the crusade had achieved little, Edward returned with his European reputation much enhanced and his personal experience much extended. Edward's commitment to crusade, his desire to lead another crusade (discussed in October 1290 at the height of his power) and the parliamentary grant of a subsidy, albeit reluctant, shows that the idea of crusading was far from *passé* in the late thirteenth century.

With Edward's contingent was one Tebaldo Visconti, who led a group of crusaders from the Low Countries. In September 1271 he was elected Pope

[44] M. Prestwich, *Edward I* (London, 1988), 66–86; F.M. Powicke, *King Henry III and the Lord Edward*, II (Oxford, 1947), 597–617; S. Lloyd, 'The Lord Edward's Crusade, 1270–2: Its Setting and Significance', in J. Gillingham and J.C. Holt, eds, *War and Government in the Middle Ages* (Woodbridge, 1984), 120–32; B. Hamilton, 'Eleanor of Castile and the Crusading Movement', in B. Arbel, ed., *Intercultural Contacts in the Medieval Mediterranean* (London, 1996), 92–103; L. Lockhart, 'The Relations Between Edward I and Edward II of England and the Mongol Il-khans of Persia', *Iran*, 6 (1968), 23–31.

Gregory X, and in January 1272 left Acre for Italy. Crusading was to be at the top of the agenda during his pontificate (1271–6). Whilst in Acre Edward had paid for the construction of a mural tower that he entrusted to the keeping of the confraternity of St Edward of Acre that he founded. At least one of his barons, Hanno l'Estrange from Knockin in Shropshire, stayed on and died in Syria. In October 1272 he married Isabella, heiress of Beirut, the daughter of the younger John of Ibelin. Edward retained an interest in the Holy Land, corresponding with the Mongol Il-khans of Persia in 1282 for an alliance against the Mamelukes, but his commitments at home meant that he was never able to crusade in the East again.

PLANS FOR A JOINT LATIN–GREEK CRUSADE, 1274–6[45]

On 24 June 1274 a Greek delegation arrived at the Council of Lyons and the formal union of the Greek and Latin churches was signed on 6 July. In the names of Michael VIII and his son Andronikos, the envoys accepted the papal primacy and the *filioque* ('and from the Son') clause, and pledged obedience to Gregory X. Charles of Anjou was informed that the union of churches had been completed and was ordered to continue the truce with Michael VIII. Charles's hope of leading a crusade to capture Constantinople was thwarted. Michael VIII was determined to impose the union on his recalcitrant subjects, especially on Mount Athos and in the provinces, and it was at this time that much damage was inflicted on the Athonite monasteries by the agents of the emperor. Opponents of the union, even members of the imperial family, were imprisoned. The Council had also decreed a poll tax of 1d. per year throughout Christendom, and a tenth on clerical incomes for six years that was to finance future crusading; Christendom was divided into twenty-six tax districts to systematise collections.

In diplomatic exchanges following the Council, it was agreed that Michael VIII would allow a crusade free passage through his empire, that the crusade would clear the way across Asia Minor and restore territory to the Greeks that had been lost to the Turks, and that the Greeks would participate in a campaign to recapture the Holy Land. Envoys from the Mongol Il-khan of Persia had proposed joint operations in Syria at the Council of Lyons, and as Michael VIII was the father-in-law of the Il-khan co-operation was more likely. It was hoped, too, that Rudolf of Habsburg and Charles of Anjou would join the crusade one that was in many respects a re-run of the First Crusade. It was certainly conceived on a grand scale. The death of Gregory X at Arezzo on 10 January 1276 ended these bold plans.

---

[45] See references in note 44; also D.J. Geanakoplos, *Emperor Michael VIII Palaeologus and the West* (Cambridge, Mass., 1959), 277–304; V. Laurent, 'La croisade et la question d'orient sous le pontificat de Gregoire X', *Revue historique du sud-est europeen*, 22 (1945), 106–37, and 'Gregoire X et le projet d'une ligue antiturque', *Echos d'Orient*, 37 (1938), 257–73.

CRUSADE AGAINST THE ARAGONESE, 1283[46]

Martin IV declared this crusade on 13 January 1283 against Peter II of Aragon and his supporters who had entered the war against the Angevins in Sicily following the revolt of the Sicilian Vespers. It was preached in Italy and France. Despite this early moral boost to the Angevin cause it did nothing to avoid a long war. The War of the Sicilian Vespers was to drag on until 1302 (see next entry), distracting attention from the losses of major towns in Latin Syria and making any response by France, Naples and the papacy to the Mamelukes impossible.

CRUSADE AGAINST FREDERICK OF SICILY, 1298, 1299 AND 1302[47]

The final round of the War of the Sicilian Vespers saw Boniface VIII throw papal support behind the Angevins in a final clearance of the Aragonese from Calabria but not from Sicily. Frederick, the younger brother of James II of Aragon, refused to carry out his brother's agreement to withdraw from Sicily and instead had himself crowned king of Sicily in March 1296. The Treaty of Caltabellota in September 1302 recognised Frederick's position in the island, a position from which the crusaders were uable to dislodge him.

CRUSADE AGAINST THE COLONNA CARDINALS, 1298[48]

Coming to the fore in the 1290s the Colonna family were rivals of the Caetani, the family of Boniface VIII, for lands and influence at the papal court. Following the seizure of a papal treasure convoy near Ninfa by Stephen Colonna in May 1297, relations rapidly deteriorated and disagreement concerning Colonna family lands induced the Colonna cardinals to appeal to a general council to judge Boniface VIII. The questionable succession of Boniface to Celestine V, who had resigned voluntarily and then had been imprisoned by his successor, provided ammunition to the Colonna who were also supporters of Frederick of Aragon and thus posed a direct and immediate threat to the position of the Pope from within the College of cardinals. Boniface deposed the Colonna cardinals and in December 1297 extended the crusade against the Sicilian rebels to them. In the summer of 1298 the family's lands and possessions, including the castle of Colonna, were seized and their town of Palestrina razed to the ground; only flight to the French court saved their lives. This was a particular use of crusade in what was essentially a family dispute, and it roused much criticism of the misuse of crusading ideology and funding.

---

[46] Runciman, *The Sicilian Vespers*, 228–41; Housley, *The Italian Crusades*, 20–2, 73, 84, 99, 129.
[47] Housley, *The Italian Crusades*, 20, 23.
[48] Housley, *The Italian Crusades*, 23, 54, 58, 132–8; Housley, *The Later Crusades*, 292–3; T.S.R. Boase, *Boniface VIII* (London, 1933), 159–85.

THE JUBILEE YEAR AND THE 'CRUSADE' OF THE GENOESE WOMEN, 1300[49]

Pope Boniface VIII (1294–1303) announced the first Holy Year (Anno Santo) in February 1300, promising a general indulgence for a hundred years to all pilgrims who visited Rome and its shrines in that year. Two hundred thousand pilgrims flocked to Rome, including Isabelle of Villehardouin, princess of Achaea, who married Philip of Savoy there. Boniface brought pressure to bear on Charles II of Naples to accept this marriage of his vassal Isabelle and showed that papal interest in the Frankish states in Greece was active. However, the occasion was not used for the discussion of crusade to the Holy Land, perhaps because virtually no major ruler appeared in Rome or perhaps because Boniface was said not to to be interested in crusading. Nonetheless, the atmosphere of the Holy Year moved a number of noble Genoese ladies to collect money and excite enthusiasm for a crusade. It is said that the women worked together regardless of the Ghibelline and Guelf divisions so evident in Genoese society since the 1240s, and that they even intended to go on crusade themselves. To this end they had special suits of armour made for them that are now on display at the Royal Armouries in Turin. Nothing appears to have come of this excitement, although it does show that crusading continued to arouse particular passions and that it was emerging as a worthy charitable cause by the end of the thirteenth century.

THE HOSPITALLER *PASSAGIUM* AND THE *PASTOREAUX* OR SHEPHERDS' CRUSADE, 1309[50]

The movement was a manifestation of crusade enthusiasm amongst the peasantry in England, north-eastern France and parts of Germany. Although stimulated by the preaching of the Hospitaller *passagium*, it sought to retain general crusades open to all-comers rather than specific, specialised campaigns with discrete objectives manned by professional soldiery. The destination of the Hospitaller *passagium* was unknown at the time of its departure and alarmed those with interest in the Aegean and Mediterranean, especially the Venetians and Lusignans. In fact, the Grand Master, Fulk of Vilaret, directed it to complete the subjugation of Rhodes; general, that is non-Hospitaller, participation was not expected or wanted.

Like that of 1320, the *pastoreaux* (see p. 190) sought to revive popular participation in crusading in the face of current trends to limit crusading to warriors signed up for a specific objective. It attracted much criticism from clerical writers for violence and disorganisation. Some 30,000 people are supposed to have

---

[49] Boase, *Baniface VIII*, 231–66; C. Manenti and M. Bollen, eds., *Castles in Italy* (Cologne, 2000), 234; H. Kessler and J. Zacharias, *Rome 1300* (New Haven, 2000).
[50] N. Housley, *The Avignon Papacy and the Crusades* (Oxford, 1986), 144–5; Setton, ed., *A History of the Crusades*, III, 284–6.

arrived in Avignon in July 1309, whilst German contingents sought passage down the Danube, with the idea that the Hospitallers would find a use for these zealous participants. It was dispersed peaceably. Like similar movements in 1251 and 1320 it showed the considerable popular enthusiasm for crusading.

CRUSADE AGAINST THE VENETIANS, 1309[51]

The dispute over rival candidates to succeed Azzo VIII Este (d. 1308) as ruler of Ferrara – one backed by Clement V, the other by the Venetians – resulted in the preaching of a crusade against Venice throughout Italy in June 1309. There was minor military action on the borders of the Romagna, but Robert of Naples, concerned to protect trade with Venice, confined himself to detaining Venetian merchants in his kingdom. The dispute was in no one's interest and Venice backed down in 1310. However, this minor crusade against a loyal daughter of the Church showed the lengths to which crusades in Italy would go to protect papal interests.

CRUSADE AGAINST FREDERICK OF MONTEFELTRO, 1320[52]

Crusade proclaimed by John XXII on 8 December 1321 to regain possession of towns in the March of Ancona and Duchy of Spoleto occupied by the count of Montefeltro and his brothers. The Malatesta of Rimini and the commune of Perugia drove out Frederick, killed him at Orvieto, and captured his brothers.

THREE FRENCH PLANS FOR CRUSADE, 1317, 1323 AND 1333[53]

With the move of the papacy from Italy to Avignon in 1307 relations between it and the kings of France became closer. Sponsoring and supporting a crusade was part and parcel of being a pope or a king, and both parties took the duty

---

[51] Housley, *The Later Crusades*, 243.
[52] Housley, *The Italian Crusades*, 25, 41, 112.
[53] J. Delaville le Roulx, *La France en Orient au XIVe siècle* (2 vols, Paris, 1886); Housley, *The Avignon Papacy and the Crusades, passim*; Housley, *The Later Crusades*, 30–7; N. Housley, 'The Franco-Papal Crusade Negotiations of 1322–3', *Papers of the British School at Rome*, 48, new series 35 (1980), 164–85; A. Atiya, *The Crusades in the Later Middle Ages* (1938; 2nd edn, New York, 1970), 95–128; S. Schein, 'Philip IV and the Crusade: A Reconsideration', in P. Edbury, ed., *Crusade and Settlement* (Cardiff, 1985), 121–6; C.J. Tyerman, 'Sed Nihil Fecit? The Last Capetians and the Recovery of the Holy Land, in J. Gillingham and J.C. Holt, eds., *War and Government in the Middle Ages* (Woodbridge, 1984), 170–81; C.J. Tyerman,' 'Philip V of France, the Assemblies of 1319–20 and the Crusade', 57 (1984), 15–34; C.J. Tyerman, Philip VI and the Recovery of the Holy Land', *English Historical Review*, 100 (1985), 25–51, *Bulletin of the Institute of Historical Research*, 'Marino Sanudo Torsello and the Lost Crusade: Lobbying in the Fourteenth Century', *Transactions of the Royal Historical Society*, Ser. 5, 32 (1982); C.J. Tyerman, *England and the Crusades 1095–1588* (Oxford, 1988), 247–51; T.S.R. Boase, ed., *The Cilician Kingdom of Armenia* (Edinburgh,1978).

seriously. In the eyes of the popes the kings of France were more closely associated than other monarchs with the crusade to the Holy Land and were its natural leaders, especially after the canonisation of Louis IX, the crusader king par excellence, in 1297. The fact that none of these crusade proposals actually materialised into a crusade, and that the financial mechanism behind crusading had so developed in the thirteenth century that those planning a crusade might actually benefit, should not lead us to think that these proposals were insincere or that they intended to make crusade planning into a cash cow for the French monarchy.

The crusade discussions of these years were informed by the growing number of appeals from the kings of Cilician (or Lesser) Armenia, threatened as they were by increasing attacks from Mamelukes, Mongols and Ottoman Turks. Armenia, which was eventually overrun by the Mamelukes in 1375, thus formed a central plank in the planning of these crusades. The discussions were also informed by a growing body of publications that provided analyses of the ideal crusade and practical advice on how this was to be achieved. Such early propagandists included the Franciscans Hethoum, a former king of Armenia, and Ramon Lull; civil servants like Peter Dubois, William Durand and William of Nogaret; and the Venetian merchant Marino Sanudo Torsello. Planning in order to ensure success became an essential part of the crusade and perhaps ensured that none of these crusade plans would develop beyond the drawing board. Against this background the propagandists and planners of these Capetian-Valois crusade proposals were some of the best informed ever, even if the proposals were overwhelmed by events.

The nature of the crusade was changing too. The concept of the *passagium particulare* was emerging; a limited specific campaign with professional warriors to clear the way for a general crusade, or *passagium generale*, that would follow in a year. The latter, however, often did not happen and the *passagium particulare* was to become the new crusade. The role of the poor crusader was reduced, if not entirely removed, in the discussions and planning around the ideal crusade; but this was not without opposition from would-be popular crusaders, as was shown by the *pastoreaux* of 1309 and 1320 (see pp. 187 and 190).

The crusades of Philip V (1317–22) and Charles IV (1322–8) failed to raise the funding that was thought essential, and both petered out in what seemed almost outrageous requests for money from John XXII who, in 1324, turned his attention to dealing with Ludwig IV of Bavaria and his threat to the papal states.

The first Valois king, Philip VI (1328–50), had taken the cross at Paris on 1 October 1331 and proposed to lead a seaborne crusade himself in August 1336 to liberate Jerusalem. Whether the destination was Egypt or Syria was not yet specified. By 1333 he had induced many French nobles to take the cross and had persuaded John XXII to authorise the preaching of a crusade and to levy a tax of a tenth on the clergy of Christendom for six years.

A lack of organisational skills on Philip's part, and a lack of adequate finance, prevented serious military preparations being put in hand, and the deteriorating relationship with Edward III of England meant that the project was abandoned in March 1336 with papal approval. This failure produced much disappointment and many cynical observations. It is from this time that French crusaders begin to participate in numbers in the Baltic crusades. Indeed, these annual expeditions became so popular with French knights that Charles V banned their participation in 1376. The failure of this crusade to materialise signalled the end of old-style crusading; it was neither financially viable nor politically possible.

THE *PASTOREAUX* OR SHEPHERDS' CRUSADE, 1320[54]

Unlike the *pastoreaux* of 1309 this was confined to France, but like it it sprang from an awareness of the crusade discussions at the court of Philip V and an eagerness to participate in some way; this movement of common people looked backwards to earlier crusades and contained an element of the People's Crusade about it. It rapidly turned to acts of violence and robbery of clerics and Jews, and was dispersed by a mixture of persuasion and force. It did, however, show the continued appeal of crusade to the East amongst common people.

TWO ANTI-GHIBELLINE CRUSADES, 1321–2[55]

Two further crusades of the sort preached against Frederick of Montefeltro were preached against the Matteo Visconti in December 1321, and renewed in 1325, and against the Estensi and their supporters in Ferrara in February 1322. The kings of France refused support to these crusades. It was Angevin forces that carried out the fighting and the aim was to bolster the Guelf position in northern Italy.

CRUSADE AGAINST LUDWIG IV OF BAVARIA, 1328[56]

Often seen as the last struggle between the empire and the papacy, its origins lay in the double election to the German kingship of Frederick II of Austria (1230–46) and Ludwig of Bavaria (1294–1347) in 1314 after the death of the German emperor Henry VII at Buonconvento on 24 August 1313. Henry's death ended three years of war with the Guelf communes of northern Italy and with the Angevins of Naples; the Guelf interest seemed about to preponderate in Italy once more.

Pope John XXII (1316–34) deposed the imperial vicar in Italy appointed by

---

[54] M. Barber, 'The Pastoreaux of 1320', *Journal of Ecclesiastical History*, 32, (1981), 143–66; Cohn, *Popular Protest in Late Medieval Europe*, 35–6.

[55] Housley, *The Italian Crusades*, 26–8.

[56] H.S. Offler, 'Empire and Papacy: The Last Struggle', *Transaction of the Royal Historical Society*, Series 5, 6 (1956), 21–47; W. Ullmann, *A Short History of the Papacy in the Middle Ages* (London, 1972) 284–6; Housley *The Later Crusades*, 15, 28, 49, 154–6; L. Green, *Castuccio Castracani* (Oxford, 1986), 205–15, 224–58; B. Gebhardt, ed., *Handbuch der deutschen Geschichte*, I (9th edn, Munich, 1970), 518–54.

Louis and appointed instead Robert of Naples. With his victory over Frederick at Muhldorf in September 1322 Ludwig established himself as the effective emperor-elect. Pope John continued to reject his claim and on 23 March 1324 excommunicated him for heresy on the dubious political grounds of his support for the Ghibellines. He freed his subjects from obedience to Ludwig and dubbed him *Ludovicus Bavaricus*, a diminutive title corresponding to his new position. In May Ludwig replied with counter-claims of heresy against the Pope for his support of the spiritual Franciscans.

In February 1326 Ludwig entered Italy and by his presence swung the balance of power in favour of his Ghibelline supporters like Castruccio Castracani (d. 1330). Ludwig received the Iron Crown of Lombardy in Milan on 31 May 1327 and was crowned emperor in Rome by the Roman commune on 11 January 1328. At this juncture John XXII declared a crusade against Ludwig. Ludwig was forced to abandon Rome in August due to shortage of food and money, and he withdrew to Lucca and Pisa. In 1328 he declared the Pope deposed, and set up an Italian antipope. He continued in Italy until 1330. The crusade was renewed against him in 1329, but his mercenary forces were too small to inflict a serious defeat on Robert of Naples. Ludwig did not return to Italy. He died on a bear hunt near Munich in the autumn of 1347.

CRUSADE AGAINST THE CATALAN GRAND COMPANY, 1330[57]

In 1308 the last Burgundian ruler of the Duchy of Athens, Guy II, died without heirs. The succession passed to his nephew, Walter (Gautier) of Brienne, the son of Guy's sister Isabelle and Hugh of Brienne, count of Lecce. In 1310 Walter had employed the Catalan Grand Company to operate in Thessaly, but a dispute over pay was settled at the battle of Halmyros, 15 March 1311, in which Walter and a large proportion of the knighthood of Frankish Greece were killed. The Catalans took over the duchy in the name of Aragon and the Briennist claim passed to his young son Walter II, who became the ward of his grandfather Walter of Chatillon, the constable of France. From August 1331 to the late summer of 1332 Walter II of Brienne sought to regain the duchy of Athens by military force, basing himself on Patras. The campaign achieved very little beyond the occupation of Arta, Vonitza and the island of Leukas (Santa Maura). Walter II of Brienne, as a prominent French noble in the service of the Angevins of Naples, to whom he was related, was clearly seen as deserving of papal support, whilst it was desirable in the interest of stability in Frankish Greece that his opponents the Catalans, with their background of regrettable violence, Aragonese connections, and use of Turkish mercenaries, should be subjugated. Prior to Walter's departure from Brindisi the Church threw its

---

[57] Housley, *The Later Crusades*, 120, 139; K. Setton, *Catalan Domination of Athens* 1311–88 (New York, 1948; revised edn, London, 1975), 38–51; Setton, ed., *A History of the Crusades*, III, 167–215.

weight behind him. In June 1330 Pope John XXII had a crusade preached against the Catalans in southern Italy and Greece, stipulating a campaign of one year's duration; at the same time he instructed the Latin clergy in Greece to excommunicate the Catalan Company.

Walter II of Brienne ruled Florence as despot for one year in 1342, saw service with the French at Crecy in 1346 and was killed at Poitiers in 1356.

THE NAVAL LEAGUE, 1333[58]

In December 1331, as part of the gathering information for his proposed crusade, Philip VI of France had asked the Venetians for their advice on the essential elements for a successful crusade. They offered to supply 100 galleys at the king's expense and to provide substantial naval support at their own expense should the proposed crusade actually get underway.

In the meantime the Turks of the emirate of Aydin had seized Smyrna from the Genoese in 1329 and used it as a base to intensify their raids throughout the Aegean. Rendezvousing at Rhodes in September 1332, representatives from Byzantium and Venice met with Helion of Villeneuve, the master of the Hospitallers on Rhodes, and agreed to maintain a naval flotilla of twenty galleys for five years to assemble at Negroponte (Chalkis) on 15 April 1333.

Nothing had been achieved by that date except the accession of the League of France, as a forerunner of Philip's crusade, and Cyprus. The preaching for Philip's crusade had begun in 1333 and the League could benefit from the moral high ground by attaching itself to that endeavour. However, the ships were present in Negroponte by midsummer 1334. Under the command of Pietro Zeno, the Venetian baili of Negroponte, it gained a signal victory over a Turkish fleet off Adramyttium (Edremit).

The League ceased to function after this victory, and Turkish raids resumed in the following year. Pope John XXII had been a keen supporter of the League and he was the first Pope to finance four papal galleys for the protection of Christians in the Aegean, perhaps the lasting outcome of the League.

THE HOLY LEAGUE OF CLEMENT VI, 1343[59]

In response to appeals from Hugh IV of Cyprus, and in the light of general concern over increasing Turkish piracy and razzias (plundering raids) from the

[58] Setton, *The Papacy and the Levant*, I, 180–2; Housley, *The Later Crusades*, 36; A. Laiou, 'Marino Sanudo Torsello, Byzantium and the Turks: The Background to the Anti-Turkish league of 1332–34', *Speculum*, 45 (1970), 374–92; A. Luttrell, 'The Crusade in the Fourteenth Century', in J. Hale *et al.*, eds, *Europe in the Late Middle Ages* (London, 1965), 122–54; A. Luttrell, 'The Hospitallers of Rhodes Confront the Turks, 1306–1421', in P. Gallagher, ed., *Christians, Jews and Other Worlds* (Lanham, Md., 1988), 80–116.

[59] See references in note 60; Setton, *The Papacy and the Levant*, I 177–94; Atiya, *The Crusades in the Later Middle Ages*, 111–12, 290–300; Housley, *The Later Crusades*, 59–61.

Venetian colonies and the Frankish states in the Aegean, Clement VI authorised the preaching of a crusade against the Turks in the bull *Insurgentibus contra fidem* of 29 September 1343. In the following December a three-year tithe on ecclesiastical incomes was to be collected to pay for the crusade. The crusade was designed to stop or reduce naval raids by the Turkish emirates of western Asia Minor, and so it was aimed at Smyrna (Izmir) the principal port of the emirate of Aydin. This crusade took the form of a naval league, a revival of an idea of Pope John of 1334 and a major departure in ways of thinking of crusading, bringing this particular organisation very much under papal direction and at the same time exploiting the versatility of ships and their objectives. In this case the objective was clearly defined, and a time limit of one summer's sailing imposed.

Since the days of Pope John XXII the papacy had maintained four galleys in the East for defence against the Turks; it now placed these under the command of the Genoese Martino Zaccaria, who had been one of the lords of Chios until its recapture by the Greeks in 1329. He also appointed Henry of Asti, the titular Latin patriarch of Constantinople, as legate; he was given strict instructions to ensure that Zaccaria made for Smyrna with no diversions. The members of the league were Cyprus, the Hospitallers of Rhodes, the Venetians and the Pope, although there was some Genoese participation.

The fleet was variously estimated as consisting of twenty-four or twenty-seven galleys; the Pope and the king of Cyrpus contributed four each, the Hospitallers six, and presumably the Venetians (with some ships from Negroponte) made up the balance. The fleet was to assemble in the harbour of Negroponte (Chalkis) on All Saints' Day 1343. On 13 May 1343 the fleet destroyed sixty Turkish vessels off Pallene (Kassandra), the westernmost prong of the Chalkidiki peninsula.

On 28 October the fleet landed at Smyrna, taking Umar Pasha, the emir of Aydin (1334–48), completely by surprise. The port of Smyrna and the lower town was captured, but the citadel remained in the hands of the Turks for some time. Umar Pasha besieged the town in turn and on 17 January 1345 surprised the crusade leadership as they were celebrating a victory mass and slaughtered them. Pope Clement and his correspondents rejoiced at the good news of the initial capture of Smyrna. Indeed, it was the first positive crusading news to be received from the East in a generation. Crosses were seen in the sky by some pious folk and even the tragic massacre of the league's leadership on St Antony's Day in Smyrna was seen as inspirational in the place and manner of their death. Nonetheless, the Latins in Smyrna were hanging on by the teeth in 1345.

CRUSADE OF HUMBERT OF VIENNOIS, 1345–7[60]

Humbert II, dauphin of Viennois, was a devout man and an actor on the European stage eager to make his mark as a crusader. He had considered joining

[60] Atiya, *The Crusades in the Later Middle Ages*, 301–18; Housley, *The Later Crusades*, 60–1; Setton, *The Papacy and the Levant*, I, 194–214; R. Kaeuper and E. Kennedy, eds, *The Book of Chivalry of*

a crusade to the Canary Islands, but in May 1345 after receiving the news of the massacre of St Antony's Day he offered himself as a leader of the crusade. Clement VI appointed him commander of the Christian army against the Turks and gave him a papal banner. Preaching for the crusade was intensified in the summer of 1345 and produced many recruits. There was a delay of nearly a year before Humbert arrived at Smyrna. In that time many would-be crusaders had made their own way to Smyrna whilst during Humbert's time there many thousands were to arrive from Europe.

Humbert left Avignon in late August and arrived in Venice on 24 October 1345 where he consulted with the Venetians over conditions in the East. He was supplied with two galleys that took him to Negroponte, where he arrived on 25 December. There he stayed until June 1346 to finalise his preparations, recommending the temporary cessation of Chios by the Byzantines as a base of operations for three years and putting together a fleet of twenty-six galleys. He also found time to canvas Church union to Anna of Savoy, the Byzantine empress. Whilst in Negroponte a Genoese fleet of twenty-nine galleys commanded by Simone Vignoso seized some of Humbert's war chest and war materials. It would not join him, but sailed on to recapture Chios and to seize the towns of old and new Phocaea on the Turkish mainland.

Arriving in Smyrna in early July, Humbert fortified the lower town, carried out raids against the Turks and dealt with the shortage of funds to pay the galley crews from his own pocket. He found great difficulty in obtaining the compliance of Venetian and Cypriot contingents in Smyrna. In November Clement wrote to Humbert of the difficulty of collecting volunteers and, more important, cash to send East due to the war between France and England; in the same month there were instructions on the negotiations of a possible truce with Umar Pasha. In March 1346 Clement gave permission to Humbert to return from crusade, even though he had not served for three years. In May 1347 he returned to Venice, having secured no truce with the Turks. In July 1349 the childless and widowed Humbert took the Dominican habit, with the son of Duke John of Normandy becoming dauphin.

The crusade had not lived up to its high expectations. However, it confirmed that the new form of crusading warfare was to be naval; that it was to be defensive, aimed at containing the advance of the Turks; and that the focus of crusading endeavour was to be Greece and the Aegean. The position that Humbert found himself in necessitated frequent consultation with Pope Clement; the resulting archive makes this one of the best-documented crusades of the whole crusading movement. The holy league was extended to 1351 when shortage of funding, and a fear on the part of the Hospitallers that the defence of Smyrna was going to pass totally to them, led to a winding down of the league and the end of the preaching of the crusade. Nonetheless, Smyrna remained beleaguered,

---

Geoffroi de Charny (Philadelphia, 1996), written by a participant who did not make light of the hazards of crusading.

NARRATIVE OUTLINE OF THE CRUSADES

but in Christian hands, serving as a forward naval base for the Hospitallers until 1402 when Timur seized it. The papacy paid 6,000 florins each year for its defence, and the popes regularly appointed and paid for the captains of Smyrna as need arose.

CRUSADE AGAINST FRANCESCO ORDELAFFI, 1355[61]

From 1353 two papal legations were sent to reassert control of the Papal States in central Italy, and to ensure the efficient raising of revenue from them. One of these legates, Bertrand du Poulet, encountered opposition from Francesco Ordelaffi, lord of Cesena and Forli, who had already been pronounced a heretic in October 1354 for his stubborn resistance to papal authority. In December 1355 Innocent IV declared a crusade against Ordelaffi. Angevin troops were used with some success against him and his lands through 1356, but Bernardo Visconti, the hot-blooded brother of Galeazzo II, sent mercenary troops, enabling Ordelaffi to prolong his resistance until 1357 when some semblance of papal control of the Romagna was restored.

CRUSADE OF PETER I DE LUSIGNAN, 1362–5[62]

Peter succeeded his father Hugh IV as king of Cyprus and titular king of Jerusalem on 10 October 1359, although it was not until Easter Sunday 1360 that he was crowned king of Jerusalem in Famagusta by the papal legate Peter Thomas. Peter I had allegedly founded the Order of the Sword, dedicated to the recovery of the Holy Land. In 1361 his forces had occupied the port of Satalia (Antalya) and cleared Turkish shipping from the seas north of Cyprus. From 1362 to 1365 he became the first Cypriot king to visit the courts of Western Europe. He left Paphos on 24 October 1362 and arrived in Venice on 5 December. It appears that he was seeking papal authorisation for a new crusade and possibly to gain substantial numbers of recruits. He arrived in Avignon in March 1363. On 31 March Urban V ordered the preaching of a crusade for the recovery of Jerusalem to be ready for March 1365, and with his own hands gave the cross to Peter I and to John II of France, whom he named as captain-general of the new crusade. The Treaty of Bretigny of 1360 between France and England had made many mercenaries unemployed and Pope Urban V hoped that many of these would find employment on the crusade, thus reducing the disorder that they caused in France. In the event, western recruitment was disappointing and most of the participants came from Cyprus. Royal leadership was lacking in France.

[61] Housley, *The Later Crusades*, 245; Housley, *The Avignon Papacy and the Crusades*, 75–7.
[62] Setton, *The Papacy and the Levant*, I, 224–84; Atiya, *The Crusades in the Later Middle Ages*, 319–78; P.M. Holt, ed., *The Eastern Mediterranean Lands in the Period of the Crusades* (Warminster, 1977), 90–105; P. Edbury, *The Kingdom of Cyprus and the Crusades, 1191–1374* (Cambridge, 1991), 141–79; G. Hill, *A History of Cyprus*, II (Cambridge, 1948), 308–69.

John II died on 8 April 1364. His son and successor, Charles V (1364–80) spent the first six years of his reign overcoming rebellion and establishing his position in France.

Peter I left Venice on 27 June 1365 to return to Cyprus. At the time the crusader flotilla was assembling in Rhodes; no one knew the destination of the crusade. Alexandria was declared the objective and in this Peter followed the precedent of the Fifth Crusade and the first crusade of Louis IX, in which it was intended to use the resources of Egypt to conquer Jerusalem at leisure. Interestingly, in 1311 Henry II of Cyprus had urged an attack on Egypt as a means to liberate Jerusalem. Though not original in his objective, his capture and sack of Alexandria on 10 October 1365 dealt the most severe blow that the Mamelukes had received at the hands of crusaders. After a week of plundering and destruction the crusade army left Alexandria on Thursday 16 October. Alexandria had been destroyed as a commercial centre for the foreseeable future. It seems that Peter hoped to restore the trading position of Famagusta at Alexandria's expense. Certainly increasing numbers of Venetian and Genoese merchants traded direct with Alexandria, by-passing Cyprus. Certainly, too, Peter's destruction of Alexandria aroused Genoese and Venetian ire against him, and they imposed trade embargoes with Cyprus. Peter was now the toast of Christendom, and his achievement compared to the capture of Jerusalem in 1099. The poet Petrarch praised him, but his crusade had certainly increased the likelihood of Egyptian retaliation on Cyprus and Rhodes.

From December 1367 to September 1368 Peter paid his second visit to Europe, this time being lionised in Italy and purchasing weapons at the Venetian arsenal with the intention of invading Cilician Armenia, where he had been offered the throne. On 17 January 1369 he was murdered in his bed by courtiers disaffected by his cruelty and paranoia. The succession of his infant son Peter II led to attacks upon his island by the Genoese and the negation of the achievements of this old-style crusader.

CRUSADE OF AMADEO VI OF SAVOY TO THRACE AND BULGARIA, 1366[63]

Once dubbed an escapade rather than a crusade, Amadeo's expedition was not without one notable outcome since he recaptured Gallipoli from the Turks. They had occupied this Dardanelles port in 1354, their first foothold in Europe, and had used it to introduce troops into the Balkans. They took a number of important Byzantine towns to the north of Constantinople, Demotika and Adrianople in 1361, and Philippopolis in 1363, alarming both Louis I the Great, Angevin king of Hungary, and John V of Byzantium.

[63] Setton, *The Papacy and the Levant*, I, 285–326; Atiya, *The Crusades in the Later Middle Ages*, 379–97; E. Cox, *The Green Count of Savoy* (Princeton, 1967), 177–239; N. Iorga, *Philippe de Mezieres (1327–1405) et la croisade au XIVe siècle* (Paris, 1896), 163–75.

Although present at Avignon on 31 March 1363 when Peter I and John II of France received the cross, Amadeo did not take the cross at that time. This he did probably on 19 January 1364 with the intention of joining Peter of Lusignan's expedition. At the same time, at Avignon, he formed the Order of the Collar for fifteen knights to commemorate the fifteen joys of the Virgin Mary and commissioned Italian jewellers to make the requisite fifteen collars. Thirteen of these knights accompanied Amadeo on his crusade. In March 1365 he received the prestigious jewelled Golden Rose from the hands of Urban V, the mark of a zealous son of the Church.

The death of John II in April 1364, and the ever-present threat from discharged mercenary bands, caused Amadeo to put his crusade plans aside, but the resounding news of Peter I's victory at Alexandria prompted action. In January 1366 he met with Urban V to explain what had been achieved since 1364 and persuaded the Pope to leave the crusade bull of 1364 in force. He appointed his wife regent for his lands during his absence. Both Genoa and Venice were unwilling to provide transport for a new crusade following the difficulties that had been caused to their commercial interests by the sack of Alexandria, but they became much more amenable when they learned that the Balkans was the object of Amadeo's crusade. Genoa, Marseilles and Venice contributed to the twenty ships that comprised Amadeo's flotilla. Amadeo sailed with the Venetians, and the ships from Genoa and Marseilles were to join Amadeo in the Venetian harbour of Korone in the south-west Peloponnese.

On 21 June 1366 Amadeo left Venice and on 19 July arrived in Korone. The combined fleet left for Negroponte on 27 July, where it arrived on 2 August. Here he learned that Louis of Hungary, expected to join him in the Balkans campaign, was campaigning in his own right against the Bulgarians, whilst John V was a virtual prisoner of the Bulgarians. After this disappointment, and with difficulties of maintaining discipline in his army, he proceeded to the north Aegean on 15 August.

On 22 August the expedition arrived at Gallipoli and by 26 August the town had been captured. He left a garrison with a captain and an administrator there until June 1367, when he handed the town back to the Byzantines. By 4 September he was in Constantinople and about 8 October took up quarters at Sozopolis on the Black Sea from where he opened negotiations with the Bulgarians for the release of John V; this was not secured until 28 January 1367. The crusade had by now been abandoned. Amadeo began his return from Constantinople on 9 June 1367. At Gallipoli on 13 June he handed the town over to the Greeks and by 29 July he was back in Venice.

THE GREAT SCHISM AND THE CRUSADES, 1382, 1383 AND 1387[64]

The Great Schism in the papacy (1378–1417) occurred after the death of Gregory XI on 27 March 1378 in Rome, soon after he had brought the papal curia back to Rome after seventy-three years in Avignon. On 9 April Urban VI (1378–89) was elected Gregory's successor, but the majority of his cardinals, who were French, abandoned him due to his reform policy, his refusal to quit Rome for Avignon and his apparent lack of respect for his cardinals. The cardinals rejected early suggestions of a general council to settle the matter since they claimed that there was no legitimate Pope to summon such a council. On 9 August 1378 they elected another Pope, Clement VII (1378–94), who removed to Avignon and constituted a new college of cardinals.

Appeals to both popes to step down were unavailing. France, Scotland, Aragon, Castile, Navarre and Naples (at first) supported the Avignonese popes. England, Germany Scandinavia, Bohemia, Genoa and Venice supported the Roman popes, whilst the Hospitallers produced Grandmasters of both the Avignonese and Roman persuasions.

It is sometimes said that during these years of schism the papacy lost the leadership of the crusades. This is not true. No one questioned the right and duty of a Pope, whether in Avignon or in Rome, to call a crusade. Housley has noted that it is perhaps surprising that this power was not invoked more often than it was in these years, so that combatants in the Hundred Years War became crusaders for one Pope or the other. Certainly the kings of both France and England suggested crusading as a means of healing the schism, although this never materialised. There were, however, four campaigns that were crusades for or against Urbanists or Clementists, and a fifth campaign in Greece that was not which a crusade but which enjoyed papal support.

In 1382 Clement VII granted crusade indulgences to French knights who fought against the Urbanist ruler of Naples, Charles of Durazzo, who had seized the throne from the Clementist Queen Joanna in 1381 with the support of Urban VI. In the following year Henry Despenser, bishop of Norwich, obtained bulls from Urban VI to lead a crusade to Flanders against the schismatic opponents of the Pope and ended by gaining some limited success in supporting an Urbanist revolt against Charles VI of France, who had invaded Flanders whilst Henry was seeking parliamentary backing for his proposed campaign. In 1387 John of Gaunt led a crusade against the Clementist Henry of Trastamara in order to conquer Castile, which he claimed in right of his second wife Constance of Castile (d. 1394).

In 1390 and 1391 Clement VII backed an abortive attempt by Amadeo VII of Savoy to gain the principality of Achaea from the seven-year-old claimant Louis

---

[64] W. Ullmann, *The Origins of the Great Schism* (London, 1948); A. Goodman, *John of Gaunt* (London, 1992), 94–7, 111–43; Housley, *The Later Crusades*, 248. Setton, ed., *A History of the Crusades*, III, 152–6; Riley-Smith, *The Crusades: A Short History*, 230.

II of Anjou. Amadeo claimed the principality as grandson of Philip of Savoy, husband of Isabelle of Villehardouin and prince of Achaea, 1301–6. Urban VI claimed the principality for himself on the grounds that the principality had reverted to him following the death of his vassal Charles II of Naples. Real power in the principality lay with Peter of San-Superan, the commander of the Navarrese Company, who was styling himself vicar-general of the Morea by 1386 and after 1396 prince of Achaea.

The final political crusade summoned during the schism was the crusade against Ladislas of Naples for his occupation of Rome. The Pisan Pope John XXIII issued indulgences in 1411. The preaching of the crusade in Prague in May 1412 convinced many Hussites of the corruption of the papacy. In 1409 the Council of Pisa had elected its own Pope as a way of ending the schism. From 1409 to 1415 there were three popes in Christendom: of Avignonese, Pisan and Roman obedience.

CRUSADE OF LOUIS II DE BOURBON AGAINST MAHDIA 1390[65]

This crusade was an example of Avignonese and Romanist co-operation; conceived by Romanist Genoa, executed by Avignonese French crusaders with a mixture of English, Catalans and Flemings and blessed by both popes; only the placing of the fleet before departure threatened to strain the co-operative mood. An attack on the Barbary pirates was conceived by Genoa in the wake of its seizure of the island of Jerba in 1388. The Genoese approached Charles VI of France for military support just after the truce of 1389 in the Anglo-French war released many knights and mercenaries for a crusade. Charles agreed that his uncle Louis II of Clermont, duke of Burgundy, who was also a claimant to the principality of Achaea, should lead the expedition. Both Clement VII and Boniface IX recognised the expedition as a crusade, harking back to the last crusade of St Louis in 1270.

A fleet of twenty-two galleys sailed from Genoa in July 1390 and later that month successfully landed at Mahdia, which it then began to besiege. The siege dragged on for ten weeks, during which time three Muslim relieving armies were held at bay. At the end of that period a ten-year truce was signed. The crusade was generally reckoned a great success, but it had achieved nothing other than to finance itself and on the way home it drove out the Catalan garrisons of Cagliari and Oglistra on Sardinia and replaced them with Genoese troops.

---

[65] L. Mirot, 'Une Expedition française en Tunisie au XIVe siècle: Le siege de Mahdia (1390)', *Revue des études historiques*, 47 (1931), 357–406; Setton, *The Papacy and the Levant*, I, 330–40; Atiya, *The Crusades in the Later Middle Ages*, 1970, 398–434; Housley, *The Later Crusades*, 286–7; Setton, ed., *A History of the Crusades*, III, 481–3.

CRUSADE TO NICOPOLIS, 1396[66]

The advance of the Ottoman Turks into the northern Balkans alarmed Sigismund of Hungary who in 1395 sought help from Charles VI of France. During 1395 both Benedict XIII in Avignon and Boniface IX in Rome issued bulls for a crusade; another example of the schism not vitiating a crusade that had wide support. The response of the French nobility was enthusiastic, especially from the Duchy of Burgundy. The duke's son and eventual successor, John of Nevers, also known as John the Fearless (b. 1371), was elected leader of the expedition. The noble participants saw themselves as the flower of French chivalry and agreed before their departure that they should insist on forming the vanguard in any battle. The assembly point was Dijon.

The crusaders left Dijon between 20 and 30 April 1396, crossed the Rhine south of Strassburg and joined the Danube in western Bavaria, following it to Regensburg (Ratisbon) where they took ships down the Danube, making their rendezvous with the Hungarians and other European contingents in Buda sometime in July. Sigismund advised the crusaders to take a defensive stance, using Hungarian strong points to await the Turks. The crusade leadership would have none of this. They crossed the Danube at Orsova and entered Bulgaria, where they seized the towns of Vidin and Rahova, killing Turks and Orthodox Christians indiscriminately. On 10 September they arrived at Nicopolis (Nicopol) and began to besiege it.

Bayezid I broke off his siege of Constantinople and marched direct to the relief of Nicopolis where he arrived on 24 September. Battle was joined on the following day when the Burgundian and French knights threw away any advantage they might have possessed by charging uphill against well-entrenched Turkish positions, strengthened by a field of stakes in front. The charge degenerated into a rout. John of Nevers and 3,000 crusaders were captured. Many were sold into slavery, the noblest being released on payment of heavy ransoms. The lessons of pride and sinfulness were not lost on the West. It was a catastrophe that left Hungary at the mercy of the Ottoman Turks whenever they should choose to advance northwards along the Danube. For the immediate future Bayezid resumed the blockade of Constantinople and sent troops to plunder and raid in what was left of Frankish Greece.

[66] Atiya, *The Crusades in the Later Middle Ages*, 435–62; A. Atiya, *The Crusade of Nicopolis* (London, 1934); R. Rosetti, 'The Battle of Nicopolis (1396)', *Slavonic Review*, 25 (1937), 629ff.; Housley, *The Later Crusades*, 76–81, 354–5, 401–2; Setton, *The Papacy and the Levant*, I, 341–69; Setton, ed., *A History of the Crusades*, III, 23–6, 82–5, 261, 265: Riley-Smith, *The Crusades: A Short History*, 231–2; R. Vaughan, *Philip the Bold* (London, 1962), 59–78.

CRUSADE OF MARCHAL BOUCICAUT TO CONSTANTINOPLE, 1399[67]

The worsening situation in Constantinople produced a flood of embassies from Manuel II Palaiologos to the courts of Western Europe. In April 1398, March 1399 and January 1400 Boniface IX preached crusades in aid of Constantinople. The response was disappointing. Charles VI of France ordered his marshal, John II Boucicaut, a survivor from the Nicopolis campaign, to sail to the beleaguered city with 1,000 men, four ships and two galleys. The flotilla left Aigues-Mortes in June 1399 and arrived in Constantinople sometime in September.

His anonymous biographer described Boucicaut as a one-man crusade. He led destructive raids against Turkish towns in Bithynia and on the Black Sea coast, but all to no avail. On 10 December 1399 he left Constantinople for France, bringing with him the emperor Manuel II who was to stay in Western Europe until 1402 soliciting aid from the various courts that he visited. Hoping to take advantage of the Turkish defeat by Timur at Ankara in 1402, Boucicaut returned to the East in 1403/4, campaigning in Messenia in south-west Greece, the Cyclades, Cyprus and Syria. This colourful piratical expedition achieved little in broader crusading terms.

ANTI-HUSSITE CRUSADES, 1420–31[68]

During the fourteenth century Bohemia emerged from being a frontier province of Christendom to being an integral part of the Holy Roman Empire, and from 1306 a kingdom. The rulers of Bohemia had encouraged German colonists since the thirteenth century, and they had played a major role in founding towns and developing the economic infrastructure of the country. Charles IV of Luxembourg, both as king of Bohemia and Holy Roman Emperor (1346–78), sought the integration of Bohemia into Western Europe. This was achieved at some cost, and the feeling amongst many Czechs was that they were treated as underdogs by foreign interlopers, many of them clerics.

Alongside this was a growing reform movement that sought a simpler faith and saw in the papacy a corrupting influence. John Hus (c. 1369–1415), who was not even the most radical of its preachers, did not found the religious reform but as rector of Prague University in 1409 became the figurehead of the movement. After his death he became its martyr, uniting the disparate strands of Hussitism. At Constance he was accused of abusing his position to shelter radical preachers. He was a disciple of Wycliffe and introduced his doctrines to the religious reformers of Bohemia. Not only were its rejection of papal authority and the demand for communion in both kinds classed as heretical but the violent actions

---

[67] Setton, *The Papacy and the Levant*, I, 370–404.
[68] Setton, ed., *A History of the Crusades*, III, 586–646; M. Lambert, *Medieval Heresy* (2nd edn., Oxford, 1992), 284–348; H. Kaminsky, *A History of the Hussite Revolution* (Berkele, 1967).

of the Hussites loosened the bonds of political authority and social structure, something that no ruler could tolerate for long.

Hus was invited to the Church Council at Constance in 1414, where he was arrested and burnt as a heretic in July 1415. Support for him and his teaching embraced all levels of society. In September the Hussites asserted that the burning of Hus was wrong and thereby rejected the judgment of the Church Council. It was becoming a Czech national movement and leading to violent encounters with Catholic German communities. The accession of Sigismund, king of Hungary (1387) and Germany (1411), as king of Bohemia in 1419 led to negotiations by which the Hussites sought to impose their religious doctrines and to gain a better position for Czechs. Their distrust of Sigismund stemmed from the uncertain role he had played in the condemnation of Hus. In 1420 Sigismund decided to take military action; Martin V, who declared a crusade on his behalf, supported him.

Five crusades in all were waged in Bohemia: those of 1420, 1421, 1422, 1427 and 1431. They achieved nothing other than to unite the disparate Hussite groups and to ensure their survival. They marked a new descent into savagery. Eventually an accommodation reached at the Compactata of Iglau (Jihlava) on 5 July 1436 was confirmed at the Council of Basel and secured the recognition of Sigismund by the Bohemians. The violence and dislocation in Bohemia distracted attention from the advance of the Turks and did nothing to strengthen a region so vital for resistance to the Turks as they moved against Hungary.

CRUSADE TO VARNA, 1444[69]

During 1442 Pope Eugenius IV was negotiating and planning to send a flotilla to the Dardanelles to prevent Turkish reinforcements moving up to Constantinople and also to co-ordinate activities with a Hungarian army led by John Hunyadi to advance into Wallachia and thus relieve pressure on the beleaguered city of Constantinople. The Venetians refused to provide ships because they thought the scheme impractical and feared for Turkish reprisals on their trade in the Aegean. They were also suspicious of the intentions of a resurgent Hungary to their cities and ports along the Dalmatian coast. There was then no naval expedition in 1443.

In September 1443 a force of Poles and Hungarians, with a smattering of mercenaries and volunteers from Western Europe, crossed the Danube and penetrated deep into Ottoman territory, arriving at Belgrade in January 1444. The revolt of Ibrahim Bey of Karaman in Anatolia limited the options for the Ottoman sultan, Murad II (1421–44), who offered a ten-year truce to Vladsislav Jagiellon, king of Hungary (1440–4). This was ratified on 1 August 1444 at

---

[69] Setton, *The Papacy and the Levant*, II, 82–107; Setton, ed., *A History of the Crusades*, VI, 276–310; Housley, *The Later Crusades*, 85–90.

Szeged, but then repudiated within three days as Murad marched off to campaign in Anatolia.

In July the promised fleet arrived at Gallipoli. It consisted of twenty-two ships provided by the Holy See, Burgundy, Venice and Ragusa. The Hungarian and Polish army crossed the Danube on 20 September. There was no co-ordination between them and the fleet, which contributed nothing to the developing land campaign. The two armies met at Varna on 10 November 1444. Losses were terrible on both sides and the battle was drawn, but it was the Christian army that collapsed and had to withdraw.

Many have seen this operation as the last chance to clear the Turks from the Balkans. The Christian withdrawal sealed the fate of Constantinople.

THE FALL OF CONSTANTINOPLE AND THE CRUSADES, 1453–60[70]

On 29 June news reached Venice of the fall of Constantinople to the Ottoman Turks on Tuesday, 29 May 1453. On 8 July it was known in Rome where fears of a Turkish attack on the city took no time to spread. Although there had been little practical help for the beleaguered Byzantines, the news sent shock waves across Europe and triggered the preaching of a crusade to recover the lost city. As the Ottoman threat to Christian powers in Hungary, in Frankish Greece and even in Italy developed, so, it has been noted, did the recovery of Constantinople replace that of Jerusalem as the goal of crusades.

On 30 September Pope Nicholas V called for a new crusade, which was confirmed by Pope Calixtus III on 15 May 1455, with a departure date set for 1 March 1456. Only in Hungary was there any practical response. John Hunyadi advanced from Buda and relieved the siege of Belgrade. In 1457 sixteen papal galleys occupied the islands of the northern Sporades, opposite the Dardanelles, Samothrace, Thasos and Limnos, but despite very up-beat reports none of this could be described as a crusade to recover Constantinople. In 1460 a three-year crusade preached by Pius II failed to elicit a response.

THE CRUSADE OF PIUS II, 1464[71]

Against the disappointing response to crusading bulls in the 1450s, the conquest of Greece by the Ottomans, all but complete by 1460, and the stillborn three-year crusade against the Turks that he had authorised on 14 January 1460, Pius II (1458–64), who had laboured for a crusade since before the fall of Constantinople, proposed to lead by example. Despite being in his sixtieth year and in poor health, he proposed to lead a crusade against the Turks himself. He took the

---

[70] Setton, *The Papacy and the Levant*, II, 138–60; Riley–Smith, *The Crusades: A Short History*, 235–6.
[71] Setton, *The Papacy and the Levant*, II, 196–270; Riley-Smith, *The Crusades: A Short History*, 236.

cross in Rome on 18 June 1464 and immediately left for Ancona where he expected to meet with a small fleet promised by the Venetians. The promised aid did not arrive until after Pius had died. Between 1502 and 1508 Bernardo il Pinturicchio painted a fresco series illustrating the life of Pius II in the Piccolomini Library at Siena. It was his last major commission. One of these frescoes depicts an idealised version of Pius launching his crusade at Ancona. Despite the busy scene full of ships and people the town contained few crusaders and the harbour was bare. There was no crusade to lead. His poor health broke down completely and 15 August 1464 he died in Ancona.

THE ANTI-TURKISH CRUSADE, 1480[72]

Sultan Mehmed II (1444–6 and 1451–81) ordered two campaigns for 1480; one was the conquest of Rhodes that was abandoned in August after a three-month siege, the other the conquest of southern Italy.

On 18 August 1480 Otranto was captured and garrisoned and preparations made for further conquests in 1481. Pope Sixtus IV proclaimed a crusade to recapture the town, and that was achieved by a Papal and Neapolitan fleet on 10 September 1481. No crusade was called to assist the Hospitallers on Rhodes, either now or in the siege of 1522.

THE WALDENSIAN CRUSADE IN THE DAUPHINE, 1487–8[73]

If we discount the Spanish Armada of 1588 – certainly a crusade and certainly aimed at heretics in England, but with much wider goals beyond the extirpation of heresy: namely the replacement of an English monarch and the incorporation of England within the Spanish Empire – then the anti-Hussite crusades were the last major crusades against heretics, and this was the last crusade intended to remove heresy from an area.

Beginning in the twelfth century as a group of reformers, the Waldenses received the sacraments from orthodox Catholic clergy but denied that these were the only vehicles of grace and as time went by came to criticise the clergy for their many vices. They seemed to have aroused their Catholic neighbours, as on this occasion. The crusade was authorised by Innocent VIII in April 1487. It was preached in the diocese of Cremona, but, although directed at Piedmont, Savoy and the Dauphine, it was only carried through in the latter area. It was essentially a small-scale event. It was characterised by violence and rapine and achieved nothing.

---

[72] Housley, *The Later Crusades*, 111–12.
[73] E. Cameron, *Waldenses* (Oxford, 2000), 193–200.

CRUSADES IN THE IBERIAN PENINSULA[74]

(Entries followed by 'SC' in parentheses in the chronological table, Part II, refer specifically to these crusades)

The manifest destiny of the Christian states of northern Spain to reconquer the lands lost to the Moors in the eighth century has been a prominent part of the Spanish historical tradition since the thirteenth century. In part, the origins of this view of the Reconquista lay in crusading propaganda, but by the nineteenth century the history had become an enduring part of the Spanish national myth with the slant on the emergence of Castile. With hindsight, too, lost Christian lands had not only been reoccupied but Christianity had been reimposed and the Jews and the Moriscoes expelled soon after 1492. It is beguiling to see it as one long connected historical process, and this view still holds sway.

According to this processual account it all began with the military activities of the three Christian principalities of Asturias, Navarre and the Spanish March (later Catalonia) established by Charlemagne around 800. The inhabitants of these lands were largely untouched by Islamic culture to the south of the Duero

[74] D.W. Lomax, *The Reconquest of Spain* (London, 1978); A. Mackay, *Spain in the Middle Ages 1000–1500: From Frontier to Empire* (London, 1977), 1–94: G. Jackson, *The Making of Medieval Spain* (London, 1972); B.F. Reilley, *The Medieval Spains* (Cambridge, 1993); D. Lomax and D. Mackenzie, eds, *God and Man in Medieval Spain* (Warminster, 1989); R.I. Burns, *The Crusader Kingdom of Valencia* (2 vols, Cambridge, Mass., 1967); R.I. Burns and P.E. Chevedden, *Negotiating Cultures: Bi-lingual Surrender Treaties in Muslim – Crusader Spain* (Leiden, 1999); R. Bartlett and A. Mackay, eds, *Medieval Frontier Societies* (Oxford, 1989), 49–76, 127–150 and 217–44; R. Fletcher, *The Episcopate in the Kingdom of Leon in the Twelfth Century* (Oxford, 1978), 1–30, 217; R. Fletcher, *St James's Catapult* (Oxford, 1984); R. Fletcher, *Moorish Spain* (London, 1992); R. Fletcher, *In Search of El Cid* (London, 1989); S. Barton and R. Fletcher, *The World of El Cid: Chronicles of the Spanish Reconquest* (Manchester, 2000); R. Hamilton and J. Perry, *The Poem of the Cid: A Bilingual Edition with Parallel Text* (Harmondsworth, 1984); C. David, *The Conquest of Lisbon* (New York [1936], 2000); Olivia Constable, *Medieval Iberia: Readings from Christian, Muslim and Jewish Sources* (Philadelphia, 1997); P.K. Hitti, *History of the Arabs* (9th edn, London, 1968), 493–590; H. Kennedy, *Muslim Spain and Portugal* (London, 1996); Salma Khadra Jayyusi, ed., *The Legacy of Muslim Spain* (Leiden, 1992); J. Dodds, ed., *Al-Andalus: The Art of Islamic Spain* (New York, 1992); O. Constable, *Trade and Traders in Muslim Spain* (Cambridge, 1994); T. Glick, *From Muslim Fortress to Christian Castle* (Manchester, 1995); J. Kritzeck, *Peter the Venerable and Islam* (Princeton, 1964); V. Mann, *et al.*, eds, *Convivencia: Jews, Muslims and Christians in Medieval Spain* (New York, 1992); P. Lineham, *History and the Historians of Medieval Spain* (Oxford, 1993), 95–127, 206, 245, 294 and 311; Setton, ed., *A History of the Crusades*, I, 31–9, and III, 396–456; Riley-Smith, *The Crusades: A Short History*, 139–41, 165–6, 221–4, 237–8; Housley, *The Later Crusades*, 267–321; E. Lourie, 'A Society Organised for War: Medieval Spain', *Past and Present*, 35 (1966), 54–76; R.I. Burns, 'Immigrants from Islam: The Use of Muslims as Settlers in Thirteenth-century Aragon', *American Historical Review*, 80 (1975); A.J. Forey, 'The Military Orders and the Spanish Reconquest in the Twelfth and Thirteenth Centuries', *Traditio*, 40 (1984), 197–234; R. Fletcher, 'Reconquest and Crusade in Spain, c.1050–1150' *Transactions of the Royal Historical Society*, Series 5, 37 (1987), 31–47; J. Williams, 'The Making of a Crusade: The Genoese Anti-Muslim Attacks in Spain, 1146–8', *Journal of Medieval History*, 23 (1997), 29–53. See also references under the Second Crusade on p. 147.

and Ebro valleys. Moved by memory of the glory of the former Visigothic kingdom and the duty to recapture lands lost to the Moors, these northern kingdoms began their expansion in the eleventh century. The success of these early military expeditions, like that the later crusades, was measured in the extent of land siezed and the number of towns and cities captured. Furthermore, the expeditions were discussed in religious and military terms. However, there was little or nothing that was concerted about these campaigns until the Barbastro campaign of 1063–4.

Some, following Carl Erdmann, see this campaign as the first crusade ever and many as a crusade in all but name.[75] Certainly, the campaign accepted that violence should be used against the enemies of Christ and Christendom, and this, thirty-five years before the capture of Jerusalem in 1099, seemed to justify such an interpretation. William VIII, duke of Aquitaine (1058–85), led an international force of French, Aragonese and Catalan knights working in concert to recover the Christian city of Barbastro that had been in Muslim hands since the early days of the conquest just after 711. A Truce of God was declared in Catalonia to ensure internal peace for the expedition, and Pope Alexander II had granted an indulgence to the participants. Although it was certainly regarded as a holy war it was no true crusade according to the 1095 model. As Professor Riley-Smith has pointed out, there was no sense of pilgrimage about the expedition, the participants had taken no vow and no formal papal authorisation had been given.[76]

These instinctive crusaders became crusaders indeed during the time of the First Crusade, when Urban II treated the fight against the Moors of Spain as essentially the same as the war against the Turks in the East. Thus runs the conventional tale, but when did war in a vaguely Christian cause in the Iberian Peninsula become a fully fledged crusade? What was the spirit of Reconquista? What did it derive from or contribute to ideas of crusade? Was the frontier between Christian, Muslim and Jew in the Iberian Peninsula an impermeable one that could only be closed with the complete conquest and expulsion of the non-Christian groups? In the myth, Reconquista seems to smack of perpetual crusade lasting 700 years and coming to a triumphant conclusion with the fall of Granada on 2 January 1492. But individual papal bulls authorised recruitment for particular crusading campaigns in Spain, especially those dependent on help from southern French knights. There was no perpetual crusade as such, nor anything comparable to the recruitment for the Baltic crusades in the thirteenth and fourteenth centuries (see pp. 213–24). In the myth too, the beginning of the Reconquista is given as 719 with the defeat of a Muslim army by the Asturians at Covadonga, but the period of Christian territorial expansion could be fitted into the century and a half from the late eleventh century to the mid-thirteenth century, with the survival of the emirate of Granada down to 1492 as something

---

[75] Erdmann, *The Origin of the Idea of Crusade*, 174.
[76] J. Riley-Smith, *What Were the Crusades?* (London, 1977; 2nd edn, 2000), 74–5.

of a historical aberration. It is also instructive that the literature on crusade in Spain is relatively thin when compared with that on crusades to the East, to the Baltic and against the political and heretical enemies of the Church; the Reconquista, it would seem, is much more a part of national history than of international crusading history.

By contrast, Moorish Spain has attracted many sympathetic studies and major museum exhibitions, especially in 1992, the 500th anniversary of the fall of Granada.

The Muslim conquest of the Iberian Peninsula was the last of the Arab wars of conquest that had begun with the invasion of Syria in 634. In the spring of 711 an army of 7,000 men crossed from North Africa into Spain. Their ranks were filled with recently converted Berbers. They were led by a Berber commander, Tariq ibn-Ziyad, who gave his name to the landing place Jabal Tariq (Gibraltar). On 19 July 711 he won a decisive victory over Roderick, the Visigothic king, at the mouth of the Barbate River (modern Salado). Roderick was a usurper and had been deserted in the battle by key elements of his army. He was killed in the battle and no other ruler came forward to resist the advance of Islam in the peninsula that became something resembling a triumphal progress. Within two months Tariq had conquered half of the Iberian Peninsula. By 718 the Arabs had advanced to the Ebro, captured Saragossa and mounted raids across the Pyrenees. Iberia south of the Ebro became the westernmost province of the Ummayad caliphate. An advance beyond the Pyrenees was repulsed by Charles Martel and the Merovingians at the battle of Poitiers/Tours in October 732. With hindsight the Christian victory can be seen as a turning point, but at the time raids into southern France continued well into the century.

In 750 the Abbasids had replaced the Ummayad caliphate in Damascus in a bloody coup. One of the very few Umayyad refugees chased across the Mediterranean by Abbasid agents arrived in Spain in 755. Within two years Abd-al-Rahman, with Berber backing, drove the Abbasid governors from Spain and established an independent emirate (after 929 a caliphate), based on Cordova, which he strove to make into a worthy religious capital for western Islam, a rival to the great shrines of Islam in Jerusalem and Mecca. In essence he tried to make Muslim Spain one kingdom, naming it Al-Andalus, but the Umayyads could not repress the racial, tribal and dynastic fault lines that ran through Muslim society in the peninsula and that would bring chaos to Al-Andalus when there was no longer a strong ruler to resist these centrifugal tendencies. Large numbers of native Christians became arabised and were known as 'mozarabs'.

By 1000 Muslim rule in Spain was at its height; the Christian kingdoms of the north were beaten into tributary status, with Barcelona and Leon sacked in 985 and 988 respectively and the new church of Saint James of Compostela razed in 997. The Christian captives taken on these expeditions were led to Cordova bearing the doors and bells from Christian churches destroyed in the north. Many of these captives were set to work on building the extension of the great mosque at Cordoba. However, with the death of al-Mansur in 1002, the strong protector of the Caliph Hisham II (d. 1009), the Umayyad Caliphate fell into civil war and anarchy. There were nine chaliphs in the next twenty years. In 1031 the last Umayyad Caliph, Hisham III, was deposed. Some twenty petty states emerged in the political confusion, based around the major urban centres of Muslim Spain.

These minor rulers were known as *muluk al-tawāif* by the Arabs and as *reyes de taifas*, or 'party kings', by their Spanish neighbours. The Christian kingdoms of the north soon learned to participate in the rivalries and conflicts of their Muslim neighbours, and to exploit them by offering military assistance in return for tribute payments in gold known as *parias*. These payments were enormous, and occasionally colossal: 10,000 dinars a year would secure a military alliance, whilst in 1085 the ruler of Valencia paid 600 dinars a day for Christian troops to protect him from his own subjects. The northern Christian kingdoms were transformed from some of the poorest to among the richest kingdoms in Christendom, able to endow churches and monasteries, to develop towns, commerce and the infrastructure of their kingdoms, to send magnificent donations to Cluny, and to attract foreign princesses as their brides. Kings south of the Pyrenees were thus drawn more into the mainstream of western Christendom, and gained in confidence and ambition.

It was not only Spanish kings who operated these protection rackets; some of their knights did as well. The most famous of these was Rodrigo Diaz de Bivar, known as El Cid (*c.* 1043–99), who sold his services to both Christian and Muslim alike and was killed defending his own kingdom of Valencia against the Almoravids from Morocco. The system began to break down in the 1080s. On 25 May 1085, Alfonso VI of Leon (1065–1109) captured Toledo, the former Visigothic capital of Spain. Much was made of this restoration at the time.

Originally, however, Alfonso had intended to maintain the Muslim ruler in place; this had necessitated not just the siege of his capital Toledo but also the unsuccessful siege of Saragossa (1081–5), to which the dissidents in Toledo had appealed. Muslim lives and property were guaranteed in Toledo and they could come and go as they pleased. Any Muslims who did not wish to remain in Toledo were allowed to depart with their property intact. This was to set a pattern for later Christian conquests of major towns from the Muslims.

The fall of Toledo not only opened up Al-Andalus to Christian attack but also showed the fundamentalist Muslim rulers of Morocco that after three centuries Islam was in a precarious position in the Iberian Peninsula. From now on, as Lomax has pointed out, successive rulers of Morocco – Almoravids (1086), Almohads (1146) and Marinids (1275) – invaded Spain.[77] When they were strong they regained lands conquered by the Christians and when they were weak the Christian advance began again. More important than this military ebb and flow was the very presence of the Moroccans in the peninsula. This led, within a

[77] Lomax, *The Reconquest of Spain*, 68–70, 112–22, 164.

quarter of a century, to the declaration of crusades against them; reconquista was changing to crusade. In 1086 al-Mu'tamid, the ruler of Seville (1069–91), invited the Almoravid ruler Yusuf ibn-Tashufin (1061–1106) to intervene in Spain. The offer was accepted, and in numbers and speed redolent of Tariq's invasion in 711 the Almoravid troops crossed the Straits of Gibraltar to Spain. On 23 October 1086 they won a decisive victory over Alfonso VI at Sagrajas (Zalaca) near Badajoz and over the next twenty years reunited Al-Andalus under Almoravid leadership, thus bringing to an end the *parias* payments, with severe economic consequences for the northern Christian monarchies. The defeat at Sagrajas also seems to have inflamed hostility against Muslims and Islam on the Christian side. Alfonso VI appealed to his French relatives by marriage for help, and over the next fifty years many French expeditions campaigned in the Ebro valley.

One result of the defeat of Sagrajas was the reconciliation of Alfonso VI with Rodrigo Diaz de Bivar who had been in exile since 1081. He encouraged Rodrigo to exploit the political situation in and around Valencia, still occupied by Alfonso's client king from Toledo. The Cid succeeded in capturing the town on 16 June 1094 by playing local Muslim and Almoravid groups off against each other. In December he defeated an Almoravid army in open battle at Cuert de Pueblo, thus exploding the myth of Almoravid invincibility. He was to defeat them again at Bairen in January 1097 and followed up this victory by capturing a number of the dependent towns of Valencia. His widow, Dona Jimena (d. 1116) resisted a siege of Valencia in 1101 and Alfonso VI razed the town when he relieved the siege in 1102. The exploits of the Cid in and around Valencia prevented an Almoravid advance up the eastern coast of Spain and limited the area of their dominance. His wealth, military prowess and reputation as the first Christian victor over the Almoravids began to pass into legend within a century of his death on 10 July 1099, turning him into a Christian Castilian paladin and a model crusader.

Although both Urban II and Paschal II were aware that the wars against the Muslims in Spain had many points in common with the First Crusade, and that Spanish warriors should not be recruited for expeditions to the East but encouraged to fight in defence of their homelands, it was not until an encyclical letter of Calixtus II, published on 2 April 1123, that the wars with the Muslims of Spain were accorded crusade status (see 'Crusade of Calixtus II' on p. 145). Fletcher has drawn attention to the marked differences between a sermon preached in 1113 by Diego Gelmirez, archbishop of Compostela, which is essentially a call to a last-ditch defence against Almoravid attacks along the Ebro, and a sermon of 1124 that he preached as papal legate in Spain urging an aggressive campaign against the Moors for the triumph of Christianity and promising full remission of sins for those *milites Christi* who responded to the call.[78] Their property and families were to receive protection during their absence, and they

---

[78] Fletcher, *St James's Catapult*, 298–9.

were identifiable as fighting in the Christian cause by the cross upon their clothing. This was crusade preaching, and the difference was brought about by the encyclical of 1123; reconquista had become crusading reconquista. Warriors from France, Normandy and England had already fought in Spain in the years after Sagrajas; now they could campaign there as crusaders. It is in the twelfth century that St James of Compostela became St James the Moor-slayer (Santiago Matamoros) and the patron saint of Spanish crusading. It is as such that he is depicted on a tympanum in the cathedral of Santiago de Compostela sculpted about 1200.

Unity there was not amongst the Christian kingdoms of northern Spain; Kingdoms that had divided and then coalesced over time. In the eleventh century Sancho III of Navarre controlled much of northern Spain, but he divided his lands between his sons as rulers of Castile and Aragon. Cut off from Muslim territory by these two kingdoms, the rump of Navarre did not participate in the Reconquista. With the death of Sancho IV in 1076 Navarre ceased to be a thorn in the side of Aragon and Castile and became in time an appanage of the county of Champagne. In 1037 Leon-Asturias had been absorbed into the new Kingdom of Castile, just as in 925 Asturias-Galicia had become part of the crown of Leon. In 1109 Alfonso VI of Castile and Leon tried to unite his kingdom with Aragon by arranging the marriage of his widowed daughter Urraca to Alfonso I, 'the Battler' of Aragon (1102–34), but the marriage was dissolved due to consanguinity. In 1162 Barcelona became part of the Kingdom of Aragon. This union dated from the marriage of Ramon Berenguer IV of Barcelona to Petronilla the daughter of King Ramiro II of Aragon in 1137. Their son Alfonso II became king of Aragon in 1162. Alfonso VI of Castile-Leon had married his younger daughter Teresa to Henry of Burgundy. First Henry then their son Afonso Henriques ruled Portugal as counts, founding the new Kingdom of Portugal in 1139.

These were the three political units that were to persist to modern times and were to extend their territories tenfold in the next century. Jackson has drawn attention to the self-confidence of these kingdoms in the crusading phase of the Reconquista, their long-term planning ability, and their rivalry in acquiring new territory – but within defined spheres of activity.[79] Portugal's target was the Algarve (Treaty of Zamora, 1143), whilst Castile-Leon and Aragon-Catalonia laid down their areas of expansion in a series of treaties agreed at Tudilen (1151), Cazorla (1179) and Almizra (1244). The expansion was not all one way. Factional fighting and royal minorities slowed down the process. There were many offensive campaigns, comprising long-distance raids into Muslim territory, capturing and losing individual towns, building frontier castles, recruiting frontier militias and winning or losing the occasional battle. There was the usual ebb and flow, but this time the ebbs brought forth crusades, authorised by the Pope. Thus, following the defeat of Alfonso VIII of Castile by the Almohads at Alarcos on 19 July 1195, Pope Celestine III had authorised a crusade, and Innocent III had

---

[79]   Jackson, *The Making of Medieval Spain*, 78.

done likewise in 1212 after the loss of the castle of Salvatierra. In general, however, the problem for these kingdoms was to be one of assimilating their conquests rather than in gaining them.

Despite the continual nature of fighting and the involvement of warriors from outside the peninsula the Reconquista was not a perpetual crusade of the type to be seen in the Baltic (see pp. 213–24); individual Spanish crusades were authorised by the Pope. Crusades were proclaimed for Spain in 1123, 1147, 1193, 1197, 1210, 1212, 1221 and 1229, with the crusading status of the Spanish campaigns being suspended during the recruitment for the Fifth Crusade. During the Second, Third and Fifth crusades (see pp. 147–50, 151–5 and 169–71 respectively) fleets heading for the East from northern Europe assisted the rulers of Portugal in capturing Lisbon (1147), Sives and Alvor (1189) and Alcazar (1217). These interventions were, however, accidental rather than a concerted part of the Spanish crusade.

Crusading privileges were also granted to those who assisted the military orders. Both the Templars and the Hospitallers had a major presence in Spain from the early twelfth century, but the defence of the ever-expanding frontiers was beyond their capabilities. New military orders were founded in Iberia, all of them militarised from their inception, all of them modelled on the two inter-national military orders, and all of them eventually to be subsumed in the orders of Calatrava and Santiago by the beginning of the thirteenth century. They were the Order of Calatrava (1158), the Order of St James (Santiago) (1170), the short-lived Order of Montjoy (Montegaudio) (1175), and the Order of St Julian of Pereiro (1176, known as Alcantara from 1218). Other orders were founded in the thirteenth and fourteenth centuries, generally interpreted as showing the enduring and important role that such religious corporations played in Spain. These later orders were St George of Afama (1201), Santa Maria de España (1270s), the Order of Montesa (1317) and the Order of Christ in Portugal (1319).

On 5 April 1212 Innocent III authorised the preaching of a crusade in Spain across France, instructing his bishops to emphasise the disaster that the fall of Salvatierra was for Christendom as a whole. Christian kings were to suspend their disputes, and trade and congress with the Muslims was forbidden. Recruit-ment for the crusade was widespread, although mainly French and Spanish. Duke Leopold VI of Austria was to arrive too late for the victory. Alfonso VIII of Castile, not bothering to fortify his cities, gambled everything on a decisive victory over the Almohads. This he achieved on Tuesday, 16 July 1212 at Las Navas de Tolosa. In its immediate aftermath the towns of Vilches, Ferrol, Banos, Tolosa, Baeza and Ubeda were captured. The Almohad Empire broke up. In the next forty years Muslim territory in Spain was reduced to the emirate of Granada south of the Guadalquivir River, and this was under Christian suzer-ainty. James I of Aragon, 'the Conqueror' (1213–76), whom Gregory IX invited to lead the papal forces in Italy against Frederick II, and Ferdinand III of Castile (1217–52), were the leading rulers in the peninsula during this period. The expan-sion may be easily followed on a map leaping from river valley to river valley. The Balearic islands were captured by Aragon between 1229 and 1235: Majorca

(1229), Minorca (1231) and Ibiza (1235). The Aragonese added Burriana (1233), Valencia (1238), Murcia (1243) and Jativa (1244). The Castilians captured Cordoba (1236), Jaen (1246), Seville (1248) and Cadiz (1265). Al-Andalus was reduced to some 13,500 square miles of territory of the emirate of Granada, containing the major urban centres of Ronda (1485), Malaga (1487), Almeira (1490) and Granada (1492), and thus it was to remain until 1492.

The involvement of Peter III of Aragon (I of Sicily) (1276–85) in the Sicilian Vespers of 1282 showed how quiescent the Spanish kingdoms were at that time. As a result of this entanglement, in January 1283 Peter III of Aragon had a crusade preached against him for his assumption of the Sicilian throne in right of his wife Constance of Hohenstaufen. In May 1285 a crusading army led by Philip III of France and King James of Majorca invaded Aragon and laid siege to Gerona. Following an outbreak of plague and the destruction of the French fleet by the Catalan admiral Roger de Lluria, the crusade disbanded in September 1285 and the armies went home. History had gone full circle, now the king of Spain might be the object of a crusade and not the meritorious champion.

Finally, it is still a matter of debate as to the extent to which Muslims, Jews and Christians created a unique culture of tolerance in medieval Spain – whether it is the Spain of Al-Andalus, of the Taifa states, or of the expanded Christian kingdoms. Works tend to range from the inspirational and positive, intent on providing a positive image of Islam in a world threatened by Islamic fundamentalism, to the more sober judgments based upon contemporary events and opinions. Sadly so much of the evidence is anecdotal and the events do not permit the model of peaceful symbiosis. Following 1992, and the quincentenary of the fall of Granada, many exhibitions in New York focused on the cultural achievements of Spanish Islam and the European scholars attracted to Al-Andalus in the search for Greek scientific and philosophical texts. Yet it is impossible to demonstrate conclusively that multiculturism and cultural borrowings really did lead to tolerance and understanding, anymore than it is possible to demonstrate today that travel really does broaden the mind. It is a complex issue.

First the Spanish experience was definitely not unique. The crusader states in Syria, Greece and Cyprus produced examples of multicultural but segregated societies, as did the Norman Kingdom of Sicily. In the first three cases the settlers were in a minority and the experiment was due to end within a century or two in each case. Public buildings in Spain were certainly as much, if not considerably more, influenced by the Gothic style emanating from France than by the Moorish style emanating from Cordoba. It was a style that sat well with crusading ideals and Christian practice. The acquisition of classical text from Arabic translations, translated into romance and then re-translated into Latin, may be just a source of essential knowledge rather than an admission of the superiority of the culture that made this transmission possible; it may also reflect upon the paucity of knowledge of Greek in the medieval West that did not acquire its texts through the medium of Byzantium. The translation of the Koran commissioned by Peter the Venerable, abbot of Cluny (c. 1092–1156), on his visit to Spain in

1142 was sought in order that Peter might refute the errors of Islam not to increase his or Christendom's understanding of the tenets of Islam or the philosophical basis of the religion. The translators or re-translators that Peter commissioned were the Englishman Robert Ketton and the German cleric Hermann of Carinthia, both in Toledo seeking texts of Greek philosophy and technology and, where possible, Arabic commentaries upon them.

It has been said that Muslim and Christian were simply not interested in one another and made no sense to each other, despite the clothes and language of the mozarabs way back in the eighth century. There most certainly was a cultural mix of Muslim, Christian and Jew in early medieval Spain, but the latter two groups were very much the *riyah* in a political sense and any advance in the Muslim political hierarchy was accompanied by conversion to Islam. Equally, the rise of Christian Spain was marked by a distrust of the minority groups, who from 1250 onwards were subjects of Aragon, Castile or Portugal. This distrust came about because in the south of the Peninsula it was the Christians who at first were the minority group, and years of fighting did not contribute to tolerance. Anti-Jewish pogroms had not been a feature of crusading in Spain, but from the fifteenth century anti-Semitic attitudes increased. In 1492 Muslims and Jews were expelled from the Peninsula, and converts – be they *conversos* (Jews) or *moriscos* (Muslims) – were subjected to examination by the Inquisition to see just how sound their conversion had been and just how reliable they were, as subjects. Multicultural they were, but tolerant they were not.

THE NORTHERN CRUSADES[80]

(Entries followed by 'BC' in parentheses in the chronological table, Part II, refer specifically to this movement).

Like the Spanish crusades of reconquest the crusades in north-eastern Europe had the most profound and long-lasting impact on Europe in the Middle Ages,

---

[80] M.M. Postan, *The Cambridge Economic History of Europe*, I (Cambridge, 1966), and 449–86; A.P. Vlasto, *The Entry of the Slavs into Christendom* (Cambridge, 1970), 142–54; A. Wieczorek and H.-M. Hinz, eds, *Europas Mitte um 1000* (3 vols, Stuttgart, 2000), for the Ottonian background, references and artefacts; F.L. Carsten, *The Origins of Prussia* (Oxford, 1954), 1–88; A.V. Murray, ed., *Crusade and Conversion on the Baltic Frontier 1150–1500* (Aldershot, 2001); J.W. Thompson, 'The German Church and the Conversion of the Baltic Slavs', *American Journal of Theology*, 20 (1916), 205–30, 372–89; F. Lotter, 'The Crusading Idea and the Conquest of the Regions East of the Elbe', in R. Bartlett and A. Mackay, eds, *Medieval Frontier Societies* (Oxford, 1989), 267–307; W. Urban, 'The Organization of the Defence of the Livonian Frontier in the Thirteenth Century', *Speculum*, 58 (1973), 525–32; W. Urban, 'The Wendish Princes and the Drang nach dem Osten', *Journal of Baltic Studies*, 9 (1978), 225–44; W. Urban, 'The Diplomacy of the Teutonic Knights at the Curia', *Journal of Baltic Studies*, 9 (1978), 116–28; M. Giedroye, 'The Arrival of Christianity in Lithuania: Baptism and Survival (1341–1387)', *Oxford Slavonic Papers*, 22 (1989), 34–57; Jordan, *Henry the Lion* 66–88; E. Christiansen, *The Northern Crusades* (London, 1980); Z. Hunyadi and J. Laszlovsky, eds, *The Crusades and the Military Orders* (Budapest, 2001), 417–500; M. Burleigh, *Prussian Society and the German Order* (Cambridge,

adding territory, trade routes, resources and Christian souls to Christendom. Unlike other crusades, however, they developed out of earlier missionary activity and combined conversion and conquest in a blend that was not found in any other crusading endeavour. Equally, the student must be careful not to be beguiled by the simple black and white picture of *Der Drang nach Osten* in which technologically advanced, rich and sophisticated Germans Christianise and civilise their Slav neighbours.

The Slav-German interaction is much more complicated.[81] Indeed, for a period after 1162 it is the Danish monarchy that dominates the Wendish lands leaving Germans dominant in the Church. The Baltic crusades were never solely a German endeavour. The establishment of the Teutonic Knights in Prussia in 1226 might lend credence to this view, but the Danes were active in the period 1167 to their collapse in 1225, when the German emperors were weak or distracted and the Wends themselves were to form a significant component of crusaders against the pagan Estonians. The Swedes brought Christianity to Finland, the Poles to Pomerania, and Russian princes and Orthodox missionaries were active in both Estonia and Finland. Nonetheless, by the 1860s the Baltic crusades were seen in processual terms as the start of Germany's timeless and historic mission to civilise and settle the Slavic lands of the East and the expression *Der Drang nach Osten* was given currency. Within forty years this simplistic model was used by the Nazis to justify their territorial designs on Czechoslovakia, Poland and Russia, and it is not entirely absent from textbooks today.

Around the middle of the tenth century German colonisation and occupation of lands occupied by the pagan Slavs between the Elbe and Oder rivers and the Baltic began. In 937 Otto I had established two margraves between the middle Elbe and the Oder, and between 948 and 968 he founded six bishoprics along the Elbe, Saale and Havel rivers to Christianise the local Slav tribes. The Wends or pagan Slavs were made up of a number of loose tribal confederations; the Abodrites were the most westerly, living in Nordalbingia (Holsatia), and made up of Abodrites, Wagrians, Polabians and Warnabians and with their pagan shrine at Rethra. On Rugen Island were the Rugians or Rani, who were notorious Baltic pirates with a central shrine at Arkona. On the mainland opposite Rugen

---

1984); M. Burleigh, *Germany Turns Towards the East* (Cambridge, 1988), 3–10; K. Hampe, *Der Zug nach dem Osten* (4th edn, Leipzig, 1937); R. Kotzschke, *Geschichte der ostdeutschen Kolonisation* (Leipzig, 1937); R. Kotzschke, *Quellen zur Geschichte der ostdeutschen Kolonisation* (Leipzig, 1937); A. Forey, *The Military Orders from the Twelfth to the Early Fourteenth Centuries* (London, 1992), 17–22, 32–9; R. Bartlett, 'The Conversion of a Pagan Society in the Middle Ages', *History*, 70 (1985), 185–201; R. Fletcher, *The Conversion of Europe* (London, 1997), 417–507; Setton, ed., *A History of the Crusades*, III, 545–85; Riley-Smith, *The Crusades: A Short History*, 161–4, 212–15; B. Hamilton, *The Christian World in the Middle Ages* (Stroud, 2003), 39–41; Housley, *The Later Crusades*, 322–75; E. Siberry, *Criticism of Crusading* (Oxford, 1985), 19–20, 156–7, 215–16, 219. There is a copious German literature on this subject to which reference is made in the articles cited.

[81] See the articles by William Urban in note 80.

down to Havelburg in the south-west was the Liutzi confederation composed of the four tribes of Redarii, Kissini, Circipani and Tolensani, whilst in the upper reaches of the Elbe, in Lusatia, were the Sorbs or northern Serbians who still exist as an ethnic group in Spreewald today. Some way east of the Oder River were the Pomeranians. North and east of the Vistula lay the confederations of the Prussians, the Lithuanians, the Letts or Latvians, and the Kurs or Curonians who inhabited the shores of the Gulf of Riga. Wendish paganism had attracted only cursory attention from Charlemagne who had encountered formidable difficulties in Christianising the Saxons in the late eighth century. Ironically, the descendants of Charlemagne's Saxon converts were now becoming missionaries and conquerors themselves.

Expansion into the area was organized by local rulers and was accompanied by forced conversions to Christianity, slave raiding, murder, and what has since been dubbed ethnic cleansing. This mix of missionary activity and conquest was encouraged by the Saxon or Ottonian dynasty (919–1002), which had founded the minster church of Magdeburg in 937 and had contained the Magyar threat to Western Europe at the battle of the Lechfeld near Augsburg on 10 August 955. Emboldened by news of the decisive defeat of Otto II by the Arabs at Capo Colonna, south of Crotone, in Calabria in 982 and by his continued absence in Italy, the Wends revolted in the following year and brought a temporary halt to German expansion into their lands for at least a generation; German settlements and churches were abandoned, three bishoprics at Havelburg, Brandenburg and Oldenburg burned and even Hamburg was raided and burned. Historians have drawn parallels with the revolt of the Saxons in 788 following the Frankish defeat at Roncevalles. Through the 980s and 990s there were revolts, with one serious uprising in 1018 described by Helmold as the second major Slav revolt.

By the beginning of the eleventh century the pagans north-east of the Elbe and in the Baltic could be seen by Western Christians as increasingly obdurate and backward. Obdurate because substantial areas of the formerly pagan North and East were Christianised: Moravia (822–67), Bohemia (900–32), Poland (966–1000), the Rus (988), the Magyars (997–1001), Norway (1016–30) and Denmark (985–1035). In Sweden missionaries had been active since the days of St Anskar (d. 865), but the country was not completely Christianised until the 1150s. Backward because principalities and rudimentary governmental organisation became established in Bohemia, Moravia and Poland by the end of the tenth century, in contrast with the apparent tribal disorder of the Wends.

However much this model might suit German chroniclers, for their part the Wends were enjoying increasing prosperity and were creating substantial prosperous towns in their territory. Although the Wendish nobility might be receptive, the bulk of their subjects resisted Christianity, which they saw as the German religion with Jesus as the *teutonicus deus*. They were not immune to Christian preaching and influences nor to the need to establish a *modus vivendi* with their German neighbours. Their numerous revolts in the tenth and eleventh centuries come at times of imperial weakness and seem to have been directed against the Empire and its visible emissary the Church more than at their German neighbours. Thus Slavs warn German rulers of impending attacks on Lübeck, Slavs fight in German and Danish armies and vice versa, and Christian Slav rulers acknowledge German overlordship and rule pagan subjects. In 1066 they rebelled again, killing their Christian ruler Gottschalk who had spent most of his life in German and Anglo-Danish court environments. His career illustrated both the inroads of Christianity and the political accommodations that might be made between Germans and Wends. The picture is a complex one.

By 1120 the Wends were becoming increasingly isolated in their pagan practices as the Poles conquered neighbouring pagan Pomerania and sponsored the missionary activities there of Otto, bishop of Bamberg. The role of focused, energetic and able bishops in the northern crusades is evident from the start. It was usual for a prominent bishop to encourage missionaries rather than missionaries to act on their own initiative. Between 1122 and his death in 1139 Otto carried on active missionary work in Pomerania. The next year a diocese was established there with the Pole Adalbert as its first bishop. In tandem with Otto's work there was a resumption of missionary activity in the Elbe region in the two decades after 1120, attempting to destroy pagan sites and to re-establish churches destroyed between 983 and 1066.

Between 1126 and 1134 Norbert of Xanten (c. 1080–1134), the founder of the Premonstratensian Order, was archbishop of Magdeburg and tried unsuccessfully to convert the Wends, who might worship the German god alongside their tribal god, a practice unacceptable to missionaries of the day. Christianisation proceeded alongside the seizure of land from the western Slavs by wealthy and ambitious rulers like Albert the Bear, margrave of Brandenburg (1134–70), and Adolph I (1124–30) and II (1130–64) of Schauenburg, counts of Holstein, who had both imperial support and the resources to encourage and the power to protect merchants and farmers settling east of the Elbe in the years before the Wendish crusade. Despite all this the Wends continued to be seen as a threat to Germans west of the Elbe. Their destruction of Hamburg in 983 was not forgotten, especially when the unexpected success of the First Crusade provided a growing confidence in the treatment of pagans and an intolerance of their very existence within and on the confines of Christendom.

Baltic crusading may be divided into five broad periods. The campaigns of the first period were directed against the Wendish confederations between the Elbe and the Oder. It involved Danish and Saxon rulers, sometimes fighting in alliance but more often with their own agendas. Broadly speaking it occupied the years 1147 to 1185. Then come the Livonian and Estonian crusades of 1198–1290, the Prussian crusades of 1230–83, the Lithuanian crusades, 1280–1435, and finally the incursions of the Teutonic Knights against Novgorod beginning about 1243 and continuing to the end of the fifteenth century.

At the time of the preaching of the Second Crusade clerical opinion in central Germany sought to link crusading with wars of defence against a perceived Wendish threat. Despite increasing missionary work the Wends were still pagan and lands that had received missionaries and produced martyrs were to all intents Christian lands that should be brought under proper Christian organisation and direction. Any war against the pagans was thus a just war, a defensive war. The anonymous *Magdeburger Aufruf* of 1108 had appealed to Christendom, without noticeable effect, in terms redolent of Urban II's speech at Clermont of 1095 to mount a crusade to recover Christian lands east of the Elbe now occupied by pagans.[82] There was no hint of conversion accompanying the proposed expedition at this stage. Sixty years later the chronicler Helmold of Bossau followed just this line with his emphasis on defence against Wendish aggression on lands formerly in Christian hands. Yet missions and their success in the 1120s and 1130s had a prominent place in his account.

In late 1146 Bernard of Clairvaux preached the Second Crusade in Germany and, as we have seen, persuaded Conrad III to take the cross on 27 December 1146. Recruitment amongst the Saxon nobility was disappointing. It seemed that the Welfs and the Hohenstaufen could not go on crusade together. On 13 March 1147 at Frankfurt Bernard was persuaded by an influential group headed by Henry the Lion of Saxony, Albert the Bear and Adolph II of Schauenburg to allow the north Germans to attack the pagan Slavs in lieu of joining the general crusade. He conferred with Pope Eugenius III, who in the bull *Divina dispensatione*, issued on 13 April 1147, extended the same crusading privileges to those who wished to fight against the Wends in the defence of northern Christendom as those proceeding on the second crusade were given. Bishop Anselm of Havelburg was appointed legate to the crusade, which wore the same cross as those proceeding to the East. Bernard, in his enthusiasm for the movement, urged that there should be no truce until the pagans were either baptised or dead, by which he seems to have meant that the Wends, if they accepted Christianity, would be allowed to continue in their existing tribal units with their own chiefs.

The first Baltic crusade set out in the summer of 1147 with Saxon, Polish and Danish contingents and two Danish fleets. One force under Henry the Lion attacked Dobin in Nordalbingia whilst the other army under margrave Albert headed eastwards to Demmin in Liutizia. Neither town was captured. The western Wends raided Lübeck, burning some merchant ships there. Albert prepared to attack the Christian town of Stettin, but the attack was called off on the religious persuasion of the inhabitants being known. However, Wagria and Polabia were occupied by the Saxons, the Wendish ruler Niklot acknowledged Saxon overlordship, slaves were taken, prisoners freed and a pagan shrine destroyed at Malchow. This was quite an achievement for a raid in force, but in terms of a crusade it was nugatory. Paganism had not been destroyed; indeed, the pagan ruler Niklot had been confirmed in his position. Bernard of Clairvaux received his due measure of censure for the failure of the wider crusade and the crusade leadership were blamed for their greed. In the wake of the crusade

---

[82]   L. and J. Riley-Smith, eds, *The Crusades: Idea and Reality* (London, 1981), 74–7, for the text.

influential marcher lords like Albert the Bear recruited and organised German settlers from the Rhineland and the Low Countries to colonise the Slav lands across the Elbe, thus bringing pressure on the Slavs to accept German rather than Slav law and to pay taxes and dues to German lords or to withdraw from their former lands, usually the most productive in the region. Their sorry plight is recorded in the pages of Helmold.

After 1147 warfare against the Wends seems to have been regarded as crusading, without a crusade actually being proclaimed for any of the particular campaigns. It was as if the bull *Divina dispensatione* was still in force. Certainly there was no papal corrective to this popular perception, and there were congratulatory letters from the Pope to mark significant military victories. The Baltic crusades became perpetual annual campaigns underpinned by the papal bulls of 1195 and 1198. Celestine III granted full crusading privileges to all who took the vow to join the Dvina campaign, and this was reiterated by Innocent III three years later. From 1204 the idea of perpetual crusading in the north was given wide currency when Innocent III authorised Albert of Buxhövden's annual recruitment drives. Although they became to be regarded as second-rate crusades, something of the poor man's crusade, they were effective nonetheless. The events of this period were in essence a power struggle between Danish, Saxon and Slav rulers and between Latin and Orthodox missionaries; something of the struggle to maintain the Latin Empire of Constantinople had its counterpart in northern Europe.

Although the proclamation of a northern crusade in 1147 had owed much to Henry the Lion it was the Danes who were to make the most striking gains from the first period of the Baltic crusades. The Danes sought to eliminate the pirates of Rugen that had devastated and depopulated the Danish coast and carried off many Danes into slavery. Their method of warfare was a series of Viking style raids devastating crops, destroying settlements and slowly wearing down the Rugians. Their inhabitants abandoned many prosperous Slav settlements like Usedom, Wollin and Kammin. The Slavs attempted to maintain control of the Baltic coastline, especially river mouths, and adopted a strategy of making counter-raids on the Danish coasts. For their part, by 1170 the Danes had constructed coastal towers as centres of resistance and refuge and set up regular naval patrols to watch for raiders. In 1160 and 1164 Valdemar I of Denmark (1157–82) and Henry the Lion of Saxony co-operated in joint campaigns. In 1169 the Danes had subdued the Rugians, reduced their ruler to tributary status, carried off much plunder and introduced Danish Cistercian and Premonstratensian monks into the region. Danish success was symbolised by the surrender of the main Rugian shrine at Arkona in 1168 and the baptism of its defenders.

When Henry the Lion fell from power in 1181 the Slavs who had been his tributaries turned to Valdemar's son, Canute VI (1182–1202), to secure protection from Danish raids; significantly they did not use Henry's removal as an opportunity to revolt. During the 1160s Henry the Lion was falling behind the Danes in his conquest and exploitation of Slav territory. His policy of turning out Slavs from the most productive parts of their lands and of exterminating the native ruling dynasties led to a serious revolt in 1164, in which he needed Danish support. In 1169 he fell out with Valdemar over his exclusion from any share in the booty from the Rugians. The Danish campaign had been marked by signal naval victories. One off Falster in December 1172 ensured the security of the Danish coast from further raids whilst that at Greifswalder Bodden on 19 May 1184 destroyed the Luitzian–Pomeranian fleet and thus secured merchant contact with the Dvina and the Russia trade and placed the whole of the Slav littoral up to the Oder at the mercy of the Danes. This was essentially the end of the first Baltic crusading endeavour.

As the Slavs of the region became Christian so they paid tithes to the German and Danish ecclesiastical hierarchy of the region and were themselves to take part in crusades to the east against the Estonians. The region was controlled by a series of castles from Dobin to Kolobrzeg, controlling passage of the main rivers of the region: the Warnow, the Peene, the Oder and the Perseto.

It was not until 1171 that a second crusading bull was granted to the northern crusaders. Pope Alexander III's crusade bull, *Non parum animus noster*, laid down a programme for the conversion of the east Baltic heathens, the Livonians and the Estonians. These peoples occupied the land between the Dvina and the Gulf of Finland, roughly from modern Riga to Revel. He seemed neither to know nor care that the subjugation of the Wends was still in process. It was only after the captivity of one missionary bishop to the Livonians and the murder of another, Bishop Berthold, in 1198 that Pope Innocent III authorised the preaching of a Livonian crusade; in October of the same year he wrote to the German clergy urging them to go to the aid of the Livonian Church.

The immensely able Albert of Buxhövden (Buxtehövden) responded. Albert was consecrated bishop of Livonia in 1199 by his uncle Hartwig II, archbishop of Hamburg-Bremen, in whose church he had previously been a canon. He was active, tough and a considerable organiser. He was confident in the support of Innocent III, or at least of his tacit approval. In the spring of 1200 he left with twenty-three ships containing crusaders, German colonists, clerics, and merchants in the Russia trade to sail to the mouth of the Dvina to see what was left of the missionary centre at Uxkull and to secure the German position in that river valley, vital as a starting point both for missionary work amongst the Livonians and for the trade route east to Novgorod. By 1200 Albert had established the new town of Riga and based the first diocese in Livonia there, transferring the see from the former minster at Uxkull. Riga was very much a frontier town in the making; the Livonians attacked it regularly in 1202, 1204 and 1206.

By 1202 his brother Dietrich, with his support, had established the Order of the Sword Brothers, also known as the Fratres Militiae Christi. This was a small order of knighthood (never more than 120). Albert's relations with the Order were problematic at first. It was not until 1211 that they swore personal allegiance to him and became a part of the bishop's household. Their task was to use their swords to create the right environment for missionary work to take place. They acted as the backbone of any crusading campaigns, bolstering the resolve of German and Danish crusaders as well as Slav converts in the army. They also formed the core garrison of the strong points that Albert rapidly planted across Livonia. Their achievements in subduing Livonia and Estonia were considerable.

Albert and his clergy were certainly active missionaries. Every year from 1204, when Innocent III had authorised a permanent crusade in the Baltic lands, up to 1224 Albert returned to Hamburg-Bremen with selected converts to advertise his work, enlist settlers for the new lands, and recruit both individual crusaders and knights for his Order of Sword Brothers. Each year there were summer campaigns, followed by consolidation in the winter. By 1208 these annual campaigns had all but worn down the Livonians, who were prepared to acquiesce. Thereafter the Livonians needed protection from raiders from Estonia to the north and pagan Lithuania to the south. Castles were again the answer, and were built well forward from Livonia settlements, being designed to shelter patrols and provide a rapid response to raiders withdrawing homewards laden with booty and slow-moving captives. Within a quarter of a century the Sword Brothers had gained an unsavoury reputation for violence and ruthlessness in this regard. In 1207, with the support of Innocent III and Valdemar II of Denmark, Albert secured Livonia as an imperial fief, and in 1215 at the Fourth Lateran Council secured the independence of Riga from the archbishop of Hamburg-Bremen by placing his diocese directly under the Pope. Four years later Honorius III gave him ecclesiastical authority over Livonia and Estonia. Albert was creating a German ecclesiastical state of his own and appointing his kin to key ecclesiastical positions within it; in 1220 he secured the appointment of his brother Hermann as bishop of Dorpat. This forward policy did not proceed without the concern and eventual opposition of Valdemar II of Denmark, who had his own designs on Estonia. In 1220 he blockaded Lübeck to prevent German settlers from travelling to Riga. This clipped Albert's wings for a few years. In 1221 he had to acknowledge the ecclesiastical supremacy of the Danish archbishop of Lund, but within two years subordination had been replaced by co-operation.

By the time of Albert's death in 1229 the Livonians could be considered as Christianised as any scattered rural population could be. Furthermore, most of southern Estonia had been conquered after the battle of Fellin in September 1217. By 1220 Valdemar II (1202–41) had brought Danish campaigns in northern Estonia, which had begun in 1196, to a successful conclusion. By 1240 frontiers had been established in Estonia between the German-dominated lands and the Danes based on Reval and the Russian ruler of Novgorod. To the south between Pomerania and Livonia remained the pagan lands of the Prussians and the Lithuanians. Their subjection was to be the task of the Teutonic Knights.

Even before Albert's death, but certainly by 1234, the Sword Brothers, despite their military successes, had gained an unsavoury reputation for rapaciousness and brutality. In that year they were reported to have killed numbers of converts, including missionary workers recruited by the papal legate William of Sabina/

Modena, to have heaped their bodies in a pile, with one corpse atop the pile said to represent the Pope, and to have refused permission for their burial. They resisted local bishops when their landed interests clashed and were said to recruit pagans and Russians to defend those interests. They paid scant attention to the papal legates sent to normalise conditions in the region. Clearly they were out of the control of the Church, and at a time when the papacy and Frederick II were at loggerheads this defiance could not be tolerated if the papacy was to justify its claims in German lands and to provide adequate support to its legatine commissions operating in the newly converted territories. In 1236 the cruelty and exactions of the Sword Brothers provoked a revolt amongst the Lithuanians, who virtually annihilated their tormentors at Saule. The following year Gregory IX took advantage of this setback to incorporate the remnant within the Teutonic Order. The defence of Livonia also became the responsibility of the Teutonic Knights at this time.

The Teutonic Knights (see p. 353) had been founded at Acre in 1198, but sought other fields for their activities as the Latin position in the Holy Land diminished. Almost from their beginning they had developed interests in Armenia and in 1225 were invited by Conrad, duke of Mazovia, to defend his lands against Prussian attacks. These last had been provoked by the missionary activity of a certain Bishop Christian on the lower Vistula. Christian followed the example of Albert of Buxhövden in founding his own version of the Sword Brothers, the so-called Fratres Militiae Christi de Livonia contra Prutenos, also known as the Knights of Dobryzn from the castle that Christian had assigned to them.

Attempts to penetrate Prussia were very limited in scope and provoked serious counter raids on the part of the Prussians. The Order stood well with the German Emperor Frederick II, who not only made it many grants of land in his dominions but also promoted its fourth grandmaster, Hermann of Salza (1209–39), to the rank of prince of the empire in 1215. In 1226, by the Bull of Rimini, he granted the Order the yet-to-be-conquered land of Prussia to hold as an imperial fief. The Order also stood well in the papal curia and in 1230, by consummate negotiations there, secured the authorisation of Gregory IX for their proposed conquest of Prussia.

The conquest of Prussia proceeded between 1230 and 1249 with the Teutonic Knights avoiding any involvement with Mongol advances into Poland and Hungary. One major setback came in August 1242. In 1240 the Knights were persuaded by the legate William of Modena to participate in a crusade against the schismatic or Orthodox Christians of Novgorod. Attitudes to Greek Christians had hardened in Latin lands since the settlement of westerners in the former Byzantine Empire after the Fourth Crusade, and the Orthodox rite was banned in the new lands of the East. It was also hoped that the movements of the Mongols might distract the prince of Novgorod.

At first the lands around Pskov were occupied, but in 1242 Prince Alexander Nevsky drove the Germans back from his lands and defeated the Teutonic Knights on 5 April 1242 in the so-called 'battle on the ice' on Lake Chud (Peipus).

The victory – immortalised in the 1938 film *Alexander Nevsky* by Sergei Eisenstein – was not as crushing as depicted on celluloid, but it did lead to a revolt in Prussia against the Knights and their harsh exploitative rule. Lessons were learned and, in 1249, at the peace of Christburg (Dierzgo) brokered by the Church between the Knights and the Prussian princes, the rights of converts were generously defined subject to there being no apostasy or revolt. The native princes were given a role in the new order in return for fighting in support of the Knights.

From the mid-1250s until the 1380s the Knights undertook the conquest and Christianisation of the Lithuanians. The latter were powerful and well organised and had taken advantage of Mongol destruction in western Russia to occupy territory there. The first campaign was the conquest of Samland between 1254 and 1256, and the founding of Königsberg in 1255. However, the Lithuanians fought hard and defeated the Teutonic Knights in three major battles at Schoden (1259), Durben (1260) and Karusen (1270). Encouraged by this the native Prussians revolted in 1260. The revolts were contained by 1277, but Prussia was not finally pacified until 1293 when the native Prussians lost the freedoms and privileges conceded to them at Christburg in 1249. German law was enforced over native law. The clergy and Church hierarchy were German and the land of Prussia passed firmly into German ownership, as the native Prussian aristocracy were judged contumacious and denied a place in the new order.

The Teutonic Order had been active since its foundation in finding a role for itself that did not depend entirely on the defence and care of pilgrims to the Holy Land. In 1291 it moved its headquarters from Acre to Venice, and in 1309 transferred them to Marienburg (Malbork) in Prussia.

The Order invited distinguished visitors to pass a season on crusade in Lithuania. During the fourteenth century to spend time in this way was popular amongst knights in England and France, and a sort of crusading tourism developed that could offer opportunities for fighting in both summer and winter. Young men could gain a reputation for bravery, some chose to be knighted there and have their armorial bearings painted on the walls of Königsberg cathedral, and all shared in the fellowship of the feasts of honour (*Ehrentisch*). Chaucer's knight had spent time on the *Reissen*, as did Henry, duke of Lancaster, in 1351 and 1352. The last *Reise* seems to have been held in 1423. Were these knightly guests (*Gäste*) of the Teutonic Knights crusaders or mere adventurers? There seems to have been no papal authorisation for the crusade against the Lithuanians in the fourteenth century. Clement IV (1265–8) seems to have been the last pope to give overt support to the crusading expeditions of the Teutonic Knights. Yet these latter-day participants regarded themselves as crusaders, who took vows and received spiritual rewards and were regarded as engaged in a holy war by chroniclers like Peter of Dusburg and writers like Geoffrey Chaucer. It has often been argued that this is another example of perpetual crusade basing its existence on crusading bulls issued in the thirteenth century, and in the absence to the contrary this must remain the best explanation. Certainly no pope objected to the enterprise of the Teutonic Knights except when they became engaged in a short war with the archbishop of Riga from 1298 to 1299.

In 1386 Wladislaw II Jagiello, king of Lithuania, married Jadwiga/Jagaila, queen regnant of Poland, thus uniting the two countries and ensuring that Lithuania became a Catholic country. The *raison d'être* for the crusades might have been removed, but the Teutonic Knights continued to wrest lands from the new kingdom. In 1346 they had purchased Estonia from Valdemar IV of Denmark. In 1398 they occupied the island of Gotland, and in 1405 seized Samogitia to ensure that they possessed an uninterrupted coastline from Memel to Riga to Reval. Their days of eastward expansion were coming to an end. On 15 July 1410 they suffered a major defeat at the hands of the Poles and the Lithuanians at Tannenberg. In 1415 both Poles and Teutonic Knights brought their respective territorial claims to the general church council at Constance and between 1454 and 1466 fought the Thirteen Years War over possessions in Prussia. They agreed to frontier adjustments in Samogitia and Prussia at the two treaties of Thorn (Torun) in 1411 and 1466, and in 1423 at the peace of Lake Melno ceded Samogitia back to the Poles.

Finland was conquered and Christianised by the Swedes. There were Orthodox missionaries functioning in Karelia and Tavastia and gaining some converts to the Greek rite in the early decades of the thirteenth century, and the princes of Novgorod were eager to limit Swedish influence. In all there were three Finnish crusades. Eric IX Jedvardsson supposedly led the first crusade from 1155 to 1159, resulting in the conversion of the Suomi in south-western Finland. This expedition was probably just a small-scale raid exaggerated into great deeds for the purposes of missionary propaganda by the author of the fourteenth century *Vita Sancti Erici*. In 1237 Gregory IX authorised a crusade against the Tavastians for refusing Latin Christianity. King Berger Magnusson led this crusade from 1238 to 1239. He succeeded in subduing the Suomi and the Tavastians, introducing Dominican missionaries at Turku (Abo) and building strong points as centres of Swedish settlement at Turku and Tavastehus that might collect tolls from merchants using the Gulf of Finland route to the Russian fur trade. Furthermore, it seems he established a Swedish settlement at the south-western end of the Gulf of Finland near the site of modern St Petersburg. In 1240 Alexander Nevsky decisively defeated the Swedes on the Neva River and forced them to give up their stronghold. In 1257 a crusade was approved by Pope Alexander VI to subdue the Karelians and sever any links that they might have with Novgorod. Nothing seems to have come of this until the third crusade of 1292–3 led by Torgils Knutsson. During the 1340s St Brdifet of Sweden (*c.* 1303–73) urged her cousin Magnus IV of Sweden (1319–65) to give up his fruitless attempts to conquer Christian Denmark in order to crusade against the heathen Karelians. Her monitions were received in visions and passed on to the king via his queen, in whose household Bridget served. Much weight was given to Bridget's vision, but she could not be persuaded to preach a crusade or join such an expedition. Latin Christianisation of Finland might be said to have been completed by 1300. Only the nomadic Lapps living north of the Gulf of Bothnia within the Arctic Circle persisted in their paganism well into the nineteenth century; their shamans were a source of wonder to those merchants trading with them. The Swedes were to be locked into border wars with the Russians from the thirteenth century to the eighteenth. For them this was to be the legacy of the Baltic crusades.

III
BRIEF BIOGRAPHIES OF
CRUSADING FIGURES

ADHEMAR OF MONTEIL, BISHOP OF PUY (d. 1098)

From a noble family from Valence, he became bishop of Puy in 1077 and made a pilgrimage to the East, 1086–7. Urban II designated him as papal legate to the First Crusade. He was a promoter of the Gregorian reform and a unifying figure on crusade, who appeared in many visions after his death. The fasts, processions and prayers that he proclaimed at times of difficulty united the crusaders and galvanised them to face the challenges to come. He strove hard to implement Urban's policy in relation to the Greek Church in Palestine in correspondence with Symeon II, patriarch of Jerusalem. His death at Antioch on 1 August 1098 led to a crisis for the crusade and a change in its guiding policies.

AGNES OF COURTENAY, COUNTESS OF JAFFA AND ASCALON (b. c. 1134–85)

Married to Amalric, count of Jaffa and Ascalon in 1157, she had borne him Sibyl and the future Baldwin IV by 1161. As a condition of his becoming king in 1163 the barons of the kingdom forced him to renounce his wife, technically on grounds of consanguinity. No blame was attached to her, the children of the marriage were declared legitimate and she retained her title of countess. Soon after she married Hugh of Ibelin (d. 1169), to whom she may have been betrothed before her marriage to Amalric. The whole bizarre incident seems to have been concerned with the fear that Agnes might exercise her patronage as queen to favour those who had been displaced from the former county of Edessa, for she was the daughter of Joscelin II of Courtenay, the last non-titular count (d. 1159). She received a bad press from the chroniclers and was reckoned a baleful influence on the affairs of the kingdom during the reign of her son, when she became queen mother at his court and a wielder of considerable power. She is said to have persuaded her daughter Sibyl to marry Guy of Lusignan rather than Baldwin of Ibelin, and in 1180 to have secured the appointment of her lover Heraclius as patriarch.

AL-ASHRAF KHALIL/AL-ASRAF SALAH-AD-DIN KHALIL (d. 1294)

Mameluke sultan (1290–4) who completed the expulsion of the Franks from Palestine with the capture of Acre on 18 May 1291.

AL-KAMIL/AL-MALIK AL-KAMIL I MASIR-AD-DIN (d. 1238)

Ayyubid sultan in Egypt (1218–38) who negotiated with Frederick II in 1228 for the surrender of Jerusalem, Bethlehem and Nazareth to the crusaders for a period of ten years.

ALBERT OF AACHEN/AIX-LA-CHAPELLE

Chancellor of the Church at Aachen, he did not particpate in the First Crusade but wrote one of the most valuable accounts of that expedition full of anecdote and intriguing observations gleaned from pilgrims and returning crusaders. As such he emphasised the bravery of the men of Lorraine, and that of Godfrey of Bouillon in particular. His work, *Liber Christianae expeditionis pro ereptione, emundatione, restitutione sanctae Hierosolymitanae ecclesiae* shows signs of incompleteness and contains material on the Latin Kingdom of Jerusalem as well. It was probably written by the 1120s and certainly by the 1140s. It may have been begun as early as 1100 or as late as 1119.

ALEXIOS I KOMNENOS (1057–18 August 1118)

He seized the Byzantine throne in a revolt against Nikephoros III in 1081. He was largely responsible for consolidating the Empire, defending it against Norman, Pechneg and Seljuk attack. He introduced fiscal and administrative changes as well as creating a number of new titles with which to reward his supporters. He called for military help from the West that resulted in the First Crusade. His dealings with the crusaders were much criticised by western chroniclers.

AMALRIC/AMAURY I (1136–11 July 1174)

Lord of Jaffa and Ascalon and second son of Fulk and Melisende, he succeeded his brother Baldwin III as king of Jerusalem on 18 February 1163. He was forced by the barons of the kingdom to divorce his wife, Agnes of Courtenay, as a condition of his accession. He continued his brother's policy of seeking Byzantine military assistance to stem the advance of Nur ed-Din. The price was the suzerainty of Byzantium over the kingdom and took the tangible form of a Byzantine bride, Maria Komnene (1167), a joint campaign in Egypt in 1169 and a state visit to Constantinople in 1171. This pro-Byzantine policy ended with Amalric's death.

ANNA KOMNENE (1083–1153/4)

The eldest daughter of Alexios I, she was thirteen at the time of the First Crusade. Exiled from court in 1118 after a failed coup to place her husband Nikephoros Bryennos on the throne. She wrote her history of her father's principate in fourteen books, known as the *Alexiad*, between 1143 and her death. Books 10–14 deal with the Crusades, but her testimony is flawed in part by defective memory and by her uncritical approach to her father. Recently it has been suggested that her work reveals more about Byzantine attitudes to the Second Crusade rather than the First. Nonetheless her work is the only Byzantine history of the First Crusade and as such the prime source for Byzantine attitudes to the First Crusade.

ANONYMOUS AUTHOR OF THE *GESTA FRANCORUM*

The anonymous author of the *Gesta Francorum et aliorum Hierosolimitanorum* was a literate Norman knight from south Italy, a supporter of Bohemond and an eyewitness of the events of the First Crusade. His account, written in 1101, is fundamental in that it influenced every other contemporary account of the crusade, subsequent authors either copying it like Peter Tudebode or basing their own accounts upon it.

ANSELM, COUNT OF RIBEMONT (d. 1099)

Took the cross in 1095 and was killed during the siege of Archas in February or March 1099. Two letters detailing events of the crusade up to July 1098 that he wrote to Manasses, archbishop of Rheims, survive.

BALDRIC/BAUDRI OF BOURGEIL OR OF DOL (*c.* 1045–7 January 1130)

From 1089 to 1107 he was prior and abbot of the Benedictine abbey of St Peter at Bourgeil. He was then elected archbishop of Dol in Brittany. He was present at the Council of Clermont but did not go on crusade. In 1110 he wrote the *Historia Hierosolymitana* in four books. He relied heavily on the anonymous *Gesta*, but gave a strong theological emphasis to his account, stressing the brotherhood of all Christians and the expedition itself as the epitome of the spiritual and temporal orders, the *sacrdotium* and the *regnum*.

BALDWIN/BAUDOUIN OF BOULOGNE/BALDWIN I OF JERUSALEM (d. 1118)

Son of Eustace II, count of Boulogne, and brother of Godfrey of Bouillon, he was in the contingent led by his brother. He left the army in March 1098 on the invitation of Thoros of Edessa on whose murder in March he took control of the town and set up the county of Edessa. On the death of his brother in 1100 he became king of Jerusalem. He was largely responsible for founding the Kingdom of Jerusalem in terms of its territory, its government and its relations with both the Latin patriarch and the other Latin principalities in the East. He died on 2 April 1118 at al-Arish returning from campaign in Egypt.

BALDWIN/BAUDOUIN OF COURTENAY/BALDWIN II OF ROMANIA (1217–73)

On his brother's death in 1228 Louis IX of France proposed that the experienced warrior John of Brienne should become Latin emperor and attempt to revive the flagging fortunes of the Latin Empire. Baldwin was to marry John's daughter Mary and his eventual succession safeguarded. He and his consort spent considerable time in the late 1230s and 1240s seeking military and financial support in the West, selling relics like the Crown of Thorns to this end. He became emperor in 1240. He was expelled from Constantinople in July 1261 and sought refuge in the West, becoming a papal pensioner. In 1267, by the Treaty of Viterbo, he passed his suzerainty of the principality of Achaea to Charles of Anjou.

BALDWIN/BAUDOUIN OF FLANDERS/BALDWIN I OF ROMANIA (1172–1205/6)

As Count Baldin IX of Flanders and the VI of Hainault he led the largest contingent on the Fourth Crusade. He was elected Latin emperor of Constantinople on 9 May 1204 and seems to have tried to reconcile the Greeks to Latin rule. He was captured by the Bulgarians in Thrace in 1205. News of his death in captivity reached Constantinople in July 1206.

BALDWIN/BAUDOUIN OF BOURCQ/OF LE BOURG/BALDWIN II OF JERUSALEM (d. 1131)

Son of Hugh, count of Rethel, and cousin, through his mother Ida, of Godfrey of Bouillon and Baldwin of Boulogne, he served in Godfrey's contingent. His succession to Baldwin I was unanimously accepted despite a deputation having been sent to Eustace III of Boulogne to invite him to succeed his brother. Eustace turned back on his journey east when he heard of Baldwin's coronation. He sponsored a castle-building programme and was active in exerting the suzerainty of Jerusalem over the other crusader states.

BALDWIN/BAUDOUIN III (1130–10 February 1163)

The son of Melisende and Fulk of Anjou, he was included with them in the tripartite succession devised by Baldwin II in 1131. He succeeded his father in November 1143 but had to deal with the political intrigues of his mother, eager not to lose her position as queen of Jerusalem. The increasing threat from Nur ed-Din caused him to court Byzantine help, and in 1158 he married Manuel I's niece Theodora. He died childless and was succeeded by his younger brother Amalric.

BALDWIN/BAUDOUIN IV (1161–May 1185)

The only son of Amalric and Agnes of Courtenay (d. 1185), he had William of Tyre as his tutor. He succeeded his father as king of Jerusalem in 1174. Subsequently known as the 'Leper king', his leprosy had not been formally diagnosed at that time. He was crowned on 15 July, the seventy-fifth anniversary of the capture of Jerusalem, with Raymond III of Tripoli as regent.

His leprosy seems to have been diagnosed by 1176, when he came of age and could rule in his own right. He sent embassies to the West to seek a suitable husband for his sister Sibyl – a man who could take on the rule of the kingdom when he himself became incapacitated and provide it with male heirs. The succession became a major issue during his reign. He undertook military campaigns until well into the 1180s, despite occasionally being too ill to ride and having to resort to a litter. A recent notion that he wore a gilded face mask is incorrect.

BALDWIN/BAUDOUIN V (1177–August 1186)

The only child of Baldwin IV's sister Sibyl. His father, William Longsword of Montferrat, had died in 1177. On 20 November 1183 he was crowned joint ruler with the ailing Baldwin IV. On the latter's death he became king, with Raymond III of Tripoli as regent. On his early death at Acre in 1186 he was succeeded by his stepfather, his mother Sibyl's second husband Guy of Lusignan.

BAYBARS I/AL-MALIK AZ-ZAHIR RUKN AD-DIN BAYBARS AL-BUNDUQARI (1233–1 July 1277)

A Kipchak Turk by origin, he was moved from his homeland north of the Black Sea on being sold into slavery sometime in the early 1240s He distinguished himself at the battle of Nablus against the Mongols in September 1260 and almost immediately seized power as Mameluke sultan in a coup. He held the Mongols at bay, drove the Assassins from Syria, extended his territories at the expense of the Seljuks in Anatolia, and between 1265 and 1271 conducted annual campaigns in Palestine seizing Atlit, Haifa, Jaffa and Antioch (May 1268). He sought to emulate Saladin and was a great patron of buildings in Cairo and Damascus, where he died reputedly drinking a poisoned draft that he had prepared for someone else.

BERNARD OF CLAIRVAUX (1090–20 August 1153)

Descended from Burgundian nobility he became a monk at Citeaux in 1113. Two years later he founded the daughter house of Clairvaux and became its abbot. He had an abiding interest in the Latin East and drew up and secured the acceptance of the Rule of the Templars at the Council of Troyes in 1128, later corresponding with Queen Melisende. Pope Eugenius III (1145–53) was a former pupil and worked closely with Bernard, enhancing his standing as an international religious figure. He virtually launched the Second Crusade on his own and devised its strategy as a crusade on three fronts. Its failure fatally damaged his reputation. He was canonised in 1174.

BOHEMOND/BOHEMUND OF TARANTO (*c.* 1047–5 or 7 March 1111)

The most experienced military leader of the First Crusade and one with some knowledge of the Byzantine Empire and perhaps of the Greek language. Anna Komnene gave him a reputation for cunning and duplicity. He was the son of Robert Guiscard (*c.* 1015–85) by his first wife, Alberada of Buonalbergo, and joined with his father on campaign against the Greeks in Epirus from 1081 to 1085. His father passed him over as heir to the duchy of Apulia in favour of his half-brother Roger Borsa. He took the cross in September 1096 whilst besieging Amalfi, and led his own Norman contingent eastwards. He set himself as prince of Antioch in 1098. He was prisoner of the Danishmend Turks from 1100 to 1103. He toured Europe between 1105 and 1107 raising support for an attack on Byzantium that might have some claim to have been the first political crusade. So great was his reputation as a crusader that he was given Constance, a daughter of Philip I of France (1060–1108), as his wife. Defeated by Alexios I he acknowledged Byzantine suzerainty over Antioch, but never returned to his principality, retiring instead to Apulia. He died at Bari and was buried in the church of San Sabino at Canossa di Puglia, believed to be modelled on the church of the Hagia Apostoloi in Constantinople.

BOHEMOND II, PRINCE OF ANTIOCH (*c.* 1109/10–February 1130)

He was the son of Bohemond and Constance of France. After the disaster of the Field of Blood in 1119 he was summoned to Antioch. However, as a minor he remained in southern Italy and Baldwin II of Jerusalem assumed the regency of Antioch until he should come of age. In November 1126 he came to Antioch, was invested with the principality and was married to Alice the second daughter of Baldwin II. Their daughter Constance became the heiress of Antioch. He followed a forward policy in Cilicia and was killed fighting the Danishmend Turks near Mamistra. His widow approached Zengi to help her stay in power, but she was confined to Latakia and Jabala by Baldwin II who became regent for his granddaughter.

BONIFACE OF MONTFERRAT, KING OF THESSALONIKA (*c.* 1152–4 September 1207)

The brother of Conrad and the military leader of the Fourth Crusade, he may have been responsible for introducing the future Alexios IV to the crusade through his cousin Philip of Swabia with whom Alexios had taken refuge in 1201. After the fall of Constantinople he married Margaret of Hungary, the widow of Isaac II Angelos. Disappointed not to be chosen the first Latin emperor of Constantinople. He established himself at Thessalonika to which he asserted a claim through his brother, Conrad. In late 1204 he initiated a successful campaign to conquer Thessaly and central Greece, culminating at the siege of

Nauplia in 1205. He laid the basis for the subsequent Latin principalities in Greece, but his reputation for rapaciousness outlived his positive achievements. He was killed near Mosynopolis, fighting against the Bulgarians, who sent his head to their leader Kalojan.

CHARLES I OF ANJOU (March 1226–7 January 1285)

Brother of Louis IX of France who participated in both Louis' crusades. In 1266, with papal backing, he took over the Hohenstaufen lands in southern Italy and Sicily and set about extending his rule into Frankish Greece and the restored Byzantine Empire. To this end, by the Treaty of Viterbo of 24 May 1267, he offered to restore Baldwin II to Constantinople in return for suzerainty over Achaea. His plans were put on hold by the Union of Churches at the Council of Lyons in 1274. His proposed expedition to recapture Constantinople in 1282 was foiled by the revolt of the Sicilian Vespers, which embroiled him in war for the rest of his life to hold on to his Sicilian kingdom.

CONRAD III OF HOHENSTAUFEN (1093–15 February 1152)

Sometimes erroneously labelled 'emperor', Conrad became king of Germany in 1138 but was never formally crowned Holy Roman Emperor. His hostility to Roger II, king of Sicily (1130–54), led to a close relationship with Byzantium that was sealed by the marriage of his sister-in-law, Bertha of Salzbach (d. *c.* 1160), to the emperor Manuel I in 1142. It is sometimes suggested that he was not welcome by the papacy on crusade, but this is erroneous. Bernard of Clairvaux took considerable trouble to recruit him and to provide an outlet for the crusading ambitions of Henry the Lion in the Baltic. The strained relations of Conrad and Henry meant that the two could not crusade together. Conrad led the German contingent on the Second Crusade in 1147. Defeated in Anatolia, he spent some-time being nursed back to health in Constantinople before sailing to Palestine in February 1148. He returned to Germany via Thessalonika, where he is thought to have concluded an alliance against Roger II with Manuel that was never activated due to preoccupations in Germany.

CONRAD OF MONTFERRAT, CLAIMANT OF THE KINGDOM OF JERUSALEM (d. 28 April 1192)

He was the son of William IV Longsword of Montferrat (d. 1177), who had been the husband of Sibyl and father to Baldwin V. Conrad, along with the rest of the Montferrat family, had opposed Frederick Barbarossa in northern Italy at the behest of Manuel I in 1179. In 1186 he was invited to Constantinople, where one year later he married Theodora, the sister of Isaac II Angelos, and was created Caesar. His brief career in Byzantium was to lay the basis of his brother Boniface's claim to Thessalonika at the time of the Fourth Crusade. Sometime between June and September 1187 he abandoned his wife and sailed to Tyre, where he took the lead in defending the city against Saladin. He refused both to admit Guy of Lusignan to the city and to recognise him as king of Jerusalem. In 1190 he married Isabel, the daughter of Amalric and his second wife Maria Komnene. Isabel was the step-sister of Baldwin IV and the aunt of Baldwin V. Through his marriage he strengthened his claim to the throne of Jerusalem. His ability and drive were widely recognised. On April 16 he was chosen by Richard I in consultation with the barons of the kingdom to replace Guy of Lusignan, whose kingship of Jerusalem was deemed to have lapsed with the death of his wife Sibyl. Within twelve days he was struck down by Ismaili Assassins at Acre before his claim could be regularised by coronation.

DAIMBERT/DAIBERT OF PISA (d. 14 May 1107)

Bishop of Pisa sometime before 1088, he became the first archbishop on the promotion of the diocese to metropolitan status in 1092. He was a supporter of the reform movement and had accompanied Urban II on his preaching tour in France after the Council of Clermont. It is possible, but by no means certain, that Urban appointed him as legate in succession to Adhemar. His high-handed actions in Jerusalem in December 1099 may be difficult to understand without legatine authority. However, the appointment of Maurice of Porto as legate in 1101 and Daimbert's own references to himself make his legatine authority doubtful. Daimbert led a Pisan fleet of 120 ships to the East that arrived at Latakia in September 1099 in time to take part in the siege. He thus represented not only his own interests but those of his native city as well, and hence his claim to half of Jaffa. He arrived in Jerusalem in December 1099 too late to participate in the discussions on the rulership of Jerusalem. He secured the dismissal of Arnold of Choques as patriarch of Jerusalem and was himself enthroned on 25 December 1099. He established his position as overlord of Godfrey of Bouillon and Bohemond, but was unable to sustain this position with Baldwin I who accused him of treason and secured his deposition in the winter of 1100. He fled to Antioch whence he returned to Italy with Bohemond in 1105. Paschal II confirmed him as patriarch of Jerusalem, but he died at Messina on his way back to Jerusalem.

EL CID/RODRIGRO DIAZ OF VIVAR (c. 1045–July 1099)

During the 1060s he was a household knight at the Court of Castile. He was dismissed in 1081 for taking too independent a line in exacting protection money from the taifa kings. He sold his services as a mercenary to both Christian and Muslim rulers. Brought back to court after the defeat of the Castilians at Sagrajas in 1086 he again fell from favour in 1089. Therafter he functioned as an independent adventurer attempting to carve out a principality for himself around Valencia, which he succeeded in capturing from the Moors in 1094 and where he died peacefully in 1099.

ENRICO DANDOLO, DOGE OF VENICE (*c.* 1107–1 June 1205)

From a prosperous merchant family active in the Byzantine trade, he was elected doge on 21 June 1192. He supported the approach from the leadership of the Fourth Crusade for the Venetians to supply ships. Blind and in his nineties, he led the Venetian contingent on that crusade and was integral to the setting up of the Latin Empire of Constantinople, where he died and was buried in Hagia Sophia.

EUSTACE III OF BOLOGNE (d. 1125)

Eldest son of Eustace II of Boulogne and brother of Godfrey of Bouillon and Baldwin of Boulogne, with whom he went on the First Crusade. He became count of Boulogne in 1093. He returned home after the capture of Jerusalem. In 1118 he was invited to succeed his brother Baldwin as king of Jerusalem. He travelled east, but turned back in Apulia when he heard of the accession of Baldwin Le Bourg. Not long before he died he became a monk at Rumilly.

FREDERICK I BARBAROSSA (*c.* 1125–10 June 1190)

He became king of Germany in 1152 on the death of his uncle Conrad III and was crowned Holy Roman Emperor at Rome on 18 June 1155. As Frederick III, duke of Swabia, he had taken part in the Second Crusade. His ambitions to secure Italy for his empire involved him in conflict with the papacy and Byzantium. Both the latter subsidised and supported the Lombard League that effectively fought against Frederick from 1165 to 1179. In 1189 he led a German army on crusade. He stopped short of an attack on Constantinople and passed through Anatolia without incident. He was drowned swimming across the Saleph River, and his crusade army broke up therafter.

FREDERICK II HOHENSTAUFEN (26 December 1194–13 December 1250)

The premature death of his father Henry VI in 1197, having united Sicily and Germany, led to his hereditary succession to the Kingdom of Sicily (1198–1250) under the guardianship of Pope Innocent III – but not to the elective Holy Roman Empire. Most of his reign was committed to restoring the unity lost at his father's death and was to involve bitter conflicts with the papacy. The spin-off of this conflict was support for the Nicaean Greeks in their struggle to regain Constantinople from the Latin Empire and a series of excommunications that were to impugn some of the real achievements of Frederick in Palestine. Frederick became king of Germany in 1212 and was crowned emperor in 1215, at the same time taking the cross. He did not participate in the Fifth Crusade, and his eventual departure on crusade was delayed until 1228 by which time he had become king of Jerusalem in right of his wife Yolanda, the daughter of Maria (daughter of Isabel and Conrad of Montferrat) and John of Brienne. Frederick negotiated the return of territory around Jerusalem in a ten-year truce negotiated with al-Kamil. His attempts to rule the kingdom through baillis in the name of his young son Conrad V (1228–54), following the death of Maria, led to violent disputes with the Ibelin family. Frederick II, following his excommunication and deposition in 1245, was himself the object of a crusade declared by Innocent VI.

FULCHER/FOUCHER OF CHARTRES (c. 1058–1128)

He was a priest from Chartres who attended the Council of Clermont and joined the First Crusade – initially as chaplain to Stephen of Blois and then, in October 1097, to Baldwin of Boulogne. He accompanied the latter to Edessa and so was not a witness of the siege of either Antioch or Jerusalem. The first version of his *Historia Hierosolymitana* was written between 1100 and 1106; a final version was produced in 1127. It is full of detail, including mention of the use of carrier pigeons, and paints a very positive account of Franco-Syrian relations. He is not to be confused with a knight of the same name who had joined Peter the Hermit in 1096, then served under Bohemond, and then joined Baldwin in Edessa where he became lord of Saruj.

FULK V OF ANJOU AND MAINE, KING OF JERUSALEM
(1092–10 November 1143)

Son of Fulk IV, he inherited Anjou in 1109 and gained Maine by marriage. His son Geoffrey married Matilda, daughter of Henry I of England, and he was thus well known on the international stage. He spent 1120–1 fighting in the Holy Land with a hundred knights, and in 1128 was approached by Baldwin II as a suitable husband for his daughter Melisende. After negotiations to protect his own interest as king of Jerusalem in his own right on the death of Baldwin, the marriage took place in 1129 as soon as Fulk had arrived in Palestine. On his deathbed Baldwin bequeathed the succession three ways: to Melisende, Fulk and Baldwin III jointly. Despite difficulties with Melisende, Fulk continued Baldwin's castle-building programme, protected Antioch against Byzantine aggression, and did what he could to contain the Zengid threat. He died as a result of a fall during a hunt when his saddle fractured his skull. His link to Jerusalem was to be used by the patriarch Heraclius to appeal to his grandson Henry II of England in 1185.

GEOFFREY OF VILLEHARDOUIN, CRUSADER AND CHRONICLER
(c. 1150–c. 1212/18)

Marshal of Champagne by 1200 and a major organiser and participant in the Fourth Crusade. He became marshal of Romania and stayed in the Latin Empire of Constantinople until his death. He was the uncle of Geoffrey of Villehardouin, prince of Achaea. He wrote the primary chronicle of the Fourth Crusade, ending his account with the death of Boniface of Montferrat on 4 September 1207.

GEOFFREY OF VILLEHARDOUIN, PRINCE OF ACHAEA (1170/5–1228)

Nephew of Geoffrey the chronicler, he had left the ranks of the Fourth Crusade in May 1203 to sail direct to Syria, and came thence to Greece in November 1204 on hearing of the capture of Constantinople. Wintering in Messenia, he learned of the ease with which southern Greece might be captured. In February 1205 he went to the army of Boniface of Montferrat, then beginning the siege of Nauplia. There he persuaded William of Champlitte, a neighbour of his uncles from Champagne, to join him, and with Boniface's blessing undertook the conquest of the Morea. After rapid early successes the complete subjugation of the Morea was to drag on until 1249. Champlitte became the first prince of Achaea in 1205. In 1209 Geoffrey took over. His two sons, Geoffrey II (1228–46) and William (1246–78), ruled as princes of Achaea until the male line ran out; the interest then passed to the Angevins of Naples by the Treaty of Viterbo in 1267.

GODFREY OF BOUILLON/OF LORRAINE/OF LOWER LOTHARINGIA (*c.* 1060–1100)

Second son of Eustace II of Boulogne and Ida, the daughter of Godfrey, duke of Lower Lorraine, he made his career within the Empire and became duke of Lower Lorraine in 1087. He led his own contingent on the First Crusade and was brave, if not always intelligent in his tactics. He was elected the first Latin ruler of Jerusalem on 22 July 1099, but refused to be crowned as such preferring instead the title of advocate (*avoué*) or protector of the Holy Sepulchre. He died unexpectedly on 18 July 1100. In the twelfth century he became idolised as the perfect crusader, an image that persisted and gained currency in Tasso's *Gerusalemme Liberata* in the late sixteenth century.

GREGORY VII/HILDEBRAND, POPE (1020/5–25 May 1085)

From a poor background in Tuscany, he became chaplain to Gregory VI (1045–6) and shared his exile in Germany in 1046. Under Leo IX (1049–55) he was appointed adminstrator of the patrimony of St Peter and as such established himself at the centre of the papacy, becoming something of a pope-maker. He was unanimously elected Pope on 22 April 1073. He was a reformer – indeed, the whole eleventh-century reform movement is sometimes named after him – and an advocate of centralisation in papal organisation. In crusade terms his pontificate may have made substantial contributions to later crusade ideology, although this is difficult to substantiate. In 1074 he considered raising an army to assist the Byzantines against the Turks, but these thoughts never reached the planning stage. He was responsible for giving new meaning to the term *militia Christi*, transferring the term from the spiritual warriors or monks to actual warriors who fought in defence of the Church.

GUIBERT OF NOGENT (1053–1125)

Descended from a noble Picard family he was elected abbot of Nogent-sous-Coucy in 1104. He was probably not present at the Council of Clermont and did not go on crusade. He relied upon the anonymous *Gesta* for his details, but his analysis of the events was his own. He emphasised the ill-treatment of pilgrims by the Muslims, centralised Jerusalem in his narrative and chose the role of the Franks as the new chosen people of God as his theme.

GUY OF LUSIGNAN (*c.* 1129–April 1194)

From a noble Poitevin family with crusading antecedents, Guy was summoned to the East by his brothers Geoffrey and Almaric (Amaury/Aimery), who had been in the East since 1174, as a possible consort for the widowed sister and heiress of Baldwin IV, Sibyl. Guy was not an ideal suitor, but a speedy marriage might be one way that Baldwin IV could counter any coup brewing in his kingdom that hinged upon a marriage with Sibyl. Guy and Sibyl were married at Easter 1180. In 1186 Sibyl and he took over the kingship from the dead Baldwin V, and the following year Guy led the field army of Jerusalem to its catastrophic defeat at Hattin. In 1188, released by Saladin and rebuffed by Conrad of Montferrat from Tyre, Guy boldly started the siege of Acre. On Sibyl's death in 1190 his right to the throne came to an end. In the crisis of the year any claims of his daughter Melisende were bypassed in favour of the claim of the able Conrad of Montferrat. Guy was recompensed with the island of Cyprus. He died in Nicosia, where he was buried, and was succeeded by his brother Almaric (d. 1205).

HENRY OF CHAMPAGNE (d. 10 September 1197)

Had come east with a French contingent on the Third Crusade and distinguished himself at the siege of Acre. On the death of Conrad of Montferrat in April 1192, Richard I proposed that Isabel, Conrad's widow, should marry Henry. The wedding took place in haste in May. Although elected to the crown of Jerusalem, Henry never seems to have used the royal title. He effectively resisted Muslim attacks and was said to have visited the Assassins at al-Khaif. He died childless as a result of an accidental fall from his window in Acre. His crown was offered to Alaric of Lusignan, and his brother Thibaut inherited his county of Champagne.

HENRY OF ANGRE/OF FLANDERS/OF HAINAULT, LATIN EMPEROR OF CONSTANTINOPLE (*c.* 1174–11 June 1216)

He was the younger brother of Baldwin of Flanders, with whom he joined the Fourth Crusade. He was regent during his brother's captivity in 1205, and when his death was confirmed was crowned Latin emperor on 20 August 1206. He took the offensive against both the Bulgarians and the Greeks of Nicaea, set about establishing imperial suzerainty over the developing Latin principalities in Greece and tried to reconcile the majority Greek population to Latin rule. He died suddenly at Thessalonika amidst rumours of poisoning, of which his Bulgarian wife was unjustly accused. He enjoyed a good reputation with both Greeks and Latins, and with hindsight his reign was the last opportunity for the Latin Empire to establish itself as a viable polity.

HERACLIUS, PATRIARCH OF JERUSALEM (d. summer 1190)

Ernoul records that he was born in the Auvergne and came to the East after he had become a priest. He was archdeacon of Jerusalem from 1169 to 1175 and archbishop of Caesarea from 1175 to 1180, when he became patriarch, appointed by the influence of Agnes of Courtenay, who was said to be his lover. In 1184 and 1185 he visited the courts of Western Europe seeking military aid for the crusader states. In 1185 he offered the kingship of Jerusalem to Henry II of England and, incidentally, consecrated the new Hospitaller church at Clerkenwell. In 1186 he crowned Sibyl and Guy of Lusignan. He was not present at Hattin, for which he was accused of cowardice, but may have been in charge of the defence of Jerusalem. He was allowed to leave with Queen Sibyl for Tripoli. He participated in the siege of Acre, where he died of plague in the summer of 1190. As the last actual Latin patriarch, and as a supporter of Guy of Lusignan, he has suffered at the hands of chroniclers, being accused of immorality, illiteracy and cowardice. Nevertheless, he was a considerable force for stability at a time of crisis in the last years of the Latin kingdom.

HUGH/HUGUES OF PAYNS (d. 1136)

He was the lord of Martigny in Burgundy, with close links of some kind to the counts of Champagne. He came east in 1115, and by 1118 had set about organising a company of knights to protect pilgrims on the Jaffa–Jerusalem road. Already known as the master of the Knights of the Temple, he visited Europe in 1127 to raise money and recruits for a proposed attack on Damascus. With St Bernard's help and advice he attended the Council of Troyes in 1128 and secured the recognition of the Templars as a military religious order, for which Bernard supplied the rule and helped with publicity. He returned to the East in 1130 and set about organising the new Order, of which he was the first Grandmaster.

HUGH OF VERMONDOIS/HUGH THE GREAT (c. 1057–18 October 1101)

Brother of King Philip I of France, who became count of Vermondois in right of his wife in 1080. he led his own contingent on crusade and is remembered for sending an embassy to announce his approach to Constantinople to lay down the ground rules for his reception. He was sent as ambassador to Alexios I to announce the capture of Antioch, but did not return to the crusade thereafter. He took part in the crusade of 1101, dying of wounds at Tarsus on 18 October 1101.

IBELIN FAMILY

This was a family of international significance, and the most powerful family in both the Kingdom of Jerusalem and that of Cyprus under the Lusignans. Ability, good luck, good propaganda, and good marriages marked out their rise. The first known member of the family was Barisan (d. 1150), constable of Jaffa in 1115. In 1141 he received the fortress and lordship of Gath (Ibelin) from King Fulk, from which the family later derived its name. He had three sons, all of whom made or aspired to good marriages within the nobility of the Kingdom of Jerusalem; his eldest son Hugh (d. 1169) married Agnes of Courtenay in 1163, his youngest son Balian married the widow of Amalric I in 1177. The Ibelins were now numbered amongst the leading nobles of the Kingdom of Jerusalem. The middle son, Baldwin of Mirabel, had ambitions of marrying Amalric's daughter, Sybil, but this came to nothing. In 1187 Baldwin chose exile in Antioch rather than service under Guy of Lusignan, and died there in 1187/8. His brother Balian supported Conrad of Montferrat after Sybil's death in 1190; he seems to have died in 1193. Balian's son John, the 'Old Lord of Beirut' was constable of the kingdom, 1194–1200, when he exhanged the office for the lordship of Beirut. Unlike his predecessors, he was very wealthy. He paid for the refortification of Beirut and built a large palace there. Here he established what was virtually an autonomous principality. He was regent of the kingdom (1205–10), and died at Acre in 1236 in the habit of a Templar. His nephew John of Jaffa (1215–66) is perhaps the best known of the Ibelins. He organised the resistance to Frederick II on Cyprus in 1230s, for which he was celebrated by Philip of Novara, and wrote *Le Livre des Assises* – the main source about the High Court of Jerusalem, completed in 1265/6. By the late thirteenth century Ibelin daughters were marrying into the Cypriot ruling family, and their kinsfolk were the uncles, seneschals and regents of various Lusignan kings; others filled important bishoprics in Cyprus.

IBN AL-ATHIR/IZZ AD-DIN IBN AL-ATHIR (1160–1233)

Many consider him the greatest Arab historian of the crusader period, covering as he did the careers of Zengi, Nur ed-Din and Saladin. Based in Mosul, he was sympathetic to the Zengids. His chronology is sometimes inexact and he relied upon Ibn al-Qalanisi for his account of the First Crusade. The whole is contained in a world history from pre-Islamic times down to 1231, the *Kitab al-Kamil fi-al-Tàrikh* or Summary of History.

IBN AL-QALANISI/ ABU YA'LA HAMZA IBN ASAD AT-TAMINI (*c.* 1073–1160)

An eyewitness of the First and Second crusades from the point of view of Damascus, where he lived and wrote. His history of Damascus from 974 to 1160, the *Dhail tàrikh Dimashq*, is the first Muslim account of the crusades.

IBN JUBAYR/ABU 'L-HUSAYN MUHAMMAD IBN AHMAD IBN JUBAYR (1145–1217)

A scholar, poet and the secretary to the governor of Granada, originally from Valencia, undertook a pilgrimage to Mecca and Medina between February 1183 and April 1185. His travelogue, *Rahlat al-Kinani*, recounts his impressions and experiences in the Kingdom of Jerusalem and the Kingdom of Sicily.

IBN MUNQIDH/USAMA IBN MUNQIDH (1095–1188)

An emir of Shaizar who travelled widely on official business to Cairo, Damascus and Jerusalem, where he clearly received privileged treatment. His *Kitab al-I'tibar* is a book of instruction and amusement and not, strictly speaking, a memoir or autobiography. It is much cited on Franco-Muslim relations, but the reliability of the anecdotes has been questioned. He also wrote the *Kitab al'Asa* (Book of the Sticks), another collection of anecdotes, which only survives as a fragment.

INNOCENT III (1160–1216)

Born Lothario of Segni into a noble family, he was educated at Paris and Bologna, became a cardinal in 1190, and was elected Pope on 8 January 1198 and crowned six weeks later on 21 February. Of all the popes he was the one who had the most profound influence on the development and definition of crusade. Immediately on assuming office he put the preparation of the Fourth Crusade in train, originally aimed at Egypt. He did his best to protect the interests of the new Latin Church in the Latin Empire, and hoped that it would bring about the union of the Greek and Latin churches. His pontificate saw the introduction of political crusading and crusades against heretics. It was he who introduced the purchase of crusade indulgences in order to finance crusades, and he who tried to place crusade finance on a regular footing. For the preparation of the Fifth Crusade he allowed a period of three years, beginning in 1213. His pontificate is generally seen as the apogee of papal monarchy, and he made the authority of the papacy felt from the Balkans to Georgia, having a profound influence on the development of the kingdoms of Bulgaria and Cilician Armenia.

ISABEL/ISABEAU/ISABELLA, QUEEN OF JERUSALEM (*c.* 1171–1205)

She was the daughter of King Amalric (1163–74) and his second wife Maria Komnene (d.1217), whom he married in 1167. She and her mother lived quietly during the reign of her half-brother Baldwin IV but, after the death of her half-sister Sibyl in October 1190, she became the heiress of the Kingdom of Jerusalem. Between then and November 1190 she was persuaded to divorce her first husband Humphrey of Toron and to marry Conrad of Montferrat in order to strengthen his claim to the kingdom. After his assassination in 1192 she married Henry of Champagne for much the same reason, and on his death in 1197 became the wife of the next king, Amalric II, the brother of Guy of Lusignan. Her married life had been at the behest of others to strengthen the dynastic chain of the Kingdom of Jerusalem.

JAMES/JACQUES OF VITRY, BISHOP OF ACRE (1160/70–1 May 1240)

Educated at Paris, he was a canon of the Church of St Nicholas at Oignies near Liège. He was bishop of Acre from 1216 to 1228 and as such participated in the Fifth Crusade, 1218–21. In 1228 he became cardinal bishop of Tusculum. Seven of his letters survive, some of which provide interesting insights into the society in the Latin east.

JOHN OF BRIENNE (*c.* 1170–23 March 1237)

From a great French noble family with close connections to crusading and the Latin East, John enjoyed a high reputation as a trusted and able warrior and ruler. He was, however, a younger son and his choice by Philip Augustus as consort for Maria, heiress to the Kingdom of Jerusalem, in 1210, was said to have been greeted with dismay. Nonetheless, Philip's son Louis IX often proposed him for and supported him in his many roles in the East. As king of Jerusalem he took an active part in the Fifth Crusade and was chosen as overall commander in 1218. From 1210 to 1225 he was king of Jerusalem in right of his wife Maria, the daughter of Isabel and her second husband Conrad of Montferrat. When Maria died he ruled on behalf of their daughter Yolanda. She married Frederick II in 1225, and John was expelled the kingdom rather peremptorily. For the next three years he commanded the papal armies in Italy opposed to his hated son-in-law. In 1228 he was invited to Constantinople to hold things together during the minority of Baldwin II. By the Treaty of Perugia in 1229 he agreed to go, provided he should become Latin emperor with Baldwin's right of succession guaranteed on John's death. He was anointed emperor in Constantinople in 1231 and mounted an effective defence of the city until his death.

JOHN OF JOINVILLE (b. 1224)

Scion of a distinguished Champagnard noble family with crusading antecedents, he was present on crusade with Louis IX between 1249 and 1254. His familiarity with the Villehardouin family induced him to write an account of the crusade after the fashion of Geoffrey of Villehardouin's account of the Fourth Crusade; this he produced in his old age between 1272 and 1309.

JOSCELIN/JOCELYN I OF COURTENAY, COUNT OF EDESSA (d. 1131)

From a noble family from the Île de France and a cousin of Baldwin Le Bourg, he came to the East possibly in 1101 and received the fief of Turbessel (Tellbashir) in the county of Edessa from Baldwin. He relinquished this in 1113 and received the lordship of Tiberias from Baldwin I of Jerusalem. He supported his cousin for the kingship of Jerusalem in 1118; as a reward he received the county of Edessa when Baldwin II vacated it to become king of Jerusalem. He was a captive in Muslim hands from 1122–1123. He and his descendants were among the greatest nobles in the Latin East.

JOSCELIN/JOCELYN II OF COURTENAY (1113–59)

Succeeded his father as count of Edessa in 1131. His alliance with the Artuqids against Zengi led to the fall of Edessa in 1144, and his attempt to retake it in 1146 resulted in the complete destruction of the city. In May 1150 he was ambushed and captured on his way to Antioch. He was blinded and died in captivity at Aleppo. He thus left his lands leaderless, and his widow Beatrice sold the county of Edessa to Manuel I. Through his daughter Agnes he was the grandfather of the future Baldwin IV. His son Joscelin III became titular count and moved to the court of Jerusalem where, as uncle of Baldwin IV, he assumed a leading position and subsequently became one of the guardians of Baldwin V. It was Joscelyn III who was responsible for surrendering Acre to Saladin in October 1187.

KALOJAN/JOHANNITZA (d. October 1207)

He was ruler or khan of the Bulgarians from 1197 to 1207 and an implacable enemy of the Byzantines. He gained a crown from Innocent III in 1204, but he assumed the title of emperor (tsar) of the Bulgars and Vlachs. After friendly approaches to the Latin conquerors of Constantinople, he turned against them and spread terror in their ranks by his violent and ruthless opposition to their early attempts at expansion in Thrace. After the death of Boniface of Montferrat he attacked Thessalonika and was murdered during the siege by the chief of his Cuman allies.

KARBUQA/KERBOGHA/CURBARAM/CORBAGATH, EMIR AND ATABEG OF MOSUL

He was one of the Seljuk military commanders who emerged from the dissension following the death of Malikshah in 1092 with his own power base in Mosul and as a powerbroker in the disputes of Dukak and Ridwan. What is known of him comes largely from Latin writers. He was a poor military leader. He delayed his approach to Antioch by besieging Edessa for three weeks in May 1098. His uncompromising approach to the crusaders in Antioch ended in his memorable defeat on 28 June 1098. His campaign was noteworthy for his interview with Peter the Hermit and for the dreams and warnings of his mother these entering the crusading chronicles. His defeat marked the end of any resistance to the crusaders from local Arab rulers.

KILIJ ARSLAN I (d. 1107)

After the death of his father, Suleiman ben Kulumush, he was brought up at the court of Malikshah, whence he escaped on the latter's death in 1092, and established himself as Seljuk sultan at Nicaea. He thought he had dealt with the crusade threat when he wiped out the crusade of Peter the Hermit at Civetot, after which he campaigned against the Danishmends in eastern Turkey and where he was surprised to learn of the arrival of the crusade army at his capital in May 1097. Defated at Dorylaion, he moved his capital to Konya (Iconion). The crusaders knew him by his patrynomic Soloman (Suleiman).

KILIJ ARSLAN II (c. 1115–92)

Seljuk sultan at Konya from 1155 and involved with efforts to frustrate the forward policy pursued by Manuel I in the East in 1158 and 1159. He brought the Danishmend Turks under Seljuk control and defeated Byzantine attempts to undo this at Myriokephalon in 1176. Thereafter he sought to gain control of the Maeander valley from the Greeks.

LOUIS VII OF FRANCE (c. 1120–18 September 1180)

In 1131 he was crowned joint ruler with his father Louis VI, becoming sole ruler on his father's death in 1137. In the same year he married Eleanor of Aquitaine. He led the French contingent on the Second Crusade (1147–9), and repudiated his wife in 1152 – partly because of her alleged misbehaviour with her uncle Raymond of Antioch.

LOUIS IX OF FRANCE (25 April 1214–25 August 1270)

He became king on the death of his father in November 1226, and married Margaret of Provence on 29 May 1234. He dealt with the Albigensian revolt, the revolt of his own baronage and the war with the English. Deeply religious, he sponsored John of Brienne as king of Jerusalem, the commander of papal forces in Italy against Frederick II, and finally as Latin emperor of Constantinople. He financed Baldwin II and bought many religious relics from him, including the Crown of Thorns for which he built Sainte Chapelle to house this most precious relic. He led the Seventh Crusade from 1248 to 1254, and an expedition to Tunis in July 1270, where he died. He was canonised by Boniface VIII on 11 August 1297.

MALIKSHAH/MALIK-SHAH/JALIL-AD-DIN MALIK-SHAH (August 1055–November 1092)

Third of the great Seljuk sultans, in succession to his grandfather Tughril Bey (1038–63) and his father Alp-Arslan (1063–72), he held the Abbasid caliphate together suppressing centrifugal tendencies amongst local governors and Turks on the borders of Byzantium. He was a great patron, building the Thursday mosque in his capital Isfahan and sponsoring the poet and philosopher Umar Khayyam. His sudden death at Baghdad was followed by a period of Muslim disunity in the regions through which the First Crusade passed.

MANUEL I KOMNENOS (28 November 1118–24 September 1180)

Recognised in both East and West as a pro-western (Latinophile) emperor. He sought closer ties with the rulers of the West and, like his father John II (1118–45), recognition of the Byzantine position in the East as protector of the Christians there. From the start there was a strong imperial presence in Syria. He bought up the remaining fortresses of Edessa, and dealt with the passage of the Second Crusade, very much as his grandfather had dealt with the First. The collapse of the Second Crusade made a Byzantine protectorate much more acceptable to the Christian states in Syria than in the time of his father. In 1158 and 1159 he brought Cilicia and Antioch back in the Byzantine fold, took Maria of Antioch as his second wife in 1161, and from 1167 to 1171 he co-operated with the Kingdom of Jerusalem in joint operations against Egypt and Damascus. There were certain tangible gains: a Greek patriarch in Antioch, Greek canons at the Holy Sepulchre and the redecoration of the Church of the Nativity at Bethlehem by Byzantine craftsmen. During his reign relations with Venice worsened. His successors changed policy from a pro-western stance to co-operation with Saladin.

MELISENDE/MELISSENDA, QUEEN OF JERUSALEM (d. 11 September 1161)

The eldest of four daughters of Baldwin II and his Armenian wife Morphia, she was married to Fulk V of Anjou in 1129 as part of her father's plans to secure the succession. Fulk was eager to receive the crown in his own right rather than as Melisende's consort. On his deathbed Baldwin bequeathed the succession three ways: to Fulk, Melisende and their infant son the future Baldwin III. Melisende was a forceful character with a thirst for political power. Fulk tried to cut her out of power, and this led to a revolt on her behalf by her cousin Hugh of Le Puiset, count of Jaffa, in 1134. The queen's party represented the old royal line. The couple were reconciled by 1136. She was regent for her son from 1143 and refused to hand over power on his coming of age, stirring up virtual civil war between 1150 and 1152. William of Tyre mentions her piety and her great patronage of the arts, especially of books. The most famous work with which she was associated is the psalter that bears her name, now in the British Museum, combining Byzantine and western-style iconography. She made bequests to many churches in the kingdom and founded the nunnery at Bethany, installing her youngest sister Yveta as abbess.

NUR ED-DIN/NUR-AD-DIN MAHMUD BIN ZANGI (February 1118– 15 May 1174)

Took over the Syrian portion of his father Zengi's territory, and from his capital Aleppo attacked the principality of Antioch. He captured Damascus in 1154 and set about denying the crusading states any control of Egypt by suppressing the Fatimids (1169–71). In 1159 he concluded an alliance with Manuel I and the Danishmends against the Seljuks of Rum. By the time of his death he had virtually surrounded the crusader states with his territory, providing a unified base from which to continue the attack. He was the first Muslim ruler to use a conscious jihad ideology against the crusaders, with the intention of expelling them from Syria–Palestine. In 1149 he had symbolically bathed in the Mediterranean after a successful campaign within the principality of Antioch, whilst the wooden *minbar* (pulpit, made of wood or stone, often elaborately carved, from which the Khutba or Friday sermon was preached in a mosque) that he had made in Damascus in 1168 for installation in Jerusalem was a clear demonstration of this intention. Saladin, who was the clear legatee of Nur ed-Din, eventually installed it in the al-Aqsa mosque. In Muslim historiography it is Nur ed-Din rather than Saladin who is seen as the model mujahad.

PELAGIUS OF OPORTO, PAPAL LEGATE IN THE LEVANT (d. 1230)

Pelagius Galvani was a Spanish cleric who was one of the few non-Italians who entered the *Curia* under Innocent III as cardinal-deacon (1205–10), cardinal-priest (1210–13) and finally as cardinal-bishop of Albano (1213–30). He was a controversial figure with a reputation for arrogance and lack of tact in his relations with the secular rulers of the Latin East, and he was the curial expert on the relations of the Latin Church with eastern-rite Christians. He was part of an inner circle working with Innocent III, who had appointed him legate to the

Latin Empire of Constantinople (1213–14). There he had held seminars to win over the Greek clergy, but at the same time had alienated them by closing the Greek churches in the city and dressing in red clothes with gilded shoes, one of the first accounts of the appearance of an apostolic legate. In 1215, at the Fourth Lateran Council, he urged the payment of tithes by eastern Christians of the non-Latin rites. He was popular with the Latin clergy of the East and was invited to become patriarch of Antioch in 1217 by the chapter of Antioch on the death of Peter of Ivrea. This he had to refuse when Pope Honorius III appointed him papal legate to the Fifth Crusade (1218–22). He joined the crusade in September 1218. He interfered in military decisions and quarrelled with John of Brienne over strategy at Damietta. He excommunicated Bohemond IV of Antioch for his treatment of the Hospitallers, and it was feared by Honorius that Antioch might be lost to the Latin cause. In 1222 he drew up the constitution for the Latin Church in Cyprus.

PETER THE HERMIT (c. 1050–1115)

Originally a hermit or wandering monk from Picardy, he became one the charismatic preachers of the First Crusade. Anna Komnene thought that Peter had devised the idea of crusade whilst on a pilgrimage to Jerusalem, but there is no foundation for either of these assertions. He led the Popular crusade, and after its destruction at Civetot in 1096 he joined the contingent of Godfrey of Bouillon with the remnants. He tried to desert at Antioch but was brought back, restoring his reputation by leading an embassy to meet Kerbogha. After the capture of Jerusalem he returned to France and became prior of the Augustinian house at Noirmoutier. After his death many legends grew up around him.

PETER THE VENERABLE (c. 1092–1156)

He entered Cluny as a monk in 1109 and was elected its eighth abbot in 1122. He travelled widely, visiting England twice, Rome eight times, and Spain twice in 1126 and 1142. On the latter visit he commissioned the first translation of the Koran into Latin, using two of the finest translators of Arabic working in Toledo, Robert of Ketton and Hermann of Carinthia. He had the translation checked by a Muslim named Muhammad. His concern was partly to refute the errors of Islam and partly to use this to evangelise amongst the Muslims of Spain. In this he was ahead of his times and clearly feared criticism from his contemporaries – for example, Bernard of Clairvaux.

PHILIP II AUGUSTUS (21 August 1165–14 July 1223)

He came to the French throne in 1179 and has the reputation of being one of the great Capetian kings. His relationship with Richard I on crusade, and his dogged policy of capturing Plantagenet lands in France, has overshadowed Philip the crusader. He was in Palestine from 20 April to 31 July 1191. During that time he played a major role in the siege of Acre.

RAMON LULL (*c.* 1235–*c.* 1316)

A Franciscan scholar, missionary and mystic who founded the college of Miramar (1276) to teach Arabic to intending missionaries. He travelled widely in Africa and Asia, and on one of these missionary journeys was stoned to death by Muslims at Bugia in Algeria.

RAYMOND OF AGUILERS/AGUILLERS/AGILES

Nothing is known of this man other than that he was a canon of Puy and the chaplain to Raymond of Toulouse, whom he accompanied on the First Crusade. During the course of the crusade he wrote the *Historia Francorum qui ceperunt Iherusalem*, which may have been completed by 1102 but certainly before 1105. It was composed for the bishop of Viviers and contains more material on miracles, especially the finding of the Holy Lance at Antioch, and on the poor crusaders than do other chronicles of the crusade.

RAYMOND OF POITIERS, PRINCE OF ANTIOCH (*c.* 1098–29 June 1149)

He was the younger son of William IX of Aquitaine. In 1135 he was sought out in England by ambassadors of Fulk of Jerusalem as a husband for Constance, the heiress of Antioch (b. 1128). In 1136 they were married and he became prince of Antioch in her right. Their daughter Margueritte/Maria (b.1140s) was to wed Manuel I in 1161. The 1136 marriage had been a deliberate rejection of Byzantine overtures on the part of the Franks of Antioch, and Raymond was subject to Byzantine pressure from the start of his reign. He was forced to acknowledge Byzantine suzerainty in 1137 in terms that went beyond the Treaty of Devol of 1108, and he visited Constantinople in 1145. During the Second Crusade he fell out with Louis VII and took the part of his niece Eleanor of Aquitaine. He died fighting the forces of Nur ed-Din and Damascus at Inab, and his skull was made into a drinking cup by Nur ed-Din.

RAYMOND IV COUNT OF TOULOUSE/RAYMOND OF SAINT-GILLES (1042–28 February 1105)

He was the oldest and wealthiest of the leaders of the First Crusade, one of the first to take the cross at Clermont and the leader of the Provençal army. He became count of Toulouse in 1088, and had fought against the Moors in Spain in the preceding year. He was often known from his favourite residence at Saint-Gilles. Despite his status and clear desire to be the leader of the crusade, he seems to have gained the least from it in material terms. He was left to carve out a power base around Tripoli and died during the siege of that town.

REYNALD/REGINALD OF CHATILLON (d. 4/5 July 1187)

A French noble who came to the East during the Second Crusade, being first mentioned at the siege of Ascalon. He stayed on in the East, and in 1152 married Constance, the widowed cousin of Baldwin III and princess of Antioch. He became prince in her right and guardian of her sons. As prince he provoked the Byzantines by raiding Cyprus in alliance with the Armenians and quarrelled with his own baronage and the patriarch of Antioch. In 1158 he made humble submission to Manuel I. In 1161 he was captured whilst raiding into the territory of Aleppo and was imprisoned there until 1176. During his captivity his wife died, and he lost the title of prince when his ward came of age in 1163. On his release from prison he was made lord of Hebron and married Stephanie of Transjordan (Outre-Jordan), controlling the south and east of the Kingdom of Jerusalem. From there he attacked the *haj* caravan from Damascus and raided Muslim shipping and ports on the Red Sea, even proposing a seaborne attack on Mecca. His activities provoked Saladin to attack the Kingdom of Jerusalem in 1183 and 1187. He was captured at the battle of Hattin and was said to have been executed by Saladin personally for his affront to Islam. He supported Sibyl and King Guy, and has received a bad press from both William of Tyre and the Muslim chroniclers. His dedication to the Kingdom of Jerusalem was never in doubt, however.

RICHARD I, LIONHEART (8 September 1157–6 April 1199)

Richard took the cross to fulfil his father's crusading vow. A brilliant soldier and tactician, the confrontation of Richard and Saladin dominates perceptions of the crusaders and Muslims and has done so since the 1190s. Richard left his lands in 1190 and arrived at Acre on 6 June 1191. Acre fell in July, and in September he defeated Saladin at Arsuf and captured Jaffa. Twice he came within ten miles of Jerusalem but failed to capture it. His decision to secure Ascalon rather than Jerusalem emphasised the importance of Egypt in crusade strategic thinking. He stabilised the rump crusader states along the coast, and sorted out the difficult issue of the kingship of Jerusalem.

ROBERT I, COUNT OF FLANDERS/ROBERT THE FRISIAN (*c.* 1013–12 October 1093)

He succeeded his father Baldwin VI as count of Flanders in 1070. Sometime between 1087 and 1090 he made a pilgrimage to Jerusalem. Returning via Constantinople, he met with Alexios I and promised to send 500 Flemish knights to his aid. He was once thought to have received a letter from Alexios I detailing the holy relics housed in Constantinople (but interestingly not the Holy Lance) and the vices and cruelty of the Turks. This letter has been shown to be spurious and to have been written after the success of the First Crusade. His son Robert II (d. 4 December 1111) took part in the First Crusade and returned to Flanders after the capture of Jerusalem.

ROBERT THE MONK/OF RHEIMS

He was a monk at Marmoutier and later became abbot of Saint Remi at Rheims. He finished the nine books of his *Historia Iherosolimitana* at the request of his abbot Bernard (d.1107). He relied upon the anonymous *Gesta* for his information since he was not present on the First Crusade but emphasised the divine initiative behind the crusade. He attended the Council of Clermont but did not mention it in his history.

ROGER OF SALERNO, PRINCE REGENT OF ANTIOCH (d. 28 June 1119)

The nephew of Tancred, he succeeded his uncle as regent of Antioch for Bohemond's son Bohemond. He consolidated his uncle's expansion of the principality and strengthened relations with the count of Edessa by marrying Cecilia, the sister of Baldwin Le Bourg. He was killed fighting at the battle of the Field of Blood.

SALADIN/AL-MALIK AN-NASIR I SALAH-AD-DIN YUSUF IBN AYYUB (1137–4 March 1193)

A Kurd born in Takrit, whose father was in the service of Zengi. He joined his uncle, Shirkuh, on campaign in Egypt during the 1160s, and in 1169 became both commander of Nur ed-Din's army of Egypt and vizier of Egypt as well. The last years of Nur ed-Din were clouded by the latter's suspicion of his protégé. From 1174 to 1186 he united Syria and Palestine to his Egyptian possessions, occupying Aleppo (1183) and Mosul (1186), and establishing the Ayyubid dynasty in place of the Zengids. He then turned against the crusader states in a conscious evocation of the jihad begun by Nur ed-Din. He gambled much on his success against the Franks as a means of legitimising and consolidating his authority. Having annihilated the field army of the Kingdom of Jerusalem at Hattin on 4 July 1187, he failed to take Tyre and lost much of the Palestinian coastline to Richard I during the Third Crusade. From that time he has enjoyed a high reputation in the West, but not so in Islam where his grave in Damascus was largely neglected until visited by Kaiser Wihelm II in 1898. He was an able rather than a great general, and this showed in his campaign against Richard I.

STEPHEN OF BLOIS (d. 17/18 May 1102)

He was the eldest son of Thibaut III of Champagne. Nothing is known of him until his marriage to Adela, the daughter of William the Conqueror, in 1081. He succeeded his father as count in 1088 and took the cross for the First Crusade in 1096. Two of the letters that he wrote to his wife whilst on crusade survive and show him as a charming man of feeling and imagination. He was much impressed by the size and fortifications of the cities of Constantinople, Nicaea and Antioch. His personal relations with Alexios I were good. He fled from Antioch on 2 June 1098, the day before the city was captured. He met Alexios I at Philomelion and warned him not to proceed to Antioch to support a cause that was already lost. For this he was branded a renegade and a European coward, a view shared by his wife. He returned on the 1101 crusade. When this broke up in Anatolia he returned to Constantinople, and in February 1102 travelled to Palestine by ship. He was killed at the battle of Ramla.

SIBYL/SIBYLLA (c. 1158–25 July 1190)

She was the daughter of Amalric and Agnes of Courtenay and sister of Baldwin IV, and thus heiress of the Kingdom of Jerusalem. Baldwin's leprosy meant that her marriage to a suitable husband who could take over the government was of paramount importance. In the autumn of 1176 she was married to William Longsword of Montferrat, who was created count of Jaffa and Ascalon. He died the following June, leaving her pregnant with the future Baldwin V and countess in her own right. Planning for her second marriage was forestalled when her mother, Agnes of Courtenay, persuaded her to marry Guy of Lusignan in October 1180. He became count of Jaffa and stepfather of the future Baldwin V. Despite Guy's military incompetence and unacceptability to the Jerusalem baronage, the couple seem to have been genuinely fond of each other. She bore him four daughters. In 1186, Sibyl used the funeral of her son to have herself crowned queen in her own right. This forestalled a coup by Raymond III of Tripoli. Guy became king as her consort. This action was not popular with the baronage, many of whom refused him homage. After the fall of Jerusalem she was allowed to go to Tripoli. Her husband was released from captivity in 1188. After they were refused admission to Tyre by Conrad of Montferrat they began the siege of Acre, where she died during an epidemic.

TANCRED, REGENT OF ANTIOCH (c. 1075–12 December 1112)

He was a nephew of Bohemond, with whom he shared command of the Norman force from southern Italy. He took Tarsos and Mamistra in September 1097 and played an active role in the sieges of Antioch and Jerusalem. He left his uncle at Antioch and led an Italian–Norman contingent on to Jerusalem. He captured Nazareth as part of the siege of Jerusalem, but when Jerusalem fell he was unable to prevent the massacre of the Muslim refugees in the al-Aqsa mosque whom he had taken under his protection. Godfrey of Bouillon enfeoffed him with Tiberias and Galilee in 1100. The following year he was succeeded as lord of Tiberias by Hugh of St Omer, when he returned to Antioch as regent during Bohemond's captivity (1101–3) and during his later absence in the West (1105–12). He expanded the principality enormously, threatening both Aleppo in the east and Shaizar to the south and occupying much of Cilicia at Byzantine expense. He refused to implement the Treaty of Devol when called upon to do so by Alexios I following Bohemond's death. He was succeeded in the principality of Antioch by his nephew Roger of Salerno. He was not just an able warrior. Ralph of Caen, in the *Gesta Tancredi*, depicted him as a thoughtful crusader racked with guilt for his violent past. In 1100 he founded a Benedictine monastery on Mount Tabor, the site of the Transfiguration, and between 1100 and 1107 he sponsored the rebuilding of the ruined Byzantine Church of the Annunciation at Nazareth.

URBAN II (*c.* 1042–29 July 1099)

Born Odo of Lagery (Eudes of Chatillon), he studied under St Bruno at Rheims and became archdeacon of Auxerre before entering Cluny as a monk in 1070. He became prior there before being summoned to Rome by Gregory VII as cardinal bishop of Ostia in 1078. He served as legate in France and in Germany. He was elected Pope in March 1088. In 1095 he presided at the councils at Piacenza and Clermont, essentially concerned with simony and clerical celibacy. At the former he received a request for help against the Turks from Alexios I and translated this into a call for an armed pilgrimage, thus initiating the crusade movement. His attitude to the Eastern Church was a conciliatory one designed to end the schism between the churches. The death of his legate Adhemar of Le Puy ended this dream, whilst he himself died before he heard of the capture of Jerusalem.

WILLIAM OF BURES, LORD OF TIBERIAS (d. 1147)

He was one of the few Franks mentioned by name by ibn-Munqidh as a principal lord of the Franks and as an amusing travelling companion. He and his brother Godfrey were in the East by 1115. He was in great favour with Baldwin II who granted him the lordship of Tiberias, the largest fief in the Kingdom of Jerusalem, in 1119 when Joscelin of Courtenay vacated it to become count of Edessa. He was constable of the kingdom and regent for the king during his captivity in 1123. From 1127 to 1128 he was in Europe negotiating with Fulk V of Anjou for the hand of Melisende. He founded the Hospital of St Julian at Tiberias, this later passing to the Hospitallers.

WILLIAM II, ARCHBISHOP OF TYRE (*c.* 1130–September 1185)

Born in Palestine, he studied at Paris and Bologna. He returned to the Kingdom of Jerusalem in 1164 and became tutor to the future Baldwin IV. He became chancellor of the kingdom in 1174 and archbishop of Tyre in 1175. He was twice sent as ambassador to Manuel I, and attended the Lateran Council of 1179. He wrote a history of Islam that does not survive. His *Historia rerum in partibus tranmarinis gestsarum*, completed in 1184, has every claim to be the first history of the Kingdom of Jerusalem. The patriarch Heraclius excommunicated him in Holy Week 1184 for unknown reasons. The year of his death is uncertain; the years 1184, 1185 and 1186 have been variously cited, with the date in September gaining the widest acceptance. He is not to be confused with the first Latin archbishop of Tyre, William I (1028–*c.* 1134), an Englishman.

ZENGI/ZANGI/ZANKI/ 'IMAD-AD-DIN ZANGI BIN AQ SONQUR (1085–14 September 1146)

A Seljuk Turk with a reputation for ruthlessness, whose father Aq Sonqur was governor of Aleppo (1086–94) for Malikshah. In 1127 Zengi was appointed governor of Mosul, from whence he set about expanding his territory in Syria and Kurdistan at the expense of Muslim rivals. Almost all his campaigns were directed against Muslims, and he remained on good terms with the Franks as need dictated. His capture of Edessa in 1144 was a by-product of one of these campaigns rather than a deliberate jihad – in this case against the Artuqids who had turned to Joscelin II of Courtenay for support. Nonetheless, thereafter he was seen as the first Muslim ruler to have fought a jihad against the Franks and the originator of the counter-crusade. He was murdered by his own bodyguard in Mosul, and his territory was divided between his two sons – broadly a split between Iraq and Syria.

IV
HISTORIOGRAPHY, OR
WHAT HISTORIANS HAVE
SAID ABOUT THE CRUSADES

The *Historia rerum in partibus transmarinis gestarum* of William II, archbishop of Tyre, completed by 1184, is not just a major primary source for the history of crusading and the crusader states in the twelfth century – it also has every claim to be regarded as their first analytical history. That apart, what might be regarded as general studies of the crusades in the context of modern history began in the late fifteenth century and, like those in the sixteenth and seventeenth centuries, relied heavily on the writings of the archbishop of Tyre. These histories used primary source materials, but they used them selectively to talk of Holy War (*bellum sacrum*), and their emphasis was upon prominent individuals and upon battles and the intrigues of high politics.

For those writing during the Reformation and the Counter-Reformation, the fierce controversies between Protestant and Catholic have to be borne in mind in the models of the crusades that were presented – an evil arm of the papacy or a meritorious and laudable endeavour. All too often their emphasis was upon partisan judgment, if not always upon integrity. Some of the earliest examples of these histories are: Benedetto, Accolti, *De bello a christianis contra barbaros gesto pro Christi sepulcro et Judaica recuperanda* (1461, printed Venice, 1532); B.J. Herold, *De bello sacro* (Basel 1560); Reinier Steinhemius, *Chronicon Hierosolmi-tanum, id est de bello sacro historia* (Helmstadt, 1584); Heinrich Meibomius, *Chronologia ad historiam belli sacri* (Helmstadt, 1584); J. Lipsius, *De cruce* (Antwerp, 1595); A. Mossi, *Breve descrizione dell'aquisto di Terra Santa* (Florence, 1601); and Michele Zappullo, *Historia di Quattro principali citta del mondo, Gerusalemme, Roma, Napoli e Venezia* (Vicenza, 1603).

Western European interest in the crusades in the sixteenth century arose not only from the different perspectives on the development and use of the powers of the papacy but also from a growing awareness of the threat posed by the Ottoman Turks to Christian polities in central Europe and in the wider Mediterranean Sea. Crusading was then just a distant memory and, in the con-text of the Turks and of Barbary corsairs, many felt that something like it should be revived again. Herein lies the origin of Torquato Tasso's epic poem *Gerusale-mme liberata*, published in Ferrara in 1581 and the subject of many pirated editions thereafter. For his information on the First Crusade, Tasso is thought to have used Accolti's work supplemented with the newly available texts (see below), and to have embellished them with numerous sub-plots to suit his literary and religious purposes. Tasso lionised Godfrey of Bouillon as the ideal military leader, and placed him in the forefront of crusading writing for nearly two cen-turies. It is also noteworthy that historians turned their attention to the rise of the Turkish threat itself, as in Richard Knolles' *A General History of the Turks to the Present Year* (London, 1603). Gibbon was to use both these volumes in the writing of his own *History*, but doubted their value in an enlightened age which required from the historian some tincture of philosophy and criticism. His evaluation of these early works is as good today as in 1776.

Thomas Fuller's *The History of the Holy Warre* (1631, 3rd edn 1647, 4th edn 1651) is perhaps the best known of these early histories and fairly representative of them. It is written from a particular religious standpoint, in this case Calvinist. Its content is firmly centred on individual leaders, both Christian and Muslim, and it focuses on battles and high intrigue. Fuller consulted Bongar's edition of crusading documents that had been published in 1611, but used one main source printed therein, William of Tyre, and took his material selectively from that. There is no attempt at synthesis and little in the way of balance; like his fellows Fuller emphasises the triumph of Christianity against its enemies. However, his book does provide a loose chronology of sorts and it does include topics that were later incorporated in the canon of crusader history such as the international military orders, the Northern and the Albigensian crusades. It is noteworthy that neither Fuller nor any of the other early histories use the term 'crusade'.

French scholars led the field in crusading history in the seventeenth century.[1] The first general history of the crusades explicitly to use that word in its title seems to have been *L'Histoire des croisades* by A. de Clermont, which was published in Lyons in 1638.[2] The better known *L'Histoire des Croisades pour la délivrance de la Terre sainte* (Paris, 1675) by the Jesuit Louis Maimbourg (1610–86) is, however, often accorded primacy of place. By the late seventeenth-century usage of the term, 'crusade' was becoming common although by no means exclusive. Although the words *croisade* and *croisad* are occasionally found in French and English in the late sixteenth century it was not until 1750 that the words *croisades, crusades* and *Kreuzzüge* had firmly established themselves in the historical usage of their respective languages. In the latter half of the seventeenth century the expansionist ambitions of Louis XIV inspired both Maimbourg to glorify the Sun King through the Crusades, that he brought up to the Ottoman threat of his own day, and Charles de Fresne du Cange (1610–88) to work up the history of earlier French expansion in the Balkans. He wrote *l'Histoire de l'empire de Constantinople sous les empereurs français jusqu'à la conquête des Turcs* (Paris, 1657), the first serious study of the Fourth Crusade and the Frankish settlements in Greece. He also researched and wrote *Les familles d'Outremer*, which was not published until edited by E.G. Rey in 1869; it provided the genealogies of French settlers in the East following the first crusade. Both books are still of value today. R. Saulger, *Histoire Nouvelle des Anciens Ducs et Autres Souverains de L'Archipel* (Paris, 1699), produced the first serious history of the Franks settled in the Cyclades with marginal notes to his sources.

During the sixteenth and seventeenth centuries editions of some of the western sources for crusading were published for the first time. Robert the Monk's *Bellum Christianum principum, praecipue Gallarum, contra Saracenum, anno salutatis MLXXXXVIII pro terra sancta gestam* (Basel, 1533) and William of Tyre's *Historia belli sacri verisssima* (Basel, 1564) became the most important historical

[1] Sorbonne Exhibition Catalogue, *Byzance Retrouvee, Erudits et Voyageurs Français [xvi–xviii siècles]* (Paris, 2001).
[2] H. Mayer, *Bibliographie zur Geschichte der Kreuzzüge* (Hanover, 1960), No. 1884. I have not been able to locate a copy of de Clermont's history.

sources used in the writing of the history of the Crusades at that time. In a class of its own, and addressing the problems of editing original sources from unpublished manuscripts, is Jacques Bongars' *Gesta Dei per Francos* (2 vols, Hanover, 1611). For the first time all the major western sources for the First Crusade were made available in Volume 1, together with a new edition of William of Tyre, Jacques de Vitry's *Historia hierosolmitana*, and Marino Sanudo's crusading propaganda from the fourteenth century in Volume 2. It took an altogether wider view of crusading than just the First Crusade and was to remain the basis for nineteenth-century editions and the collection of sources. Perhaps the first monumental collection of source material built upon Bongars' work and produced texts of most of the French medieval chroniclers and historians of the Middle Ages, including Suger, Odo of Deuil and Orderic Vitalis, appeared with André and François Duchesne's *Historiae francorum scriptores coactenei, ab ipsius gentis origine ad Philippi IV tempora* ... (5 vols, Paris, 1636–49). Gibbon appears not to have consulted Fuller, but he did make full use of the work of both Bongars and the Duchesne brothers in his own monumental History.

The historians of the eighteenth century were to bring both a critical faculty and a sense of historical integrity to their sources, and with this the use of the footnote. However, writing within the Enlightenment tradition, with its basis in human progress based upon reason, they were to adopt a wholly negative approach to the priest-ridden Byzantine Empire; an approach which was to exercise its baleful influence down to the 1920s, if not later. Equally the Middle Ages were seen as barbarous, fanatical and cruel; the so-called sacred war was now seen as the height of human folly and a barbarian onslaught on Islamic cultures. Examples of such writing are F.M.A. de Voltaire, 'Histoire des Croisades', published in the Paris *Mercure* in 1750 and 1751, and which he later incorporated in *l'Essai sur les moeurs*; Denis Diderot's entry on 'Croisades' in the *Encyclopedie*, Volume 2; Jean Baptiste Mailly, *L'Esprit des Croisades* (4 vols, Dijon, 1780); and Edward Gibbon, *The History of the Decline and Fall of the Roman Empire*, Volume 6 (London, 1788). Voltaire addressed broader issues of the folly and ignorance of mankind, rather than a formal history of the Crusades. Diderot (1713–84), who based his short notice of the Crusades upon Voltaire's work, likewise did not overburden his work with historical details and gave no chronological markers for the Crusades nor any numerical ordering; rather, he implied that they should be studied as a movement and suggested a classification according to their aim – 'soit pour le recouvrement des lieux saints, soit pour l'extirpation de l'heresie et du paganisme'.[3] Gibbon, on the other hand, focused on the clash of religions and cultures involved in the Crusades and which underscored his account of them. As far as I know he was the first to assign numbers to the Crusades, from the First to the Seventh, to see them unequivocally as a movement, and in chapter LXI to attempt a general assessment of the consequences

---

[3] J. Lough and J. Proust, eds, *Diderot, Encyclopedie*, II (Lettres B–C) (Paris, 1976), 523.

of the crusades on both East and West in which violence, fanaticism and folly provide the underlying themes for the view that the Crusades were a failed and flawed endeavour; a view that has continued to hold ground in some quarters to this day. His theme was the Roman Empire and as such he dealt with the first four crusades at some length as germane to his grand work, limiting his comments on the other crusades to aphorisms.

Despite the distaste of the *philosophes* for facts, the work of publishing source materials continued in the eighteenth century. G.D. Mansi's *Sacrorum concili- orum nova et amplissima collectio* (31 vols, Florence and Venice, 1759–98) contained much material on crusading, whilst a number of independent scholars were making reliable texts of Byzantine sources available for the first time. From early in the century the Benedictine community of St Maur conceived an ambitious project for the publication of all the known literary sources for the history of France and of the Latin Orient down to 1500. Dom Martin Bouquet edited the first compilation, *Recueil des historiens des Gaules et de la France* (13 vols, Geneva, 1781), which contained material up to 1060. It was also planned to edit the eastern sources for the history of the Crusades, and the task was entrusted to Dom Berthereau (1732–95) in 1770. The project was interrupted by Berthereau's death and by the Revolutionary and Napoleonic Wars that diverted both attention and resources. The Maurist projects were to be taken forward to completion in the nineteenth century (see pp. 261–3).

Reference works on diplomatic, palaeography and medieval Greek and Latin were also becoming available with Charles du Fresne Du Cange's *Glossarium ad Scriptores Mediae et Infimae Graecitatis* (2 vols, Leiden, 1688) and his *Glossarium ad Scriptores Mediae et Infimae Latinitatis* (6 vols, Basel, 1752). As we have seen, Du Cange and Saulger, influenced by the expansionist policies of Louis XIV, had also produced a work on the Frankish conquest of the Morea after the Fourth Crusade. It is perhaps interesting to note that at the end of the seventeenth century the Fourth Crusade and its aftermath was attracting relatively more attention in scholarly publications than the other crusades. In part this was due to the significance of the Ottoman Empire in European politics and the consequent attraction that the area exerted on intrepid travellers like Bernard Randolph (1671–9), Jacob Spon of Lyons and George Wheler (1675–6), all of whom travelled in Greece in the years indicated and noted Frankish remains where appropriate.[4]

In a century that witnessed the voyages of Bougainville, Cook and Dampier there arose the desire to measure, describe and evaluate the physical remains of antiquity. Some of these accounts were of value to the historians of the Crusades, such as those of Jean Baptiste Bourguignon d'Anville's maps and

---

[4] B. Randolph, *The Present State of the Morea called anciently Peloponnesus* (London, 1680); B. Randolph, *The Present State of the Islands of the Archipelago* (Oxford, 1687; reprinted Athens, 1983); J. Spon, *Voyage d'Italie, de Grèce et du Levant* (Lyons, 1676); G. Wheler, *A Journey into Greece* (London, 1682).

memoirs on Greece and Jerusalem, published in Paris in 1747 and 1757; Carsten Niebuhr's *Description de l'Arabie* (Copenhagen, 1771), and *Voyage en Arabie* (2 vols, Amsterdam, 1776–80); and Dawkins and Woods, drawings of Baalbek and Palmyra (London, 1757) – all of which were cited by Gibbon in his chapters on the Crusades.

The nineteenth-century study of the Crusades was dominated by French and German scholarship, aided by the publication of source material on a monumental scale, building on the work of Bongars and the Maurist Fathers. In the early nineteenth century the political and diplomatic interests of Western European powers began to focus once again on the eastern Mediterranean. The Revolutionary and Napoleonic Wars had seen military action in Egypt and in Acre, together with increasing diplomatic activity in Greece and Albania; all areas directly associated with former crusading activity. Emergent nationalism in Greece, Syria and Egypt led to direct West European involvement in the region, and with it an impetus to know something of its geography, history and ethnography. Two direct results of this involvement were the publications by two men directly involved with diplomatic missions to the Levant: in the 1830s the journals of the travels of William Martin Leake, undertaken in Greece between 1801 and 1805, were published in London,[5] and F.C.H.L. Pouqueville's *Voyage en Morée, à Constantinople, en Albanie et dans plusiers autres parties de L'Empire Ottoman* (3 vols, Paris 1805). Unlike British topographers, who were firmly based in the location of classical sites, Pouqueville went on, in the late 1820s, to produce a study of the French settlements in Greece in his *Mémoire sur les établissements français au Levant depuis l'an 500 jusqu'à la fin du XVIIe siècle.*

As the rationalism of the Enlightenment gave way to Romanticism the Middle Ages were seen in a more positive light, marked by an interest in Catholicism and folklore and seen physically in the so-called Gothic revival. It was ground in which the study of the Crusades flourished. The first half of the century witnessed the work of scholars of prodigious energy and wide interests in the achievements of Buchon, Michaud, Migne and Wilken.

Two general studies of the crusades, F. Wilken, *Geschichte der Kreuzzuge nach morgenlandischen und abendlandischen Berichten* (7 vols, Leipzig, 1807–32) and J.F. Michaud, *Histoire des Croisades* (7 vols, Paris, 1812–22), placed sources – both western and eastern – at the centre of crusading studies, and the scanty nature of the latter became evident and provided an impetus to revive the work of the Maurist Fathers shelved in 1794. Both attempted to evaluate the evidence at their disposal in an impartial light; but both provided a model for Christian West versus the Islamic East, centred the Crusades firmly on the Holy Land and, incidentally, opened the rivalry between French and German historical scholarship in the nineteenth century. Of the two studies Wilken was more judicious in the use of his source material and was the first to use Arabic sources, but

[5] W. Leake, *Travels in the Morea* (3 vols, London, 1830; reprinted Amsterdam, 1968), and *Travels in Northern Greece* (4 vols, London, 1835, reprinted Amsterdam, 1968, and New York, 2003).

Michaud's became the more popular study with an English translation of the body of the text without the sources being published in 1854 by William Robson; an abridgement in one volume for young people by B. Poujoulat was published in Tours in 1883. Both studies reflect the romanticism of their generation; indeed, in 1877 an edition of Michaud illustrated with one hundred prints by the celebrated Gustave Doré was published.[6] Both have long been superseded, but their approach and the interpretative model that they provided were to cast a long shadow.[7] Both provided their readers with source materials; Wilken in the last four volumes of his study and Michaud, perhaps more notably, in the *Bibliotheque des Croisades* (4 vols, Paris, 1829) in which he sought to provide his readers with all the known sources for the Crusades, including the reissue of the work of Bongars and the Duchesne brothers and, in Volume 4, under Wilken's influence, translations from Arabic sources in the French Royal Library. The sources were categorised by their nature and format and represent a major achievement. However, some of the material was abridged and, apart from extracts from Nicetas Choniates, the sources for the Fourth Crusade are largely ignored. This reflected the interests of Michaud, but it also provided an opportunity for another industrious French scholar to fill the gap. This was J.A.C. Buchon who set the study of the Fourth Crusade and its aftermath on something like the footing that the First Crusade had enjoyed over the previous two centuries; the study of Frankish Greece had a platform from which it could expand. His major work was *Collection des chroniques nationals françaises écrites en langue vulgaire du XIIIe au Xvie siècle* (46 vols, Paris, 1826–8), in which he inserted material relevant to the Fourth Crusade and the Latin states in Greece, such as the chronicles of Villehardouin and Clari and the Catalan chronicle of Ramon Muntaner, together with a new and accessible edition of du Cange's history published in 1657. He went on to make contributions of his own to the history of Frankish Greece and its surviving monuments with *Recherches et materiaux pour servir a une histoire de la domination Française . . . dans les Provins démembrés de l'Empire Grec* (Paris, 1840), *Nouvelles Recherches historique sur la Principauté de Morée et ses Hautes Baronnies . . . 1334–1470* (Paris, 1843), *Recherches historiques sur la Principauté franque de Morée et ses hautes baronies . . . de l'an 1205 a l'an 1333* (Paris 1846), and *Atlas de Nouvelles recherches de historiques sur la Principauté Morée . . .* (Paris, n.d. = 1 846).

France in the 1830s and 1840s was engaged in creating a modern *outremer* in North Africa. In this expansionist mood King Louis Philippe (1830–48) sought to celebrate the achievement of French noble families who had a hand in creating the first *outremer* after the First Crusade. In 1839 work began on the Crusader Gallery at Versailles.[8] When it was opened in 1840 some sixty families were commemorated with painted coats of arms and charter evidence. Such was the

[6] R. Gervaso, ed., *Storia delle Crociata illustrata da Gustave Doré* (3 vols, Milan, 1978).
[7] A reprint of Michaud abridged into one volume by Robert Delort was produced in 1970.
[8] C. Constans and J. Richard, *Les Salles des Croisades* (Paris, 2002).

outcry from those families who felt slighted by their omission that the gallery was closed. Following further research and the submission of many forged charters the gallery, now extended to four galleries was reopened in 1843 – this time with 250 families commemorated. Work in the twentieth century has shown that many of these claims were spurious and based upon ingeniously faked documentation, the authenticity of which came to a head in 1989. Nonetheless, it did show the interest and the cherished tradition of French crusading in the mid-nineteenth century and the impetus that it gave to research into the Crusades – in particular to the western settlements in mainland Greece. It is interesting that the accession to the Greek throne of Othon I from the Bavarian Wittlesbach family in 1833 provoked no such interest in the Fourth Crusade amongst German historians; rather it induced more of a concentration upon Greek culture in its classical and Byzantine forms. Reliable texts of Byzantine historians became available, with the so-called Bonn Corpus or *Corpus Scriptorum Historiae Byzantinae* (Bonn, 1828–97) begun by Barthold Georg Niebuhr in 1828.

Increasing specialisation and professionalism marked publication on the Crusades in the latter half of the nineteenth century; besides general studies that had their own particular emphasis on the crusader states or the impact of the Crusades upon Islam, a number of specialised monographs were written that focused upon the architecture of the Crusades, the Kingdom of Jerusalem, and upon a selected crusade or individual crusader. New areas began to be applied to crusading history, especially numismatics, sphragistiks, epigraphy, archaeology, architectural history and geography. In addition, new tools became available with the publication of a variety of archive collections with direct or tangential bearing on the Crusades. This was the most important development of all and its results were and are essential supports to the study of crusading. An early example of a history displaying these characteristics was H. Prutz, *Kulturgeschichte der Kreuzzüge* (Berlin, 1883).

In 1841 the Academie des Inscriptions et Belles-Lettres in Paris revived the Benedictine plan for the publication of all the known sources of the Crusades, and between then and 1906 produced sixteen folio volumes known as *Recueil des Historiens des Croisades* (abbreviated to RHC): *Historiens Occidentaux* (5 vols, Paris, 1844–95), *Lois* (2 vols, Paris, 1841–3), *Historiens Orientaux* (5 vols, Paris, 1872–1906), *Historiens Grecs* (2 vols, Paris, 1875–81), and *Documents Armeniens* (2 vols, Paris, 1869–1906). For the first time major and minor chronicles were available for convenient comparison, detailed introductions provided contexts for the material, and a series of appendices made available related and important texts and chronological tables, especially in the volumes dealing with the laws of the crusader states. For western, Greek and Armenian sources texts were provided, together with a French translation. The Arabic sources presented the most serious problems to the translators who, building on the work of Berthereau, provided extracts and sought to convey the meaning of the texts rather than provide exact translations. Today historians use more accurate editions of many of the texts provided in this monumental collection, but it is by no means surpassed for its encyclopaedic coverage. It took forward the sources published by both Michaud and Wilken, who produced materials that supported their arguments and provided the sources intended as a historical resource for use by future generations. In its chronological coverage of material it extended the current perception of crusading and pointed to the crusade movement continuing into the seventeenth century.

The history of the Crusades is in part a history of those European countries that participated in the movement or were affected by it. As such, the monumental national collections of sources published in the latter part of the nineteenth century almost always had some direct bearing on the Crusades and the Latin Orient. First off the mark was the *Monumenta Germaniae Historica* (MGH), planned as the publication of Die Gesellschaft für Deutschlands altere Geschichtskunde (Society for the Study of Early German History), a private historical society founded in Frankfurt in 1818 and of which Wilken was a founder member. Its first publication appeared in 1826 with Einhard's *Life of Charlemagne*. The series continues today, its longevity due to the size of its task and the nature of its organisation. In 1875 it ceased to be a private learned society but came in part under state control, with a Zentraldirektion based in Berlin. In 1935 it became a Reichinstitut. Since 1949 it has been based in Munich, and since 1963 it has been incorporated and funded by the Bavarian state government. Those chronicles dealing with Conrad III, Frederick I Barbarossa and Frederick II Hohenstaufen are prime sources for relations between the empire, the papacy, and the Holy Land. Its editors established new standards – and high ones at that – for the collation, editing and discussion of manuscripts that have had and continue to have a direct influence on modern scholarship.

Other European countries imitated the German example in the age of nationalism, but their aims were for selective publication rather than attempting the completeness implicit in the German programme. These included the British Rolls Series (1848–1911), the first volume of which was suggestively titled *Monumenta Historica Britannica* (1848), and the Greek *Monumenta Hellenicae Historica* edited by K.N. Sathas (1880–90). Of these latter, the first contained material on Richard I and the Third Crusade and the second a selection of documents on Venetian settlements in Greece after the Fourth Crusade. In the same vein, but this time emphasising the multinational culture of the Habsburg Empire, two Austrian scholars produced reliable editions of select documents from the Venetian archives, then under Habsburg rule, as Volumes 12 and 13 of a series entitled 'Fontes Rerum Austriacarum'. This was G.L.F. Tafel and G.M. Thomas, *Urkunden zur Alteren Handels-und Staatsgeschichte der Republik Venedig* (3 vols, Wien, 1856–7). Following Italian independence, G.M. Thomas went on to collaborate with R. Predelli in the production of *Diplomatarium Veneto-Levantium sive acta et diplomata res Venetas, Graecas atque Levantinas illustrantia, 1300–1451* (2 vols, Venice, 1880–99). Both these works revealed the value of the archives of the Italian city-states for the history of the Crusades and inaugurated a series of records publication still continuing in Italy today.

In 1875 Comte Paul Riant founded the Societé de l'Orient Latin, with offices in Geneva and Paris. This was the first society to be concerned with crusading history, and it brought together fellow researchers from France, Germany and Britain. Its aims were the publication, discussion and dissemination of relevant source materials. The *Archives de l'Orient Latin* (2 vols, Paris, 1881–4) was replaced as the organ of this new society in 1893 by *Revue de l'Orient Latin*, which ceased publication after twelve volumes in 1911 having drawn attention to charter evidence for the Crusades and acted as a first resource for current crusading publications. Riant also published *Exuviae sacrae Constantinopolitanae* (2 vols, Geneva, 1877–8) under the auspices of the Society; it brought together source materials on the Fourth Crusade, especially those concerned with the removal of religious relics from Byzantium to the West.

The nineteenth-century enthusiasm for travel and travel writing brought a rigorous topographical and cultural aspect to the study of crusading. The Palestine Exploration Fund (founded in 1864) sponsored a series of cartographic surveys of Palestine conducted by C.R. Conder, E. Hull and H.H. Kitchener in the 1880s; not only were reliable maps produced but also a series of memoirs on archaeology, geology and place-names. The Fund is, however, most noted for its financing and publication of the Palestine Pilgrims' Text Society Library (13 vols, London, 1890–7). This provided translations of pilgrim journeys, and observations on the geography of the Holy Land and Jerusalem from the fourth to the fourteenth century, and included accounts by Muslim travellers as well as a translation of an Arabic life of Saladin. Other important collections included Titus Tobler and Augustus Molinier, *Itinera hierosolymitana et descriptiones Terrae Sanctae bellis sacris anteriora et latina lingua exarata* (2 vols, Geneva, 1879–85), and H. Michelant and G. Raynaud, *Itineraires a Jerusalem et descriptions de la Terre Sainte* (Geneva, 1885). Both works were published under the auspices of the Societé de l'Orient Latin. More specifically, M.J. de Goeje collected and published the works of Arab geographers in *Bibliotheca Geographarum Arabicorum* (8 vols, Leiden, 1870–94), and topographical material was published by E.G. Rey, *Recherches geographiques et historiques sur la domination des Latins en orient* (Paris, 1877), and by C.R. Conder, *Medieval Topography of Palestine* (London, 1881). R. Röhricht, too, published numerous articles on the topography of Syria in *Zeitschrift des deutschen Palastinavereins* in the years 1887 to 1895, and in 1890 published his *Biblioteca Geographica Palestinae* which catalogued in chronological order all material dealing with the Holy Land written between 333 and 1878. It is still the starting point for research and has been reprinted many times.

The line between historical geography and archaeology is a fine one. Pioneers of archaeological work concerned with crusading sites were Mas-Latrie, Rey, Conder and Gerola. In the main their work was non-excavational fieldwork, locating and identifying sites and employing the new medium of photography. In this last field Gerola excelled, leaving a lasting record of the fortifications of Crete and Rhodes. In particular the monuments of the crusaders in Syria and

Cyprus, their castles and churches, were studied. Count Louis de Mas Latrie made early progress in the use of architecture and inscriptions with his *Monuments français de l'île de Chypre* (Paris, 1850) and *Inscriptions de Chypre et Constantinople* (Paris, 1850). His early work on architecture was amplified and massively extended by Camille Enlart's *L'Art gothique et la Renaissance en Chypre* (Paris, 1899), still a classic for the medieval buildings of the island. E.G. Rey's *Études sur les monuments de l'architecture militaire des croises* (Paris, 1871) laid the foundations for the later work of Deschamps. Best known to Anglophones, but now much criticised for its interpretation, is the work carried out by T.E. Lawrence in 1908, published as *Crusader Castles* (2 vols, London, 1936).

The Crusades were intimately involved with the Church and the papacy. Two collections are of particular note in this respect. The first, a monument to private enterprise and cheap publication, is the *Patrologia Latina* (218 vols, Paris, 1844–55); the second is the *Patrologia Graeca* (166 vols, Paris, 1857–66) of Abbe Jacques-Paul Migne. If not always as accurate as modern editions of many of the texts, the series made available a huge number of texts germane to the Crusades and the idea of crusading. Both series have been recently reissued in print and in electronic forms. The first attempt at ordering papal records and the keeping of a register of papal correspondence dates from the pontificate of Innocent III (1198–1216). The wealth of the papal archives for the medieval historian was previewed in the summaries published by A. Potthast, *Regista Pontificum Romanorum inde ab anoo post Christum natum MCXCVIII ad annum MCCCIV* (2 vols, Berlin, 1875–6). With the opening of the Vatican Archives in 1881 the École Française d'Athènes et de Rome sought to capitalise on this pioneering work and undertook the publication of the registers of the correspondence of the popes of the thirteenth and fourteenth centuries – work that revealed that this period did not so much witness the decline of the Crusades but rather the golden age of crusading. The Bibliotheque des Écoles Française d'Athènes et de Rome (BEFAR) comprised two series: Deuxième Serie, Registres et Lettres des Papes du XIIIe siècle (1884–1960) beginning with Gregory IX (1227–41), and the Troisième Serie, Registres et Lettres des papes du XIVe siècle (1899–). The first series comprised those registers already in print – namely, those of Innocent III published by Migne in *Patrologia Latina*, Volumes 214–17 (Paris, 1855), and now in the process of being superseded by O. Hägender and A. Haidacher of the Austrian Institute in Rome (1968–), and those of Honorius III calendared by P. Pressutti (2 vols, Rome, 1888–95).

The historical studies produced by scholars in the late nineteenth century were both prodigious and professional, making full use of the printed sources available, as well as discovering hitherto untapped sources. Specialisation and concentration on detail were at the forefront and most of the materials then produced, although dated, are still useful – especially with the broadening approach to crusading in the latter part of the twentieth century. The works cited here are selective but representative. Reinhold Röhricht wrote widely on crusading history, both general overviews of the crusade movement and also extensive articles on topography and monographs focusing on the First Crusade and the crusades of the thirteenth century. He was one of the first historians to publish an extensive corpus of articles in which he discussed the sources interpreted in the widest possible terms. His writings are found somewhat indigestible today, but his dedication, productivity, and focus leave all crusading historians in his debt. His contemporary, Gustave Schlumberger, was not just a numismatist and sigillographer, work for which he is perhaps best remembered today, but he was also a prolific writer on crusading history. He wrote some of the early specialised monographs such as *Renaud de Chatillon* (Paris, 1898), *Expédition des 'Almugarves' ou Routiers Catalans en orient, 1302–1311* (Paris, 1902), and *Les campagnes du Roi Amaury Ier . . . en Égypte* (Paris, 1906). He gathered a personal collection and pioneered the study of the seals and coins of the crusader states, defining them in the broadest terms to encompass Greece and Cyprus in addition to the Holy Land. His *Numismatique de l'Orient Latin* (Paris, 1878) is still used today. In a long publishing career he exemplified all the changes that made the late nineteenth century so significant in the development of crusading studies: an inclusive approach to the Crusades, specialised monographs and journal articles, generalisation supported by detailed analysis and a willingness to extend the sources beyond the written record.

Apart from his archaeological contribution to crusading studies, Louis de Mas Latrie laid the foundations of Cypriot studies with his *Historie de l'île de Chypre sous le règne des princes de la maison de Lusignan* (3 vols, Paris, 1852–62). Interest, too, was focused for the first time on the relationship of Byzantium and the Crusades, a development in which Schlumberger too had a hand; A. Thiener and F. Miklosich, eds, *Monumenta spectantia ad unionem ecclesiarum Graecae et Romanae* (Vienna, 1872); F. Miklosich and J. Müller, eds, *Acta et diplomata Graeca medii aevi sacra et profana* (6 vols, Vienna, 1862–90); B.Kugler, *Boemund und Tankred Fürsten von Antiochen* (Tübingen, 1862); C. Neumann, *Griechische Geschichtschrieber und Geschichtsquellen im 12 Jahrhundert* (Leipzig 1888); W. Norden, *Das Papsttum und Byzanz* (Berlin, 1903); and F. Chalandon's *Essai sur le Règne d'Alexis I Comnène* (Paris, 1900). W.B. Stevenson examined for the first time the Crusades as part of the history of the Muslim Near East in the twelfth and thirteenth centuries in his *The Crusaders in the East* (Cambridge, 1907), and Wilhelm Heyd examined commerce and its ramifications in *Geschichte des Levantshandels im Mittelalter* (2 vols, Stuttgart, 1879), better known in the French translation by Furcy Reinaud, *Historie du commerce du Levant au moyen-âge* (2 vols, Paris, 1885–6). Other works concentrated on the First Crusade, all of them appearing with critical evaluations of the sources as a standard feature. Heinrich von Sybil, *Geschichte des ersten Kreuzzugs* (Dusseldorf, 1841) went through three editions by 1900, becoming the model for crusading history, worthy of a pupil of Leopold von Ranke. Its analysis of source material was translated into English by Lady Duff Cooper and published as *The History and Literature of the Crusades* (London, 1861). Other notable studies of the First Crusade include J.F.A. Peyre, *Histoire de la Première croisade* (Paris, 1859); R. Röhricht *Geschichte des ersten Kreuzzüges* (Innsbruck, 1901); T. Wolff, *Die*

Bauernkreuzzüge (Tübingen, 1891); and Heinrich Hagenmeyer, *Peter der Eremite* (Leipzig, 1879), *Der Kreuzzugsbriefe aus dem Jahren 1088–1100* (Innsbruck, 1901), and *Chronologie de la première croisade 1094–1100* (Paris, 1901), which first appeared in serial form in the *Revue de l'Orient latin*, Volumes VI to VIII (1898–1901). Apart from the First Crusade, other individual crusades were the subject of monographs: B. Kugler, *Studien zur Geschichte des zweiten Kreuzzüges* (Stuttgart, 1866); Edward Pears, *The Fall of Constantinople* (London, 1885); Karl Hopf, *Geschichte Griechenlands*, in Ersch-Gruber *Encyklopädie*, Volumes LXXXV–LXXXVI (Leipzig, 1867–8); R. Röhricht, *Studien zur Geschichte des fünften Kreuzzüges* (Innsbruck, 1891), and his *Die Kreuzfahrt Friedrich II* (Berlin, 1872). Kugler's monograph still remains the only monograph on the Second Crusade, whilst the others have all provided springboards for further work in the twentieth century.

The Latin Kingdom of Jerusalem also attracted attention for the first time with the works of Röhricht, *Geschichte des Königreichs Jerusalem* (Innsbruck, 1898), and his edition of all the extant charters of the kingdom in his *Regesta Regni Hierosolymitani* (Innsbruck, 1893–1904); C.R. Conder, *The Latin Kingdom of Jerusalem* (London, 1897); and Hagenmayer's 'Chronologie du royaume de Jerusalem', *Revue de l'Orient latin*, vols IX–XII (1902–11). The international military orders, although not crusaders in the strict sense of the term, were intimately bound up with crusading and they too began to be studied: F.C. Woodhouse, *The Military Religious Orders* (London, 1879); H. Prutz, *Entwicklung und Untergang der Templerherrenordens* (Berlin, 1888); and J. Delaville Le Roulx, *Les Hospitaliers en Terre sainte et à Chypre 1100–1310* (Paris, 1910), and *Les Hospitaliers a Rhodes jusqùa la mort de Philibert de Nailhac, 1310–1421* (Paris, 1913). Less original, but more widely available, was the popular study in English by T.A. Archer and C.L. Kingsford, *The Crusades. The Story of the Latin Kingdom of Jerusalem* (London, 1895); crusading had reached the general educated public with a desire for the facts behind the allusive references to crusades in Walter Scott's novels and Tennyson's *Marmion*.

The late nineteenth century witnessed the publication of works of reference for the public library. The Crusades appeared in a number of encyclopaedia entries firmly anchored in history, but also emphasising the grand crusades as distinct events. Perhaps the first such entry was Philipp Schaft's article in the *Schaff-Herzog Encyclopaedia of Religious Knowledge* (3 vols, New York, 1882–4), followed by those in the *Encyclopaedia Britannica* written by Ernest Barker (1911) and in the *Catholic Encyclopaedia* written by Louis Bréhier (1912), both with excellent bibliographical summaries. All three articles are available on websites today; proof that not all old things are useless. By this time too the first considerable North American historian of the Crusades, Dana C. Munro, had made his mark. The history of crusading in the nineteenth century had belonged to the French and the Germans. By the beginning of the twentieth century crusading had become a distinct and specialised area of study, with a considerable academic infrastructure in the form of monographs, atlases, chronologies and glossaries. This firm foundation was to be amplified and built upon over the next century and was to see the primacy in crusading studies pass to American, British and Israeli historians.

The twentieth century has produced a number of prominent overviews of the Crusades. First in the field was René Grousset, who focused on the Crusades in the Holy Land in his *Histoire des Croisades* (3 vols, Paris, 1934–6) and placed them within a model of French colonial expansion, thereby sparking off a debate on the very existence and nature of medieval colonialism. In the post-colonial period of the 1960s the Israeli historian Joshua Prawer took up this debate. For him the crusader principalities were explicit examples of medieval colonialism. French tastes, traditions and language were imposed on a native culture, resulting in political and legal segregation and in artistic terms the emergence of a Franco-Byzantine style termed 'crusader art'. This view was most forcefully set out in *The Latin Kingdom of Jerusalem: European Colonialism in the Middle Ages* (London, 1972; reprinted as *Crusaders' Kingdom*, London, 2000). The debate engendered by this book moved crusader studies forward, especially in terms of the constitutional history of the Latin Kingdom of Jerusalem from the point where it had been left by John La Monte's study, *Feudal Monarchy in the Latin Kingdom of Jerusalem, 1100–1291* (Cambridge, Mass., 1932). The colonial model has weathered well in political terms. However, during the 1990s art historians, who see the artistic world as showing numerous examples of cultural intersection, have challenged the segregationist approach.

Sir Steven Runciman produced perhaps the most enduring of the general studies with *A History of the Crusades* (3 vols, Cambridge, 1951–4). It is a fundamental study since it set the parameters of debate and future research. It is now a classic work. Its urbane unhurried tone, its polished prose, and its judicious and objective approach not only established the reputation of the English in crusading studies but also provided a gateway to a whole generation of undergraduates. Runciman might be criticised for his reliance on RHC for his Arabic sources and for his pro-Byzantine standpoint, but for many undergraduates, perhaps to the despair of their tutors, it still remains a first port of call despite its half-century. This is a tribute to the robust standards set by Runciman and the enduring appeal of well-written narrative history.

In a consciously analytical vein K.M. Setton oversaw the work of over sixty specialists in *A History of the Crusades* (6 vols, University of Pennsylvania Press, 1955–89), in which a broad view of crusades and crusading was adopted with useful summaries of the state of knowledge at the time each chapter was written. Frequently referred to as 'the Wisconsin History' (from the current publishers) or 'the Pennsylvania History' (after the original one), the work is uneven in parts and at times dated, but it remains the starting point for all aspects of crusading history with fine maps, bibliographies and toponymic details. By twentieth-century standards these three studies rank as being monumental.

Single-volume histories of special merit and influence developed upon and around them. Most notable are H.E. Mayer, *Geschichte der Kreuzzüge* (Stuttgart,

1965, 9th edn 2000; English translation, 2nd edn, Oxford, 1988); C. Morrison, *Que sais-je? Les Croisades* (Paris, 1969); and Jean Richard, *Histoire des Croisades* (Paris, 1996; English translation, Cambridge, 1999). Most of these adopted a traditional view of crusading history, focusing almost entirely on expeditions to liberate or to defend the Holy Land and generally following a chronological sequence.

During the 1970s the pluralist view of crusading developed, concentrating on the papal authorisation of crusade, its preaching and recruitment. This extended studies of the Crusades to all its manifestations, whether they were major expeditions to the East or directed against heretics, political enemies of the Church and the papacy, pagans and peasants. The principal publicist for this view has been Jonathan Riley-Smith in his *What were the Crusades?* (London, 1971; 2nd edn, 2000). The view influenced the later volumes of the Wisconsin History and may be seen expressed most explicitly in N. Housley, *The Later Crusades* (London, 1992); Jonathan Riley-Smith, ed., *The New Oxford Illustrated History of the Crusades* (Oxford, 1995); Michel Balard, *Croisades et Orient Latin* (Paris, 2001); and in the two-volume collection of essays presented to Jonathan Riley-Smith on his sixty-fifth birthday. The wide-ranging scope of these essays accurately reflects the state and concerns of crusading historians in the twenty-first century. Today most crusade historians are pluralists in their approach to the subject.[9] Crusading history forms a part of virtually all history syllabuses in western institutions of Higher Education. It is brought to the wider public by means of television, radio and film. Few people are unaware of the Crusades, and in the current world political climate a proper understanding of them, stripped of partisan nonsense, is more important than it ever has been.

By the beginning of the twentieth century crusading history had crossed many academic disciplines. One of the most significant was the work of Carl Erdmann, which brought crusading into the world of ideas and sought to explain the idea of crusading and the motivation of crusaders (see p. 298). This interdisciplinary approach was to grow, especially from the 1970s onwards. Today crusading history is approached from many standpoints, both theoretical and practical: as a part of the history of medieval western Europe, the Middle East or of Islam, the Baltic or the Aegean, or as part of the disciplines of religious history, economic history, gender history and art history. There has been a plethora of studies examining the ideology of crusading, the crusade experience, their cost and financing, crusading prosopography and genealogy, European approaches towards Muslims and vice versa, ethnicity and gender, assimilation and acculturation, crusade propaganda and criticism, and, of course, the technicalities of crusading warfare. Old evidence has been looked at in a fresh and critical way. Three studies might be singled out here, the first re-examining pilgrimage; the second the economic origins of crusading, the home pressures, lack of

---

[9] M. Bull and N. Honsley, eds, *The Experience of Crusading* (2 vols, Cambridge, 2003).

adaptability and violence of pilgrims, and the application of modern economic theories of industrial organisation and behaviour to the Crusades; and the third, injuries and their surgical treatment in the crusades.[10] Much of this reflects the expanding agenda of history during the twentieth century, the phenomenal range of reference involved with crusading history, and the value of the interdisciplinary approach. Archaeology, too, has added much to the dynamic of crusade settlement and the study of cultural artefacts. All of the major crusades, and some lesser-known ones too, have received modern monographs since the 1980s. These works are all listed in the bibliographical references in Part 7.

By the 1930s crusading studies had become sufficiently distinct and self-conscious for the production of occasional review articles discussing the state of the subject area, together with suggestions for further research, co-operative endeavours and the like. They provided benchmarks for the development of the subject, and were often seen as such by their authors. Book reviews might also fulfil this purpose and came increasingly to do so with the publication of the large general histories of the Crusades, as too did obituary notices by the end of the twentieth century.[11] The students of crusading were taking stock and setting targets in the best traditions of modern academe.

Bibliographical aids with some claim to completeness became available in the latter half of the twentieth century. In particular, Hans Eberhard Meyer produced the *Bibliographie zur Geschichte der Kreuzzüge* (Hanover, 1960), a valuable resource that he sought to supplement in 'Literaturbericht über die Geschichte der Kreuzzüge (1958–67)' in *Historische Zeitschrift*, Sonderheft 3 (1969), 642ff.; and in K. Setton, ed., *A History of the Crusades*, VI (Madison, 1989), 511–664. The amount of new publication, both in paper and online, has made this task of completeness almost impossible, but *The International Medieval Bibliography* produced at the University of Leeds since 1967 and now available in print, on CD-Rom and online, may now be consulted for the development and diversity of crusading studies in the last thirty years. The reviews section in the journal

---

[10] G. Anderson, *et al.*, 'An Economic Interpretation of the Medieval Crusades', *Journal of European Economic History*, 21 (1992), 339–63; M.-L. Favreau-Lilie, 'The German Empire and Palestine: German Pilgrimages to Jerusalem between the 12th and 16th Century', *Journal of Medieval History*, 21 (1995), 321–41; P. Mitchell, *Medicine in the Crusades; Warfare, Wounds and the Medieval Surgeon* (Cambridge, 2004).

[11] T. Boase, 'Recent Developments in Crusading Historiography', *History*, 22 (1937–8), 110–25; J. La Monte, 'Some Problems in Crusading History', *Speculum*, 15 (1942), 57–75; J. Brundage, 'Recent Crusade Historiography: Some Observations and Suggestions', *Catholic Historical Review*, 49 (1964), 493–507; H. Mayer, 'America and the Crusades', *Proceeding of the American Philosophical Society*, 125 (1981), 38–45; G. Constable, 'The Historiography of the Crusades', in A. Laiou and R. Parviz-Mottahedeh, eds, *The Crusades from the Perspective of Byzantium and the Muslim World* (Washington, DC, 2000), 1–22. See also F. Duncalf's review of Grousset, *American Historical Review*, 41 (1935–6), 124–6; H. Mayer's review of Ehrenkreutz, *Speculum*, 49 (1974), 724–7, and the obituaries of Prawer (*Guardian*, 4 May 1990) and Runciman (*Independent*; 2 November 2000).

Crusades that was launched in 2002 by the Society for the Study of the Crusades and the Latin East may supplement this.

Current debates on the future of crusading study focus on the Crusades as part and parcel of Medieval European history, and at the same time on the perceived Eurocentric nature of past work and upon the use and incorporation of the widest range of source materials possible. This last is a direct legacy from the French Annales School that developed from the 1930s onwards. To some extent this bias was inevitable, given that many have seen the Crusades as a defining moment in European history and some as the first step to globalisation. Yet what about the Levant? The excellent study by Carole Hillenbrand, *The Crusades: Islamic Perspectives* (Edinburgh, 1999), shows just what can be done, but there has yet to appear an Islamic academic study of the Crusades. What there is to date follows the western model for crusading studies. This is a source of regret. From the viewpoint of western scholarship, has ignorance of the Arabic language skewed views and perceptions? Is it possible to study the Crusades and the crusading states without knowledge of Arabic and Turkish? The answer to both questions is clearly 'yes', but is it acceptable in an emerging global culture? Currently these are the counsels of perfection as European school curricula squeeze out even knowledge of Greek and Latin and thus endanger the future of medieval studies in general, let alone that of the Crusades.

V
BRIEF BIOGRAPHIES OF CRUSADE HISTORIANS

Except for Accolti, Fuller and Lipsius, most of the authors listed for the sixteenth century and the early seventeenth have scant biographical detail. Thus for Johannes Basileus Herold (1544–67), Reinier Steinheimius (1541–95) and Heinrich Meibomius (1638–1704) there are just their dates of birth and death, and for A. de Clermont, Mossi, Saulger and Zappullo there is not even that.

ACCOLTI, BENEDETTO (1416–66)

Professor of Law at Florence and secretary of the Republic, co-authored with his brother Leonardo the first attempt at a history of the Crusades in 1452; first published in Venice 1532. It was not a particularly historical approach and was concerned almost entirely with the First Crusade and the heroic role of Godfrey of Bouillon. Nonetheless it was very popular and was reprinted as late as 1731. It is said to have been Tasso's main inspiration for *Gerusalemme Liberata* (earliest version 1564).

BARKER, SIR ERNEST (1874–1960)

Oxford philosopher and historian who specialised in political thought and Byzantine social and political theory. His succinct account of the Crusades in the 1911 edition of the *Encyclopaedia Britannica*, and the broad insights expressed there, shows the very real value of crusading history written by Byzantinists.

BONGARS, JACQUES, SEIGNEUR OF BAULDRY AND LA CHESNAYE (1554–1612)

A Huguenot, he studied in Germany and visited Constantinople. He was a classicist who produced two notable translations of Justin (1581) and of the letters of Aristaenetus (1597). From 1581 he was in the service of Henry of Navarre (later Henry IV), serving as a diplomat in England and Germany (1593–1610). On his retirement he brought together for the first time in 1611 the principal western sources of the Crusades in two folio volumes entitled *Gesta Dei per Francos*, a title he borrowed from Guibert of Nogent's twelfth-century chronicle of the First Crusade. The compilation remained influential until the publication of RHC in the nineteenth century, and is still the main working text for Marino Sanudo's *Liber Secretorum Fidelium Crucis* (c. 1318–21).

BRÉHIER, LOUIS (1868–1951)

A distinguished French Byzantinist best known for *Le Monde Byzantin* (3 vols, Paris, 1946–50). He was particularly interested in symbolism in religious art. In 1907 he produced *Les Croisades, L'Eglise et L'Orient au Moyen Age*, which went through five editions by 1928. Five years later, in 1912, he wrote a short overview of the Crusades for *The Catholic Encyclopaedia*. Today the presence of this article on the Internet makes it the first introduction to crusading history for many.

BUCHON, JEAN ALEXANDRE C. (1791–1846)

Known as Alexandre, he was born on 21 May 1791 and was a traveller journalist, prolific editor, and the historian who edited the major chronicles associated with the Fourth Crusade and the Frankish settlements in Greece. His work on Greece, although of immense importance to the study of the area as a whole, was but a small portion of his output which consisted of *Collection des chroniques nationals françaises ecrites en langue vulgaire du XIIIe au XVIe siècles* (46 vols, Paris, 1826–8), *Histoire populaire des Français* (Paris, 1834), *Pantheon Literaire* (38 vols, Paris, 1835–43), journals from his various travels in Ireland, Greece, the Ionian Islands, the Cyclades undertaken at various times between 1820 and 1845. He was instrumental in the preservation of many heraldic carvings unearthed in Chalkis in the 1830s and 1840s; these may still be seen in the museum there. He died on 29 April 1846.

CONDER, CLAUDE REIGNIER (1868–1909)

Conder combined professional soldiering and scholarship. He was the discoverer of the site of ancient Kadesh. As an officer in the Royal Engineers he participated with Kitchener in the survey of western Palestine (1870–88), and combined his topographical and historical skills in the first academic history of the Latin Kingdom of Jerusalem.

DELAVILLE LE ROULX, JOSEPH MARIE ANTOINE (1855–1911)

A prolific writer on crusading whose bibliography reflected the concerns of the late nineteenth century. His work on the Hospitallers built upon that of Bossio and the abbe Vertot in the eighteenth century and set it on a secure historical footing. His major publications were *Cartulaire general de l'ordre des Hospitalers de St-Jean de Jerusalem (1100–1310)* (4 vols, Paris, 1894–1906), *Les Hospitaliers en Terre Sainte et à Chypre (1100–1310)* (Paris, 1904) and *Les Hospitaliers à Rhodes jusqu'a la mort de Philibert de Naillac (1310–1420)* (Paris,1913); all of which bar the first have been superseded in the twentieth century.

DU CANGE, CHARLES DU FRESNE, SIEUR (1610–88)[1]

Born in Amiens, du Cange was a private scholar of wide historical interests who is best known for his *La lexiicographique du latin medievale et ses rapports avec les recherches actuelles sur la civilisation du Moyen-Âge* (Paris, 1678). He wrote under the patronage of Louis XIV and Colbert, and the topics of some of his work may be fitted into this imperial and expansionist ideology. He produced a text and translation of Villehardouin's chronicle and incorporated it in his *Histoire de l'empire de Constantinople sous les empereurs français* (1657). He published texts and translations of the Byzantine historians Kinnamos and Nicetas Akominatos for the Byzantine du Louvre series, and in 1680

---

[1] Jean-Michel Speiser, 'Du Cange and Byzantium', in R., Cormack and E. Jeffreys, eds, *Through the Looking Glass* (Aldershot, 2000), 199–210.

published his *Historia Byzantina*. Much of his work on genealogy and heraldry remained unpublished in his lifetime, most notably *Les familles d'Outremer*, written in 1657 and published by E.G. Rey in 1869 (Paris, Imprimerie imperiale).

ENLART, CAMILLE (1862–1927)[2]

Born in Boulogne, whose museum now houses his private archaeological collection, Enlart was assistant librarian to the École des Beaux Arts (1891), and in 1903 he became curator of the Musée de Sculpture Comparée. His research was based around the influence of French gothic architecture in the eastern Mediterranean and his *L'Art gothique* (1899), based on fieldwork carried out in Cyprus in 1896, is a model of comprehensiveness and thoroughness. Like Schlumberger, he was responsible for introducing cultural history to the study of the Crusades.

ERDMANN, CARL (1898–1945)[3]

As a member of the Prussian Institute in Rome, Erdmann established his reputation as a historian with two works on the papacy in the Iberian Peninsula based on his doctoral research: *Papsturkunden in Portugal* (Berlin, 1927) and *Das Papsttum und Portugal im ersten Jahrhundert der portuguessichen Geschichte* (Berlin, 1928). In 1934 he joined the University of Berlin, but his anti-Nazi views held up his academic career. In the same year he became a staff member (Mitarbeiter) of the Monumenta Germaniae Historica, a post he held until his death. He was one of the most effective and productive members of that formidable body, contributing to some twenty editions of charters and letters, especially those of Henry IV, emperor of Germany (1050–1106). His groundbreaking work, *Die Entstehung des Kreuzzugsgedankens*, was published in 1935. For the first time it focused attention on the evolution of the idea of crusade and the motivation of crusaders. It is still a fundamental book for crusading studies. The so-called Erdmann thesis has set the parameters of debate for seventy years. In 1977 it was translated into English by Marshall Baldwin and Walter Goffart as *The Origin of the Idea of Crusade*. He was conscripted into the German army in September 1943 and served as an interpreter in the Balkans. He died of typhus at Zagreb on 7 May 1945 and was buried in the military cemetery there.

FULLER, THOMAS (1608–61)

Fuller was an English Protestant clergyman and royalist who produced the first English history of the crusades in 1631. His line was strongly anti-Catholic, but

---

[2] Nicola Coldstream, 'Camille Enlart and the Gothic Architecture of Cyprus', in D. Hunt, ed., *Gothic Art and the Renaissance in Cyprus by Camille Enlart* (London, 1987), 1–10.
[3] An appreciation and bibliography of his work is included in Friedrich Baethgen, ed., C. *Erdmann, Forschungen zu politischen Ideenwelt des Frühmittelalters aus dem Nachlass des Verfassers* (Berlin 1951).

he did take a broad view of crusading to include the Albigensian crusade and he did include a very inexact map. His work is more anecdotal than historical, but it does have marginal notes from which it is clear that he used Bongar's edition of western crusade texts. He also published *A History of Cambridge University* (London, 1655) and *Worthies of England* (London, 1662), on which his reputation as a wit is largely based.

GEROLA, GUISEPPE (1877–1938)[4]

On completion of his doctoral studies in medieval history at the University of Freiburg im Breisgau in 1899, Gerola was invited by the Venice Institute to participate with Friedrich Halbherr in the recording of the medieval monuments of Crete, following the Ottoman withdrawal from the island. The work was conducted between 1900 and 1902. To supplement written descriptions of the monuments and transcripts of the inscriptions everything was photographed. The photographic archive is invaluable today in the assessment of the condition of the monuments. Gerola was a fast-working and accurate field archaeologist. In 1911 he was invited to conduct a similar survey of the Dodecanese, newly acquired as a colonial possession by Italy from the Ottomans. His work on Rhodes, conducted in a little over a fortnight, is of enormous value today in the assessment of the state of the monuments. His work shows the value of photography as applied to medieval sites. His later work concentrated on the restoration of Hospitaller monuments in Rhodes city, and from this came an overview of the Italian contribution to military architecture on Rhodes. His photographic archive is in the possession of the Italian Archaeological School in Athens.

GIBBON, EDWARD (1737–94)

Born in Putney, Gibbon spent much of the late 1750s and 1760s, and the late 1780s, in Geneva, Rome and Lausanne. It was during a visit to Rome in 1764 that he conceived the idea for his classic study *History of the Decline and Fall of the Roman Empire*, which appeared in 1776 (Volume I), 1781 (Volumes II–III) and 1788 (Volumes IV–VI). On the death of his father in 1774 Gibbon lived in London, entering into literary society there, and from 1774 to 1782 sitting as a Member of Parliament. His reputation for learning was prodigious in English circles, but his treatment of the early Christian Church and the Byzantine Empire has been subject to severe revisions in the last two centuries.

---

[4] S. Curuni and L. Donati, *Creta Veneziana* (Venice, 1988); G. Gerola, 'I Monumenti mediovali delle tredici Sporadi', *Annuario Scuola Archaeologica Italiana di Athene*, 1 (Athens, 1914).

GROUSSET, RENÉ (1885–1952)[5]

Born Grenoble, and a graduate of the University of Montpelier, where he was the student of Joseph Calmette. After military service in the First World War he became director of the Cernuschi Museum in Paris and curator of its Asiatic art collection. In 1946 he was appointed to the Academie française. His two most important works were *Histoire des Croisades* (3 vols, Paris, 1934–6), which was much criticised in the Anglo-Saxon academic world, and *L'Empire des Steppes* (Paris, 1939).

HAGENMEYER, HEINRICH (1834–1915)

The first major publication on the Crusades written by this German Protestant clergyman and professor at Nancy was *Peter der Eremite. Ein kritischer Beitrag zur Geschichte des ersten Kruezzüges* (Leipzig, 1879). He was concerned with producing critical editions of Latin crusader texts improving upon those made available in RHC. To this end he edited the chronicles of Ekkehard, abbot of Aura (Tubingen, 1877), the Anonymous *Gesta* (Heidelberg, 1890), Walter the Chancellor (Innsbruck, 1896), and Fulcher of Chartres (Heidelberg, 1913). He is best known for his *Chronologie de la première croisade* (Paris, 1901), and for *Die kreuzzugsbriefe aus den Jahren 1088–1100* (Innsbruck, 1901) in which he established the authenticity of various letters from and to crusaders, the texts of which he published for the first time. Both books have been reprinted in the 1970s and both are of use today. In 1897 he exposed the so-called letter of Alexios I to Robert of Flanders as spurious (*Byzantinizsche Zeitschrift* 6).

KREY, AUGUST C. (1887–1961)

An American academic, who in the best tradition of his generation was concerned with the effective teaching of history both in schools and universities. His publications reflect that interest. He is best remembered for his collection of source material in translation for undergraduate students of the First Crusade (Princeton, 1921, reprinted 1958) and for his translation of William of Tyre with Emily Babcock (New York, 1943).

KUGLER, BERNHARD VON (1837–98)

An academic who spent his academic life at Tübingen University. In a series of articles he did early work on crusade letters which was built upon by Hagenmayer, on sources for a biography of Godfrey of Bouillon, and on the Second Crusade. His major works are *Boemund und Tankred, Fürsten von Antiochien. Ein beitrag zur geschichte der Normannen in Syrien* (Tübingen, 1862), *Studien zur zweite Kreuzzüge* (Stuttgart, 1866), and *Albert von Aachen* (Stuttgart, 1885).

---

[5] S. Halperin, ed., *Some Twentieth Century Historians* (Chicago, 1961), 201–25.

LA MONTE, JOHN LIFE (1902–49)

During the 1930s and early 1940s he wrote many articles on the baronage of the Kingdom of Jerusalem and one important monograph on its constitutional history, *The Feudal Monarchy in the Latin Kingdom of Jerusalem* (New York, 1932). His health broke down in the early 1940s, curtailing his scholarly output. Just what was lost to scholarship could be seen at the 1938 meeting of the American Historical Association in Chicago where he set out various avenues for the future of crusading research and publication. All of this is contained in two important review articles on the state and potential for crusading studies. In one he resurrected and publicised the idea of Frederic Duncalf (b. 1882) for a collaborative history of the Crusades by American scholars, this eventually being realised with the multi-volume Pennsylvania/Wisconsin History.[6] In collaboration with Merton Hubert he translated Philip of Novara on Frederick II and the Ibelins (New York, 1936) and Ambroise's account of the Third Crusade in verse (New York, 1941).

LIPSIUS, JUSTUS (1547–1606)

He was a Flemish humanist and classicist who occupied the chairs of History and Philosophy at Jena (1572), of History and Law at Leiden (1578), and of History and Latin at Louvain (1592). He was best known for his editions of Tacitus and Seneca. His work on the Crusades is epigrammatic and moral in tone, and heavily reliant of William of Tyre.

MAIMBOURG, LOUIS (1610–86)

He was a prolific French church historian born at Nancy on 10 January 1610. He entered the Society of Jesus in 1626 and won fame as a preacher and staunch opponent of Protestantism and Jansenism. He was also a trenchant supporter of the Gallican Church, for which he was expelled from the Jesuits in 1682. Louis XIV granted him a pension and he lived the remainder of his life at the abbey of St Victor near Paris. His many books, written from 1673, deal with Arianism, Lutheranism, Iconoclasm and the Eastern Schism. These works, including his *Histoire des Croisades* (Paris, 1675), are beautifully written but have a clear partisan agenda that did not always respect the facts.

MAS-LATRIE, JACQUES MARIE JOSEPH LOUIS COMTE DE (1815–97)

An independent scholar who used archaeology and geography in the service of history, particularly the history of Lusignan Cyprus. Following an article on

---

[6] 'Recent Developments in Crusading Historiography', *History*, 22 (1937–8), 110–25, and 'Some Problems in Crusading History', *Speculum*, 15 (1940), 57–75.

Lusignan coins and seals to be found in the national collections in Paris, 'Un voyage archeologique en Orient' in 1845–46, sponsored by the Ministry of Education, he focused his attention on the gothic (French) monuments of Cyprus. This led to a series of articles on the buildings of Cyprus in general and of Nicosia in particular, Frankish inscriptions in Cyprus and Constantinople and the influence of geography on the history of Cyprus produced between 1847 and 1850. His major work was the *Histoire de l'île de Chypre sous le règne des princes de la maison de Lusignan* (3 vols, Paris, 1852–62). In the tradition of Michaud and Wilken, he followed this up with the publication of hitherto unknown documents dealing with the history of Lusignan Cyprus in articles in the *Bibliotheque de l'École des Chartes* (1871–82), and in particular documents dealing with the Genoese involvement in the island in the *Archives de l'Orient Latin* in 1881. His work, although now superseded, is still consulted by those concerned with the protection of Cypriot heritage; it exercised considerable influence on that of Enlart.

MICHAUD, JOSEPH-FRANÇOIS (1767–1839)

Born in Bourg-en Bresse on 19 June 1767, he was a journalist and historian and a member of the publishing house Michaud Freres. As a royalist he suffered much during the Revolutionary and Napoleonic periods, which he spent in hiding in the Jura. However, he was given permission by Napoleon to consult the Imperial archives in 1811, and with the return of the Bourbons in 1813 and 1815 he became lecteur du Roi and was well-connected within the Parisian literary world. He instituted the *Biographie Universelle Anciens et Modernes* (82 vols, Paris, 1811–62), but it was his history of the Crusades for which he is best remembered. His history emphasised the religious motivation of the First Crusade and stressed its importance in defining western Christendom. He spent the 1820s and 1830s in revising his great work, first by publishing the sources on which his history had been based (1829) and then in visiting the Holy Land 'not to reform the errors of his life but to correct the errors in his history'.[7] As a member of the Academy français (1813) and the Academy of Belles-Lettres (1837), he was prominent as a supporter for the RHC project. He died on 30 September 1839.

MIGNE, ABBÉ JACQUES-PAUL (1800–75)[8]

He was the archetypical self-made man of the mid-nineteenth century, almost a model for the novels of Balzac and Dickens. As a poor priest from the Auvergne ordained in 1824, he appreciated the technological and marketing techniques that could make available large amounts of technical scholarly literature at affordable prices. Although often in trouble with the Catholic authorities in Paris

---

[7] G.P. Gooch, *History and Historians of the Nineteenth Century* (2nd edn, London, 1952), 157–8.
[8] R.H. Bloch, *God's Plagiarist* (Chicago, 1994).

he established a religious publishing empire worth over 3 million francs at the time of his death. He moved to Paris in 1833 and founded the Ateliers catholique, which published ten newspapers and over a thousand volumes of theological literature between 1840 and 1870. He is best known for the Patrologia series that made accessible in 384 volumes many Greek and Latin texts not available elsewhere. The quality of the textual editing is much criticised, but the very scope of the texts that were published makes the works still valuable today.

MILLS, CHARLES (1788–1826)

This English barrister and historian abandoned the law to concentrate upon his historical writing. The results – *The History of Muhammadism* (London, 1817) and *The History of the Crusades* (London 1820) – were some of the earliest serious overviews to be published in English, though lacking in the consideration of the primary sources in Michaud and Wilken.

MUNRO, DANA CARLETON (1866–1933)

Like his near contemporary Krey, Munro was a historian concerned with historical education in the United States. The majority of his writings were textbooks concerned with medieval survey courses. He was much respected as an inspirational teacher. He wrote two principal monographs, *The Speech of Urban II at Clermont* (New York, 1906) and *The Kingdom of the Crusaders* (New York, 1935; reprinted Port Washington, 1966), seen through the press by Krey.

PRAWER, JOSHUA (1927–90)

Born in Bedzin (Poland), he emigrated to Palestine in 1936. He entered the Hebrew University, Jerusalem, as a lecturer in 1947 and became Professor of Medieval History there in 1958. He was the founder and inspirer of Israeli crusading studies, and his many important and controversial books include: *The Latin Kingdom of Jerusalem* (London, 1972), *Crusader Institutions* (Oxford, 1980) and the *History of the Jews in the Latin Kingdom of Jerusalem* (Oxford, 1988). He was interested in the interface of history and archaeology. In 1999 he was honoured by having a street named after him in Jerusalem, one that led to the remains of a crusader village.

PRUTZ, HANS (1843–1928)

This Munich-based historian was the first to publish a cultural history of the Crusades that went beyond the events of the Crusades themselves. He had been involved in excavations at Tyre in the mid-1870s and went on to make serious contributions to the study of the international military orders and the Malta archives. His major contribution in this field was his work on the financial operation of the Hospitallers and the Templars, in which he complemented the work of J. Delaville le Roulx.

REY, EMMANUEL GUILLAUME (b. 1837)

This topographer and historian was concerned with the interface between history and archaeology, and as such reflected the growing contribution of archaeology in crusading studies from the 1870s up to the present day. During the late 1870s Rey was himself involved in fieldwork in Antioch, Acre and Edessa. His writings were concerned with the life in the crusader states and with the families that were established in the lordships of Outremer. This led him to publish du Cange's unpublished work on this subject in 1869. His major works include: *Essai sur la domination franque en Syrie Durant le moyen-âge* (Paris, 1866), *Études sur les monuments de l'architecture des croises en Syrie et dans l'ile de Chypre* (Paris, 1871), *Récherches geographique et historique sur la domination des Latins en Orient* (Paris, 1877), and *Les colonies franques de Syrie au XIIe et XIIe siècles* (Paris, 1883).

RIANT, PAUL EDOUARD DIDIER, COMTE (1836–88)

This private scholar wrote widely on all aspects of the Crusades. It was he who had the vision to found the Societe de l'Orient Latin in 1875. This defined crusading as a distinct subject for study and sowed the seed for a truly international community of scholars engaged in its pursuit. As such his publications reflect the current issues in crusading history at that time, such as the authenticity of crusading letters, charter evidence for the Crusades and the crusader settlements, the spurious letters of Alexios I to Robert of Flanders.[9] He was interested in the transfer of relics to the West after the Fourth Crusade, and in his major work, *Exuviae sacrae Constantinopolitanae* (2 vols, Geneva, 1877–8), he edited a number of lesser accounts of that crusade by Gunther of Pairis and the Anonymous of Halberstadt. His large library was acquired by Harvard University in 1899.[10]

RÖHRICHT, REINHARD (1842–1905)

A teacher in the Luisenstadt Realschule (1870s) and the Humboltgymnasium (1880s), Röhricht's output was prodigious in both book and article form. He wrote overview histories of the Crusades and studies of individual crusades, focusing scholarly attention on the golden age of crusading in the thirteenth

---

[9] 'Inventaire des letters historiques des croisades', *AOL*, 1 (1881); 'Les archives des établissements latins d'Orient, *AOL*, 1 (1881); *Alexii I Comneni Romanorum imperatoris ad Robertum I Flandriae comitem epistola spuria* (Geneva, 1879).

[10] L de German and L. Palain, *Catalogue de la bibliotheque de feu M. le comte Riant* (2 vols, Paris, 1899).

century. His use of pilgrim texts and geographical material was innovative, whilst his edition of the charters of the Latin Kingdom of Jerusalem, for which he is best remembered today, set high technical standards and is still in use and recently reprinted. In may ways this scholar deserves the title of 'father of modern crusade studies'.

RUNCIMAN, JAMES COCHRAN STEVENSON (1903–2000)

Sir Steven was a distinguished British Byzantinist and international scholar, who could claim to be the first and only postgraduate student of J.B. Bury (1861–1927). During his life time he was acclaimed as the greatest living narrative historian. Nowhere is this seen better than in his *History of the Crusades* (3 vols, Cambridge, 1951–4), a fundamental study that set out the parameters for future debate. For him the whole crusading movement was a vast fiasco, and the crusaders compared to the armies of Genghis Khan in their destructiveness. Other books from his considerable list of publications, with special relevance to crusading history were, *The Sicilian Vespers* (Cambridge, 1958), *The Fall of Constantinople, 1453* (Cambridge, 1965), and *Mistra* (London, 1980). All his books are beautifully written and a joy to read. He was knighted in 1958 and paid the compliment of having a street named after him in Mistra. He has left a verbal biography in the 1987 television programme for Channel 4, *Bridge to the East*, and a partial autobiographical memoir, *A Traveller's Alphabet* (London, 1991).

SCHAFF, PHILIPP (1819–93)

Swiss pastor and Church historian who emigrated to the United States in 1864. Here he became involved in Protestant publishing activities on a large scale. He produced an influential encyclopaedia article on crusading that has had amazing longevity due to its use on the web.

SCHLUMBERGER, GUSTAVE (1844–1929)

He was a prolific writer of both books and articles on Byzantine and crusading history.[11] He is celebrated for bringing the material culture of the Byzantine and crusader worlds to the assistance of historians in his two treatises on coins and on seals. His *Numismatique de l'Orient Latin* (Paris, 1878) relied upon verbal descriptions and did not employ any illustrations. It did, however, consider crusading states in both Greece and Cyprus as well as in Syria. *Sigillographie de l'empire byzantin* (Paris, 1884) was sumptuously illustrated and considered the Byzantine influence on crusader seal design. He went on, in a series of studies of

---

[11] A. Blanchet and G. Millet, eds, *Mélanges offerts a M. Gustave Schlumerger a l'occasion du Quatre-Vingtième Anniversaire de sa Naissance* (2 vols, Paris, 1924), I, xvii–xxxi, has a bibliography of Schlumberger's work.

Byzantine emperors, to use objects to illuminate political and administrative history.

SETTON, KENNETH MEYER (1914–2000)

In 1950 he succeeded La Monte at the University of Pennsylvania. He went on to become Professor of History at the Institute for Advance Study, Princeton and the general editor of the collaborative work, *A History of the Crusades* (6 vols, Madison, 1955–89). His own original work, published as *Catalan Domination of Athens, 1311–1388* (1948; revised London, 1975) and *The Papacy and the Levant, 1204–1571* (4 vols, Philadelphia, 1976–84), produced much new material on the later crusades that is still being assimilated.

SMAIL, RAYMOND CHARLES 'OTTO' (1913–86)

He was an outstanding and inspirational Cambridge historian from 1948 until his retirement in 1980. His two main works, *Crusading Warfare* (Cambridge, 1956) and *The Crusaders in Syria and the Holy Land* (London, 1973), were well written, magisterial in approach, and provoked thought on all levels not just on crusading. His study on warfare set the parameters for future debate on the subject.

SYBIL, HEINRICH VON (1817–95)[12]

A pupil of von Ranke and a German nationalist historian, he was the first professor of History at Munich, the department of which he established. His anti-Catholic stance made his position in Bavaria difficult and he moved to a chair at Bonn University. He is best remembered for his considerable work on French and German history in the eighteenth and nineteenth centuries, but his forays into crusading history were profound – especially his source criticism applied to the First and Second crusades, which were thought worthy of publication and imitation in England.

TASSO, TORQUATO (1544–95)

Late Renaissance poet and courtier whose unsettled vagabond life was often troubled by bouts of poor health and mental instability. In *Gerusalemme liberata* he attempted to revive the ancient epic tradition according to the recently rediscovered *Poetics* of Aristotle, anchored in the events of the First Crusade and interspersed with various interludes of courtly love. The poem became the obsession of his life, with parts of it written in the 1560s and, according to his own

---

[12] C. Varentrapp, *Vortrage und Abandlungen von Heinrich von Sybil* (Munich, 1897); Gooch, *History and Historians of the Nineteenth Century*, 131–7.

lights, never finished to perfection. It went through many pirated editions and even became something of a historical source in the eighteenth century, being cited by Gibbon.

WILKEN, FRIEDRICH AUGUST (1777–1840)[13]

A historian and orientalist who was born in Ratzeburg on 23 May 1777. He was well connected with the Prussian royal family, to which he served as a tutor from 1803 to 1809. He was Oberbibliothekar of the Royal Library in Berlin, and from 1817 until his death was Professor of History at the Humboldt University, in which he served as rector, 1821–2. Best known for his history of the Crusades and for his use therein of Arabic and Syriac sources for the first time. This work was seminal and made a difference to the way people viewed the Crusades. His other publications show the range of his interests in East–West relations, which to some extent underpinned his approach to the crusades. These include *Über die verfassung, den Ursprung und die Geschichte der Afghanen* (Berlin, 1818–19), *Über die Partheyen der rennbahn vornehmlich Byzantinischen Kaiserthum* (Berlin, 1827), *Geschichte der Königlichen Bibliothek zu Berlin* (Berlin, 1828), *Über die verhaltnisse der Russen zum Byzantischen Rieche in dem Zeitraum vom neunten bis zum zwölften Jahrhundert* (Berlin, 1829), and *Über die Venetianisch Consulin zu Alexandrien im 15 und 16 Jahrhundert* (Berlin, 1831). He died on 24 December 1840.

[13] Adam Stoll, *Freidrich Wilken* (Berlin, 1896).

VI
CRUSADES, CRUSADING AND
THE CRUSADER STATES

WHAT WAS A CRUSADE?

The term 'crusade' is a modern not a medieval term. Its application as a title for the crusade movement seems to be no earlier than 1638 in Western Europe. Muslim sources did not distinguish between western pilgrims, crusaders, or settlers, labelling them all as Franks (al-Franj). It is only in the twentieth century that the literal term for crusade, al-salibiyyun, enters Arabic historical writing. Interestingly, Arabic, Romance and Germanic words for 'crusade' derive etymologically from their word for 'cross', and thus emphasise the symbol of the cross in crusading activity.[1]

From the days of Gibbon there has been general agreement that the Crusades represented a turning point in European history, defining the nature of European identity and telling us as much about European medieval history as about the history of the Middle East. Until the present century this has led to a Eurocentric approach to crusading history. In the same vein Jewish historians thought that the Crusades exercised a profound influence on Jewish culture in Europe, and since the 1960s have traced the roots of the Holocaust back to the First Crusade.[2] Since the 1960s a debate regarding the unambiguous definition of the term 'crusade' has developed between the so-called traditionalists and the pluralists. The former hold that only those expeditions aimed at the recovery or defence of the Holy Land should be considered crusades, whilst the latter maintain that all expeditions authorised by the papacy with the concomitant crusade privileges, preaching and recruitment should be considered crusades.[3] The first approach privileges place – that is, the Holy Land – as the destination that made a true crusade. The second approach emphasises the procedural and organisational nature of crusading expeditions regardless of their destination. This book is written from a pluralist viewpoint.

Nearly half a century later we need more than ever to anchor crusades into an historical context, since the term is misused and distorted in the media. Today 'crusade' means many things to many people, usually associated with moral or emotive issues. By analogy with the perceived spirit of the medieval crusades, the term has undergone considerable extension in the twentieth century. It has been applied to both individual motivation and, more often, to movements with positive, quite often moral outcomes usually restricted to the confines of one nation – for example, the crusade against drugs, pornography and slavery, or for green issues, family values and widening participation in education and the

---

[1] See A. de Clermont, *Histoire des Croisades* (Paris, 1638); C. Hillenbrand, *The Crusades: Islamic Perspectives* (Edinburgh, 1999), 31.

[2] I. Abrahams, *Jewish Life in the Middle Ages* (London, 1896), 16, 157, 185, 335–8, 424–8; D. Nirenberg, 'The Rhineland Massacres of the Jews in the First Crusade: Memories Medieval and Modern' in G. Althoff, J. Fried and P. Geary, eds, *Medieval Concepts of the Past* (Cambridge, 2002), 279–310.

[3] J. Riley-Smith, *What Were the Crusades?* (London, 1977).

like.[4] Indeed, since 1989 crusades history has been included in the UK National Curriculum for History (Key Stage 3), with the agenda of cultural diversity, religious rights and cultural conflict. In the same vein an EU project for secondary schools across the European community, and extending to those in Turkey, Cyprus, Israel and the Arabic-speaking countries of the Middle East, is co-ordinated by the Graf-Zeppelin-Gymnasium in Friedrichshafen.[5]

From the 1930s the image of a crusader was used as the logo for the *Daily Express* newspapers, with implications of truth and the courage to address the issues of the day. For many this image was their first contact with the crusades. More recently the satirical journal *Private Eye* has adopted the image of the crusader as its banner head; his battered sword and bemused expression still bear the message of a commitment to publish the truth. One of the earliest examples of the term 'crusader' applied to the self-perceived right cause was its use in the early eighteenth century by a group of anti-Habsburg Hungarian nobles who dubbed themselves 'the crusaders' (*kurucz*). Perhaps the best-known modern use of the term 'crusade' was its application by General Dwight D. Eisenhower in the specific context of the allied war effort during the Second World War; campaigns conducted overseas by a group of allies fighting for 'decency, democracy and liberty' against enemies that might reasonably be castigated as evil.[6] The use of the term 'evil' is to make an emotive assessment of prior guilt and provides a powerful negative image of those so described. The perceived nature of the other, the enemy, is important in the definition and function of crusade and counter-crusade. Indeed, on 23 February 1998 Osama Bin Laden used the rhetoric of crusade in his Declaration of the World Islamic Front for Jihad Against the Jews and Crusaders, the latter including the House of Saud.[7] Islamists are not alone in adopting this loose application of crusade to describe any tension or conflict between western and Middle Eastern interests. Once again, as the western media highlights the militancy of Islam, the simplistic model of the inevitable clash between the worlds of the western liberal democracies and of Islam is coming to

---

[4] L. Filler, *The Crusade Against Slavery* (New York, 1960); Z. Yongming, *Anti-Drug Crusades in Twentieth-Century China* (New York, 2000); L. Zurcher, *Citizens for Decency: Antipornography Crusade for Status Defense* (Austen, 1976); J. Noel, *Canada Dry: Temperance Crusades before Confederation* (Toronto, 1995) *inter alia*. What was once a North American usage has now been adopted in the United Kingdom; see W. Keegan, 'The Crusading Chancellor', *The Tablet*, 4 December 2004, 6–9, brings many of these strands together.

[5] P. Kernaghan, *The Crusades: Cultural Conflict*, Cambridge History Programmes, Key Stage 3, (Cambridge, 1993) F. MacDonald, *The Crusades: Teacher Notes* (London, 1992) <http://www.gzg.fn.bw.schule.de/stafer/frank1.htm>

[6] D. D. Eisenhower, *Crusade in Europe* (London, 1948); Herbert Parmet, *Eisenhower and the American Crusades* (New York, 1976).

[7] J. Riley-Smith, 'Islam and the Crusades in History and Imagination, 8 November 1898–11 September 2002', *Crusades*, 2 (2003), 151–68; Channel Five 1.00 p.m. News, 14 March 2004; *The Times* 18 March 2004, T2, 3, and 31 May 2004, 4–5; Islamist website:http//alsaha.fares.net (30 May 2004); N. Ferguson, *Colossus: The Rise and Fall of the American Empire* (London, 2004), 119–20.

the fore. Sadly this value-laden model conceals the fact that Muslims are the principal victims of violence in the Middle East, and that many of these killings are perpetrated by Muslims against other Muslims. It is a perspective that does little to bring about peace and stability in this troubled region of the earth. However, it is a model that has a long pedigree; it may be traced back to Herodotus in the fifth century BCE and continued by the Greek and Roman biographers of Alexander the Great. Gibbon in the eighteenth century, Wilken and Michaud in the nineteenth century and Grousset and Atiya in the twentieth century have applied it to the history of the Crusades.[8]

Crusading and its history certainly do have a significant part in East–West relations, and its perceived legacy may well be more of a hindrance than help.[9] The Crusades were a potent mix of ethnic and religious wars; initially expansive, but in their latter phase defensive, the longer the movement persisted the more potent was the religious symbolism attached to it. In the post-colonial period, and especially since the rise of the Islamist movement in the 1980s, the Crusades have come to be seen as an instrument of imperialist oppression. On 12 March 2000 Pope John Paul II (1978–2005) issued an official apology, couched in general terms, for all sins in the service of truth, including sins against Jews, Muslims and minorities. The Crusades were not specifically mentioned, only by implication, since it would have been inappropriate for a pope to criticise the actions of his predecessors who lived in times when human rights and personal religious freedom were unknown concepts.[10] Building bridges is generally a laudable activity, but these are not the materials to use. The crusaders acted under the conditions of their own time, and their deeds and motives were never black and white. However misguided and anachronistic this process of 'truth and reconciliation' may be thought to be, it does show how emotive the Crusades are today in one of the world's flashpoints. It is certainly fertile ground for liberal Catholics at one end of the spectrum and for the publicists of both western and Islamic fundamentalists at the other. All of this distorts history. Little of it is helpful in the historical consideration of what constituted a crusade, but it does serve to highlight how relevant crusading history is today and how important is an understanding of those ideas and events if we are to avert what Samuel P. Huntington predicts as a clash of civilisations as a scenario for global conflict.[11]

The medieval terminology for 'crusade' and 'crusaders' in both Latin and French was neither precise nor consistent. A crusade was often seen as a

---

[8] E. Said, *Covering Islam* (London, 1981; reprinted 1997), xi–xxxiii, 36–68; A. Atiya, *Crusade, Commerce and Culture* (Oxford, 1962), 17–91.

[9] J. Phillips, 'Why a Crusade will Lead to a Jihad', *Independent*, 18 September, 2001.

[10] L. Accatoli, *When A Pope Asks Forgiveness* (New York, 1998), <http://biblia.com/islam/crusades.htm>

[11] S. Huntington, *The Clash of Civilizations and the Remaking of World Order* (New York, 1996); see E. Qureshi and M. Sells, eds, *The New Crusades: Constructing the Muslim Enemy* (New York, 2003), 1–47 and *passim*, for a discussion of the clash-of-civilisations hypothesis and its impact on US foreign policy makers.

pilgrimage, an *iter* or *peregrinatio*, and its participants as *peregrini*. This latter term was used frequently up to and during the Fourth Crusade, when the term *crucesignati* also seems to have become common. The more vague expressions of a passage or general passage (*passagium generale*), an expedition of the cross (*expeditio crucis*), or the business of Jesus Christ (*negotium Jhesu Christi*) were also much used in papal letters and amongst chroniclers of the Crusades. During the late thirteenth century – especially during the pontificate of Gregory X (1271–6) – *passagium generale* came to distinguish a major expedition from a *passagium particulare*, an altogether smaller enterprise with a limited aim, usually an advance party to prepare the way for a *passagium generale*. 'Holy war' (*Bellum sacrum* or *guerre sainte*) became a popular term that held the field until well into the seventeenth century amongst commentators who could perceive the various crusading campaigns as a movement with certain common characteristics. By the late twelfth century, and increasingly during the thirteenth century in the pages of Monstrelet, Villehardouin and Joinville, vernacular expressions like *croiserie* and *croisement* (crusade), *croize* and *croisse* (crusader), *firent croise* (make crusaders), and *se croizer* (to take the cross) enter the vocabulary; yet as late as 1375 Philippe de Mezieres (1327–1405), the chancellor of Cyprus, referred to crusade as '*la sainte passage*'.[12] Just as the language of crusade took a long time to develop so did the concept of crusading. The concept of crusade was not fully developed in the mind of Urban II in 1095. It was to evolve and develop in the following centuries. Certainly by the thirteenth century contemporaries knew what a crusade and a crusader was; they were people engaged in a holy activity sanctioned by the Pope and marked with a cross as a public symbol of their obligations.

This lack of crusade terminology for at least the first century of the crusade movement is undeniable, and its absence has affronted modern sensibilities with their need to empathise with the common man and not to privilege statements by popes and canon lawyers. The absence of verbal images of a crusade amongst participants has led Christopher Tyerman in his radical and thought-provoking study, *The Invention of the Crusades* (London, 1998), to question the existence of crusading as such in the twelfth century and certainly the First Crusade as the precursor of a movement. If contemporaries had no word for 'crusade' how could they possess, let alone explain, the concept? Canon lawyers laid out the criteria for crusading in the thirteenth century when crusading had reached its most diverse range of expression. According to Tyerman generations of crusade historians have employed these criteria to classify one war as a crusade and another as just a holy war. Is this wrong? Popes and canon lawyers indulged in it, and contemporaries did seem able to distinguish in their scale of values between

---

[12] A. Greimas, *Dictionnaire de l'ancien français* (2nd edn Paris, 1992); L. Stone, W. Rothwell and T. Reid, eds, *Anglo-Norman Dictionary*, Fascicle 2 (London, 1981); G. Coopland, ed., *Philippe de Mezieres, Le Songe du Vieil Pelerin* (2 vols, Cambridge, 1969), I, 250, amongst many other references.

campaigns against the Muslims in Sicily and Spain and campaigns in the Holy Land. Contemporaries, Tyerman argues, saw only holy wars in the tradition of other proposals and campaigns in the eleventh century. Yet the response to Urban's appeal reached all economic groups in society, and the response was much greater numerically and much broader socially and in gender terms than that of previous holy wars in the eleventh century. One effect of Tyerman's thesis would be to downgrade the revolution of the First Crusade and to elevate the holy wars of the eleventh century from 'proto-crusades' to crusades, and although at first sight this might remove an ugly adjective from crusade text-books it would also have the effect of undervaluing the very real response and assessment of the First Crusade by contemporaries. It is perhaps to expect too much that in the early days of crusading emphasis should have been placed on distinguishing pilgrimage from crusade, when the former was central to the latter and so perceived by contemporaries. The introspections of eleventh-century men and women have left few records, but we do have a record of their actions and responses to Urban's appeal of 1095, and of what they went on to endure and to achieve. Did they do this for nothing other than another holy war on a par with the Hastings campaign of 1066? This is a question we must ask ourselves. As we shall see there was a discernible difference in the preaching of a holy war as a commendable act and the preaching of the first Spanish crusade in 1123 (see p. 206). The deliberate borrowings of Pope Calixtus II from Urban's appeal of 1095 would suggest that he saw the significance of what Urban had set in train and sought to emulate it. Perhaps the place that the First Crusade has on under-graduate syllabuses, based on the traditional evaluation of it as a blueprint for later crusading campaigns, is not so far amiss. If verbal images of crusade in the twelfth century are lacking the artistic image of the crusader, the *miles Christi*, certainly spoke to some. In our multicultural society should all Christian holy wars be classed as crusades, including those fought by the East Roman Empire, or should we persist with the by now traditional classification? More recently, in what traditionalists would see as a loose use of terminology, the Byzantine emperor Heraklios (610–41) has been dubbed as the first crusader. This is unhelpful and stems from the post-modernist perspective that everything is rela-tive and ultimately everything means nothing. The debate continues, and just like the motivation of crusaders (see pp. 317–18) is a question that must be confronted by all students of crusading and resolved to their own satisfaction.

Today we see no war as holy.[13] Yet from the Council of Clermont in 1095 crusading was advertised as a particular form of holy war, with appropriate rewards for the participants – especially the casualties. A holy war was not the same operation as a just war, but it had to have all the attributes of such a war; it had to be a just war, but one that was religiously and theologically orientated around the perceived division of existence into the *civitas divina* and *civitas*

---

[13] This was the theme of the exhibition *Die Kreuzzüge* in Mainz, 2 April to 30 July 2004.

terrena.[14] It was sanctioned by God, and here the ideas and perceptions of the moment became linked to signs of God's will in terms of natural and supernatural occurrences and, of course, victory. To the victors belong not only the spoils but also the holy war, the just war. This is evident in the accounts of the First Crusade after its unlooked-for success in reaching and capturing Jerusalem in 1099. At the planning stage, however, the ideas of St Augustine of Hippo (354–430) were brought into play.

Ostensibly Christianity was a pacific religion, and many – like the canon lawyer Gratian – continued to think so in the twelfth century; it had been so publicised up until its recognition and reception into the Roman Empire during the fourth century BCE. References to war in the New Testament are very few compared to those in the Old Testament, and their message is equivocal. With the recognition of Christianity and its sponsorship by the Roman emperors the stance of Christian apologists like Ambrose and Augustine had to accommodate wars in defence of imperial territory and the role of the Christian as soldier rather than pacifist. Augustine was by far the most influential writer in this respect. In *The City of God* (*De civitate Dei*), and in his numerous tracts against the Manichaeans and the Donatists, Augustine argued that war was sometimes the lesser of two evils and could be both legal and justified if it were fought under strictly controlled conditions. These conditions may be summarised as a just cause, leading to declaration by a legitimate authority, and finally it must be waged with right intention, which is without breach of Christian ideas of love and charity. Augustine's arguments clearly played a significant part in the thinking of Urban II as he made his way to Clermont in the late summer and autumn of 1095. It was not, however, the first time that they had been used. Isidore of Seville had summarised the first two criteria in a sentence which was enshrined in canon law: 'That war is lawful and just which is waged upon command in order to recover property or to repel attack'.

Popes Urban II (1088–99) and Eugenius III (1145–53), who declared the First and the Second crusades respectively, placed the papacy at the centre of the new movement and were instrumental in defining it. Their successor Innocent III (1198–1216) felt the need to reassert the role of the papacy at the centre of crusade planning, logistics and leadership after the debacle of the Fourth Crusade. Other popes, such as Urban IV, John XXII and Pius II, also felt the need to reassert the papal position at the heart of crusading. The appeal of Pope Urban II made at Clermont on 28 November 1095 drew on the passion-rousing idea of the evil enemy by denigrating the "pagans", barbarians, and strange race from 'Persia' who had killed, raped, robbed and abused the Christians of the East. The Christian faithful were to right these evil deeds, but the idea of recovering the patrimony of Christ by war seems to have developed during the First Crusade

---

[14] J.T. Johnson, *The Holy War Idea in Western and Islamic Traditions* (Penn State, 1979), 29–76; T.P. Murphy, ed., *The Holy War* (Columbus, 1976); and F.H. Russell, *The Just War in the Middle Ages* (Cambridge, 1975), 16–39.

itself. By publicly taking the penitential vow of the pilgrim and by marching to Jerusalem they were to succour their eastern brothers and recover Jerusalem into Christian hands. The ideas of penitence and violence, pilgrimage and military expedition had been linked together in a new and appealing concept that was to become known as crusade. In return for their vows the crusaders were to receive protection for their families and their interests while they were absent; most important of all they were to get full remission of their sins in return for their participation in the expedition. This, at least, seems to have been what crusaders themselves understood. On occasion they wrote of their dead comrades as enjoying Paradise or glorying in eternal life.[15] Urban, for his part, seems to have offered commutation of penance rather than remission of sins. Already, within months of Clermont, crusading had developed as an idea and this sort of organic development was to be a feature of the crusading movement. The essential elements were to remain papal authorisation, the crusader's vow and the granting of indulgence.

After the success of the First Crusade western commentators wrote up Pope Urban's words in terms of a defining moment of western history. Despite the hindsight of their evaluations there is no doubt that Urban's words spoke to the ideas and concerns of his audience, and the response that it produced showed that people in the West were willing and able to conceptualise and to mount such a great undertaking. Whatever might be judged about the greed and violence of individual crusaders their motivation and focus was not in doubt. The exact words that Urban used are unknown to us and probably will remain so. However, the sense of his appeal has come down to us in five reports, three of which were those of eyewitnesses, which are discussed below. A start date for the expedition was fixed for August 1096. Leadership was to rest in the hands of Adhemar, bishop of Le Puys, as papal legate, and Raymond IV of St Gilles, count of Toulouse, for military matters. Thus far, then, we have papal proclamation of a holy war, papal leadership implicit in the appointment of a legate, pilgrim vows taken by participants who receive a cloth cross as a mark of their status, and vaguely defined indulgences for the next world, together with some legal safeguards in this. The costs were to be borne by the participants themselves, and the object of the journey was Jerusalem.

The next development in crusading ideology was the issue of a papal letter proclaiming a crusade with written, and therefore defined, crusading privileges. It was addressed to the metropolitans of a given area and through them authorised the preaching of a crusade in the name of the Pope. The first of such encyclical letters to summon a crusade seems to have been those issued by Pope Calixtus II in April 1123 calling for crusades to both Spain and the Holy Land.[16] However, it is the encyclical letter *Quantum predecessors*, issued by Pope Eugenius III on 1 December 1145 (reissued on 1 March 1146), that was the first crusade encyclical

---

[15] I.S. Robinson, *The Papacy, 1073–1198: Continuity and Change* (Cambridge, 1990), 344–5.

[16] J. Riley-Smith, *The Crusades: A Short History* (London, 1987), 91–2.

to set out clearly and unequivocally the indulgences to be enjoyed by crusaders in full (see pp. 294–5). Death on crusade was equated to martyrdom and guaranteed direct entry to paradise; a guideline for the comportment and behaviour of crusaders was also offered. The provisions were broadly similar to those made by Urban fifty years before; however, they conceded the general interpretation of those earlier provisions and tightly defined them. Eugenius' appeal was in response to the fall of Edessa to the forces of Zengi on 24 December 1144. This was to be the first of many such letters in the twelfth and thirteenth centuries to proclaim a crusade. The relationship of Eugenius' original encyclical and the plans of Louis VII of France's for an expedition to the Holy Land (a crusade?), that had been announced at the Christmas court at Bourges in 1145, is unclear. However, with the advice and support of Bernard of Clairvaux the reissue of the encyclical gave papal backing to Louis' plans, authorised Bernard to preach the crusade north of the Alps and firmly established the idea that all expeditions claiming to be crusades – no matter who had envisaged them – had to have papal authorisation and approval to proceed. Within fifty years of Urban's appeal at Clermont papal backing and leadership of crusading was firmly established and the manner in which crusades were declared or approved by encyclical letter laid down. Crusading was emerging as a papal instrument for intervention in the secular political world, but so far it had been concerned with matters in the East, with the liberation and defence of the Holy Land.

The question of how a crusade, an expedition called and willed by God, could fail in the military sense vexed preachers and theologians after the unlooked-for success of the First Crusade and certainly invited comparisons. Priestly logic put a Christian gloss on disaster and turned to the books of Joshua and Judges, where the moral standing of the warrior was linked to success in the conquest of the Promised Land.[17] People could not make proper sense of military failure upon military failure unless such failure was linked to divine anger or divine displeasure at accumulated sin. The relevance of the two biblical texts to crusading was obvious, and success seemed to be linked to the moral standing of a crusader before his maker. Penitential attitudes and awareness of sin remained strong well into the thirteenth century. However, from the outset of the thirteenth century the scope of crusading was extended to the perceived enemies of the Church within Europe. This was to result in a plethora of smaller crusades with limited goals, easier to organise and direct than the major expeditions to the East.

Success of some sort was generally achieved and the campaigns seen in a more pragmatic political way. The *passagium particulare*, a small expedition of professional warriors with discrete goals, was used increasingly to combat the growing Turkish threat in the Aegean. By the mid-thirteenth century crusading itself, together with the devastating advent of the Mongols in eastern Europe and the

---

[17]   W. Cook and R. Herzman, *The Medieval World View* (2nd edn, Oxford, 2004), 5.

travels and reports of the Franciscan emissaries into Asia, had brought Europeans into contact with the wider world and given them an awareness that there were more religious practices than just the polarity between Christians and Muslims. Outside of the Iberian Peninsula the chivalry and manners of the Muslims came to be written of with some respect and an attempt made at understanding them. Brutality shown to those who had not experienced the word of the Christian God came to be questioned, most notably in the poems of Wolfram von Eschenbach in the decades before 1220 and in the missionary agendas of St Francis and Raymond Lull. As crusading moved its objectives (or had them moved by events) from the liberation and defence of the Holy Land to the liberation and defence of Europe itself, so crusades called in defence of Christendom became more strategic in their approach but still pan-European in their appeal. The moral standing of the warrior had been subsumed in the knightly ethics of chivalry. The Christian knight was *ipso facto* moral and upright, and what there was of moral laxity applied to the inhabitants of Europe as a whole.

Can we consider as crusades those directed at heretics, pagans and individual enemies of the popes, or was it the connection with Jerusalem that distinguished crusades from other forms of warfare organised by the Church? Diderot answered an unequivocal affirmative in his *Encyclopédie* article of 1751, and Fuller had given very brief notice of the Albigensian crusade in 1631; later commentators, however, especially in the influential and widespread encyclopaedia articles of the period 1895–1912, suggested that the Crusades were directed at the liberation of the Holy Land and could be fitted into the period 1095 to 1291, with crusades like the Fourth Crusade, the Albigensian crusade and the Italian crusades of the fourteenth century interpreted as deviations from the norm. The debate over the definition of 'crusade' came to the fore in the 1970s and 1980s, in part in response to Mayer's appeal and his own preference for a narrow definition focused on the Holy Land. In his influential book *What were the Crusades?* Jonathan Riley-Smith took a broad or pluralist view of crusading. He demonstrated that to the papal *Curia*, and to those crusaders in the thirteenth century who took advantage of the practice of commutation to change the terms of their vow from help to the Holy Land to participation in a European campaign, the expeditions to Spain, the Baltic and against heretics and schismatics – and even against lay powers – were regarded as essentially the same as crusades to Jerusalem. His work has been expanded upon with detailed investigation of the criticism of crusading and the political crusades in Italy.[18] Campaigns against the enemies of the faith, whether Muslims, heretics or schismatics, were seen as legitimate crusades by popes and canonists – and this as early as 1130.

---

[18] H. Mayer, *The Crusades* (Oxford, 1972, 2nd edn 1988), 312, n. 108; Riley-Smith, *What Were the Crusades?*, 14, 24–33; J. Riley-Smith, *The Oxford Illustrated History of the Crusades* (Oxford, 1995), 4–12; E. Siberry, *Criticism of Crusading 1095–1274* (Oxford, 1985); N. Housley, in P. Edbury, *Crusade and Settlement* (Cardiff, 1985), 17–36. See also, The First Political Crusade 1135?, p. 167, this volume.

This broader view of crusading has now become the norm. In the ninth edition of *Die Kreuzzuge*, Professor Mayer has adopted this view too, devoting over fifty pages to Frankish Greece, Cyprus and the crusades of Louis IX.[19] Along with this broad view of crusading came the realisation that crusade was a continuous process and was not just confined to the nine numbered crusades of Edward Gibbon; rather, it was also applicable to groups going to Spain or the Holy Land at other times, but still in response to a papal appeal – thus the crusade of 1101. Crusading did not end in 1291 with the extinction of the crusader states in Syria but continued, with publicists for crusading writing in the late sixteenth century. Just when the last crusade took place is a matter of opinion with, as we have seen, many candidates in the twentieth century that claimed to have direct links with what had gone before.

THE IDEA OF CRUSADE

The historic origins of the Crusades are complex and still ill-understood.[20] To attempt to understand them involves some knowledge of the social and economic development of western Europe in the eleventh century that made long-distance campaigning both able to be envisaged and possible, of the religious reform that placed the papacy at the centre of political life and promoted ideas of a personal relationship with God through a heightened awareness of sin and the need for penitence, and finally that brought about the ability to engage in long-distance travel for large numbers of people either as pilgrims to Compostela, Jerusalem and Rome or as crusaders and mercenaries to Spain, Italy and the East. In all this there was an increasing confidence and certainty in many western Christians, tantamount to awareness that the individual could make a difference. With hindsight, contemporaries saw Urban's appeal at Clermont as the beginning of the crusade movement. Today we follow them in this evaluation. What Urban actually said at Clermont doesn't survive; there are only garbled accounts from memory written down after the unlooked-for success of the First Crusade. It cannot be said with any certainty whether Urban asked for military aid for Byzantium, the liberation of Jerusalem, or for both objectives. Ultimately what it was believed that he said became more important than what he actually said. It was a movement originating in western Christendom in the eleventh century, a

---

[19] H. Mayer, *Geschichte der Kreuzzuge* (9th edn, Stuttgart, 2000), 172–88, 210–38, compared to just four pages in the 1965 edition.

[20] The fundamental study that has directed debate since its publication in 1935 is C. Erdmann, *The Origins of the Idea of Crusade* (1935; Princeton, 1977); J. Gilchrist, 'The Erdmann Thesis and the Canon Law, 1083–1114' in P. Edbury, ed., *Crusade and Settlement* (Cardiff, 1985), 37–45. P. Alphandéry and A. Dupront, *La Chrétienté et L'Idée de Croisade* (2 vols, Paris, 1954–9), has focused on the theological developments, and J.A. Brundage, *Medieval Canon Law and the Crusader* (London, 1969), on the legal side. Jean Flori, *La Guerre saint, La formation de l'idée de croisade dans l'Occident chrétien* (Paris, 2001), gives a modern overview with an excellent bibliography.

movement with the Pope at its heart and one whose broad appeal and enthusiastic uptake surprised Pope Urban II.

Byzantium was central to the crusading movement. It had been the first Christian adversary of Islam and had maintained this stance by war and diplomacy over many centuries, beginning in the seventh century. Muslim perceptions of Byzantines were to profoundly influence their later relationships with the crusader states. Byzantine support and understanding of crusade were essential to success. The appeal for help by Alexios I at Piacenza in March 1095 might be argued to have prompted Urban to preach the crusade in the first place. Yet, although there were striking parallels between Byzantine and western holy war and the imposition of penance on troops who had shed blood, the idea of crusade originated in Latin Christendom. This combination of pilgrimage, penance and holy war was alien to Byzantine thinking, as indeed was the very concept of killing being enjoined by a priest. Since the seventh century the Byzantine army had fought wars with the Persians, Muslims, Avars and Slavs in defence of the God-protected empire. The silver *nomisma hexagrammon* (double *miliaresion*) was first coined in 615, at a time when the empire was almost prostrate before Persia, and bore the invocation 'God help the Romans (*Deus adiuta Romanis*)'.[21] The special relationship of empire and God permeated all aspects of Byzantine life, including war. If all wars fought in defence of the empire might be regarded as holy wars in a general sense, the soldiers who were killed on these campaigns were not looked upon as martyrs. Certainly there was the case of the sixty martyrs of Gaza, a Byzantine garrison killed in the aftermath of the fall of Jerusalem to the Muslims in 636; but these seem to have stood in isolation.[22] Indeed, the attempts of Nikephoros II Phokas (963–9) to persuade his patriarch to grant the martyr's crown to his troops killed on campaign got nowhere. It was also the case that St Basil of Caesarea (330–79) had urged soldiers who had killed whilst campaigning to abstain from full participation in the Liturgy for three years. This remained intrinsic to Byzantine perceptions of defensive wars: necessary but regrettable.[23] During the ninth and tenth centuries, with Byzantine recovery in Cilicia, Cyprus, Crete and Thrace, the military saints became a popular theme for religious art and a reaffirmation of divine assistance in imperial warfare.[24] The astonishingly successful campaign that Heraklios mounted against the Persians from 626 to 629, resulting in the return of the True Cross to Jerusalem in 630,

---

[21] W. Wroth, *Catalogue of Imperial Byzantine Coins in the British Museum*, I (London, 1908), 195, plate XXIII, 19–21, contrasting with the *Victoria Augg* of the gold coinage.

[22] H. Delahaye, 'Passio sanctorum sexaginta martyrum', *Analecta Bollandiana*, 23 (1904), 289–307; J. Pargoire, 'Les LX soldats martyrs de Gaza', *Echos d'Orient*, 8 (1905), 40–3.

[23] J. Harris, *Byzantium and the Crusades* (London, 2003), 102–3, for the examples cited; J. Chrysotomides, 'Byzantine Concepts of War and Peace', in A. Hartmann and B. Heuser eds, *War, Peace and World Orders in European History* (London, 2001), 91–101; G. Dennis, 'Defenders of the Christian People: Holy War in Byzantium', in A. Laiou and R. Parviz-Mottahedeh, eds, *The Crusades from the Perspective of Byzantium and the Muslim World* (Washington, DC, 2001), 31–9.

[24] C. Walter, *The Warrior Saints in Byzantine Art and Tradition* (Aldershot, 2003).

was financed by massive loans from the Church, and may have been seen in terms of the confrontation of David and Goliath if one interpretation of a set of silver plates in the Metropolitan Museum of New York is correct.[25] These anecdotes suggest that there was something of the holy war about all Byzantine military operations, but that those singled out for particular mention for whatever reason were viewed within a traditional biblical framework.

Disaster was shortly to return as the weakened Byzantine and Persian empires lost territory in the Near East to the emergent Muslim forces from Arabia. The Greek inhabitants of the empire saw themselves as Romaioi and, in biblical terms, as the new Chosen People of God. As Walter has pointed out, this role as the new Israelites precluded discussion of the morality of war and the nature of just war so prevalent in the West. Their defeats at the hands of Islam from the seventh to ninth centuries, and in particular the loss of Egypt and Syria in the years 636 to 642, were explained in terms of God's anger with the Chosen People. Whittow has pointed out the link between military disasters and liturgical change in Constantinople as a means of making the empire pleasing to God.[26] A very similar problem was to face Latin theologians – both those on crusade faced with difficult tactics and those at home faced with explaining the military failure of crusades. The Byzantine Empire had continued the military traditions of the Late Roman Empire and used a professional full- and part-time army. In the eleventh century mercenary forces had replaced that professional force of native recruits. Some of these mercenaries came from Scandinavia, England and Normandy, yet none of these international warriors seem to have been regarded as holy warriors, let alone crusaders, either in the East or in their homelands. Alexios I was both surprised and challenged by the number of crusading armies that arrived at Constantinople in 1096/7, and by their composition. A successful emperor might be a David to his opponent's Goliath, but there was no equivalent in Byzantine history to an army composed of armed penitential pilgrims prepared to fight and to die in expiation of their past sins. Whatever help he had asked for at Piacenza in March 1095 this was apparently not it. Byzantium was familiar with holy war and with pilgrimage, but not with crusade. This was something new, something western, and something with which ultimately they would fail to come to terms.

Just why the mass movement took place in the years after 1095 and not a century or a half-century earlier or later, demands an examination of various complex social and economic developments of the eleventh century. It is generally agreed that between the eighth and eleventh centuries population growth became more prolonged, the contraction of the early Middle Ages was reversed and population increase took place, possibly doubling in the course of the three

---

[25] M.M. Mango, *Silver from Early Byzantium* (Baltimore, 1986); G. Regan, *First Crusader: Byzantium's Holy Wars* (London, 2003), has dubbed Heraklios a crusader, but this is not generally accepted.

[26] M. Whittow, *The Making of Byzantium, 600–1025* (London, 1996), 134–6.

centuries mentioned. The evidence is largely circumstantial and any attempt at quantification is little more than guesswork. It is unlikely that the European population increased in all areas at the same time; there were probably fluctuations caused by the incidence of war, famine and disease. Nonetheless, in broad terms, according to McEvedy and Jones, Europe's population stood at 36 million in the year 1000, equal to the best level of the classical period, and during the eleventh century rose by a further 20 per cent. From around 800 the population increase in north-west Europe overtook that in the Mediterranean. The increase continued at accelerated rates throughout the twelfth and thirteenth centuries, despite a high mortality rate and a low life expectancy. More land in cultivation and more food supported this increase. There were technical advances in agriculture, such as the development of the horse collar, and the subsequent use of horses in ploughing, the general acceptance of three-field rotation rather than two, and the increase of animal husbandry all enlarged the area of cultivation, increased the food supply and improved diet.[27] It may be that there was a slight lowering of age on marriage. Even a decrease of two years can substantially increase the population, and it may be that assarting or the taking in of new lands allowed sons to set up families of their own without awaiting the death or incapacity of their parents and thus contributed to the increase of births over deaths. Lynn White has drawn attention to the importance of the spring planting of legumes – peas, chickpeas, lentils and broad beans – made possible by the three-field system. These vegetable proteins, especially peas, were a perfect supplement to the grains. He has attributed the new exuberance of Europe to these new types of food; for him, from the tenth century onwards, Europe was full of beans.[28] Population there was, as well as the surpluses of hay and oats for the feeding of horses, and – perhaps impossible to measure – a changed attitude to challenges and possibilities.

Until the analysis of Jonathan Riley-Smith on the First Crusade, of Jean Longnon on the Fourth, and of James Powell on the Fifth, it used to be thought that the Crusades were stocked with younger sons eager to carve out a patrimony in the East.[29] Their analysis, however, has shown that this was not the case. To be sure many may have hoped for material gains, but many family contingents went on crusade – lords with their heirs as well as their younger sons, many with established positions in their homelands and, therefore, likely to return home if they survived the rigours of crusade. The thrill of warfare may have led many to take the vow, but with it too was a religious motive that had particular poignancy at the end of the eleventh century.

[27] C. McEvedy and R. Jones, *Atlas of World Population History* (London, 1978), 22–5; N.J.G. Pounds, *An Economic History of Medieval Europe* (London, 1974), 90–159.
[28] L. White, *Medieval technology and Social Change* (Oxford, 1962), 69–76.
[29] J. Riley-Smith, *The First Crusaders, 1095–1131* (Cambridge, 1997); J. Longnon, *Les Campagnons de Villehardouin* (Geneva, 1978); J. Powell, *The Anatomy of a Crusade 1213–1221* (Philadelphia, 1986), 207–58.

The anonymous knight who wrote the *Gesta Francorum* was in no doubt that Pope Urban's sermon at Clermont spoke to the hearts and minds of his contemporaries: 'there was a great stirring of heart throughout all the Frankish lands, so that if any man, with all his heart and all his mind, really wanted to follow God and faithfully to bear the cross after him, he could make no delay in taking the road to the Holy Sepulchre as quickly as possible'.[30] The roots of this lay enthusiasm for the First Crusade lay in the religious revival that took place in the years from 950 to 1100. A fundamental study in this respect was Carl Erdmann's *Die Entstehung des Kreuzzugsgedankens* (Stuttgart, 1935); this postulated a direct link between the reform movement and the Crusades.[31] This affected not just the political stance of the papacy but also involved people of all social classes in Western Europe, many of them the poor. All were concerned with leading a holy life. Robert Moore sees in the reform movement the birth of Europe, since it was known about and discussed all over Western Christendom; certainly a distinctive Latin Christian culture had emerged by the end of the eleventh century from which crusading was to derive and to which it was to contribute.[32] Dissatisfaction with the Church was evident and may well have been sparked off by the Magyar, Muslim and Norse attacks on Europe in the ninth century that showed up God's people as somehow displeasing to him. The response, not unfamiliar today, was an ordering and standardisation of practices. Despite the inevitable gap between promise and performance, Church law and custom was to be collected and codified in authoritative texts. Monastic reform placed a new emphasis on the dignity and purity of the monastic life, enforcing the traditional Benedictine precepts of poverty, chastity and obedience. The elaborate ritual of Cluny was to provoke a reaction with the foundation of the Carthusian Order in 1083. The emphasis of this order was personal spirituality, to be fostered by reading, contemplation and working alone in the garden attached to each individual cell. The magnificence of Cluny was shunned. Many of the secular clergy, the canons who served in cathedrals, collegiate foundations and baptismal churches were encouraged to shun private property and marriage and to return to a common life in a college with its own dormitory and refectory. Diocesan bishops urged this move, and some were to impose it by force. The Church was to be hierarchically organised and was to intervene in all aspects of life and thought. The increasing appointment of monk-bishops during the eleventh century, and the tendency for monks to occupy the papal office in the latter half of that century, is a measure of the efficacy and achievement of the reform movement. All his flock knew the reputation of the parish priest. His deficiencies were difficult to conceal. His life came under scrutiny, since there should be

---

[30] R. Hill, ed., *Gesta Francorum et aliorum Hierosolimitanorum* (Oxford, 1962), 1.
[31] English translation by M. Baldwin and J.W. Goffart, *The Origin of the Idea of Crusade* (Princeton, 1977).
[32] R.I. Moore, *The Origins of European Dissent* (London, 1977), 53; R.I. Moore, *The First European Revolution, c. 970–1215* (Oxford, 2000), 3.

something of the holy about it and with it a desire to eradicate simony and to enforce clerical celibacy; paying for ecclesiastical office and clerical marriages had become almost customary. Criticism of the clergy was one thing, but there was clearly a desire amongst many laymen to amend their own lives. Imitating the apostolic life too might reform the life of the laity. But what was the apostolic life, and what if this desire for personal spirituality was at variance with authority and the precepts of the Church? Robert Moore has drawn attention to the growth and vigour of the popular dimension of the reform movement, such as the Paterenes who developed in the 1060s around the Church of Milan whose clergy were vigorously opposed to reform.[33]

The Reform movement also had a profound effect on the papacy's political stance in Christendom.[34] Many non-Gregorian reformers like Peter Damian, cardinal bishop of Ostia (1007–72), saw the Church's task as one of moral regeneration rather than the reordering of society. They appreciated the benefits of a strong monarchy and saw that the clergy had a community of interest with kings. Peter's death in 1072 left the field open to Gregory VII (1073–85) who saw just this re-ordering as the only path to complete reform. Like many revolution-aries he appealed to the past and set in train a study of the old laws and canons of the Church that had bearing on the powers of the Holy See. In 1075 the fundamentals of this work were set out in the twenty-seven propositions of the so-called *Dictatus Papae.*, inserted in the second volume of the letters of Gregory VII.[35] The Pope could depose and restore bishops, absolve subjects of their allegiance, alone use the imperial insignia, depose kings and emperors, and appoint legates with precedence over bishops. These were just some of the twenty-seven points by which the papacy placed itself at the centre of the life of Christendom and could exercise authority in all aspects of Christian life. These were not just the thoughts of Gregory, but his references to the ideas of his predecessors Leo IX (1049–54), Nicholas II (1058–61) and Alexander II (1061–73) show that this was the working out of ideas of the Reform movement for a complete change in society. It was, of course, not a simple struggle of good and evil. The Reform popes were glad of the solid support of the Saxon Church in their struggles with the German emperors, yet the Saxon Church was the most corrupt one in Germany. So much for western Christendom. However, there were no clear ideas about how the papacy should broach its claims towards other churches, usually the preserve of ecumenical councils, at least up until the last one held in 787 at Nicaea, according to Orthodox reckoning, or in 870 at Constantinople according to western ideas. Leo IX's attempt to explain papal primacy to Michael Kerularios in 1054 had resulted in mutual recriminations and a rift between the churches of the Western and Eastern communities. That

[33] Moore, *The Origins of European Dissent*, 48–81; 57 for the Paterenes.
[34] C. Morris, *The Papal Monarchy: The Western Church from 1050 to 1250* (Oxford, 1989), 109–33; Robinson, *The Papacy 1073–1198*, 293–321.
[35] E. Caspar, ed., *Gregorii VII Registrum, MGH. Epistolae Selectae*, II (1920–3), 201–8.

apart, the reformed papacy was prepared to intervene in eastern affairs. Gregory VII had proposed a stillborn military expedition to aid the Byzantines in 1074, and seven years later supported the Norman invasion of Albania – even going so far as to excommunicate Alexios I. There was then an ideology, ability and a will to intervene in the East.

Claims were one thing, but the popes lacked fighting men to enforce them. The use of Church funds to employ mercenaries was looked upon with disapproba- tion – most notably in 1082 when Gregory VII sought to use the treasures of Canossa to employ Wibert to attack Ravenna. At the same time, Gregory sought fighting men by developing the idea of the *milites sancti Petri ad servicium beati Petri*, mingling terms that had both military and spiritual connotations. Expres- sions like *milites Christi* had long been in use as a term for bishops or for monks waging the spiritual war, whilst *christiana militia* was a broad term for the Church or Christendom. With Gregory VII there is more than just a change in language and its use; there is also a sea-change in ideas and concepts. Erdmann has seen this development as an important step towards the idea of crusade, involving as it did the direct interweaving of religious symbolism with military action. The *milites* might be seen as the supporters of the Pope, often in further- ance of their own objectives. They were scattered thinly from Normandy to Sicily. In return for a papal banner, that might just guarantee victory, their cause gained much in moral standing. Gregory also promised spiritual rewards in terms of the forgiveness of sins for those he persuaded to join this or that cam- paign. In 1095 Urban II used the idea to appeal to the military aristocracy as *milites Christi*. It came at a time when his dispute with Emperor Henry IV (1050–1106) had intensified, and it served to focus attention on the Pope as the leader of Christendom and able to raise an army from the community of Christendom to defend the Christians of the East and to liberate the most sacred of Christian holy places. By this sermon the Pope emphasised that he, not the emperor, was the leader of Christendom; yet in the latter half of the twelfth century the German emperors were to stake their claim for the leadership of the Crusades.[36]

One manifestation of the reform was the Peace of God movement, reinforced by the Truce of God that sought to limit days on which fighting might take place and to restrict violence on the clergy, women, children and the poor. Con- temporaries noted the novelty of the movement, and its activity mainly in southern France.[37] It was the Church's response to outbreaks of violence amongst the military aristocracy in the face of the late Carolingian and Capetian monarchy's inability to keep the peace. Twenty-six peace councils were recorded

[36] Erdmann, *The Origin of the Idea of Crusade*, 159, 201–28; L. and J. Riley-Smith, *The Crusades: Idea and Reality* (London, 1983), 7–9.

[37] T. Head and R. Landes, eds, *The Peace of God: Social Violence and Religious Response in France Around the Years 1100* (Ithaca, 1992), 26–7, for link with crusades; Moore, *The First European Revolution*, 8–10.

between 989 and 1038. The clergy, usually bearing relics, convened them, and the miracles recorded at these meetings attested divine approval. All social groups, with the participation of common people being particularly noted, attended them. They swore on the relics to defend each other, the Church and the poor. Notorious breakers of the peace were excommunicated. The movement was complex, but from the point of view of the Crusades it has been argued that it was an essential forerunner. In the 1930s Mackinney, and later Erdmann, emphasised popular participation in the Peace movement – participation without which the movement could not have functioned – and stressed that without it there would have been no First Crusade.[38] 'An inactive population was transformed into a positive ally of the Church and of social reform.'[39] Peace was seen as not only essential to the functioning of the community but also as a sign of purity itself on a par with the rooting out of simony and clerical marriage.[40] Furthermore, the Truce of God gave the military aristocracy a place in Christian society by the limitations imposed upon violence, whilst at the same time accepting the place of violence in society. Urban II, in Fulcher of Chartres, account, drew upon the Peace movement in his sermon at Clermont in 1095 when he urged men 'who are accustomed to wantonly wage private war against the faithful [to] march upon the infidels in a war which should be begun now and be finished in victory. Let those who have long been robbers now be soldiers of Christ. Let those who once fought against brothers and relatives now rightfully fight against barbarians.'[41] This theme has also been found in a charter of Saint-Père, Chartres, by H.E.J. Cowdrey.[42]

Finally, a society focused on sin and repentance and the need to make atonement had witnessed the rise in the making of penitential pilgrimages. We have only to note that in the 1390s Chaucer's Wife of Bath on pilgrimage to Canterbury (St Thomas Becket) had already undertaken pilgrimages to Rome (St Peter), Boulogne (St Martin), Compostela (St James), Cologne (The Magi), and three times to Jerusalem to appreciate the variety of the major European pilgrimage destinations and to gain an impression of the priority of Jerusalem amongst them all.[43] The use of the relics of local saints during the Peace movement serves to remind us that medieval man did not have to travel far to indulge in the cult of relics and that relics occupied a central place in Christian activity.

---

[38] L. Mackinney, 'The People and Public Opinion in the Eleventh Century Peace Movement', *Speculum*, 5 (1930), 181–206; Erdmann, *The Origins of the Idea of Crusade*, 57–94.

[39] Mackinney, 'The People and Public Opinion in the Eleventh Century Peace Movement', 204.

[40] R.I. Moore, 'Family, Community and Cult on the Eve of the Gregorian Reform', *Transactions of the Royal Historical Society*, Series 5, 30 (1980), 49–69.

[41] F.R. Ryan and H. Fink, trans., *Fulcher of Chartres, A History of the Expedition to Jerusalem* (Talahassee, 1969), 66–7.

[42] H.E.J. Cowdrey, 'Pope Urban II's Preaching of the First Crusade', *History*, 55 (1970), 177–88, esp. 182.

[43] F.N. Robinson, ed., *The Works of Geoffrey Chaucer* (2nd edn, Oxford, 1955), 21; 'General Prologue', *Canterbury Tales*, lines 463–6.

Penance as a means of mitigating divine judgment after death was neither new in the eleventh century nor unique to Christianity. Likewise, pilgrimage might be so described; it is evident from the second century AD and found in both Judaism and Islam. Yet there is a noticeable increase in the number of pilgrims in the eleventh century and a broadening of the social spectrum from which pilgrims came.[44] For many generations great European sinners had sought absolution in pilgrimage. Just as sanguinary Anglo-Saxon kings had sought to end their days at the shrine of St Peter in Rome in the eighth and ninth centuries, so men like Fulk III Nerra of Anjou (987–1040), whose by-name suggests that he had a lot for which to atone, made three pilgrimages to Jerusalem in the years after 1000. That is a significant date, since the Byzantine reconquest of Crete and Cyprus and the Christianisation of Hungary made two routes from Europe to the East open for travel once again. Mass pilgrimage was a feature of the eleventh century. In 1027 Abbot Richard of Verdun took a large group of pilgrims to Jerusalem, as did Liebert, bishop of Cambrai, in 1054. In 1064 came the great German pilgrimage, with numbers variously estimated between 7,000 and 12,000 members. Grossly exaggerated as these numbers may be, the commitment to Jerusalem pilgrimage by a wide range of people cannot be doubted. Nor can the accessibility of the Holy Land, the reverence for Jerusalem, knowledge of its shrines and relics, especially the True Cross, and an awareness of the hazards of the journey thence. Urban II is credited with linking the ideas of penance, indulgence, pilgrimage and war. Since a common motive for most crusaders would have been to make a pilgrimage to Jerusalem, it is perhaps no wonder that *peregrinatio* (pilgrimage) was the favoured descriptor of what we call the First Crusade.

THE PROTO-CRUSADES, OR THE PREHISTORY OF CRUSADING

The so-called proto-crusades were part of a wider war with Islam for control of the Mediterranean basin. They also constituted a process by which the church laid aside its objection to the use of violence. Not all these campaigns progressed beyond the planning stage, but they did mark a change in ideas and beliefs in the decades before the First Crusade. Erdmann noted the resemblance of these campaigns to a crusade and judged them as crucial in the development of the idea of crusade.[45]

In 1011/12 Pope Sergius IV is supposed to have issued an encyclical calling for a military expedition to Jerusalem to right the wrongs caused by Caliph al-Hakim's destruction of the Church of the Holy Sepulchre in 1009. Nothing came of the proposal, if indeed it was ever made. Erdmann accepted the

---

[44] J. France, N. Bulst and P. Reynolds, eds, *Rodulfus Glaber Opera*. (Oxford, 1989), 36–7, 96–7, 136–7, and 60 = 1 and 212–15 on Fulk Nerra.

[45] Erdmann, *The Origin of the Idea of Crusade*, 113–17, 136, 194–9, 288–9; H.E. Cowdrey, 'The Genesis of the Crusades: The Springs of Western Ideas', in T. Murphy, ed., *The Holy War* (Columbus, 1976), 9–32.

authenticity of the encyclical letter and saw it as the first evidence of papal leadership of a campaign to the East. However, Gieysztor has suggested convincingly that it was a late eleventh-century forgery, produced at Moissac about the time of the Council of Clermont, to give a firm historical basis for the ideas preached by Urban and to place Jerusalem and the abuse of its shrines by the Muslims at the centre of western Christian consciousness.[46]

In 1053 Pope Leo IX personally led a campaign against the Norman invaders of the Patrimony of St Peter. This was most definitely papal militarism at its most noticeable. It ended in defeat at Civitate. Leo's contemporaries and indeed Leo himself, censured this action. The one consolation that Leo had was a vision of the slain being admitted to paradise.[47]

The Barbastro campaign of 1063–4 has been called a crusade in all but name, largely because of the substantiated involvement of French knights in a Spanish campaign, fighting under a papal banner, at a time when the peace of God had been declared in Catalonia as a direct spiritual aid to the warfare against the Moors (see p. 206). If the international component of the force has been overemphasised, since it is likely that French warriors had served in Spain before this campaign, and the outcome in the form of the temporary seizure of Barbastro exaggerated, a papal willingness to be associated with war was not in doubt. There was most definitely no evidence of direct papal sponsorship of this campaign, either that it was preached in France and Italy or that funds were raised in those areas at papal behest.

In 1074 Pope Gregory VII mulled over the idea of leading a campaign to aid the eastern Christians, followed by a pilgrimage to Jerusalem. These cogitations emanated from appeals from Emperor Michael VII and from emissaries from Cilician Armenia detailing the collapse of the eastern frontier consequent on the defeat of the Greeks at Manzikert in 1071. However, it only received scant attention in his letters and never got to the planning stage.[48]

Two naval expeditions mounted by the Pisans had an aura of campaigns in the public interest. The plunder seized from the Muslims of Palermo (1063) and from the sack of Mahdia (1087) provided funds for the building of a new cathedral in Pisa.[49]

A series of campaigns – the Norman invasion of Sicily in 1059, the Norman attack on Harold of England in 1066 and the invasion of Byzantine territory in the Balkans by Robert Guiscard in 1080 – were all fought under the banner of St Peter (*vexillum sancti Petri*) granted by the Pope of the day to confer the status

---

[46] A. Gieysztor, 'The Genesis of the Crusades: The Encyclical of Sergius IV (1009–1012)', *Medievalia et Humanistica*, 5 (1948), 3–23, and 6 (1949), 3–34.

[47] Morris, *The Papal Monarchy*, 145.

[48] H.E.J. Cowdrey, 'Pope Gregory VII's Crusading Plans', in B.Z. Kedar *et al.*, eds, *Outremer: Studies in the History of the Crusading Kingdom of Jerusalem Presented to Joshua Prawer* (Jerusalem, 1982), 27–40; Erdmann, *The Origin of the Idea of Crusade*, 160–9.

[49] H.E. Cowdrey, 'The Mahdia Campaign 1087', *English Historical Review*, 92 (1977); K. Setton, ed., *A History of the Crusades*, I (6 vols, Madison, 1969–89), 40–53.

of holy war on the campaigns about to be undertaken. What this banner looked like is unknown, but it did carry implications of papal overlordship of the conquered territories, subsequently not acknowledged by the conquerors concerned.[50] A whole mass of cross currents and anecdotes in the eleventh century, then, but a sure indication of a willingness and ability to conceive of war on an international scale against enemies reckoned to be outside the embrace of Christendom. And a readiness to be involved in war and especially war against the Muslims of the Mediterranean region.

WHAT DID THE WEST KNOW OF ISLAM AT THE TIME OF THE CRUSADES, AND VICE VERSA?[51]

It seems incredible in our multicultural society that on the eve of the Crusades knowledge of Islam in the ruling circles of Western Europe was so limited, if not non-existent. There was certainly no idea that Jerusalem was as much a holy city for Muslims as for Christians. This awareness had to wait until the late twelfth century and the negotiations between Richard I and Saladin. In 1095 Urban II's characterisation of Muslims as subhuman went unchallenged. He denigrated them as ravishers of women, murderers of Christians and polluters of Christian churches, violent, rapacious, and aggressive. It was not until 1142 that something like the first research project on Islam was instituted when Peter the Venerable (c. 1092–1153), abbot of Cluny, commissioned a translation of the Koran into Latin from western Christian scholars resident and studying in Toledo. This was no disinterested work of scholarship; Peter wished the translation made in order to refute the theological errors of Islam. The translation was ready by 1143 and his tract 'Against the Abhominable Heresy or Sect of the Saracens' was finished by 1144. His support for crusading had never wavered, but here he suggested that Muslims could be won over to Christian belief by preaching. According to him they were in error, but only because they had never heard the true word (see p. 360 for a different Byzantine perspective).[52] Nonetheless, he was apprehensive of the reaction of his fellow churchmen like Bernard of Clairvaux to this project. As Maxime Rodinson has observed, there was nothing

[50] Erdmann, *The Origin of the Idea of Crusade*, 182–200.
[51] R. Southern, *Western Views of Islam in the Middle Ages* (Cambridge, Mass., 1962); N. Daniel, *The Cultural Barrier* (Edinburgh, 1975); N. Daniel, *The Arabs and Medieval Europe* (2nd edn, London, 1979); W. Watt, *The Influence of Islam on Medieval Europe* (Edinburgh, 1972); R. Fletcher, *The Cross and the Crescent* (London, 2003); K. Sema'an, ed., *Islam and the Medieval West* (New York, 1980); D. Munro, 'The Western Attitude Toward Islam During the Period of the Crusades', *Speculum*, 6 (1931), 329–43; W. Comfort, 'The Saracens in the French Epic', *Publications of the Modern Language Association of America*, 55 (1940), 628–59; B. Hamilton, 'Knowing the Enemy: Western Understanding of Islam at the Time of the Crusades', *Journal of the Royal Asiatic Society*, 3rd Series, 7 (1997), 373–87.
[52] J. Kritzeck, *Peter the Venerable and Islam* (Princeton, 1964), 220–91.

approaching the complete separation of scholarship from religious dogmatism until the modern world.[53]

Yet Muslims had been in contact with Christian Europeans since the seventh century on the Byzantine frontier and had made annual attacks on Constantinople itself between 674 and 678, with a year-long siege from 717 to 718 and an attempted naval assault in 904. From 711 Christians had lost territory to Islam in Spain, and in 732 Muslims were poised to capture Poitiers. The Carolingians and the Ottonians were in occasional diplomatic contact with the Muslim rulers of Al-Andalus. Sometime around 800 Charlemagne had received an elephant as a diplomatic gift from Harun al-Raschid and housed it at Aachen. From the ninth century to the fifteenth, the Christian kingdoms of Spain were in permanent contact with their Muslim enemies and neighbours. Between 826 and 860 Arab pirates made sporadic raids along the Italian coast, including the sacking of Benevento and St Peter's in Rome. Southern France, Sardinia, Corsica and the Balearic islands had also suffered from pirate attacks. Sicily, Crete and Cyprus were occupied. There seems to have been no especial rancour directed at these Muslim aggressors, any more than that directed against Vikings and Magyars. They were all seen as instruments of God's anger with his people. The Venerable Bede noted their aggression and their defeat at Poitiers, but no more.[54] Equally, no Christian chronicler of the tenth century has anything to say about the religion of either the Magyars or the Vikings. Comparative religion was of no interest: the Muslims were not distinguished from the other pagan aggressors from without Christendom.

From the book of Genesis there was some knowledge amongst biblical scholars like Isidore of Seville and Bede about the ethnic origin of the Arabs. Like the Jews they were supposed to be the descendants of Hagar, the Egyptian wife of Abraham, whom he repudiated, and their son Ishmael.[55] Hence references to Hagarenes and Ishmaelites; but just why the Arabs were known as Saracens was not securely known since they were most definitely not descended from Abraham's other wife Sarah. Ralph Glaber, writing around 1040, provides the first awareness of Islamic religion in northern Europe. In his account of the capture and ransom of St Mayol (Majolus), abbot of Cluny, in 972 at La Garde-Fresnet, he mentions that the Muslims respected the Holy Book of the Christians and regarded Muhammad as the descendant of Ishmael and also as the ultimate fulfilment of Old Testmant prophecies.[56]

In Spain and Sicily there were positive links between Christian and Muslim. Mozarabs, or native Christians who took to the Arabic language, culture, and lifestyle with enthusiasm, enjoyed Arabic poetry and philosophical speculation,

---

[53] M. Rodinson, *Europe and the Mystique of Islam* (London, 1988), 95.
[54] W. Plummer, *Bedae Historia Ecclesiastica* (2 vols, Oxford, 1896), II, 339.
[55] Genesis, chs 8 and 17.
[56] France *et al.*, eds, *Rodulfus Glaber Opera*, 18–23, discussed in Southern, *Western Views of Islam in the Middle Ages*, 1962, 28, n.25.

but they rejected Islam and indeed provided martyrs at Cordoba in the early 950s when their enthusiasm for discussion went too far. Study and manners were one thing, but they were pursued within the limits of Muslim tolerance and patronage. This should provide some restraint on the enthusiasts for the so-called 'la Convivencia' of Al-Andalus. It was not a simple distinction between tolerance and learning in Spain and ignorance elsewhere in Europe. In Sicily and Spain Muslims and Christians might live together as neighbours, but they did not pray together and they maintained their distinctive cultures. La Convivencia was bi- or tri-cultural, but not multicultural. From at least the middle of the eleventh century some western scholars were attracted to Spain to study Muslim philosophy,[57] scientific literature and, through them, its Greek sources. They sought hard, practical facts on mathematics, medicine and alchemy. Their enthusiasm did not extend to Islam or the ethnography of their Muslim hosts. With the capture of Toledo by the king of Leon in 1085 that city became a centre for the transmission of Greek and Muslim learning to the north. Not only was it a Christian-held city but also it was within the cultural orbit of Cordoba and had bilingual Arabs within its walls to assist with translation. It was to remain a centre for this process of translation and transmission throughout the twelfth century. Also during the twelfth century, the Italian commercial republics opened emporia in Muslim lands and they too became an avenue for the transmission of knowledge and ideas. Leonardo Fibonacci (*filius Bonacci*) of Pisa is credited with the introduction of Arabic numerals to Europe with the publication of his *Liber abaci* in 1202. Fibonacci learned his mathematics whilst at his father's trade counter in Bugia in Algeria. The potential to learn a great deal about Muslim history, philosophy and culture was there even at the time of the summoning of the First Crusade, but the Christian world-view of the time could not adopt such an approach. It appeared that the rulers in the West were just not interested, and were satisfied with stereotypical images of the other that marked them off from west European Christians. Intolerance of Semites, Jews or Muslims was the norm, from which it would have been both dangerous and uncomfortable to depart. Basically this is correct, but they could do no other being men of their time.

The epic French poem *The Song of Roland* is a convenient starting point for western attitudes to Muslims and Islam, possibly on the eve of the First Crusade. It may have been written as early as 1093, but certainly no later than the first half of the twelfth century. Its theme is the death of Charlemagne's nephew Roland in 778 whilst returning home after a campaign against the Moors in Spain in which the city of Zaragossa was sacked. The Moors are viewed as savage and lewd, easily bribed by the promise of sexual favours (verse 3398). They are treated as pagans to be forcibly converted or to die. The synagogues and mosques (*les*

---

[57] Watt, *The Influence of Islam on Medieval Europe*, 58–71; Fletcher, *The Cross and the Crescent*, 116–30.

mahumeries, verse 3662) are vandalised and, in the search for idols, to be smashed with hammers (verses 3657–3700). Charlemagne has authorised the attack, and God is clearly on the side of the French, signified by a change from darkness to dawn as the French return home (verses 3657–9). There is much here that is a parallel to the negative image of Islam given by the chroniclers of the First Crusade.[58]

The stereotypes cast a long shadow right down to the eighteenth century. They were in the main the product of writers about the First Crusade during the twelfth century. It was they who reported Urban's speech at Clermont that portrayed the Muslims in emotive and violent language. These clichés have been succinctly summarised by Watt.[59] Muslims were violent and cruel. Muslims were pagans and idolaters. Later, when a little more was known, their religion was declared false, as it was bound to be given the mindset of Christendom. The division of Islam into Sunni and Shīite was one plank in this argument, an argument that Muslim writers turned on the Christians themselves. Muhammad was variously described as the god of the Muslims, a false prophet, or the antichrist heralding the end of the world. Guibert of Nogent was certain that the Muslims did not regard Muhammad as a god, but as a good man who had passed on the divine law to them. For Guibert he was a profane man about whom he could discover nothing from the writings of the doctors of the Church, and whom he thought was some form of Christian heretic preaching extreme monophysitism.[60] A distorted understanding of Muslim polygamy and the attributes of their paradise leads to the descriptors 'licentious', 'sensuous' and 'immoral'. Interestingly, the Muslims were polluters. They destroyed churches and polluted the land where Christ had walked by their very presence. There was clearly no concept of the place of both Christ and Jerusalem in Muslim theology. Gone is the moderate observational approach of Ralph Glaber. Muslims were now the enemies of Christ, and appropriate rhetoric was produced. For Guibert Muslims were barbarians speaking a strange language; for him they represented the other, despite the process of translation currently going forward in Spain. It was in such attitudes that the Crusades defined Western Europe.

Byzantines, too, proved fairly resistant to acquiring knowledge of Muslim culture, although there were translators of Arabic available at the Byzantine court, diplomatic missions to Muslim rulers, a (possible) Greek translation of the Koran available by the end of the ninth century, and a mosque for Arab traders in Constantinople by the time of the First Crusade. They too were Christians and could brook no rival to their religious traditions and beliefs. They included Arabs amongst the peoples who might have heard the teaching of the Apostles

---

[58] G. Brault, *The Song of Roland: An Analytical Edition* (2 vols, Philadelphia, 1978).
[59] Watt, *The Influence of Islam on Medieval Europe*, 72–7.
[60] R. Levine, trans., *The Deeds of God Through the Franks: A Translation of Gurbert de Nogent's 'Gesta Dei per Francos'* (London, 1997), 32.

and had rejected it. In Byzantine literature Muslims were described as fierce warriors, but also as lustful, and variously as polygamists and as sodomites. Their religion emphasised the material at the expense of the spiritual. Their concept of God could not be reconciled with either the Trinity or the Incarnation. Theological tracts apart, the emperor was the protector of the Holy Places and the Christians in Abbasid and Fatimid territory and as such had to tread warily regarding any form of missionary work in Muslim lands. This was to lead to difficulties between the emperor and ecclesiastics. There might not have been missions, but there were some Muslim converts to Orthodoxy who were resettled within the empire. The Church required them to anathematise the Muslim God, Muhammad and the Caliph; a practice the Emperor Manuel I was eager to discontinue. Just as in western polemic the Muslims or Arabs were described as a whole rather than as one at a time.[61] As we shall see, the crusader settlements in the East and the proliferation of Christian and Muslim captives brought closer personal contacts – and at this level there were to be a few modifications to the stereotypical. But by the time of the Crusades, the Christian communities of Europe had created a powerful negative image of Muslims and Islam that was to fuel Europe's myth of the Orient for centuries to come.[62]

Equally, Muslims condemned the westerners as being composed of 72 different races (hence disunited) and barbarians, who were violent and bloodthirsty. It is interesting that this polemic has also cast a long shadow and was taken up by western writers in the eighteenth century. When it came to brutality in the twelfth and thirteenth centuries there was little to choose between the crusaders and their Muslim adversaries. Despite notable exceptions like Ibn Munqidh, they tended to shun contact with the West. Muslim rulers did not encourage Christian missionaries to enter their territories, as the failure of the preaching of St Francis in Egypt in 1219 revealed. Travel within Christendom was not only hazardous for Muslims but was also officially discouraged unless no other route was practicable. Whereas western painters, musicians and tradesmen are found at the Ottoman court by the end of the sixteenth century, there was no reciprocal patronage in the West. The Muslim discovery of Europe was to be postponed to the eighteenth and nineteenth centuries.[63]

---

[61] J. Meyendorff, 'Byzantine Views of Islam', *Dumbarton Oaks Papers*, 18 (1964), 113–32; S. Vryonis, 'Byzantine Attitudes Towards Islam During the Late Middle Ages', *Greek, Roman and Byzantine Studies*, 12 (1971), 263–86; E. Jeffreys, 'The Image of the Arabs in Byzantine Literature', *Seventeenth International Congress of Byzantine Studies Major Papers* (New Rochelle, 1986), 305–23.

[62] R. Kabbani, *Europe's Myth of Orient* (London, 1986).

[63] B. Lewis, *The Muslim Discovery of Europe* (London, 1982).

THE MECHANISMS OF CRUSADING

Preaching[64]

Urban II certainly touched a chord with those gathered at Clermont in November 1095, provoking the response '*Deus le vult, Deus le vult.*' However, if the announcement of the proposed expedition had been limited to this event the crusade would have been small indeed, and quite possibly stillborn. As Erdmann emphasised, the popular element in the crusade was essential and to tap this preaching the crusade across France, Flanders, the Rhineland and Lombardy had to take place. Urban was just as aware of this as Erdmann 840 years later. For six months he remained in southern and central France preaching the crusade himself. Religious events and gatherings were the venues for such preaching to take place, and from them word of mouth would take the message further, if in garbled form. Urban could not be everywhere, and from the start he urged the bishops to preach the crusade within their dioceses. The response to this injunction was patchy and depended on the character and interests of the individual diocesans. Many did so, like Hugh of Die, or organised preaching within their dioceses.

Both the Pope and the bishops did not shun the services of popular preachers, holy men thrown up by the effect of the Reform movement on lay society, commissioning Robert d'Arbrissel and Vitalis of Mortain to preach in the Loire valley. Others like Peter the Hermit took it upon themselves to preach the cross. These men probably preached in the vernacular, rather than in the Latin and French preferred by their ecclesiastical colleagues, and used homely images familiar to their audience. Guibert, abbot of Nogent, disapproved of Peter and his doings; he probably reflects the stance of many of the regular clergy, who preferred ecclesiastical authority to popular endorsement. Nonetheless, these charismatic holy men certainly had a profound effect, as can be seen from the size and diversity of the so-called peasants' crusade that left Western Europe in April 1096. According to Orderic Vitalis Peter set out with about 15,000 men, including a number of eminent French knights.[65] It should be remembered that the majority of these so-called peasant recruits would have been free men, and probably from towns since it would have been virtually impossible for the villein to absent himself from service on the land except by recognition payments or substitution. It may well be the effect of these preachers on the religious enthusiasm of their audiences that made the First Crusade the first and only mass

---

[64] P.J. Cole, *The Preaching of the Crusades to the Holy Land, 1095–1270* (Cambridge, Mass., 1991); C.T. Maier, *Preaching the Crusades: Mendicant Friars and the Cross in the Thirteenth Century* (Cambridge, 1994); C.T. Maier, *Crusade Propaganda and Ideology: Model Sermons for the Preaching of the Cross* (Cambridge, 2000).

[65] Chibnall, trans., *The Ecclesiastical History of Orderic Vitalis*, V (6 vols, Oxford 1978; reprinted 2002), 29.

crusade – impressive in numbers but not entirely desirable from the point of view of military efficiency. To exert even minimal control over recruitment, authorised preachers and preaching places would be the way forward for the papacy.

St Bernard of Clairvaux was largely responsible for preaching the Second Crusade. Pope Eugenius gave him legatine authority to do so, and his identity with the crusade ensured that he attracted his full share of blame for its failure. Recruitment was aimed at kings and took place mainly in the setting of courts and diets. Although preoccupied with the Roman commune and the activities of Roger of Sicily, Eugenius made a progress into Burgundy, presumably preaching as he went, and backed this up with letters to the towns in the imperial territories in Italy. There had been impromptu preaching in support of an expedition to the East by Geoffrey of Langres at the Christmas court at Bourges in 1145, but this was the work of a loyal royalist and not part of any papal preaching campaign. William of Tyre noted that Eugenius appointed a plethora of preachers to announce the new crusade; but William was not in the West, and if there were such preachers they followed in the wake of Bernard and are unknown to us. The only preacher to attract attention other than Bernard was the renegade Cistercian monk Radulph/Rodulf, who stirred up anti-Jewish sentiment in the Rhineland and whom Bernard was at pains to silence.

The Third and Fourth crusades were proclaimed in bulls addressed to the rulers of Europe, and their organisation took place much more at private meetings of royal and noble warriors entrusting committees or individuals to perform essential tasks, negotiations and research. Important decisions were arrived at during discreet meetings at tournaments and at conveniently located Cistercian monasteries.

Preachers there were, but in the main their names have not come down to us. Just as with the Second Crusade, the Cistercian Order played a prominent part. North of the Alps the Cistercians Henry, cardinal legate of Albano, and Baldwin of Canterbury were active alongside Joscius, Archbishop of Tyre. Concerning Archbishop Baldwin of Canterbury, who actually died at Acre in November 1190, his preaching tour in Wales in March 1188 in the company of Gerald of Wales, archdeacon of Brecknock and failed candidate to the See of St David, has left a number of informative vignettes recorded by Gerald. The preaching party received hospitality, advice and company from local nobles, monastic communities, clergy and bishops. At Haverfordwest: 'It appeared wonderful and miraculous that, although the archdeacon addressed them both in the Latin and French tongues, those persons who understood neither of those languages were equally affected and flocked in great numbers to the cross'. At Usk they spoke through an interpreter and recruited many of the most notorious thieves and murderers to the cross. The business of the cross was publicly proclaimed at Llandaff, and the English and Welsh stood in two separate groups to hear the sermon. Donations were made for the service of the cross and at St Clare twelve archers from the garrison there were signed with the cross as a punishment for the murder of a youth. Gerald placed due emphasis on the restraining hand of friends and wives on would-be crusaders and the tendency of many about to take the cross to consult with their wives who then dissuaded them.[66] Interestingly James of Vitry was to preach the crusade to the women of Genoa in September 1216, who seem to have had considerable effect on the recruitment of their menfolk.[67]

For the Fourth Crusade both Geoffrey of Villehardouin and Ralph of Coggeshall recorded the name of Fulk of Neuilly as a particularly effective preacher, held in high esteem for his learning, piety and miracle working by his audiences and renowned for castigating the sins of his congregation to raise money for the crusade.[68] There was also Martin, abbot of the Cistercian monastery of Pairis, near Basel, whose crusade sermon at Basel encapsulated the appeal of crusading since the days of Urban II. He emphasised the centrality of the Holy Land for the Christian, the call of Christ and the sure reward of eternal life for those who answered it, along with a bettering of their lot in the land of milk and honey. There can be no doubt that there was a strong religious side to the Fourth Crusade, despite the thoughts of those modern cynics who might doubt the sincerity of Doge Dandolo's tears in St Mark's Venice in April 1201.[69] By the end of the twelfth century raising money for crusading had become an additional task for crusade preachers, alongside the gaining of recruits and the dispensing of crosses.

The sermon of Martin of Pairis is unusual in that there is some record of what he said, and of the structure of his address at Basel. His better-known contemporary Fulk of Neuilly has left no record of his sermons. For the rest of crusade preaching in the late eleventh and twelfth centuries there is quite simply no record in the narrative sources of what was said. Sadly, there is no record of what Urban II said – either at Clermont or in any of his preaching tours. Equally, there is no account of Peter the Hermit's words, except that they were inspirational. None of the crusade sermons of Bernard of Clairvaux survive. Even Gerald of Wales, who recorded where he preached the cross in 1188, does not tell us what he said, only that he preached in Latin or French and used interpreters as they were available. It may be surmised, however, that the theme of penitence to make the crusaders acceptable in the eyes of Christ was strong, as was the related theme of crusaders taking up the cross for Christ who had once taken it up for them.

Like crusade finance and papal archives, Innocent III was also concerned with the systematisation and organisation of crusade preaching. Most of this took

---

[66] T. Wright, ed., *The Historical Works of Giraldus Cambrensis* (London, 1913), 331–3, 338, 368, 371, 383, 388, 397–9.

[67] Powell, *Anatomy of a Crusade 1213–1221*, 67–8.

[68] M.R.B. Shaw, *Joinville and Villehardouin: Chronicles of the Crusades* (Harmondsworth, 1963), 29; A. Andrea, *Contemporary Sources for the Fourth Crusade* (Leiden, 2000), 277–8.

[69] A. Andrea, trans., *The Capture of Constantinople: The 'Hystoria Constantinopolitana' of Gunther of Pairis* (Philadelphia, 1997), 68–72; also in L. and J. Riley-Smith, *The Crusades: Idea and Reality*, 69–71, and discussed in J. Phillips, *The Fourth Crusade and the Sack of Constantinople* (London, 2004), 26–38.

place in 1213 in the preparatory period to what we call the Fifth Crusade. It was now that pilgrimage and crusade became clearly differentiated and ecclesiastical authority restored in the preaching of crusade. Europe was divided up into regions for crusade preaching, and prominent individuals, usually bishops or abbots, were entrusted with that preaching, commissioned by Innocent himself, who personally oversaw preaching in Italy.[70] This was a major step forward, with a move towards close control being exercised from the centre; but, as Christoph Maier has pointed out:

> With the [crusade] movement growing and moving into new theatres of war against heretics, non-Christian peoples in the Baltic and political enemies of the papacy crusade propaganda undertaken by individually commissioned preachers and the resident secular clergy had become desperately inadequate. The building up of an effective propaganda machinery for the crusades was only possible with the help of the many well-trained Franciscan and Dominican preachers and thanks to the hierarchic structure of the two orders which allowed them to spread information quickly and effectively over large geographical areas. Their efforts made it possible for the papacy to control crusade propaganda and carefully allocate the resources of people and money for the many crusades organised in Europe throughout the thirteenth century.[71]

The rapid growth and success of the mendicant orders across Christendom during the 1220s, and their status as non-enclosed orders, gave them a huge advantage over the Cistercians,[72] whose primary vocation was cloistered and contemplative, when it came to crusade preaching. Both their saintly founders had been involved in crusading: Francis at Damietta in 1219, when he sought to convert al-Kamil, and Dominic, who was the head of a religious community at Prouille in the Languedoc between 1211 and 1219, receiving endowments from Albigensian crusaders. During the 1230s the mendicant friars gained the trust of Pope Gregory IX who used them as his agents in his disputes and negotiations with Frederick II. Their wide journeying in the Near East and Far East meant that they were a prime source of knowledge for eastern crusade strategy and were able to impart something of the crusade experience to their audiences. It has been said that they were the nearest that the Middle Ages had to a mass medium.[73] From the 1230s onwards they preached every thirteenth-century and early

---

[70] Powell, *Anatomy of a Crusade 1213–1221*, 51–65; L. and J. Riley-Smith, *The Crusades: Idea and Reality*, 118–36.

[71] Maier, *Crusade Propaganda and Ideology*, 8, and more generally discussed by the same author in *Preaching the Crusades*.

[72] C.H. Lawrence, *The Friars* (London, 1994), *passim*, but 185–7 for preaching the Crusades.

[73] G. Steier, 'Bettelorden-Predigt als Massenmedium', in G. Heinzle, ed., *Litterarische Interessens-bilddung im Mittelalter* (Stuttgart, 1993), 314–36, cited by Maier, *Crusade Propaganda and Ideology*, 7.

fourteenth-century crusade, but in a less target-orientated age there is no record of the numbers of crusaders who took the cross from their hands. It is from this period that numbers of model sermons, some of them for the preaching of the cross, survive. It is doubtful whether any of them were actually preached, and as models they were able to be adapted to a wide range of non-crusading scenarios, but they do make an important contribution to the understanding of crusade propaganda that was based on the devotional and the penitential aspect of participation in wars authorised and supported by God. From the 1320s the controversy between the conventual and spiritual Franciscans over the absolute poverty of Christ and his apostles weakened the Friars minor and led to a clash between the spirituals and Pope John XXII in 1323. As a result, that trust between the Franciscans and the papacy was breached and the papal *Curia* came to rely more on the Dominicans for the preaching of the crusades.

Motivation

As we are unable to penetrate the minds of medieval crusaders all that can be said about motivation is generalised and vague. It is a question that fascinates and yet cannot be answered in any definite way. It asks us to ponder common humanity across time and to consider how and why medieval people were different from ourselves in their responses to the great issues of their day, and to evaluate whether any perceived differences were due to mindset (religiosity and sense of sin), to environment (no mass media and hence no broad world-view other than the Christian cosmos), or to opportunity (limits imposed by wealth, gender and status).

Piety was at the root of all crusading vows and penance was fundamental to those who voluntarily took the cross.[74] The absolution of all sins confessed and the guarantee of life eternal were very powerful enticements indeed, especially for those whose penance had been postponed or neglected. In addition, there was strong social approbation for those who took the cross. The *negotium Jhesu Christi* – that is, aiding the Christians of the East and liberating the Christian holy places – was so important that the crusader was assigned a special status, and his family and property were protected in his absence, together with a moratorium on any debts that he may have contracted. The inducements might be appealing, but the failure to fulfil a crusader vow was a very serious matter indeed and would certainly result in infamy, dishonour, excommunication, and hounding by the Church. The branding of Stephen of Blois as a European coward was a fate for the eminent and privileged. Of all this there is no doubt, whatever weight might be given to wanderlust, curiosity, boredom with the daily round, travel for health, family honour, a wish to impress one's neighbours, a zeal for charity, the idealism of love for one's enemies, a desire to kill infidels or make

---

[74] M. Bull, *Knightly Piety and the Lay Response to the First Crusade* (Oxford, 1993), 155–203; J. Riley-Smith, 'Crusading as an Act of Love', *History*, 65 (1980), 177–92.

material gains on the way. All of these motives can be pieced together from the available evidence. Just as crusades were armed pilgrimages so the motivation for pilgrimage may usefully be considered in this respect.[75]

Recruitment

Just as we do not know the number of recruits garnered by the mendicants for the crusades so any discussion of the numbers of crusaders on any particular crusade must rely on plausible estimates – that is, guesswork. It should be said at the outset that few of us are good at visualising numbers of people. Most of us are aware that 600–3,000 people attended our school, or some hundreds are in our university department, or so many thousands in our university. In this we are little different than our medieval forebears.

Both Byzantine and western chroniclers relied upon impressionistic language to convey the idea of very large numbers on the First Crusade. For Anna Komnene they were 'More numerous than grains of sand and the stars', whilst Fulcher considered them 'a countless number', and Guibert of Nogent 'the whole of Christendom capable of bearing arms'.[76] Orderic Vitalis alone, writing forty years after the event, gives a figure for the followers of Peter the Hermit, although he does list the diverse contingents leaving the West, which lays bare another problem. Compounding the difficulties of guesswork is the processual nature of crusading. Different groups leaving at different times meeting up and joining forces. Thus Anna Komnene recorded the arrival of a certain count Raoul with 15,000 followers in Constantinople, travelling independently of Bohemond and Godfrey whom he supported in attacks on the Greeks.[77] Apart from the different contingents on the First Crusade, including Byzantine reinforcements, crusading was an ongoing movement not just confined to the main armies on the eight numbered expeditions. Concomitant with this were the late starters, the non-showers who had taken the cross, and participants for whom there is no record of their taking the cross, let alone the deserters and the casualties who were all non-quantified or quantifiable factors of prime importance.

The diverse theatres of operation during the Second Crusade – the East, Spain and the Baltic – further complicate the whole question. Of all the crusades only the first crusade and its follow-up in 1101 could be described as mass movements. The sources cited serve to confirm this view but give no idea as to the proportions of military effectives to non-combatants. Apart from the 15,000 following Peter the Hermit, unmentioned until Orderic Vitalis wrote in 1135, the numbers following Gottschalk, Folkmar and Emicho of Leinigen on the so-called peasants'

---

[75]   D. Webb, *Medieval European Pilgrimage* (London, 2002), 44–77.

[76]   Ryan and Fink, trans., *Fulcher of Chartres, A History of the Expedition to Jerusalem*, I, 9, p. 73; Dawes, E.A.S., trans., *The Alexiad of the Princess Anna Comnena* (London, 1928; reissued 1967), 249, 261, 262, 268; Levine, trans., *The Deeds of God Through the Franks*, 27.

[77]   Dawes, trans., *The Alexiad*, 261–2, discussed in S. Runciman, *A History of the Crusades*, I (3 vols, Cambridge, 1951–4), 152–3.

or popular crusade in 1096 are completely unknown. Guibert described the followers of Peter 'as poor in resources but copious in number'.

During the twelfth century the organisers of crusades sought to limit participation to professional warriors. The participation of kings on the Second and Third crusades tended to limit such recruitment, whilst the change to sea transport rather than overland marches both increased the cost of passage and limited the availability of space for non-combatants. There was also a greater emphasis on discipline and the maintenance of order, this provoking amazed responses from an Armenian witness to Barbarossa's progress.[78] This is evident too in Villehardouin's account of the Fourth Crusade. Frederick Barbarossa imposed a property qualification on participants in his crusade expedition, and was constantly sending unsuitable recruits home.[79] Certainly there was a trend to streamlining, and specialisation, and the chronicles of the thirteenth-century crusades focus their attention on the families and relationships of participants with little or no mention of camp followers, who occasionally appear in incidental stories. Some of the Italian crusades were very localised affairs preached and recruited locally.

It is, then, impossible to estimate the numbers on crusades. However, this does not prevent students asking the question. Below are given some of the medieval observations on numbers on crusade, with some modern estimates that illustrate historical approaches to medieval numbers.

For the First Crusade there was no consensus on numbers amongst the chroniclers. The anonymous author of the *Gesta Francorum* does not mention figures or impressions of numbers at all. The impressions of Anna Komnene, Fulcher, Guibert and Orderic Vitalis have been cited above. As the crusading army came together for the first time at Nicaea in May 1097, Fulcher estimated that it was 600,000 strong, of whom 100,000 (16.6 per cent) had basic military equipment; Ekkehard of Aura and Albert of Aachen both give the strength as 300,000 combatants.[80] Raymond d'Aguilers recorded that at the start of the siege of Antioch the army consisted of 100,000 effectives, and that the army that arrived at Jerusalem consisted of 1,200 or 1,500 knights and 12,000 foot soldiers; he also records that at the battle of Ascalon on 12 August 1099 the Frankish army of 1,200 knights and 9,000 infantrymen was opposed to an Egyptian army of 3,000.[81] In September 1099 Daimbert of Pisa, Raymond of Toulouse, Robert of Normandy and Robert of Flanders wrote to Urban II (d. 1099), stating that the army at Ascalon was 20,000 strong.[82]

[78] P. Munz, *Frederick Barbarossa* (London, 1969), 387, n.3.
[79] Munz, *Frederick Barbarossa*, 387 and n.2.
[80] J. France, *Victory in the East: A Military History of the First Crusade* (Cambridge, 1994), 127, for discussion and references.
[81] Hill, J.H. and L.L., trans., *Raymond d'Aguilers, Historia Francorum Qui Ceperunt Iherusalem*, (Philadelphia, 1968), 31, 125, 134.
[82] H. Hagenmeyer, *Die Kreuzzugsbriefe aus dem Jahren 1088–1100* (Innsbruck, 1901; reprinted New York, 1973), 161–5.

Three estimates of the numbers involved have been attempted in the last half century by Steven Runciman, Jonathan Riley-Smith and John France; they show something of the workings in these matters, conservative and plausible:

> The actual size of the crusading armies can only be conjectured. Medieval estimates are always exaggerated: but Peter the Hermit's rabble, including its many non-combatants, probably approached twenty thousand. The chief crusading armies, Raymond's, Godfrey's and the northern French, each numbered well over ten thousand, including non-combatants. Bohemond's was a little smaller; and there were other lesser groups. But in all from sixty to a hundred thousand persons must have entered the Empire from the West between the summer of 1096 and the spring of 1097.[83]

> Leaving aside the great numbers on the third wave of the crusade [the so-called crusade of 1101] the following figures can be suggested very tentatively. A fair, perhaps too conservative, estimate of the numbers on the second wave that gathered before Nicaea in June 1097 would be 43,000. Crusaders continued to overtake and join the army right up to the fall of Jerusalem and beyond, even though the total in the army had fallen to 15,000. We might add 3,000 for late departures. The armies of the first wave were at least as large, possibly larger, than those of the second. So a guess for them would be 45,000 persons. This gives us a total of 91,000, of whom perhaps 7,000 would have been knights. We then have to take into account the substantial number who took the cross but did not leave; perhaps 45,000 or 50 per cent of the total number departing would be reasonable. So we end with a figure of 136,000, of which less than 10 per cent would have been knights.[84]

> A round figure of the order of 20,000 survivors seems likely of whom fewer than 20,000 would have been knights. In the light of all they had gone through and all the attritions they had faced an overall loss rate of 3:1 would appear reasonable. That would have fallen rather more heavily on the followers than on the knights and lords; they might have been more at risk in battle but battle losses were only a fraction of total losses and their superior wealth must have meant they were less exposed though never immune, to malnutrition and its attendant risks. So a likely figure for the army at its greatest would be around the 50,000–60,000 mark including non-combatants . . . It has already been noted that the main force of the People's Crusade was of the order of 20,000, of whom about 3,000 survived to march on, so a total of 70,000–80,000 reached Asia Minor at one time or another.[85]

---

[83]   Runciman, *A History of the Crusades*, I 169; further discussion on pp. 336–41.
[84]   Riley-Smith, *The Crusades: A Short History*, 11.
[85]   France, *Victory in the East*, 141–2; the whole problem of numbers is discussed on pp. 122–42.

For the Second Crusade there is only the impressionistic account of Otto of Freising, who recorded that 'in a short time you might have seen the whole earth at peace and countless numbers from Gaul and from Germany accepting crosses and undertaking military service against the enemies of the Cross', and again, Conrad III 'drew after him so great a throng that the rivers seemed scarcely to suffice for navigation, or the extent of the plains for marching'.[86] Odo of Deuil has nothing to say on numbers in the army of Louis VII. Conrad divided his army at Nicaea, sending 14,000 men with Otto of Freising along the longer coast road while he led the remainder, including all non-combatants, by the inland road. At Dorylaion he was attacked, and, as William of Tyre records, 'Of seventy thousand mailed knights and many companies of foot soldiers, countless in number, barely a tenth part escaped.' If the figures are in doubt the proportion of losses has generally been accepted. The force with Otto was also virtually annihilated and he had to proceed to the East by sea.[87] It is perhaps not surprising that no modern estimates have been made.

The same is true for the Third and Fourth Crusades, for which there is some anecdotal evidence that is difficult to use to estimate overall numbers since so many separate contingents made their way to Syria. Richard I was joined on his journey through France and at Messina by various contingents, and yet his crusade is often represented as a discrete crusade. Two such discreet crusade groups were the German and the English, each with 100,000 in their respective ranks, it is said, as they crossed the Save River with Frederick Barbarossa or crossed the Rhône at Lyons with Richard I.[88] At Marseilles Richard awaited a fleet of over 114 ships from England.[89] Philip I Augustus had contracted with the Genoese for 5,850 marks for the transport of 650 knights, 1,300 squires and their horses with food and fodder for eight months, and wine for four months.[90] Unlike in the Plantagenet and Hohenstaufen crusades, the French contingents travelled separately, intending to meet up in the Holy Land; thus Henry, duke of Burgundy, arrived there separately with 500 knights and 4,000 foot soldiers. Previously, in March 1188, William II of Sicily had sent 500 knights to the aid of the Kingdom of Jerusalem. Certainly much more evidence was becoming

[86] C.C. Mierow, trans., *The Deeds of Frederick Barbarossa by Otto of Freising and his continuator Rahewin* (New York, 1953; reissued 1966), 78–9.

[87] Babcock, E.A. and Krey, A.C., trans., *A History of the Deeds Done Beyond the Sea by William Archbishop of Tyre*, II (New York, 1943), 171–2; C.C. Mierow, trans., *The Two Cities: A Chronicle of Universal History in the year 1146 by Otto Bishop of Freising* (New York, 1928), 16.

[88] Arnold of Lübeck, cited by Runciman, *A History of the Crusades*, III, 11, n.4; Ansbert confines himself to comments of the 'infinite number' variety, but he does list the principal nobles who accompanied Frederick – see *Historia de Expeditione Frederici I Imperatoris*, in A. Chroust, ed., *Quellen zur Geschichte des Kreuzzuges Kaiser Friedrichs I* (MGH, Scriptores reum Germanicarum new series 6, Berlin, 1928), 15–22; M.J. Hubert and J. La Monte, trans., *The Crusade of Richard Lion-Heart by Ambroise* (New York, 1941), line 419.

[89] C. Tyerman, *England and the Crusades 1095–1588* (Oxford, 1988), 80–2.

[90] C. Imperiale di Sant'Angelo, ed., *Codice diplomatico della repubblica di genova* (3 vols, Genoa, 1936–42), II, 366–8.

available from official and legal sources to supplement the chroniclers' estimates, but it is not helpful in talking of overall numbers with so many groups involved.

The planners of the Fourth Crusade tried to muster and transport their army as one complete force that would rendezvous at Venice in April 1202 and proceed eastwards together. The crusade was to be entirely seaborne, unlike any previous crusade. The planning and conceptualisation of the crusade was strikingly new and clearly acceptable and plausible to the Venetians, who agreed to provide all the transport required and to join in the expedition themselves with fifty galleys led by the doge himself. In April 1201 it was estimated that the total force for the crusade would be 4,500 knights, 9,000 squires and 20,000 foot sergeants, together with 4,500 horses. The total cost was to be 85,000 marks, at the rate of 5 marks per horse and 2 marks per man; the total estimated force for the crusade was 33,500. As Villehardouin recorded, not all these crusaders kept the rendezvous in Venice; many, an unknown number, chose to sail from other ports. In part it must have been sheer frustration at the failure of this revolutionary crusade plan that led Geoffrey of Villehardouin to dub those absconders 'traitors'.

If so little that is definite can be said about numbers, three crusades have been examined from the point of view of the known participants looking at their family, political and kinship links. This approach is not entirely new, but it has benefited from new work and especially from the application of computer technology.[91] Much that is useful, quantifiable and revealing emerges from these studies. Firstly, crusading was an activity for free men. Any lingering notional ideas about camp followers and the surge of serfs and villeins joining the peasants' or popular contingent of the First Crusade must be jettisoned with this in mind. Secondly, only a very small proportion of the total population of western Christendom participated in the Crusades. This is not surprising, given the numbers bound to the soil. However, it is noteworthy how much better the rich and the notable faired in the numerous setbacks on the various crusades when compared to the poor, who usually were the principal casualties in the disasters of the First and Second crusades.

Riley-Smith has shown the importance of the kin group, both on crusade and in the recruitment for and financing of the expedition. 'Women probably played the same positive role in the transmission of support from one family to another as they did with respect to monastic reform . . . a woman is often to be found at the junction between her own family, which produces many crusaders, and the one she has married into, in which the only recruits are associated with her in one way or another.'[92] This is one of the most unexpected findings of his work, along with the establishment of family traditions of crusading and pride in the crusading record of forebears that seem to have been well-established by 1140.

---

[91] R. Röhricht, *Studien zur geschichte des fünften Kreuzzüges* (Innsbruck, 1891), 79–135; Riley-Smith, *The First Crusaders 1095–1131*; Longnon, *Les Compagnons de Villehardouin*; Powell, *Anatomy of a Crusade 1213–1221*, 67–88, 207–58.

[92] Riley-Smith, *The First Crusaders*, 98.

Relatives in the Church became particularly evident on the eve of departure, either seeking endowments for a particular religious house or to give their spiritual support. His work on the families of the counts of Burgundy, of the Montlhery, the Le Puiset, and the Lusignans as descendants of Almodis of La Marche is particularly illuminating and important, and should be consulted in the work cited. Kin groups were to be found on crusade with no plethora of younger sons, but often fathers and sons. Longnon has found the same pattern amongst the warriors on the Fourth Crusade, where many family groups were to be found and kinship ties and bonds of loyalty played a significant role. The well-established position of many of the participants would seem to preclude settlement in the East. Powell has found that 16 per cent of German bishops went on the Fifth Crusade and 29 per cent of them had relatives on the crusade. Of the knights participating, 26 per cent of the French, 17 per cent of the German and 20 per cent of the English had relatives. Crusading was definitely not the preserve of the landless younger sons. The geographical spread of those participating in the three crusades would seem to enlarge through time, from being a mainly French affair in 1096 to embracing most of Western Europe from York to Cassino and from Rodez to Kuenring by 1217.

Backsliding on crusader vows was an issue right from the start. During the First Crusade Anselm, bishop of Ribemont, who was killed at Arqah in April 1099, urged that those who had taken crusader vows in the archdiocese of Rheims should be forced to fulfil them, presumably by the moral pressure of their neighbours.[93] In 1123 the First Lateran Council imposed an interdict on the lands of those who did not fulfil their crusading vows, and in 1215 the Fourth Lateran Council increased the penalty to excommunication. Failure to raise the appropriate funds for participation was not deemed an adequate excuse by the early thirteenth century.

Logistics

Mounting a crusade was no easy task and the time given for preparation was often short, allowing no leeway for political events, depressed economic conditions or poor harvests. In the twelfth century many proposed expeditions never got beyond the planning stage, and those that did happen usually ran into difficulties of finance and supply. By comparison with the First Crusade, which seemed to surmount all these difficulties, the crusades of the twelfth century seemed to wallow in the sins of the participants.[94] Yet it was also acknowledged that God helped those who helped themselves, and in 1199 the financing of crusade by the Church was introduced. In 1213 a substantial lead-in period of four years prior to a crusade was declared.

---

[93] Hagenmeyer, *Die Kreuzzugsbriefe aus dem Jahren 1088–1100*, 144–6, 156–60.
[94] It was of course more apparent than real since there were many who did not fulfil their vow due to lack of funding and who were the subject of Anselm of Ribemont's letters.

For men of means it has been estimated that a pilgrimage to Jerusalem in the eleventh century needed at least one year's income; on this basis a crusade might well require four or five times the income from an average knightly estate.[95] Planning embraced family or comital contingents, not the expedition as a whole, which did not come together as one large army until the siege of Nicaea in May 1097. Provision was left largely, if not entirely, to the individual participant. Gerald of Wales records that in 1188, for a wealthy prince with sufficient determination like Rhys ap Gruffydd, it took just fifteen days to make the necessary preparations for so distant a journey – until his wife's objection put a stop to his plans.[96] Length of campaign, distance over which supplies had to be transported and individual needs dictated what resources and rations were to be committed.

It must not be thought that Jerusalem was a far-away place about which nothing was known; some information was available regarding the length of the journey and the territories through which the armies must pass. Quite early on, as preparations for the First Crusade were underway, there was an idea that the campaign would take about three years. Crusade leaders like Peter the Hermit and Robert of Flanders had both gone on pilgrimage to Jerusalem via Constantinople, and some comital families (like those of Robert of Normandy) had relatives who had also made the pilgrimage to Jerusalem; others had relatives who had served as mercenaries in the Byzantine army.[97] The main pilgrimage route from the West through Hungary and the Balkans was also well known. The quality and reliability of this knowledge improved through time and the development of the crusade movement.

Negotiation with the relevant Christian rulers whose kingdoms lay along the land route was essential, especially since the efforts to raise sufficient money chests by the leaders before departure suggest that the purchase of supplies was one of the major expenses that they anticipated. Those travelling via Norman Italy seemed to have been well received, and their hosts given warning of their arrival. As regards Hungary and Byzantium, however, rulers were often only apprised of the approach of crusade armies by rumour and by the despatch of ambassadors asking permission to cross their realms just when the armies arrived at the borders. This gave little time for the agreement of a route of passage, or the provision of markets or supply dumps along that agreed route. It totally failed to appreciate that rulers of other countries might have preoccupations and agendas of their own. Whatever this tells us about the motivation and single-mindedness of the crusaders their resentment at attempts to keep them to a confined route suggests little or no understanding of either the enormity or the nature of the demand that a crusading army would have placed on local resources, and the

[95] J. Sumption, *Pilgrimage* (London, 1975), 169, 205–6; Riley-Smith, *The Crusades: A Short History*, 12.
[96] T. Wright, trans., *The Historical Works of Giraldus Cambrensis* (London, 1913), 332–3.
[97] France, *Victory in the East*, 98–102.

considerable organisational pressures that were placed on host communities. Those who had taken inadequate preparation for their journey were not slow to note the failings of the host communities. It is as if large numbers of small-scale expeditions are joined together in a huge mass, the like of which had not been experienced before, yet behaving as if they were discrete war bands limited in size and objective. There was clearly surprise that their approach might excite distrust and suspicion as to their intentions.

Except by reading inferentially, the western sources tell us little or nothing about the commissariat – especially pack animals, wagons, remounts, iron for horseshoes,[98] fodder and other supplies (particularly water) that were essential to the success of the crusade. Apart from Bohemond, who had campaigned in the Balkans from 1081 to 1085, none of the principal leaders – or indeed any one in the West – would have had experience of campaigning for such a long time with such a large army over such considerable distances from home and in such differing terrains. Preparation was left to each individual. Although Urban had suggested that God would provide what was necessary, he had carefully syn-chronised the departure of the First Crusade on 15 August 1096 with the harvest. Yet the people's crusade that had departed before the harvest in April 1096 did not run into difficulties until it crossed into the Byzantine Empire. Loss of its wagon train and cash had made it desperate, and its sudden appearance in the Empire had left the authorities with insufficient time to provide adequate sup-plies. Once they had mustered as one large army and marched into Asia Minor, the difficulties that the crusaders of 1096 and 1147 encountered, with regard to supplies of food, water and fodder, were predictable and should have been antici-pated by the leadership; indeed, they had all been discussed in Byzantine military manuals for generations, from the sixth century to the tenth. These had consist-ently recommended that soldiers should take twenty or thirty days' supplies with them on campaign.[99] This precaution the crusaders seem to have ignored, or were incapable of providing. Conrad III spectacularly ignored it on the Second Crusade, which that was bedevilled by food and water shortages soon after its departure from Nicaea. Indeed, his catastrophic defeat near Dorylaion was in part due to the dehydration of his thirsty army. Some of this might well have been avoided with forethought and begs the question of the quality of leadership on the Second Crusade.

Food was always a problem, and reliance seems to have been placed on local markets in Christian territory and upon foraging in hostile territories or when local markets failed to deliver adequate supplies. This problem meant that armies

---

[98] Richard I purchased 50,000 horseshoes from the ironworks of the Forest of Dean for his crusade; see J. Gillingham, *Richard I* (London, 1999), 114.

[99] Byzantine didactic military handbooks had a long tradition and may be said to originate with the work of Aeneas Tacticus in the fourth century BC. J. Haldon, *Warfare, State and Society in the Byzantine World, 565–1204* (London, 1999), 166–83; G.T. Dennis, *Three Byzantine Military Treatises* (Washington, 1985), 159, 161, 215, 225, 285.

had to keep on the move. The fifteen-month siege of Antioch was to pose particular problems, with foraging parties having to range ever further from camp and thus expose themselves to Turkish attack. Some roamed as far as 40–50 miles from base and others travelled to Edessa and Cyprus.[100] In the absence of tinned or dried foods it is perhaps difficult to see what other provision could have been made. Through the Balkans the Byzantine authorities had provided food dumps at regular intervals. These seem to have been provided without too much difficulty. It was expecting much of Hungarian and Byzantine communities on the line of march to provide adequate resources, and this often led to violence and disagreements. Peter the Hermit and his following had passed peacefully through Hungary, presumably sustained by supplies loaded in his wagon train of 2,000 wagons. Most of these wagons, including the contingent's war chest, had been lost at Nish. Now desperate for food and lacking the money to buy supplies, Albert of Aachen described how the force with Peter the Hermit gathered the harvest around the village of Bela Palanka after its inhabitants had deserted it, whilst Odo of Deuil recounts the resentment in the army of Louis VII as it followed the route of Conrad III through the Balkans, a route that had already been eaten up by the German crusaders. Manuel's refusal to provide supplies to the French camp at Chalcedon brought Louis VII to agree to restore any recaptured Byzantine territory to the Empire. Interestingly, it forced the Franks to eat the supplies that they had laid aside for their journey. This is the first direct mention of such rations. Odo of Deuil also mentions that the German crusaders were each to gather eight days' supplies for the march from Nicaea to Iconium.[101] There seems to have been a lack of political will to co-ordinate and to consult. This was to improve, but, as John France has observed, for the leaders of the First Crusade co-operative action was something of which none of them had any real experience.[102] This was equally true of Conrad III and Louis VII.

The change to seaborne crusading in the late twelfth century involved planning as to the provision of supply, now the responsibility of the provider of the ships. Good planning could obviate distress. This was shown by the voyage to the East of Adelaide of Salerno in 1115, who stocked her flotilla with grain, wine, oil and salt meat as well as with well-filled treasure chests and reinforcements of knights and foot soldiers.[103] Adelaide was wealthy and could rely on the nautical expertise of the Normans of south Italy. With seaborne crusades reliable estimates of the number of combatants and animals to be transported became essential, since not just ships but horse transports had to be obtained or constructed. As in

[100]   Ryan and Fink, *Fulcher of Chartres, A History of the Expedition to Jerusalem, 1095–1127*, 95; J.H. and L.L. Hill, trans., *Raymond d'Aguilers, Historia Francorum Qui Ceperunt Iherusalem*, 53–4.
[101]   Runciman, *A History of the Crusades*, I, 126–7, and II, 263, 269; Berry, trans., *Odo of Deuil, De Profectione Ludovici VII in orientem*, 77, 91.
[102]   France, *Victory in the East*, 79.
[103]   Babcock and Krey, *A History of Deeds Done Beyond the Sea by William Archbishop of Tyre*, I, 497.

1201/2, this might involve the whole capacity of a maritime republic like Venice which put a stop on overseas trade during the construction of the fleet for the Fourth Crusade. Negotiation and information exchange seem also to have been better addressed, although mistakes could be made as with the estimated turn out for the Fourth Crusade that threatened to ruin the Venetian economy and the dogeship of Enrico Dandolo.

Byzantine military manuals had much to say on water and the danger to troops and horses if this was denied for half a day during summer campaigning.[104] At the outset members of the First Crusade seemed to be particularly negligent in securing this essential support to life. Neglecting to equip themselves with skin bottles of water, they trusted themselves to Byzantine cisterns and to the springs of villages, directing their march from settlement to settlement. None of these could be relied upon, as was illustrated by the cruel fate of the 6,000 French crusaders trapped in Xerigordon in 1097, the poor crusaders dying of thirst soon after the victory at Dorylaion, and the dried up Byzantine cisterns that confronted the crusaders in 1147. Nonetheless, they did learn. Water brought up to the front line by women during the battle at Dorylaion played a major part in the Frankish victory. The anonymous *Gesta Francorum* also records the advice given by the inhabitants of Iconium (Konya) to equip themselves with skins full of water (*utres plenos aqua*) on the first part of their journey to Heraklea (Eregli), which would consist of a full day's march with no water and hence no settlements.[105] After the fall of Antioch in 1098 the early discussions regarding the march to Jerusalem set November as the month for departure precisely because the crusaders had learned the lessons of waterless summer marches. Yet problems with water supply were to remain a problem right through the twelfth century. The army of the Kingdom of Jerusalem was to suffer defeat twice due to being surrounded with no water – first in 1113 and finally in 1187 at the disastrous debacle of Hattin.

For all that food shortages were recorded more than thirst, and the acts of cannibalism perpetrated at Marra were recorded in a matter-of-fact way and do not seem to have elicited any particular acts of penance.[106] The chroniclers cited poverty as the cause of starvation consequent on the dearth of supplies. Food was to be had but at a price. Certainly it was disproportionate numbers of the poor who suffered and died from malnutrition. Those who could not afford tents died from exposure to the elements.[107] Prices of supplies became prohibitive in

---

[104] Dennis, *Three Byzantine Military Treatises*, 159, 225, 285.

[105] Hill, *ed.*, *Gesta Francorum et aliorum Hierosolimitanorum*, 19, 23.

[106] Fink and Ryan, *Fulcher of Chartres, A History of the Expedition to Jerusalem, 1095–1127*, 112; J.H. and L.L. Hill, trans., *Raymond d'Aguilers, Historia Francorum Qui Ceperunt Iherusalem*, 81; Hill, ed., *Gesta Francorum et Aliorum Hierosolimitanorum*, 80.

[107] Fink and Ryan, *Fulcher of Chartres, A History of the Expedition to Jerusalem, 1095–1127*, 96, 131.

times of dearth.[108] Although sumpters were accused of profiteering and greed there were always those who could and would pay the prices. In the environs of Constantinople moneychangers were available in the markets set up for the Second Crusade to facilitate purchases, and these offered tempting targets for the indigents. Violence offered to these, however, seemed to imperil the very provision of the market.[109] It was expected that if a market was provided then the safety of the traders should be guaranteed. In less sophisticated towns bartering was acceptable, especially the swords and shields of the crusaders.

The enterprise that the presence of a crusading army might stimulate is well noted by Guibert of Nogent: 'the clever Armenians and Syrians, when they saw that the army's food was running out [at Antioch], . . . travelled about among all the places that they knew, bought grain and brought it back to the army that was suffering from lack of supplies. They sold the grain at inordinate prices, so that the amount of grain a single ass could carry brought eight of their besants . . . approximately 120 sous.'[110]

Once the crusaders had reached Antioch, and thereafter on their advance to Jerusalem, enterprising merchants brought ships with supplies from Cyprus and Italy. These set up markets, but only supplied the wealthy; and starvation continued amongst the poor.[111] Everything was paid for. On the second and third day after the capture of Jerusalem on 15 July 1099 markets were set up for the sale of provisions found in the city. Even the poor did not go wanting since they had earned money clearing the dead from the city and so could afford to purchase what they needed.[112]

The only wagons mentioned on the crusade were the 2,000 with Peter the Hermit, mentioned by Albert of Aachen, but there were certainly others as may be inferred from the eagerness with which Bohemond's army seized oxen and mules at Kastoria on their way to Constantinople. In view of the problem of transport across the Bosphoros and the narrow mountain tracks that were to be traversed, these may not have proceeded into Asia Minor, although Odo of Deuil mentions two- and four-horse carts being transported on boats down the Danube. He also talks of the delays caused by wagons breaking down and suggests that their usefulness was limited, except to give a sense of well being.[113] Pack animals too were present and recorded as perishing for lack of fodder or falling

[108]   J.H. and L.L. Hill, trans., *Raymond d'Aguilers, Historia Francorum Qui Ceperunt Iherusalem*, 35, 59; Fink and Ryan, *Fulcher of Chartres, A History of the Expedition to Jerusalem, 1095–1127*, 96; Hill, ed., *Gesta Francorum et Aliorum Hierosolimitanorum*, 90.

[109]   Berry, trans., *Odo of Deuil, De Profectione Ludovici VII in orientem*, 73–7.

[110]   Levine, *The Deeds of God Through the Franks*, 78.

[111]   Levine, *The Deeds of God Through the Franks*, 99, and 103, where prices and availability of foodstuffs in Antioch are mentioned.

[112]   Babcock and Krey, *A History of Deeds Done Beyond the Sea by William Archbishop of Tyre*, I, 377.

[113]   Berry, trans. *Odo of Deuil, De Profectione Ludovici VII in orientem*, 25.

from mountain tracks, but there is no indication of their numbers except that they were diminishing rapidly.[114]

Sheep and cattle were also seized on the journey eastwards as food on the hoof; when these were not available feeble and dying horses were consumed. Both crusaders and Turks sought to deny each other pasture facilities, or to run off each other's herds and flocks as they came upon them and thus to deprive each other of food resources. Sheep seem to have been hardier than sumpter animals, horses and cows. Such animals can only be driven in lines and their presence would have served to both extend the line of march and to slow it down. Providing fodder and pasture for these animals was essential to maintain their well-being. Suitable pasture cannot have been easy to find en route, and once in Turkish territory it often had to be fought for, since both Turks and crusaders sought to deny one another pasture. Given the high volume of waste products produced by large concentration of animals, an extensive area for grazing was required for any stay longer than three days. This necessity must have presented considerable scouting and security problems to any crusading army. Horses seem to have been particularly prone to injury and disease. It is reckoned that none of the horses and mules that left the West in 1096 actually survived to reach Syria – hence the pressure to buy local breeds of animals. They were protected whenever possible and replaced when opportunity arose, horses even being bought from the emirs of Homs and Tripoli in 1098.[115]

Those without resources were at extreme risk on crusade, and a well-stocked war chest was clearly a desideratum – a point not lost on Alexios I, who rewarded the crusading army after the fall of Nicaea with gold (*nomisma/bezant*) or copper (*tetarteron*) coins according to their status.[116]

The raising of cash for crusading was left to each individual participant according to his means and his needs. This was to be the case right through the Crusades, despite the introduction of official taxation for crusade funding in the late twelfth century. The remission of interest payments for crusaders may have exacerbated the raising of loans, but the practice of gifts in which an interest payment was included was one way round this impasse. Clearly crusading in the Baltic, in the Languedoc or in Spain would not have been so expensive as a Holy Land crusade since rations and transport costs would have been less; but the other expenses remained. It was not only food, equipment, war horses, remounts, transport and retainers that were required for the noble contemplating a crusade; cash was also needed to finance all these activities in a manner appropriate to their status. Unforeseen expenses such as gift exchange, ransom, compensation

[114] Fink and Ryan, *Fulcher of Chartres, A History of the Expedition to Jerusalem, 1095–1127*, 88; *De Profectione Ludovici VII in orientem*, 105, 117.

[115] J.H. and L.L. Hill, trans., *Raymond d'Aguilers, Historia Francorum Qui Ceperunt Iherusalem*, 84; Hill, ed., *Gesta Francorum et Aliorum Hierosolimitanorum*, 81–3.

[116] Fink and Ryan, *Fulcher of Chartres, A History of the Expedition to Jerusalem, 1095–1127*, 80, 83; the Anonymous author of the *Gesta* records that only the poor pilgrims received alms (p.18).

and emoluments to specialised craftsmen might also arise on crusade. Raymond d'Aguilers has recorded all of these exigencies as experienced by Raymond of Toulouse: gifts to the king of Slavonia, compensation to his followers for the loss of horses, contributions to the construction of siege works at Antioch, the purchase of remounts from Shaizar, a gift of 5,000 *solidi* and two Arabian horses to Tancred, and payments to artisans for the construction of siege engines at Jerusalem.[117] Raymond of Toulouse had also sought to use his considerable resources to buy the loyalty of the of the crusade army for the final march on Jerusalem.[118] It appears that only such a wealthy ruler as Raymond of Toulouse could finance crusading activity from income; for the rest the selling or mortgaging of land and/or seigniorial rights raised the cash required to supplement any dues procured from tenants. Sometimes pack animals were included in the purchase price too. Charters provide the evidence for most of these transactions. They often include rights for the redemption of the property, or at least enjoyment of the usufruct for the term of the seller's life should they return from crusade. The Church, usually a bishop or a religious house, was the vehicle that turned land and rights into hard cash. That an institution existed that could provide funds on this scale by the end of the eleventh century made the crusade viable at that time, and it is noteworthy that such means of capital accumulation were available in Western Europe by the end of the eleventh century. Italian merchants did not figure in the financing of the Crusades in the early twelfth century; they were to come much later, and certainly after the papacy had taken steps to regularise and equalise the funding of crusading (see pp. 333–7). It also meant that crusading was an occupation for free men and women only.

The sums raised were occasionally paid in gold, but more often in silver pennies (*deniers/denarii*) recorded as 10,000 silver marks (for the pawn of Normandy by William Rufus), 1,000 pieces of silver raised by Godfrey of Bouillon from the Jewish communities of Cologne and Mainz, or 2,000 *solidi* of Lyons for the mortgage of a property to Cluny.[119] The marks that Robert Curthouse received for Normandy were made up of 16 million pennies (payable in four instalments), whilst 2,000 *solidi* came to 24,000. There was no easy or convenient way to transport such sums. It was usually transported in chests or barrels in wagons – at least that is where Peter the Hermit kept his funds. Quite how this money was transported over mountain ranges and kept secure in the tents of a besieging army is never explained or mentioned. Sometimes it was lost. Stephen of Blois lost much money when a vessel sunk in the harbour at Bari and, as we have seen, Peter the Hermit lost all his funds, together with his wagon train, at Nish.[120] It is

[117] J.H. and L.L. Hill, trans., *Raymond d'Aguilars, Historia Francorum Qui Ceperunt Iherusalem*, 18, 36, 46, 84, 92, 124.
[118] J.H. and L.L. Hill, trans., *Raymond d'Aguilars, Historia Francorum Qui Ceperunt Iherusalem*, 80.
[119] Examples from France, *Victory in the East*, 84–7.
[120] Fink and Ryan, *Fulcher of Chartres, A History of the Expedition to Jerusalem, 1095–1127*, 76, and see p. 328 above.

mentioned that Bohemond kept accounts of his expenditure on crusade and that Raymond withdrew cash from his treasury.[121] There were also opportunities to increase funding on the march itself. Alexios I had been generous in his gifts to the crusading leadership, just as his grandson Manuel I was to be to Louis VII and Conrad III. There was booty both in precious objects and in kind to be obtained from captured camps, towns and farmsteads, provided they were outside Byzantine territory. Fulcher of Chartres gives the most embellished accounts of the spoils obtained in this way.[122] All in all it is amazing what funding could be raised in such a short time, and how it could be husbanded and used in emergencies.

In the context of the siege of Arqah Raymond d'Aguilars wrote:

> The king of Tripoli offered us fifteen thousand gold pieces of Saracen money plus horses, she-mules, many garments and even more of such rewards in succeeding years. To give this offer meaning one gold piece was equivalent to eight or nine *solidi*. Our money in circulation included Pictavini (Poitou), Cartensis (Chartres), Manses (Le Mans), Luccenses (Lucca), Valanzani (Valence), Melgoriensis (Melgueil) and Pogesi (Le Puys), the last named being two for one of the others.[123]

Of these seven different types of coin current in the Latin East the coins of Lucca and Valence predominate by far in the coin hoards that have been found. Possibly they were the preferred currencies of the Latin states until such time as they minted their own coins sometime before 1100.[124] As the crusaders moved east they moved from their own silver standard economies to the gold standard economies of the Byzantine and Muslim East. Raymond reflects this and gives the rate of gold to silver exchange. Curiously Raymond does not mention Byzantine coinage. Whatever the religious motivation and commitment of the crusaders, the Crusades were fuelled by cash. Even so famous a warrior as Bohemond threatened to withdraw from the siege of Antioch because his limited personal wealth seemed inadequate to support both him and his followers during a protracted siege. Nothing came of the threat, but its basis – lack of cash – seems to have been accepted as a reason for withdrawal by an honourable man.[125]

Good logistics may have been beyond the planners of the early crusades, but poor logistics had a deleterious affect upon discipline. Food shortages usually provoked rioting as when the Lombard contingent, deprived of markets outside

[121] J.H. and L.L Hill, trans., *Raymond d'Aguilars, Historia Francorum Qui Ceperunt Iherusalem*, 124.

[122] Fink and Ryan, *Fulcher of Chartres, A History of the Expedition to Jerusalem, 1095–1127*, 106, 122, 127.

[123] J.H. and L.L. Hill, trans., *Raymond d'Aguilars, Historia Francorum Qui Ceperunt Iherusalem*, 91.

[124] D. Metcalf, *Coinage of the Crusades and the Latin East* (London, 1983), 2–6.

[125] J.H. and L.L. Hill, trans., *Raymond d'Aguilars, Historia Francorum Qui Ceperunt Iherusalem*, 35.

Constantinople, broke into the Blachernae palace and killed one of Alexios I's prized pet lions. Anselm, archbishop of Milan, and Albert, count of Biandrate, succeeded in restoring order on their own – but it was a deplorable incident.[126] Lack of discipline had been a regrettable feature of the early crusades. It was by no means confined to the poor, but was exacerbated by the presence of large numbers of non-combatants. If Alexios I had been dismayed by the composition of the crusading hosts as they had arrived at Constantinople this may in part be due to the warnings in Byzantine military manuals against too many non-combatants on any military expedition.[127] It was not until the end of the twelfth century that steps were taken to limit their numbers on crusades.

The change to seaborne crusades limited the space available, and what was available was assigned to fighting men. Mercenaries were used increasingly and professionalism was replacing weight of numbers. Those recruited by the preaching of crusade by Baldwin of Canterbury in 1188 and Fulk of Neuilly in 1201 seem, with a few exceptions, to have been mainly nobles and knights. The leaders of the crusades tried to oversee recruitment and to exclude non-combatants. Their households provided the basis of such recruitment, with mercenaries hired by contract. For the latter there was to be pay as well as the spiritual rewards and protection of property. Prince Edward in 1270 issued contracts of service in which 100 marks were paid to each hired knight for one year's service.[128] Priests there had to be for the spiritual needs of the warriors, but ordinances issued by Henry II for the conduct of crusaders in 1188 forbade women to take part in the proposed crusade, except for 'laundresses of good repute'.[129] Godliness and cleanliness were the requirements for any non-combatants wishing to go as pilgrims on crusade. Whatever crusade leaders might lay down and achieve for their own followers, crusading remained very attractive to men and women of all classes, who could not be dissuaded from participating despite the official introduction and endorsement of redemption payments in the early thirteenth century.[130] Non-combatants were to found on all crusading expeditions in the thirteenth and fourteenth centuries. From about the 1190s discipline too was generally tightened up, with recourse to public execution for defaulters, thieves and looters. The discipline imposed by Frederick Barbarossa excited Muslim observers to wonder at the manner in which he treated his men; but such measures were not lacking from the Fourth Crusade either. Undisciplined looting, although it never disappeared, became something associated with the poor in the pages of the chroniclers, and in particular with the *pastoreaux* of 1251 and 1320.

---

[126]   Runciman, *A History of the Crusades*, II, 20.
[127]   Dennis, ed., *Three Byzantine Military Treatises*, 287–8; Dawes, trans., *The Alexiad of the Princess Anna Comnena*, 249–50.
[128]   M. Prestwich, *Edward I* (London, 1988), 68–71; H. Richardson and G. Sayles, *The Governance of Medieval England* (Edinburgh, 1963), 463–5.
[129]   Roger of Howden, *Gesta Regis Henrici Secundi*, ed. W. Stubbs (2 vols, London, 1867), II, 30–2, cited by W.L. Warren, *Henry II* (London, 1973), 607.
[130]   Riley-Smith, *What Were the Crusades?*, 67.

Financing the Crusades; the official approach[131]

From its inception the resources of the participants financed crusading, and this approach continued throughout the crusading movement. As pilgrims, the crusaders were expected to pay for themselves. Lack of funds prevented many from fulfilling their crusading vows. However, many of the lords who sought to crusade spent their time and their resources in defending their rights and property or threatening that of others. They thus had accumulated little capital. Both Urban II and Eugenius III had laid down that intending crusaders might pledge or sell their lands and possessions (such as mills, ovens, rents, advowsons, court dues, fairs and serfs) to the Church to raise money, and had excused crusaders from paying interest on debts while they were on crusade. Both these procedures were accepted in canon and civil law by the end of the twelfth century and remained the normal resort of those funding an individual crusade to the Holy Land.[132] In the early twelfth century only the existence of monastic credit allowed crusading to function in this way. Precious metals in candelabra, sacred vessels and crucifixes might be coined to supplement the monastic treasuries. If lenders could not charge interest on loans to crusaders they did enjoy the income of a property whilst it was mortgaged, and this might more than have made up for their outlay. However, this *laissez-faire* approach had revealed weaknesses from the start and within fifty years was proving totally inadequate to meet the spiralling cost of crusading, with the need to charter ships and to hire mercenaries and specialist troops like crossbowmen. What the pious members of the First Crusade had borne and seen as the chastisement of God, later crusading leaders were not prepared to endure. Lack of financial resources was holding back the recruitment of the right sort of crusader, the knight. Innocent III was aware of this when he observed to the Lateran Council in 1215: 'If the money be not wanting, the men will not be wanting.'[133] With the involvement of monarchs in crusade some sort of official financial provision for crusading was implemented.

In 1146 Louis VII raised a general levy on all his subjects to raise money for his crusade. The word 'levy' is generally used because it is not clear whether it was a form of feudal aid or a general tax to ward off a threat to the kingdom, like the Danegeld last collected in 926. It is not known what percentage of income and possessions was demanded, but it was asked of all, both clergy and laity, and, according to Ralph of Diceto, was most unpopular.[134] It did not raise anything

---

[131]   G. Constable, 'The Financing of the Crusades', in B. Kedar, *et al.*, eds, *Outremer* (1982), 64–88; M. Purcell, *Papal Crusading Policy 1244–1291* (Leiden, 1975), 99–156; Setton, ed., *A History of the Crusades*, VI, 116–49; Riley-Smith, *What Were the Crusades?*, 45–9; L. and J. Riley-Smith, *The Crusades: Idea and Reality*, 143–52.

[132]   Brundage, *Medieval Canon Law and the Crusade*, 175–87; Constable 'The Financing of the Crusades', 72–3.

[133]   Cited in Setton, ed., *A History of the Crusades*, VI, 117.

[134]   W. Stubbs, ed., *The Historical Works of Master Ralph of Diceto* (2 vols, London, 1876), I, 256–7, cited by Constable, 'The Financing of the Crusades', 67.

like enough money since once away from France Louis made frequent requests for more money to be sent him, presumably from income from the royal demesne. Conrad III did not resort to any levy and presumably sought to pay for his crusade from imperial income alone.

In 1166 Louis VII raised the first tax to provide financial aid for the Holy Land. It was levied at the rate of a penny in the pound (0.4 per cent) on the incomes and possessions of all his subjects for five years. The proceeds were to be sent to the Holy Land. He persuaded Henry II to follow suit; he set his levy at two pence in the pound. Other similar levies were made both in France and England in 1183 and 1185. The levies were, however, to raise cash for the Holy Land not to finance a crusade. Taxation was applied to crusading in 1188 when people in England and in France were required to give a tenth of their income and movable goods (10 per cent). Those who had taken the cross were exempt. Collection was on a parish basis, with excommunication threatened on those who did not comply. A check on the honesty of self-assessment was to be made at the time of payment by four or six law-worthy parishioners.[135] The money was to be got together in homes between Christmas 1188 and the 2 February 1189, and delivered to the parish church in the days thereafter. It was known as the 'Saladin Tithe'. Its heaviness and the precedence it set made it unpopular. Philip II Augustus suspended it in France, but in Angevin territory there was no remission; it was thought to have raised £70,000 in England alone. At his death Henry's treasury was thought to contain £90,000 (135,000 marks), certainly sufficient for 25,000 marks to be sent to Philip II in the opening months of Richard I's reign. However, vast sums were needed.[136] By 1270 the financing of the crusade of Prince Edward had become a matter for a parliamentary grant. Edward had taken the cross before the parliament at Northampton in 1268 and thereafter negotiated with the representatives of the laity to grant a tax to supplement the funds raised by the Church. In 1270 a subsidy of one-twentieth was granted by the knights and burgesses in parliament and expected to raise £31,000.[137]

On 31 December 1199, in the encyclical *Graves orientalis terrae*, Innocent III instituted direct taxation of the whole Church as the basis for the funding of crusades. This first direct tax was set at a fortieth of clerical incomes (2.5 per cent).[138] For the French clergy this represented a substantial reduction of a tax of 11/30ths (36 per cent) imposed on their incomes earlier in the year at the council of Dijon. It proved difficult to collect, and caused so many disputes with religious orders over exemptions that Innocent III did not repeat it in April 1213 when he proclaimed the Fifth Crusade in the encyclical *Quia maior*.[139] In

[135]   L. and J. Riley-Smith, *The Crusades: Idea and Reality*, 144.
[136]   Tyerman, *England and the Crusades*, 66–83, discusses the preparations in England.
[137]   Prestwich, *Edward I*, 72.
[138]   L. and J. Riley-Smith, *The Crusades: Idea and Reality*, 144–8.
[139]   L. and J. Riley-Smith, *The Crusades: Idea and Reality*, 118–24.

the encyclical *ad Liberandum*, issued on 30 November 1215, a general tax of a twentieth of all clerical incomes was imposed for a period of three years.[140] Direct clerical taxation was to be the main source for the funding of crusades in the later Middle Ages. At first it was collected on a diocesan basis with cathedral clergy involved, but in 1213 papal collectors or procurators were instituted, thus centralising the fund-raising process. The procurators were urged to deposit the money collected in a religious house and render annual accounts to the Pope. After 1228 the self-assessment by the clergy was abandoned in favour of the assessment of tax liability by the papal collectors. Clerical taxation for the crusades was here to stay, with taxes imposed at regular intervals: 1225, one-tenth (10 per cent) in France and one-fifth (20 per cent) in England, 1245 a levy of one-twentieth (5 per cent), 1263, one-hundredth (1 per cent) and in 1274 one-tenth (10 per cent) for five years. Popes oversaw the distribution of funds, either directly to rulers and others organising crusades in the West or sent eastwards by means of the military orders for financial supply once the crusade had departed. In 1274 at the Second Council of Lyons all Christendom was organised into twenty-six tax districts, with collectors and sub-collectors in each. In addition a tax of a tenth (10 per cent) for six years was imposed on the clergy, with no exemptions allowed.

Donations from the pious had been a part of crusade funding from the start, and these had helped fill the war chest of Peter the Hermit. Indeed, the sending of alms to the Holy Land was in place before the 1090s. William of Tyre recorded that the citizens of Amalfi had a well-developed system for collecting money and transmitting it to the abbot of St Mary of the Latins, the Benedictine house and hostel that Amalfian merchants had founded in 1071.[141] Throughout the crusading period donations continued to be made and continued to be important. In 1215 Innocent was able to set aside 3,000 marks derived from alms for the expenses of the proposed crusade, having previously sent an undisclosed sum from the same source for the Holy Land.[142] In his proclamation of the Fifth Crusade in April 1213 Innocent III made provision for the convenient and secure donation of money to aid the Holy Land by decreeing that chests locked with three keys should be placed in all churches 'where a general procession gathers'.[143] Despite these official measures the individual crusader was still reliant on his family or his own resources in his journey to the Holy Land. They did, however, receive certain tax exemption for crusaders, and these were thought to have stimulated recruitment to the Third Crusade according to Roger of Howden.[144] For all that, just like the levies of the Capetians and Plantagenets the

[140] L. and J. Riley-Smith, *The Crusades: Idea and Reality*, 124–9.
[141] Babcock and Krey, *A History of Deeds Done Beyond the Sea by William Archbishop of Tyre*, II, 243.
[142] L. and J. Riley-Smith, *The Crusades: Idea and Reality*, 126.
[143] L. and J. Riley-Smith, *The Crusades: Idea and Reality*, 124.
[144] Warren, *Henry II*, 377–8, 607–8; Gillingham, *Richard I*, 89, 114.

monies gathered by the papal legates were paid to the leaders of a crusade and were of little assistance in meeting the immediate expenses of the intending crusader.

The expenses faced by the crusade leadership were enormous. The expenses of Louis IX from 1250 to 1253 were well in excess of 1,053,000 *livres* of Paris and were expended on the costs of the royal households while overseas, transport, both ship rental and pack animals, costs of soldiers and craftsmen, building works and the ransoms of captives, including 167,102 *livres* for Louis himself.[145]

Legacies too were encouraged. Small sums might be collected through the new system of papal collectors, but large endowments tended to go to the international military orders or to religious houses in the East.[146] From 1198, with the founding of the Order of the Most Holy Trinity, the so-called Trinitarians, Mathurins or Red Friars, whose income and endowments were in part dedicated to the ransom of captives in the hands of infidels, another order worthy of legacies from those with crusading interest was available.

Plenary indulgences went back to the roots of the Crusades and may have originated with them. Remission of time in purgatory had been a reward of the crusaders from the start. It expanded from partial to complete remission of sins confessed in the first half of the twelfth century, and by the early thirteenth century was applicable to all geographical areas of crusading, not just the Holy Land. Crusaders in the Balkans, the Baltic, the Iberian Peninsula and the Languedoc received indulgences on the same terms. Innovation in this context came in 1213 when the preaching of crusade was once again aimed at the broadest spectrum of society to embrace women, the aged and the infirm. Procurators were encouraged to accept crusading vows from those they might deem unsuitable, with the idea that these would either pay for a substitute to go on crusade or redeem their vows with cash payments. They were entitled to the benefits of crusade indulgence just as those who actually went on crusade. They probably did not enjoy the crusader privilege of freedom from interest on debts, but this is not clear. Any substitutes who went in their place also enjoyed the indulgence. This innovation was very popular indeed. Matthew Paris described crusade recruitment in England in 1241. He noted that women, old men, the sick and disabled, and children took the cross, with the intention of gaining the promised remission of sins rather than with any serious intention of participating in the proposed crusade.[147] Indulgences were changing from a reward for those who endured the hardships of an armed pilgrimage and fulfilled their crusader vows to a means of financing the Crusades, merit that could be bought and not earned. The procurators oversaw the taking of vows and their redemption. This would

---

[145] L. and J. Riley-Smith, *The Crusades: Idea and Reality*, 148–52.

[146] L. and J. Riley-Smith, *The Crusades: Idea and Reality*, 173–7, where two crusaders' wills are translated. Tyerman, *England and the Crusades*, 46, 105–6, 205.

[147] H. Luard, ed., *Matthew Paris, Chronica Majora*, IV (London, 1877), 134, cited and discussed in S. Shahar, *Growing Old in the Middle Ages* (London, 1995), 2.

obviate fraud since the selling of false indulgences was a fact condemned at the Lateran Council of 1215 and was to be condemned again by popes through the fourteenth century. Redemption might be extended to the commutation of vows to provide support for a crusading enterprise deemed more urgent by the Pope. Thus in November 1239 Gregory X tried to persuade Richard of Cornwall to commute his crusading vow and to give the grant he had received for his own crusade to finance a proposed crusade to aid the Latin Empire of Constantinople. This proposal had no appeal for Richard, who continued with preparations for his own crusade.[148]

Those whose credit was good could avail themselves of increasing and improving financial facilities during the thirteenth century. Italian banking families with their networks of branches were able and willing to extend credit. The Florentine banking firm of Acciaiuoli were closely associated with the Angevins of Naples, making substantial loans for their crusades against the Hohenstaufen in Italy and for their campaigns in the Morea after 1267. So closely were their interests linked to a stable Angevin rule that as soon as the revolt of the Sicilian Vespers broke in March 1282 they advanced 15,000 ounces of gold (*onzi*) and 5,000 florins. In the 1330s they were to reduce the huge debts owed them by the Angevins by accepting lands and other resources in the principality of Achaea. Edward I received loans from the Riccardi of Lucca, both in Acre and on his way back to England. They were to remain bankers to the English crown until their collapse in 1294. In 1250 Louis IX was able to raise ransom money at Damietta from a floating Templar bank, the sum repayable in Acre.[149]

Diplomacy and the Crusades

Diplomacy, or the conduct of relations between kingdoms and foreign potentates by accredited representatives, was well documented in the Old Testament and did not cease with the end of the Roman Empire in the West. Popes and the Holy Roman Emperors kept up contacts with the Byzantine Empire and with a variety of rulers in Western Europe. During the period of the Crusades, however, a broader group of rulers, dukes and counts became involved, with a wider spectrum of cultures than previously encountered, and their skills and perceptions in this respect were developed and honed. In our sound-bite culture crusading might be seen as the first step to globalisation on the part of Western Europeans, and for many commentators in the twentieth century 'there is a clear continuous line from the crusades to the aggressive imperialism of the western European powers in the Levant and North Africa in the nineteenth century'.[150]

---

[148] Purcell, *Papal Crusading Policy 1244–1291*, 99–135, on commutation in general.

[149] C. della Berardenga, *Gli Acciaioli di Firenze* (2 vols, Florence, 1962), I, 31; Setton, *The Papacy and the Levant*, 159–62; Shaw, trans., *Joinville and Villehardouin: Chronicles of the Crusades*, 258–9, 267; R. Kaeuper, *Bankers to the Crown: The Riccardi of Lucca and Edward I* (Princeton, 1973), 3, 81–2, 105.

[150] Setton, ed., *A History of the Crusades*, VI, 38.

Certainly experience of crusading, and especially the establishment of the crusader states, involved a change in that outlook that had condemned any dealings, other than violent ones, with Muslims and had castigated the Byzantines for maintaining diplomatic relations with Muslim rulers. In broad terms negotiations and treaties with Muslim rulers developed during the twelfth century and by the thirteenth century had become almost common form. The talks between representatives of Richard I and Saladin in 1192 and those of Frederick II and al-Kamil in 1229 were accepted, if some of the details were much criticised.[151] During the passage of the Second Crusade and the preparation for the Third Crusade, suspicions as to Byzantine intentions in their dealings with Seljuk rulers were rife. Knowledge of Alexios III's treaty with Saladin were well known in the West by 1188 and may have decided Richard I and Philip II to take the sea route to Palestine. A decade later these long-held suspicions may have contributed to that mindset, present throughout the twelfth century that Constantinople should be in reliable western control. Certainly the presence of mosques in Constantinople was a cause for comment and a target for vandalism during the Fourth Crusade. All that apart, it did appear that crusading broadened the mind. Experience and sophistication meant that by the middle of the thirteenth century language skills were acquired, embassies sent across Asia, marriage alliances sealed with Armenian and Cuman princesses, and treaties and trade links fostered with Muslim powers.

One of the prime developments was a sea-change in attitude from one with a difficulty about co-operation and the sharing of information with foreign allies to one in which mutual interests could be shared and negotiated around. Knowledge of other cultures, their resources and ways of doing business, was gained through time and familiarity, and the degree of trust and openness that was appropriate to each was appreciated. The usual stuff of diplomacy was truces, safe conducts, exchange of prisoners, military assistance and the arrangement of marriage alliances.

Details of the personnel, diplomatic instructions and accreditation can only be gained by inference from the sources. Sometimes embassies are assumed to have taken place, as with Urban II's presumed embassy to Alexios I informing him of the First Crusade. Were agreements to buy horses in Shaizar in 1099 diplomacy or less formal dealings? Just where diplomacy begins and personal approaches end is not always clear. All crusades began with some form of diplomatic exchange or negotiation with the Pope, be it from the Byzantine emperor, the rulers of the crusader states or more personal representations like that of Gebhard of Bremen in his dispute with the peasants of Stedingen in the 1230s. Alexios I had asked Urban II for military aid via his embassy to the Council of Piacenza in March 1095. His approach to the Pope was to an individual with some concern and awareness of the Christians of the East and their plight, as

---

[151]   P. Holt, *The Crusader States and their Neighbours* (London, 2004), 79–88.

well as to someone with an interest in the union of the Greek and Latin churches. According to legend, Peter the Hermit had encouraged the Orthodox patriarch of Jerusalem, Simeon II, to appeal for help to Urban II, thus beginning a tradition of patriarchal appeals for crusades.[152]

Crusading armies about to take the land route to the East negotiated their passage with the appropriate rulers. This had caused trouble for some crusade contingents during the First Crusade, but those led by the so-called princes announced their approach by embassy, for which those sent by Hugh of Vermondois and by Bohemond have left some record. During the course of the twelfth century such missions became the norm, with Frederick Barbarossa taking particular care in this respect in 1188.

The first accredited mission from a crusade on campaign took place on 27 June 1098 when Peter the Hermit and a certain Herluin were sent to the camp of Kerbogha outside Antioch to ask what he was doing there and to bid him be gone. Not surprisingly the embassy was unsuccessful, but if Herluin was an interpreter, as we are told, here was a Frank with a good working knowledge of Turkish.[153] The second mission came soon afterwards in July 1098 when Hugh of Vermondois was sent from Antioch to Constantinople to ask Alexios for military assistance and to offer him Antioch in return.[154] The Byzantine reinforcements did not materialise and Hugh did not return to the crusade army. In September the crusade leadership, apparently inspired by Bohemond and Daimbert, wrote to Urban urging him to come to Antioch and lead his crusade to Jerusalem. If and how this letter was sent to the West is unknown, but it was more a letter of information and jubilation than a serious diplomatic mission. Thereafter there came negotiations with the emirs of coastal territories through which the crusaders were to pass on their march to Jerusalem, and the purchase of horses and supplies. In the late summer of 1099 Godfrey of Bouillon and Patriarch Daimbert sent a letter asking for reinforcements to Italy (Genoa only?) by the hands of two Genoese sea captains, William Embriaco and his brother Primus, who had arrived in Jaffa earlier in the summer. In 1100 Raymond of Toulouse had gone to Constantinople to gain Alexios' permission and support for his territorial expansion around Homs, Tripoli and Tortosa. This was more the last resort of one of the most prominent crusaders who had lost out in the setting up of crusader states. He left his wife and child in Latakia, and his mission was more that of a suppliant and guest than a diplomatic mission. If much of this might be thought semantics it does suggest certain informality.

In 1111 Baldwin, in the light of ignorance of the former Byzantine metropolitan

---

[152]   E. Blake and C. Morris, 'A Hermit Goes to War: Peter and the Origins of the First Crusade', in W. Shiels, ed., *Studies in Church History*, 22 (1985), 79–100, discussed in J. Phillips, *Defenders of the Holy Land: Relations Between the Latin East and the West, 1119–1187* (Oxford, 1996), 16.

[153]   Hill, ed., *Gesta Francorum*, 66–7.

[154]   Fink and Ryan, *Fulcher of Chartres, History of the Expedition to Jerusalem*, 107–12.

structure, sent envoys to Paschal II to ask that all towns that he might conquer should be subject to the Church of Jerusalem. This was one of the first recorded embassies from the crusader states to the West that in turn provoked embassies from the patriarch of Antioch defending the rights of his church.[155] In 1112 the first embassy from a crusader state to negotiate a marriage alliance with a western ruler was sent by Baldwin I to Roger II of Sicily for the hand of Roger's mother Adelaide. Baldwin needed money and had instructed his ambassadors to agree to any terms, and the Normans overlooked Baldwin's questionable divorce of his first wife, the Armenian princess Arda, in order to gain a claim to the crown of Jerusalem should the 37-year-old Adelaide fail to provide Baldwin with an heir. The negotiations were duplicitous on both sides and ended in divorce in 1116.[156]

Jonathan Phillips has reviewed the various embassies sent to the West in the period 1119 to 1187.[157] Some, like the missions of 1127 to Fulk V of Anjou and of 1178 to Hugh III of Burgundy, were to negotiate marriage settlements; the majority, however, were to seek military help, which was essentially endorsement of another crusade. Such were the missions of 1120, 1127, 1145, 1166, 1169 and 1173. Bishops, or the masters of the Templars or Hospitallers, usually headed these embassies. When Baldwin II sent envoys to Calixtus II in 1120 they also contacted the Venetians. This set a precedent for seeking help from appropriate rulers and communes in addition to embassies to the Pope. In 1127 and 1128, Hugh of Payns was in the West to secure formal recognition of his new order of the Templars, but he also travelled widely in France and Flanders recruiting troops for a proposed attack on Damascus. In 1145 the emissary Hugh, bishop of Jabala, approached both Eugenius III and Louis VII; again, in 1184 and 1185 in the run up to the Third Crusade, Heraclius, patriarch of Jerusalem, made a formal appeal to Pope Lucius III and then went on the courts of Philip Augustus and Henry II. This was the first time the patriarch of Jerusalem had been used to voice an appeal, and his embassy included the two masters of the military orders to emphasise the parlous state of the Kingdom of Jerusalem. The Pope might endorse a crusade by his proclamation, but there was no constraint on spreading the word or seeking other aid by direct approach to suitable western rulers.

Embassies also went the other way from Rome to Jerusalem. Generally these were legatine commissions, sent east with a specific ecclesiastical mission to address. That apart, these could not help but be fact-finding missions – although it seems that the popes relied upon missions from the East to keep them abreast of political and military developments. The number, dates, purpose, and

[155] Babcock and Krey, *A History of Deeds Done Beyond the Sea by William Archbishop of Tyre*, I, 508–13.
[156] Babcock and Krey, *A History of Deeds Done Beyond the Sea by William Archbishop of Tyre*, I, 496–7.
[157] Phillips, *Defenders of the Holy Land, passim*, esp. 14–20, 239–42, 252–64, on which this section is based.

personnel of these missions are not securely known, especially in the two decades after the First Crusade. Even the status of so prominent a figure as Daimbert (Dagobert), first archbishop of Pisa and later patriarch of Jerusalem, is unclear. Many accept that Urban II appointed him as his legate to succeed Adhemar (d. 1 August 1098), but this is only a possibility given the problems confronting the Church in Jerusalem that a legate would have attempted to resolve. Daimbert may have come east in 1100/1 as the leader of the Pisan fleet that carried out piratical raids on Byzantine territory in the Ionian Islands and then became a substantial naval presence that facilitated his election as patriarch of Jerusalem. Nonetheless, his letters to the West were a source of information for Urban's successor Paschal II, who appointed Maurice of Porto legate in April 1100.[158] In 1160 Alexander III sent legates to Jerusalem to ensure the kingdom's support for him in the struggle against the antipope Victor IV (1159–64). Legates *a latere* continued to be appointed to each major crusade expedition throughout the crusade movement.

Diplomatic exchanges with Byzantium continued throughout the life of the crusader states and beyond, but it is the dealings with non-Christian powers that the most profound change in mentality is noticeable, a tribute to the perceptions and adaptability of the crusaders. Even before Jerusalem had been besieged peaceful contact had been made with local Muslim rulers, but thereafter truces and alliances were arranged and the self-interests of individual rulers, Christian or Muslim, crossed racial and religious barriers. In 1108 Baldwin Le Bourg of Edessa, who had been a prisoner since his defeat at the battle of Hauran in 1104, formed an alliance with his captor Chavli to assist the latter to defend himself against an army sent against him by the sultan. To contain the threat of Chavli on his own lands around Aleppo, Ridwan formed an alliance with his erstwhile enemy Tancred, regent of Antioch. The spectacle was presented of two Christian and Muslim alliances opposed to each other.

According to Ibn Jubayr the Franks permitted a mosque in both Acre and Tyre after their capture in 1104 and 1124 respectively. He also recorded the peaceful co-operative exploitation of the land around Banyas by Franks and Muslims. In the same region he even lodged in Château Neuf on his journey to Acre.[159] In 1154 Nur ed-Din secured a safe conduct for ibn-Munqidh and his family to travel from Egypt via Acre in a Frankish ship; although all did not go well in Acre itself, these commitments were honoured to the letter.[160] Later ibn-Munqidh was to travel from Acre to Tiberias in the company of William Bures, lord of Tiberias, suggesting at the same time that such travel arrangements were not uncommon and that no stigma was attached to such relationships that were

---

[158] Hagenmeyer, *Die Kreuzzugsbriefe aus dem Jahren, 1088–1100*, 167–73, 176–8.

[159] R. Broadhurst, trans., *The Travels of Ibn Jubayr* (London, 1952), 315, 318, 321.

[160] P. Hitti, trans., *The Memoirs of an Arab-Syrian Gentleman and Warrior, Usama ibn Munqidh* (New York, 2003), 60–1, 166.

not felt to be incompatible with the general state of hostilities. From 1192 onwards considerable details survive of negotiations between the leaders of the major crusades of 1190, 1217, 1229 and 1250 and their Muslim opponents.[161] Truces, alliances, safe conducts, and ransoms became the accepted stuff of these negotiations.

The western belief that somewhere beyond the eastern confines of Islam lay a friendly Christian power went back to the twelfth century and the legend of Prester John that was first recorded by Otto, bishop of Freising. Legend and reality came together with the Mongol raids into Hungary and Poland in 1241 and 1242. The Mongols were definitely a power, but were they capable of being harnessed to Christian objectives in the Levant? These new horizons were explored when Pope Innocent IV sent a series of diplomatic missions to sound out the possibility of an alliance with the khan of the Mongols against the Muslims of Syria and Egypt. Four missions are recorded in the 1240s: first the Franciscan John of Piano Carpini, then the Dominican Andrew of Longjumeau, later the two Dominicans Anscelin and Simon of St Quentin, and finally the Franciscan Dominic of Aragon who travelled to Cilician Armenia. All four envoys had returned to Rome between mid-1247 and the summer of 1248, with much information but no alliance. In 1248 Louis IX received two Mongol ambassadors in Cyprus. These were apparently sent to co-ordinate Louis' own planned attack on Egypt with a proposed Mongol attack on Baghdad. Nothing came of this in military terms, but it does say much for Mongol knowledge of western plans in the Levant. Hopes were raised and early in 1249 Louis sent ambassadors of his own back with the returning Mongol embassy. The envoys were Andrew of Carcassone, Andrew of Longjumeau and his brother Guy – all Dominicans. Andrew reported the failure to gain an alliance to Louis in 1251. Two years later Louis also sponsored the mission of the Franciscan William of Rubruck to Kharakorum; this, though, this was a Christian mission rather than a diplomatic embassy. William reported back to Louis in 1255. The European outlook had been greatly extended by these travels. Commerce also benefited for a while from the so-called *pax mongolica*, as the later career of the Polo family in China was to demonstrate. The prospect of Mongol aid to the crusades was extinguished, though, with the crushing defeat of the Mongol army at 'Ain Jalut on 3 September 1260.[162]

---

[161] Gillingham, *Richard I*, 210–21; Powell, *Anatomy of a Crusade 1213–1221*, 188–91; D. Abulafia, *Frederick II, a Medieval Emperor* (London, 1988), 180–8; J. Richard, *Saint Louis, Crusader King of France* (1983; Eng edn, Cambridge, 1992), 128–33.

[162] J.R.S. Phillips, *The Medieval Expansion of Europe* (Oxford, 1988), 123–7; C. Beazeley, *The Dawn of Modern Geography*, II (London, 1901), 275–391; B. Hamilton, 'Prester John and the Three Kings of Cologne', in H. Mayr-Harting and R. Moore, eds, *Studies in Medieval History presented to R.H.C. Davis* (London, 1985), 177–91; P. Jackson and D. Morgan, eds, *The Mission of Friar William of Rubruck* (London, 1990); C. Dawson, ed., *Mission to Asia* (New York, 1966).

WOMEN AND THE CRUSADES[163]

By combining the ideas of pilgrimage and holy war Urban II brought together two contrasting concepts. If warriors were needed for a war of liberation could non-combatants be prevented from participating in what was also penitential pilgrimage with attractive spiritual rewards? Papal authority and the needs of the moment led to a fudged outcome, making others like husbands and priests responsible for turning away eager women pilgrims. This was no small order, and many women participated in the crusading movement. The age of the Crusades was not gender-blind; women fighting or wearing armour was seen as unnatural. Accounts of women crusaders wearing armour come only from Byzantine and Muslim sources and were designed to highlight the barbarism of the Franks rather than the initiative of their women. Fighting was a male activity, and warriors spent their whole lives from their childhood perfecting the profession of arms. This formed no part in the upbringing of women, who were assigned a supporting role. This is not to say that military logistics were beyond the understanding of women, since there were noble women who did command castle garrisons or even the resources of a kingdom; examples are Matilda of England and Melisende of Jerusalem. But it was in other ways that the contribution of women to crusading were viewed. The positive moral influence women might exert on their men was fully appreciated, both in the camp as well as at home when the decision to crusade was being discussed. Yet the supposed sinful proclivities of the daughters of Eve were not overlooked.

Given embedded notions of the inferiority and moral weakness of the female sex, it is not surprising that misogynistic clerical chroniclers of the Crusades should have a negative view of crusading women. Right from the start Urban II had forbidden women to go on crusade except with their husbands or brothers, or with special permission. This gave them some identity and status in the crusading army and might go some way to protect them from molestation or unwanted

---

[163] S. Edgington and S. Lambert, eds, *Gendering the Crusades* (Cardiff, 2001), has wide-ranging and original contributions; D. Baker, ed., *Medieval Women* (Oxford, 1978), 143–84; J. Brundage, 'Prostitution, Miscegenation and Sexual Purity on the First Crusade', in Edbury, ed., *Crusade and Settlement* (1985), 57–64; J. Brundage, 'The Crusader's Wife: A Canonistic Quandary', *Studia Gratiana*, 12 (1967), 425–41; J. Brundage, 'The Crusader's Wife Revisited', *Studia Gratiana*, 14 (1967), 241–52; S. Farmer, 'Persuasive Voices: Clerical Images of Medieval Wives', *Speculum*, 61 (1986), 517–43; R. Mazeika, 'Nowhere was the Fragility of their Sex Apparent: Women Warriors in the Baltic Crusade Chronicles', in A. Murray, ed., *From Clermont to Jerusalem* (Turnhout, 1998), 229–48; H. Nicholson, 'Women on the Third Crusade', *Journal of Medieval History*, 23 (1997), 335–49; J. Powell, 'The Role of Women in the Fifth Crusade' in B. Kedar, ed., *The Horns of Hattin* (Jerusalem, 1992), 294–301; M. Purcell, 'Women Crusaders: A Temporary Canonical Aberration?', in L. Frappell, ed., *Principalities, Powers and Estates* (Adelaide, 1979), 57–67; J. Riley-Smith, 'Family Traditions and Participation in the Second Crusade', in M. Gervers, ed., *The Second Crusade and the Cistercians* (New York, 1992), 101–8. For a general discussion of women in knightly culture, see J. Bumke, *Courtly Culture* (New York, 2000), 325–59.

attention. In 1188, in the period of preparation for the Third Crusade, Ralph Niger reflected the concern of his royal master, Henry II, to reduce non-combatants by urging that women, clerics, the old and the poor should not proceed on crusade. Practical proposals to reduce the numbers of non-combatants seem to have been a peculiarly English concern. Ralph thought it best for women to stay at home where they couldn't imperil or hinder a military campaign and to consider joining their husbands as settlers when the outcome of a campaign was known.[164] Some of this sprang from concern over the fate of western women captured during crusade. Death or slavery was the normal outcome, but rape was common, especially on the capture of a town; gang rape was not unknown, being used as a means to taunt opponents when armies were at a standoff. The violation of women captives was not just a western male concern, as was illustrated in the pages of Usamma Ibn Munqidh and by the legendary gratitude of an emir for the courteous and considerate treatment of his pregnant wife by Baldwin of Boulogne.[165]

There was an element of gratuitous interest in sexual relations among some of the male commentators. Albert of Aachen devoted considerable space to the sexual tastes of the nun from the convent of St Mary of Trier. She had been captured by the Turks from Peter the Hermit's contingent in late 1096, and was presumably from the upper class since she was recognised amongst the liberated captives from Nicaea by the nobleman Henry of Castle Ascha. Within one day she fled her liberators and their easy penance to be with her Turkish master/ravisher/lover. Lessons on lewdness, unchastity and lust were drawn, but no understanding was shown of the difficulties captive women might experience on return to their own society. Orderic Vitalis recorded how Adela, the wife of Stephen of Blois, nagged him to participate in the crusade of 1101 – nagging that did not stop even during sexual intercourse. Then there were the alleged sexual improprieties of Eleanor of Aquitaine, wife of Louis VII of France, and her uncle Raymond of Antioch during the Second Crusade, commented upon by both William of Tyre and John of Salisbury.[166] Prostitutes were present on most crusades and a certain tolerance seems to have been extended towards them. On the whole little was written about them. It was during extended siege operations such as at Antioch in 1098, Acre in 1192 and Damietta in 1218 that the prostitutes and their pimps seemed to be most active and most visible. In times of difficulty during these operations a period of penance was declared to allow the army to set itself right with God, and the prostitutes – the cause of Divine wrath – were

[164] L. Schmugge, ed., *Radulfus Niger, De Re Militari et Triplici Via Pergrinationis Ierosolimitane* (Berlin, 1977), 224–7, section 59; this section, on women, is translated in E. Hallam, ed., *Chronicles of the Crusades* (London, 1989), 168.

[165] Babcock and Krey, *A History of Deeds Done Beyond the Sea by William Archbishop of Tyre*, I, 429–30; Hitti, trans., *Memoirs an Arab-Syrian Gentleman and Warrior*, 61, 100, 164.

[166] Conveniently published together in translation by Hallam, ed., *Chronicles of the Crusades*, 73, 97, 140–3.

expelled from the camp for its duration and forced to find quarters elsewhere.[167] Adultery was a concern in patriarchal societies, both Christian and Muslim. In the twelfth century the Catholic Church was trying to sacramentalise marriage and to regularise marriage ceremonies. In this context clerical writers might well take a strong line on sexual relations outside marriage. Their attitude to prostitution might be explained both in terms of the needs of the army and in the function of prostitutes outside kinship links and property rights. Nonetheless, there was a gap between what was acceptable in the clerical and secular worlds.

Women who did not go on crusade still played an important part in the recruitment process by bringing an awareness of the crusading tradition from one family to another by marriage, agreeing to the sale or mortgage of patrimonial lands to finance the crusade of husband or son, consenting to the absence of a spouse for an extended period, administering lands and rights during that absence and waiting chastely for his subsequent return. If a husband did not return his legal death might not be assumed until the passage of a period of time varying from five to one hundred years according to the Church court concerned. Lives and property might be left in limbo, unless secular mores differed here from the decrees of the Church courts. In an age when love and marriage more often than not did not go together, the close links of affection, support, and shared strength between a wife and crusader spouse may be seen in two pieces of monumental sculpture surviving from the twelfth and thirteenth centuries: the sculpture of a departing or returning crusader being embraced by his wife from Belval Priory, Lorraine, now in the Musée des Beaux Arts, Nancy, and the tomb figures of Count Otto of Botenlauben and his wife Beatrix of Courtenay in the church of Frauenroth. Otto had participated in the crusade of Henry VI in 1197 and was a well-known minnesinger.[168] From 1213, with the administering of the crusade vow to all-comers, preachers such as James of Vitry targeted wealthy and noble women. On his visit to Genoa in the summer of 1216 he recruited many women of high status and wealth whose redemption of their vows would make a considerable contribution to crusading funds and whose enthusiasm might well prompt their husbands to take the cross.

From the outset of the crusade movement the agreement of a wife to her husband's absence was crucial. Emphasis in canon law was placed on the rights and duties of the marriage bed and the prolonged absence of a sexual partner was not lightly endured. Urban II had urged that newly married couples should not be separated from their wives by taking crusade vows, and those that did should do so only after thought and discussion with their wife and priest. Some women certainly did urge their men to participate in the Crusades, but there were many who objected. Gerald of Wales records a number of examples

[167] Levine, *The Deeds of God through the Franks*, 87–8; Hubert and La Monte, trans., *The Crusade of Richard Lion-Heart by Ambroise*, 233, 277.
[168] Full length 'photographs' appear in Riley-Smith, ed., *The Oxford Illustrated History of the Crusades*, 69; H. J. Kotzur, ed., *Die Kreuzzge* (Mainz, 2004), 318–19.

of backsliding in Wales due to a wife's objection, of which the most famous was Gwendolyn's aborting of the crusade plans of her husband Rhys 'by female artifices'.[169] Whether objections of this kind were becoming more common during the course of the twelfth century is not clear, but certainly in 1213 Innocent III went against the traditions of canon law and decreed that a wife's objections to her husband taking the cross should no longer be regarded as an impediment – just as in the army of an earthly king so in the service of the King of Kings.[170]

Crusading women – that is, women actually on crusade – appear fitfully in the chronicles, either suffering from the rigours of the climate and the terrain, especially if pregnant, or providing support services for their men, boosting morale, comforting the sick and wounded, washing heads and nit-picking, washing clothes, bringing up supplies of arrows or stones, and especially in the provision of water to thirsty warriors in the battle line.[171] Surprisingly, the presence of pregnant women on a penitential pilgrimage did not excite the attention of the clerical chroniclers. In Europe water fetching seems to have been a female task, or at least one usually left to women. It seems to have come east with them. The image of women carrying water crops up over and over again. Was it a topos? Yet it is found not only in Christian chronicles but also in Muslim accounts of the Franks. The anonymous author of the *Gesta Francorum* described how, at the battle of Dorylaion on 1 July 1097, 'The women in our camp were a great help to us that day, for they brought up water for the fighting men to drink, and gallantly encouraged those who were fighting and defending them.'[172] Richard the Pilgrim, in his poem the *Chanson d'Antioche*, described a moment on the passage of the First Crusade across Anatolia when 'Tancred's knights were thirsting for water. Then the women and young girls, their countrywomen, came to them in their hour of need. Rolling up their sleeves and casting aside their long dresses, they carried water to the brave knights in pots, pans and even golden bowls.'[173] Separated by distance, culture, and the passage of half a century, ibn-Munqidh described how a Frankish woman following her husband on the road to Jerusalem carrying a small wooden jar containing water defended herself with this jar and inflicted facial wounds on an Arab warrior who had just killed her husband.[174] Virtually nothing is recorded regarding gathering firewood or the preparation of food. In the travelling households of the princes cooking was the job of male

[169] Wright, *The Historical Works of Giraldus Cambrensis*, 333.
[170] L. and J. Riley-Smith, *The Crusades: Idea and Reality*, 131–2.
[171] Hubert and La Monte, trans., *The Crusade of Richard Lionheart by Ambroise*, 233; Levine, *The Deeds of God Through the Franks*, 103, who has something to say about women in the army of Kerbogha; Ryan and Fink, trans., *Fulcher of Chartres, A History of the Expedition to Jerusalem*, 241, for women's role in the defence of Jaffa in 1123; see also notes 114–16.
[172] Hill, ed. and trans., *Gesta Francorum*, 19; Guibert recounts the same incident and stresses the morale-boosting presence of the women (Levine, *The Deeds of God Through the Franks*, 66).
[173] Hallam, *Chronicles of the Crusades*, 76.
[174] Hitti, *Memoirs of an Arab-Syrian Gentleman and Warrior*, 158.

cooks. Much is written of dearth, so presumably this meant that food preparation was not onerous for most participants on a crusade. Women crusaders would seem to have had an important but ancillary role with the army on campaign; but some of them did participate in the fighting.

Usually women were drawn into fighting by the necessity of the moment – for example, the need to defend the camp or the town walls. Thus the women of Jaffa brought stones and water to their menfolk on the walls during the Egyptian siege of 1123, and Margaret of Beverley helped defend the walls of Jerusalem in 1187 wearing a cooking pot as a helmet and bringing water to the men. In 1245 the women of Elbing manned the walls of their town girt with swords to deter an impending attack from the Duke of Pomerania and the Prussian pagans. On the Baltic crusades women fulfilled all the ancillary roles of their sisters in the East, but also took on a more sanguinary role in their own defence.[175] On the attacking side women brought up stones and earth to fill in moats for siege engines to be rolled up, and often met their death in this way. The story of the heroic death of a woman doing this work at the siege of Acre in 1190, whose dying wish was to speed up the work by having her corpse thrown into the ditch, elicited considerable admiration among the Franks – just as the female archer in a green mantle killed at the same siege impressed Saladin, who became the owner of her wooden bow.[176]

Apart from a few exceptions women crusaders are anonymous. They were there fulfilling an important role that could not be denied them. They sustained casualties in all the crusades of the first century of the movement. Depending on the force of their personality and the political circumstances, some women were to figure prominently as rulers, regents and wives in the various crusading states. These will be discussed in the relevant section (see pp. 420–41).

CRUSADING WARFARE[177]

Warfare was the dominant concern of the crusading leadership and of the rulers of the crusading states. Suitable fighting men were always in short supply,

---

[175] Rasa Mazeika article cited in note 163 above.
[176] Ryan and Fink, *Fulcher of Chartres, A History of the Expedition to Jerusalem, 1095–1127*, 241; R. Finucane, *Soldiers of the Faith* (London, 1977), 178–9; Hallam, *Chronicles of the Crusades*, 182–3; F. Gabrieli, *Arab Historians of the Crusades* (London, 1969), 218.
[177] R. Smail, *Crusading Warfare* (Cambridge, 1956), is a fundamental study; C. Marshall, *Warfare in the Latin East, 1192–1291* (Cambridge, 1992); R. Rodgers: *Latin Siege Warfare in the Twelfth Century* (Oxford, 1992); P. Edbury, 'Warfare in the Latin East' in M. Keen, ed., *Medieval Warfare: A History* (Oxford, 1999), 89–112; J. France, 'Crusading Warfare and Its Adaptation to Eastern Conditions in the Twelfth Century', *Mediterranean Historical Review*, 15 (2000), 49–66; Hillenbrand, *The Crusades: Islamic Perspectives*, 431–510; H. Nicolson and D. Nicolle, *God's Warriors: Crusaders, Saracens and the Battle for Jerusalem* (Oxford, 2005); J. France, *Western Warfare in the Age of the Crusades* (London, 1999); P. Contamine, *War in the Middle Ages* (Oxford, 1984); V. Parry and M. Yapp, eds, *War, Technology and Society in the Middle East*

dictating both the strategic concepts and the tactics that might be adopted. War materials of any sort – horses, weapons, metal and wood – were also in short supply, and especially singled out for seizure on the capitulation of towns or on raids. Whenever possible pitched battles were avoided as too costly in men and horses. Knights, who were liable for military service between the ages of fifteen and sixty, spent their whole lives perfecting themselves as warriors, and any losses were difficult to replace in terms of lost skills. It was essential to conserve both, and the disastrous defeats at the Field of Blood (1119), Hattin (1187) and La Forbie (1244) showed just what lost battles might mean to a kingdom that could not recruit additional manpower quickly or conveniently. In 1187 King Guy had stripped the castles of his kingdom of their garrisons in order to make up the largest field army the Kingdom of Jerusalem had ever seen. His defeat at Hattin meant that the castles surrendered quickly to Saladin since they lacked the garrisons to mount a credible defence.

Pitched battles were rare since they involved mutual exposure to danger and the vagaries of chance. Since the days of Vegetius it was appreciated that general engagements were hazardous, a state of affairs that might be exacerbated by a whole host of imponderables, often beyond the control of commanders. They were also costly in men and horses.[178] Siege warfare generally accompanied the major crusading campaigns and formed a prominent part in the military careers of Nur ed-Din, Saladin and Baybars. During sieges foot soldiers, technicians skilled in constructing and operating siege engines and sappers were at a premium. Fortunately such skilled operatives were available in the naval flotillas that accompanied such expeditions. As in the West, the mounted knight remained central to concepts of the conduct of warfare (see p. 423). Their mobility meant that raids for livestock or other booty, or to extract protection money from client Muslim rulers such as the emir of Shaizar, were by far the most common form of military activity; they were both profitable and, in the main, light in casualties. These might be conducted on the initiative of individual lords or the masters of the military orders, and may have little bearing on the policies of the ruling

---

(London, 1975), 97–112; K. de Vries, *Medieval Military Technology* (New York, 1992); D. Nicolle, *Arms and Armour of the Crusading Era, 1050–1350* (2 vols, London, 1986); M. de Riquer, *L'Arnes del Cavalier* (Barcelona, 1968); W. Karcheski and T. Richardson, *The Medieval Armour from Rhodes* (Leeds, 2000); J. Prawer, *The Latin Kingdom of Jerusalem* (London, 1972), 280–351; J. Prawer, *Crusader Institutions* (Oxford, 1988) 484–500; D. Nicolle, *Hattin 1187, Saladin's Greatest Victory* (Oxford, 1993); D. Ayalon, 'Studies in the Structure of the Mameluk Army', *Bulletin of the School of Oriental and African Studies*, 15 (1953), 203ff., 448ff., and 16 (1954), 133ff.; D. Pringle, ed., *T.E. Lawrence: Crusader Castles* (Oxford, 1988); D. Pringle, *Secular Buildings in the Crusader Kingdom of Jerusalem* (Cambridge, 1997); D. Pringle, *Fortification and Settlement in Crusader Palestine* (Aldershot, 2000); H. Kennedy, *Crusader Castles* (London, 1994); P. Deschamps, *Les Chateaux des Croises en Terre Sainte* (3 vols, Paris, 1934–73); brief summaries with plans and photographs contained in P. Deschamps, *Terre Sainte Romane* (Paris, 1990), 11–162; W. Muller-Wiener, *Castles of the Crusaders* (London, 1966); D. Pringle, *The Red Tower* (al-burj all-Ahmar) (London, 1986); K. Molin, *Unknown Crusader Castles* (London, 2001).

[178] N. Milner, trans, *Vegetius: Epitome of Military Science* (Liverpool, 1993), 61–109.

princes and effects not envisaged at the time. For all that, it should not be forgotten that it was by siege warfare that the crusader states were established, and that in siege warfare they were extinguished between 1188 and 1291.

The campaigning season fell between late March and mid-November. Military service was unconditional within the boundaries of the principality in which the knight held his fief (see p. 423). Although winter campaigns did occur they were generally avoided. They were remembered as fraught with difficulties and suffering for the combatants, such as the Damascus campaign of 1129, and regretted as infringing upon time that warriors might spend on their estates with their families, having perhaps been absent for the previous eight months.

In what follows, the difference between Christian and Muslim armies, the castle-building programme, and the evolution of the military orders will be discussed. Details of arms, armour and other equipment, and the sources by which such information is derived, have been assembled, illustrated and discussed in the works of David Nicolle and Carole Hillenbrand, and to these the reader is referred.

In the main the wars of the Crusades were conducted in Syria-Palestine. The enemies that opposed the crusaders were the Seljuk Turks and the Fatimids, and later the Ayyubids and Mamelukes of Egypt. Egyptian warriors were very similarly equipped and armed as the crusaders. By 1000 they wore armour in battle, and the range of weaponry at their disposal was similar: straight swords, javelins, pikes, maces, axes and crossbows. They produced military manuals, possessed a good and developing siege capability as well as a navy, and were generally a well-organised opponent. However, the first enemy that the crusaders encountered in May 1097 were the Seljuk Turks, who used a method of fighting unknown in Europe, or at least forgotten since the days of the Magyars. Their strength lay in their light cavalry, suitable both for long-distance raiding and harassing columns on the march. In particular their mounted archers, who swooped into the attack, fired a hail of arrows with fearsome accuracy and then sped away. Their arrows might not be able to penetrate the mail of the western knights, but they could kill their horses and thus eliminate them militarily. Such tactics often lured the crusading knights – those still mounted that is – into a brave but disorganised pursuit into a well-prepared ambush, where the narrow straight swords of the Turkish cavalry might come into play in close-quarter fighting. There was a wide range of arrowheads for particular tasks; the diversity may be seen in those found at Vadum Jabob, Acre and Belvoir, dating from the twelfth and thirteenth centuries.[179] The Turks possessed armour too, but generally lighter protection suited their mode of fighting. The bows that they used were composite ones made of horn, and it has been suggested that they had developed a light crossbow too. Turkish mounts were lighter than those of the crusaders, but better suited to the climate and the terrain. It is unclear whether the bulk of the Turks

[179] S. Rozenberg, ed., *Knights of the Holy Land: The Crusades Kingdom of Jerusalem* (Jerusalem, 1999), 154, plates 8 and 9.

CRUSADING AND THE CRUSADER STATES

had remounts. It was this tactical use of mounted archers that was new to the crusaders – one that threatened to break up the ranks of their armoured knights and to leave little opportunity for the mass charge of their heavy horses to have an effect. One year later, facing the army of Kerbogha at Antioch, and this time with most of their knights fighting on foot, the crusaders demonstrated that they had learned much about Turkish warfare in their passage across Anatolia. They presented an army with a unified command, Bohemond; a high moral motivation to win or to die; and one that was well disciplined, able to keep its formations, and determined to come to grips with their enemy at close quarters as soon as possible. In this they were successful and able to exploit the weaknesses in Kerbogha's command structure.[180] The crusaders could learn and adapt.

Light cavalry and the process of raid and counter-raid were to remain a problem for the crusaders in the Kingdom of Jerusalem. In any raid, Muslim or Christian, things might go wrong due to forewarning or just bad luck. Generally they coped and were no mean raiders themselves, as ibn-Munqidh made clear. Despite some lamentable exceptions, highlighted by the Christian chroniclers, their best military leaders could match the best Muslim leadership. And it must not be forgotten that the Kingdom of Jerusalem existed for nearly two centuries and that as late as the 1260s its leaders enjoyed a reputation amongst the Mongols as formidable warriors who would dispute possession of the battlefield until the end.[181] Western accounts record crusading armies as confronted by huge Muslim forces, but this seems to have little behind it – at least until the thirteenth century.

From the mid-1890s interest was focused on the Frankish castles in the Latin Kingdom. The initial debate was concerned with their source of inspiration: western or Byzantine. It limited itself to the last phase of crusader castle-building at such sites as Belvoir and Krak des Chevaliers, seeing therein the source for the western concentric castles. Serious fieldwork and excavation have replaced these grand debates. The model of separate, distinct and independent development has replaced the model of *lux ex oriente* at that time so favoured by prehistorians and perhaps rather too conveniently adopted by medievalists. After all, who needed to travel to the Levant to appreciate concentricity and round towers when so many Iron Age hill forts survived in France and England, and examples of Roman town defences with square, round and multiangular towers were to hand? This does not mean that the Franks did not learn in the Holy Land. They were nothing if not adaptable, and they repaired existing structures, using local materials and local craftsmen and labour. Nonetheless, the great crusading stone castles are one of the enduring images of the Crusades and wrongly seen as a symbol of defence and defiance. The dating of the building, rebuilding and enlargements of the castles is not always precisely known. The castles of the Kingdom of Jerusalem were slighted either by Saladin in 1188 and 1189 or by the

---

[180] France, *Victory in the East*, 145–9, 286–96.
[181] P. Jackson, 'The Crisis in the Holy Land in 1260', *English Historical Review*, 95 (1980), 496–7.

Mamelukes in the 1260s. Some of the best surviving examples are to be sought in North Syria and Cilician Armenia.

Castle-building in the Latin Kingdom may be conveniently divided into four periods: broadly 1099–1125, 1125–65, 1165–87, and thirteenth-century structures. The structures erected in these periods did not have distinctive diagnostic forms and features. A type associated with period 1, a square keep surrounded by a rectangular curtain wall, can be found being constructed during period 2 – thus the castles built around Ascalon, at Ibelin, Bethgibelin, Blanche Garde and Darum by Fulk of Anjou from 1137 to 1142. The elongated plan of some of the castles of period 2 may be found contemporary with concentric castles – thus Le Chastellet in 1178. The functions of these various structures differed in their inception, and their locations not surprisingly reflected the military, economic and social conditions of the time. During the first period relatively few castles were built. Those that were built were constructed for either attack or defence. The latter were usually reconstructed Byzantine fortifications in long-established settlement sites. Those with an offensive purpose were sited to tighten control, that at the Muslim harbour town of Tyre being an example. It was surrounded by Chastel Neuf at Hunin (1106–7) Toron or Tibnin (1106–7) and Casal Imbert (c. 1123). King Fulk constructed similar structures around Ascalon some twenty to thirty years later. The earliest crusader work at Krak belongs to 1110 and guarded the approach to Tripoli from the Orontes Valley, whilst Montreal (1115) was built on the emerging frontier to threaten the main route from Damascus to Egypt and Mecca. Some of these early fortifications were little more than free-standing towers, such as those built for the siege of Antioch in 1098. They were built quickly, but they had the potential to be developed into larger structures with the addition of a walled bailey at a later date.

The second period corresponded to a period of general military security following the destruction of Jerash in 1119 and the capture of Tyre in 1124. A ring of small castles, completed with the construction of Gaza from 1149 to 1150, neutralised the Fatimid garrison in Ascalon. During this period there was only one major Muslim incursion – that against Nablus in 1137. It was during this phase that the majority of crusader castles were constructed. Most of these castles were built in the interior of the kingdom and reflected economic, political and social realities; they encouraged the growth of settlement, made a social statement about the builder, and acted as administrative centres with an eye to agricultural and commercial development. In form they adapted themselves to natural contours and features, elongated in shape with extensive bailies and curtain walls. The principal castles of this period were Acre, Akkar, Banyas, Belmont Caesarea, Castrum Regis (later Montfort), Chastel Blanc (Safita), Gibelet, Jaffa, Jerusalem, Kerak of Moab (1142), Mirabel, Nablus, Saone, Subeibe (Nimrud) (1132, 1156) and Tyre. Many were built inside major towns and all had dominating tower keeps. The castle at Saone (Sahayun), developed from its Byzantine nucleus of small fortress and rock-cut ditch in the 1120s, is perhaps the best surviving example of this type. Pringle has listed around ninety freestanding towers in crusader Palestine; some of these are urban tower houses in the coastal cities and others form part of fortified churches and monasteries.[182] These provided other forms of defensive structures.

The third period marked a response to military threat, beginning with the capture of Banyas by Nur ed-Din in 1164 and continuing with regular incursions and sieges up to 1189. The castles of this period were fortresses indeed, built to withstand the latest siege techniques and located to interdict and intercept raiders. Some sites, such as the castle at Darum originally built as a small fort to the south of Ascalon in 1141, were substantially rebuilt and enlarged during the 1170s. Others like Belvoir, Safed, and La Fève (al-Fule) were constructed between 1168 and the early 1170s. The intensity behind these building operations can be seen in the construction of Le Chastellet at Jacob's Ford (Vadum Jacobi) in eight months; the cost of hiring masons to hew the stone was reckoned at 80,000 dinars. The castle was captured and destroyed by Saladin in 1179. Developed Muslim siege techniques, especially more powerful trebuchets, produced the concentric castle, just as the development of sling warfare in the late Iron Age had produced the multivallate hill forts of northern Europe; they were both attempts to distance the inhabitants from projectiles. The castle at Belvoir, refortified by the Hospitallers in 1168, is the earliest datable concentric castle. It is one of the most impressive remains and illustrates the thought and planning behind these castles.

The walls of these period 3 castles were extremely thick, their magazines and cisterns capacious, and their overall form compact. They were built ultimately for defence in areas threatened by razzias (plundering raids) and invasions, and to that extent they represent a change in the mentality of crusader castle-builders. But castles were nothing on their own without an adequate garrison and without a field army. Garrisons were stripped to the bare minimum and beyond to fill the ranks of the field army, as at Hattin, or to mount local expeditions, as that to the Springs of Cresson in May 1187. Ernoul, who was then serving as a squire of Balian of Ibelin, has a story of their arrival at the castle of La Fève on 1 May 1188. The castle was empty of human beings except for two men, both so seriously wounded that they could not speak. They walked all over the castle unchallenged. As they left a wounded knight approached the castle and told them that on the previous day the whole garrison had left, together with those from Caco (Qaqun) and Nazareth, under the command of the master of the Temple, Gerard of Ridefort, to intercept a party of Muslim raiders. They had been wiped out.[183] This vignette explains how Saladin was able to secure the surrender of most of the castles in the kingdom without long sieges after the destruction of the field army at Hattin.

---

[182] D. Pringle, 'Towers in Crusader Palestine' (1994), reprinted in Pringle, *Fortification and Settlement in Crusader Palestine* (2000), essay VIII.

[183] L. de Mas-Latrie, ed., *Chroniqued'Ernoul* (Paris, 1871), 145–6, cited and discussed in Smail, *Crusading Warfare*, 104–5.

The castles most associated with crusading in the minds of visitors to Israel and Lebanon were those built or rebuilt in the thirteenth century. These are the most impressive of the surviving castles, incorporating the developments of period 3. Such were the castles at Atlit (1217–18), Krak des Chevaliers (where the present structure dates from the first part of the thirteenth century), Margat, and Montfort (Starkenberg) (1226–7, 1240). The by-name of 'Atlit, *castrum peregrinorum*, or Chastel Pelerin, preserves the background of the builders. The massive fortifications at Caesarea were rebuilt by Louis IX in 1251 and incorporate a moat designed to make sapping impossible. There was also castle building in Cyprus, Cilician Armenia and the mainland and islands of Greece. The range and the forms of these structures approximate to those of period 2, outlined above, and demonstrate the continuity of such structures in the Frankish Levant.

Perhaps the greatest military innovation of the crusader period was the foundation of the international military orders. These were to outlast the Kingdom of Jerusalem: the Templars until 1312, whilst the Hospitallers and the German order still exist today in reinvigorated and reinvented forms. Their members were to appear in all crusading theatres of warfare. In the Frankish principalities of Syria–Palestine they were not technically crusaders, although in other crusading endeavours they seem to have participated as crusaders in their own right. By the 1180s they garrisoned the majority of the castles of the Kingdom of Jerusalem, and their hold on these was to increase in the early thirteenth century. Their troops were under the direction of their respective grandmasters and, although vital to any major campaign conducted by the Frankish rulers, their aid might come in return for political influence or economic advantage. They were by far and away the most important means of channelling western economic support to the East and developed financial procedures for doing this, including the floating bank that helped amass the enormous ransom that Louis IX had to pay at Damietta.

The development of the orders, and especially their militarisation in the 1120s and 1130s, brought together religion and warfare, knighthood and monasticism in an innovative and appealing way, building on the appeal and ideas that Urban II had set in train. Knighthood was justified ethically and morally in a new way. The spiritualisation of warfare was one of the effects of the Gregorian Reform movement. It replaced the pragmatism that had justified the existence of knights hitherto and laid the foundations of the chivalrous ideal that was to develop over the next three centuries.[184]

[184] A. Forey, *The Military Orders from the Twelfth the Early Fourteenth Centuries* (London, 1991); M. Barber, 'The Origins of the Order of the Temple', *Studia Monastica*, 12 (1970), 219–40; M. Barber, *The New Knighthood: A History of the Order of the Temple* (Cambridge, 1994); P. Partner, *The Knights Templar and Their Myth* (Oxford, 1981; revised 1990); H. Nicholson, *Templars, Hospitallers and Teutonic Knights: Images of the Military Orders, 1128–1291* (Leicester, 1995); H. Nicholson, *The Knights Hospitaller* (Woodbridge, 2001); D. Seward, *The Monks of War: The Military Religious Orders* (Harmondsworth, 1972; revised 1995); J. Riley-Smith, *The Knights of St. John in Jerusalem and Cyprus, c.1050–1310* (London, 1967); A. Luttrell, *The*

From the start the papacy had realised the value of these monks of war. The earliest bull granting privileges to the Hospitallers was issued by Paschal II in 1113 (*Pie postulatio voluntatis*), and that to the Templars by Innocent II in 1139 (*omne datum optimum*).[185] They were exempted from Episcopal jurisdiction, answering directly to the Pope, and they were exempted from the payment of tithes on their demesnes lands. They were held in high esteem by the landowning classes of the West, and were endowed liberally by them during the twelfth century. This extended their financial base and represented another way in which western society supported the crusading movement. Their positive image was such that the redoubtable John of Ibelin chose to die in the habit of a Templar in 1236 in Acre. Their military exploits became the stuff of legend. On capture, their Muslim captors usually executed them; this showed that their military significance and contribution was not lost on their enemies. Praised in the generality by the western nobility, their ruthless exploitation of their rights and privileges made them bad neighbours. They would not make concessions on anything that they felt was theirs. In 1154 in Jerusalem they are reported by William of Tyre to have shot arrows into the cloister of the canons of the Church of the Holy Sepulchre with whom they were in dispute.[186] Both in the East and in Europe they alienated the local clergy, the clerical hierarchy, the kings of Armenia, and each other when their interests clashed over castle and estate ownership.

The earliest of the orders was the Knights of St John of Jerusalem, the Knights Hospitaller or Hospitallers. Their origins lay with an Amalfitan foundation of the Church of St Mary of the Latins and a hospital of St John nearby. The hospital was dedicated to the care and support of poor and ailing pilgrims. The foundations were made in the late 1060s. Early twelfth-century popes granted privileges and encouraged donations and recruitment. The Hospitallers were militarised in the 1130s, and certainly by 1136 when King Fulk granted them the castle of Beit Jabrin (Gibelin). Overall they were to hold some fifty-six castles in the Kingdom of Jerusalem. Their function was protecting pilgrims as they moved to and from the holy places of the kingdom. Their military and medical role was an essential element in the promotion and defence of the crusader states. They appear to have been a richer order than the Templars or Teutonic Knights. On the suppression of the Templars in 1312 most of their landed estates outside of France passed to the Hospitallers. They also appear to have been more innovative, or at least wary not to be left behind by developments

---

Hospitallers in Cyprus, Rhodes, Greece and the West, 1291–1440 (London, 1978); A. Luttrell, *Latin Greece, The Hospitallers and the Crusades 1291–1440* (London, 1982); E. Kollias, *The Medieval City of Rhodes and the Palace of the Grand Master* (2nd edn, Athens, 1998); M. Barber, ed., *The Military Orders 1: Fighting for the Faith and Caring for the Sick* (Aldershot, 1994); H. Nicholson, ed., *The Military Orders 2: Welfare and Warfare* (Aldershot, 1998); Z. Hunyadi and J. Laslovsky, eds, *The Crusades and the Military Orders* (Budapest, 2001).

[185] Prawer, *The Latin Kingdom of Jerusalem*, 257, n.10.
[186] Riley-Smith, *The Knights of St. John in Jerusalem and Cyprus*, 398–9.

in crusade thinking in the late thirteenth century. After the loss of Acre in 1291 the Hospitallers withdrew to Cyprus for a while, and between 1306 and 1310 set about the conquest of Rhodes, this remaining the headquarters of their order until 1522. During the fourteenth and fifteenth centuries they formed the backbone of the various naval crusading initiatives, capturing Smyrna in 1343 and providing money, arms and military advice to a variety of small military theatres throughout Greece and the Aegean in efforts to resist Ottoman expansion.[187]

In 1119 a small group of knights – there were only nine in 1128 – took vows of poverty, chastity and obedience before the Latin patriarch of Jerusalem and were given temporary accommodation in the former Aqsa mosque, deemed to be the Temple of Solomon. The motivation of the group was said to be the slaughter of a large number of pilgrims (possibly as many as 300) travelling from Jerusalem to Jordan at Easter 1119. Hugh of Payns was the founder member and soon to be the first grandmaster when the Council of Troyes gave the order a formal existence within the Church and authorised its rule. The rule was written by St Bernard who had been instrumental in guiding Hugh through the intricacies of the Church council. Thereafter donations and recruits came in rapidly, helped by the unstinted support of Bernard. The new order was thus able to make substantial loans to Louis VII during the Second Crusade. It participated in the siege of Damascus in 1129 and thereafter in all the main campaigns mounted by the crusader states, as well as razzias of their own. The first castle granted to them seems to have been with the grant of the town of Gaza in 1152. Overall they garrisoned between twenty-five and thirty castles. Their reputation stood high throughout the twelfth and thirteenth centuries. Their castles at Tortosa and Castel Pelerin held out for two months after the fall of Acre, and they maintained a garrison on the island of Ruad off Tortosa from 1291 to 1302. After 1291 their headquarters was on Cyprus. They adapted badly to the loss of the Holy Land and seemed unable to find a new role for themselves. In October 1307 all Templars in the Kingdom of France were arrested, and over the next few years this policy was adopted in the other kingdoms of the West. On 6 May 1312 the order was dissolved at the Council of Vienne and its properties and endowments were used to re-endow the Hospitallers. Their violent demise gave rise to fabulous stories of magic and the occult that are strill thriving today.

German princes participating in the Third Crusade established a German hospital at Acre in 1190. The new order, the Teutonic Order of St Mary, received papal recognition in 1191, confirmed in 1199. The new order was militarised by 1197. In 1220 they established a hospital in Jerusalem, but the extent to which this hospital existed in the twelfth century and the extent to which it was linked to the 1190 fouundation have been the subject of much debate. The order received rights in the Baltic area in 1231, but it was only in 1291 that it finally abandoned the Holy Land. It transferred its headquarters to Venice and in 1309 relocated

---

[187] J. Rosser, 'Byzantine Isles of Refuge in the Chronicle of Galaxeidi', in P. Lock and G. Sanders, eds, *The Archaeology of Medieval Greece* (Oxford, 1996), 139–46.

them to Marienburg in Prussia. It was in the Baltic that the Teutonic Knights were to demonstrate their continued relevance to Christendom.

Other lesser orders were founded in imitation of the Hospitallers and Templars in the Holy Land: the Order of St Lazarus for Leper knights (c. 1142) and the Order of St Thomas of Acre during the Third Crusade. In Spain two distinct military orders were established: the Order of Calatrava (1150s) and the Order of Mountjoy (1175). The military orders brought dedication, discipline and order to their vocation. They were valued highly as soldiers and thought worthy of reduplication in all areas of crusading endeavour.

CRUSADING SONGS AND POEMS[188]

Music formed an important part in church services and in civic ritual. Music and song were thus an important part of the lives of the crusaders. On crusade itself satirical songs could form a source of diversion and entertainment and, perhaps more importantly, an escape mechanism allowing complete divorce from what was happening around them. It could provide encouragement on the march. Sadly, there are no traces of what music was composed and sung on the early crusades themselves. Guibert of Nogent noted that on the departure of the people's crusade 'Everyone sang of battle, but did not say that they would fight', and William of Tyre recorded that scurrilous songs were composed and sung on the First Crusade about the sex life of Arnold of Choques, soon to be the future Latin patriarch of Jerusalem.[189] These scanty references show that lyric songs did exist independent of the troubadour influence.

Crusader song, as attested by the numerous CD compilations, is associated with the troubadour lyric tradition. This originated in the courts of southern France ('Occitania' in the eleventh century), possibly strongly influenced by Moorish love songs from Spain. The first known troubadour is variously given as either a certain Guillem of Peiteus (1071–1137) or the better-known William IX of Aquitaine (1071–1126), himself a crusader. During the twelfth and thirteenth centuries the troubadour tradition and its lyrics spread to the courts of northern France and the Christian kingdoms of Spain, Sicily and Italy, creating an international culture of lyrical love songs with their emphasis on the erotic and the devices of hidden love.[190] Courtly love provided the model for western romance

---

[188] M. Routledge, 'Songs', in and Riley-Smith, ed., *The Oxford Illustrated History of the Crusades*, 91–111; J. Bedier and P. Aubrey, eds, *Chansons de Croisade* (Paris, 1909); N. Daniel, *Heroes and Saracens: An Interpretataion of the Chansons de Geste* (Edinburgh, 1984); D. Trotter, *Medieval French Literature and the Crusades* (Geneva, 1988); F.-W. Wentlaff-Eggebert, *Kreuzzugsdichtiung des Mittelalters* (Berlin, 1960); F. Akehurst and J. Davis, eds, *A Handbook of the Troubadours* (Berkeley, 1995); L. Patterson, *The World of the Troubadours* (Cambridge, 1993).

[189] Levine, *The Deeds of God Through the Franks* 47; Babcock and Krey, *A History of Deeds Done Beyond the Sea by William Archbishop of Tyre*, I,300.

[190] Known as *trouvère* in northern France. The link between troubadours and the German Minnesinger tradition is hotly debated, often reflecting national tensions at the time of any particular study.

and was a major influence on poets from Petrarch and Dante to Boccaccio and Chaucer. As C.S. Lewis has observed, '[the troubadors] effected a change which has left no corner of our ethics, our imagination, or our daily life untouched . . . Compared with this revolution, the Renaissance is a mere ripple on the surface of literature.'[191]

Troubadors relied upon court patronage, if indeed they were not the patrons themselves. This was the very milieu of crusaders. They came from all social groups – monarchs, nobles, clergy, townsmen and former *jongleurs* (itinerant dancing jugglers), but being a troubador was primarily an aristocratic activity and the better ones were assumed to be noblemen even if they were not. The period associated with troubador creation was the one and a half centuries from 1150 to 1300, although it is interesting to note that the earliest recorded *trouvère* work was a song from the Second Crusade.[192]

It has been estimated that in total 2,500 songs (250 with melodies), composed by 460 troubadours, have survived, compared with 2,000 songs (1,500 with melodies) by 200 *trouvères*.[193] Of these only a small proportion, about 1.4 per cent, are crusade songs bearing directly on the Crusades: thirty-five in Occitan and twenty-nine in Old French.[194] These were the most common languages of composition, but songs also exist in early Spanish, Catalan and German.

The best-known crusaders who were also troubadours were William IX of Aquitaine (1071–1126), Richard I of England (1157–99), Raimbaut of Vaqueiras (*c.* 1155–1207?), Conon of Bethune (1150–1219), Thibaut of Champagne (1201–53) and Emperor Frederick II (1194–1250). Most of their compositions were not related to crusading at all but rather to the repertoire of knightly honour, the finest woman in the world and songs of separation from a loved one. Very occasionally there is some historical fodder as when the Provençal Raimbaut tells of his lord and patron Boniface of Montferrat. Both were participants in the Fourth Crusade, and Raimbaut may have died alongside Boniface in the Rhodope Mountains in September 1207. He depicted Boniface as the model knight, but also provided insights into the marquis' character not apparent in the chronicles of Geoffrey of Villehardouin or Robert of Clari. He viewed the conquest of Constantinople in 1204 as an essential part of the war against Islam, and also saw Boniface as having a family claim to the Kingdom of Thessalonika.[195] In the songs of Conon of Bethune, the spokesman for the crusaders at Constantinople in 1203/4, there are accounts of earlier triumphs against Islam in Spain, themes on the divine protection of crusaders, and poetic

[191] C.S. Lewis, *The Allegory of Love* (Oxford, 1936), 4.
[192] U. Holmes, *A History of Old French Literature from the Origins to 1300* (New York, 1948), 198.
[193] H. van der Werf, *The Chansons of the Troubadours and Trouvères* (Utrecht, 1972), 15.
[194] P. Bec, *La Lyrique française au moyen age (XIIe–XIIIe siècles)* (2 vols, Paris, 1977–8), I, 152.
[195] J. Linskill, ed., *The Poems of the Troubadour Raimbaut de Vaqueiras* (Paris, 1964), 218–53, 301–44; see also Lock, *The Franks in the Aegean*, 20, 44, 47, 176.

depictions of the Holy Land as a topographical icon of Christ and the moral and uplifting effects a visit has on the crusader. One of the best examples of this latter genre is the *Palästinalied* of Walter von der Vogelwiede (*c.* 1170–*c.* 1230), who was not a crusader but a professional performer.

As musical history and entertainment they are outstanding and occupy a fundamental position in the history of the language of love, but as a source for the Crusades they are very disappointing and scarcely illustrate the massive support that crusading enjoyed amongst contemporaries.

CRUSADES FROM A BYZANTINE PERSPECTIVE[196]

The East Roman Empire (or to use an anachronistic seventeenth-century French term, the Byzantine Empire) was in every sense the heir and embodiment of the Roman Empire. Its emperor and many of his subjects regarded the Byzantine *oikumene* as coterminous with the bounds of civilisation, just as the former Roman Empire had been so conceived. The resources of the Roman Empire had been formally divided into an eastern and western half by Theodosius I in 395, each with its own emperor. Practically, this division had taken shape with the Tetrarchy (another modern term) of four rulers instituted by Diocletian in 293. Constantine the Great's refounding of Byzantium as Constantinople in 324 was merely the establishment of a capital for his own tetrarchy and in no sense an attempt to replace the city of Rome. However, following the sack of Rome in 410 Constantinople became commonly referred to as New Rome and after 476 was the capital of the Roman Empire. With the deposition of the last emperor of the western half of the Roman Empire in 476 the integrity of the Empire was

---

[196] G. Ostrogorsky, *History of the Byzantine State* (2nd edn, Oxford, 1968), 320–50, provides the classic account; S. Runciman, *The Eastern Schism* (Oxford, 1955); P. Charanis, 'Byzantium, the West and the Origins of the First Crusade', *Byzantion*, 19 (1949), 17–36; S. Vryonis, *The Decline of Medieval Hellenism in Asia Minor and the Process of Islamization from the Eleventh Though the Fifteenth Century* (Berkeley, 1971); S. Vryonis, 'Byzantium, the Social Basis for Decline in the Eleventh Century', *Greek, Roman and Byzantine Studies*, 2 (1959), 159–75; J. Shephard,'When Greek meets Greek: Alexius Comneneus and Bohemond in 1097–98', *Byzantine and Modern Greek Studies*, 12 (1988), 185–277; J. Shepard, 'Cross-Purposes: Alexius Comneneus and the First Crusade', in J. Phillips, ed., *The First Crusade: Origins and Impact* (Manchester, 1997), 107–29; P. Magdalino, *The Byzantine Background to the First Crusade* (Toronto, 1996), available electronically at http://www.deremilitari.org/RESOURCES/ARTICLES/magdalino.htm; D. Baker, ed., *Relations Between East and West in the Middle Ages* (Edinburgh, 1973); J. Howard-Johnston, ed., *Byzantium and the West, c.800–c.1200* (Amsterdam, 1988); M. Angold, *The Byzantine Empire 1025–1204: A Political History* (London, 1984); R.-J. Lilie, *Byzantium and the Crusader States 1096–1204* (Oxford, 1993); Lillie Harris, *Byzantium and the Crusades*; Laiou and Parviz-Mottahedeh, eds, *The Crusades from the Perspective of Byzantium and the Muslim World*; C. Brand, *Byzantium Confronts the West 1180–1204* (Princeton, 1968); C. Brand, 'The Byzantines and Saladin 1185–1192: Opponents of the Third Crusade', *Speculum*, 37 (1962), 167–81; C. Brand, 'A Byzantine Plan for the Fourth Crusade', *Speculum*, 43 (1968), 462–75; J. Herrin, 'The Collapse of the Byzantine Empire in the Twelfth Century', *Birmingham Historical Journal*, 12 (1970), 188–203.

restored and that emperor's rights and authority passed to his eastern colleague. These claims were serious claims and had been given some reality by Justinian I's programme of reconquest in Italy and North Africa in the 530s, by the plan of the emperor Maurice (582–602) in 597 to restore Rome as the second city of the Empire, by papal co-operation with Byzantium against both Saracens and Normans in the tenth and early eleventh centuries, and by the continued Byzantine naval and military presence in Italy down to 1071.

Constantine I the Great's (306–37) conversion to Christianity and his protection and endowment of that religion substantially increased the power of the emperors in what was the first Christian polity. The emperor was the king of kings, divinely appointed and answerable to God alone for the protection of the Christian *oikumene* and its capital. Christians everywhere were, in theory, under his protection, as were the holy places and the Christian artefacts located by Constantine the Great and his mother Helena. It was the emperor as vicegerent of God, and not the patriarch, who summoned and presided over Church councils and appointed and dismissed its patriarchs and leading ecclesiastics. After 652 only two of the five patriarchates remained under any semblance of direct Byzantine control: Constantinople and Rome. Of these Rome was accorded the primacy of honour because of its dual foundation by Peter and Paul and because of the historic status of the city itself. After 476 the Roman emperor was not present in Rome, but he maintained close links with the bishop of Rome whom he treated as a loyal ecclesiastical functionary and supporter in the defence of the Christian *oikumene* and of the beliefs of its inhabitants. The development of the Reform papacy in the eleventh century, with its advocacy of the doctrine of the two swords and of papal primacy, by which all the world was to be judged by the bishop of Rome, was bound to lead to tensions. By the end of the eleventh century, popes and the western emperors whom they crowned were in dispute over their respective Universalist claims in what has traditionally been known as the Investiture Controversy.[197] Universalism was at the very centre of Byzantine imperialism. Neither the Byzantine emperor nor his patriarch could concede anything to a reformed and strident papacy that regarded the Orthodox Church as a church in schism rather than vice versa. Geographical distance might moderate the asperity of the diplomatic language of letters but it could also exacerbate misunderstanding. The Pope, the man who summoned crusades, and the Byzantine emperor, the ruler of the lands through which those crusaders must pass, were likely to disagree over fundamental issues.

Politically, too, tensions developed with the re-establishment of the idea of the Western Roman Empire by Charlemagne and Pope Leo I in Rome on Christmas Day 800. The Byzantine king of kings might be prepared to accord an honoured place in his virtual family of kings to a particularly favoured 'brother' or 'son' from amongst the rulers of the western kingdoms, and to overawe their

---

[197] Morris, *The Papal Monarchy*, 109–33, 154–81.

representatives with imperial ceremonial and costly gifts, but the breaking of the unity of the God-protected empire by a western barbarian was too much to stomach. The imperial title of Charlemagne and his successors was simply ignored in favour of that of King of the Franks. To the Byzantine courtiers it appeared that the western world-view and that of their own did not accord. Perhaps the westerners did not know how to behave. There were to be a number of conspicuous examples of this during the crusades of the twelfth century, and particular difficulties when kings of Germany and western emperors like Conrad III, Frederick I Barbarossa, and Frederick II went on crusade.

By virtue of its geographic position, a 400-year tradition of military conflict and diplomatic exchanges with Islam, and historic claims to territory from Constantinople to Caesarea and Carthage, Byzantium was both central and crucial to any crusading expedition in the twelfth century. Yet from the start cultural and ideological, political and religious differences between the Greek East and the Germanic West intruded themselves. These were to be exacerbated by language and the habits of mind that go with it. Although the coinage of Byzantium was to be produced with Latin inscriptions down to 1453, the official language of the Empire was Greek and had been so since the early seventh century. It was primarily as Greeks and not as fellow Christians or Romans that the crusaders knew the Byzantine emperor and his subjects. The word 'Greek' (Graecas), and especially its diminutive 'Greekling' (Graeculus), rapidly became pejorative, both mocking in tone and deeply offensive to the Byzantine court.

It may well be claimed that Byzantium started the crusade movement in the West by appealing to Pope Urban II for military assistance at the Council of Piacenza in March 1095. It is likely that this was an appeal for mercenaries to fight in an offensive against the Seljuks of Rum. There is considerable evidence that the Byzantine emperors had been seeking increasing numbers of western mercenary contingents in the years after 1070. Approaches were made to likely western pilgrims returning home through Constantinople. Such had been Alexios I's approach to Robert of Flanders in 1089/90 that had resulted in the recruitment of 500 Frankish mercenaries. There had also been appeals to Gregory VII in 1074 as well as to Urban in 1095. It was the interpretation that the Pope put on these appeals that generated a crusade rather than a mercenary force.

At the beginning of the eleventh century the reputation of the Byzantine armed forces stood high. They were, however, a major expense to the Byzantine treasury and one of the many factors contributing to the devaluation of the gold *nomismata* beginning under Constantine IX Monomachos (1042–55). One solution was to reduce the defence budget, and this policy was introduced under Constantine X Doukas (1059–67). The peasant militias of the various themes were run down, military installations were not maintained, and the former fleet was reduced in favour of contracting out naval activities to the Genoese, Pisans and Venetians. The field army was largely manned with mercenary soldiers, recruited from within the Empire, from its neighbours or from abroad. These mercenaries would provide their own equipment, require no land allotments for their support and possibly more amenable to long range military campaigns, should these prove necessary. Diplomacy and a system of alliances were to be the first resort and military force the last. Despite initial difficulties in 1064 and 1065 this policy could and did work satisfactorily as was to be shown by the defeat of the Norman in the Balkans in 1085 and 1108, by the annihilation of the Pechnegs in 1091 and 1122, the mustering of fleets of 100–150 ships in the 1170s and 1180s and by the Byzantine protectorate exercised over the crusader states in the middle of the twelfth century. But it could be handicapped by the abilities of individual military leaders or by lack of political will at the centre. Palace revolutions and rebellions had witnessed nine rulers in the fifty years before the First Crusade. This was especially important because the change of strategy and the reduction of military districts focused more attention on the emperor and his imperial general staff as commanders of the field army.

Mercenaries had been a feature of the late Roman army and their use carried on into the Byzantine armed forces. During the tenth and eleventh centuries they were recruited from Cumans, Pechnegs, Russians, Scandinavians, Germans, English, Normans and Franks. During the thirteenth century Seljuk and Ottoman Turks and Catalans were to be used as well. The political circumstances of the lands of origin might influence the volume of recruitment, thus the proportion of mercenaries from England rose in the years after the Norman Conquest of 1066. It does appear, however, that the troubles caused by the Pechnegs and the Seljuk Turks from the 1040s onwards, both Turkic peoples, led to a preference for mercenaries from the West. These western recruits brought with them their own military precepts and techniques and usually fought under their own western leaders. However, they fought under Byzantine generals and they waged war according to Byzantine direction and strategy not according to Christian belief.

By the 1090s when Alexios I made his appeals for mercenaries to Robert of Flanders and Urban II, the Pechneg threat had been contained and a campaign of reconquest against the Seljuks of Rum may have been in the planning stage. Western mercenaries were a familiar feature of Byzantine military society, and western methods of warfare were well known. For their part the mercenaries helped foster some awareness of Byzantium in their families back home in the West. It was mercenaries that Alexios I expected; soldiers to be commanded by him and used in the furtherance of his imperial designs. What arrived at Constantinople in 1096 and 1097 was a crusade, an army on pilgrimage to liberate Jerusalem under the command of the Pope. During the twelfth century the relationship of this western military endeavour and Byzantine agendas was to be worked out.

Byzantium was central to the success of any crusade that took the overland route to the East. Large numbers of crusaders passed through Constantinople in 1096, 1097, 1101, 1147, 1189/90 and 1203/4. On each of the crusades of the twelfth century the Byzantine emperors and their provincial officials provided supply dumps, oversaw the relations of crusaders with their host communities, entertained and housed many of the crusade leaders, gave practical and strategic advice, provided guides through the former territories of the Empire now in Seljuk hands, and gave substantial military support in the form of specialised equipment for sieges, professional troops and experienced commanders. Anna Komnene attests that her father had particular concern for the well-being of the crusaders. All of the western chroniclers of the twelfth-century crusades attest to the variety of Byzantine support on offer. All also criticise the support in terms of quality, quantity and motivation. The markets were too few and the supplies inadequate. The guides were ignorant or treacherous. The emperor was too concerned with the defence of the Empire, distrustful of the crusaders, and not sufficiently focused on the ideology and objectives of the Crusades. Some of these comments arose from ignorance, self-obsessive religiosity, or downright prejudice. There was no awareness of the strains imposed and the suspicions aroused by such large numbers camped outside Constantinople demanding to be fed, or any appreciation of the organization that seems to have dealt with disputes and prevented them from getting more serious. What had caused the clerical writers of western crusade chronicles to attempt to write Byzantium out of the picture?

From the start the crusaders clearly expected too much from Byzantium, but in part this negative attitude towards the Greeks was a psychological defence mechanism, a sort of reverse cultural snobbery. Byzantium was richer, grander and more sophisticated than the courts, towns and cities of home. Those who were recieved at the Byzantine court were left in no doubt about this. The ceremonial was awesome, the receptions lavish, and the gifts that they might receive attested to the wealth of the emperor. Yet they too had their pride. Constantinople was the largest city by far in Christian Europe and its Graeco-Roman heritage was evident for all to see. It was a capital city that sucked in the resources of empire in a way that was unfamiliar to western visitors. Conducted tours of the city were available for those with a mind to look, and those crusaders who did marvelled at the amenities of the city. Luxury and Byzantium had long been equated in the western mind, providing silks, bronze doors, religious relics and artists in mosaic to the courts and churches of the West. It was probably this perception that helped raise crusader expectations.

In the crusade chronicles that appeared in the twelfth century the Byzantines were variously dubbed as treacherous, effeminate, lazy and lacking in honour. This image originated with Norman writers like the anonymous author of the *Gesta Francorum* and proved a compelling model against which to judge Byzantine dealings with the crusaders. Marc Carrier has argued persuasively that this reaction was grounded in differing views of honour.[198] That of the crusade

---

[198]   Marc Carrier, 'Perfidious and Effeminate Greeks: The Representation of Byzantine Ceremonial in the Western Chronicles of the Crusades (1096–1204)', *Annuario dell'Instituto Romeno di Cultura e Ricerza Umanistica Venezia 2002*, 23pp (available electronically: http://www.callisto. si.usherb.ca/Byzance.htm), on which this paragraph is based.

leadership was grounded in Germanic views of honour based on courage, loyalty and manliness, primarily shown in battle.[199] For the Byzantines negotiation and diplomacy were the basis of dealing with an enemy, and might well involve deceit.[200] Honour, on the other hand, was measured by position in the hierarchy of court office. It was in their reception at the imperial court that these differences manifested themselves for the crusade leadership. They did not or could not come to terms with the use of eunuchs at the Byzantine court. It was eunuchs that introduced them into the imperial presence and were clearly an affront to western masculinity. Proskynesis, or prostration before the emperor, was also a humiliating experience and one to be avoided if at all possible, whilst the perceived dishonour in taking an oath to the emperor occupied much ink in the pages of the chroniclers. Carrier cites many examples of crusaders behaving badly at the Byzantine court; I quote two examples from the time of the First Crusade. 'Anna Comnena recounts the famous case of the French knight, from the suite of Godfrey of Bouillon, who dared sit on the imperial throne while in audience with Alexius I. After he had been reprimanded for his audacity and questioned on his motives, the knight simply retorted by putting into question the emperor's honor ... [and] ... Tancred snubbed the emperor's gifts and demanded the imperial tent instead.'[201] On the other hand Bohemond, with more familiarity with Byzantine ways than his fellow leaders, was prepared to take the oath that the emperor requested and may have hoped to have overall command of the crusade conferred upon by Alexios. This did not happen. His change of stance after his seizure of Antioch is reflected in the strictures of the anonymous *Gesta Francorum*.[202] Stephen of Blois was delighted with his own reception by Alexios, who apparently showered him with gifts and regarded him as more important than any of the other crusaders. Raymond of Toulouse's reputation suffered because he sought to respect the rights of the emperor and became linked with the suspicions that surrounded the emperor in the anti-Byzantine propaganda of the Normans.[203]

The nature of anti-Byzantine comments, and some reasons for them amongst the First Crusaders, is clear enough. Yet just how widespread was this anti-Greek

---

[199] Dawes, trans, *The Alexiad of the Princess Anna Comnena*, 264, using the words of the Frank who sat on the emperor's throne for a Byzantine comment on this; see 310 for Byzantine diplomacy.

[200] D. Obolensky, 'The Principles and Methods of Byzantine Diplomacy', *Actes du XIIe congrès International d'Ètudes Byzantines*, I (Belgrade, 1963), 45–61; J. Shepard and S. Franklin, eds, *Byzantine Diplomacy* (Aldershot, 1992), for essays reflecting the various manifestations of this diplomacy in all periods, especially marriage alliances and honorary kinship with the imperial family.

[201] Carrier, 'Perfidious and Effeminate Greeks', 14–15.

[202] Shepard, 'When Greek meets Greek'; K. Wolf, 'Crusade and Narrative: Bohemond and the *Gesta Francorum*', *Journal of Medieval History*, 17 (1991), 207–16; Hill, ed. and trans., *Gesta Francorum et aliorum Hierosolinctounorum*, 12, 44–5.

[203] Hagenmayer, *Die Kreuzzugsbriefe aus den Jahren 1088–1100*, 138; J. Hill, 'Raymond of Saint Gilles in Urban's Plan of Greek and Latin Friendship', *Speculum*, 26 (1951), 265–70.

feeling in the West? The chroniclers of the First Crusade, as distinct from Odo of Deuil, pay relatively little attention to the crusader–Byzantine relationship. The First Crusade had been summoned as a war of protection for Constantinople and as an act of brotherly love for fellow Christians, the orthodox Greeks. Was it rather the stresses and strains of the journey to the East that provoked these hostile reactions to the Byzantines and their emperor?[204] Odo of Deuil's account of the crusade of Louis VII is full of anti-Greek comments, from his reception by Manuel I, to his treatment by Greek guides on the march and by Byzantine officials at Atalya.[205] On the other hand this Graecophobia is not evident in the work of Conrad III's half-brother Otto of Freising. Indeed Conrad, who had as much to complain about regarding the inadequacies of Greek guides, took time out from crusading to recuperate in Constantinople from late 1147 to the spring of 1148. Here he was personally cared for by Manuel I, who was married to Conrad's sister-in-law, Bertha of Salzbach. It was now, or in October 1148 on his return from crusade, that Conrad and Manuel agreed a formal alliance against Roger II of Sicily.[206] Clearly the rulers of two empires with mutual interests in Italy could find much about which to agree.

Anna Komnene makes clear that suspicion of potential crusade attacks were present from the first arrival of large numbers of crusaders at Constantinople and that Alexios' handling of the crusader leadership was designed to minimise this threat.[207] In this he was completely successful. Although the armies of Godfrey of Bouillon and Raymond of Toulouse had resorted to fighting and pillaging on their approach to Constantinople, and although some western leaders might find little honour in the receptions, gifts, adoptive sonships and oath-takings, no outright attack on the city happened in either 1096/7 or in 1101. There were two regrettable outbreaks of violence at Constantinople itself, but that was all: the first when Peter the Hermit's followers looted the suburbs of Constantinople and were reported stripping the lead off roofs; the second in March 1101 when elements of the Lombard contingent had rioted in Constantinople, broke into the Blachernae Palace and killed one of Alexios' favourite lions in the menagerie there. The response to these acts was the acceptance of an apology and the speedy transport of the contingents concerned across the Bosphoros.

The first mention of a possible attack on Constantinople by crusaders comes with the arrival of the German and French armies outside the city in September and October 1147. It occurs in both Byzantine and western sources.[208] Manuel I

---

[204] W. Daly, 'Christian Fraternity, the Crusaders, and the Security of Constantinople, 1097–1204: The Precarious Survival of an Ideal', *Medieval Studies*, 22 (1960), 43–91.

[205] V. Berry, ed. and trans., *Odo of Deuil, De Profectione Ludovici VII in orientem* (New York, 1948), 25–7, 59–61, 81, 83 and 133.

[206] T. Reuter, 'The Non-Crusade of 1149–50', in J. Phillips and M. Hoch, eds, *The Second Crusade: Scope and Consequences* (Manchester, 2001), 150–63.

[207] Dawes, trans., *The Alexiad of the Princess Anna Comnena*, 258–68.

[208] P. Magdalino, *The Empire of Manuel I Komnenos, 1143–1180* (Cambridge, 1993), 46–61.

(1143–80) had definitely not asked for such an expedition, as his grandfather had done in 1095, and the repair of the walls of Constantinople that he put in hand showed his concern for safeguarding the city from western crusading armies. There were the same expectations of Byzantine support for a crusade as in 1096/7, but this time kings were leading the campaign and they could not be treated as dukes and counts had been fifty years before. Odo of Deuil records that some of Louis VII's advisers urged him to set up base in Thrace and await the arrival of the forces of Roger II of Sicily, who was then attacking the Byzantine cities of Thebes and Corinth. The reasons for such a move were not just the treatment of the French on their passage through the Balkans but the designs of the Byzantines on Antioch.[209] According to Otto of Freising there was a prophecy current in the West that Louis would capture both Constantinople and Babylon.[210] After the Germans had crossed into Asia Minor an anonymous poet, conventionally known as 'Manganeios Prodromos', addressed an encomium to Manuel in which he accused Conrad of wishing to storm Constantinople and instal a Latin patriarch, almost a prospectus for the Fourth Crusade.[211] Nonetheless, despite the destruction of a monastery near Adrianople and damage to the Philopation palace outside Constantinople there was no attack on the city itself.

Looking back from the perspective of the fall of Constantinople to the Fourth Crusade in April 1204 it is tempting to see it as the culmination of a process of ideas first formed in 1097. However, there was nothing inevitable about such an attack. For the next thirty years, apart from Roger II of Sicily's plans for an attack on Constantinople in 1150,[212] the Byzantines continued to exercise a protectorate over the crusader states and to have earned the good opinion of the West as a Christian ally against Islam. All of this was to change in April 1182 when Andronikos I Komnenos (1183–5), then regent for John II, sought to bolster his political position by allowing a mob to massacre western merchants in Constantinople. In the same year he sanctioned the murder of Renier of Montferrat, the most distinguished Latin in Constantinople. Pope Lucius III sent a fact-finding mission to Andronikos in December 1182, but Byzantine-western relations definitely took a turn for the worse at this point. The Byzantines were now definitely distrusted and hated in the West, especially by the Genoese, Pisan and Venetians who had suffered the most in the massacres. Any lingering presumption of Byzantine good faith took a further knock during the passage of the crusade of Frederick Barbarossa from July 1189 to March 1190.

At that time it was discovered that Isaac II Angelos (1185–95) had diplomatic relations with Saladin, whilst his headstrong conduct convinced many of Frederick's advisers that Isaac was intent on breaking up the crusade itself. All of

[209] Berry, ed., and trans., *Odo of Deuil, De Profectione Ludovici VII in orientem*, 59, 68–71.
[210] Mierow, trans., *The Deeds of Frederick Barbarossa by Otto of Freising and his Continuator Rahewin*, 25–6.
[211] Magdalino, *The Empire of Manuel I Komnenos, 1143–1180*, 48.
[212] See Reuter, 'The Non-Crusade of 1149–50', Phillips, *Defenders of the Holy Land*, 114–18.

this was accompanied with rumours of vats of poison provided by Saladin and intensified by the imprisonment of Frederick's envoys. In December 1189 Frederick sounded out the Serbs for a possible military alliance to capture Constantinople, and an assault on the city was on the brink of taking place. Nothing happened on this occasion. Agreements were reached and the Germans passed on their way; but the idea of Constantinople in reliable Latin hands, once formed, would not go away.[213] It is possible, but debatable, that the German emperor Henry VI (1190–7) contemplated the capture of Constantinople in 1194/5. Following his coronation as king of Sicily at Palermo on Christmas day 1194 he demanded the cession of territory between Dyracchium and Thessalonika, tribute from Alexios III, and an agreement that the Byzantines would provide naval support for his proposed crusade. Any such plans were aborted by Henry's death in September 1197.[214] Before leaving the twelfth century it is time to look at Byzantine relations with the crusader states set up in the East after 1098/9.

The setting up of crusader states had not been part of Urban's plan for the liberation of Jerusalem, but the possibility of crusaders seizing former Byzantine territory had been present in Byzantine thinking from the first. That is why Alexios I was at such pains to exact 'the customary oath of the Latins'[215] to return all former Byzantine possessions in both 1097 and 1101. In 1097 Tatikios and a small Byzantine army accompanied the crusaders to garrison the surrendered towns. Despite a dip in morale when Nicaea surrendered directly to the Greeks, the crusaders had fulfilled all Byzantine expectations regarding the return of reconquered towns up to and including the capture of Comana in September 1097, one month before the army arrived at Antioch. The crusaders never challenged the legitimacy of the oaths that they swore to Alexios, and for many it appeared that he had succeeded in turning the motley crusade into a Byzantine mercenary force.

There is no doubt, as Jonathan Shepard has argued, that Alexios I and the first crusaders were at cross purposes. Just what constituted former possessions was left vague. Was it recent losses after, say, 1071 or what had constituted Byzantine territory before the Arab expansion in the 630s, including Jerusalem itself? The latter seems to have been the case: a Pisan–Byzantine treaty of 1111 recognized Byzantine claims in Syria and Palestine up to the Egyptian frontier whilst the campaigns of John and Manuel I suggested an assumed suzerainty over the crusader states.[216] Of these the most important for the control of north Syria was Antioch, lost to the Byzantines as recently as 1084. Sometime in March 1099

---

[213] Brand, *Byzantium Confronts the West 1180–1204*, 66–7, 176–88; Brand, 'The Byzantines and Saladin, 1185–1192: Opponents of the Third Crusade', 167–81.

[214] Ostrogorsky, *History of the Byzantine State*, 412–13, and references. The 'German tax' (το αλαμανιχον) was levied in the Empire.

[215] Dawes, trans., *The Alexiad of the Princess Anna Comnena*, 266.

[216] Lilie, *Byzantium and the Crusader States 1096–1204*, 20–4; J.L. La Monte, 'To What Extent was the Byzantine Empire the Suzerain of the Latin Crusading States?', *Byzantion*, 7 (1932), 253–64.

a Byzantine embassy had been rebuffed when it demanded the return of Antioch from Bohemond. Yet when Baldwin of Boulogne had set himself up as ruler of Edessa in March 1098 there had been no demand for restitution from the Byzantines. Edessa was as important strategically for any advance into Mesopotamia as Antioch was for the control of North Syria.

It was not just a difference of strategic intent that accounted for the different reaction of the Byzantines to the recovery of different parts of their former provinces. At its heart lay the universal claim of the Byzantine emperor to be the protector both of Christians and the Christian Holy Places and of artefacts under Muslim control. Antioch was the city where the followers of Christ were first called 'Christians' (Acts 11.26). It was the seat of a patriarchate, supposedly founded by St Peter, and had been recognised as such at the Council of Nicaea in 325 alongside Alexandria and Rome. It hosted two important church synods in 325 and 341. Thus, apart from its strategic situation, it was an essential part of the *oikumene* and for its religious associations should be returned to the emperor, the protector of Christians. Edessa, on the other hand, had no such pretensions despite its Christian cathedral. Its most precious relics – the *mandylion* and the letter to Abgar that had accompanied it – had been removed to Constantinople for safe keeping in 944. It was therefore just a place, though a strategically important place; however, it did not figure in Byzantine military plans in 1098. Both the concentration of holy relics in Constantinople from the tenth century onwards and the imperial claims of the Christian protectorate were vitally important in the Byzantine world-view.

The replacement of the emperor by various Christian potentates as the effective protectors of the Christians of Syria and Palestine could not be easily tolerated – hence the row over Antioch. Matters were exacerbated in 1100 when the resident Greek patriarch, John IV the Oxite, fled to Constantinople for imperial protection on the appointment of a Latin patriarch, Bernard of Valence, in his stead. The prominent place that the city occupied in Anna Komnene's account of the crusade and its aftermath attests to its significance in Byzantine eyes. Its loss to Bohemond coloured her whole assessment of Alexios' dealings with the crusaders from one of qualified success to one of failure.

The lower town of Antioch surrendered on 3 June 1098, and on the 28 June with the defeat of Kerbogha's relieving force the crusaders had complete control of the city, including the citadel. Success had been achieved without any Byzantine assistance. Tatikios had been persuaded to leave the army during the siege. Alexios I, who had left Constantinople in June 1098 with an army to reinforce the crusaders, had turned back at Philomelion influenced by the dire reports of Stephen of Blois and the other 'ropedancers' of Antioch. For Bohemond and his supporters this was used to demonstrate that Alexios was both unable and unwilling to support the crusaders, and had thus broken the terms of the oaths of 1097 and had forfeited any right to the return of recaptured places. For others like Raymond of Toulouse the oath still held and Antioch should be returned to Alexios. The outcome of the discussions was the abandonment of any idea of military or political co-operation with the Byzantines. This was summed up in the letter that the crusade leadership addressed to Urban II from Antioch on 11 September 1098 urging him to come east himself and lead the crusade that he had launched.[217] For Alexios, after due representations had been made in March 1099, force might be used to recover the city, and in 1100 a military expedition was sent to Cilicia to prepare the way for such an assault.

Nothing came of this proposed offensive measure. Bohemond took the fight to the Balkans. From 1105 he was in Europe recruiting for a crusade that in 1107/8 resulted in the siege of Dyrrachium at the western end of the Via Egnatia. Here Alexios besieged the besiegers and in September 1108 forced Bohemond to agree to the Treaty of Devol (Deabolis). Anna Komnene gives the text in full.[218] The emperor was acknowledged as overlord of Antioch, which Bohemond held as the emperor's vassal (lizios). The emperor should have the appointment of the patriarch, but in practice this led to the existence of two patriarchs – one resident in Constantinople and a Latin patriarch in Antioch itself. Legally the Byzantines seemed to have triumphed. Byzantine suzerainty had been accepted, but in practice Bohemond returned to Apulia and no attempt was made to ensure that his regent Tancred compiled with the treaty. The question of the suzerainty over the crusader states was to remain an issue for Alexios' successors, John II (1118–43) and Manuel I Komnenos (1143–80). For nearly twenty years other military preoccupations were to distract John II from any reckoning with the crusader states: wars with the Seljuk sultanate of Iconium, Pechnegs (1122), Serbs (1122–3), Venetians (1125–6), Hungarians (1128), the Danishmend emirate of Melitene (1130–5), diplomatic exchanges with the emperor Lothar III (1125–37) against the Normans in Italy (1135–7), and the subjection of the Cilician Kingdom of Lesser Armenia (1137). John established that Cilicia was to be a Byzantine not a Frankish protectorate with an Orthodox clerical hierarchy. At the end of the Cilician campaign in August 1137 John II marched to Antioch and on 29 August began the siege of the city.

Raymond II of Antioch was too weak to resist the siege for long, and John II was aware of the risk of war with the crusader states as a whole. Within weeks a compromise was agreed on the basis of the Treaty of Devol of 1108. Raymond recognised the Byzantine position in Cilicia and agreed to hand over Antioch to John on condition that he was given a principality encompassing Aleppo, Homs, Shaizar and Emessa (Homs). The imperial banner now flew over Antioch, and the Byzantine army withdrew into winter quarters in Cilicia until the campaign season of March 1138 when it would return to capture the towns promised to Raymond. The Byzantines failed to take either Aleppo or Shaizar, but the emir of Shaizar was forced to return a jewelled cross that had been taken from Romanos IV at Manzikert in 1071. In the meantime, March 1138, Innocent II had condemned Byzantine aggression in North Syria and called upon all western

[217] Hagenmayer, ed., *Die Kreuzzugsbreife aus den Jahren 1088–1100*, 161–5.
[218] Dawes, trans., *The Alexiad of the Princess Anna Comnena*, 348–57.

mercenaries in the Byzantine army to resign their posts. After a triumphal parade in Antioch the emperor accepted excuses for delay in handing over Antioch and returned to Constantinople.[219]

Three years later (1142–3) John II mounted a second campaign to secure Antioch. He marched first to Turbessel in the county of Edessa and obtained hostages from Joscelin II of Courtenay against any interference in the emperor's dealings with Raymond of Antioch; he then marched towards Antioch, arriving there on 25 September. Negotiations were opened with both Raymond II and Fulk of Jerusalem, both of them hinting at Byzantine suzerainty over the respective principality and kingdom. Diplomatic delays ensued and the Byzantine army moved to winter quarters in Cilicia where on 8 April 1143 John died of septicaemia as a result of a hunting accident. His son and heir Manuel I withdrew to Constantinople to secure his position, and the crusader states were granted respite from recognising the suzerainty of Byzantium.[220]

Manuel did not forget Antioch and in 1144/5 sent a combined naval and land expedition against Cilicia and Antioch. This secured the former for the Byzantines and posed a sufficient threat to Raymond II that prevented him from sending any assistance to Edessa, then under attack by Zengi of Mosul. Manuel was distracted by the need to secure his own imperial position in Constantinople, by war with the Normans of Italy from 1146 to 1157 (including an invasion of Italy from 1155 to 1157), and by the passage of the Second Crusade in 1147. It was to be ten years before he would be able to campaign in Syria. He was different from his father and grandfather in that he was interested in western culture, employed Normans and Franks at his court and generally gained a reputation as a Latinophile.[221]

Following the failure of the Second Crusade and the absence of concrete western military support for the crusader states, the latter were thrown into the arms of Byzantium, the only state with a military force capable of operating in Syria at will and one that elicited respect from their Muslim opponents. For his part, Manuel was prepared to take a more circumspect approach to his relations with the West in general and the crusader states in particular. The death of Raymond II of Antioch in battle in June 1149, and the subsequent capture of Joscelin II of Edessa by Turkomans in May 1150, placed the rule of these north Syrian principalities in the hands of regents. Manuel I was not slow to exploit these problems. In 1150 he proposed a consort of his own for the widowed Constance of Antioch, in the person of the Caesar John Roger, a Norman from southern Italy long-established at the Byzantine court. Constance rejected his suit and to the annoyance of both Manuel and Baldwin III of Jerusalem married Reynald of Chatillon three years later. In the spring of 1150 Manuel bought the rump of the county of Edessa from Joscelin's wife, Beatrice, and with the help of

---

[219] Lilie, *Byzantium and the Crusader States, 1096–1204*, 120–34.

[220] R.-J. Lilie, *Byzantium and the Crusader States, 1096–1204*, 134–41.

[221] N. Oikonomides, *Hommes D'Affaires Grecs et latines à Constantinople* (Paris, 1979).

Baldwin III of Jerusalem installed a Greek garrison in Turbessel (Tell Bashir). Although Turbessel was lost by the summer of 1151 he had established the principle of Byzantine suzerainty over Edessa.

From 1157 to 1158 Manuel campaigned in person in Cilicia. At his head-quarters at Mopsuestia he received first Reynaud of Chatillon, who appeared as a penitent and received pardon for his attack on Cyprus in 1156 and for his support for Thoros in Cilicia. Reynaud acknowledged Byzantine suzerainty of Antioch. He agreed to hand over the citadel when required and to replace the Latin patriarch with a Greek nominated by Manuel. He also promised to provide military support to Manuel on request. Baldwin III of Jerusalem came next and spent ten days with Manuel. The subject of their discussions is unknown, but Manuel may have seen in Baldwin someone with whom he could deal regarding the crusader states as a whole. Finally, the Armenian rebel Thoros came in from the hills and made his peace with Manuel, restoring those parts of Cilicia he had seized from 1143 onwards. The campaign was rounded off on 12 April 1159 by a triumphal entry into Antioch that demonstrated both Byzantine military strength and the suzerainty of Byzantium in the region. In May, alarmed by the presence of a Byzantine army at Antioch, Nur ed-Din concluded a truce with the Franks, after which Manuel returned to Constantinople. The crusader states were dependent on Byzantine support for their survival, and a series of marriage alliances demonstrated this reality: Baldwin III and the emperor's niece Theo-dora had married in Jerusalem in September 1158; Manuel I and Maria of Antioch in December 1161; Amalric of Jerusalem with Maria Komnene, the daughter of Manuel's nephew in August 1167; Manuel's great-nephew Isaac Komnenos was married to a daughter of Thoros, sometime before the latter's death in 1168; and Manuel's great-niece Thoedora with Bohemond III of Anti-och in 1177. Throughout the 1160s Manuel was very much the power-broker in Syria. Fear of Byzantine intervention exercised some restraint on Nur ed-Din, Manuel paid for the restoration of the Church of the Nativity at Bethlehem and in 1165 had also paid the ransom of Bohemond III, after which Bohemond paid a visit to Constantinople and on his return to Antioch installed Athansios as Greek patriarch. Despite all this, with hindsight, Manuel's campaign of 1157–8 was the last time a full imperial field army campaigned in Syria.[222]

The marriage negotiations with Amalric had included plans for a joint Jerusa-lemite-Byzantine campign to conquer and partition Egypt. If this succeeded there would have been no doubt in either East or West that Byzantium was indeed the suzerain of the crusader states. However, after the failure of the siege of Damietta (20 October to 21 December 1169), the Byzantine claims were seen as hollow and meaningless in military terms. This was confirmed in 1177 when a Byzantine fleet of 150 ships arrived at Acre for an attack on Egypt that had to be postponed due to the domestic politics of the crusader states. In 1171 Amalric

---

[222] Lilie, *Byzantium and the Crusader States, 1096–1204*, 176–83; Magdalino, *The Empire of Manuel I Komnenos, 1143–1180*, 66–76.

had visited Constantinople to arrange another alliance for an attack on Egypt. This was renewed on Amalric's death in 1174 with the regency for his successor Baldwin IV. Postponements had followed on the Byzantine side due to shortage of troops, but in 1177 the Byzantine suzerain could not force the expedition through. During the 1170s Manuel became preoccupied with the Venetians and the resurgent Seljuk sultanate of Iconion under Kilij Arslan II (1155–92). Manuel's order for the arrest of all Venetians in the Empire on 12 March 1171 seemed to signal the end of any special relationship with the West, whilst his defeat by Kilij Arslan at Myriokephalon on 17 September 1176 meant loss of prestige and the effective end of the Byzantine protectorate.[223]

The death of Manuel I ushered in a period of twenty years of political instability in Byzantium. Palace revolutions in 1183, 1185 and 1195 brought to power emperors who were more concerned to secure their own position internally in Constantinople than to have a care for the needs of the Empire and its people. The disbandment of the fleet in 1182 resulted in the increase of piracy along the sea lanes of the Empire, whilst the massacre of Pisan and Genoese merchants in Constantinople in April of the same year made the city unsafe for westerners and seemed to be ushering in a policy of isolation from the West. In the absence of clear direction from the emperors Byzantium was ceasing to be an international player and in danger of becoming a political victim. This tone is evident in the pages of the historian Nicetas Choniates as he sought to explain the disaster of 1204.[224]

Operating as if isolated from the West soon led to confrontation with the West. The truce with Saladin negotiated in 1181 brought Byzantium in line with the crusader states that had made their own peace the year before and no more. However, alliances negotiated in 1183 and 1188 were trumpeted in the West as the height of duplicitous behaviour and led to a return of the negative view of the Greeks current in the Norman propaganda of the early twelfth century. Even the truce of 1181 was so interpreted.

There was a cooling too in the crusader states towards Byzantium. Renewed Seljuk pressure on the Byzantine lands in Anatolia ensured that Byzantine military assistance or intereference in Syria was a very remote possibility indeed. Relations between Byzantium and Antioch became strained. The will to co-operate dissipated quickly. In 1180 Bohemond III divorced his Byzantine consort and over the next three years intervened in Cilicia, capturing Tarsus in 1181 and in 1183 holding the Byzantine governor of Cilicia, Isaac Komnenos, to ransom. In the light of this weakness Byzantium made treaty arrangements with Saladin in 1183 and 1188. It is unlikely that the aim was to regain their footing in Antioch; rather, it was probably to ensure the protection of the Christian Holy Places. In return Saladin funded the building of a new mosque in Constantinople

---

[223] Lilie, *Byzantium and the Crusader States, 1096–1204*, 210–20.

[224] H. Magoulias, trans., *O City of Byzantium: Annals of Niketas Choniates* (Detroit, 1984), 321–3, 334, 354.

that was to be one of the first targets of crusader incendiarism in 1203. Possibly too there was an agreement to disrupt, or at least to offer assistance, to the Third Crusade. This so-called Byzantine treachery was made much of in the West. Rumours of poisoned supplies prepared for westerners travelling within the Empire were rife. Those who were able to go on crusade by sea, like Philip II Augustus of France and Richard I, avoided Constantinople. Frederick I Barbarossa, who had to follow the land route, felt sufficiently frustrated and provoked to make serious preparations for an attack on the city in late 1189 (see p. 153).[225]

Byzantine weakness became apparent as the 1180s progressed. The Norman seizure and sack of Thessalonika, the second city of the empire, in June 1185 showed that Byzantium could not ensure its territorial integrity, even for a major city within three days, march of Constantinople itself. The empire was in danger of becoming an early version of the 'sickman of Europe' and one that western leaders might well exploit to their own advantage. Important parts of the empire simply broke away and the emperor seemed unable to prevent this. On his release in 1184, and possibly with Frankish backing, Isaac Komnenos set himself up as independent ruler in Cyprus (1184–91). This centrifugalism was to continue in western Anatolia where a variety of strong men established themselves in Phila-delphia (Theodore Mankaphas), Miletos (Sabas Asidenos), and in the Maeander Valley (Manuel Mavrozomes) as the protectors and rulers of regions that lacked governance from the centre. They were to last into the early thirteenth century until a ruler with a will to reassert Byzantine unity reintegrated their lands into the rump Byzantine empire of Nicaea. The first-ever Byzantine territory to be seized deliberately by a crusader was the island of Cyprus, which had developed as an exporter of necessities to the crusader states in the twelfth century and which was rapidly conquered by Richard I of England in 1191. Both then and in 1204 westerners were exploiting and becoming a part of this process of Byzantine centrifugalism.

The capture of Constantinople on 12 April 1204 ushered in fifty-seven years of Byzantium in so-called safe Latin hands. The Fourth Crusade had not set out to capture Constantinople as part of its original aims. However, both Christians and Muslims saw Constantinople as a vital base for the recovery or defence of Syria. This was to form a consistent theme of papal correspondence from 1204 until well into the 1270s. Against this background it was the proposals of the envoys of Alexios, exiled son of the deposed emperor Isaac II Angelos, to the cash-strapped crusaders at Zara in late December 1202 that settled the mat-ter. In return for their support to place Alexios on the Byzantine throne, he promised a sum of 200,000 marks, a Byzantine army of 10,000 men for one year, and thereafter, for the term of his life, a garrison of 500 men to help defend the Christian position in the Holy Land. In addition, on becoming emperor he

[225] Lilie, *Byzantium and the Crusader States, 1096–1204*, 222–45.

would acknowledge the papal overlordship of the Christian Church and bring the Greek Church into conformity with it.[226] At this stage there was no thought of establishing a western state in Constantinople, merely of re-endowing the crusade by the restoration of the rightful ruler who would adopt a pro-western stance. Alexios joined the crusade army and confirmed the agreement at Corfu in May 1203.

The Latin empire was not conceived until March 1204, eight months after Alexios IV had been crowned as co-emperor with his father Isaac II Angelos. The terms of the treaty had not been met, despite hostile representations from the crusaders, eager to be underway. In February Alexios IV had been murdered and his place as emperor taken by Alexios V Murtzouphlos, who stirred up anti-Latin feeling in the city. The crusaders were in a desperate position. They resolved to capture Constantinople and set up a Latin emperor chosen from among their ranks. The city was captured on 12 April, and between then and November various steps were taken to secure and stabilise the empire. It was a very *ad hoc* affair.

Nonetheless, it was seen as the heir to Byzantium, not just in Latin-occupied Constantinople but also in the wider crusader states. In August 1204 Bohemond IV of Antioch performed homage for his principality to Marie of Champagne, the wife of Baldwin I, the Latin emperor. Contrary to expectations the Latin empire of Constantinople did nothing to aid the recovery of the Kingdom of Jerusalem. Neither a Latin emperor nor a Latin patriarch could bring about the union of the Latin and Orthodox churches. Worse still, little was achieved to win the loyalty and support of the majority Greek population for the new order. The Latin emperor's control over his Latin nobility was limited indeed. The princes of Achaea were more powerful than he, and in 1236 equipped a fleet of 120 ships to protect Constantinople from Greek attack. Apart from this, however, they were intent on securing their own wealth and status rather than maintaining the empire. It was William of Villehardouin's personal involvement with the Greeks of Epiros that led to the defeat at the battle of Pelagonia in 1259. From 1216 until 1230, when John of Brienne became co-emperor with the young Baldwin II, there was no effective leadership from the Latin emperor. From the mid-1230s the empire sought help from the rulers of the West in terms of cash, mercenaries or a crusade. Baldwin II was frequently absent from Constantinople trying to raise such support. Its cause was unpopular in the West and the Pope's request to commute crusader vows for cash for the Latin empire or to crusade in person in the empire produced little effective assistance. The Venetians set up an unrivalled commercial predominance in the city and seemed set fair to monopolise the Black Sea trade. It was in defence of these interests that the Venetians left Constantinople virtually defenceless in July 1261 when the Greeks entered the city almost unopposed and brought an end to the Latin empire. The Franks in

---

[226] Shaw, trans., *Joinville and Villehardouin: Chronicles of the Crusades*, 40.

the empire had become just one element amongst Bulgars, Epirote Greeks and Nicene Greeks, all seeking to dominate the region and none being sufficiently strong to knock out the others definitively. Worse still, within five years of the empire's establishment none of the interested parties could co-operate or work together to maintain the Latin empire. It was, as the anonymous annalist of Santa Justina at Padua noted, but 'the shadow of a great name'.[227]

As soon as news reached Rome of the fall of Constantinople to the Greeks Urban IV (1261–4) declared a crusade against Michael VIII Palaiologos and his supporters. For the first time Constantinople was the declared target of a crusade. Nothing happened immediately until Charles I of Naples took up the challenge in the late 1260s. The restored Byzantine empire, although united under one emperor in its various parts in Thrace, Macedonia and the Morea, was militarily weak. Michael VIII had to rely upon statecraft. He did not turn his back on the West as his predecessors had done in the 1190s. Rather, he engaged fully with it. He formed treaties with the Venetians in 1265 and 1277 that increased their privileges, assuaged any rancour they might have felt at the loss of their favoured position in Latin Constantinople and persuaded them not to support any proposals Charles I might advance for an anti-Byzantine alliance. In July 1274 at the Council of Lyons, through his envoys, he accepted the union of the Greek and Latin churches and promised to participate in any future crusade proposals. At the same time he became a son of the Church, protected by Gregory X, and with the crusade proclamation of 1261 dropped. This checked Charles of Anjou's anti-Byzantine crusade in its tracks. Michael seems to have done much to be seen to enforce the union. It was now, and not during the Latin occupation as Greek tradition would have it, that the recalcitrant monasteries on Athos suffered much damage at imperial hands. By 1281 it appeared that the unionist policy was stalling because of native Greek opposition, especially that of the monks. Pope Martin IV excommunicated Michael and relaunched the crusade against him. At the treaty of Orvieto on 3 July 1281 Martin brokered a Venetian–Angevin alliance to restore the Latin empire. A serious threat brought forth serious counter measures. It was now that the Byzantines fomented and subsidised the revolt of the Sicilians against Charles that escalated, with Aragonese involvement, into the War of the Sicilian Vespers that was to last until 1302.[228]

On 27 July 1302 the first recorded encounter between the Byzantines and the Ottoman Turks took place at the battle of Baphaeon. Two years later Pope Benedict IX wrote to Andronikos II warning him that some Byzantine territory might be seized to help mount an effective resistance to the Turks. With the Ottomans a new element was entering Mediterranean politics and warfare that, with hindsight, was to change the nature of crusade and Byzantium's place

[227] Lock, *The Franks in the Aegean*, 35–67, 283.
[228] D. J. Geanakoplos, *Emperor Michael VIII Palaeologus and the West* (Cambridge, Mass., 1959), 138–60, 189, 367; Runciman, *The Sicilian Vespers*; Setton, *The Papacy and the Levant*, I, 123–62.

within it. However, for the next decade a series of unsuccessful plans for the seizure of Constantinople were rehearsed. Therafter naval campaigns – either grand ones labelled 'Holy Leagues' or smaller expeditions funded by the Hospitallers or individuals – sought to check the spread of Ottoman power by protecting or restoring Byzantine territory occupied by the Turks. Such were the expeditions of 1334, 1344, 1365 and 1366. In 1396 the Crusade of Nicopolis, and in 1404 the Crusade of Varna, aimed to protect Constantinople from the Turks. Both ended in disaster. Byzantium was now the object of protection by crusading endeavour.[229] The defence of the Orthodox Christians that Urban II had half proposed in 1095 before changing the focus to the liberation of Jerusalem was now a reality. Crusading, with Byzantium at its centre, had come full circle.

CRUSADES FROM AN ARMENIAN PERSPECTIVE[230]

Unlike their relations with the Byzantines, crusade and Armenian chroniclers wrote positively of one another. The crusaders and the Armenians thought well of each other, intermarried, and co-operated militarily and economically against both Muslims and Byzantines. This relationship was carried on with the Armenians settled in Cilician or Lesser Armenia,[231] and, during the Fourth Crusade, with those Armenian groups settled in Bithynia. These were all settlers from the Armenian diaspora of the mid-eleventh century that had transplanted them

---

[229] Setton, *The Papacy and the Levant*, I, 163–370; N. Housley, *The Later Crusades* (Oxford, 1992), 80–150; A. Atiya, *The Crusade of Nicopolis* (London, 1934).

[230] C. Toumanoff, 'Armenia and Georgia', in J. Hussey, ed., *The Cambridge Medieval History*, IV (Cambridge, 1966), 593–637; S. der Nersessian, *The Armenians* (London, 1969) S. der Nersessian, *Armenia and the Byzantine Empire* (Cambridge, Mass., 1947); P. Charanis, *The Armenians and the Byzantine Empire* (Lisbon, 1964); R.G. Hovannistan, ed., The Armenian People, I (New York, 1997); C. Walker, *Armenia: The Survival of a Nation* (2nd edn, London, 1990), 19–34; C. Burney and D. Lang, *The Peoples of the Hills* (London, 1971), 183–266; S. der Nersessian, 'Between East and West: Armenia and its Divided History', in D. Talbot-Rice, ed., *The Dark Ages* (London, 1965), 63–82; S. der Nersessian, 'The Kingdom of Cilician Armenia', in Setton ed., *A History of the Crusades*, II, 630–59; R. Thomson, 'The Crusaders through Armenian Eyes', in Laiou and Parviz-Mottahedeh, eds, *The Crusades from the Perspective of Byzantium and the Muslim World*, 71–82; W.H. Rüdt-Collenberg, The *Rupenides, Hethumides and Lusignans. The Structure of the Armeno-Cilician Dynasties* (Lisbon 1963) N. Iorga, *Brève histoire de la Petite Arménie* (Paris, 1930); T.S.R. Boase, ed., *The Cilician Kingdom of Armenia* (Edinburgh, 1978); A.E. Dostourian, trans., *Armenia and the Crusades, 10th to 12th Centuries: The Chronicle of Matthew of Edessa* (London, 1993); G. Burger, ed., *Hethoum, A Lytell Cronycle, Richard Pynson's Translation (c. 1520) of La Fleur des histoires de la terre d'Orient (c. 1307)* (Toronto, 1988); L. Alishan, *Léon le Magnifique premier roi de Sissouan ou de l'Arméno-Cilicie* (Venice, 1888); R. Thomson, *A Bibliography of Classical Armenian Literature to AD 1500* (Turnhout, 1995); R. Thomson, 'The Concept of "history" in Medieval Armenian Historians', in A. Eastmond, ed., *Eastern Approaches to Byzantium* (Aldershot, 2001), 89–100; J.H. Forse, 'Armenians and the First Crusade', *Journal of Medieval History*, 17 (1991), 13–22; B. Hamilton, 'The Armenian Church and the Papacy at the Time of the Crusades', *Eastern Churches Review*, 10 (1978), 61–87.

[231] Also known as Armenia in Exile, Little Armenia, New Armenia, Armeno-Cilicia, and Sisuan.

from their homeland in Greater Armenia in one of the most significant mass migrations of medieval times.

Greater Armenia is a mountainous region bounded on the north by the Pontic range and to the south by the Taurus Mountains. It is famous for its horses and its horsemen. The Armenian plateau is cut by numerous valleys running east–west and giving excellent access to both Cappadocia in the west and Iran to the east. The sources of the Tigris and Euphrates lie in Armenia too and allow access into Mesopotamia. It is a strategically important area. From the time of Pompey the Great (106–48 BC), who established Roman domination in Asia Minor, it was a battleground between Romans and Persians, neither of whom could afford to concede control to the other.

It was the Greek geographer Hekataeos of Miletos who first noted the Armenians (Armenoi), who called themselves 'Hayk', as living in the region of the headwaters of the Tigris and Euphrates in 550 BC; a century later they were mentioned by Herodotos, who thought that they had emigrated thence from Phrygia. It was Alexander the Great (d. 323 BC) who brought the area into the Greek and Mediterranean world. Pompey the Great gave the region its name of Greater Armenia during the Mithridatic Wars (66–62 BC); he failed to settle the matter of its control with the Persians and thus turned it into a battleground. In 387 Byzantines and Persians created spheres of influence in Armenia, an arrangement that lasted, with modifications, down to the seventh century and the conflicts of the two empires with Islam.

In the meantime Armeno-Byzantine relations worsened due to Byzantine pressure and persecution of the Armenian Church. The Armenians consider themselves to be the first Christian nation. They had adopted Christianity officially sometime between 294 and 301, at least a decade before Constantine I's supposed edict of toleration for the Roman Empire. In 374 they rejected the authority of the bishop of Caesarea and within twenty years had established a native church hierarchy of their own with a patriarch (Katholikos), and with the Liturgy and the scriptures in Armenian rather than Syriac. In 451 representatives of the Armenian Church did not attend the Council of Chalcedon and had not adopted the definition of the the dual nature of Christ worked out there. Although they adhered to the teaching of Cyril of Alexandria (d. 444) in describing Christ as having one nature, they did not deny the humanity of Christ and had not entered into communion with the other anti-Chalcedonian churches of the East. Nonetheless, the Byzantines classed them as Monophysites and schismatics. It was this religious difference that cut them off from both Greeks and Muslims and to some extent facilitated the relationship with the crusaders. From the twelfth century the Armenian Church was united to that of Rome.

Despite this negative image Armenians were cosmopolitan and culturally adaptable.[232] Some of them played a prominent role in the Byzantine Empire

---

[232] The use of Armenian, Greek and Latin variants for names and toponyms can cause problems for the unwary: for example, Lwon, Leon, or Leo.

and were an important minority in its towns and cities. They had been Hellenised since the fourth century BC and posed no threat to the values of the Byzantines except in their anti-Chalcedonian theological position. From the seventh century onwards refugees fleeing from Muslim attacks bolstered their numbers. So much so that Armenians were settled en masse in depopulated parts of the empire like Macedonia and Thrace; after the reconquest of Cilicia and North Syria by Nikephoros Phokas, they were settled in those areas too. Their cavalrymen were valued in the army. On accepting Greek Orthodoxy many Armenians became prominent generals, ecclesiastics, and even emperors. Many Armenian chieftains were appointed governors of towns such as Melitene, Marash, Birejik and Edessa, where Thoros was governor in 1098.

In 652 Muslim suzerainty was recognised by the Armenians and Armenia became a battleground between Byzantines and Muslims. From 1000, for the next fifty years, the Byzantines gradually took over Armenia seeking to turn it into a buffer zone with Islam and at the same time protect the approaches to Asia Minor. Armenian princes and notables were bribed, bullied and coerced into accepting land grants in Cappadocia within the empire in return for handing over their territories in Armenia itself. Armenians were transplanted with their leaders. By 1050 the policy seemed to be working tolerably well, although Seljuk campaigns in the land continued and, indeed, were stepped up after 1047. Following their defeat at Manzikert in 1071 the Byzantines had to abandon their forward policy in Armenia and relinquished any control they had once exercised. The number of Armenian refugees increased rapidly, and they sought out the settlements of those who had forcibly been relocated before. They fled to the Kingdom of Georgia and to all parts of Byzantine Anatolia, and in particular to Cilicia where there was already a substantial settlement of Armenians from earlier in the eleventh century and where some sort of Armenian government was establishing itself. Cilician Armenia was an important commercial and strategic area. The mountain passes to and from Anatolia (the Cilician Gates) and to and from Syria (the Syrian gates) lay in its territory. It was on the caravan route from Mesopotamia and Syria to Constantinople and Iconion, and its harbours provided facilities for onward transport by sea and close links to Cyprus. After 1071 control of this area was disputed with the Seljuks. In 1074 the Armenians, as well as the Byzantines, had sent an embassy to Gregory VII asking for help. At different times over the next thirty years Seljuks or Armenians, depending on circumstances, controlled different parts of Cilicia. Pressures caused by the Armenians in Cappadocia had led to the liquidation of the Armenian leadership there in 1079/80 by the Byzantine authorities. In turn this produced further displacements of Armenians from Cappadocia to Cilicia – this time Armenians with reasons to distrust the Greeks. This was very much the state of affairs when the army of the First Crusade approached that region in 1098.

Within Cilician Armenia the family of the Roupenids sought political power from their base in the Amanus Mountains in the east of the country. From 1070 to 1218 they transformed their position from 'lords of the mountains' to kings of

Armenia. Their rivals were the Hethoumid clan of Lampron and Barbaron in the west. The Hethoumids were loyal allies of the Komnenoi and generally inclined to accept Byzantine suzerainty. As Rüdt-Collenberg has pointed out, the right of succession was not well defined and pretenders to the crown might invoke various customs to suit their particular case. Claimants might apply Latin custom (succession in the female line), Arab custom (brothers before sons), Greek and Armenian custom (elective with no rights of primogeniture, but a tendency to co-kingship for an heir). Around 1250 the translation of the Assises of Antioch attempted to formalise Latin practice for the kingdom, although Mongol suzerainty tended to make this a dead letter.[233] In 1226 the marriage between Isabel the daughter and heiress of Leon II/I and Hethoum, heir to the Hethoumids, ended the dispute between the clans by creating the royal line of the Hethoumids (1226–1373).

The Armenians welcomed the crusaders as liberators, provided facilities for food and refreshment and offered much practical advice for their onward journey to Antioch. During the extended siege of Antioch the Armenians brought supplies to the crusader camp, although they were much criticised for the high prices that they charged. Indeed, Firouz, who betrayed Antioch to the crusaders, was an Armenian. During the passage of the First Crusade Franco-Armenian relations were friendly, although this was to change as the Franks established themselves in Syria and Mesopotamia. Armenian brigands preyed upon their neighbours. When their raids went too far they attracted punitive expeditons from the Danishmends to the north and from the Franks to the south and east.

The first crusader state to be established was the county of Edessa, where Baldwin of Boulogne established himself after the murder of his Armenian benefactor Thoros (Theodore) in 1098. Thoros' death signalled the end of any joint Armenian–Frankish power sharing. The Franks were to rule Edessa. By 1118 Baldwin and his successor Baldwin Le Bourg had captured all Armenian possessions in the wider Edessa region. Soon after his establishment in Antioch Bohemond tried to sieze territory from Cilician Armenia, ostensibly from the few remaining allies of Alexios I. He captured Germanikeia, Mamistra, Adana and Tarsos, but failed to take Marash. The Armenians tailored their military assistance to the crusaders according to their own political interests and military readiness. Thus in 1108 Armenian troops assisted Roger of Antioch at the siege of Azaz, though at other times they held aloof from the Franks. In 1131, following the death of Bohemond II of Antioch near Mamistra the previous year, the towns of Adana, Mamistra and Tarsos were regained by the Armenians. This in turn led to a counter-attack by Raymond of Antioch and a short period of captivity for Leon I (1129–37) in Antioch.

The attempts by John II Komnenos and his son Manuel I to reassert Byzantine supremacy in Cilicia and north Syria naturally drew the Armenians and the

---

[233] Rüdt-Collenberg, *The Rupenides, Hethumides and Lusignans: The Structure of the Armeno-Cilician Dynasties*, 27–8.

Franks together against a common Byzantine threat. Imperial field armies campaigned in Cilicia in 1136–8, 1142–3 and finally in 1157–8, basing themselves at Mopsuestia. By the winter of 1137–8 Cilician Armenia was once again a Byzantine province and Leon I and his family were prisoners in Constantinople. The escape of his surviving son and heir Thoros in 1145 led to revolt in Cilicia, an ongoing guerrilla war from strongholds in the Amanus mountains, and co-operation with Reynald of Chatillon in a raid on Cyprus in 1156. Both Reynald and Thoros made their humble submissions to Manuel in 1157, and Thoros (d. 1175) was integrated into the Byzantine dispositions for the province of Cilicia.

The Byzantine defeat at Myriokephalon in 1176 spelt the end of the Byzantine suzerainty in Cilician Armenia. Roupenid ambitions would have their headway. With the death of Manuel I in 1180, and the period of instability that followed in Byzantine politics, the rulers of Cilician Armenia (Roupen III and Leon II) opened negotiations with the papacy for Church union and with the Holy Roman Emperor for political recognition. On 6 January 1198 Thoros' grandson Leon (Lewon) II (1187–98) was crowned king of Armenia at Tarsos as Leon I (1198–1219) by the papal and imperial legate Conrad of Wittelsbach, archbishop of Mainz.[234] Henry VI provided the royal insignia and the Byzantine emperor Alexios III Angelos provided the crown, thus recognising the elevation in status of Armenia from province to kingdom. Leon I was now the equal in status of the princes and kings of Antioch, Jerusalem and Cyprus. With the loss of Edessa (1144) and Jerusalem (1187) the Frankish states of north Syria were drawn to the Armenians who in their turn, suffering from attacks from Kilij Arslan II from Iconion, had mutual interests in working together.

Leon II/I had opportunities to extend Armenian control over Antioch itself, when, following the death of Raymond, heir to Antioch, in 1197, the issue of the Antiochene inheritance was disputed. Raymond's son was Raymond Roupen, Leon's great-nephew, but his succession was opposed by the Templars and by the commune of Antioch. The war of succession in Antioch between Raymond Roupen and Bohemond of Tripoli seemed to be resolved in the favour of the Armenians when Raymond was crowned in 1216, only to be deposed by Bohemond in 1219, bringing to an end any hope of Armenian suzerainty over Antioch.

During the Fourth Crusade, hundreds of miles north-west of Cilicia, some of the descendants of the Armenian diaspora settled in Phrygia and Troad were massacred by Greeks. In April 1205 Henry of Flanders, the brother of the Latin emperor Baldwin, had campaigned against the Greeks of Nicaea and occupied Adramyttium. He had been assisted by the Armenians who lived in the region and dared not remain behind on his withdrawal for fear of reprisals. Some 20,000

---

[234] The date of the coronation is disputed; some place it as early as 1196, others as late as 1199. During the thirteenth century Sis (Kozan) replaced Tarsos as the most important town in Cilicia.

Armenians came with him on foot, men, women and children. Once in Thrace they became separated from the Latin army and were massacred by the Greek inhabitants.[235]

On Leon I's death in 1219 his younger daughter Isabel was declared his heiress and was married to Philip, fourth son of Bohemond IV of Antioch, in the hope of ensuring stability within Cilicia and peace with Antioch. This caused offence in Acre by denying the rights of her elder sister, Rita/Stephanie, the wife of John of Brienne of Jerusalem. Philip's strong Latinising trends in the Church and court of Cilicia were unpopular. He was deposed and murdered in 1225. The next year Isabel was persuaded to marry Hethoum, the son and heir of the regent Constantine of Lampron, thus uniting the factions of Hethoumids and Roupenids. The reigns of Leon I (1198–1219) and of Hethoum I (1226–70), and Leon II (1270–89), are often seen as the golden age of Cilician Armenia, with internal peace, good commercial links with the West, and, in the main, peaceful relations with the Franks of Syria. Internal political stability was their great contribution: three kings in one century (1187–1289) contrasts with the nineteen rulers who were either murdered or forced to abdicate in the period from 1127–89 and 1289–1373.[236] Freedom from Turkish and Mameluke aggression was bought at the price of Mongol overlordship.

Cilicia had marked its turn to the West in the coronation of 1198. The Armenians were Christians and not polygamists. Divorce was allowed, but they seem to have followed the Greek practice of making no more than two marriages in a lifetime. Their princesses were thus entirely acceptable for consorts for Byzantine and Frankish nobles. There had been frequent marriages between Frankish rulers and Armenian princesses, beginning with the marriage of Baldwin of Boulogne to Morphia/Arda, the daughter of Gabriel of Melitene, about 1100 (divorced 1109). Sometime before 1104 Joscelin of Courtenay, count of Edessa, married the Roupenid princess, Beatrice (d. 1122). In 1195 Leon II/I had married his niece Alice to Raymond of Antioch, the heir of Bohemond III. The daughters of Leon I had married John of Brienne, king of Jerusalem, in 1214 and Philip of Antioch in 1219. In 1237 Hethoum I married his sister Stephanie to Henry I of Cyprus (1218–53), and in 1254 his daughter Sibyl to Bohemond VI of Antioch. After Bohemond's death in 1275 Sibyl acted as regent for her son Bohemond VII (1275–87). The Ibelins of Jaffa and Cyprus had also taken Armenian wives, and help had been forthcoming from Armenia in their struggle with Emperor Frederick II. If Philip of Antioch had offended his Armenian subjects in 1225, this was not because his Latinising policies were entirely new but because they were too much too soon. There was much Latin influence in Armenian culture, art and religious practice. Indeed the only surviving text of the Assises of Antioch is an Armenian translation undertaken by Hethoum's brother, Sempad the Constable, as a new basis for the law of Cilician Armenia.

---

[235]   Shaw, trans., *Joinville and Villehardouin: Chronicles of the Crusades* 127–8.
[236]   Rüdt-Collenberg, *The Rupenides, Hethumides and Lusignans*, 25.

In 1245 the Armenians in Cilicia acknowledged Mongol overlordship as the price for protection from Turkish and Mameluke attack. To some extent this was to remove them from the Latin Mediteranean world they had done so much to embrace. Hethoum I was absent on embassy to Karakorum from 1253 to 1256, just as his brother Sempad had been from 1247 to 1250. In 1260 the Mongols attacked Syria in alliance with Hethoum and Bohemond IV; both received additions to their territory as a result. News of the death of the Great Khan Mongke in 1259 deflected Mongol interest in Syria and allowed the Mamelukes to regain Syria and Palestine and attack both Antioch and Cilician Armenia. In 1266 Baybars led a devastating raid into Armenia, taking 40,000 captives into slavery. Two years later, in May 1268, he captured Antioch, massacred the inhabitants and destroyed the city. Alongside the rump of the Kingdom of Jerusalem at Acre, Cilicia and Cyprus were now the only Christian states in the East. Cilicia was now at the forefront of Mameluke aggression and its own plans for expansion rapidly became a thing of the past. Armenian reliance on the Mongols increased. On 30 October 1281 the Mamelukes defeated a joint expedition of Armenians, Franks and Mongols at Homs. The Hospitallers, too, in 1300 and 1305, carried out naval raids into Armenia to forestall a Mameluke takeover of the Armenian coast and its harbours. The conversion of the Il-khans to Islam in 1304 turned an erstwhile protector into another enemy alongside the Seljuks and the Mamelukes. In 1335 the Mamelukes invaded Armenia to forestall crusade preparations being carried on in Cyprus, and in 1337 secured the port of Ayas on the Gulf of Alexandretta from which they could threaten Cypriot trade with the West. Not only was Armenia a target for external aggression but also its leadership was to be substantially weakened by succession disputes.

When Leon IV (1320–41), the last direct descendant of Hethoum I, was assassinated as a result of factional disputes on 28 August 1341, he died childless. The next twenty years witnessed succession disputes between those who upheld the true royal line and those who followed the female line. His immediate successor was his cousin Constantine II (1342–4), usually known as Guy in Frankish circles. He was the grandson of Leon II, through his mother Isabelle and through his father Amaury of Tyre, the grandson of Hugh III, king of Cyprus. The Lusignan family were thus involved in the affairs of the kingdom and eager to defend or destroy its harbours to prevent their use by Mameluke pirates. They provided occasional military support and carried out tactical raids on the seaports of Cilicia to deny them to the Mamelukes. In 1366 Peter I Lusignan of Cyprus (1358–69) sent expeditions to relieve Korykos from Turkish attack and to garrison Antalya (Antalya). In October 1367 he planned a joint attack on Ayas with Constantine V of Armenia (1364–73). The latter did not keep the arrangement and the attack failed. In the same month Peter declared himself king of Armenia in opposition to Constantine, but this had little effect on the security of Armenia except that in the long term it was to provide titular western kings once the kingdom had passed to Mameluke control. On 13 April 1375 Sis (Kozan) fell to the Mamelukes and the last Armenian king of Cilician Armenia, Leon V

(1373–93), was led a captive to Cairo. He eventually died a papal pensioner in Paris on 29 November 1393. In 1374 the titular kingship of Armenia passed to John I of Cyprus and in 1438 to Philip of Savoy and, through him, to the House of Savoy.

CRUSADING AND THE ITALIAN CITY REPUBLICS[237]

The Italian commercial republics concerned with crusading and trade in the eastern Mediterranean were Genoa, Pisa and Venice. Amalfi, Gaeta and Naples,

[237] W. Heyd, *Le colonie commerciali degli Italiani in oriente nel medio evo* (2 vols, 2nd Venice, 1866–8); W. Heyd, *Histoire du Commerce du Levant au Moyen Age*, trans. F. Raymaud), (2 vols, 2nd edn, Leipzig, 1936), I, 131–90, 310–59; R. Lopez, 'The Trade of Medieval Europe: The South', in M. Postan and E. Miller, eds, *Cambridge Economic History of Europe*, II (2nd edn, Cambridge, 1987), 306–79; C. Cahen, 'Notes sur l'histoire des Croisades et de L'Orient latin, III, L'Orient latin et commerce du Levant', *Bulletin de Faculté des Lettres de Strasbourg*, 29 (1950–1), 328–46; Prawer, *The Latin Kingdom of Jerusalem*, 85–93, 391–402; Prawer, *Crusader Institutions*, 217–49; Setton, ed., *A History of the Crusades*, V, 379–451; J. Riley-Smith, 'Government in Latin Syria and the Commercial Privileges of Foreign Merchants', in D. Baker, ed., *Relations Between East and West in the Middle Ages* (Edinburgh, 1973), 109–32; M. Balard, 'Amalfi et Byzance (Xe–XIIe siècles)', *Travaux et mémoires*, 6 (1976), 85–95; M. Frazer, 'Church Doors and the Gates of Paradise: Byzantine Bronze Doors in Italy', *Dumbarton Oaks Papers*, 27 (1973), 145–62; A. Citarella, 'The Relations of Amalfi with the Arab World before the Crusades', *Speculum*, 42 (1967), 277–312; C. Verlinden, *L'Esclavage dans L'Europe médiévale*, II (Ghent, 1977); M.-L. Heers, 'Les Gænois et le commerce de l'alun à la fin du Moyen Age', *Revue d'histoire économique et sociale*, 32 (1954), 31–53; M. Balard, *La Romanie Génoise* (2 vols, Genoa, 1978); M. Balard, 'The Genoese in the Aegean (1204–1566)', in B. Arbel, B. Hamilton and D. Jacoby, eds, *Latins and Greeks in the Eastern Mediterranean After 1204* (London, 1989), 158–74; G. Day, *Genoa's Response to Byzantium, 1155–1204* (Urbana, 1988); F. Lane, *Venice, A Maritime Republic* (Baltimore, 1973), 30–85; F. Thiriet, *La Romanie Vénitienne au Moyen Age* (Paris, 1975); D. Jacoby, *Studies on the Crusader States and on Venetian Expansion* (Aldershot, 1989); D. Jacoby, 'New Venetian Evidence on Crusader Acre', in P. Edbury and J. Phillips, eds, *The Experience of Crusading*, II (Cambridge, 2003), 240–56; E. Zachariadou, *Trade and Crusade: Venetian Crete and the Emirates of Menteshe and Aydin (1300–1415)* (Venice, 1983); A. Pertusi, ed., *Venezia e il Levante Fino al Secolo XV* (2 vols, Florence, 1973); essays by Jacoby, Robbert and Stahl in E. Kittell and T. Madden, eds, *Medieval and Renaissance Venice* (Urbana, 1999), 27–68, 124–40; E. Byrne, 'Commercial Contracts of the Genoese in the Syrian Trade of the Twelfth Century', *Quarterly Journal of Economics*, 31 (1916), 128–70; E. Byrne, 'Genoese Trade with Syria in the Twelfth and Thirteenth Century', *American Historical Review*, 25 (1919–20), 191–219; E. Byrne, 'The Genoese Colonies in Syria', in L. Paetow, ed., *The Crusades and Other Historical Essays* (New York, 1928), 139–82; E. Byrne, *Genoese Shipping in the Twelfth and Thirteenth Centuries* (Cambridge, Mass., 1930); S. Epstein, *Genoa and the Genoese 958–1528* (Chapel Hill, 1996); C. Marshall, 'The Crusading Motivation of the Italian City Republics in the Latin East, c.1096–1104', *Rivista di Bizantinistica*, 1 (1991), 15pp. [available electronically at <http://www.deremilitari.org/RESOURCES/ARTICLES/marshall2.htm>; L.T. Belgrano and C. Imperiale di Sant'Angelo, eds, *Annali genovesi di Caffaro e de'suoi continuatori dal MXCIX al MCCXCIIII* (5 vols, Rome, 1890–1901), esp. vol 1; G. Tafel and F. Thomas, *Urkunden zur älteren Handels- und Staats geschichte der Republik Venedig* (3 vols, Vienna, 1856–7; reprinted Amsterdam, 1964); R. Lopez and I. Raymond, *Medieval Trade in the Mediterranean World* (London, 1955); A. Stahl, 'Italian Sources for the Coinage of Cilician Armenia', *Armenian*

but particularly the merchants of Amalfi, had had close commercial links with Byzantium from at least the ninth century and had founded a hospital there in 1070. The Amalfitans and Venetians had also developed commercial links with the Muslims of North Africa during the tenth century. In 1073 Amalfi had acknowledged the overlordship of Roger Guiscard, count of Apulia, and thereafter had come uneasily under Norman domination. In 1173 the city was fully incorporated in the Norman Kingdom of Sicily. This change from nominal Byzantine suzerainty to Norman control had led to a gradual transference of Amalfitan privileges in Constantinople to the Venetians, the naval allies of the Byzantines. During the first half of the 1080s the Venetians were actively engaged in resisting Guiscard's invasion of the Balkan provinces of Byzantium and therefore the more worthy of increased trading privileges within the Byzantine Empire. On occasion Amalfi revolted against Norman control. Indeed, in August 1096, when Bohemond was said to have heard of the First Crusade for the first time, he was engaged in the siege of Amalfi; he called this off to make his own crusade preparations. Amalfi did not cease to be a commercial centre and its merchants continued to have a hand in southern Italian and Levantine trade, but by the time of the First Crusade it had lost what predominance it once had in Byzantine and Levantine trade and its Genoese and Pisan rivals from northern Italy were even penetrating the commercial network of southern Italy and challenging it in home waters.

Fleets from Genoa, Pisa and Venice played a vital role in the establishment and in the supply and maintenance of the crusading states, both in the Levant and later in the Aegean. Chronologically, from a crusading point of view, Italian involvement in the ports of the crusader states will be taken first, but it should be borne in mind that the trade with these ports never came close to challenging the position of either Constantinople and the Aegean or Alexandria in the Italian commercial trading network. Both in volume and in significance Constantinople and the Aegean remained the predominant zone of Italian commercial interests. The bloody 'War of St Sabas' in Acre between Genoese and Venetians from 1256 to 1258 was but an extension of the open war for dominance of the Constantinopolitan and Aegean trade routes.

Broadly speaking, in the twelfth century it was the Genoese and Pisans who concentrated on the crusader states, with occasional piratical attacks on Byzantine harbours and shipping as opportunity presented. The Venetians did not ignore the opportunities of the emergent crusader states, but they sought to build up their control of the Adriatic sea lanes and their predominance in the Aegean trade. This was the focus of their attention throughout the twelfth century. With the loss of Latin control in Constantinople in 1261 the Genoese sought to extend

---

NumismaticJournal, 15 (1989), 59–66; A. Stahl, *The Venetian Tornesello: A Medieval Coinage* (New York, 1985); A. Evans, ed., *Francesco Balducci Pegalotti, La Practica della Mercatura* (Cambridge, Mass., 1936; reprinted New York, 1970); J. Dotson, trans., *Merchant Culture in Fourteenth Century Venice: The Zibaldone da Canal* (New York, 1994).

their commercial interests there by siding with the Greeks, whilst the Venetians opposed them at every opportunity. That apart, sailors and ships from Genoa, Pisa and Venice had been involved in crusading right from the start, and both the Genoese and the Pisans had participated in the so-called proto-crusades. Each year all three cities had fleets of varying size sailing at some time in the waters of Syria-Palestine. Along with the Byzantines on Cyprus and the Armenians in Cilicia, they had played a crucial role in transporting supplies to the emergent crusader states during the twelfth century. Indeed, they were the essential lifelines for those emergent principalities. None of them had a navy and were totally reliant on whatever provision the Italians could offer. Just as the Byzantines had purchased Venetian naval support with commercial privileges, so the rulers of the crusader states did likewise. It was absolutely essential that they should control the harbours of their new principalities – not just for pilgrims and control of any import-export trade from their hinterlands but in order to survive as political entities and to ensure links with the West to obtain supplies of food and men.

Without Italian naval support to challenge the Egyptian fleet the ports could not be won and the long-term future of the crusader principalities could not be guaranteed. The more serious the game the higher the stakes; the commercial concessions gained by the Italians were eventually to undermine the financial stability of the crusader states. At the outset, though, their assistance was essential. The Italian republics were commercial rivals. They attacked each other's shipping as chance offered and they sought to cut each other out of any advantage; but their motives could pass muster with the crusade motivation of their fellow Latins on land. Urban II had approached the Genoese to provide naval support to the First Crusade and this they had agreed to do, equipping a fleet of twelve ships that did not leave for the East until the summer of 1097. The Genoese annalist and politician Caffaro di Caschifellone (c. 1080–1166) participated in the fleet action at Caesarea in 1101 and again during the Second Crusade in the capture of Almeira and Tortosa in Spain in 1147 and 1148. He was in doubt that Genoese participation in the First Crusade was a defining moment in Genoese history. Equally, Calixtus II had written to the Venetians in 1123 requesting their participation in a proposed crusade.

The outline of their involvement is soon told. A fleet of thirteen Genoese ships had arrived at St Simeon, the port of Antioch, in November 1097 bringing food and military equipment. In June 1098 these ships withdrew to ports in Cilicia on the news of the approach of Kerbogha. With them travelled the so-called 'rope dancers' of Antioch who were to go on from Antalya to meet Alexios I at Philomelion. Elements of the Genoese fleet and some English ships that had arrived at St Simeon in May 1098 were to accompany the march along the coast to Jerusalem, providing some protection from naval attack by the Egyptian fleet. In June 1099 six ships, including two Genoese vessels commanded by William Embriaco, put in at Jaffa and, being forced to abandon their ships on the approach of an Egyptian squadron, joined in the siege of Jerusalem and constructed the necessary siege engines. In the first decade of the twelfth century the

Genoese played a prominent role in securing the harbours of the coastal principalities for the crusaders and were rewarded with commercial concessions in each
of the towns captured. From late 1097 they had secured and organised the port
of St Simeon during the siege of Antioch. In July 1098 Bohemond rewarded
them and secured their support for his seizure of Antioch by granting them a
commercial quarter in Antioch. At the beginning of August 1100 a fleet of
twenty-six galleys and four ships set sail from Genoa with Caffaro on board. On
arrival at St Simeon they sought confirmation of Bohemond's charter from his
regent Tancred, who extended the privileges by granting exemption from import-
export taxes. After wintering in Antioch the fleet sailed south. They captured
Arsuf and Caesarea in May in the service of Baldwin I of Jerusalem. In October
1101 the fleet sailed home, taking with them the late antique green glass bowl
found in Caesarea back to their cathedral of San Lorenzo where it may still be
seen. It was known as the green basin or, more suggestively, as the Holy Grail.
Some ships remained behind and helped Raymond of Toulouse capture Tortosa
in March 1102. In the spring of 1103 they participated in the capture of Latakia
(Laodicea) from the Byzantines by Tancred, regent of Antioch, an earlier attack
by the Pisans, prompted by Bohemond, having been abandoned in September
1099 due to pressure from other crusade leaders intent on the capture of
Jerusalem. The Genoese fleets had made vital contributions to securing the
harbours of the Kingdom of Jerusalem. They assisted in the capture of the ports
of Arsuf (1101), Caesarea (1101), Ghibelet (Jebail) (1103–4), Acre (1104) and
Beirut (1110) by Baldwin I of Jerusalem who granted them market rights in each
port as well as a one-third share of the spoils. And in March 1109 they obliged
their Provençal neighbour by bringing Raymond of Toulouse's son and heir,
Bertram of St Gilles, to his inheritance in the East and co-operated with him in
the capture of Tripoli, for which they received one-third of the town.

A Pisan fleet of 120 ships anchored at St Simeon in July 1099, having left its
homeport the previous year. On the voyage out it had raided Byzantine islands in
the Ionian Sea and in the southern Cyclades, and had defeated a Byzantine fleet
off Rhodes. With them was Daimbert, archbishop of Pisa. Bohemond persuaded
him to use his fleet to expel the Byzantine garrison from Latakia, perhaps as
a preliminary of securing the other ports of Maraclea and Valania, also in
Byzantine hands. This attack was abandoned after pressure from Raymond of
Toulouse. By early 1100 the Pisans based themselves at Jaffa, which they repaired
and refortified. Their presence ensured not only the quiescence of the Muslim
rulers of Acre, Arsuf, Ascalon and Caesarea but also ensured that Daimbert's
claim to the patriarchate of Jerusalem was accepted without too much opposition from Godfrey of Bouillon. It was probably from Daimbert as patriarch and
now lord of Jaffa that the Pisans received a commercial quarter and privileges in
Jaffa, a vital port for access to Jerusalem. In April 1100 the Pisan squadron sailed
home, not only weakening Daimbert's bargaining position but also leaving the
way clear for the Genoese to assume the dominant role in the naval actions of the
Kingdom of Jerusalem. The Genoese might have eclipsed the Pisans, but they did

not expunge them from a share in the Levantine trade. Eight years later the Pisans contributed ships for Tancred's campaign in Cilician Armenia in return for extended commercial concessions in the principality of Antioch. Pisan ships, too, formed part of the Byzantine fleet that supported King Amalric's campaign to Egypt in 1168 and 1169.

The Venetians sent three fleets to the East in the early years of the crusader conquest and settlement. The first was a private enterprise adventure led by John Michiel, the son of the doge. His fleet of thirty vessels left Venice in July 1099 and arrived at Jaffa one year later having defeated a Pisan fleet off Rhodes. It assisted in the capture of Caifas (Haifa) in the late summer of 1100. In return the Venetians received toll exemptions and commercial quarters in both Jaffa and Haifa. In 1110 a fleet of 100 ships participated in the capture of Sidon, alongside a naval flotilla from Norway commanded by King Sigurd. In August 1122 a Venetian fleet of 120 ships flying a papal banner and with the sign of the cross on its sails left Venice under the command of the doge, Domenico Michiel himself. It destroyed the Egyptian fleet off Ascalon in May 1123, thus facilitating the siege of Tyre by land and sea from February to July 1124. The Venetian naval contribution had been significant, and the commercial privileges it received were summarised after the fall of Tyre in the so-called *pactum Warmundi*, confirmed by Baldwin II in May 1125 after his release from captivity.[238] Ships from Genoa, Pisa, Venice and England participated in the siege of Acre during the Third Crusade, but the role of the Italian republics was a limited one except in the scramble to reclaim commercial quarters and privileges.

The presence of English ships at St Simeon in 1098 and of Norwegian ships at Sidon in 1110 should alert us to the fact that there were always other ships and seamen involved in the Levant than the three major Italian republics of Genoa, Pisa and Venice. To be sure these cities sent fleets to the coast of Syria-Palestine on an annual basis, but the merchants of Ancona, Amalfi, Gaeta and Naples continued to have an interest along with the other merchants from the Norman Kingdom of Sicily. A warfleet sent by William II of Sicily in the spring of 1188 protected the ports of Antioch, Tripoli and Tyre from Muslim conquest. Ships from Catalonia and Provence also traded with the crusader states and with the Aegean.

All these foreign communes enjoyed commercial quarters, tax concessions and other rights legally conceded in charters by the local Frankish rulers. The Genoese had commercial enclaves in Acre, Arsuf, Antioch, Beirut, Caesarea, Ghibelet (Jebail), Jaffa, Latakia, St Simeon, Tripoli and Tyre; the Venetians in Acre, Antioch, Ascalon, Seleucia, Tripoli and Tyre. Tyre was their headquarters until the fall of the Kingdom of Jerusalem in 1187. Both Genoese and Venetians had streets for markets in the city of Jerusalem. The Amalfitans were established

---

[238] Tafel and Thomas eds, *Urkunden zur älteren Handels-und Staatsgeschichte der Republik Venedig*, I, 140–7.

in Acre and Latakia. The merchants of Marseilles had establishments in Acre, Jaffa, Jebail and Tyre, and the Catalans of Barcelona in Tyre.[239]

The commercial quarters varied considerably in size and physical make up. Some were never exploited despite the concession on parchment. The basic components seem to have been a church, an oven, a market (*funda, fundaco funduq*), a bathhouse, warehouses and other houses. Depending on topography there might be specified wharfs for their use (*cathena*). It was not until the 'War of St Sabas' from 1256 to 1258 that the Genoese and Venetians began to wall off their own commercial quarters; possibly, therefore, they were unwalled up to that time. As regards dealings amongst themselves, the merchants had the right to use their own weights and measures and to be subject to the laws of their homeland. For capital crimes and in any suits brought against natives they were subject to the law of the host principality. Legal complications arose when an Italian merchant married into a local Christian family and thereby owned or occupied real estate outside the commercial quarter and then tried to extend his immunities to his new property outside the commercial enclave. The question then arose as to whom their dues and legal responsibility belonged. They were also exempt from the import-export dues paid by native merchants, and they had the right to recover their own ships and cargoes in case of shipwreck.

The exports from Acre from the mid-thirteenth century have been given in a tariff list and include silk, cotton, thread from Damascus, wool carpets, linen, buckram, pottery, leather goods, beams and rafters, a varety of fruits and vegetables, including shallots from Ascalon, frankincense, liquorice, cinnamon, emery, lavender, black pepper, ginger and clove. Spices, perfumes and dyestuffs were clearly important. Some of these goods were intended as ship provisions – some for onward transport to Egypt.[240]

Ships coming to Syria-Palestine from Europe were entering the fringe of the gold standard economies of Byzantium and Islam. Before the thirteenth century, with an emerging market for western textiles and metal products in the East, ships often sailed eastwards with a cargo of gold, or silver to exchange for gold, to make purchases and transporting pilgrims for high fares to offset the cost. Occasionally, too, they brought timber and other military materials. In the East they bought silk, glass, sugar, perfumes, black pepper and balsam. Bulkier imports had to await the development of larger round ships in the thirteenth century.

The Fourth Crusade of 1204 was to place Constantinople and the Aegean and Black Sea trades into western hands for just over half a century, turning western dominance of the carrying trade between East and West into something amounting to paper control. From at least the sixth century onwards both Amalfi and Venice had been parts of the Byzantine Empire and their merchants were closely

---

[239] Runciman, *A History of the Crusades*, II, 294.
[240] The list in Latin is printed in Setton, ed., *A History of the Crusades*, V, 400, n. 172. It is translated and discussed in Prawer, *The Latin Kingdom of Jerusalem*, 402.

integrated into the Byzantine commercial system. By the tenth century the Almalfitans appeared to have a commercial quarter in Constantinople. Their links with the imperial court were such that they had founded a Benedictine monastery on Mount Athos by 983. Its merchants had overseen the manufacture of bronze doors for the cathedral of Amalfi and for the monastery at Monte Cassino at Constantinopolitan foundries in the first part of the eleventh century.[241] Amalfi was to forfeit this favoured position in the decades after 1071 as its political situation in Italy led it into ever-closer links with the Normans. Finally, in 1147, all Amalfitan trading posts within the empire were closed down by imperial order. It was the Venetians who benefited, increasing their own privileges in a series of chrysobulls issued in 992, 1082, 1126 and 1187. They came to almost monopolise the carrying trade between Constantinople, the Aegean and the West, trading at considerable advantage to local merchants due to their exemption from import-export duties. They owed their privileges to the naval support that they gave to the empire, but these privileges led to considerable resentment amongst native merchants and, of course, their commercial rivals in Genoa and Pisa.[242]

The chrysobull of 1082 was the real foundation of Venetian commercial dominance in the Aegean. Immediately west of the Amalfitan quarter, which they were to absorb in 1147, they were given their own permanent quarters or *embolon*. This was centred on the church of St Akindynos and contained three wharfs, some shops and houses and an oven. The Venetians had the right of trading free of duty, not just in Constantinople but in a number of important towns in Syria and Anatolia and also at Durazzo (Dyrrachium), Avlona, Boudonitza, Corfu, Modon, Coron, Nauplion, Corinth, Athens, Thebes, Negroponte (Chalkis), Demetrias, Thessalonika and the coastal towns of Thrace. Like other western merchants, they were banned from entering or trading in the Black Sea, and their merchants were not self-governing as in Syria-Palestine and Cyprus but remained subject to Byzantine law. The Venetians were the most privileged traders in the empire. Local merchants were keen to deal with them since those selling to the Venetians were exempt from the *kommerkion* (in Latin, *commercium* – an import/export tax) on that transaction.

The commercial concessions made to the Venetians do not seem to have harmed the Byzantine economy, which showed signs of rapid expansion during the eleventh and twelfth centuries.[243] Nonetheless they were unpopular with local merchants and clamping down on these privileges did occasionally take place. In 1119 John II Komnenos refused to renew the grant of 1082. In return the Venetians made devastating attacks along the Dalmatian coast and on the

---

[241] L. Bonsall, 'The Benedictine Monastery of St. Mary on Athos', *Eastern Churches Review*, 2 (1969), 262–7; H. Bloch, *Monte Cassino in the Middle Ages*, I (Cambridge, Mass., 1986), 139–63.

[242] Lock, *Franks in the Aegean*, 135–60, for further details on what follows on the Aegean trade.

[243] M. Hendy, *The Economy, Fiscal Administration and Coinage of Byzantium* (London, 1989), essays I and II.

Ionian Islands in 1122 and 1123; in 1125 they destroyed the harbour at Modon before the privileges were confirmed in 1126. The violent seizure of Venetian merchants and their property in Constantinople on 12 March 1171 resulted in fourteen years of naval raids and reprisals before a settlement over damages incurred in 1171 was reached in 1185; it was another two years before the commercial concessions were confirmed in 1187. In the midst of these years of uncertainty, in 1182, there had been the massacre of western merchants in Constantinople that had affected the Genoese and Pisans but not the Venetians, who were excluded from the Constantinopolitan trade at the time.

In 1111 the Pisans gained a commercial quarter in Constantinople and in 1155 the Genoese too received similar concessions. These commercial rivals from the western Mediterranean were late arrivals on the Aegean trading scene, but they wasted no time in gaining imperial favour. It was a Genoese flotilla that brought Agnes-Anna from France as the bride of Alexios II in 1179 and a Pisan vessel that brought the fugitive Alexios Angelos from Constantinople to Ancona in late 1201. Genoese merchants established a trading post at Thebes before 1169, fifteen years before the Venetians set up formal trading quarters there. Nonetheless, around 1170 the Rabbi Benjamin of Tudela noted merchants from Genoa, Pisa and Venice trading in silk at Thebes, Negroponte and Halmyros in central Greece.[244] The Venetians resented these interlopers. In 1162 they allied with the Pisans in an attack on the Genoese *embolon*, and in March 1196 a Venetian fleet cruising off Abydos expelled Pisan corsairs from the harbour, occupied it for themselves, and sought to dissuade the emperor from extending Pisan commercial privileges.

Venetian responsibility for the diversion of the Fourth Crusade has never been proven and rests on circumstantial evidence. Certainly the Venetians were the great winners. Their privileges were confrmed by the Latin Empire and they seemed set fair to exclude their commercial rivals from Genoa and Pisa, some of whom had fought on the Byzantine side in 1204. They also could enter the Black Sea trade, a privilege never extended to foreign merchants in the days of the Byzantine Empire. They had received a one-third share of the lands of the Byzantine Empire and now set up a colonial administration in Crete, castellans in Modon and Coron and a bailli in Negroponte. Between 1207 and 1212 six Venetian noble families, with official sanction, sought to set up dukedoms in the Cyclades, some of which survived into the sixteenth century. Genoese corsairs had intercepted an envoy from the new Latin Empire somewhere in the Adriatic in 1204, relieving him of jewels and other precious gifts sent from Constantinople for Innocent III. Genoa was placed under interdict pending the return of the gifts. Genoese corsairs also set up fortified bases in the Ionian Islands, Crete, and, until 1206 in Modon, from whence they preyed upon Pisan and Venetian shipping. The Aegean was now integrated into the Italian dominated Mediterranean

---

[244] M. Adler, ed. and trans., *The Itinerary of Benjamin of Tudela* (London, 1907), 11.

economy and as such it was becoming a battleground for the rival commercial republics.

The Genoese and Pisans had been virtually excluded from Aegean trade after 1204 and their only way back was by forming an alliance with Michael VIII Palaiologos. On 13 March 1261 the treaty of Nymphaion was negotiated. In return for a fleet of fifty ships to support a Greek attack on Constantinople the Genoese were promised free trade throughout the empire, and trading quarters on Chios and Lesbos and in the port of Smyrna (Izmir). In the same year a Genoese merchant, Manuale Zaccaria, was granted the monopoly of the alum mines around Phocaea (Foggia). This was the source of the best-quality alum in the Aegean and made a fortune for the Zaccaria family before the grant was extended to Genoese investors in general in 1304. On 25 July 1261 Constantinople fell once again into Greek hands and the Genoese replaced the Venetians as most favoured merchants in the Aegean and in the Black Sea trade that had been opened up to western traders since 1204 – trade renowned for its corn, alum and slaves from the Kaffa region and for mineral resources around Trebizond. It was this access to the Black Sea that helped sustain the importance of Constantinople as a mercantile centre. In 1267 the Genoese were granted a substantial self-governing trading quarter in Galata (Pera) on the northern shore of the Golden Horn across from Constantinople, which during the early fourteenth century they fortified to resist Venetian raids. Like the Genoese in 1204, the Venetians could only take reprisals. The Venetians were re-admitted to the Constantinople trade in 1268, but their position was only a shadow of what it had been before 1261. With the extension of commercial sailings to Flanders by both the Genoese and the Venetians in the 1270s eastern luxury items took on a new importance for their respective economies.

Four Veneto-Genoese wars resulted, pursued as fleet actions and piracy in the Aegean, conflict in the commercial quarters of Syria, and by land wars in Italy itself: 1258–70, 1294–9, 1350–1 and 1375–81. Major naval battles were fought off Acre in 1258, by Settepozzi (Spetsopoulos) near Nauplion in 1263, off Trapani in Sicily in 1268, and again off Kastro near Negroponte in 1350. The Venetians came off better in all the set-piece battles but found dealing with Genoese corsairs both difficult and expensive. Not only were these wars destructive of property, shipping and trade but while the big players were occupied with each other, new players came on the scene. The Ottoman Turks seized much of the coastlands of Anatolia and became a force in their own right in the Aegean, occupying Smyrna in 1300 and threatening the harbours and trade routes of both the Venetians and the Genoese. From 1311 the Catalan Grand Company had seized power in the Duchy of Athens and Thebes, threatened Venetian commercial interests in central Greece and provided harbours for Catalan merchants from Barcelona. In this period, too, Pisa ceased to be a prominent commercial power. It never recovered from the destruction of its fleet by the Genoese in a naval battle fought at Maloria, just 10 miles south-west of the mouth of the Arno in August 1284. The Arno River, too, was beginning the process of silting up and altering its course; by the fifteenth century this was to disable Pisa as a galley port.

The latter half of the fourteenth century and on into the fifteenth century saw both the Genoese and the Venetians purchasing, conquering or leasing islands and other territories around the Aegean to prevent them falling into Byzantine or Turkish hands. The Venetians were active participants alongside the Hospitallers in the various naval leagues from the 1330s onwards. Both cities contributed ships to the Holy League that captured Smyrna in 1344, and two years later the Genoese captain Simone Vignoso captured the island of Chios from the Greeks in order to protect Smyrna and secure the valuable mastic production for Genoese mechants. The Genoese contributed some military support in the defence of Constantinople in 1453, and the Venetians were to continue as active participants in the naval leagues up to the battle of Lepanto in 1571 and beyond. Their possessions in Crete were not finally to fall to the Ottomans until 1669.

The Aegean was a transit zone for the products of the East, and possibly became more important as such after the loss of Acre in 1291 and the Mongol conquests of the thirteenth century that focused attention on the Black Sea ports as a point of contact with trade routes to China. High-priced items from the East coming through the Aegean included spices of every kind, from camphor, cinnamon and mace to pepper and rhubarb, porcelain, gems and silks. Local products that were exported westwards included foodstuffs like apricots, oranges, walnuts, figs, raisins, the heavy red wines of Chios and Monemvasia and high-quality olives and olive oil. Recently Professor Jacoby has drawn attention not just to the importance of foodstuffs in general but to the importance of Cretan cheeses in particular in the long-distance trade.[245] Raw materials included mastic from Chios, the dentifrice of the rich, valonia for leather tanning, raw silk, cotton, dyestuffs like cochineal (grana) from Corinth, alum from the Black Sea, Phocaea and the Peloponnese, and carborundum from Naxos, an essential industrial grinding agent.

In 1126 when John II Komnenos confirmed the chrysobull of 1082 to the Venetians he extended their commercial privileges to the island of Cyprus. If they had a commercial quarter it was probably at Limassol where resident Latins were noted when Richard I anchored there in May 1191. The Venetians seem to have lost their privileges at the same time as the Byzantines lost the island. The Lusignans did not grant the Venetians any commercial privileges until 1306. That dynasty seemed to favour the Genoese, who had substantially aided Henry I of Cyprus and his Ibelin advisers in their war with Emperor Frederick II and had received as a reward commercial privileges of free trade and freedom from duties in 1231, confirmed in 1232. Their trading centre was at Famagusta, with a *podesta* (chief magistrate) in overall charge. Disputes between the Genoese and their Lusignan hosts were frequent, especially over the legal and commercial

---

[245] D. Jacoby, 'Cretan Cheese: A Neglected Aspect of Venetian Medieval Trade', in E. Kittell and T. Madden, eds, *Medieval and Renaissance Venice* (Urbana, 1999), 49–68.

rights of the Genoese citizens. Just who qualified as Genoese citizens was the point at issue: natives of Genoa or their subjects in the Aegean and Black Sea possessions? In 1343 and 1344, and again in 1364 and 1365, the two parties were on the brink of open war; this was settled by the confirmation of the privileges of 1232 and the exile of Cypriot officials who had offended Genoese sensibilities. There were also disputes with their Genoese rivals. In 1344 and 1368 there was open fighting on the streets of Famagusta between Venetians and Genoese. Perhaps as latecomers, the Venetians and the Lusignans tended to be mutually supportive. The Venetians provided transport and hospitality on Peter's visit to Italy from 1362 to 1363, and Peter I had provided aid to the Venetians in suppressing the Cretan revolt of 1363–4. However, when Peter sacked Alexandria in October 1365 and brought about the disruption of Italian trade with the Mamelukes, there was a cooling of relations with the Italian maritime republics. In 1373 and 1374 the Genoese invaded Cyprus and occupied Famagusta, but they failed to take Kyrenia. Ostensibly to avenge the murder of Peter I in 1369 and with the support of his widow Eleanor of Aragon, they hoped to control the island through a puppet ruler of their own choosing. The Lusignan dynasty was substantially weakened by these events, but they were to last as rulers of Cyprus until 1489 when the island passed to Venice, under whose control it remained until the Ottoman conquest in 1571. The last century of the Lusignans was marked by political intrigue on a grand scale, involving the Catalans, Genoese and the Venetians. It was resolved in the marriage of James II (1460–73) who, after much diplomatic and financial pressure from the Venetian senate, had married Catherine Cornara (1454–1510), the daughter of a Venetian patrician in 1472. On his death on 6 July 1473 he left his kingdom to his wife and their unborn child – if it was a son. Catherine ruled as regent for her baby son James III (1473–4), and then, after his premature death, alone until 1489 when she was persuaded to abdicate and cede her kingdom to Venice. This she did and retired to Venice.[246]

Except in times of famine Cyprus is a fertile island and had managed to send cereals and fruit to the army of the First Crusade at Antioch. Cyprus was a convenient entrepôt both for the pilgrim trade to Palestine and as a manufactory of high-priced goods like sugar and perfume that were made in Syria-Palestine; after 1291, however, these were firmly under Muslim control. It was less than 90 miles from the Syrian coast and enjoyed a climate that could produce and process sugar-cane. Of the sugar mills and refineries that have been explored by archaeologists, three were on Cyprus at Kolossi, Kouklia (Old Paphos) and Episkopi, one on Rhodes at Haraki and one in Syria at Khirbat Manawat near Acre.[247] In March 2005 Italian archaeologists located a perfumery at Nicosia complete with oil presses and unguent bottles whose residues indicate that oil was mixed with

[246] P. Edbury, *The Kingdom of Cyprus and the Crusades; 1191–1374* (Cambridge, 1991), 3, 65, 155–68; G. Hill, *A History of Cyprus*; III (Cambridge, 1948), 634–756.

[247] A. Boas, *Crusader Archaeology* (London, 1999), 81.

cinnamon or lavender.[248] Sugar and perfumes were the products the Italian merchants wanted from the island, and it may have been that under their organising genius Cypriots were industrialising the manufacturing processes involved to become the centre for satisfying the western demand for these items.

Trade with the Mamelukes of Alexandria was a less certain enterprise. During the planning stage of the Crusades the Pope imposed embargoes on trade with the Muslims, especially in naval materials like cordage, metals, timber and tar. These restrictions were enforced as far as they could be at the time, as much by the commercial republics themselves against renegade merchants as by others the Hospitallers (such as) with a naval capacity. Illicit trading apart, the Italians and the Egyptians might well find themselves on opposing sides, especially in their provision of naval support for the crusader states. The Venetians had negotiated with the Ayyubids sometime before the Fifth Crusade and had renewed the agreement in 1254 with the Mamelukes. It is unclear how long these arrangements lasted. Were they only for the lifetime of the Egyptian sultan concerned? In Egypt the Italians were occasional visitors rather than a settled element of the population. There was no provision for commercial quarters as such, only the right to a market (*funduq*), temporary accommodation in the vicinity of that market, and protection under the law. There was certainly no idea of the Italian merchants forming a self-governing entity. Voyages and trade depended very much on trade developments elsewhere in the Italian trading zones and on the political and military situation of the time. Crusade action in the years 1217–18, and 1249–50 certainly dirsrupted trade, as did the sack of Alexandria by Peter I of Cyprus in 1365. The resentment of both Genoese and Venetians at this action shows that Alexandria was a valued, if occasional, destination. The same sorts of raw materials came from Egypt as from the other Levantine destinations, although ivory was particularly noted. Alexandria could be visited as part of the triangle of trade on the return journey to the home city from Constantinople, Cyprus or Acre.

The influence that the Italian merchants were able to exert in Acre, Famagusta, Constantinople and the Aegean shows, amongst other things, that their numbers were not insignificant. Once again we enter the realms of estimations. It has been reckoned, not without disagreement, that there were between 10,000 and 15,000 Latins and their dependants resident in Constantinople in 1203/4. The number of Latins in the Aegean area was also increasing in the later Middle Ages.

The Italian merchants made a reality of eastern promise in the shopping baskets of Europe. They brought sugar to the European diet and introduced a sense of smelling nice to what there was of personal hygiene. Their marketing may have contributed to the mystique of the East, an idea that still pervades our Christmas stockings with dates, sugared almonds, sugared figs and Turkish Delight. On balance the Venetians outstripped their rivals from Genoa and Pisa

---

[248]   I thank my student Mirko Lezzi for drawing my attention to this news item on BBC Radio 4.

in the extent of their privileges and in their concept of their role in the East. They, after all, were the only one of the three commercial republics to produce a colonial coinage for their Levantine possessions,[249] and it was they who emerged as a naval power in the struggle against Ottoman domination of the Mediterranean Sea. All might be regarded as crusaders, and their great contribution was their knowledge of the sea and of ships. If, on occasion, the demands of trade and of crusade were in danger of being confused no one doubted the sincerity and self-sacrifice of Doge Enrico Dandolo when, at the age of 97, he took the cross in St Mark's, Venice, in April 1201.

CRUSADES FROM A JEWISH PERSPECTIVE[250]

The Jewish pogroms associated with the First Crusade have formed an important part in Jewish identity and memory and have been subsumed into the debate on the origins of racial prejudice that resulted in the Holocaust of the twentieth century.

There are three surviving Jewish accounts of the passage of the First Crusade: the *Eliezer bar Nathan Chronicle*, the *Soloman bar Simson Chronicle* and the *Mainz Anonymous*, also known as the, *Narrative of the Old Persecutions*. These Hebrew chronicles complement and extend the Christian narratives of the crusade, and, as Robert Chazan has noted, have 'adopted a style that is more realistic, more human, more conflicted and ultimately more historical' than

---

[249] Stahl, *The Venetian Tornesello*; A. Stahl, 'The Coinage of Venice in the Age of Enrico Dandolo', in E. Kittell and T. Madden, eds, *Medieval and Renaissance Venice* (Urbana, 1999), 124–40.

[250] M. Cohen, *Under Crescent and Cross: The Jews in the Middle Ages* (Princeton, 1994); R. Chazan, *European Jewry and the First Crusade* (Berkeley, 1987); R. Chazan, *God, Humanity and History: The Hebrew First Crusade Narratives* (Berkeley, 2000); S. Eidelberg, ed. and trans., *The Jews and the Crusaders: The Hebrew Chronicles of the First and Second Crusades* (Madison, 1977); Prawer, *The History of the Jews in the Latin Kingdom of Jerusalem*; R. Moore, *The Formation of a Persecuting Society* (Oxford, 1987); J. Cohen, *The Friars and the Jews. The Evolution of Medieval Anti-Judaism* (Ithaca, 1982); R. Dobson, *The Jews of Medieval York and the Massacre of March 1190* (York, 1974); N. Glob, 'New Light on the Persecution of French Jews at the Time of the First Crusade', *Proceedings of the American Academy for Jewish Research*, 34 (1966), 1–63; J. Riley-Smith, 'The First Crusade and the Persecution of the Jews', in W. Shiels, ed., *Studies in Church History 21: Persecution and Toleration* (Oxford, 1984), 51–72; R. Chazan, 'The Emperor Frederick I, the Third Crusade and the Jews', *Viator*, 8 (1977); M. Barber, 'Lepers, Jews and Muslims. The Plot to Overthrow Christendom in 1321', *History*, 66 (1981), 1–17. For information on contemporary Jewish communites, not always with reference to the Crusades, see Adler, *The Itinerary of Benjamin of Tudela*; A. Sharf, *Byzantine Jewry* (London, 1971); S. Bowman, *The Jews of Byzantium 1204–1453* (Alabama, 1985); H. Richardson, *The English Jewry under Angevin Kings* (London, 1960); R. Chazan, *Medieval Jewry in Northern France* (Baltimore, 1973); W. Jordan, *The French Monarchy and the Jews* (Philadelphia, 1989); G. Kisch, *The Jews in Medieval Germany* (Chicago, 1949); I. Elbogen, A. Freimann and H. Tykocinskij, eds, *Germania Judaica* (2 vols, Tubingen, 1963–8); J. Sola, G. Armistead and J. Silverman, eds, *Hispania Judaica* (2 vols, Barcelona, 1985); B. Lewis, *The Jews of Islam* (London, 1984).

previous Jewish narrative.[251] Only the *Soloman bar Simson Chronicle* has a date: 1140. The dating of the other two chronicles is problematic. They all share an awareness of the crusading fervour as it developed in northern Europe, of the novelty of the undertaking and the inherent danger to the Jewish communities. The central role of Urban II was not noted or understood. The *Mainz Anonymous* linked the various pogroms to the recruitment process itself, noting that the French pogroms took place alongside the assembly of Peter the Hermit's contingent, and similarly, but later, in the Rhineland where the stimulus to crusade resulted from the passage of Peter the Hermit's army. In the Rhineland, Peter – and later Godfrey of Bouillon – had passed through rapidly, extracting financial contributions from the Jewish communities – but no more. The pogroms there were attributed to the followers of Emicho of Leinigen in which the townsmen, the neighbours of the Jews, assisted them.

In his chronicle Rabbi Eliezer bar Nathan recorded that:

> There arose an arrogant people, a people of strange speech, a nation bitter and impetuous, Frenchmen and Germans, from all directions. They decided to set out for the Holy City, there to seek their house of idolatry, banish the Ishmaelites and conquer the land for themselves. They decorated themselves prominently with their signs by marking themselves upon their garments with their sign – a horizontal line over a vertical one – every man and woman whose heart yearned to go there, until their ranks swelled so that the number of men, women and children exceeded a locust horde.[252]

Jewish attitudes to the Crusades in the twelfth century were conditioned by Christian anti-Semitism, a persistent element in the social and cultural lives of the people of Christendom. According to many Jewish historians of differing historical periods, like Robert Chazan and Daniel Goldhagen, anti-Semitism should be given a central place in the history of Christendom and not just in that of the Crusades in the twelfth century.[253] Whereas persecution is bound up with every monotheistic religion, anti-Semitism is intrinsically linked to Christianity and might be seen as fundamental to Christian theology and teaching. Nonetheless, Jews were recognised as part of God's creation and as part of the divine plan for the universe. Their forcible conversion or slaughter was forbidden by canon law. All in all they were regarded as almost a separate human species.

This is perhaps most clearly expressed in the sermons of John Chrysostom (*c.* 347–407), patriarch of Constantinople, doctor of the Church and saint. His anti-Semitic sermons belong to the period 386–98 when he was patriarch of Antioch and faced with a questioning of their faith by many Christians and with

---

251   Chazan, *God, Humanity and History*, 187.
252   Eidelberg, ed. and trans., *The Jews and the Crusades*, 79.
253   R. Chazan, *Medieval Stereotypes and Modern Anti-Semitism* (Berkeley, 1997); D. Goldhagen, *Hitler's Willing Executioners* (New York, 1996), 49–53.

growing numbers of converts from Christianity to Judaism. In his sermon *Adversus Judaeos* he established many of the traditions later associated with Christian anti-Semitism. It was clear that Jews and Christians shared a common religious tradition. Yet, if the teaching of the Jew Jesus was correct – that Christianity had superseded Judaism – why had not all Jews become Christians and why did Judaism persist? The tensions come out in John's sermon in which he attributes the persistence of Judaism to wilful rejection of the revealed truth due to lack of reason. He does not, however, urge any violence against the Jews of Antioch; his objections are passionate but they are theological. They focus on the rejection of Jesus:

> Where Christ-killers gather the cross is ridiculed, God blasphemed, the Father unacknowledged, the Son insulted, the grace of the Spirit rejected . . . If the Jewish rites are holy, and venerable, our way of life must be false. But if our way is true, as indeed it is, theirs is fraudulent. I am not speaking of the Scriptures. Far from it! For they lead on to Christ. I am speaking of their present impiety and madness.[254]

Certainly acts of violence had been perpetrated against Jews in the pre-Christian period. Leaving aside the record of the Old Testament, there had been riots against Jews by the majority Greek population in Alexandria in AD 38 and again in 66. These attacks were more in the nature of anti-Jewish attacks rather than anti-Semitic violence, and might be seen as similar to the anti-Christian attacks by pagans in Ephesos, Rome and elsewhere in the first century AD, or the anti-pagan attacks by Christians as evidenced by the destruction of the Mithraeum at Carrawburgh in the fourth century.

It was with the triumph of Christianity in the Roman Empire that Jews were deprived of civic rights, and anti-Semitism may be said to have replaced anti-Judaism. In 415 it was declared that no new synagogues were to be built within the empire. In 438 the Theodosian Code forbade Jews to marry Christians, own Christian slaves or to convert any other slaves that they might possess to Judaism. In 526 the Code of Justinian excluded Jews from the civil service and the legal profession, and took away their right to make wills, inherit property or to bring actions in the law courts. These laws, and the attitudes behind them of which John Chrysostom was a mouthpiece, cast a long shadow over medieval Europe. Christianity and law were the two fundamental bequests of the Roman Empire. These particular laws formed the economic and social framework in which Jews were expected to operate and sanctioned the perception of Jews as the other, strangers and outsiders to Latin and Greek Christians alike. Christian teaching and Roman legislation had laid the basis for European anti-Semitism. It is interesting to note that it had been the Roman emperor Hadrian who had first

---

[254] Cited in D. Berger, ed., *History and Hate: The Dimensions of Anti-Semitism* (Philadelphia, 1986), 69.

banned Jewish habitation in Jerusalem around 138. This ban was lifted after the Muslim conquest of 638, reimposed after the crusader conquest of 1099, and lifted again after 1192. The crusaders neither knew nor cared that the Western Wall was Jewry's holiest shrine. The Jews, however, were understood not to be heretics and could practise their religion even if oppressed in other activities.

The economic growth in Europe in the tenth and eleventh centuries that permitted the Crusades to be launched at all is still ill understood. It is clear, however, that Jewish immigrants (probably from Byzantine territory?) were encouraged by local rulers to settle in some towns in northern Europe in order to foster economic growth. Some of the charters that emergent Jewish communities purchased in the late tenth century down to the 1080s have survived.[255] These make clear that these Ashkenazic or north European Jews were both recent immigrants and a tiny minority in most of the towns in which they settled. It was a case of privileges bought, usually royal protection and the right to build a synagogue, that allowed them to function as subjects on sufferance; they did not enjoy the rights and protections of native subjects. Herein lay a fatal weakness to their protection and safety when attacked by members of the crusading armies in 1096. In northern and central Europe violence to the Jews did not provoke the same reaction from the authorities as damage to the persons and property of their Christian subjects.

The religious reform movement of the eleventh century had emphasised the workings of the Holy Spirit and through it prompted thought on individual spirituality. The excitement and religious zeal associated with the twelfth-century crusades certainly seemed to have excited some of its participants to violence against the enemy in their midst; that is, the Jews of Christendom. Robert Moore has charted some instances of changing attitudes to the Jews in events prior to 1096 associated with Christian relations with Muslims and linking Jews with Muslims as the perceived enemies of Christendom – the one within and the other without the borders of Christendom. From 1010 to 1012 there were attacks on the Jewish communities of Limoges, Mainz and Rouen associated with rumours (true as it turned out) that the Church of the Holy Sepulchre in Jerusalem had been sacked. In 1063 the Jews of Narbonne were attacked in connection with the Barbastro campaign. The local authorities were ineffective. Both the sheriff and the archbishop opposed the violence but failed to quell it, offering only half-hearted protection to the Jews. Finally, the late eleventh-century *Song of Roland* has Charlemagne ordering the destruction of the synagogues and mosques of Saragossa and the forced conversion of both Jews and Muslims (lines 3658–71).[256]

It was in this context that popular anti-Semitism developed, bringing violence

---

[255] There were Jews in the Rhineland in 321 when the emperor Constantine wrote to the magistrates of Cologne regarding Jewish recruitment into the citizen militia. These settlers probably came as part of the Roman army. The first record of Jews in that area in the Middle Ages is 962.

[256] Moore, *The Formation of a Persecuting Society*, 27–45.

to a number of Jewish communities across Europe from the Seine to the Danube between December 1095 and July 1096. It was associated with the popular crusades inspired by Peter the Hermit in the areas between the Seine and the Rhine, and with that led by Count Emicho of Leiningen in the upper Rhineland. It used to be thought that this was the work of the lower orders of society acting without the restraints of noble leadership, but this model cannot be sustained since there were significant knightly elements present in both contingents The motivation for the attacks has produced considerable discussion, with reasons ranging from early manifestations of the Holocaust, to financial extortion and plunder to purchase supplies, the desire to baptise the Jews regardless of financial gain, and as a bad boys' bonding activity. None of these reasons need be mutually exclusive except the first. Both Jewish and Christian writers agreed that the attacks were caused by a desire to revenge the crucifixion of Christ, in whatever forms that revenge might take. The attacks were limited and random. The city authorities opposed them on the grounds of public order. The bishops sought to uphold canon law by forbidding forced baptisms. However, it was where those secular and Episcopal powers were ineffective that violence occurred – hence the random nature of the attacks. In Hungary and in Byzantine territory the authorities took a firm stance towards the crusaders, either dispersing disorderly groups or policing their progress carefully; the result was no anti-Semitic attacks.

The Jewries of Cologne, Mainz and Worms were destroyed, along with their religious books and artefacts. It was in these three towns that the bulk of the casualties were sustained. Between 700 and 1300 Jews perished in Mainz. There were attacks in Rouen and Trier, with some casualties but no figures, whilst violence in Metz, Speyer and Regensburg left, respectively, 22, 11 and no persons reported dead as a result. There was clearly no intention to wipe out the Jewish race as a whole from the path of the crusade. Violence occurred where there was opportunity, where the authorities were weak or ineffective. There was nothing in these sad tales, either in scale or intent, to rival the Nazi Holocaust of the twentieth century. Without that hindsight, as Professor Riley-Smith has noted, it was anti-Jewish violence on a new scale; rumours of it preceded the crusading armies to the Holy Land and dirges to the memory of the martyrs are recited to this day.

It is difficult to come to grips with the casualties since the Christian chroniclers mention the violence as a regrettable aside to the main crusade narrative and the Jewish chroniclers emphasise the aspect of forced conversions in language redolent of the disasters of the Old Testament. However, there were new synagogues and *mik-voth* at Cologne, Speyer and Worms by the 1120s. The Jewish communities in those towns clearly felt sufficiently secure to build within a generation of the pogroms.[257]

---

[257] Christian architects were commissioned to design some of these synagogues, hence their Romanesque or Gothic features in arches, windows and doors. A fine example of this is the Altneusynagogue in Prague built *c.* 1270.

The consequence of the attacks in 1096 has been variously assessed. Israel Abrahams, in his popular and influential book on *Jewish Life in the Middle Ages* (London, 1896; 2nd edn 1932), saw it as ushering in a total transformation of Jewish life. According to him the destruction of schools and houses led to wandering scholars and tinkers, which in turn led to a change from daily food distributions to the poor to a tradition of hospitality for the itinerant Jew. It also resulted in the early betrothal of daughters before the crusaders could seize dowries.[258] In the 1970s Jewish scholars such as Alexander Shapiro and Arno Meyer saw the First Crusade as the first Holocaust; that is, as a manifestation of the *shoah*.[259] This view is misleading, although still not uncommon. There are considerable disjunctions of scale and intent between this first pogrom in European history and the eliminationist anti-Semitism of the Nazis. Interestingly, the Jüdisches Museum, Berlin, has nothing whatever to say in its exhibitions about the First Crusade or later ones. Rather, it focuses on the large-scale massacres in German-speaking lands during the period of the Black Death (1349–53) and later plague outbreaks as a fundamental turning point in Jewish persecution. The root of these anti-Semitic attacks lay in accusations of Jews being polluters and deliberate poisoners of town water supplies. The proportion of Jews to Christians dying as a result of the plague outbreaks is much disputed.[260]

The capture of Jerusalem on 15 July 1099 was effected through a breach in the wall in the Jewish quarter in the north-east of the city. It ended with the massacre of Muslims, native Christians and Jews. The crusaders seemed to be living up to their reputation, but these casualties – although directed at Muslims – were the result of ignorance and the inability to distinguish one from another in the heat of the moment. It should be noted that when Tiberias, Tyre and Ascalon surrendered to the crusaders in 1099, 1124 and 1153 respectively, the Jewish communities continued to exist in all three towns, as did the rural Jews in the villages of the Galilee region. When Saladin destroyed Ascalon in 1191 many of the Jews there moved to Jerusalem. The Jewish and Muslim survivors in 1099, having removed the dead from the city, were themselves expelled. This stimulated the growth of Jewries in Alexandria, Cairo and Damascus. It was unthinkable that the killers of Christ should be allowed to live in Jerusalem where he had been crucified and buried. Jews were virtually segregated in the Kingdom of Jerusalem. They might perform menial tasks such as tanning and dyeing. Jewish physicians seemed to have been preferred by westerners; this patronage was viewed in a very negative light by the authorities in Acre in 1261, fearing what it might suggest about the efficacy of the Christian religion. Jews might participate in commerce and could appear as witnesses and bring actions in the courts of burgesses, but very much on Latin terms. They were not called upon to serve in

---

[258] Abrahams, *Jewish Life in the Middle Ages*, 16, 157, 335–8, 224–8.
[259] See discussion by Nirenberg, 'The Rhineland Massacres of the Jews in the First Crusade: Memories Medieval and Modern', (Cambridge, 2002), 279–310.
[260] S. Cohn, *The Black Death Transformed* (London, 2002), 232–3, for discussion and references.

the armies of the crusader states since their loyalty was suspect. Surprisingly, the success of the First Crusade had a marked effect on the Jews of Western Europe. Although pilgrimage had not been an institutionalised part of Jewish religion after the destruction of the Second Temple in AD 70, the number of Jewish visitors to the holy places from Europe seemed to have increased during the twelfth century, showing in an unexpected way how the crusader states brought Jerusalem firmly into Christendom. Indeed, a new genre in Hebrew literature emerged at this time with the writing of Hebrew itineraries to Palestine written by Jews for Jews. It was during the crusader period too, and as a direct result of it, that the appellation 'Edom', the metaphor for the persecutor of Jews, was transferred from Byzantium to western Christendom, then seen as the main contestant with Islam for possession of the Jewish holy places. The Italian commercial republics dominated the maritime trade of the crusader states, but Jewish merchants sometimes appeared in partnership with them. They were by no means excluded from the commercial life of the East.[261]

Blood was shed in the anti-Jewish riots associated with the preaching of the Second Crusade. These anti-Semitic attacks were associated with the preaching of the renegade Cistercian monk Radulph. This time St Bernard of Clairvaux nipped the outbreaks in the bud. In August 1145 he drove Radulph away from Sully and Carenatan to the Rhineland, and in September/October preached against him in Cologne, Mainz, Worms and Speyer, putting him into custody in Mainz and then arranging for him to be readmitted to his cloister. He sought to defuse the anti-Semitic feelings of his congregations by pointing out the failure of the popular elements on crusade in 1096, and attributed this to their greed; that is, their plundering of the Jews. However erroneous he may have been in linking anti-Semitic attacks on the popular element alone, he seems to have been effective in limiting the anti-Jewish attacks. No casualty figures have survived, but there was nothing on the scale of the violence of 1096.

Later in the twelfth century both William of Newburgh and the Peterborough Chronicle recorded the spread of irrational stories of the crucifixion of Christian boys by the Jews in order to revenge themselves on Christ. These stories seemed to have been in circulation as early as 1136. Also in England, and linked to it, were stories of Jewish ritual murders of Christian youths in Norwich (1144 and 1235), Gloucester (1168), Bury St Edmunds (1182), Bristol (1183), Winchester (1192) and Lincoln (1255). There is no evidence of any Jewish involvement in these murders or of any wider plot. Similar murder stories appeared on the continent about the same time as in England, but do not appear to have been so common: Wurzburg (1147), Blois (1171) and Bacharach (1284).[262] Perhaps

---

[261] Prawer, *The History of the Jews in the Latin Kingdom of Jerusalem, passim.*

[262] Many of these so-called victims of Jewish ritual murder were canonised, and their shrines were much visited in the Middle Ages; e.g. St William of Norwich (1132–44) in Norwich cathedral and St Werner of Oberwesel (1271–84) in the Wernerkappelle, Bacharach.

these were attempts to explain paedophile murders in a way acceptable to all except the Jewish community.

Crusading and anti-Semitic violence were a potent mix. This seems to be the case in England as much as anywhere else in Christian Europe. Jews had been introduced into England from Rouen by William I after 1066 and ever since had been closely linked to the crown. All Jewish properties were registered and the crown took a percentage of their commercial and financial transactions. Violence against the Jews was not in the royal interest, and the limited involvement of the English in the First and Second crusades may have contributed towards the absence of anti-Jewish attacks. However, with the absence of Richard I in France, and as preparations were underway for the Third Crusade, there was a spate of violent attacks on Jewish persons and properties in London (September 1189), Norwich (February 1190) and York (March 1190). These consisted of the usual baiting of Jews, arson attacks, murder, accompanied by the flight of the Jews to the royal strongholds in the cities concerned, ineffective support from the local authorities and the Jewish suicides. The loss of life was considerable, and his ineffective agents felt the anger of the king.[263] By contrast, little is heard of anti-Semitic attacks in Germany associated with the crusades of either Frederick I Barbarossa or of Henry VI, other than some anti-Jewish riots in Speyer in 1195.

From the thirteenth century the situation was to change in degree if not in nature. The Jews were being stigmatised as unclean and as defilers of the host. For this perceived rejection of Christ numbers were burned as heretics, an equation that seems new in anti-Semitic propaganda. Their separation from Christian society became more formalised. The Fourth Lateran Council of 1215 emphasised the conversion, where possible, of the Jews of Christendom; in this the new preaching orders, particularly the Franciscans, were to take a lead. The Order has been blamed for spate of new Jewish stories dealing with desecrations of the host and the forcible circumcision of Christian boys. Jews, like lepers, were not allowed to touch food in markets unless they purchased it. This equation of Jews with lepers seems to have been a new idea. It is to this time too that the desecration of Jewish cemeteries began to be mentioned for the first time. Jews were also to wear distinctive badges on their clothing. These could be of any shape or colour, as laid down by the Christian communities in which they dwelt. There were to be local expulsions of Jews from some of the towns of Germany during the fourteenth century, and even from countries as a whole (England 1291, France 1326 and Spain 1492), with ghettoisation introduced during the sixteenth century for Jews in the cities of Europe.

There were still occasional mass acts of violence against Jewish communities. Those of 1251 and 1320 were both associated with the *pastoreaux*. The

---

[263] Dobson, *The Jews of Medieval York and the Massacre of March 1190*; J. Lilley et al., *The Jewish Burial Ground at Jewbury* (York, 1994), 302–10; V. Lipman, *The Jews of Medieval Norwich* (London, 1967), 57–64.

Franciscans had effectively diabolised the Jews in popular culture. Very few persons in medieval Europe may have actually come across Jews face to face, but the familiar stories of the Passion plays, with their visual depictions of Jews, and references to their desecration of the host and of ritual murders, had produced a more persuasive reality of the medieval Jew than any actual Jewish behaviour.[264]

It is impossible to quantify the consequences of crusader violence against the Jews. It is not known how many Jews were actually resident in Europe. Estimates vary between 30,000 and 50,000 *in toto*. In terms of loss of life it is reckoned between 3,000 and 5,000, or 1 per cent, were casualties of the First Crusade, most of these perishing as a result of the assault on Jerusalem. For the other crusades put together a total of 1,000 casualties has been put forward. Any estimates of the material and cultural damage are not available.[265] It is very much as a direct result of the twentieth-century Holocaust that we look on the Jews and the Crusades in these terms. Regrettable and anachronistic as it is, it seems unavoidable.

CRUSADES FROM A MUSLIM PERSPECTIVE[266]

Islam is still relatively unknown, or at least ill understood, in the West. Both to the frustration of many Muslims and the bewilderment of western audiences, the

---

[264] B. Glassman, *Anti-Semitic Stereotypes Without Jews: Images of the Jew in England, 1290–1700* (Detroit, 1975), 11–14.

[265] S. Katz, *The Holocaust in Historical Context*, I (Oxford, 1994), 334–5.

[266] Hillenbrand, *The Crusades. Islamic Perspectives*; J. Saunders, *A History of Medieval Islam* (London, 1972; reprinted 1996); M. Rodgers, *The Making of the Past: The Spread of Islam* (Oxford, 1976); B. Spuler, *The Muslim World, A Historical Survey* (3 Parts, Leiden, 1960–9); Setton, ed., *A History of the Crusades*, I, 181–276; P. Holt, A. Lambton and B. Lewis, eds, *The Cambridge History of Islam* (4 vols, Cambridge, 1980); Esposito, ed., *The Oxford History of Islam* (Oxford, 1999), esp. pp. 305–46; B. Lewis, ed., *The World of Islam* (London, 1976); C. Bosworth, *The New Islamic Dynasties* (Edinburgh, 1996); R. Roolvink, *Historical Atlas of the Muslim Peoples* (Amsterdam, n.d. = 1956); A. Ducellier *et al.*, *Le Moyen Age en Orient: Byzance et Islam* (Paris, 1990); C. Cahen, *Pre-Ottoman Turkey* (London, 1968); M. Shatzmiller, ed., *Crusaders and Muslims in Twelfth Century Syria* (Leiden, 1993); P. Hitti, *A History of the Arabs* (London, 1939, 9th edn 1968), 617–709; P. Holt, ed., *The Eastern Mediterranean Lands in the Period of the Crusades* (Warminster, 1977); P. Holt, *The Age of the Crusades. The Near East from the Eleventh Century to 1517* (London, 1986); Holt, *The Crusader States and Their Neighbours*; H. Dajani-Shakeel and R. Messier, eds, *The Jihad and its Time* (Ann Arbor, 1991); R. Peters, *The Jihad in Medieval and Modern Islam* (Leiden, 1977); Laiou and R. Parviz-Mottahedeh, eds, *The Crusades from the Perspective of Byzantium and the Muslim World*; A. Maalouf, *The Crusades Through Arab Eyes* (London, 1984); Z. Haddad, 'The Crusaders Through Muslim Eyes', *The Muslim World*, 73 (1983), 234–52; F. Michau, 'Croisades et croises vus par les historiens arabes chrétiens d'Egypte', in R. Curiel and R. Gyselen, eds, *Itineraires d'Orient. Hommages a Claude Cahen* (Burges-Sur-Yvette, 1994), 169–87; B. Lewis, *The Assassins* (London, 1967; reprinted 1999); W. Bartlett, *The Assassins* (Stroud, 2001); W. Madelung and P. Walker, eds, *The Advent of the Fatimids* (London, 2000); E. Ashtor, *A Social and Economic History of the Near East in the Middle Ages* (London, 1976); Parry and Yapp, eds, *War, Technology and Society in the Middle East*; J. Schacht and C. Bosworth, eds, *The Legacy of Islam* (2nd edn, Oxford, 1974);

---

media have emphasised the tensions within Islam as it confronts the global, commercialised world and focused attention upon poverty, tyranny and violence. All of this naturally affects our perceptions of the past. Islam is an enormous topic that can only be touched upon here in terms of its relationship with the Crusades – primarily to the extent that the disunity of Islam contributed to the success of the First Crusade, together with the Muslim counter-crusade and jihad, and the legacy of the Crusades within Islam. This is a Eurocentric point of view, and I would maintain that as someone brought up in a western, Latin Christian tradition it could be no other. However, from the time of the Enlightenment such a point of departure has not always been unfair in its perceptions of Islam; rather the reverse. The Enlightenment provided the model of Islamic civilisation confronted by western barbarism. In this it accepted Islam on its own terms as one all-embracing and unified culture and political system. Certainly it is seen as the opponent of Christendom for the control of the Mediterranean world, but it was often given the benefit of the doubt when its religious and political systems did not match up to legal and political theory in a way that the actions of the Pope or the western emperor would not have been condoned. These benign generalisations often fudge the behaviour and expectations of peoples in a particular time and place.

At first sight, from the perspective of the early twenty-first century, the Muslim world that confronted the crusaders seems to have been more civilised, less vicious, and more tolerant than its western counterpart. In our age of globalisation

---

R. Hillenbrand, *Islamic Art and Architecture* (London, 1999); J. Hoag, *Islamic Architecture* (1975; English edn London, 1979); V. Enderlein *et al.*, *Museum of Islamic Art, State Museums of Berlin* (Berlin, 2003); J. Gierlichs and A. Hagedorn, eds, *Islamic Art in Germany* (Mainz, 2004); T. Insoll, *The Archaeology of Islam* (Oxford, 1999) M. Lyons and P. Jackson, *Saladin, The Politics of Holy War* (Cambridge, 1982); A. Ehrenkreutz, *Saladin* (Albany, 1972), and review by H. Mayer in *Speculum*, 49 (1974), 724–7; Y. Lev, *Saladin in Egypt* (Leiden, 1999); H. Gibb, 'The Achievement of Saladin', *Bulletin of the John Rylands Library*, 25 (1952); Brand, 'The Byzantines and Saladin: Opponents of the Third Crusade'; P. Thorau, *The Lion of Egypt: Sultan Baybars I and the Near East in the Thirteenth Century* (London, 1974); R. Humphreys, *From Saladin to the Mongols* (Albany, 1977); R. Humphreys, *Islamic History* (Princeton, 1991; revised edn London, 1995); B. Lewis and P. Holt, eds, *Historians of the Middle East* (Oxford, 1962); D. Morgan, ed., *Medieval Historical Writing in the Christian and Islamic Worlds* (London, 1982); C. Robinson, *Islamic Historiography* (Cambridge, 2003). Useful translations of Muslim sources are: B. Lewis, *Islam from the Prophet Muhammad to the Capture of Constantinople* (2 vols, Oxford, 1987); Gabrieli, *Arab Historians of the Crusades*; H. Gibb, *The Damascus Chronicle of the Crusades* (London, 1932; reprinted New York, 2002); Hitti, *The Memoirs of an Arab-Syrian Gentleman*, also available in G. Potter, *The Autobiography of Ousama* (London, 1929); Broadhurst, *The Travels of Ibn Jubayr*; D. Richards, *The Rare and Excellent History of Saladin* (Aldershot, 2001), also available in an earlier trans. by C.W. Wilson, *'Saladin' or What Befell Sultan Yusuf by Beha-ed-Din* in Palestine Pilgrim Text Society, 13 (London, 1897; reprinted New York, 1971); H. Masse, *Imad-ed-Din Conquete de La Syrie et la Palestine par Saladin* (Paris, 1972); U. and M. Lyons and J. Riley-Smith, *Ayyubids, Mamelukes and Crusaders. Selections from the Tafakh al-dawal wal-Muluk* (2 vols, Cambridge, 1971); J. Boyle, *Genghis Khan: The History of the World Conqueror* (2 vols, Manchester, 1958; reprinted 1997).

and relativism that seeks multiculturism in the apparent relationship of super-ficially similar artefacts (rosary, *komboloi* or *tespih* [a Levantine fidget toy in the form of a string of beads used to pass the time], amulet, crucifix), and in religious festivals that mark life's transitions, medieval Islam may be easily ideal-ised. In geographical terms its global reach was extensive. The contribution of its scholars to the sciences, medicine, mathematics, astronomy, and cartography was considerable. In the wake of the capture of Toledo by the Christians in 1085 cultural contacts allowed the translation into Latin of Greek scientific and philo-sophical texts that had been formerly translated from Greek and Syriac. This not only enriched western science but also shed a very positive light on the assimila-tive if not the acculturative qualities of Islam. The Koran's emphasis upon clean-liness and the bath culture taken over from the Greeks and Romans resonates with modern concerns for personal hygiene. Muslim traditions for the conduct of war forbade looting and the killing of women and children and seem to present a stark contrast to the aspirations of the eleventh-century peace councils in west-ern Europe. There were no forced conversions to Islam for Jews and Christians. No bloodbath when Saladin captured Jerusalem in 1187 to compare with the crusade onslaught of 1099. Muslim culture appears to have been inclusive and enabling rather than exclusive and devisive. It is to centres such as Cordoba, Palermo and, after 1453, Istanbul (Constantinople) that we look for cross-cultural exchanges. The languages of Islam, Arabic, Persian and Turkish were assimilated, given an Arabic script, and treated on an equal footing. Hellenistic, Byzantine and Iranian cultures were used and adapted. In central and eastern Turkey the Byzantine double-headed eagle was as appealing to rulers as it was in northern Europe and was used in building decoration, tile design, and as a famil-iar device on coins.[267] The art of the Ottoman court used all the artistic and craft traditions of its empire and its neighbours.[268] All the great conquerors – Saladin (d. 1194), Baybars I (d. 1277), Timur (d. 1405) and Suleyman the Magnificent (d. 1566) – sought to display themselves as exemplars of taste, and in their use and appreciation of Chinese porcelain they had a common passion. Yet it is in the western tradition that these rulers were extolled. European rulers and col-lectors commissioned medals and portaits of Suleyman within his lifetime.[269] Christopher Marlowe's *Tamburlaine* (1587–8) was a box-office success with Eliz-abethan theatregoers, with its rags to riches theme interlaced with thwarted love, sadism and a high body count. At a time when Saladin was all but forgotten in Muslim historiography, Sir Walter Scott's *Talisman* (Edinburgh, 1825) painted him as a perfect chivalrous paladin, Stanley Lane-Poole idolised him in his biography of 1898, and the visit of Kaiser Wilhelm II (1888–1918) to Damascus

---

[267] D. Roxburgh, ed., *Turks: A Journey of a Thousand Years, 600–1600* (London, 2005), 109, 118, 120, 128–9.

[268] Roxburgh, ed., *Turks*, 260–375.

[269] Roxburgh, ed., *Turks*, 316–17, 448.

in November of the same year rescued his tomb from neglect.[270] Perhaps it is in western perceptions that Islam is still taken at the face value of its classical age and judged accordingly against modern criteria, whilst the world of the crusaders is deemed to be embedded in the past and thus subjected to different standards of analysis.

Lack of knowledge of the Arabic language among western crusade historians, and the Eurocentric nature of crusade historiography, may be academically regrettable amongst western scholars and perhaps used to accuse them of a lingering moral and cultural superiority that characterised the work of scholars of the nineteenth century.[271] Perhaps this is unavoidable. Western scholars may advocate, and indeed embrace, the study of Arabic and Ottoman Turkish, but Muslim scholars have done little to redress the balance, either in making available texts in translation or in providing a new model for crusade studies – and this at a time when the rhetoric of crusade is becoming a contemporary issue amongst extremists in both the Muslim and western worlds. Current political correctness has identified Islamophobia and Arabophobia as appropriate labels for any critics of non-Turkish Islam. Perhaps when neo-conservatists draw stark contrasts between the behaviour of those two sons of Takrit, Saladin (b. 1137) and Saddam Hussein (b. 1937), it is another way of talking about the challenges posed to Islam by the values and ethos of global commercialisation. But just how valid were the global traits of civilization and restraint that the Enlightenment attributed to Islam, a model that has cast a long shadow in comparison with crusade behaviour?

There does not appear to have been a blanket animosity for the West amongst Muslim writers, such as was to manifest itself in Europe with regard to Islam by the end of the eleventh century. The crusaders derived their moral will to fight from the religious propaganda of the papacy that stigmatised Islam in terms of infidels, pagans and idolators. Within Islam the crusaders were given a linguistic not a religious descriptor. The crusaders (as well as westerners in general) were known as *al-Ifranj/al-Franj* (Franks), Norman French being the language of the so-called crusader states and thus reflecting the leading role that the French played in the crusade movement. The relationship with the crusaders was essentially one of war. Any lasting peace was impossible since each clung to mutually exclusive religious ideologies that sought to possess the holy places of their religions for themselves. Once a strong Muslim ruler had established himself in the region the conquest and retention of these places was to invest their conquerors with much prestige and political capital. Saladin (1137–93) gambled much on the success of his campaign to recapture Jerusalem in 1187, and had much to lose

[270] S. Lane-Poole, *Saladin and the Fall of the Kingdom of Jerusalem* (London, 1898); Riley-Smith, 'Islam and the Crusades in History and Imagination, 8 November 1898–11 September 2002'. See J. Sweetman, *Oriental Obsession* (Cambridge, 1988), 112–210 for Islamic inspiration on British and American art, architecture and design in the nineteenth century.
[271] Lane-Poole, *Saladin and the Fall of the Kingdom of Jerusalem*, iii–xiii.

should he fail.[272] At first the Franks were just one more pawn in an already overcrowded political chessboard, and were not distinguished from the Byzantines. It was the length and the religious nature of their occupation that gradually provoked an Islamic reaction. In terms of significance to Islam they pale into insignificance besides the Mongols; one has only to contrast the relative ease with which the former crusader states were absorbed in the thirteenth century with the cultural and artistic contributions of the Mongol khanate. In the literature of the West the crusade literature is a genre of its own. In the literatures of Egypt and Iraq they received relatively little attention, and that usually compiled in the thirteenth century. In the literature of Iran they are scarcely mentioned at all.

Bad behaviour seemed to know no religious bounds. The rulers and warriors of Islam were no less vicious or ruthless than their crusading counterparts. As successful rulers they could be no other. They sought to be feared rather than loved in the pursuit of their political purposes, and it should come as no surprise that jihad was not at the forefront of their thoughts. Zengi spent his time in attacking his Muslim neighbours rather than the crusader states, with which he sought to remain on good terms. It is only with his attack on Edessa that later writers saw him as the founder of the counter-crusade. As many examples of violence may be plucked from the annals of Islam as from those of the West. Dynastic coups, as in 661 and 750, were accompanied by extreme violence in an attempt to wipe out the opposition. Louis IX and his fellow captives were appalled by the bloodshed that accompanied seizure of power by the Mamelukes at Damietta in 1250. The course of the slave revolt by East African slaves in the saltpetre mines of the Basra region (869–73), known as the Zanj rebellion, showed no mercy to captives and non-combatants and was suppressed as harshly as in any other slave-owning society. Violence, too, was exercised as much against Shīʿite enclaves as against infidels. Both Zengi and Nur ed-Din had a reputation for ruthlessness and violence. If they were not loved they were certainly feared and respected. Many are the folk tales of loyal servants carrying out Zengi's orders to the letter, even if it meant waiting years holding a loaf of bread by a Euphrates ferry station for his return. Ibn Athir (1160–1233) eulogised Zengi for these very qualities.[273] Saladin's first thought on attacking Jerusalem was to take it by force. It was only the prevalence of wiser counsels that pointed out that should he not offer terms the defenders of the city would fight to the end; thus a more conciliatory line was taken. Saladin's humanity and magnanimity on this occasion was almost immediately written up to demonstrate the superiority

---

[272] A taste of this may be read in Ibn al-Athir's hostile comment on Saladin's failure to take Tyre in November 1187: 'The sole responsibility for Tyre's resistance lies with Saladin ... Failure accompanied by firm conduct is preferable to success acquired with feebleness and lassitude, and makes the king less to blame in men's judgement'; cited from Gabrieli, *Arab Historians of the Crusades*, 180.

[273] Gabrieli, *Arab Historians of the Crusades*, 50–5.

of Muslim over Christian conduct, with direct reference to the events of 1099.[274] Control of troops after a hard-pressed siege was as much a problem for Muslim commanders as for Christians. Both Ibn al-Qalanisi's (1073–1160) account of the capture of Edessa on 23 December 1144 and the eyewitness account of Abu al-Fida (fl. 1300) of the sacking of Tripoli in April 1289 and the capture of Acre in June 1291 show the problem well.[275] The victory parade of the Mameluke sultan al-Ashraf Salah-ad-Din Khalil (1290–4) in Acre in June 1291, celebrating the final removal of the Franks from Palestine, featured a display of scalps from dead Franks.[276] Neither side hesitated to slaughter captives if justified by security or military necessity. All of this may seem like pleading from relativism – the violence of one side excuses the violence of the other. Certainly there was an element of tit for tat. However, it is worth noting that no side occupied the moral high ground, despite the trend in western universities in the 1960s and 1970s to view Islam in just this ethical light and to contrast it favourably with the acts of violence of the crusaders, especially two incidents that were long-remembered in Islam: the massacre in the al-Aqsa mosque of the Muslim refugees who had surrendered to Tancred in July 1099 and the slaughter of 3,000 prisoners from the Muslim garrison at Acre by Richard I in August 1191.

Islam was riven in almost as many facets as could be imagined. It was ethnically, geographically, politically and religiously divided. It was not a monolithic whole. This division undoubtedly assisted the warriors of the First Crusade and the survival of the so-called crusader states. In the next three paragraphs advantage is taken to explore these divisions and to outline some background material on Islam.

During the period of the Crusades the Muslim world may be divided geographically into the west (North Africa and Spain), the central lands (Anatolia, Syria, Egypt and Iraq) and the east (Iran, the Caucasus, central Asia, northern India, and parts of the Indonesian archipelago). Between the eleventh and thirteenth centuries the crusades erupted into the western and central parts of the Muslim world: in Syria (1098), in Spain (1063) and in North Africa (1217, 1250, 1270). These were but a small part of the world of Islam, but they were areas that had formerly been parts of the Hellenistic, Roman and Byzantine empires. The Arab Muslims adopted the urban culture of these areas as the focus of their own settlements, and replicated Roman town planning in the founding of new towns: the agora became the *suq*, the bathhouse the *hammam*, and the road network more adapted to the exploitation of shade and the use of the camel rather than

[274] *Arab Historians of the Crusades*, 140–6; Hillenbrand, *The Crusades: Islamic Perspectives*, 316.
[275] Gabrieli, *Arab Historians of the Crusades*, 49–50, 342, 344–6, and 349 for the account of Abu al-Mahasin (1411–69) of the massacre of Franks who had surrendered under terms of safe conduct.
[276] Hillenbrand, *The Crusades: Islamic Perspectives*, 240, citing D. Little, 'The Fall of Akka in 690/1291: the Muslim Version', in M. Sharon, ed., *Studies in Islamic History and Civilisation in Honour of Professor David Ayalon* (Jerusalem, 1986), 159–82.

the wheel. The Byzantine dome became the model for mosque construction, with an eager rivalling of Christian architects in the size and magnificence of dome construction and decoration. The Roman *castella* became the basis for Muslim fortifications and palaces, just as they had in Western Europe. On buildings and artefacts vine scrollwork might replace Christian motifs, but there was much in the material culture of the western parts of Islam and that of the West that was shared. The world of Islam into which the crusaders intruded themselves was not entirely unfamiliar.

In addition it was ethnically and religiously divided. Islam was composed of many ethnic groups with differing cultural backgrounds and expectations: Arabs and Turks, Iranians, Pathans and Indians. It was with the first two ethnic groups that the crusaders dealt. There were three primary religio-political sects: Sunni, Shia, and Kharij. The members of all three sects were Muslims, and all agreed that there should be one caliph but disagreed as to how he should be selected. The caliph was the political successor of Muhammad. He defended the faith, suppressed heresy, warred against unbelievers and extended the boundaries of the *Dar-al-Islam*. The office was in many respects like that of the Holy Roman Emperor in the West.[277] For Sunni Muslims the caliph was the spiritual leader (imam) of Islam. However, the very existence of these sects threatened the political authority of the caliphate and provided fertile ground both for rebellion and the multiplication of new sects. The Sunni accepted that divine revelation was complete with the last prophet Muhammad, and accepted the legitimacy of the four elective caliphs, with Mu'wayya as caliph and imam through his kinship with the house of Quarysh, the clan to which Muhammad had belonged. The Shīites agreed that succession should be hereditary, but limited to the direct descendants of Ali (d. 660), the son-in-law and cousin of the prophet, and his wife Fatima. For them revelation was not yet completed. With the death of Ali's younger son al-Hussein in a skirmish at Karbala on the Euphrates in 680, the Shīites lacked a leader descended from the prophet; however, they remained a political force both as the opponents of the supposed false leadership and with their own imamate. Their opposition to the hereditary basis of the Ummayad caliphs was a factor in their overthrow in 750. The Shīites, however, were unable to secure the succession of a descendant of Ali and had to make do with the descendants of Muhammad's uncle al-Abbas. Of the twelve Shīte imams, of whom the last nine were descendants of al-Hussein, the twelfth – Muhammad al-Muntazar – 'disappeared' in the cave of the great mosque at Samarra in 878. He became the hidden or expected imam who will reappear as the Messiah or al-Mahdi prior to the end of the world. Following the murder of Ali in 660 the Kharijites advocated that the caliph might be elected from any worthy Muslim and that he might be deposed should he prove sinful. Islam was therefore not one body politic. Shīites ruled in Egypt from 909 until the Sunni Saladin overthrew them in 1171.

---

[277] T. Arnold, *The Caliphate* (Oxford, 1924), 9–41, summarised in Hitti, *History of the Arabs*, 185, who is followed here.

From 945 until 1055, when the Seljuks replaced them as *de facto* Controllers of the Abbasid caliphs, a Persian Shīite clan, the Buwayids, controlled both Baghdad and the caliph. They adopted the title 'amr al-Umara', or supreme commander, to justify their position – just as the Seljah protectors of the caliphs were to adopt the title 'sultan'. The crusaders came across Sunnite Turks and Arabs in Anatolia and Syria and Shīites in Egypt, and amongst the mountains of Lebanon they had dealings with a minority Shīite sect, the Ismailis, who claimed that Ismail (d. 760) was the seventh and last imam, and with an offshoot of that sect, the Assassins of al-Khaif in Syria.[278]

There was no agreed principle of succession to rulership in the Islamic world. Political power tended to follow dynastic lines, but within that framework all relatives who could might exert a claim or carve out a principality. Thus on the death of Zengi in 1146, of Nur ed-Din (1174) and Saladin (1193), the hard won unity that they had achieved was jeopardised until a strong man came to the top once again. This was a fundamental weakness and one that was to create many minor emirates, given the nature of Islamic expansion. Good as this was for artistic patronage it was a disaster in terms of presenting a united front. Personal ambition outstripped the dictates of Islam. This was to lead to violent coups and occasionally, as at the time of the First Crusade, to divisions in the Islamic body politic. In terms of the caliphal dynasties, following the death of the Prophet Muhammad in 632, the succession passed to the four righteous caliphs who were either the Companions of the Prophet – Abu Bakr (632–4), Umar (634–44) and Uthman (644–56) – or a member of his family – in this case his cousin, step-brother, and son-in-law Ali (656–60). Ali could not exert his authority over Mu'awiya, the governor of Syria, who had organised the campaigns against the Byzantines since 640. After Ali's murder in the mosque at Kufa in 661 his son al-Hasan (d. 685) was persuaded to resign the caliphate and Mu'awiya took his place. Mu'awiya sought to legitimise his position by emphasising his kinship to the former caliph, Uthman. This was to remain a weakness for the Umayyad dynasty (661–750). Nonetheless, it was with this dynasty that the notion of hereditary rulership took hold. They moved the capital of the Islamic Empire from Medina to Damascus. It was they who gave Islam a material identity and thus established much that we accept as Islamic culture today. In 698 they introduced an Islamic coinage in both gold (the dinar) and silver (the dirhem) with Arabic religious inscriptions, thus replacing the currencies of Byzantium and Persia then still current in Muslim areas. Arabic became the official language of Muslim administration, replacing Greek. Indeed, the speed with which Arabic took hold in former Byzantine provinces has been a source of debate and may reflect how imperfectly Hellenised such areas really were in the seventh century. It was they who sponsored the collection of an authorised version of the Koran in Arabic. It

[278] Hitti, *History of the Arabs*, 429–49; M. Ruthven, *Islam: A Very Short Introduction* (Oxford, 1997), 51–6.

was in this period that the greatest religious monuments of Islam were built: the Dome of the Rock in Jerusalem (685–91) and the Great Mosque in Damascus (706–14). They strengthened Sunni religious orthodoxy by sponsoring the foundation of *madrasas* (centres for the study of the Koran), the *hadith* (traditions) and the Sharia (religious law). The Abbasids (750–1258) replaced the Umayyads as caliphs in 750 in a bloody coup in which all members of the Umayyad clan were killed.[279] The Abbasids based their claim on clan descent from al-Abbas, the uncle of the prophet Muhammad. They established their capital at Baghdad and in the thirty years from 830 sought to build a new administrative centre at Samarra on the Tigris. Muslim arts and sciences derived much from non-Arab sources, particularly Hellenistic, Iranian, Turkish and Byzantine influences, some of which may be read in the *Tales of a Thousand and One Nights* written for the Caliph Harun al-Raschid (786–809). Between 800 and 1000 the Abbasids sponsored a massive programme of translations from Greek, Syriac and Persian into Arabic. The taste of the patrons was for scientific works dealing with astronomy, geography, mathematics, mechanics, medicine and philosophy rather than the literary, historical and religious corpus that had been made obsolete by the new religion of Islam.[280] They also founded the first Islamic hospital and a university in Baghdad in the 840s, apparently building on Byzantine models.[281] The dynasty lost effective political power in 945 when the Shïite Buwayid clan gained control of Baghdad. Buwayid ascendancy was lost with the entry of the Seljuk Turks into Baghdad in 1055 and the establishment of their leader, Tughril Bey, as sultan or protector of the caliph. The establishment of the sultanate meant that the caliphate took on a purely religious role that in practice it had done since 945. In 1258 the Mongols sacked Baghdad and strangled the last Abbasid caliph, al-Mustasim (1242–58). The caliphate was transferred to Cairo, where surviving members of the Abbasid family and their descendants filled the office under Mameluke patronage down to 1517. Some independent Muslim rulers did not accept the legitimacy of the Cairo caliphate and used the title themselves. The nineteenth-century tradition that the last Abbasid caliph, al-Mutawakkil III, formally passed the title to the Ottoman sultan Selim I (1512–20) in 1517 is no older than 1798, and is false. The Ottoman sultans did not regularly use the caliphal title, but seemed to have regarded it as theirs to use as the leading Muslim ruling dynasty. The sultans did, however, use it as it was convenient to their political needs and aspirations. It no longer signified any hereditary link

---

[279]   A survivor, Abd-ar-Rahman, escaped to North Africa and thence to Spain where he refounded the Umayyad caliphate.

[280]   M. Ullmann, *Islamic Medicine* (Edinburgh 1978; reprinted 1997), 7–40.

[281]   M. Dols, *Majnun: The Madman in Medieval Islamic Society* (Oxford, 1992), 45–6, 113–14; G. Makdisi, 'Muslim Institutions of Learning in Eleventh-Century Baghdad', *Bulletin of the School of Oriental and African Studies*, 24 (1961), 1–56; D. Constantelos, *Byzantine Philanthropy and Social Welfare* (New Jersey, 1968); T. Miller, *The Birth of the Hospital in the Byzantine Empire* (Baltimore, 1985).

with Muhammad's clan of the Quyarish, or with the Abbasids, but was rather a sign of God's favour.[282]

Islam was not united politically at less exalted levels of the political spectrum. Professor Bosworth has listed eighty-five principal dynasties.[283] Of these the Sunni caliphates of the Umayyads and Abbasids were challenged by the Shīite Fatimad caliphs in North Africa (909–69) and Egypt (969–1171), and by the rump Umayyad caliphate in Spain (756–1031). From the crusading perspective the following dynasties were significant: the Arabs and Berbers in Iberia (711–1492); the Great Seljuks (1037–1194), effectively divided in Anatolia and Syria at the death of Malik Shah in 1092; the Seljuks of Rum (1071–1307); the Khwarimian shahs of central Asia (1150–1231); the Ayyubids in Egypt and Syria (1171–1250); the Mamelukes (1250–1517); and the Ottomans (1300–1922). Nomad groups from central Asia and beyond also carried out long-distance destructive raids into both the world of Islam and Christendom. In 1220, at the behest of Genghis Khan (c. 1167–1227), nomadic Mongol tribes did just this, spreading a reputation for ruthlessness, slaughter and destruction before them. One group under Genghis Khan's grandson Hülegü (1256–65) set up the Il-khanid dynasty in Iran (1256–1353), whose rulers converted to Islam in 1296. Another would-be world conqueror Timur (c. 1330–1405) from Samarkand, known in the West as Tamburlaine/Timurlane, sought to fill the void created by the decline of Mongol political power. From 1386 to 1405 he mounted successful annual campaigns in central Asia, Iran and Anatolia, using Mongol tactics to secure victory. Like the Mongols before him he appeared to offer an ideal ally for the West in its conflict – first with the Mamelukes and later with the Ottomans. So much for general observations on Islam, but how did this stack up at the time of the Crusades?

As we have seen, following the death of Muhammad in 632 there was a rapid expansion in the territories subject to Islam. Within a century its adherents had reached Poitiers in central France, and in 751 defeated the Chinese at Talus in the upper Jaxartes (Syr-Darya) basin.[284] The nature of this conquest had encouraged fragmentation in local rulership and facilitated the proliferation of small clan groups ruling towns and regions. On its frontiers warriors who had fought successfully against infidels (*ghazis*), fired by the spirit of jihad, sought to raid and rule as they pleased. There had also been a dispute regarding the succession to the prophet that had produced a fundamental cleavage between Sunni and Shīite. In theory most of the Muslims in the Middle East were ruled by a Seljuk Turkish sultan owing allegiance to the orthodox Sunni caliph in Baghdad. In practice the area was one of fragmented authority with local rulers squabbling amongst themselves for local supremacy. Thus, despite its centripetal theory, centrifugalism was becoming the norm in the world of Islam by the eleventh

---

[282] Arnold, *The Caliphate*, 89–159.
[283] Bosworth, *The New Islamic Dynasties*.
[284] See Part I, p. 6.

century. This undoubtedly eased the passage of the crusaders to Jerusalem from 1097 to 1099. The crusaders would fight some of these groups; others, like the rulers of Shaizar, they would negotiate and trade with – but in all cases they could exploit the divisions.

Syria lay on the direct land route between Egypt and the cities of the Euphrates and Tigris. The Holy Land was as much the crunch point in the eleventh-century Islamic world as it had been in the days of the Old Testament prophets. The Shīite Fatimid caliphs were established in Egypt, and the Sunni Seljuk sultans were the protectors of the orthodox caliph in Baghdad and the overlords of the *ghazi* on the Byzantine frontier. Neither could afford to lose control of Syria. Between 1070 and 1075 the Seljuks captured Aleppo, Damascus and Jerusalem from the Fatimids. In 1098 the Fatimids retook Jerusalem.The coastal towns were disputed between the Byzantines, the Seljuks and the Fatimids, who in 1089 regained control of Acre, Ascalon and Tyre, the latter from their own governor or *qaudi*, ibn Abi Arqil. Incidentally, in wider Mediteranean terms, the attention that the Fatimids focused on Syria and Palestine diminished the efforts that they had previously devoted to North Africa, and certainly facilitated the Norman conquest of Sicily. Although not directed against Christians, the fighting in this area, on the pilgrimage route to Jerusalem, made life uncomfortable, not to say dangerous, for pilgrims. In 1055 the Byzantine authorities at Laodicea (Latakia) prevented Liutprand, bishop of Cambrai, from proceeding on his pilgrimage to Jerusalem because of the disturbed situation in Muslim territory. Ten years later, in 1064/5, conditions were still unstable; Bishop Gunther of Bamberg and the German pilgrims had to ward off the attacks of bandits as they proceeded to Jerusalem. Such bandits may well have come from the nomadic Tayy tribe that raided into Palestine from Transjordan.

Seljuk authority in Syria was not unified. Apart from uncontrolled raiders from the fringes of the Syrian desert, sheikhs of semi-nomadic Arab tribes tried to carve out small principalities for themselves and their families; in this they were supported by either Seljuks or Fatimids, as appropriate. The Kilab tribe gained Aleppo in 1060 only to lose it to the Seljuk-backed Uquhids in 1079. The *quadis* of Tyre and Tripoli set themselves up as independent of the Fatimids in 1070; Tyre was recaptured in 1089, but in Tripoli the family of Hasan ibn Amman retained control until its capture by the crusaders in 1109. In 1081 Ali ibn Munqidh bought Shaizar from its Orthodox bishop and set up a principality there that his great-grandson Usammah ibn Munqidh was to enjoy a century later. In 1091 Karbuqa, a Turkish adventurer, captured Mosul from the Arab Bani-'Uqayl clan and ruled it as an emir of the Seljuk empire. In this politically fragmented environment cash was often demanded from Christian pilgrims passing through the various towns. This appears to have got worse in the late eleventh century and contributed to the western perception of the ill treatment of pilgrims. However, it was not a distinction between tolerant Arabs and intolerant Turks but rather a reflection of need and opportunity. If anything the Turks were just more efficient in exploiting the pilgrim traffic than the Arabs.

The first three Seljuk sultans – Tughril Bey (1037–63), his nephew Alp Arslan I (1063–72) and Alp Arslan's son Malikshah (1072–92) – brought most of Syria and Anatolia under their rule and attempted to introduce some of the infrastructure on which to build unified authority. The greatest of these was Malikshah whose assassination in 1092 ushered in instability in the Seljuk realms and intensified the tendency to fragmentation and civil war. His brother Tutush (d. 1095) and his son Barkiyaruq (1094–1105) disputed for Malikshah's inheritance in Syria and Iran. On Tutush's death in battle in 1095 his two sons disputed the territories that their father had managed to gain in Syria: Ridwan (1095–1113) seizing Aleppo, Duqaq (1095–1103) Damascus. Ridwan further fell out with two important city governors: Janah-ad-Daulah of Homs and Yaghi-Siyan of Antioch. All of this assisted the army of the First Crusade. Kilij Arslan I (1092–1107),[285] the ruler of Rum, thought he had annihilated the crusading army at Civetot in August 1096. He then withdrew eastwards to wage war against the Danishmend Turks; this was where he was when the main crusading army invested Nicaea in May 1097. During the siege of Antioch three Muslim relieving armies approached the city and were driven off in their turn: Duqaq from Damascus in December 1197, Ridwan from Aleppo in February 1098 and Karbuqa (Kerbogha) in June 1098. They could not operate together since both Duqaq and Karbuqa hoped to gain Antioch for themselves at Ridwan's expense.

Following the fall of Jerusalem in 1099 and the aggressive and confident expansion of the crusader states in the first decade of the twelfth century, no jihad was declared against crusaders or against the westerners settled in Syria and Palestine; yet these very people were engaged in wresting land from Islam. There seemed little hope for an Islam that was fragmented, and possibly apocryphal views of the Frankish arrival coincided with the arrival of the sixth Islamic century in 1106. Yet as early as 1105 the scholar Ali bin Tahir as-Sulami an-Nahawi (1039–1106) laid out the ground rules for a jihad in terms of unity and religious purity, and called for a holy war to recover Jerusalem. His treatise seems to have attracted little attention at the time, but like Ibn al-Athir in the thirteenth century he seems to have identifed the crusade as a form of western jihad.[286] In this he was most prescient, since it was not until the time of Ibn al-Athir that it was generally appreciated that the Franks were engaged upon a holy war to keep control of their holy sites, just as the Muslims in their turn were in order to wrest them from them. Yet at first it is almost as if the concept of jihad was irrelevant to crusader–Muslim relations – at least until a sufficiently unified power base existed under Nur ed-Din and later Saladin. The commitment

---

[285] Kilij Arslan I was the son of Suleiman, the son of Kutulmush, who had brought central Anatolia into the Seljuk Empire in the 1065/70s and ruled there in the name of the Seljuks. His full patronymic was ibn Suleiman; hence the crusaders called him Soloman.

[286] N. Elisseef, 'The Reaction of the Syrian Muslims After the Foundation of the First Latin Kingdom of Jerusalem', in M. Shatzmiller, ed., *Crusaders and Muslims in Twelfth-Century Syria* (Leiden, 1993), 162–72, esp. 163.

of both these rulers to jihad is not in doubt. Nur ed-Dn had commissioned a minbar in 1168/9 to be installed in Jerusalem after the defeat of the infidels. It was eventually brought from the Great Mosque at Aleppo to the Aqsa mosque in Jerusalem on the orders of Saladin.[287] The latter had made a jihad for the recovery of Jerusalem his official policy since his seizure of Damascus on 28 October 1174, but in the period that elapsed between then and March 1187 he had spent nearly three years fighting his fellow Muslims. It was on 13 March 1187 that he formally summoned his fellow Muslims to join in a jihad against the Franks.[288] A strong Muslim leadership tended to be hostile to the Franks. However, it is misleading to suppose that Muslim unity in the late twelfth century was a reaction to the Christian presence on the Syrian coast and its hinterland. This unity would almost certainly have happened anyway since in the progress of political squabbles the strong men will eventually come out on top. Thus in 1127 Zengi emerged as atabeg of Mosul, took over the territories of many of his Muslim neighbours, and not until 1144 did he turn against his Christian neighbours, capturing Edessa. The Latins never regained this city. With hindsight, from then on they were on the defensive in the East (yet nine years later they captured Ascalon) and very aware of the emergence of powerful men in the immediate Muslim world. Just as in the West, power was acquired on dynastic lines. Two sons, Nur ed-Din in Aleppo and Safadin (d. 1149) in Mosul, succeeded Zengi on his assassination in 1146. The two brothers avoided a fratricidal war, but Nur ed-Din was prevented from occupying Mosul in 1149 when a third brother, Qutb ad-Din Maudud, was chosen ruler. Nur ed-Din had to maintain himself against the Seljuks of Rum, the Second Crusade and the Byzantine forward policy of the 1160s. He added considerably to his territories. He occupied the rump of the county of Edessa, took territory from the Armenians on the upper Euphrates and seized lands from the principality of Antioch. In 1148 he exterminated the Shīite leadership in Aleppo and in 1154 occupied Damascus. From 1164 to 1169 he contested control of Egypt with the Kingdom of Jerusalem in alliance with Byzantium. His commander Shirkuh ended the Fatimid caliphate in Egypt and reincorporated the land within the Sunni caliphate. However, his agents there showed signs of independence and thus relations between Saladin, who had assisted his uncle Shirkuh in the subjugation of Egypt, and Nur ed-Din were tense and suspicious. Not without reason, since on the latter's death in 1174 Saladin declared his independence in Egypt and sought to gain the guardianship of Nur ed-Din's son al-Malik as-Salih. He defeated the combined armies of Aleppo and Mosul at the Horns of Hammah on 13 April 1175 and within a month was formally invested with the rule of Egypt and Syria. He was not, however, recognised as the leading *mujhadin* and had not gained control over as-Salih. He was wary of the dealings of the latter and his advisers with the crusader states, and of the aggressive policy of the latter to intervene in Muslim Syria. A

[287] Hillenbrand, *The Crusades: Islamic Perspectives*, 152–61.
[288] Lyons and Jackson, *Saladin*, 239.

powerful Muslim bloc now faced the Christian states. Muslim unity had been achieved by power struggles, not by ideas of counter-crusade. Saladin's rise to power had been paralleled by the reign of the leper-king Baldwin IV (1174–85), destined for a short life with no heirs to succeed him. This resulted in power struggles within the Kingdom of Jerusalem that both weakened that kingdom internally and led to relations with the Muslims that provoked them.

Jihad or holy war derives from a view that saw the world as divided between Islam (Dar al-Islam) and the rest, the House of War (Dar al-Harb). In Islamic eschatology the whole world will be part of the Dar al-Islam before the end of time. It was thus a religious duty to expand the Dar al-Islam, and the defence of Islam was a duty enjoined upon all believers. There could be no lasting peace with the Dar al-Harb; at most a truce lasting no longer than ten years. Crusading and the existence of the crusader states should have ensured jihad, yet no jihad was declared in the aftermath of the fall of Jerusalem in 1099, and indeed for eighty-eight-years therafter. As in the Christian tradition 'holy war' can only be waged against infidels and apostates, and like the concept of holy war is a much older term than 'crusade'. Carole Hillenbrand has drawn attention to the modification of jihad theory in the tenth century following the divisions in the Abbasid caliphate. Treaty relations became possible with non-Muslim powers, the so-called House of Covenant (Dar al-'ahd). Individual warriors on the frontier might engage in an individual jihad unauthorised by the caliph.[289] Like 'crusade', 'jihad' is a term that has undergone some change of emphasis in the modern age where its generic idea of struggle has been internalised to mean the personal spiritual struggle of the Muslim to improve his religious standing with God. Although this meaning was present in the Koran, its association with warfare was to the fore right from the start; this was reinforced by the rewards promised the holy warriors (*mujahedin*) and the contrasts drawn between them and those who did not fight. Unlike crusade, however, neo-conservative commentators point out that the original meaning of jihad still has currency today.[290] Muhammad enjoined jihad on his followers. Turkish *ghazis* on the frontiers of Byzantium invoked it in the eleventh century. But it was only when a united and powerful Islam confronted the crusaders that it actually came into its own as a powerful motivating factor that enhanced the moral will to fight and to win. The victories of the Mamelukes over both Franks and Mongols justified the legitimacy of their rule and led to an elaborate jihad titulature. As the biographer of Baybars I (1260–77), Ibn abd al-Zahir (d. 1292), noted: 'he prosecuted Jihad with the utmost zeal and fought against the unbelievers, for which God rewarded him'.[291]

Certainly conflict was the basis of the relationship of the Franks in Syria with

---

[289] Hillenbrand, *The Crusades: Islamic Perspectives*, 98–9.
[290] Lewis, *The Crisis of Islam*, 29.
[291] Hillenbrand, *The Crusades: Islamic Perspectives*, 237, for the quotation, and 230–4 for discussion of the jihad titulature.

their Muslim neighbours. Yet on both sides there were apparent exceptions, even if these did not represent significant attempts to end the aggression of either side. Indeed, they did not challenge the ideological framework that Islam should be attacked or undermined or that the Frankish occupation of the holy places should be brought to an end by war. Conversions from Christianity to Islam, and vice versa, were not an unknown phenomenon in the twelfth century and seemed to have been confined to the uppermost and lowest strata of society. Fulcher of Chartres cited examples of Muslim women being baptised and starting a new life, but these presumably started out as captives.[292] Yet no record of a named Muslim's conversion has survived. Material interests rather than genuine religious conviction seem to have been the motivationg factor and from the Christian viewpoint opened a whole can of worms regarding the freeing of converted Muslim slaves, sexual liaisons and motivation. The idea of peaceful attempts to convert Muslims associated with the Mendicant Orders, and in particular Joachim of Fiori (c. 1135–1202), Francis of Assissi (c. 1181–1226) and Raymond Lull (c. 1235–c. 1315), met with general disinterest. Rather, crusade and mission were seen as connected, the one preparing the way for the other.[293] From the Muslim side both Jews and Christians might refuse conversion to Islam and continue to practise their religions openly as the so-called people of the book. In return they paid a poll-tax (jizya) and as dhimmis or non-Muslims might be subject to social discrimination or even persecution, depending on circumstances. Both sides enslaved their captives, and women were subject to sexual abuse. Freedom from slavery would follow conversion to Islam. Ibn Munqidh has many stories of Christian women marrying Muslim men, but he, like Fulcher of Chartres, has nothing to say on their social integration.[294]

Some Muslim writers – for example, Usamma Ibn Munqidh (1095–1188) in his memoirs and Ibn Jubayr of Valencia (b. 1145) in his travel journal – used their experiences of travelling in the crusader states to make comments on their own political and social systems. Ibn Jubayr was careful to sit apart from Christians whenever possible, adamant that Muslims should not stay in Christian territory unless absolutely necessary, always hoping for the destruction of the Christian states and not lacking in expletives for the Christians and their rulers, pigs and polluters.[295] He did, however, concede that the Christians were better at organising themselves and their subjects and that this in itself might pose a threat to Islam. Travelling from Tibnin (Thoron), near Tyre, to Acre he noted:

---

[292]   Fink and Ryan, *Fulcher of Chartres, A History of the Expedition to Jerusalem*, 271.
[293]   B. Kedar, *Crusade and Mission: European Approaches Towards the Muslims* (Princeton, 1984), esp. 74–84; E. Siberry, 'Missionaries and Crusaders, 1095–1274: Opponents or Allies?', *Studies in Church History*, 20 (1983), 103–10.
[294]   Hitti, *An Arab-Syrian Gentleman and Warrior*, 160; N. Christie, 'Just A Bunch of Dirty Stories? Women in the Memoirs of Usammah Ibn Munqidh', in R. Allen, ed., *Eastward Bound: Travel and Travellers 1050–1550* (Manchester, 2004), 71–87; see above, p. 312.
[295]   Broadhurst, trans., *The Travels of Ibn Jubayr*, 322–5.

We moved from Tibnin – may God destroy it – at daybreak on Monday. Our way lay through continuous farms and ordered settlements, whose inhabitants were all Muslims, living confortably with the Franks. God protect us from such temptation. They surrender half their crops to the Franks at harvest time, and pay as well a poll-tax of one dinar and five qirat for each person. Other than that they are not interfered with, save for a light tax on fruit trees. Their houses and all their effects are left in their full possession. All the coastal cities occupied by the Franks are managed in this fashion, their rural districts, the villages and farms, belonging to the Muslims. But their hearts have been seduced, for they observe how unlike them in ease and comfort are their brethren in the Muslim regions under their (Muslim) governors. This is one of the misfortunes afflicting the Muslims. The Muslim community bewails the injustice of a landlord of its own faith, and applauds the conduct of its opponent and enemy, the Frankish landlord, and is accustomed to justice from him.[296]

Perhaps the most cited source of anecdotes regarding the Franks in the East comes from Ibn Munqidh's *Book of Learning by Example (Kitab al-I tibar)*. Traditionally described as memoirs or an autobiography, it is now more appropriately described as a collection of autobiographical stories illustrating the role of fate in life, designed to instruct and to amuse, with a pronounced nostalgia for the lost days of youth. Ibn Munqidh made the usual pious pronouncements with regard to his Christian neighbours and throughout sought to demonstrate the superiority of Muslim behaviour and practice. Thus Franks do not know how to behave with regard to their women, their tables and their deportment. On the other hand there is some semblance of balance in the noting of good and bad points about the Franks, despite their lack of sexual jealousy they were brave warriors and had some of the most pious priests that Ibn Munqidh had encountered. Frankish idiosyncrecies were noted such as trial by battle and by ordeal and the forward behaviour of their women. He makes many interesting observations: on Frankish rulers and other figures like William Bures, on the smuggling of escaped Muslim slaves to safety in the villages around Acre and twice observes the superiority of acclimatized Franks to new-comers. For Ibn Munqidh Frankish and Muslim societies interacted and interlocked but the otherness of the Franks was never in doubt nor was the superiority of Islam.[297]

In 1990 Professor Kedar wrote that there was no monograph on Levantine Muslims living under Latin rule. This is still the case. The lack of archival

---

[296] Citation from Broadhurst, trans., *The Travels of Ibn Jubayr*, 316–17. Some discussion of this passage is in Maalouf, *The Crusades Through Arab Eyes*, 262–3.

[297] Hitti, trans., *An Arab-Syrian Gentleman and Warrior*, 111, 161–70; Hillenbrand, *The Crusades, Islamic Perspectives*, 259–62, 309, 347–50, 354; R. Irwin, 'An Arab-Syrian Gentleman at the Time of the Crusades Reconsidered', in J. France and W. Zajac, eds, *The Crusades and Their Sources: Essays Presented to Bernard Hamilton* (Aldershot, 1998), 71–88.

material, and the preoccupation of chroniclers with military and political events, is not conducive to such a study. Virtually nothing is known of the infrastructure by which the Muslim population was managed or controlled. They seemed to have had no formal public existence and their religion, although banned, might be practised in the breach. William of Tyre's history of the Muslim East, *Historia orientalium principum*, has not survived and is known only from citations in later works.[298] Professor Mayer has shown that between 1099 and 1110 when a town was captured the Muslims were put to the sword. With the capture of Sidon in 1110 this changed; garrisons were allowed to withdraw and the peasantry was left to cultivate the land. The villages were occupied by Muslim farmers who tilled the land under the direction of their own headman for Frankish lords who dwelt in the towns. Muslims, too, lived and traded in towns, although they were excluded from Jerusalem itself. Both Ibn Munqidh and Ibn Jubayr broadly attest these facts. As we have seen the latter painted a very positive picture of the lives of his co-religionists in the villages between Tibnin and Acre.[299] In the absence of other evidence his image has held the field. Mayer cautions, however, that the Muslims were not particularly well off, having to pay dues of 30–40 per cent on their produce and, although not subject to tithes or labour dues, might well have been subject to forced labour in the construction of castles. Muslim villagers might assist in the smuggling of escaped Muslim prisoners to safety, but they seem to have had little incentive to rebel against the Franks. Mayer cites two such incidents: one in 1113 in the Nablus area and the other at Wadi Musa in 1144, both coinciding with military operations of Muslim troops across the Jordan.[300] Necessity rather than tolerance dictated the co-existence of Franks and Muslims.

As we have seen, trade relations were maintained between Muslim rulers and the mercantile republics of the western Mediterranean. Silver and gold were brought east to purchase spices and, when not banned by the exigencies of a crusade, timber, iron and cereals as well.[301] Commercial relations governed by need and self-interest are one thing, but any assessment of cultural interactions is difficult to quantify and to assess. From Ibn Jubayr and Ibn Munqidh there are references to acclimatised westerners living in Syria who abstained from pork, adopted light clothing, enjoyed frequent baths and patronised Muslim and Jewish physicians. This 'taste for the luxuries of local life' allowed certain objects to be produced for the Christian and Muslim consumer. Such were the eighteen

---

[298] B. Kedar, 'Subjected Muslims of the Frankish Levant', in J. Powell, ed., *Muslims Under Latin Rule, 1100–1300* (Princeton, 1990), 135–74, 136–7 for citations.

[299] See p. 253 above.

[300] H. Mayer, 'Latins, Muslims and Greeks in the Latin Kingdom of Jerusalem', *History*, 63 (1978), 175–92.

[301] See p. 387 above; Hillenbrand, *The Crusades: Islamic Perspectives*, 391–408; Ashtor, *A Social and Economic History of the Near East in the Middle Ages*, 8–9, 195–200; M. Lombard, *The Golden Age of Islam* (Amsterdam, 1975), 161–204, for commodities and trade routes; D. Abulafia, 'The Role of Trade in Muslim–Christian Contact during the Middle Ages', in D. Agius and R. Hitchcock, eds, *The Arab Influence in Medieval Europe* (Reading, 1994), 1–24.

inlaid brass canteens made in Damascus in the thirteenth century. Christian themes of Madonna and child, the Nativity and the Entry into Jerusalem alternate with Muslim ornament and decorative calligraphy.[302] Yet what can be said of this behaviour other than comfort and taste? We cannot discern any deeper motive to know and to seek to understand Muslims and their religion any more than the amusing anecdotes of Ibn Muqidh can be said to reflect any sympathy with the Franks. It is no easy task to evaluate the impact that Muslim art and architecture had on westerners in the period of the Crusades. The problem of survival over the seven centuries since the fall of Acre means that we are looking at a preselected corpus of material and are unable to even guess at the number of artefacts that might once have found their way to Europe or were once owned by westerners resident in the Levant. The bulk of survivals are in cathedral treasuries and may reflect pious deposits by returning crusaders and pilgrims that endowed the objects in question with a religious significance. A prime example of this is the eleventh-century rock crystal perfume bottle from Egypt turned into the so-called fish reliquary around 1400 in the Emmerich church treasury. Such too are the so-called Hedwig glasses manufactured in Egypt or Syria in the twelfth century at Veste Coburg, the Episcopal chasuble from Bremen with the Arabic inscription 'The Almighty Sultan', and the linen cloth made in Damietta around 1097 known as 'the veil of St Anne' at Apt.[303]

When it comes to architecture the element of triumphalism is writ large. Both sides would purify and reuse the churches and mosques of each other for their own religious purposes. They might slight or reuse Byzantine or each other's fortification. The fragments of the tombs of the Latin kings of Jerusalem were reused, occasionally inverted, as decorative features in the al-Aqsa mosques and the Dome of the Rock,[304] whilst in 1291 the Gothic west door from St John's church in Acre was completely removed to be re-erected as the main entrance to the mosque of al-Nasir in Cairo. This was triumphalism and propaganda at its grandest.[305] Perhaps the strangest monuments of triumph are the two west towers of St Paul's, Worms, and those of the church at Guntersblum, together with the single west towers at Alsheim and Dittelsheim. These form a discrete group in the area between Mainz and Worms. They have been dated by dendrochronology to 1100–8, 1102, 1100–10 and 1138–48 respectively. As far as I know they are unique and may be modelled on either the Byzantine cylindrical dome or the stepped mosque tower. They are interpreted as triumphal momuments erected in the Rhineland by returning crusaders.[306]

---

[302] Hillenbrand, *Islamic Art and Architecture*, 136–7.

[303] Gierlichs and Hagedom, eds, *Islamic Art in Germany*, 12, 73–82; Hillenbrand, *Islamic Art and Architecture*, 84–5.

[304] J. Strzygowski, 'Ruins of Tombs of the Latin Kings on the Haram in Jerusalem', *Speculum*, 11 (1936), 499–509.

[305] Hillenbrand, *The Crusades: Islamic Perspectives*, 385–6.

[306] H.-J. Kotzur, Denkmäler des Triumphs', in Kotzur, ed., *Die Kreuzzuge*, 265–85.

The Muslims, like the Christians, were convinced of the truth of their religion, of their superiority, morally, intellectually and on the field of battle. They were not primarily interested in each other. As Z. Haddad has concluded, Muslim writers in the age of the Crusades rejected any possible influence in religion, ethical, moral or social values, and found little if anything to learn from the the crusaders.[307]

OUTREMER: THE FRANKISH STATES IN THE EAST[308]

It has long been known that the term 'crusader states' is a misnomer since, apart from their founders, the bulk of the Frankish population were either later

---

[307] Haddad, 'The Crusaders Through Muslim Eyes', 234–52.

[308] The bibliography for this topic is very large indeed, especially in periodical literature. What follows are the principal books and collected essays on the topic. For articles look especially in the works of Edbury, Hamilton, La Monte, Mayer, Murray, Prawer, Richard, and Riley-Smith listed in the bibliography. The Latin states are covered in all the main histories of the Crusades by Mayer (1988), Setton, ed. (1969–89), Riley-Smith (1987 and 1995), Richard (1996), and Hamilton (1998). These volumes of collected essays have major articles on all aspects of the crusader states: Holt, ed., *The Eastern Mediterranean Lands in the Period of the Crusades*; B. Hamilton, *Monastic Reform, Catharism and the Crusades* (London, 1979); B. Kedar *et al.*, eds, *Outremer: Studies in the History of the Crusading Kingdom of Jerusalem Presented to Joshua Prawer* (Jerusalem, 1982); Edbury, ed., *Crusade and Settlement*; V. Goss and C. Bornstein, eds, *The Meeting of Two Worlds* (Kalamazoo, 1986); B. Kedar, ed., *The Horns of Hattin* (London, 1992); Shatzmiller, ed., *Crusaders and Muslims in Twelfth Century Syria*; M. Balard, ed., *Autour de la premiere croisade* (Paris, 1996); Lock and Sanders, eds, *The Archaeology of Medieval Greece*; B. Kedar *et al.*, eds, *Montjoie: Studies in Crusade History in Honour of Hans Eberhard Mayer* (Aldershot, 1997); H. Mayer, ed., *Die Kreuzfahrerstaaten als multikulturelle Gesellschaft* (Munich, 1997); J. France and W. Zajac, eds, *The Crusades and their Sources: Essays Presented to Bernard Hamilton* (Aldershot, 1998); Rozenberg, ed., *Knights of the Holy Land: The Crusader Kingdom of Jerusalem*; B. Hamilton, *Crusaders, Cathars and the Holy Places* (Aldershot, 1999); M. Balard, *et al.*, eds, *Dei gesta per Francos: Crusade Studies in Honour of Jean Richard* (Aldershot, 2001); T. Madden, ed., *The Crusades* (Oxford, 2002); Edbury and Phillips, eds, *The Experience of Crusading 2: Defining the Crusader Kingdom*. The following monographs should also be consulted, virtually all have excellent bibliographies: J. La Monte, *Feudal Monarchy in the Latin Kingdom of Jerusalem* (Cambridge, Mass., 1932); R. Smail, *The Crusaders in Syria and the Holy Land* (London, 1971); A. Ben-Ami, *Social Change in a Hostile Environment* (Princeton, 1969); Prawer, *The Latin Kingdom of Jerusalem*; J. Richard, *The Latin Kingdom of Jerusalem* (2 vols, Amsterdam 1969); Prawer, *Crusader Institutions*; J. Riley-Smith, *The Feudal Nobility and the Kingdom of Jerusalem, 1174–1277* (London, 1973); S. Tibble, *Monarchy and Lordships in the Latin Kingdom of Jerusalem 1099–1291* (Oxford, 1989); P. Edbury, *John of Ibelin and the Latin Kingdom of Jerusalem* (Woodbridge, 1997); P. Edbury, ed., *Le Livre des Assises* (Boston, 2003); A. Murray, *The Crusader Kingdom of Jerusalem: A Dynastic History* (Oxford, 2000); A. Jotischky, *Crusading and the Crusader States* (London, 2004); B. Hamilton, *The Leper King and His Heirs: Baldwin IV and the Crusader Kingdom of Jerusalem* (Cambridge, 2000)); Phillips, *Defenders of the Holy land*; Lilie, *Byzantium and the Crusader States 1096–1204*; P. Holt, *The Crusader States and Their Neighbours* (London, 2004); B. Hamilton, *The Latin Church in the Crusader States* (London, 1980); A. Jotischky, *The Perfection of Solitude: Hermits and Monks in the Crusader States* (University Park, Pa., 1995); D. Pringle, *The Churches of the Crusader Kingdom of Jerusalem: A Corpus* (2 vols, Cambridge 1993, 1997; a third volume in press); Boas,

immigrants or were born in the East. Indeed, crusades were preached in the Kingdom of Jerusalem, as James of Vitry, records, and so living in a crusader state did not automatically make one a crusader. That apart, although terms like 'Frankish' or 'Latin states' may be preferable, to avoid the term 'crusader states' would be pedantic.

The chronological, geographical and governmental diversity of these states (kingdom, principality, dukedom or county) is at once apparent from the following list that gives their name in order of their foundation date: the county of Edessa (1098–1144), the principality of Antioch (1098–1263), the first Kingdom of Jerusalem (1099–1187), the county of Tripoli (1109–1289), the second Kingdom of Jerusalem or Kingdom of Acre (1187–1291), the Kingdom of Cyprus (1191–1489; then a Venetian colony until 1571), the Latin Empire of Constantinople (1204–61), the marquisate of Boudonitza (1204–1414), the principality of Achaea (1205–1429), the lordship/duchy of Athens and Thebes (1205–1460), and the duchy of the Archipelago (1207–1383). All of the last four technically acknowledged the suzerainty of the Latin emperor, and perhaps the Hospitallers on Rhodes (1306–1523) should be added too, although that polity was not a crusader state in the strict sense. All of them were terminated in violence by Muslim conquest. The Zengids, Ayyubids, Mamelukes and Ottomans variously conquered them between the twelfth and the sixteenth centuries, the driving of the Latins from the Levant being perceived as an act of legitimation.

The military and political histories of these states may be followed in the chronological table. Here the government, ecclesiastical and social history of the Kingdom of Jerusalem will be examined, as well as those states formed around the Aegean basin in the thirteenth century for which the Kingdom of Jerusalem served as a model. The four crusader states formed after 1098 around Edessa, Antioch, Jerusalem and Tripoli were autonomous and were not identical in their government; they were essentially similar however.

Of these states those in the north, Antioch and Edessa, were securely established early on. Baldwin of Boulogne was sending cash and supplies from Edessa to the crusade army besieging Antioch within weeks of taking over from the murdered Thoros. It may be that the predominance of oriental Christians in these areas helped: Antioch was primarily Greek and Edessa Armenian. Despite hostility with the Byzantines over the status of Antioch and the early loss of Edessa in 1144, there was some community of interest between the inhabitants and their conquerors at the outset. Indeed, unlike in the Kingdom of Jerusalem, Armenians, Greeks and Syrians could hold public office in both Antioch and

Crusader Archaeology; A. Boas, *Jerusalem in the Time of the Crusades* (London, 2001); R. Ellenblum, *Frankish Rural Settlement in the Latin Kingdom of Jerusalem* (Cambridge, 1998); M. Benvenisti, *The Crusaders in the Holy Land* (Jerusalem, 1970); J. Folda, *The Art of the Crusades in the Holy Land, 1098–1187* (Cambridge, 1995); Metcalf, *Coinage of the Crusaders and the Latin East*; Edbury, *The Kingdom of Cyprus and the Crusades, 1191–1374*; N. Coureas, *The Latin Church in Cyprus, 1195–1312* (Aldershot, 1997); Lock, *The Franks in the Aegean 1204–1500*.

Edessa. The Kingdom of Jerusalem was to make slow progress by comparison. Until the establishment of the county of Tripoli in 1109 it was separated from the states in north Syria by Muslim-held territory, roughly between Latakia and Acre. This made mutual support and joint action very difficult. Its control of the countryside was to remain insecure. It was subject to raids by Bedouin from the fringes of the Syrian desert, whilst the principal harbours and inland towns were still in Muslim hands and had to be captured in expensive siege operations. In addition, whilst all benefited alike from the political disunity of the Seljuk Turks in Anatolia and Syria – for some time the rulers of Aleppo and Damascus were at loggerheads and posed no military threat until 1119 – the Kingdom of Jerusalem alone had to deal with the Fatimid caliphate in Egypt. The Fatimids were effective both on land and sea and mounted three major campaigns to recapture Jerusalem in 1101, 1102 and 1105. These were withstood. To ensure communication to and supplies from the West it was essential to control the ports of Syria-Palestine and deny their use to the Fatimid navy. From their base at Ascalon the Egyptians on occasion could interdict road links between Jerusalem and its only port at Jaffa. Between 1099 and 1110, with the help of naval contingents primarily from the Italian commercial republics, all the ports of the kingdom were captured, leaving only Tyre in the north and Ascalon in the south still in Muslim hands. These were not to be taken until 1124 and 1153 respectively. The Egyptian presence in Ascalon resulted in some twenty years of conflict centred around the plains of Ramla, until that fortresss could be isolated by the construction of a series of fortresses between 1134 and 1143. On the death of Baldwin I in April 1118 the boundaries of the Kingdom of Jerusalem were essentially as they were to remain until the dissolution of the first kingdom in 1187. Despite its slow start it was to be the kings of Jerusalem who emeged as the bedrock of the Latin East and who supported the northern principalities in the twelfth century when they underwent considerable fluctuations in their fortunes in the face of a Byzantine forward policy and Muslim hostility. The Franks were not at home in the Syrian desert. It is said that their inability to exchange the horse for the camel limited their expansion to the south-west and left the desert fringes in the hands of Bedouin raiders.[309]

The crusaders were a minority amongst a Muslim majority population. This was to limit their settlement to towns, and later castles and the towns that grew up around them. In the main the countryside was left to the Muslim peasantry farming under the direction of their own headmen (*ra'is*/*rays*) for absent Frankish lords. It has been estimated that of the 20,000 who survived the First Crusade most went home in late 1099, leaving possibly 3,000 troops with Godfrey in Jerusalem – a number that fell to 200 knights and 1,000 foot soldiers by the spring of 1100 and some 300–500 knights and 3,000 to 5,000 foot in the two emerging principalities of north Syria. These were all combatants, with no

---

[309]   B. Hamilton, *The Crusades* (Stroud, 1998), 15.

information at all available for non-combatants who might have stayed on.[310] Recruitment of settlers was to be an abiding problem for the states of Outremer throughout the twelfth century. Physically it was not an attractive environment for many westerners, and from the beginning – especially after the 1140s – it was a dangerous one as well. Apart from population increase by natural means the main source of settlers were pilgrims, either those who came as religious tourists or those who formed part of the continuing crusade movement. Western pilgrims flocked to the Kingdom of Jerusalem to visit the holy sites and from their numbers new settlers were recruited, as also from those crusaders who came to fight during the twelfth century of whom some few remained as settlers. Certainly by the 1180s a second and third generation of Franks had emerged who were born in Syria, often with native Christian women as mothers, and fluent in Arabic. We have no idea of their numbers or whether their birth outstripped deaths amongst the Franks of the East. Nobles lured from the West by the prospect of a royal marriage, like Fulk of Anjou and Raymond of Poitiers, brought their own households with them, reinvigorating the noble stock of the kingdom where they did not cause offence to the older noble families. Attrition rates were high, and this accounts for the marriage market of the daughters of royal and noble households; love was not part of the bargain, the continuance of the dynasty was.

The crusader states were more or less continually at war and the recruitment of an effective army was a prime concern. As in the West this rested upon feudal tenure of land and the provision of military service. The lords and their vassals provided the army by fulfilling their feudal obligations. The principalities were divided into lordships and each lordship was further parcelled out amongst vassals as fiefs. In earlier books this process was known as sub-infeudation, and the great lords were known as tenants-in-chief and the fiefs of their vassals as sub-fiefs or arriere-fiefs. The vassals owed mounted military service as heavily mailed and armed knights (*miles/milites*), and their fiefs were intended to provide the wherewithal for them to do this. In the thirteenth century, the Hospitallers reckoned that the cost of equipping a knight came to 1,000–1,200 deniers of Tours. Some fiefs consisted of money payments alone and this reflected the urban nature of crusader society. The Church and the towns, too, provided troops for their lands. These tended to be sergeants (*serjants/serviens*), who were non-noble warriors serving as lightly mailed troops and used as either cavalry or infantry. The military service could last for up to one year, depending on need, and was unconditional within the boundaries of their respective principalities. However, military service outside the home principalities was subject to individual negotiation regarding place, duration and reward. Personal military service seems to have been the norm, with no provision for commutation to a money payment (scutage) such as had evolved in England by 1135 and which allowed the Anglo-Norman monarchs to hire mercenaries for the protection of their continental possessions. Little is known of the field armies of the north Syrian states, but in

---

[310]   France, *Victory in the East*, 133–4, 141.

the 1180s the Kingdom of Jerusalem could muster 655 knights and 5,055 sergeants in this way. The Hospitallers and Templars could provide an additional 600 knights between them. In times of crisis when a larger army was needed, recourse was had to mercenaries and to native contingents, Christian or Muslim, who served as Turcopoles (*Turcoples*) or light cavalry.[311]

La Monte has listed the most significant fiefs in Syria-Palestine; that is, those held direct from the prince. In the Kingdom of Jerusalem they were the principality of Galilee or Tiberias, the county of Jaffa and Ascalon, the county of Sidon, the principality of Montreal and Outrejordan, and the lordships of Arsur, Beirut, Blanchegarde, Caiphas, Saint Abraham and Caimont, and Toron. In the principality of Antioch they were Harenc, Margat, Saone, Cerep, and Apamea; for the county of Tripoli, Gibelet, Botron, Maraclea, Nephin, Le Puy and Tortosa; and for the county of Edessa, Mares, Ravendal Samosata and Turbessel.[312]

The Franks in the East tended to be city-dwellers, adopting the predominant form of settlement in the region since the foundation of Jericho in the Bronze Age. Commerce rather than agriculture underpinned the Latin states in the East. This, together with a concern for personal security and the need to have a viable number of Franks to support priests, might dictate this settlement pattern which was unusual in their own homelands. However, military and agricultural factors meant that they could not ignore the countryside. The land that the crusaders occupied was a devastated and depopulated one. It was essential for their survival that settlements should be re-established, and in this they met with a measure of success. Prawer has pointed out that the Franks tended to rebuild former settlements, a continuity of settlement based upon access to water and strategic positioning that was as relevant in the twelfth century as it had been in Old Testament times. In the first seventy years of the twelfth century a series of fortifications were built around which settlements grew up, and which provided both security and a market for outlying villagers. They provided not just a focus of refuge in times of war but administrative centres in more peaceful times. In other villages freestanding towers were constructed that acted both as a point of refuge and also as collection points for agricultural produce. In this colonising activity all landlords, from king to clergy, from military orders to independent lords, had a part. Muslim and Christian Syrian peasants made up the agricultural populations, tied to the land as serfs and paying between 30 and 40 per cent of their produce to their absentee Frankish lords. Except where sugar plantations and vineyards were a feature, mainly between the Beqah valley and Tyre, the serfs were exempt from labour dues on the lord's demesne because there were no manors or demesne land in the western sense since the lords were

[311] P. Edbury, 'Feudal Obligations in the Latin East', *Byzantion*, 47 (1977), 328–56; Riley-Smith, *The Feudal Nobility and the Kingdom of Jerusalem*, 21–39; Prawer, *The Latin Kingdom of Jerusalem*, 327–30, 338; Smail, *Crusading Warfare*, 88–106.

[312] J. La Monte, 'Chronology of the Latin Orient', *Bulletin of the International Committee of Historical Sciences*, 12 (1942–3), 141–202.

city-dwellers.[313] The input of the Frankish settlers may not have outlasted their military and political dominance of the region, but it was innovative in its approach.

Innovative, too, was their approach to governance, adapting western household practices to their particular needs. Whether rulership was elective or hereditary was a question very much alive at the time of the Crusades, both in Muslim as well as in Christian circles, in Europe as well as in the Middle East. The Latin settlers in Syria-Palestine undoubtedly found themselves in a hostile environment, and it was clear that if Jerusalem was to be held considerable territorial acquisitions had to be made. The personal qualities needed to mount an effective offence or defence was the prime factor in the selection of their first rulers, and to this end the leadership of a contingent of followers was essential. Military success had secured rulership for both Bohemond in Antioch and Baldwin of Boulogne in Edessa in 1098. Most of the other nobles who had gone on to Jerusalem in 1099 were intent on returning home now that they had fulfilled their vows, like Robert of Normandy and Robert of Flanders. Both Godfrey of Bouillon and Raymond of Toulouse seemed intent on remaining in the East, and both were present in Jerusalem with their households and contingents of troops. Raymond had alienated many by his attempts to carve out a principality north of the Orontes, and then by his attempt to purchase the leadership of the crusade for its push on Jerusalem and therafter delaying over the siege of Arqah. Godfrey, on the other hand, seemed free of such taints and he and his following had been the first to enter Jerusalem. On 22 July he was duly elected ruler. He declined the title of king and took instead the title of prince and advocate or protector (defensor) of the Holy Sepulchre. In doing this he showed that he shared the idea in the army that the crusaders had liberated a kingdom, but one in which God ruled rather than any ordinary mortal. There was also the notion that Jerusalem, if not all the crusader states, should be a model of the Church–king relationship as advocated by the clerical reformers, and be held as a fief of the Church. Daimbert of Pisa's installation as patriarch in December 1099 was followed by demands for control of Jerusalem and half of Jaffa. With Daimbert the investiture dispute had come East. However, Jerusalem as an ecclesiastical polity was not to happen. The departure of the Pisan fleet in September 1100 lessened his political influence and he failed to stop the nobility of Jerusalem summoning the childless Godfrey's brother, Baldwin, to assume the throne. On Baldwin I's death in 1118 there was a dispute over the succession. The throne passed to his nephew Baldwin Le Bourg, count of Edessa, rather than to his

---

[313] J. Prawer, 'Colonization Activities in the Latin Kingdom of Jerusalem', *Revue Belge de Philologie et d'Histoire*, 29 (1951), 1063–118; H. Mayer, 'Latins, Muslims and Greeks in the Latin Kingdom of Jerusalem', 175–92; Ellenblum, *Frankish Rural Settlement in the Latin Kingdom of Jerusalem*; Pringle, *Fortification and Settlement in Crusader Palestine*. The discovery of the so-called Frankish manor houses at isolated sites at Kharj al-Lawza, Karj Burj Kafriya and Kharj Salman challenges the view of Frankish settlement confined exclusively to towns and castles: see Ellenblum, *Frankish Rural Settlement*, 179–91.

direct male heir – his elder brother Eustace of Boulogne – who had returned home after the First Crusade, but whom Baldwin himself had designated as his heir on his deathbed. In 1118 the patriarch and the most powerful of the Jerusalem nobles took the pragmatic approach and offered the throne to an available and able ruler who had demonstrated his commitment to the crusader states. The hereditary principle had been set aside and those who supported Baldwin, like Joscelin of Courtenay, expected their reward. It was only with Baldwin II's own dispositions for the succession through his daughter Melisende that the crown of Jerusalem became a hereditary one with a legitimate line of succession. Frederick II Hohenstaufen was king of Jerusalem in right of his wife Isabel (Yolande), the granddaughter of Isabel and Conrad of Montferrat. By the time he arrived in Acre in 1228 his wife had died in childbirth and he was regent for his son, Conrad, the future Emperor Conrad IV (1250–4). From 1225 until 1268, with the execution of Conradin in Naples by Charles I of Anjou, the Hohenstaufen ruled the kingdom. On leaving Jerusalem in May 1229 Frederick tried to rule the kingdom on behalf of their son Conrad through baillis. This situation led to disputes between the Frankish nobles of the East and the bailli. The former regarded the Hohenstaufen as not being formally given seisen of the kingdom. This technical dispute is said to have given the Jerusalem nobility their particular penchant for legalism. The last three monarchs of the kingdom were Lusignans, jointly kings of both Cyprus and Jerusalem: Hugh III (1268–84), John I (1284–5) and Henry II (1285–91, king of Cyprus alone to 1324). They were descended from Hugh I of Cyprus (1205–18) and Alice, the daughter of Isabel and Henry of Champagne, whose claim to the kingdom had been rejected by the High Court in 1229. At a time of Mameluke and Mongol threat the political classes of the Kingdom of Jerusalem were unable to work together to exploit whatever opportunities might arise.

The rights of the crown bore very favourable comparison with regalian rights in the West. The king had the monopoly of tolls in the ports of the kingdom and in making commercial agreements with his Muslim neighbours. He had the monopoly of coinage and seems to have been able to break his vassals, often without the judgment of their peers. The royal domain (demesne) was extensive and formed the reserve from which grants were made. Godfrey could reward his followers with fiefs, revenues and concessions in ports and towns. These seem not to have been heritable but to have reverted to the crown on their death, thus re-endowing the crown. This was an element of considerable strength when compared with the alienation of the royal demesne in Western Europe.

The contingents of the various leaders of the First Crusade, and those that came east later with nobles who stayed on or came to settle for a purpose, formed the basis of the nobilities of the crusader states. Alan Murray has demonstrated that we must exercise caution in seeing the composition of these contingents as basically what they were when they left their homelands in 1096. He concludes: 'The character of the early Jerusalem nobility was determined far less by feudal and kinship ties dating from before 1096 than by events and conditions prevailing during the course of the First Crusade itself.'[314] The same might be said of the evolving nobility in the twelfth century. Self-interest rather than kinship would often direct their behaviour. They relied upon the patronage of their monarch and the latter relied upon his control of patronage to exert his authority and, by placing his followers under obligation, to ensure their loyalty. Thus there were the disputes between Fulk and Melisende in the 1130s. This was not just personal but a struggle for patronage and its rewards between the Bouillon line and the incoming Angevins. It appears, too, that the repudiation of his wife Agnes of Courtenay that Amalric I was forced to make in 1163 had more to do with concern that an ambitious and able queen might endow supporters and kinsmen from her rump county of Edessa at the expense of the Jerusalem nobility. Between 1186 and 1228 the Kingdom of Jerusalem was ruled by king-consorts, none of whom had been born in the East and all of whom had their own households and kinsmen who might hope for patronage from the new king. This led to tension between the newcomers and the native Franks.[315]

The king was advised and assisted by the Curia Regis or High Court (*haute court*). At first it consisted only of the chief vassals of the kingdom, but during the reign of Amalric I (1163–74) it was open to all vassals and rear-vassals of the kingdom. Here was an attempt to limit the growing power of the nobility by allying the crown with the lesser nobles. In practice only the leading nobles of the kingdom attended, in which case it took on the form of a royal council; but Amalric's changes did reveal the growing tensions between old and new noble families in the kingdom. The great officers of state attended. Just as in the courts of the twelfth-century West these were the household offices of seneschal or steward, the constable, the marshal, the butler and the chamberlains, together with the chancellor who headed the secretariat and kept the archives. The offices were a form of property. Thus Eudes of St Amand gave up the Marshalsea for the viscounty of Jerusalem around 1160, and John of Ibelin traded the constableship for the fief of Beirut in 1200. The king might consult the members of the *haute court*, but he was not bound to follow their advice. It also had legislative and judicial functions in that it created the various laws and acted as judge of its peers in cases that did not involve trial by battle (treason, murder and homicide). The court of Burgesses oversaw non-noble cases and might employ trial by ordeal, as witnessed by Ibn Munqidh. Just as the *haute court* might be slimmed down to act as a royal council so it might be enlarged for matters of general interest or important ceremonial purposes into a *conventus publicus et curia*

---

[314] A. Murray, 'The Army of Godfrey of Bouillon, 1096–1099: Structure and Dynamics of a Contingent on the First Crusade', *Revue Belge de Philologie et d'Histoire*, 70 (1992), 301–29, citation from 329.

[315] B. Hamilton, 'The Titular Nobility of the Latin East: the Case of Agnes of Courtenay', in P. Edbury, ed., *Crusade and Settlement* (Cardiff, 1985), 197–203; B. Hamilton, 'King Consorts of Jerusalem and their Entourages from the West from 1186 to 1250', in H. Mayer, ed., *Die Kreuzzfahrerstaaten als multikuturelle Gesellschaft* (Munich, 1997), 13–24.

generalis by the addition of the clergy and/or the burgesses. Just such a gathering was the council at Nablus that gathered on 23 January 1120, and it was in just such terms that the meeting was described by William of Tyre. With nobles, clergy and burgesses present such a gathering was in the tradition of a *parlement*, a form developing in Western Europe at the time. It can be seen that legal and constitutional developments in Jerusalem kept abreast, if not in the forefront, of similar developments in Europe. In Jerusalem, however, that development was arrested in 1187.[316]

During the twelfth century in Jerusalem, as in Western Europe, royal law codes were developed. These were known as assises, and their maintenance and safe-guarding formed an important part of the king's coronation in the thirteenth century, by which time much of the twelfth-century legislation had been lost in the upheavals following the fall of Jerusalem in 1187. In the mid-thirteenth century much of this legislation, together with what was understood to be the customary law of the kingdom, was being reconstructed and collected by Philip of Novara and John of Ibelin, lord of Jaffa in the Assises de Jérusalem.[317] The assises were declared at the Curia Regis or High Court (*haute court*) of the Kingdom. The Coronation oath mentioned specifically the legislative work of Amalric I (1162–74) and Baldwin III (1143–62). It is to their reigns that most of the assises belong, bolstering royal rights and power: the Assise of Bileis (1168), the Assise sur la ligece (*c.* 1170), Assise de Teneure, Assise de Vente, Assises des Bourgeois and the royal assise of Baldwin III. Trial by battle and trial by ordeal existed in all the crusader kingdoms in both the Levant and the Aegean and provoked surprise and interest from Greeks and Muslims alike. In the thirteenth and fourteenth centuries the Assises of Jerusalem were believed to have been copied by the other later crusader states established in Cyprus, in Constantinople and in mainland Greece.

Frankish settlers and garrisons meant the presence of Latin priests to serve their spiritual needs. From before the capture of Jerusalem a full-blown ecclesiastical establishment was in the process of evolving. The development of the secular church in the Holy Land seems to have been an *ad hoc* affair. It appears that it had been no part of Urban II's plans to set up a Latin Church in the East. His speech at Clermont is all about aid to the eastern Christians; that is, to the Orthodox Christians acknowledging one of the patriarchs of Constantinople, Antioch, Jerusalem or Alexandria. This did not include the other minority eastern Christians, namely the Armenians, Copts, Maronites and Jacobites. Little if anything was known about these separatist churches except that they were monophysite and therefore heretical; only the Armenian Catholicus had ever been in touch with Rome and that was in 1074. The behaviour of Urban's legate, Adhemar of Le Puy, was conciliatory towards the Orthodox, signalling co-operation not confiscation. Thus in late 1097 he had corresponded with

[316] H. Mayer, 'The Concordat of Nablus', *Journal of Ecclesiastical History*, 33 (1982), 531–43.
[317] Edbury, ed., *Le Livre des Assises*, for an exemplary modern edition.

Symeon II, the Greek patriarch of Jerusalem, who was in exile in Cyprus. This resulted in a joint letter to the Pope in January 1098. This showed that Adhemar recognised Symeon as the legitimate patriarch and that Symeon expected to be restored to Jerusalem by the crusaders. Yet if Urban's policy can be discerned in these actions there had also been provision made at Clermont 'that the Churches that were restored should belong to the principalities of whichever princes conquered provinces or cities from the gentiles and eliminated their religious Practices'. It has been suggested that there may have been no conflict of interest here; that this provision was intended to avoid disputes between Greeks and Latins, such as those disputes over churches then bedevilling relations between the Normans and the Greek communities in Sicily; and that Urban fully expected a strong Byzantine presence on the crusade that would receive back reconquered cities into the Orthodox fold.[318] Be that as it may, the death of Adhemar on 1 August 1098 removed the main conciliator and when, by September 1098, it was clearly understood that Alexios I would not be coming to Antioch the policy of co-operation with the Byzantines was abandoned. The leaders of the crusade wrote to Urban urging him to occupy the patriarchate of St Peter in Antioch, thus setting aside the claim of the Greek patriarch John the Oxite; this meant the end of the conciliatory policy in practice. Hamilton has adduced the anti-Greek mood of the crusading army as it advanced on Jerusalem from the fact that no Greek patriarch, neither John the Oxite nor Symeon II, accompanied it.

It is surprising that in an enterprise derived in part from the Gregorian Reform movement in the West the crusade leadership should behave in a totally pre-Gregorian fashion in the appointment of new bishops. In September 1098 Raymond of Toulouse had captured Albara and nominated his chaplain Peter of Narbonne as bishop. Albara was not a vacant Byzantine see but a new Latin creation reflecting the strategic importance of the place; it required a Latin garrison and an administrator, Peter, to run it and exercise some sort of military command there. Peter was sent to Antioch to obtain consecration from John the Oxite. Not only did this show that there was no problem about a Greek patriarch in Syria but it was an arrant case of lay interference in clerical appointments. In June 1099 Ramla, near Lydda, was captured. Again a garrison was required, and again a bishop was appointed to minister to its spiritual needs and to administer this important location between Jerusalem and Jaffa at the intersection of the road from Ascalon. This time the army chose the Norman priest Robert of Rouen as bishop. On 1 August 1099 the senior clergy present met together and elected Arnulf of Chocques (also of Rohes) as the first Latin patriarch of Jerusalem. This most impressive position had gone to the chaplain of Robert of Normandy. He was an able administrator, preacher and scholar, but his sexual peccadilloes were well-known throughout the crusade army; what is more, the

---

[318] Hamilton, *The Latin Church in the Crusader States* 1–19; J. Riley-Smith, 'The Latin Clergy and the Settlement in Palestine and Syria, 1098–1100', *The Catholic Historical Review*, 74 (1988), 539–57.

Pope had had no hand in this appointment and had to accept a *fait accompli*. After his enthronement as the first canonical patriarch on 25 December 1099, daimbert of Pisa consecrated the nominees of Bohemond of Antioch and of Baldwin of Edessa as bishops: Bartholomew of Mamistra, Benedict of Edessa, Bernard of Artah, and Roger of Tarsus. The impetus for new bishoprics and the choice of the men to fill them came from the lay rulers themselves. The early archbishops and bishops were not clerics of the first rank, either intellectually or spiritually. They had made their careers in princely households and it was as princely nominees that they held their new positions. Their primary role was administrative, economic and military, rather than spiritual. The Pope had had no hand in their appointments.

It was at least a generation before a high calibre of bishop was appointed in the Latin East in both intellectual and spiritual terms. These men were educated in the schools of Western Europe. They were aware of their place in wider Latin Christendom and also responsive to the needs of their churches men – like Aimery of Limoges, patriarch of Antioch (1140–65, 1170–96); Ralph the Englishman, bishop of Bethlehem (1156–74); Ralph of Domfront, patriarch of Antioch (1135–40); William, archbishop of Tyre (1175–84); and James of Vitry, bishop of Acre (1216–28).[319] These men sought to reverse the pre-Gregorian tendencies of the Latin Church in the East and made possible some understanding based upon their own practical experience of the diversity of eastern spirituality. Despite being displaced as patriarch of Antioch by the Greek appointee Athanasios III in 1165, Aimery displayed commendable interest in the Greek Church, Orthodox monasticism, and the churches of the Christian minorities, and it was he who established the framework for Uniate churches when he brought the Maronites into communion with Rome *c.* 1181. In the latter part of its existence the Latin secular Church had an improving episcopate that stood well within Latin Christendom as a whole. Within the East itself ecclesiastical exemptions for the various military orders, medicants and monastic communities weakened the authority of the bishops in their own dioceses. After 1187, when these were all concentrated in Acre, together with many refugee Latin bishops, all asserting their own independence from the bishop of Acre, the Latin Church became almost dysfunctional. In 1262 the offices of the Latin patriarch of Jerusalem and of the bishop of Acre were combined to create an ecclesiastical official with some authority to bring order to the chaos.

The crusaders were not ecclesiastical historians and in their first appointments had concentrated upon strategic rather than ecclesiastical concerns. The dioceses of Artah and Lydda were not former Byzantine dioceses; they merely became

---

[319] B. Hamilton, 'Ralph of Domfront, Patriarch of Antioch (1135–40)', *Nottingham Medieval Studies*, 28 (1984), 1–21; B. Hamilton, 'Aimery of Limoges, Patriarch of Antioch', in E. Elder, ed., *The Joy of Learning and the Love of God: Studies in Honor of Jean Leclercq* (Kalamzoo, 1995), 269–70; B. Hamilton, 'Ralph (d.1174)', in the *New Oxford Dictionary of National Biography* (Oxford, 2004).

suffragans of the patriarch of Antioch. Yet the patriarchates that the Latins took over were assumed to follow the former Byzantine boundaries. On paper the patriarchate of Jerusalem included four archbishoprics and seventy-four bishoprics, but by 1120 only four bishops were actually in place, reflecting the disparity between Byzantine arrangements of the seventh century and crusader reality in the twelfth. At times this created political problems, most notably with the new appointment to Tripoli in 1105. Since 1100 Raymond of Toulouse had attempted to carve out a principality for himself around the town of Tripoli. Like any prince he wanted a bishop of his own. On his deathbed in 1105, four years before Tripoli was actually captured, he appointed Hubert (Albert) of St Everard to be its first bishop. Hubert was duly installed. If there had been a Greek bishop he was either ignored or driven out. Tripoli had been a suffragan see of Tyre, but Tyre remained in Muslim hands until 1124, and Bernard of Antioch annexed Tripoli as his own suffragan see, a source of annoyance to the independent rulers of the county of Tripoli. Latin dioceses in Cilicia had a very short life, with the Latin bishops there being expelled by the Byzantine emperor by 1114. In addition, former Greek dioceses did not have the landed resources to support a Latin cathedral establishment or a Latin bishop in the style of their western colleagues. This could be a source of embarrassment and poverty for the ambitious. In 1187, however, the lands available to the Latin Church were to be drastically reduced by the conquests of Saladin.

The crusader church was not a missionising church. Its focus was in the towns where the majority of its Latin flock chose to live. Western pilgrims travelled to the Holy Land in greater numbers than ever before. As an object of western pilgrimage the Church there developed a shrine-centred religion that catered for mass pilgrimage and built large and impressive churches over or in the vicinity of the holy places associated with the life of Christ. Bernard Hamilton has emphasised that the Kingdom of Jerusalem became a Catholic country and that this was emphasised by the construction of Romanesque churches in western style with western liturgical needs, especially with the procession to the fore. In the thirty-one dioceses – fourteen of them in the Kingdom of Jerusalem, set up or taken over by the Latins – new cathedrals were constructed or old one's adapted.[320] The consecration of the new Church of the Holy Sepulchre on 15 July 1149 not only commemorated the fiftieth anniversary of the capture of Jerusalem but housed for the first time under one roof the scenes of Christ's Passion, death and resurrection. Religious tourism did provide a platform for cross-cultural intersections. Pilgrim *ampullae* (water flasks) seem to have been the favoured pilgrim souvenir from the Holy Land rather than the pilgrim badge of Western Europe. In the twelfth century these bore the names of the individual shrines where they had been acquired, but after 1187 they were all manufactured

[320] B. Hamilton, 'The Latin Church in the Crusader States', in K. Ciggaar, A. Davids and H. Teule, eds, *East and West in the Crusader States: Context, Contacts, Confrontation. Acta of the Congress held at Hermen Castle in May 1993* (Leuven, 1996), 1–20, esp. 14.

and purchased in Acre and became anonymous. Greek icons, too, found their way to the West, where they are said not only to have influenced personal religious devotions but also to have inspired Italian panel painting. It should be reiterated that pilgrims from other Christian traditions, and Muslims and Jews, were permitted to visit the holy places, and that the crusader period did witness an increase in the number of Jewish visitors from Europe.

The treatment of the Orthodox Church in Syria-Palestine changed through time. As we have seen, the clergy and army of the First Crusade had favoured ignoring or expelling the Greek clergy that they found in the churches that they had taken over. Arnulf of Chocques may have expelled the Greek monks from the the Holy Sepulchre, but the failure of the miracle of the Holy Fire in 1101 meant that his successor, Daimbert, soon brought them back.[321] Tensions though there were in the early days of the Latin settlement, it was the Greek hierarchy that were primarily affected. The bulk of the Greek clergy were left in place. Greek practice did not always accord with the Latin legalistic approach to Church organisation. In the 1220s James of Vitry experienced difficulties with Greek Church customs. He complained of the latitude given to the Greek clergy, by which he seems to have meant activities carried out by Greek priests that in the West were the preserve of bishops; such activities included the consecration of cemeteries and the service of confirmations. For all that, Orthodox spirituality did exert an influence on the western Church in the Holy Land. St Katherine's monastery on Mount Sinai continued to function as an orthodox monastery and was held in high esteem by westerners. Pilgrims visited this and other Orthodox monasteries and drew religious inspiration from what they saw there. Greek and Latin monasteries were built side by side on the Mount of Olives, Mount Tabor and Mount Carmel, and a mixed community of Greek and Latin monks seems to have been established on the latter in the 1180s.

There were relatively few new monastic foundations in the Holy Land. Security and distance from mother-houses in Western Europe may have been a factor here, but of more significance was the emphasis in the East on the importance of the holy places; a shrine-centred church and the demands of monastic solitude did not sit well together. Two Benedictine houses established in 1099/1100 were refoundations of earlier Latin shrine churches founded by the Amalfitans: Our Lady of Josaphat at the tomb of the Virgin Mary outside the eastern wall of Jerusalem had been founded in the late eleventh century, and St Mary Latin by 1023. Both received considerable royal patronage: Queen Melisende chose to be buried at the former monastery. In the first decades of the twelfth century two Benedictine nunneries were established at St Anne's in Jerusalem and at St Lazarus in Bethany, and Augustinians were placed at the Church of the Nativity in Bethlehem. New foundations seem to have come late in the day, some inspired

---

[321] For a different version of this story, see Riley-Smith, 'The Latin Clergy and the Settlement of Palestine, 1099–1100', 539–57; Jotischky, *Crusading and the Crusader States*, 141–5, for a summary of the treatment of the Greek Orthodox clergy.

by the desire to discover new sites of pilgrim interest such as the Cluniacs on Mount Tabor. The Premonstratensians established themselves at St Joseph's at Ramla and at St Samuel's at Montjoie in the 1150s, whilst in the same decade the Cistercians appear at Belmont (1157) near Tripoli and at Salvatio (site unknown) in 1161. In a countryside that had long served as a refuge for hermits, the western eremitical tradition was reintroduced between the 1120s and the 1160s by Bernard of Blois at Jubin and Elias of Narbonne in the Kedron Valley. The work of these men and others following an eremitical tradition on the boundaries of settled monasticism has been seen by Jotischky as breaking down the formal distinctions between monk and hermit, constituting something akin to unofficial reform foundations.[322] Latin monasticism in the Holy Land was vibrant and out-reaching. It did not wither on the vine but was brought to an effective end by the conquests of Saladin in 1187 and 1178. The new mendicant orders were to appear during the 1220s and to form a loyal arm of the papacy in that rich mix of ecclesiastics in Acre.[323]

The question to what extent an integrated nation evolved in the Frankish states of the East has formed a topic of debate since Louis Madelin coined the phrase 'une nation franco-syrienne' in 1916. French historians such as Grousset and Richard have stressed the positive side of this question, whilst Prawer and Smail have made a more muted assessment: cultural synthesis versus marginalisation and segregation.[324]

Linguistically and biologically the settlers and the native population remained distinct. French was the language of the Frankish minority: Norman in Antioch, Provençal in Tripoli, *langue d'oïl* in Edessa and Jerusalem. By the thirteenth century the purity of its *langue d'oïl* was something of a matter of pride. However, a second generation of Franks born in Syria could speak Arabic; Ibn Jubayr described the Christian clerks writing Arabic in the customs house at Acre, but these might have been Syrian Christians. There had always been bilinguals around, men who must have led interesting lives but about whom we know very little. Men like Herluin on the First Crusade who acted as interpreter to Peter the Hermit in his interview with Kerbogha, and the unnamed renegade Englishman who according to Matthew Paris was captured in Hungary in 1241 whilst acting as an interpreter for the Mongols. It is interesting that the leaders of the Fourth Crusade could not find one of their number who spoke Greek and were forced to rely upon Byzantine interpreters.[325]

[322]   Jotischky, *The Perfection of Solitude: Hermits and Monks in the Crusades States*.

[323]   A. Jotischky, 'The Mendicants as Missionaries and Travellers in the Near East in the Thirteenth and Fourteenth Centuries', in R. Allan, ed., *Eastward Bound* (Manchester, 2004), 88–106.

[324]   L. Madelin, 'La Syrie franque', *Revue des deux mondes*, 38 (1916), 314–58; R. Smail, *The Crusaders* (London, 1973), 182–7; and A. Murray, 'Ethnic Identity in the Crusader States: The Frankis Race and the Settlement of Outremes', in S Forde *et al.*, eds, *Concepts of National Identity in the Middle Ages* (Leeds, 1995), 59–74, for a summary of the debate.

[325]   Hill, trans., *Gesta Francorum*, 66; P. Jackson, 'The Crusade against the Mongols (1241)', *Journal of Ecclesiastical History*, 42 (1991), 1–18, esp. 8–9; Lock, *The Franks in the Aegean*, 295–6.

At the high political level marriages with Armenian or Byzantine princesses might be necessary, but the rest brought womenfolk from their homes when they could. Those who could afford it seemed to have a distinct preference for western partners. Poorer knights, sergeants and merchants intermarried with the native Christian women. Usummah ibn Munqidh, however, tells us that marriage with a Muslim could only take place if she had first been baptised. The children of such mixed marriages were known as *poulani*. They took the religion of their father, but were generally written down in the literature of the West as being characterised by indolence.

In all the crusader states in the Levant, and in Cyprus and Greece, high attrition rates of men in warfare meant that women enjoyed a position of greater possibilities for the exercise of power than their sisters in the West. They could inherit fiefs if there were no male heirs. They were the legal guardians for their children, who did not become wards of the king as in the West. If heiresses they could not just be married off at royal behest; instead they were offered a choice of three suitors of equal or superior status to themselves, none of whom they were obliged to accept.

Ibn Munqidh drew a sharp distinction between acclimatised westerners and newcomers; the latter being unfamilar with the courteous relations between Franks and distinguished Muslim visitors. Many Franks adopted a penchant for eastern customs, baths, fresh fruits and light fabrics. Items like silk, cotton, oranges, sugar that were either unknown in the West or were prohibitively expensive there as luxury items were available in quantity in their new homes. Their accommodation was the same as that of the natives: stone houses built around a courtyard secluded from the outside, with integral fireplaces and chimneys – the earliest examples of such features in houses occupied by westerners in the Middle Ages.

For the rest the legal status of Muslim and other native Christians was one of be seen but not heard. Ibn Munqidh perhaps provides the clue here; status was everything and it was better to be a distinguished Muslim visitor than a member of a powerless if useful group of native merchants or serfs. Working with *rais* (native serfs) in the running of an estate, segregating non-Catholic worship, and denying political and legal rights in the courts of the kingdom was not the stuff of integration. Murray has convincingly demonstrated the existence of a foundation myth amongst the Franks of Outremer, discernible in the pages of Fulcher of Chartres and William of Tyre. However, it was a Frankish nation that was envisaged not a Franco-Syrian one; the Franks remained a race apart from the natives of Syria-Palestine and were eager to mark their distinctiveness.

The field of crusader art is a specialist one and readers are referred to the references under Buchthal, Folda, Hunt, Kühnel and Weitzmann in the bibliography.[326] The great debate has been whether this was an area of true cultural

---

[326] Brief overviews of crusader art may be found in Setton, ed., *A History of the Crusades*, IV, the whole volume being devoted to art and architecture; Smail, *The Crusaders in Syria and Palestine* 123–81; Jotischky, *Crusading and the Crusader States*, 145–9.

intersection or an art-historical construct. In the main it seems that acculturation and assimilation were possible in the fields of art and architecture. The Melisende Psalter, executed sometime after 1136, contains western illuminated work under Byzantine inspiration, bound in a Byzantine ivory cover with Byzantine silk work on the spine. The 1160s and 1170s seem to have been a period of artistic co-operation, most notably in the Church of the Nativity at Bethlehem where Byzantine or local mosaicists were at work using Byzantine imagery and subjects in their decorative cycles. Byzantine crosses and chalices were appreciated in the West, as the large number of examples in western churches demonstrates. Much of this was booty after the Fourth Crusade, especially in the Treasury of San Marco in Venice, but some was earlier. Western pilgrims liked to purchase flasks as mementoes of their pilgrimage, and they became susceptible to the value and use of icons in their personal worship. Icons presented to the Monastery of St Katherine in Sinai by western pilgrims in the thirteenth century showed not just an adoption of a Greek spiritual device but, more often than not, a mixture of western and eastern styles in one artefact.[327] Byzantine influence on western art is not in doubt, but the relationship between western and eastern artists, between immigrant and native, is. One of the great problems is that the artists are anonymous, and sometimes their attribution to eastern or western camps is suspect. It is clear that Frankish patrons did not disdain native craftsmen, even if they denied them legal and political integration. It is all very reminiscent of Latin American craftsmen and Renaissance patrons. It is time that crusader art is reframed, as art historians have indicated for more than a decade, with the traditional Eurocentric conceptualisation of crusader art being replaced with one that privileges an intercultural perspective.[328]

The settlers in the Frankish principalities set up in Constantinople, mainland Greece, and the Aegean islands in the wake of the Fourth Crusade bore many similarities to the social condition of the Franks of Outremer. They were a tiny minority population in a landscape dominated by Greeks. After the influx of some crusaders and other settlers from the Levant to Constantinople in late 1204, there was no large-scale immigration thereafter. The continuator of William of Tyre wrote 'and I tell you if the emperor Baldwin had settled Constantinople as Guy [I, 1192–4] did the island of Cyprus [by advertising for settlers in Cilician Armenia, Antioch and Acre] he would never have lost it'.[329] The Franks in the Aegean did advertise for settlers in both Syria and the West, but Cyprus proved more attractive. This apparent failure had one advantage. It eased pressure on landed resources and allowed for an accommodation to be worked out with

---

[327] K. Weitzmann, 'Thirteenth-Century Crusader Icons on Mount Sinai', *Arts Bulletin*, 45 (1963), 179–203; K. Weitzmann, 'Icon Painting in the Crusader Kingdom', *Dumbarton Oaks Papers*, 20 (1966), 49–84.

[328] C. Farago, ed., *Reframing the Renaissance* (New Haven, 1995) for just such an approach to Latin American art in the period 1450–1650.

[329] M. Morgan, ed., *La continuation de Guillaume de Tyr (1184–1197)* (Paris, 1982), 138–9.

Greek landowners without recourse to the wholesale dispossession that was carried out in Syria and later on in Cyprus. This was possibly the single most important factor that allowed the Latins to maintain their foothold in Greece until the fifteenth cenutry.

Politically and militarily they were just one more tessera in the complex mosaic of Balkan ambitions and princedoms. From the 1230s, when the first crusades were preached to aid the Latin Empire, Constantinople proved an unpopular crusade destination and the military support that might have just tipped the balance in favour of the Franks eluded them. They were surrounded by enemies as powerful, or as weak, as themselves and were unable to knock out their rivals: Bulgarians, Epirote Greeks and the Byzantine Empire in exile at Nicaea. All three prevented their expansion, and the latter ultimately recaptured Constantinople in July 1261.

The Latin Empire was set up on 16 May 1204 when Baldwin of Flanders was crowned Baldwin I of Constantinople in the Hagia Sophia. The ritual and the regalia were designed to appeal to the Greeks of Constantinople and win their support for the new regime. In this it had some success, but the family origins of the new Latin emperors and their early signs of military weakness meant that this empire was never taken seriously. Its emperors weren't accorded imperial status during its active life down to 1261; it was after 1267 when the claims to that empire passed to powerful rulers in the West like Charles I of Anjou that this occurred. It was in theory, if not in practice, the suzerain of the other western states that grew up around the Aegean basin after 1204. However, they proved both more powerful and more enduring than their suzerain. Those in Greece established themselves on a firmer foundation and by the 1230s were sending substantial aid in men, money and ships to Constantinople, whilst the Venetian dominions in Crete, Euboea, Messenia and the Cyclades were very much Venetian-controlled territories doing the behest of the Venetian senate or direct Venetian colonies. In 1262 the anonymous annalist of the abbey of Santa Justina at Padua wrote the epitaph of the Latin Empire when he described it as 'just the shadow of a great name (tantum magni nominis umbra)'.[330]

In October 1204 Boniface of Montferrat, who had established himself as king of Thessaloinka and who saw himself as rivalling the Latin Empire, set out to conquer the Greek peninsula. His conquest of central Greece was rapid and he began the siege of Nauplia by late 1204. It was from Nauplia that William of Champlitte and Geoffrey of Villehardouin set out to acquire the rest of the Peloponnese, presumably as a fief to be held from Boniface. They had subdued the west and centre of the peninsula within a year, but the conquest of the southeast was to take until 1249 and their northern frontier with Epiros was to remain insecure. Boniface's death in Thrace in September 1207 ended any ambitions he might have had of setting up a kingdom independent of the Latin Empire. By

---

[330] Cited in Lock, *Franks in the Aegean*, 67.

1209 the principalities of central and southern Greece had acknowledged the suzerainty of the new emperor Henry (1206–16). The lordship, after 1260 duchy, of Athens and Thebes and the principality of Achaea vied for dominance in the peninsula during the first half of the thirteenth century. Success lay with the Villehardouin princes of Achaea. The magnificence of the Villehardouin court in the 1240s was described eighty years later by Marino Sanudo: 'he [Geoffrey II of Villehardouin, 1228–46] had in his court eighty knights at his service which were paid with gold ingots as well as with the necessary items of support. For that reason knights were coming to the Morea from France, Burgundy and particularly from Champagne, which was his native place.'[331] The principality received refugees from Constantinople in 1261. But two years previously its prince, William of Villehardouin (d. 1278), had been captured by Michael VIII Palaiologos and his release in 1261 was agreed only in return for the surrender of the key fortresses of Mistra, Maina and Monemvasia. From these bases the Greeks sought to recapture the Peloponnese, a task that was not completed until 1429, but was pursued sufficiently rigorously in the 1260s that William had to seek military help from the Angevins of Naples, who effectively took over the principality after his death. By the beginning of the fifteenth century the Ottoman Turks had emerged as the new power to be reckoned with in the Aegean. Western resistance to them rested primarily with the fleets of the Hospitallers and the Venetians, allied together on occasion, and reinforced by papal galleys in naval leagues, a new form of crusading expedition. Nonetheless, the Turks proceeded to capture Constantinople in 1453 and to extinguish the Latin states in Greece by 1460.

The Latins in Greece were a tiny minority amongst the majority Greek population and as such they tended to be urban dwellers, as were their compatriots in Syria. This was also to be true for the Catalans who took over the duchy of Athens and Thebes in 1311. The Greeks were Christians and their leaders could not be segregated and marginalised in quite the same way as the Muslims, Jews and oriental Christians of Syria-Palestine. Intermarriage too was a possibility, but partners from home seemed to have been the favoured option as in Syria. The Greeks in the countryside were left to their own priests and religious practices. They were the serfs who tilled the soil and paid a proportion of their crops to their lords, be they Latin or Greek. For some the arrival of the Latins had meant the possibility of stability and peace, and there was a measure of co-operation and assimilation. Their leading men served the Franks as castellans and sat on their councils. Castles were built or former Byzantine strongholds repaired, and freestanding towers were placed in villages as both centres of refuge and as collection and administrative centres. Whilst Constantinople was an important commercial centre of long standing in Venetian trading control throughout the time of the Latin Empire, the rest of Greece was incorporated into that trading

---

[331] C. Hopf, ed., *Chroniques gréco-romaines* (Berlin, 1873; reprinted Brussels, 1963), 101.

network. The twice-yearly Venetian fleets sailing to Constantinople called regularly at Negroponte (Chalkis) to collect the agricultural and natural resources of mainland Greece brought to that port.

As in the crusader states, the prince had extensive arbitrary powers and enjoyed the usual feudal dues and services. Government followed the household system of the West, and the law code or assises were said to be modelled on those of the Kingdom of Jerusalem. Each of the princes was advised by his council (*haute court*), which had both consiliar and judicial functions; but unlike those of the Kingdom of Jerusalem, Venetians, as appropriate, and Greek landowners (*archontes*) had a voice. The prince might make a judgment on his own authority. Landed estates formed the basis of imperial and princely revenues, but plunder too seems to have formed an important part of income, and this might include piratical raids at the expense of Christian shipping. This last was particularly the case with the Venetian rulers of the Cyclades.

The secular church that evolved after the conquest was an *ad hoc* development. It was not a missionising church. In Constantinople Papal legates like Pelagius concentrated upon winning over the Greek clergy to the Latin rite, but this met with no success and much tension in the city. In Greece the native clergy were left well alone; any attempts at interference by zealous archdeacons met with violence. It was also not a rich church. There was a lack of western parishioners to maintain a widespread church organisation, and what there was was confined to the principal towns. This was reflected in the very few western structures erected in Greece, confined to the principal churches at Andravida and Negroponte and the Cistercian churches at Issova and Zaraka. For the rest, Greek churches were taken over with minimal alterations. There were never the holy places of Latin Syria to encourage western pilgrims, and the nature of the conquest was in danger of reducing the Church to penury. In mainland Greece the conquest had proceeded a year or even two years before a diocesan structure was introduced, and this led to problems for churchmen gaining back the rights and revenues enjoyed by their Byzantine predecessors, even though these were often inadequate to maintain a Latin Episcopal establishment. The dispute was not finally settled until 1223. This led to some dioceses folding before that date, being too poor to support a bishop and even a truncated cathedral chapter. The Latin Church in Thessaly was brought to an end by 1211 when that area fell to the Greeks of Epiros, whilst the 1260s saw the virtual end of isolated Latin churches and monasteries in southern Greece with the raids of the Byzantines from Mistra. By the 1260s the Latin Church was virtually just holding on. It had lost an active patriarch with the recapture of Constantinople in 1261, although titular appointments were to continue until well into the nineteenth century. The standard of the early Latin bishops was not high, but ironically this was to improve considerably during the thirteenth century as papal provision to dioceses and benefices took effect. Increasingly, members of the mendicant orders were appointed to bishoprics, and this might have been in line with the poverty of some of those dioceses. Only William of Moerbecke (*c.* 1220–86), archbishop of

Corinth from 1278, took an interest in the language and literature of classical Greece when he set out to translate the whole Aristotelian corpus into Latin. From the remains of buildings, frescoes and icon painting it would seem that Latin influence was virtually non-existent in Greece.

The full spectrum of western religious orders was to be found in Frankish Greece, both male and female: Benedictines, Cistercians, Premonstratensians, Augustinians and the mendicant orders. Sadly very little is known of their early history, especially of the Benedictine and Cistercian orders. The first Franciscan foundation was said to have been made by St Francis himself at St Mary of Sisi at Eikosimia on Cephalonia.[332] Until 1263 the Franciscan houses in Greece and the Aegean formed part of the province of the Holy Land, indicating the crusading affiliation between Outremer and the Frankish states in the Aegean.[333] The Cistercians had been involved with the Fourth Crusade and with the conquest from the start, with twelve monasteries and nunneries established during the thirteenth century. It was they who chose sites in the countryside at Daphni, Issova and Zaraka. The rest were based in the principal towns of the principalities. Like the other exempt orders – the Templars and the Hospitallers – the mendicants fell foul of the local clergy with regard to mortuary fees and the like, and as in the Holy Land in the thirteenth century this elicited papal interference in the fourteenth century. Any rural presence came to an end during the 1260s. Nunneries were closed and their inmates sent to mother-houses in Italy. The Greek religious houses were left alone. It was only at Daphni that a Greek house was taken over by Latin monks, but this may have been deserted by 1205. Mount Athos, in particular, retained its status. The damage incurred there, sometimes attributed to the Franks, was in fact inflicted under Michael VIII Palaiologos as he tried to enforce the Church Union of the 1274 Council of Lyons. St Katherine's monastery on Sinai owned lands in Crete. These possessions were respected under Venetian rule, with Greek monks left in charge. The Latin Church had made little headway in Greek lands and left behind very few monuments.[334]

As in Syria-Palestine women in Frankish Greece enjoyed rights denied their sisters in the West. Second and third marriages were not uncommon in this frontier society, but women could not be forced to remarry against their will. They could hold fiefs exercise regencies and be custodians of their infant children. Following the capture of William of Villehardouin at Pelagonia in 1259, along with most of the knights of southern Greece, a parliament was summoned

---

[332] I would like to thank Nicky Tsigourakis for this reference. His forthcoming thesis on Latin monasticism in Greek lands will shed much light on this topic.

[333] J. Moorman, *A History of the Franciscan Order to 1517* (Oxford, 1968), 168.

[334] E. Brown, 'The Cistercians in the Latin Empire of Constantinople and Greece, 1204–76', *Traditio*, 14 (1958), 63–120; P. Lock, 'The Latin Secular Church in Mainland Greece', *Medieval History*, 1 (1991), 93–105; Lock, *The Franks in the Aegean*, 193–239; Lock and Sanders, eds, *The Archaeology of Medieval Greece*.

to meet at Nikli in 1261 to make arrangements for their release with Michael VIII Palaiologos. Wives represented their absent husbands at what became known as the *parlement des dames*. Nowhere in Western Europe in the thirteenth century could there be found anything to parallel this assembly.[335]

Over time the western settlers in Greece became assimilated into the majority culture. By the fifteenth century Frankish Greece came to an end, not just by Greek and Ottoman conquest but because the Latins had become Greeks in all but name. During the thirteenth century this was not the case, however, and Latins seemed to wish to keep themselves distinct. Since both Greeks and Latins were Christians there was no canonical impediment to mixed marriages, yet the Byzantine historian Nikephoros Gregoras recorded that it was the custom of the Latin nobility not to contract marriages with Greeks, and the Catalan chronicler Ramon Muntaner observed that the wealthy and knightly classes of Frankish Greece took their wives from the best French houses and did not marry a lady who did not descend from a French knight. He also noted that they prided themselves on the purity of their spoken French.[336] By 1300 it would appear that the upper levels of Frankish society sought to preserve their racial and linguistic purity. In 1311 the Catalans who took over central Greece married the widows of the men that they had slain in the battle of Halmyros; their preference too was for western women. Nonetheless, by the 1240s a generation of Franks had grown up who could speak fluent Greek and who were able to work with and trust Greeks of a similar class to their own. In 1336 Pope Benedict XII castigated those Italians and other Catholics on the island of Euboea who had married Greek women and attended Orthodox services because of a lack of Catholic partners and priests. Mixed marriages had been taking place in Constantinople since the twelfth century without attacting adverse comments. These comments only seemed to emerge at times of political tensions. The same was true of the *gasmouloi* or children of mixed parentage. They appear for the first time in the pages of the Byzantine chroniclers Akropolites and Pachymeres in the context of the Greek capture of Constantinople in 1261. They were said to have the discretion and caution of the Greeks, combined with the ardour and pride of the Latins; but whose side were they on? Interestingly, they usually served with the Greeks. In both these last anecdotes there is a distinct move of Latins into the Greek social and cultural world.[337]

---

[335] Lock, *The Franks in the Aegean*, 302–5.
[336] Lady Goodenough, trans., *The Chronicle of Muntaner* (2 vols, Hakluyt Society, London, 1920–1), II, 627.
[337] Lock, *The Franks in the Aegean*, 266–309.

WHEN DID THE CRUSADES END?[338]

Crusading ideals and values persisted for a very long time, surviving to this day as an adjunct to spin. Postmodernism, with its emphasis on relativism and the validity of all narratives of experiences, may have helped this process. The so-called pluralist approach to crusading has expanded the world of crusading enormously, adding expeditions against heretics, against Christian rulers, and against the Turks to the canon of the Crusades as originally laid down by Edward Gibbon. But if we confine the term 'crusade' to a military expedition authorised by a pope with a stated defensive objective in which participants took a vow to see the campaign through and for which they received indulgences, then perhaps, in our current state of knowledge, we should limit crusading to the fifteenth century. Certainly it might be argued that the shepherds' crusades of 1251, 1309 and 1321 should not have been included on these grounds. Yet they exemplify what ordinary people understood by crusade and might well lead us to ponder what was understood by crusade by the thousands of poor pilgrims who departed for the First Crusade in April 1096. Would they have been classed as crusaders by the definitions of crusading emerging at the end of the twelfth century?

Expeditions in the sixteenth and seventeenth centuries were backed by the papacy, and there were indulgences. However, the printing of these documents in the fifteenth and sixteenth centuries was aimed at raising money from purchasers and not seeking their personal involvement or commitment to a crusade. From the point of view of the participants, most of these were professional soldiers and mercenaries and it is unknown if any of them took a crusading vow. In this category come the naval league that won the victory at Lepanto in October 1571, the Spanish Armada of 1588, the various heroic sieges at Malta in 1565, Nicosia in 1570 and Heraklion between 1645 and 1669, the wars in the Morea waged by the Holy League of 1684–1718, and the activities of the Hospitallers on Malta until their expulsion by Napoleon in 1798. R.C. Anderson wrote about many of these campaigns,[339] with no reference to crusading, focusing on them as aspects of the history of naval warfare.

From the time of Pius II (1405–64) and of Benedetto Accolti (d. 1464) the marvellous and unexpected success of the First Crusade had become a great theme of humanist literature, held up as an example not only to would-be crusaders, if there were any, but to a much wider audience, perhaps seeking not just information and diversion but guidance in their lives. This certainly comes through in Torquato Tasso's (1544–95) *Gerusalemme Liberata* of 1581. Crusading was becoming a set of values rather than a programme for action. In this way

---

[338] Riley-Smith, *What were the Crusade,?*; Housley, *The Later Crusades*; K. Setton, *Venice, Austria and the Turks in the Seventeenth Century* (Philadelphia, 1991), who cites Paruta on p. 12; R. Black, *Benedetto Accolti and the Florentine Renaissance* (Cambridge, 1985).

[339] In his *Naval Wars in the Levant, 1559–1853* (Liverpool, 1953).

it is still with us today. If we are to believe the report of the Venetian historian Paolo Paruta to the doge and senate of Venice in February 1596, the role of the papacy in the crusading movement was becoming a mere formality. He noted that formerly the popes were central to crusading but that now they had endorsed proposed campaigns rather than summoning them and that their endorsement was valued for the sense of justice that it might bring. Paruta noted that in the past a summons from the Pope had mobilised great armies against Saracens and infidels, but that the zeal for religion had diminished. Crusading had already taken its place in the golden past, a fit subject for historical painters from Bernardo il Pinturicchio (1454–1513) to Karl Theodor von Piloty (1826–86).

CONCLUDING REMARKS

It was not uncommon in the 1950s and 1960s to see the Crusades from a long historical perspective and to write them off as unsuccessful (whatever that meant) and as a futile waste of time, and to compare the participants unfavourably with their hosts or opponents the Byzantines and the Muslims. In many ways this was a return to the view of the Enlightenment historians of the eighteenth century. Today, in current affairs, with the involvement of western troops in the Middle East, history appears to have returned to haunt the so-called 'new crusaders'. It is impossible to write the history of the Crusades without some reference, however unhistorical, to 9/11 and its aftermath. Whatever perspective and interest that we approach the Crusades from we have to make up our own minds.

For me they are a very positive series of events involving adaptation, invention and innovation on the part of a significant group in western society. Certainly they tell us as much about the history of Western Europe as the history of the Near East. The establishment of the crusader states in the Levant was no mean feat, as was their political survival for two centuries. Just as Charles Martel in 732 and the Byzantines, by their continued existence, are hailed as the bulwarks of western Christendom, so too should the crusading states share in some of that praise. They undoubtedly held up the advance of Islam into south-eastern Europe and provided something of a solution for dealing with the advance of the Ottomans from the fifteenth century onwards.

Their legacy in terms of an evolving Franco-Syrian culture, the relations between Catholic and Orthodox, the symbiosis between Franks and natives, may still form the focus of debate. The long-term contribution to the Levant may be difficult to measure, but in terms of ideas it has cast a long shadow, evident in statuary, films and logos.

It might once have been fashionable to dismiss the Crusades as violent, barbarous and cruel, based upon morally dubious grounds. We must never forget, though, that the crusaders were men of their time operating within the values of that time, and that they should not be judged by modern ethical and moral standpoints any more than their Muslim opponents should. Western saints like Bernard, Bridget and Francis were intimately involved in crusading, and in their time widely acclaimed for being so.

It is clear that the idea of crusade was an evolving idea and ideal that came a long way from the early thoughts of Gregory VII and the speech of Pope Urban II. Much of this evolution was rapid within a century of 1095. Some of it was long term and subtle, as in its contribution to western ideas of chivalry and romance and in the linking of crusader and warrior for the truth, crusade and campaign for the good – ideas current in our present use of the term.

The Crusades continue to be thought of in terms of military confrontation between Christendom and Islam. This was an important side, but it was just one side. There was of course much more to them than just warfare. Their economic, political, religious and cultural implications were enormous. It is their cross-cultural intersections that provide the most fruitful area for study today.

It was not specifically anti-Jewish or anti-Muslim feelings that generated the Crusades but the very real desire that Christian holy places should be recovered for Christendom and retained in Christian hands. If today we realise that no war is holy, and that negotiation, reconciliation and a sharing of sacred space is better than conflict and destruction, then this is no small contribution that crusading might teach the modern world.

VII
SELECT BIBLIOGRAPHY
OF PUBLICATIONS MAINLY
IN ENGLISH

I cannot claim to have read every book or article in this bibliography. The listings here are intended as a source of enlightenment and information on all topics covered in this book. Many of them provide sound qualifications to the generalisations necessarily indulged in within the main body of the text and should provide a sound basis for further work.

The bibliography is laid out as follows:

(A) Collections of sources in translation
(B) Specific sources in translation
    1   Latin and Old French sources
    2   Armenian, Greek, Jewish and Syriac sources
    3   Muslim sources
(C) Principal editions of selected western primary sources
(D) Secondary sources
    1   Bibliography
    2   Reference works
    3   Collected essays
    4   Books and articles
    5   The Crusades on the Internet

Articles by Hamilton and Mayer that have appeared in collected studies are marked by asterisks indicating the appropriate collection, which appears in bold under their names.

(A) COLLECTIONS OF SOURCES IN TRANSLATION

Allen, S.J. and Amt, Emilie, eds, *Readings in Medieval Civilizations and Cultures 8: The Crusades, A Reader* (Peterborough, Canada, 2003).

Brundage, J.A., *The Crusades, A Documentary Survey* (Milwaukee, 1962).

Hallam, E., *Chronicles of the Crusades* (London, 1989).

Housley, N., *Documents on the Later Crusades, 1274–1580* (London, 1996).

Krey, A.C., *The First Crusade: The Accounts of Eye-Witnesses and Participants* (New York, 1921; reprinted Gloucester, Mass., 1958).

Peters, E., *The First Crusade: The Chronicle of Fulcher of Chartres and Other Source Materials* (Philadelphia, 1971; 2nd edn, 1998).

Peters, E., *Christian Society and the Crusades, 1198–1229* (Philadelphia, 1971).

Régnier-Bohler, D., *Croisades et Pèlerinages, Récits, Chroniques et Voyages en Terre Sainte xiie–xvie siècle* (Paris, 1997).

Richard, J., *L'Esprit de la Croisade, Textes recueillir et présenté* (Paris, 1969).

Riley-Smith, L. and J., *Documents of Medieval History 4: The Crusades, Idea and Reality 1095–1274* (London, 1981).

(B) SPECIFIC SOURCES IN TRANSLATION

1 Latin and Old French sources

(a) The First Crusade

Bachrach, B. and D., *The Gesta Tancredi of Ralph of Caen: A History of Normans on the First Crusade* (Aldershot, 2005).

Brault, G., ed. and trans., *The Song of Roland* (2 vols, Pennsylvania, 1978).

Chibnall, M., *The Ecclesiastical History of Orderic Vitalis* (6 vols, Oxford, 1978; reprinted 2002).

Emerton, E., *The Correspondence of Pope Gregory VII: Selected Letters from the Registrum* (New York, 1932).

Grocock, C. and Siberry, J., *The Historia Vie Hierosolimitane of Gilo of Paris and a Second Anonymous Author* (Oxford, 1997).

Hill, J.H. and L.L., *Raymond d'Aguilers: Historia Francorum Qui Ceperunt Iherusalem* (Philadelphia, 1968).

Hill, J.H. and L.L., *Peter Tudebode, Historia de Hierosolymitano Itinere* (Philadelphia, 1974).

Hill, R., *Gesta Francorum et aliorum Hierosolimitanorum* (Oxford, 1962).

Levine, R., *The Deeds of God through the Franks: A Translation of Guibert de Nogent's 'Gesta Dei per Francos'* (Woodbridge, 1997).

Ryan, F.R. and Fink, H., *Fulcher of Chartres, A History of the Expedition to Jerusalem, 1095–1127* (Tallahasee, 1969; reprinted New York, 1973).

Sweetenham, C., *Robert the Monk's History of the First Crusade* (Aldershot, 2005).

A translation of Albert of Aachen, *Historia Hierosolymitana*, is being prepared by Susan Edgington.

(b) The Second Crusade

Berry, V.G., *Odo of Deuil, De Profectione Ludovici VII in orientem* (New York, 1948).

Chibnall, M., *The Historia Pontificalis of John of Salisbury* (London, 1956).

David, C.W., *De Expugnatione Lyxboniensi: The Conquest of Lisbon* (New York, 1936; reprinted 1976; reissued with a new foreword and bibliography, New York, 2000).

Loud, G.A. and Wiedemann, T., *The History of the Tyrants of Sicily by Hugo Falcandus, 1154–69* (Manchester, 1998).

Mierow, C.C., *The Two Cities: A Chronicle of Universal History to the Year 1146 by Otto Bishop of Freising* (New York, 1928).

Mierow, C.C., *The Deeds of Frederick Barabarossa by Otto of Freising and his Continuator Rahewin* (New York, 1953; reissued 1966).

Scott James, B., *The Letters of St. Bernard of Clairvaux* (London, 1953), Letters 320, 323, 391–4, 398–400, 408, 410.

(c) The Frankish principalities in Syria-Palestine

Asbridge, T.S. and Edgington, S.B., *Walter the Chancellor's The Antiochene Wars, A Translation and Commentary* (Aldershot, 1999).

Babcock, E.A. and Krey, A.C., *A History of Deeds Done Beyond the Sea by William Archbishop of Tyre* (2 vols, New York, 1943).

Shirley, J., *Crusader Syria in the Thirteenth Century, The Rothelin Continuation of the History of William of Tyre with Part of the Eracles or Acre text* (Aldershot, 1999).

Stewart, A., *Theoderich, Guide to the Holy Land* (Palestine Pilgrim Text Society 5, London, 1896; 2nd edn New York, 1986).

Stewart, A., *Jacques de Vitry, History of Jerusalem* (Palestine Pilgrim Text Society 11, London, 1896; reprinted New York, 1971).

Wilkinson, J., *Jerusalem Pilgrimage 1099–1185* (Hakluyt Society, London, 1988).

A letter of James of Vitry, bishop of Acre (1216–28), that records his impressions of Frankish society in Acre in 1216/17 has been translated by Iris Rau. Its URL is: http://www.leeds.ac.uk/history/weblearning/MedievalHistoryText Centre/James%20of%20Vitry.doc

(d) The Third Crusade

Ailes, M. and Barber, M., *Ambroise, The History of the Holy War* (Aldershot, 2003).

Edbury, P.W., *The Conquest of Jerusalem and the Third Crusade: Sources in Translation* (Aldershot, 1996).

Hubert, M.J. and La Monte, J., *The Crusade of Richard Lion-Heart by Ambroise* (New York, 1941).

Nicholson, H., *Chronicle of the Third Crusade, A translation of the Itinerarium Peregrinorum et Gesta Regis Ricardi* (Aldershot, 1997).

Thorpe, L., *Gerald of Wales, The Journey Through Wales and the Description of Wales* (Harmondsworth, 1978; reissued 2004).

Wright, T., *The Historical Works of Giraldus Cambrensis* (London, 1913).

(e) The Fourth Crusade and Frankish Greece

Andrea, A.J., *The Capture of Constantinople: The 'Hystoria Constantinopolitana' of Gunther of Pairis* (Philadelphia, 1997).
Andrea, A.J., *Contemporary Sources for the Fourth Crusade* (Leiden, 2000).
Lurier, H.E., *Crusaders as Conquerors: The Chronicle of the Morea* (New York, 1964).
McNeal, E.H., *The Conquest of Constantinople Translated from the Old French of Robert of Clari* (New York, 1936).
Marzials, F., *Memoirs of the Crusades by Villehardouin and Joinville* (London, n.d.=1908).
Powell, J.M., *The Deeds of Pope Innocent III by an Anonymous Author* (Washington, DC, 2004).
Shaw, M.R.B., *Joinville and Villehardouin: Chronicles of the Crusades* (Harmondsworth, 1963).

A new translation of Geoffrey of Villehardouin and of his continuator Henry of Valenciennes is in preparation by Peter Noble.

Goodenough, Lady, *The Chronicle of Muntaner* (2 vols, Hakluyt Society, London 1920–1).
Topping, P., *Feudal Institutions as Revealed in the Assizes of Romania, the Law Code of Frankish Greece* (Philadelphia, 1949; reprinted in P. Topping, *Studies in Latin Greece* [London, 1977], 1–192).

A translation of Marino Sanudo Torsello's *Liber Secretorum Fidelium Crucis* and the *Istoria di Romania* is in preparation by Peter Lock.

(f) Thirteenth-century crusading

Dawson, C., ed., *The Mission to Asia* (London, 1980), a reprint of *The Mongol Mission* (London, 1955).
Evans, J., *The History of St. Louis by Jean sire de Joinville* (Oxford, 1938); see also Marzials and Shaw in 1(e) above.
Gavigan, J.L., *Oliver of Paderborn, The Capture of Damietta* (Philadelphia, 1948); reprinted without the map in E. Peters, ed., *Christian Society and the Crusades 1198–1229* (Philadelphia, 1971), 49–139.
Jackson, P. and Morgan, D., eds, *The Mission of Friar William of Rubruck* (London, 1990).
Komroff, M., ed., *Contemporaries of Marco Polo* (London, 1928).
La Monte, J. and Hubert, M.J., *The Wars of Frederick II Against the Ibelins in Syria and Cyprus by Philip de Novare* (New York, 1936).
Shirley, J., *Guillaume de Machaut, The Capture of Alexandria* (Aldershot, 2001).
Wedgewood, E., *The Memoirs of the Lord of Joinville* (London, 1906).

(g) Propaganda and preaching

Brandt, W.L., *Pierre Dubois, The Recovery of the Holy Land* (New York, 1955).
Esolen, A.E., *Torquato Tasso, Jerusalem Delivered Gerusalemme liberata* (Baltimore, 2000).
Maier, C.T., *Crusade Propaganda and ideology: Model Sermons for the Preaching of the Cross* (Cambridge, 2000).

Thorpe, L., *Gerald of Wales, The Journey Through Wales and the Description of Wales* (Harmondsworth, 1978; reissued 2004).

(h) The Albigensian Crusade

Peters, E., *Heresy and Authority in Medieval Europe: Documents in Translation* (Philadelphia, 1980).
Shirley, J., *The Song of the Cathar Wars: A History of the Albigensian Crusade* (Aldershot, 1996).
Sibly, W.A. and M.D., *The History of the Albigensian Crusade: Peter of les Vaux-de-Cernay* (Woodbridge, 1998).

(i) The Baltic and Spain

Barton, S. and Fletcher, R., *The World of El Cid: Chronicles of the Spanish Reconquest* (Manchester, 2000).
Brundage, J.A., *The Chronicle of Henry of Livonia* (Madison, 1961).
Burns, R.I. and Chevedden, P.E., *Negotiating Cultures: Bi-Lingual Surrender Treaties in Muslim–Crusader Spain* (Leiden, 1999).
Hamilton, R. and Perry, J., *The Poem of the Cid: A Bilingual Edition with Parallel Text* (Harmondsworth, 1984).
Kagay, D.J., *The Usatges of Barcelona: The Fundamental Law of Catalonia* (Philadelphia, 1994).
Nelson, L.H., *The Chronicle of San Juan de la Peña: A Fourteenth-Century Official History of the Crown of Aragon* (Philadelphia, 1991).
Smith, D. and Buffery, H., *The Book of Deeds of James I of Aragon* (Ashford, 2003).
Smith, J., and Urban, W., *The Livonian Rhymed Chronicle* (Bloomington, 1977; 2nd edn, 2001).
Tschan, F.J., *The Chronicle of the Slavs by Helmold, Priest of Bosau* (New York, 1935; reissued 1963 and 1966).
Tschan, F.J., *Adam of Bremen, History of the Archbishops of Hamburg-Bremen* (New York, 1959).
Wolf, K.B., *Conquerors and Chroniclers of Early Medieval Spain* (Liverpool, 1991).

(j) The Military Orders

Barber, M. and Bate, K., *The Templars: Selected Sources Translated and Annotated* (Manchester, 2002).
Gilmour-Bryson, A., *The Trial of the Templars in Cyprus: A Complete English Edition* (Leiden, 1998).
Upton-Ward, J.M., *The Rule of the Templars* (Woodbridge, 1992).

2 Armenian, Greek, Jewish and Syriac sources

Adler, M.N., *The Itinerary of Benjamin of Tudela* (London, 1907).
Brand, C.M., *Deeds of John and Manuel Comnenus by John Kinnamos* (New York, 1976).

Burger, G., *Hetoum, A Lytell Cronycle, Richard Pynson's Translation (c.1520) of La Fleur des histories de la terre d'Orient (c.1307)* (Toronto, 1988).

Dawes, E.A.S., *The Alexiad of the Princess Anna Comnena* (London, 1928; reissued 1967).

Dawkins, R.W., *Leontios Makhairas, Recital Concerning the Sweet Land of Cyprus Entitled 'Chronicle'* (2 vols, Oxford, 1932).

Dennis, G.T., ed., *Three Byzantine Military Treatises* (Washington, 1985).

Doustourian, A.E., *Armenia and the Crusades, 10th to 12th Centuries: The Chronicle of Matthew of Edessa* (London, 1993).

Eidelberg, S., ed., *The Jews and the Crusades: The Hebrew Chronicles of the First and Second Crusades* (Madison, 1977).

Hamilton, J. and B., *Christian Dualist Heresies in the Byzantine World, c.650–c.1405: Selected Sources* (Manchester, 1998).

Jones, J.R.M., *Eustathios of Thessaloniki, The Capture of Thessaloniki* (Canberra, 1988).

Magoulias, H., *O City of Byzantium: Annals of Niketas Choniates* (Detroit, 1984).

Philippides, M., *The Fall of the Byzantine Empire: A Chronicle by George Sphrantzes, 1401–1477* (Amherst, 1980).

Sewter, E.R.A., *Michael Psellus, Fourteen Byzantine Rulers* (Harmondsworth, 1966).

Sewter, E.R.A., *The Alexiad of Anna Comnena* (Harmondsworth, 1969).

Tritton, A., 'The First and Second Crusades from an Anonymous Syriac Chronicle', *Journal of the Royal Asiatic Society* (1933), 69–101, 273–305.

3 Muslim sources

Boyle, J., *Genghis Khan: The History of the World Conqueror* (2 vols, Manchester, 1958; reprinted 1997).

Broadhurst, R., *The Travels of Ibn Jubayr* (London, 1952; reprinted New Delhi, 2003).

Gabrieli, F., *Arab Historians of the Crusades* (London, 1969).

Gibb, H., *The Damascus Chronicle of the Crusades* (London, 1932; reprinted New York, 2002).

Hitti, P., *The Memoirs of an Arab-Syrian Gentleman, Usama ibn Munqidh* (New York, 1929; reprinted 2003).

Lewis, B., *Islam from the Prophet Muhammad to the Capture of Constantinople* (2 vols, Oxford, 1987).

Masse, H., *Imad-ed-Din Conquete de La Syrie et la Palestine par Saladin* (Paris, 1972).

Lyons, U., Lyons, M.M. and Riley-Smith, J., *Ayyubids, Mamelukes and Crusaders. Selections from the Tařakh al-dawal wal-Muťuk* (2 vols, Cambridge, 1971).

Melville, C. and Lyons, M., 'Saladin's Hattin Letter', in B. Kedar, ed., *The Horns of Hattin* (Jerusalem, 1992), 208–12.

Potter, G., *The Autobiography of Ousama* (London, 1929).

Richards, D., *The Rare and Excellent History of Saladin* (Aldershot, 2001); also available in an earlier translation by C.W. Wilson as *'Saladin' or What Befell Sultan Yusuf by Beha-ed-Din* (Palestine Pilgrim Text Society 13, London, 1897; (reprinted New York, 1971).

(C) PRINCIPAL EDITIONS OF SELECTED WESTERN PRIMARY SOURCES

A guide to all the principal sources may be found in S. Runciman, *A History of the Crusades* (3 vols, Cambridge, 1951–4), I, 327–35; II, 475–90; III, 481–92.

Monumenta Germaniae historica (Hanover, Berlin and Munich, 1826–). All texts available on line at: http://www.dmgh.de/
Recueil des Historiens des Croisades (16 vols, Paris, 1841–1906).

Individual editions
Constable, G., ed., *The Letters of Peter the Venerable* (2 vols, Cambridge, Mass., 1967).
Coopland, G.W., ed., *Philippe de Mezieres, Le Songe du Vieil Pelerin* (2 vols, Cambridge, 1969).
Dietan, J.L. van, ed., *Historia* [Nicetas Choniates] (2 vols, Berlin, 1975).
Dietan, J.L. van, ed., *Nikephoros Gregoras, Rhomaïsche Geschichte, Historia Rhomaike* (3 vols, Stuttgart, 1973–88).
Edbury, P., ed., *Le Livre des Assises* (Boston, 2003).
Faral, E., ed., *Villehardouin La Conquête de Constantinople* (2 vols, Paris, 1961).
Hagenmayer, H., ed., *Anonymi gesta Francorum Hierosolimitanorum* (Heidelberg, 1890).
Hagenmayer, H., *Die Kreuzzugsbriefe aus den Jahren 1088–1100* (Innsbruck, 1901).
Hagenmayer, H., ed., *Fulcheri Carnotensis Historia Hierosolmitana (1095–1127)* (Heidelberg, 1913).
Hopf, C., ed., *Chroniques gréco-romanes inédites ou peu connues* (Berlin, 1873; reprinted Brussels, 1966).
Huygens, R.B.C., ed., *Lettres de Jacques de Vitry, Edition Critique* (Leiden, 1960).
Huygens, R.B.C., ed., *Willelmi Tyrensis Archiepiscopi Chronicon* (2 vols, Turnhout, 1986).
Lieb, B., ed., *Anne Comnène, Alexiade* (4 vols, Paris, 1937–46).
Longnon, J., ed., *Livre de la Conqueste de la Princée de l'Amorée* (Paris, 1911).
Longnon, J. ed., *Henri de Valenciennes, Histoire de L'Empereur Henri de Constantinople* (Paris, 1948).
Luard, H., ed., *Matthei Parisi Chronica Majora* (6 vols, London, 1876–80).
Mas-Latrie, L. de, ed., *Chronique d'Ernoul et de Bernard le Trésorier* (Paris, 1871).
Morgan, M.R., ed., *La continuation de Guillaume de Tyr (1184–1197)* (Paris, 1982).
Papadopoulou, E., ed., *Marin Sanudo Torsello, Istoria di Romania* (Athens, 2000).
Recoura, G., ed., *Les Assises de Romanie* (Paris, 1930).
Röhricht, R., ed., *Regesta regni Hierosolymitani* (2 vols, Innsbruck, 1893–1904).
Strehlke, E., ed., *Tabulae Ordinis Teutonici* (Berlin, 1869; reprinted Toronto, 1975).
Tafel, G.L.E. and Thomas, G.M., eds, *Urkunden zur älteren Handels- und Staatsgeschichte der Republik Venedig mit besonderer Beziehung auf Byzanz und die Levante* (3 vols, Vienna, 1856–7; reprinted Amsterdam, 1964).

(D) SECONDARY SOURCES

1 Bibliography

Atiya, A.S., *The Crusades: Historiography and Bibliography* (Bloomington and London, 1962).

Halsall, P., The Crusades: Bibliography available at http://www.unf.edu/classes/crusades/crusadesbibliography.htm

Mayer, H., *Bibliographie zur Geschichte der Kreuzzüge* (Hanover, 1960).

Mayer, H., 'Literaturbericht über die Geschicte der Kreuzzuge: Veröffentlichungen 1958–1967', *Historische Zeitschrift*, Sonderheft 3 (1969), 641–731.

Mayer, H. and McLellan, J., 'Select Bibliography of the Crusades', in K. Setton, ed., *A History of the Crusades*, VI (Madison, 1989), 511–664.

Röhricht, R., *Bibliotheca Geographica Palaestinae* (Berlin, 1890; reprinted Jerusalem, 1963 and Chippenham, Wilts, 1989).

The *Bulletin of the Society for the Study of the Crusades and the Latin East* (1981–) and the *Bulletin of the British Byzantine Society* (1975–) both provide annual updates of relevant literature and work in progress.

The *International Medieval Bibliography* (IMB), produced by the Institute of Medieval Studies, Leeds University, since 1967 is available in hard copy, stand-alone CD-Rom and online. In addition to monographs, conference proceedings, exhibition catalogues, and essay collections it lists over 300,000 articles culled from around 4,500 periodicals worldwide for the period AD 400–1500.

2 Reference works

Gibb, H.A.R., *et al.*, eds, *The Encyclopaedia of Islam* (11 vols, Leiden, 1954–2002).

Houtsma, M.T., *et al.*, eds, *E.J. Brill's First Encyclopaedia of Islam, 1913–36* (9 vols, Leiden; reprinted 1993).

Kazhdan, A., ed., *The Oxford Dictionary of Byzantium* (3 vols, New York, 1991).

Murray, A.V., ed., *An Encyclopaedia of the Crusades* (2 vols, Santa Barbara, forthcoming)

Riley-Smith, J., ed., *The Atlas of the Crusades* (London, 1991).

Roolvink, R., *Historical Atlas of the Muslim Peoples* (Amsterdam, n.d. = 1956).

Roth, C. and Wigoder, G., eds, *Encyclopaedia Judaica* (16 vols, Jerusalem, 1972).

Setton, K., ed, *A History of the Crusades* (6 vols, Madison, 1969–89), available on line at: http://libtext.library.wisc.edu/HistCrusades/About.html

Strayer, J.R., ed., *Dictionary of the Middle Ages* (13 vols, New York, 1982–9).

3 Collected essays (conference papers, collected studies or Festschriften)

Abulafia, D. and Berend, N., eds, *Medieval Frontiers: Concepts and Practices* (Aldershot, 2002).

Agius, D. and Hitchcock, R., eds, *The Arab Influence in Medieval Europe* (Reading, 1991).

Allen, R., ed., *Eastward Bound: Travel and Travellers 1050–1500* (Manchester, 2004).

Arbel, B., Hamilton, B. and Jacoby, D., eds, *Latins and Greeks in the Eastern Mediterranean after 1204* (London, 1989).

Arbel, B., ed, *Intercultural Contacts in the Medieval Mediterranean: Studies in Honour of David Jacoby* (London, 1995).

Balard, M., ed., *Autour de la premiere croisade* (Paris, 1996).

Balard, M., Kedar, B.Z. and Riley-Smith, J., eds, *Dei Gesta per Francos: Crusade Studies in Honour of Jean Richard* (Aldershot, 2001).

Boase, T., ed., *The Cilician Kingdom of Armenia* (Edinburgh, 1978).

Bull, M. and Housley, N., *The Experience of Crusading [Essays Presented to Jonathan Riley-Smith on his Sixty-fifth Birthday] 1: Western Approaches* (Cambridge, 2003).

Edbury, P., ed., *Crusade and Settlement: Papers Read at the First Conference of the Society for the Study of the Crusades and the Latin East and Presented to R.C. Smail* (Cardiff, 1985).

Edbury, P. and Phillips, J., eds, *The Experience of Crusading [Essays Presented to Jonathan Riley-Smith on his Sixty-fifth Birthday] 2: Defining the Crusader Kingdom* (Cambridge, 2003).

France, J. and Zajac, W.G., eds, *The Crusades and their Sources: Essays Presented to Bernard Hamilton* (Aldershot, 1998).

Gervers, M., ed., *The Second Crusade and the Cistercians* (New York, 1992).

Gervers, M. and Bikhazi, R.J., eds, *Conversion and Continuity: Indigenous Christian Communities in Islamic Lands, Eighth to Eighteenth Centuries* (Toronto, 1990).

Goodich, M., Menache, S. and Schein, S., eds, *Cross Cultural Convergences in the Crusader Period: Essays Presented to Aryeh Grabois on his Sixty-Fifth Birthday* (New York, 1995).

Goss, V. and Bornstein, C., eds, *The Meeting of Two Worlds: Cultural Exchange between East and West during the Period of the Crusades* (Kalamazoo, 1986).

Holt, P., ed, *The Eastern Mediterranean Lands in the Period of the Crusades* (Warminster, 1977).

Kedar, B.Z., ed., *The Horns of Hattin* (Jerusalem, 1992).

Kedar, B.Z., Mayer, H.E. and Smail, R.C., eds, *Outremer: Studies in the History of the Crusading Kingdom of Jerusalem Presented to Joshua Prawer* (Jerusalem, 1982).

Kedar, B.Z., Riley-Smith, J. and Histand, R., eds, *Montjoie: Studies in Crusade History in Honour of Hans Eberhard Mayer* (Aldershot, 1997).

Kühnel, B., ed., *The Real and the Ideal Jerusalem, Christian and Islamic Art, Studies in Honor of Bezalel Narkiss on the Occasion of his Seventieth Birthday* (Jerusalem, 1998).

Madden, T., ed, *The Crusades* (Oxford, 2002).

Mayer, H.E., ed., *Die Kreuzzfahrerstaaten als multikulturelle Gesellschaft: Einwander und Minderheiten in 12 und 13 Jahrhundert* (Munich, 1997).

Murphy, T.P., ed., *The Holy War* (Columbus, 1976).

Murray, A.V., ed., *From Clermont to Jerusalem: The Crusades and Crusader Society 1095–1500* (Turnhout, 1998).

Paetow, L.J., ed., *The Crusades and Other Historical Essays Presented to Dana C. Munro by his Former Students* (New York, 1928).

Phillips, J., ed., *The First Crusade, Origins and Impact* (Manchester, 1997).

Phillips, J. and Hoch, M., eds, *The Second Crusade: Scope and Consequences* (Manchester, 2001).

Powell, J., ed., *Muslims Under Latin Rule, 1100–1300* (Princeton, 1990).

Shatzmiller, M., ed., *Crusaders and Muslims in Twelfth-Century Syria* (Leiden, 1993).

4 Books and articles

Abrahams, L., *Jewish Life in the Middle Ages* (London, 1896; 2nd edn enlarged by Cecil Roth, 1932).

Abulafia, D., *Frederick II, a Medieval Emperor* (London, 1988).

Abulafia, D., 'The Role of Trade in Muslim–Christian Contact during the Middle Ages', in D. Agius and R. Hitchcock, eds, *The Arab Influence in Medieval Europe* (Reading, 1994), 1–24.

Adler, M., ed. and trans., *The Itinerary of Benjamin of Tudela* (London, 1907).

Akehurst, F. and Davis, J., eds, *A Handbook of the Troubadours* (Berkeley, 1995).

Alishan, L., *Léon le Magnifique premier roi de Sissouan ou de l'Arméno-Cilicie* (Venice, 1888).

Alphandéry, P. and Dupront, A., *La Chrétienté et L'Idée de Croisade* (2 vols, Paris, 1954–9).

Anderson, G., Ekelund, R., Herbert, R. and Tollison, R., 'An Economic Interpretation of the Medieval Crusades', *Journal of European Economic History*, 21 (1992), 339–63.

Andrea, A., 'Cistercian Acounts of the Fourth Crusade. Were They Anti-Venetian?', *Analecta Cisterciensia*, 41 (1985), 3–41.

Andrea, A., *Contemporary Sources for the Fourth Crusade* (Leiden, 2000).

Andrews, K., *Castles of the Morea* (Princeton, 1953; reprinted Amsterdam, 1978).

Angold, M., *The Byzantine Empire 1025–1204: A Political History* (London, 1984).

Angold, M., *Church and Society in Byzantium Under the Comneni, 1081–1261* (Cambridge, 1995).

Angold, M., *The Fourth Crusade: Event and Context* (London, 2003).

Archer, T. and Kingsford, C., *The Crusades: The Story of the Latin Kingdom of Jerusalem* (London, 1894).

Arnold, T., *The Caliphate* (Oxford, 1924).

Asbridge, T., 'The "Crusader" Community at Antioch: The Impact of Interaction with Byzantium and Islam', *Transactions of the Royal Historical Society*, Series 6, (1999), 302–25.

Asbridge, T., *The Creation of the Principality of Antioch, 1098–1130* (Woodbridge, 2000).

Asbridge, T., 'Alice of Antioch: A Case Study of Female Power in the Twelfth Century', in Edbury and Phillips, eds, *Experience of Crusading* 1 (2003), 29–47.

Asbridge, T., *The First Crusade: A New History* (London, 2004).

Ashtor, E., *A Social and Economic History of the Near East in the Middle Ages* (London, 1976).

Atiya, A., *The Crusade of Nicopolis* (London, 1934).

Atiya, A., *The Crusades in the Later Middle Ages* (1938; 2nd edn, New York, 1970).

Atiya, A., *Crusade, Commerce & Culture* (Oxford, 1962).

Ayalon, D., 'Studies in the Structure of the Mameluk Army', *Bulletin of the School of Oriental and African Studies*, 15 (1953), 203ff., 448ff. and 16 (1954), 133ff.

Baker, D., ed., *Relations Between East and West in the Middle Ages* (Edinburgh, 1973).

Balard, M., 'Amalfi et Byzance (Xe–XIIe siècles)', *Travaux et mémoires*, 6 (1976), 85–95.

Balard, M., *La Romanie Génoise* (2 vols, Genoa, 1978).

Balard, M., 'The Genoese in the Aegean (1204–1566)', in B. Arbel, B. Hamilton and D. Jacoby, eds, *Latins and Greeks in the Eastern Mediterranean After 1204* (London, 1989), 158–74.

Balard, M., *Croisades et orient latin, XIe–XIVe siècle* (Paris, 2001).

Baldwin, M., *Raymond III of Tripolis and the Fall of Jerusalem (1140–1187)* (Princeton, 1936).

Barasch, M., *Crusader Figural Sculpture in the Holy Land* (New Brunswick, 1971).

Barber, M., 'The Origins of the Order of the Temple', *Studia Monastica*, 12 (1970), 219–40.

Barber, M., *The Trial of the Templars* (Cambridge, 1978).

Barber, M., 'The Pastoreaux of 1320', *Journal of Ecclesiastical History*, 32 (1981), 143–66.

Barber, M., 'Lepers, Jews and Muslims. The Plot to Overthrow Christendom in 1321', *History*, 66 (1981), 1–17.

Barber, M., 'The Crusade of the Shepherds in 1251', in J., Sweets, ed., *Proceedings of the Tenth Annual Meeting for the Western Society for French History* (Lawrence, Kans., 1984), 1–23.

Barber, M., 'The Social Context of the Templars', *Transactions of the Royal Historical Society*, series 4, 34 (1984), 27–46.

Barber, M., *The Two Cities: Medieval Europe, 1050–1350* (London, 1992).

Barber, M., 'The Order of St. Lazarus and the Crusades', *Catholic Historical Review*, 80 (1994), 439–56.

Barber, M., *The New Knighthood: A History of the Order of the Temple* (Cambridge, 1994).

Barber, M., 'The Charitable and Medical Activities of the Hospitallers and Templars, Eleventh to Fifteenth Centuries', The Whichard Lecture, 23 March 2000, available electronically at http://www.ecu.edu/history/whichard/MBarberCharitable.html

Barker, E., 'The Crusades', in *Encyclopaedia Britannica* (11th edn, 1911); published separately as *The Crusades* (Oxford, 1923).

Bartlett, R., 'The Conversion of a Pagan Society in the Middle Ages', *History*, 70 (1985), 185–201.

Bartlett, R., *The Making of Europe: Conquest, Colonisation and Cultural Change, 950–1350* (London, 1993).

Bartlett, R. and Mackay, A., eds, *Medieval Frontier Societies* (Oxford, 1989).

Bartlett, W., *The Assassins* (Stroud, 2001).

Beazeley, C., *The Dawn of Modern Geography*, II (London, 1901).

Bec, P., *La Lyrique française au moyen age (XIIe–XIIIe siècles)* (2 vols, Paris, 1977–8).

Bedier, J. and Aubrey, P., eds, *Chansons de Croisade* (Paris, 1909).

Belgrano, L.T. and Imperiale di Sant'Angelo, C., eds, *Annali genovesi di Caffaro e de'suoi continuatori dal MXCIX al MCCXCIIII* (5 vols, Rome, 1890–1901).

Ben-Ami, A., *Social Change in a Hostile Environment* (Princeton, 1969).

Benvenisti, M., *The Crusaders in the Holy Land* (Jerusalem, 1970).

Berardenga, C della, *Gli Acciaioli di Firenze* (2 vols, Florence, 1962).

Berger, D., ed., *History and Hate: The Dimensions of Anti-Semitism* (Philadelphia, 1986).

Biddick, K., *The Shock of Medievalism* (Durham, N.C., 1998).

Biddle, M., *The Tomb of Christ* (Stroud, 1999).

Billings, M., *The Crusades* (1987; revised edn, Stroud, 2000).

Black, R., *Benedetto Accolti and the Florentine Renaissance* (Cambridge, 1985).

Blake, E., 'The Formation of the Crusade Idea', *Journal of Ecclesiastical History*, 21 (1970), 11–31.

Blake, E. and Morris, C., 'A Hermit Goes to War: Peter and the Origins of the First Crusade', in W. Shiels, ed., *Studies in Church History*, 22 (1985), 79–100.

Bloch, H., *Monte Cassino in the Middle Ages*, I (Cambridge, Mass., 1986), 139–63.

Boas, A., *Crusader Archaeology* (London, 1999).

Boas, A., *Jerusalem in the Time of the Crusades* (London, 2001).

Boase, T., 'Recent Developments in Crusading Historiography', *History*, 22 (1937–8), 110–25.

Boase, T.S.R., *Boniface VIII* (London, 1933).

Boase, T.S.R., *Castles and Churches of the Crusading Kingdom* (Oxford, 1967).

Boase, T.S.R., ed., *The Cilician Kingdom of Armenia* (Edinburgh, 1978).

Bon, A., *La Morée franque: Recherches historiques, topographiques et archéologiques sur la Principauté d'Achaie (1205–1430)* (2 vols, Paris, 1969).

Bonsall, L., 'The Benedictine Monastery of St. Mary on Athos', *Eastern Churches Review*, 2 (1969), 262–7.

Bosworth, C., *The New Islamic Dynasties* (Edinburgh, 1996).

Bowman, S., *The Jews of Byzantium 1204–1453* (Alabama, 1985).

Bradbury, J., *Philip Augustus* (London, 1998).

Brand, C., 'The Byzantines and Saladin 1185–1192: Opponents of the Third Crusade', *Speculum*, 37 (1962), 167–81.

Brand, C., *Byzantium Confronts the West 1180–1204* (Princeton, 1968).

Brand, C., 'A Byzantine Plan for the Fourth Crusade', *Speculum*, 43 (1968), 462–75.

Brand, C., 'The Fourth Crusade: Some Recent Interpretations', *Medievalia et Humanistica*, 12 (1984), 33–45.

Bréhier, L., 'The Crusades', *Catholic Encyclopaedia* 1912; available online.

Brown, E., 'The Cistercians in the Latin Empire of Constantinople and Greece, 1204–76', *Traditio*, 14 (1958), 63–120.

Brundage, J., 'An Errant Crusader: Stephen of Blois', *Traditio*, 16 (1960), 380–95.

Brundage, J., 'Recent Crusade Historiography: Some Observations and Suggestions', *Catholic Historical Review*, 49 (1964), 493–507.

Brundage, J., 'Prostitution, Miscegenation and Sexual Purity on the First Crusade' in P. Edbury, ed., *Crusade and Settlemen* (Cardiff, 1985), 57–64.

Brundage, J.A., *Medieval Canon Law and the Crusader* (London, 1969).

Brundage, J., 'The Crusader's Wife Revisited', *Studia Gratiana*, 14 (1967), 241–52.

Brundage, J., 'The Crusader's Wife: A Canonistic Quandary', *Studia Gratiana*, 12 (1967), 425–41.

Brundage, J., 'The Army of the First Crusade and the Crusade Vow', *Medieval Studies*, 33 (1971), 334–43.

Buckler, G., *Anna Comnena: A Study* (Oxford, 1929).

Buckley, J., 'The Problematical Octogenarianism of John of Brienne', *Speculum*, 32 (1957), 315–22.

Buchthal, H., *Miniature Painting in the Latin Kingdom of Jerusalem* (Oxford, 1957).

Bull, M., 'The Roots of Lay Enthusiasm for the First Crusade', *History*, 78 (1993), 353–72; reprinted in Madden, ed., *The Crusades* (2002).

Bull, M., *Knightly Piety and the Lay Response to the First Crusade* (Oxford, 1993).

Bumke, J., *Courtly Culture* (New York, 2000).

Burleigh, M., *Prussian Society and the German Order* (Cambridge, 1984).

Burleigh, M., *Germany Turns Towards the East* (Cambridge, 1988).

Burney, C. and Lang, D., *The Peoples of the Hills* (London, 1971).

Burns, R., *Monuments of Syria: An Historical Guide* (London, 1992).

Burns, R.I., 'The Catalan Company and the European Powers, 1305–1311', *Speculum*, 29 (1954), 751–71.

Burns, R.I., *The Crusader Kingdom of Valencia* (2 vols, Cambridge, Mass., 1967).

Burns, R.I., *Medieval Colonialism: The Postcrusade Exploitation of Islamic Valencia* (Princeton, 1975).

Burns, R.I., 'Immigrants from Islam: The Use of Muslims as Settlers in Thirteenth-century Aragon', *American Historical Review*, 80 (1975), 21–42.

Burns, R.I. and Chevedden, P.E., *Negotiating Cultures: Bi-lingual Surrender Treaties in Muslim – Crusader Spain* (Leiden, 1999).

Byrne, E., 'Genoese Trade with Syria in the Twelfth and Thirteenth Century', *American Historical Review*, 25 (1919–20), 191–219.

Byrne, E., 'Commercial Contracts of the Genoese in the Syrian Trade of the Twelfth Century', *Quarterly Journal of Economics*, 31 (1916), 128–70.

Byrne, E., 'The Genoese Colonies in Syria', in L. Paetow, ed., *The Crusades and Other Historical Essays* (New York, 1928), 139–82.

Byrne, E., *Genoese Shipping in the Twelfth and Thirteenth Centuries*, (Cambridge, Mass., 1930).

Cahen, C., *La Syrie du Nord a L'Époque des Croisades et la Principauté Franque d'Antioche* (Paris, 1940).

Cahen, C., 'Notes sur l'histoire des Croisades et de L'Orient latin, III, L'Orient latin et commerce du Levant', *Bulletin de Faculté des Lettres de Strasbourg*, 29 (1950–1), 328–46.

Cahen, C., 'An Introduction to the First Crusade', *Past & Present*, 6 (1954), 6–31.

Cahen, C., *Pre-Ottoman Turkey* (London, 1968).

Cameron, E., *Waldenses* (Oxford, 2000).

Carrier, M., 'Perfidious and Effeminate Greeks: The Representation of Byzantine Ceremonial in the Western Chronicles of the Crusades (1096–1204)', *Annuario dell'Instituto Romeno di Cultura e Ricerza Umanistica Venezia 2002*, 23pp. (available electronically: http://www.callisto.si.usherb.ca/Byzance.htm).

Carsten, F., *The Origins of Prussia* (Oxford, 1954).

Charanis, P., 'Byzantium, the West and the Origins of the First Crusade', *Byzantion*, 19 (1949), 17–36.

Charanis, P., *The Armenians and the Byzantine Empire* (Lisbon, 1964).

Chazan, R, *Medieval Jewry in Northern France* (Baltimore, 1973).

Chazan, R., 'The Emperor Frederick I, the Third Crusade and the Jews', *Viator*, 8 (1977).

Chazan, R., *European Jewry and the First Crusade* (Berkeley, 1987).

Chazan, R., *Medieval Stereotypes and Modern Anti-Semitism* (Berkeley, 1997).

Chazan, R., *God, Humanity and History: The Hebrew First Crusade Narratives* (Berkeley, 2000).

Christiansen, E., *The Northern Crusades* (London, 1980).

Christie, N., 'Just A Bunch of Dirty Stories? Women in the Memoirs of Usammah Ibn Munqidh', in R. Allen, ed., *Eastward Bound: Travel and Travellers 1050–1550* (Manchester, 2004), 71–87.

Citarella, A., 'The Relations of Amalfi with the Arab World before the Crusades', *Speculum*, 42 (1967), 277–312.

Clapham, A., 'The Latin Monastic Buildings of the Church of the Holy Sepulchre', *Antiquaries Journal*, 1 (1921), 3–18.

Cohen, J., *The Friars and the Jews. The Evolution of Medieval Anti-Judaism* (Ithaca, 1982).

Cohen, M., *Under Crescent and Cross: The Jews in the Middle Ages* (Princeton, 1994).

Cohn, S., *Popular Protest in Late Medieval Europe* (Manchester, 2004).

Cohn, S., *The Black Death Transformed* (London, 2002).

Cole, P., 'Oh God, the Heathen hath come into your inheritance (Ps.78.1). The Theme of Religious Pollution in Crusade Documents', in M. Shatzmiller, ed., *Crusaders and Muslims* (1993).

Cole, P., 'Purgatory and Crusade in St. Gregory's Trental', *The International History Review*, 17 (1995), 713–25.

Cole, P.J., *The Preaching of the Crusades to the Holy Land, 1095–1270* (Cambridge, Mass., 1991).

Comfort, W., 'The Saracens in the French Epic', *Publications of the Modern Language Association of America*, 55 (1940), 628–59.

Conder, C.R., *Tentwork in Palestine, A Record of Discovery and Adventure* (London, 1885).

Constable, G., 'The Second Crusade as Seen by Contemporaries', *Traditio*, 9 (1953), 213–79.

Constable, G., 'The Financing of the Crusades', in B. Kedar *et al.*, eds, *Outremer* (Jerusalem, 1982), 64–88.

Constable, G., 'Medieval Charters as a Source for the History of the Crusades', in Edbury, ed., *Crusade and Settlement* (1985); reprinted in Madden, *The Crusades* (2002).

Constable, G., 'The Crusade Project of 1150', in B. Kedar *et al.*, eds, *Montjoie: Studies in Crusade History in Honour of Hans Eberhard Mayer* (Aldershot, 1997), 67–75.

Constable, O., *Trade and Traders in Muslim Spain* (Cambridge, 1994).

Constable, O., *Medieval Iberia: Readings from Christian, Muslim and Jewish Sources* (Philadelphia, 1997).

Constantelos, D., *Byzantine Philanthropy and Social Welfare* (New Jersey, 1968).

Contamine, P., *War in the Middle Ages* (Oxford, 1984).

Costen, M., *The Cathars and the Albigensian Crusade* (Manchester, 1997).

Coureas, N., *The Latin Church in Cyprus, 1195–1312* (Aldershot, 1997).

Coureas, N. and Riley-Smith, J., eds, *Cyprus and the Crusades: Papers Given at the International Conference 'Cyprus and the Crusades', Nicosia, 6–9 September 1994* (Nicosia, 1995).

Cowdrey, H.E., 'The Mahdia Campaign 1087', *English Historical Review*, 92 (1977).

Cowdrey, H.E., 'Pope Urban II's Preaching of the First Crusade', *History*, 55 (1970), 177–88; reprinted in Madden, *The Crusades* (2002).

Cowdrey, H.E., 'The Gregorian Papacy, Byzantium and the First Crusade', in J. Howard-Johnston, ed., *Byzantium and the West c.850–c.1200* (1988), 146–69.

Cox, E., *The Green Count of Savoy* (Princeton, 1967).

Crawford, R., 'William of Tyre and the Maronites', *Speculum*, 30 (1955), 222–8.

Dajani-Shakeel, H., 'Natives and Franks in Palestine: Perceptions and Interactions', in Gervers and Bikhazi, eds, *Conversion and Continuity* (1990).

Dajani-Shakeel, H., and Messier, R., eds, *The Jihad and its Time* (Ann Arbor, 1991).

Daly, W., 'Christian Fraternity, the Crusaders and the Security of Constantinople, 1097–1204: The Precarious Survival of an Ideal', *Medieval Studies*, 22 (1960), 43–91.

Daniel, N., *The Cultural Barrier* (Edinburgh, 1975).

Daniel, N., *The Arabs and Medieval Europe* (2nd edn, London, 1979).

Daniel, N., *Heroes and Saracens: An Interpretataion of the Chansons de Geste* (Edinburgh, 1984).

Day, G., *Genoa's Response to Byzantium, 1155–1204* (Urbana, 1988).

Dehérain, H., 'Les origines de recueil des "Historiens des Croisades" ', *Journal des Savants* (1919), 260–6.

Delaville le Roulx, J., *La France en Orient au XIVe siècle* (2 vols, Paris, 1886).

Denholm-Young, N., *Richard of Cornwall* (Oxford, 1947).

Der Nersessian, S., *Armenia and the Byzantine Empire* (Cambridge, Mass., 1947).

Der Nersessian, S., 'Between East and West: Armenia and its Divided History', in D. Talbot-Rice, ed., *The Dark Ages* (London, 1965), 63–82.

Der Nersessian, S., 'The Kingdom of Cilician Armenia', in K. Setton, ed., *A History of the Crusades*, II (2nd edn, Madison, 1969), 630–59.

Der Nersessian, S., *The Armenians* (London, 1969).

Deschamps, P., *Les Chateaux des Croises en Terre Sainte* (3 vols, Paris, 1934–73).

Deschamps, P., *Terre Sainte Romane* (Paris, 1990).

DeVries, K., *Medieval Military Technology* (New York, 1992).

Dickson, G., 'The Advent of the Pastors (1251)', *Revue belge de philologie et d'histoire*, 66 (1988), 249–67.

Dobson, R., *The Jews of Medieval York and the Massacre of March 1190* (York, 1974).

Dodds, J., ed., *Al-Andalus: The Art of Islamic Spain* (New York, 1992).

Dodu, G., *Histoire des institutions monarchiques dans le royaume latin de Jérusalem, 1099–1291* (Paris, 1894).

Dols, M., *Majnun: The Madman in Medieval Islamic Society* (Oxford, 1992).

Donia, R. and Fine, J., *Bosnia and Hercegovina: A Tradition Betrayed* (London, 1994).

Dotson, J., trans., *Merchant Culture in Fourteenth Century Venice: The Zibaldone da Canal* (New York, 1994).

Ducellier, A., *et al.*, *Le Moyen Age en Orient: Byzance et Islam* (Paris, 1990).

Dunbabin, J., *Charles I of Anjou* (London, 1998).

Duncalf, F., 'The Peasants' Crusade', *American Historical Review*, 26 (1921), 440–53.

Edbury, P., 'Feudal Obligations in the Latin East', *Byzantion*, 47 (1977), 328–56.

Edbury, P., 'John of Jaffa's Title to the County of Jaffa and Ascalon', *English Historical Review*, 98 (1983), 115–33.

Edbury, P., *The Kingdom of Cyprus and the Crusades, 1191–1374* (Cambridge, 1991).

Edbury, P., 'Propaganda and Faction in the Kingdom of Jerusalem: The Background to Hattin', in Shatzmiller, ed., *Crusaders and Muslims* (1993).

Edbury, P., 'The Lyon Eracles and the Old French Continuations of William of Tyre', in Kedar *et al.*, eds, *Montjoie* (1997).

Edbury, P., *John of Ibelin and the Latin Kingdom of Jerusalem* (Woodbridge, 1997).

Edbury, P., 'Warfare in the Latin East', in M. Keen, ed., *Medieval Warfare: A History* (Oxford, 1999), 89–112.

Edbury, P. and Metcalf, D., eds, *Coinage in the Latin East. The Fourth Oxford Symposium on Coinage and Monetary History*, (BAR International Series 77 (Oxford, 1980).

Edbury, P. and Rowe, J., 'William of Tyre and the Patriarchal Elections of 1180', *English Historical Review*, 93 (1978), 1–25.

Edbury, P. and Rowe, J., *William of Tyre, Historian of the Latin East* (Cambridge, 1988).

Edgington, S. and Lambert, S., eds., *Gendering the Crusades* (Cardiff, 2001).

Edgington, S.B., *The First Crusade* (London, 1996).

Edwards, R., *The Fortifications of Armenian Cilicia* (Washington, DC., 1988).

Ehrenkreutz, A., *Saladin* (Albany, 1972).

Elbogen, I., Freimann, A., and Tykocinskij, H., eds, *Germania Judaica* (2 vols, Tubingen, 1963–8).

El-Hayek, E., 'Struggle for Survival: The Maronites of the Middle Ages', in Gervers and Bikhazi, eds, *Conversion and Continuity* (1990).

Elisséeff, N., *Nur ad-Din, un grand prince musulman de Syrie aux temps des croisades* (3 vols, Damascus, 1967).

Elisséeff, N., 'The Reaction of the Syrian Muslims After the Foundation of the First Latin Kingdom of Jerusalem', in M. Shatzmiller, ed., *Crusaders and Muslims in Twelfth-Century Syria* (Leiden, 1993), 162–72; reprinted in Madden, *The Crusades* (2002).

Ellenblum, R., 'Three Generations of Frankish Castle-Building in the Latin Kingdom of Jerusalem', in Balard, ed., *Autour de la premiere croisade* (1996).

Ellenblum, R., *Frankish Rural Settlement in the Latin Kingdom of Jerusalem* (Cambridge, 1998).

Ellenblum, R., 'Frankish and Muslim Siege Warfare and the Construction of Concentric Castles', in Balard *et al.*, eds, *Dei Gesta per Francos* (2001).

Enderlein, V., *et al.*, *Museum of Islamic Art, State Museums of Berlin* (Berlin, 2003).

Enlart, C., *Gothic Art and the Renaissance in Cyprus* (2 vols, Paris, 1899; English trans. London, 1987).

Enlart, C., *Les Monuments des croisés dans le Royaume de Jérusalem: Architecture réligieuse et civile* (2 vols, Paris, 1925–8).

Epstein, S., *Genoa and the Genoese 958–1528* (Chapel Hill, 1996).

Erdmann, C., *Die Entstehung des Kreuzzugsgedankens* (Stuttgart, 1935), trans. by M. Baldwin and W. Goffart, *The Origin of the Idea of Crusade* (Princeton, 1977).

Esposito, J., ed., *The Oxford History of Islam* (Oxford, 1999).

Evans, A., ed., *Francesco Balducci Pegalotti, La Practica della Mercatura* (Cambridge, Mass., 1936; reprinted New York, 1970).

Farmer, S., 'Persuasive Voices: Clerical Images of Medieval Wives', *Speculum*, 61 (1986), 517–43.

Favreau-Lilie, M.-L., 'The Military Orders and the Escape of the Christian Population of the Holy Land in 1291', *Journal of Medieval History*, 19 (1993), 201–27.

Favreau-Lilie, M.-L., 'The German Empire and Palestine: German Pilgrimagess to Jerusalem Between the 12th and 16th Century', *Journal of Medieval History*, 21 (1995), 321–41.

Fine, J.A., *The Bosnian Church* (New York, 1975).

Fine, J.A., *The Late Medieval Balkans* (Ann Arbor, 1987).

Finucane, R., *Soldiers of the Faith* (London, 1977).

Fletcher, R., *The Episcopate in the Kingdom of Leon in the Twelfth Century* (Oxford, 1978).

Fletcher, R., *St James's Catapult* (Oxford, 1984).

Fletcher, R., 'Reconquest and Crusade in Spain, c. 1050–1150', *Transactions of the Royal Historical Society*, Series 5, 37 (1987), 31–47; reprinted in Madden, *The Crusades* (2002).

Fletcher, R., *In Search of El Cid* (London, 1989).

Fletcher, R., *Moorish Spain* (London, 1992).

Fletcher, R., *The Conversion of Europe* (London, 1997).

Fletcher, R., *The Cross and the Crescent* (London, 2003).

Flori, J., *La Premiere Croisade, L'Occident chretien contre l'Islam* (Brussels, 1992; 2nd edn, 1997).

Flori, J., *Croisade et Chevalrie* (Brussels, 1998).

Flori, J., *Pierre L'Ermite et la Premiere Croisade* (Paris, 1999).

Flori, J., *La Guerre saint, La formation de l'idée de croisade dans l'Occident chrétien* (Paris, 2001).

Folda, J., *Crusader Manuscript Illumination at Saint-Jean d'Acre, 1275–1291* (Princeton, 1976).

Folda, J., ed., *Crusader Art in the Twelfth Century*, (BAR International Series 152 Oxford, 1982).

Folda, J., *The Nazareth Capitals and the Crusader Shrine of the Annunciation* (University Park, 1986).

Folda, J., *The Art of the Crusades in the Holy Land, 1098–1187* (Cambridge, 1995).

Forey, A., 'The Military Order of St. Thomas of Acre', *English Historical Review*, 92 (1977), 481–503.

Forey, A., 'The Military Orders in the Crusading Proposals of the Late Thirteenth Century', *Traditio*, 36 (1980), 317–45.

Forey, A., 'The Military Orders and the Spanish Reconquest in the Twelfth and Thirteenth Centuries', *Traditio*, 40 (1984), 197–234.

Forey, A., 'The Militarisation of the Hospital of St. John', *Studia Monastica*, 26 (1984), 75–89.

Forey, A., 'The Failure of the Siege of Damascus in 1148', *Journal of Medieval History*, 10 (1984), 13–23.

Forey, A., 'The Emergence of the Military Order in the Twelfth Century', *Journal of Ecclesiastical History*, 36 (1985), 175–95.

Forey, A., 'The Military Orders and Holy War against Christians in the Thirteenth Century', *English Historical Review*, 104 (1989), 1–24.

Forey, A., *The Military Orders from the Twelfth to the Early Fourteenth Centuries* (London, 1992).

Förg, L., *Die Ketzerverfolgung in Deutschland unter Gregor IX* (Berlin, 1932).

Forse, J.H., 'Armenians and the First Crusade', *Journal of Medieval History*, 17 (1991), 13–22.

France, J., 'The Crisis of the First Crusade from the Defeat of Kerbogha to the Departure from Arqa', *Byzantion*, 40 (1970), 276–308.

France, J., 'The Departure of Tatikios from the Crusading Army', *Bulletin of the Institute of Historical Research*, 44 (1971), 131–47.

France, J., 'The Election and Title of Godfrey of Bouillon', *Canadian Journal of History*, 18 (1983), 321–9.

France, J., 'Anna Comnena, the *Alexiad* and the First Crusade', *Reading Medieval Studies*, 10 (1984), 20–35.

France, J., *Victory in the East: A Military History of the First Crusade* (Cambridge, 1994).

France, J., 'Patronage and Appeal of the First Crusade', in J. Phillips, ed., *The First Crusade: Origins and Impact* (Manchester, 1997), 5–20; reprinted in Madden, *The Crusades* (2002).

France, J., *Western Warfare in the Age of the Crusades* (London, 1999).

France, J., 'Crusading Warfare and its Adaptation to Eastern Conditions in the Twelfth Century', *Mediterranean Historical Review*, 15 (2000), 49–66.

Frazer, M., 'Church Doors and the Gates of Paradise: Byzantine Bronze Doors in Italy', *Dumbarton Oaks Papers*, 27 (1973), 145–62.

Freed, J., *The Friars and German Society in the Thirteenth Century* (Cambridge, Mass., 1977).

Gadolin, A., 'Prince Bohemund's Death and Apotheosis in the Church of San Sabino, canosa di Puglia', *Byzantion*, 52 (1982), 124–53.

Gallagher, P., ed., *Christians, Jews and Other Worlds* (Lanham, Md., 1988).

Geanakoplos, D.J., *Emperor Michael VIII Palaeologus and the West* (Cambridge, Mass., 1959).

Gebhardt, B., ed., *Handbuch der deutschen Geschichte* (9th edn, Munich, 1970).

Gibb, H., 'Notes on the Arabic Materials for the History of the Early Crusades', *Bulletin of the School of Oriental and African Studies*, 7 (1933–5), 739–54.

Gibb, H., 'The Arabic Sources for the Life of Saladin', *Speculum*, 25 (1950), 58–72.

Gibb, H., 'The Armies of Saladin', *Cahiers d'histoire Égyptienne*, 4 (1951), 304–420; reprinted in H. Gibb, *Studies on the Civilization of Islam* (Boston, 1962).

Gibb, H., 'The Achievement of Saladin', *Bulletin of the John Rylands Library*, 25 (1952), 44–60.

Giedroye, M., 'The Arrival of Christianity in Lithuania: Baptism and Survival (1341–1387)', *Oxford Slavonic Papers*, 22 (1989), 34–57.

Gieysztor, A., 'The Genesis of the Crusades: The Encyclical of Sergius IV (1009–1012)', *Medievalia et Humanistica*, 5 (1948), 3–23, and 6 (1949), 3–34.

Gierlichs, J. and Hagedorn, A., eds, *Islamic Art in Germany* (Mainz, 2004).

Gilchrist, J. 'The Erdmann Thesis and the Canon Law, 1083–1114', in P. Edbury, ed., *Crusade and Settlement* (Cardiff, 1985), 37–45.

Gillingham, J., *Richard I* (London, 1999).

Glass, D., *Portals, Pilgrimage and Crusade in Western Tuscany* (Princeton, 1997).

Glassman, B., *Anti-Semitic Stereotypes Without Jews: Images of the Jew in England, 1290–1700* (Detroit, 1975).

Glick, T., *From Muslim Fortress to Christian Castle* (Manchester, 1995).

Glob, N., 'New Light on the Persecution of French Jews at the Time of the First Crusade', *Proceedings of the American Academy for Jewish Research*, 34 (1966), 1–63.

Godfrey, J., *1204: The Unholy Crusade* (Oxford, 1980).

Goodman, A., *John of Gaunt* (London, 1992).

Gouma-Peterson, T., ed., *Anna Komnene and her Times* (New York, 2000).

Green, L., *Castuccio Castracani* (Oxford, 1986).

Grousset, R., *Histoire des croisades et du royaume de Jérusalem* (3 vols, Paris, 1934–6).

Haddad, Z., 'The Crusaders Through Muslim Eyes', *The Muslim World*, 73 (1983), 234–52.

Hagenmayer, H., 'Chronologie de la Premiere Croisade 1094–110', in *Revue de L'Orient Latin*, VI (1898), 214–93, 490–549; VII (1899), 275–339, 430–503; VIII (1900), 318–44. Printed in one volume with the same title (Hildesheim, 1973).

Hagenmayer, H., ed., *Die Kreuzzugsbriefe aus dem Jahren 1088–1100* (Innsbruck, 1901; reprinted New York, 1973).

Hagenmayer, H., 'Chronologie del'histoire du royaume de Jérusalem, règne de Baudoin I (1101–1118)', *Revue de L'Orient Latin*, IX–XII (1902–11).

Hamilton, B., *The Albigensian Crusade* (London, 1974).*

Hamilton, B., 'The Cistercians in the Crusader States', in M. Pennington, ed., *One Yet Two: Monastic Tradition East and West* (Kalamazoo, 1976), 405–22.*

Hamilton, B., 'Rebuilding Zion: The Holy Places of Jerusalem in the Twelfth Century', in D. Baker, ed., *Studies in Church History*, 14 (Oxford, 1977), 105–16.*

Hamilton, B., 'The Elephant of Christ: Reynald of Chatillon', in D. Baker, ed., *Studies in Church History*, 15 (Oxford, 1978), 97–108.*

Hamilton, B., 'The Armenian Church and the Papacy at the Time of the Crusades', *Eastern Churches Review*, 10 (1978), 61–87.*

Hamilton, B., 'Women in the Crusader States: The Queens of Jerusalem, 1100–90', in D. Baker, ed., *Medieval Women* (Oxford, 1978), 143–74.**

Hamilton, B., 'A Medieval Urban Church: The Case of the Crusader States', in D. Baker, ed., *Studies in Church History*, 16 (Oxford, 1979), 159–70.**

Hamilton, B., *Monastic Reform, Catharism and the Crusades* (London, 1979), contains reprints of Hamilton articles marked.*

Hamilton, B., *The Latin Church in the Crusader States: The Secular Church* (London, 1980).

Hamilton, B., 'Ralph of Domfront, Patriarch of Antioch (1135–40)', *Nottingham Medieval Studies*, 28 (1984), 1–21.**

Hamilton, B., 'The Titular Nobility of the Latin East: The Case of Agnes of Courtenay', in P. Edbury, ed., *Crusade and Settlement* (Cardiff, 1985), 197–203.**

Hamilton, B., 'Prester John and the Three Kings of Cologne', in H. Mayr-Harting and R. Moore, eds, *Studies in Medieval History Presented to R.H.C. Davis* (London, 1985), 177–91.

Hamilton, B., *Religion in the Medieval West* (London, 1986).

Hamilton, B., 'Manuel I Comnenus and Baldwin IV of Jerusalem' in J. Chrysostomides, ed., *Kathegetria: Essays Presented to Joan Hussey* (Camberley, 1988), 353–76.**

Hamilton, B., 'Miles of Plancy and the Fief of Beirut', in B.Z. Kedar, ed., *The Horns of Hattin* (Jerusalem, 1992), 136–46.**

Hamilton, B., 'The Impact of Crusader Jerusalem on Western Christendom', *The Catholic Historical Review*, 80 (1994), 695–713.**

Hamilton, B., 'Ideals of Holiness: Crusaders, Contemplatives and Mendicants', *The International History Review*, 17 (1995), 693–712.**

Hamilton, B., 'Aimery of Limoges, Patriarch of Antioch: Ecumenist Scholar and Patron of Hermits', in E. Elder, ed., *The Joy of Learning and the Love of God: Studies in Honor of Jean Leclercq* (Kalamazoo, 1995), 269–90.**

Hamilton, B., 'The Latin Church in the Crusader States', in K. Ciggaar, A. Davids and H. Teule, eds, *East and West in the Crusader States: Context, Contacts, Confrontation. Acta of the Congress held at Hermen Castle in May 1993* (Leuwen, 1996), 1–20.**

Hamilton, B., 'King Consorts of Jerusalem and their Entourages from the West from 1186 to 1250', in Mayer, ed., *Die Kreuzfahrerstaaten* (1997), 13–24.**

Hamilton, B., 'Knowing the Enemy: Western Understanding of Islam at the Time of the Crusades', *Journal of the Royal Asiatic Society*, 3rd Series, 7 (1997), 373–87.**

Hamilton, B., *The Crusades* (Stroud, 1998).

Hamilton, B., *Crusaders, Cathars and the Holy Places* (Aldershot, 1999), contains reprints of Hamilton articles marked.**

Hamilton, B., *The Leper King and His Heirs: Baldwin IV and the Crusader Kingdom of Jerusalem* (Cambridge, 2000).

Hamilton, B., *The Christian World in the Middle Ages* (Stroud, 2003).

Hamilton, R. and Perry, J., *The Poem of the Cid, A Bilingual Edition with Parallel Text* (Harmondsworth, 1975).

Hampe, K., *Der Zug nach dem Osten* (4th edn, Leipzig, 1937).

Hansberry, J., 'The Children's Crusade', *Catholic Historical Review*, 24 (1938), 30–8.

Harper, R. and Pringle, D., *Belmont Castle: The Excavation of a Crusader Stronghold in the Kingdom of Jerusalem* (Oxford, 2000).

Harris, J., *Byzantium and the Crusades* (London, 2003).

Head, T. and Landes, R., eds, *The Peace of God: Social Violence and Religious Response in France Around the Year 1100* (Ithaca, 1992).

Heers, M.-L., 'Les Génois et le commerce de l'alun à la fin du Moyen Age', *Revue d'histoire économique et sociale*, 32 (1954), 31–53.

Hendy, M., *The Economy, Fiscal Administration and Coinage of Byzantium* (London, 1989).

Hermans, J., 'The Byzantine View of the Normans – Another Norman Myth?', *Battle*, 2 (1979), 78–92, 176–84.

Herrin, J., 'The Collapse of the Byzantine Empire in the Twelfth Century', *Birmingham Historical Journal*, 12 (1970), 188–203.

Heyd, W., *Le colonie commerciali degli Italiani in oriente nel medio evo* (2 vols, Venice, 1866–8).

Heyd, W., *Histoire du Commerce du Levant au Moyen Age*, trans. F. Raymaud (2 vols, 2nd edn, Leipzig, 1936).

Hill, J. and L., *Raymond IV Count of Toulouse* (Syracuse, 1962).

Hill, G., *A History of Cyprus* (4 vols, Cambridge, 1940–8).

Hillenbrand, C., *The Crusades: Islamic Perspectives* (Edinburgh, 1999).

Hillenbrand, R., *Islamic Art and Architecture* (London, 1999).

Hitti, P.K., *History of the Arabs* (9th edn, London, 1968).

Hoag, J., *Islamic Architecture* (1975; English edn, London, 1979).

Holmes, U., *A History of Old French Literature from the Origins to 1300* (New York, 1948).

Holt, P., *The Crusader States and Their Neighbours* (London, 2004).

Holt, P., *The Age of the Crusades. The Near East from the Eleventh Century to 1517* (London, 1986).

Holt, P., *The Crusader States and Their Neighbours* (London, 2004).

Holt, P., Lambton, A. and Lewis, B., eds, *The Cambridge History of Islam* (4 vols, Cambridge, 1980).

Hopf, C., 'Geschichte Griechenlands vom Beginn des Mittelalters bis auf unsere Zeit', in J. Ersch and J. Gruber, *Allgemeine Encyklopädie*, 85–6 (Leipzig, 1867–8; reprinted New York, 1960).

Horden, P. and Purcell, N., *The Corrupting Sea: A Study of Mediterranean History* (Oxford, 2000).

Housley, N., 'The Franco-Papal Crusade Negotiations of 1322–3', *Papers of the British School at Rome*, 48, New series 35 (1980), 164–85.

Housley, N., *The Italian Crusades* (Oxford, 1982).

Housley, N., 'Crusades Against Christians: Their Origins and Early Development, c. 1000–1216', in Edbury, ed., *Crusade and Settlement* (1985); reprinted in Madden, *The Crusades* (2002).

Housley, N., *The Avignon Papacy and the Crusades* (Oxford, 1986).

Housley, N., *The Later Crusades* (Oxford, 1992).

Housley, N., *The Crusaders* (Stroud, 2002).

Hovannistan, R.G., ed., *The Armenian People*, I (New York, 1997).

Howard-Johnston, J., ed., *Byzantium and the West, c. 800–c. 1200* (Amsterdam, 1988).

Humphreys, R., *From Saladin to the Mongols* (Albany, 1977).

Humphreys, R., *Islamic History* (Princeton, 1991; revised edn, London, 1995).

Hunt, L.-A., 'Art and Colonialism: The Mosaics of the Church of the Nativity in Bethlehem (1169) and the Problem of "Crusader" Art', *Dumbarton Oaks Papers*, 45 (1991), 69–85.

Hunyadi, Z. and Laszlovsky, J., eds, *The Crusades and the Military Orders* (Budapest, 2001).

Ileva, A., *Frankish Morea (1205–1262): Socio-cultural Interaction Between the Franks and the Local Population* (Athens, 1991).

Insoll, T., *The Archaeology of Islam* (Oxford, 1999).

Iorga, N., *Philippe de Mezieres (1327–1405) et la croisade au XIVe siècle* (Paris, 1896).

Iorga, N., *Brève histoire de la Petite Arménie* (Paris, 1930).

Irwin, R., 'An Arab-Syrian Gentleman at the Time of the Crusades Reconsidered', in

J. France and W. Zajac, eds, *The Crusades and Their Sources: Essays Presented to Bernard Hamilton* (Aldershot, 1998).

Jackson, G., *The Making of Medieval Spain* (London, 1972).

Jackson, P., 'The Crisis in the Holy Land in 1260', *English Historical Review*, 95 (1980), 480–513.

Jackson, P., 'The End of Hohenstaufen Rule in Syria', *Bulletin of the Institute of Historical Research*, 59 (1986), 20–36.

Jackson, P., 'The Crusade Against the Mongols (1241)', *Journal of Ecclesiastical History*, 42 (1991), 1–18.

Jackson, P., *The Mongols and the West, 1221–1410* (London, 2005).

Jacoby, D., *La Féodalité en Grèce médiévale: Les Assises de Romanie, application et diffusion* (Paris, 1971).

Jacoby, D., 'The Encounter of Two Societies: Western Conquerors and Byzantines in the Peloponnesus after the Fourth Crusade', *American Historical Review*, 78 (1973), 873–906.

Jacoby, D., 'Crusader Acre in the Thirteenth Century: Urban Layout and Topography', *Studi Medievali*, Series 3, 20 (1979), 1–45.

Jacoby, D., 'The Kingdom of Jerusalem and the Collapse of Hohenstaufen Power in the Levant', *Dumbarton Oaks Papers*, 40 (1986), 83–101.

Jacoby, D., *Studies on the Crusader States and on Venetian Expansion* (Aldershot, 1989).

Jacoby, D., 'Conrad, Marquis of Montferrat and the Kingdom of Jerusalem (1187–1192)', in L. Balleto, ed., *Dai feudi monferrini e dai Piemonte ai nuovi mondi oltre gli Oceani* (Genod, 1993), 187–238.

Jacoby, D., 'Cretan Cheese: A Neglected Aspect of Venetian Medieval Trade', in E. Kittell and T. Madden, eds, *Medieval and Renaissance Venice* (Urbana, 1999), 49–68.

Jacoby, D., 'New Venetian Evidence on Crusader Acre', in P. Edbury and J. Phillips, eds, *The Experience of Crusading*, II (Cambridge, 2003), 240–56.

Jayyusi, S.K., ed., *The Legacy of Muslim Spain* (Leiden, 1992).

Johnson, J.T., *The Holy War Idea in Western and Islamic Traditions* (Penn State, 1979).

Joranson, E., 'The Alleged Frankish Protectorate in Palestine', *American Historical Review*, 32 (1927), 241–61.

Joranson, E., 'The Great German Pilgrimage of 1064–1065', in Paetow, ed., *The Crusades* (1928).

Joranson, E., 'The Palestine Pilgrimage of Henry the Lion', in J. Cate and E. Anderson, eds, *Medieval and Historiographical Essays in Honor of James Westfall Thompson* (Chicago, 1938), 146–225.

Joranson, E., 'The Spurious Letter of Emperor Alexius to the Count of Flanders', *American Historical Review*, 55 (1950), 811–32.

Jordan, K., *Henry the Lion: A Biography* (Oxford, 1986).

Jordan, W., *The French Monarchy and the Jews* (Philadelphia, 1989).

Jordan, W.C., *Louis IX and the Challenge of the Crusade* (Princeton, 1979).

Jotischky, A., *The Perfection of Solitude: Hermits and Monks in the Crusader States* (University Park, Pa., 1995).

Jotischky, A., *Crusading and the Crusader States* (London, 2004).

Kaegi, W., *Byzantium and the Early Islamic Conquests* (Cambridge, 1992).

Kaeuper, R., *Bankers to the Crown: The Riccardi of Lucca and Edward I* (Princeton, 1973).

Kaeuper, R. and Kennedy, E., eds, *The Book of Chivalry of Geoffroi de Charny* (Philadelphia, 1996).

Kaminsky, H., *A History of the Hussite Revolution* (Berkeley, 1967).

Karcheski, W. and Richardson, T., *The Medieval Armour from Rhodes* (Leeds, 2000).

Katz, S., *The Holocaust in Historical Context*, I (Oxford, 1994).

Katzir, Y., 'The Patriarch of Jerusalem, Primate of the Latin Kingdom', in Edbury, ed., *Crusade and Settlement* (1985).

Kedar, B.Z., 'The Passenger List of a Crusader Ship, 1250: Towards the History of the Popular Element on the Seventh Crusade', *Studi Medievali*, 3rd series, 13 (1972), 278–9.

Kedar, B.Z., 'The General Tax of 1183 in the Crusading Kingdom: Innovation or Adaptation?', *English Historical Review*, 89 (1974), 339–45.

Kedar, B.Z, 'The Patriarch Eraclius', in Kedar *et al.*, eds, *outremer* (1982).

Kedar, B.Z., 'Gerard of Nazareth, a Neglected Twelfth-Century Writer of the Latin East: A Contribution to the Intellectual History of the Crusader States', *Dumbarton Oaks Papers*, 37 (1983), 55–77.

Kedar, B.Z., *Crusade and Mission: European Approaches Towards the Muslims* (Princeton, 1984).

Kedar, B.Z., 'Subjected Muslims of the Frankish Levant', in J. Powell, ed., *Muslims Under Latin Rule, 1100–1300* (Princeton, 1990), 135–74; reprinted in Madden, *The Crusades* (2002).

Kennan, E., 'Innocent III and the First Political Crusade', *Traditio*, 27 (1971), 231–49.

Kennedy, H., *Crusader Castles* (London, 1994).

Kennedy, H., *Muslim Spain and Portugal* (London, 1996).

Kessler, H. and Zacharias, J., *Rome 1300* (New Haven, 2000).

Kieckhefer, R., *Repression of Heresy in Medieval Germany* (Liverpool, 1979).

Kienzle, B., *Cistercians, Heresy and Crusade in Occitania 1145–1229* (Woodbridge, 2001).

Kisch, G., *The Jews in Medieval Germany* (Chicago, 1949).

Kittell, E. and Madden, T., eds, *Medieval and Renaissance Venice* (Urbana, 1999).

Knappen, M., 'Robert II of Flanders in the First Crusade', in Paetow, ed., *The Crusades* (1928).

Kotzschke, R., *Quellen zur Geschichte der ostdeutschen Kolonisation* (Leipzig, 1937).

Kotzschke, R., *Geschichte der ostdeutschen Kolonisation* (Leipzig, 1937).

Kotzur, H.-J., ed., *Die Kreuzzüge* (Mainz, 2004).

Krey, A., 'A Neglected Passage in the Gesta and its Bearing on the Literature of the First Crusade', in Paetow, ed., *The Crusades* (1928).

Krey, A., 'Urban's Crusade: Success or Failure?', *American Historical Review*, 53 (1948), 235–50.

Kritzeck, J., *Peter the Venerable and Islam* (Princeton, 1964).

Kugler, B., *Boemund und Tankred, Fursten von Antiochien* (Tubingen, 1862).

Kugler, B., *Studien zur Geschichte des Zweiten Kreuzzugs* (Stuttgart, 1866; reprinted Amsterdam, 1973).

Kühnel, B., *Crusader Art of the Twelfth Century: A Geographic, Historical or Art Historical Notion?* (Berlin, 1994).

Kühnel, G., *Wall Painting in the Latin Kingdom of Jerusalem* (Berlin, 1988).

La Monte, J., *Feudal Monarchy in the Latin Kingdom of Jerusalem* (Cambridge, Mass., 1932).

La Monte, J., 'To What Extent was the Byzantine Emperor the Suzerain of the Latin Crusading States?', *Byzantion*, 7 (1932), 253–64.

La Monte, J., 'John d'Ibelin, the Old Lord of Beirut 1177–1236', *Byzantion*, 12 (1937), 417ff.

La Monte, J., 'Some Problems in Crusading History', *Speculum*, 15 (1942), 57–75.

La Monte, J., 'The Significance of the Crusader States in Medieval History', *Byzantion*, 15 (1940–1), 300–15.

La Monte, J., 'The Lords of Le Puiset on the Crusades', *Speculum*, 17 (1942), 100–18.

La Monte, J., 'Chronology of the Latin Orient', *Bulletin of the International Committee of Historical Sciences*, 12 (1942–3), 141–202.

La Monte, J., 'The Lords of Sidon in the 12th and 13th Centuries', *Byzantion*, 17 (1944–5), 183–211.

La Monte, J., 'The Lords of Caesarea in the Period of the Crusades', *Speculum*, 22 (1947), 143–61.

Laiou, A., 'Marino Sanudo Torsello, Byzantium and the Turks: The Background to the Anti-Turkish League of 1332–34', *Speculum*, 45 (1970), 374–92.

Laiou, A. and Parviz-Mottahedeh, R., eds, *The Crusades from the Perspective of Byzantium and the Muslim World* (Washington, DC, 2001).

Lambert, M., *Medieval Heresy* (2nd edn, Oxford, 1992).

Lambert, M., *The Cathars* (Oxford, 1998).

Lane, F., *Venice, A Maritime Republic* (Baltimore, 1973).

Lane-Poole, S., *Saladin and the Fall of the Kingdom of Jerusalem* (London, 1898).

Laurent, V., 'Gregoire X et le projet d'une ligue antiturque', *Echos d'Orient*, 37 (1938), 257–73.

Laurent, V., 'La croisade et la question d'orient sous le pontificat de Gregoire X', *Revue historique du sud-est europeen*, 22 (1945), 106–37.

Law, J., *The Lords of Renaissance Italy*, (London, 1981).

Lawrence, C.H., *The Friars* (London, 1994).

Leonhardt, W., *Der Kreuzzugsplan Kaiser Heinrich VI* (Leipzig, 1913).

Lev, Y., *Saladin in Egypt* (Leiden, 1999).

Lewis, A., 'The Catalan Failure in Acculturation in Frankish Greece and the Islamic World During the Fourteenth Century', *Viator*, 11 (1980), 361–9.

Lewis, B., ed., *The World of Islam* (London, 1976).

Lewis, B., *The Assassins* (London, 1967; reprinted 1999).

Lewis, B., 'The Mongols, the Turks and the Muslim Polity', *Transactions of the Royal Historical Society*, Series 5, 18 (1968), 49ff.

Lewis, B., *The Jews of Islam* (London, 1984).

Lewis, B. and Holt, P., eds, *Historians of the Middle East* (Oxford, 1962).

Lewis, C.S., *The Allegory of Love* (Oxford, 1936).

Leyser, K., 'Money and Supplies on the First Crusade', in T. Reuter, ed., *Communications and Power in Medieval Europe: The Gregorian Revolution and Beyond* (London, 1994), 77–96.

Lilie, R.-J., *Byzanz und die Kreuzfahrerstaaten. Studien zur Politik des Byzantinischen Palästina bis zum vierten Kreuzzug (1096–1204)* (Munich, 1981); English translation as *Byzantium and the Crusader States 1096–1204* (Oxford, 1993).

Lilley, J., *et al.*, *The Jewish Burial Ground at Jewbury* (York, 1994).

Lineham, P., *History and the Historians of Medieval Spain* (Oxford, 1993).

Linskill, J., ed., *The Poems of the Troubadour Raimbaut de Vaqueiras* (Paris, 1964).

Lipman, V., *The Jews of Medieval Norwich* (London, 1967).

Little, D., 'The Fall of Akka in 690/1291: The Muslim Version', in M. Sharon, ed., *Studies in Islamic History and Civilisation in Honour of Professor David Ayalon* (Jerusalem, 1986), 159–82.

Lloyd, S., 'The Lord Edward's Crusade, 1270–2: Its Setting and Significance', in J. Gillingham and J.C. Holt, eds, *War and Government in the Middle Ages* (Woodbridge, 1984), 120–32.

Lloyd, S., *English Society and the Crusades 1216–1307* (Oxford, 1988).

Lock, P., 'The Latin Secular Church in Mainland Greece', *Medieval History*, 1 (1991), 93–105.

Lock, P., *The Franks in the Aegean* (London, 1995).

Lock, P. and Sanders, G., eds, *The Archaeology of Medieval Greece* (Oxford, 1996).

Lockhart, L., 'The Relations Between Edward I and Edward II of England and the Mongol Il-khans of Persia', *Iran*, 6 (1968), 23–31.

Loenertz, R.-J., *Byzantina et Franco-Graeca*, ed. P. Schreiner (2 vols, Rome, 1970, 1978).

Lomax, D., *The Reconquest of Spain* (London, 1978).

Lomax, D. and Mackenzie, D., eds, *God and Man in Medieval Spain* (Warminster, 1989).

Lombard, M., *The Golden Age of Islam* (Amsterdam, 1975).

Longnon, J., *L'Empire Latin de Constantinople et la Principauté de Morée* (Paris, 1949).

Longnon, J., *Les Compagnons de Villehardouin* (Geneva, 1978).

Lopez, R., 'The Trade of Medieval Europe: The South', in M. Postan and E. Miller, eds, *Cambridge Economic History of Europe*, II (2nd edn, Cambridge, 1987), 306–79.

Lopez, R. and Raymond, I., *Medieval Trade in the Mediterranean World* (London, 1955).

Lotter, F., 'The Crusading Idea and the Conquest of the Regions East of the Elbe', in R. Bartlett and A. Mackay, eds, *Medieval Frontier Societies* (Oxford, 1989), 267–307.

Lourie, E., 'A Society Organised for War: Medieval Spain', *Past and Present*, 35 (1966), 54–76.

Luttrell, A., 'The Crusade in the Fourteenth Century', in J. Hale *et al.*, eds, *Europe in the Late Middle Ages* (London, 1965), 122–54.

Luttrell, A., 'The Hospitallers' Interventions in Cilician Armenia, 1291–1375', in Boase, ed., *Cilician Armenia* (1978).

Luttrell, A., 'Gregory XI and the Turks 1370–1378', *Orientalia Christiana Periodica*, 46 (1980), 391–417.

Luttrell, A., 'Settlement on Rhodes, 1306–1366', in Edbury, ed., *Crusade and Settlement* (1985).

Luttrell, A., 'The Hospitallers in Cyprus, 1310–1378', *Kypriakai Spoudai*, 50 (1986), 155–84.

Luttrell, A., 'Rhodes and Jerusalem, 1291–1411', *Byzantinische Forschungen*, 12 (1987), 189–207.

Luttrell, A., 'The Hospitallers of Rhodes Confront the Turks, 1306–1421', in P. Gallagher, ed., *Christians, Jews and Other Worlds* (Lanham, Md., 1988), 80–116.

Luttrell, A., 'The Earliest Templars', in Balard, ed., *Autour de la premiere croisade* (1996).

Luttrell, A., 'The Earliest Hospitallers', in Kedar *et al.*, eds, *Montjoie* (1997).

Luttrell, A., *The Town of Rhodes: 1306–1356* (Rhodes, 2003).

Lyons, M. and Jackson, P., *Saladin, The Politics of Holy War* (Cambridge, 1982).

Maalouf, A., *The Crusades Through Arab Eyes* (London, 1984).

Mackay, A., *Spain in the Middle Ages 1000–1500: From Frontier to Empire* (London, 1977).

Mackinney, L., 'The People and Public Opinion in the Eleventh Century Peace Movement', *Speculum*, 5 (1930), 181–206.

McQueen, W., 'Relations between the Normans and Byzantium, 1071–1112', *Byzantion*, 56 (1986), 427–76.

Madden, T., *A Concise History of the Crusades* (New York, 1999).

Madden, T., *Enrico Dandolo and the Rise of Venice* (Baltimore, 2003).

Madelung, W. and Walker, P., eds, *The Advent of the Fatimids* (London, 2000).

Magdalino, P., *The Empire of Manuel I Komnenos, 1143–1180* (Cambridge, 1993).

Magdalino, P., *The Byzantine Background to the First Crusade* (Toronto, 1996) available electronically at http://www.deremilitari.org/RESOURCES/ARTICLES/magdalino. htm

Maier, C., *Preaching the Crusades: Mendicant Friars and the Cross in the Thirteenth Century* (Cambridge, 1994).

Maier, C., *Crusade Propaganda and Ideology: Model Sermons for the Preaching of the Cross* (Cambridge, 2000).

Maimbourg, L., *Histoire des croisades pour la deliverance de la Terre Sainte* (2 vols, Paris, 1675–6).

Makdisi, G., 'Muslim Institutions of Learning in Eleventh-Century Baghdad', *Bulletin of the School of Oriental and African Studies*, 24 (1961), 1–56.

Maltezou, C. and Schreiner, P., eds, *Bisanzio, Venezia e il mondo franco-greco (XIII–XV secolo), Atti del Colloquio Internazionale organizzato nel centenario della nascita di Raymond-Joseph Loenertz o.p., Venezia 1–2 dicembre 2000* (Venice, 2002).

Manenti, C. and Bollen, M., eds, *Castles in Italy* (Cologne, 2000).

Mann, V., *et al.*, eds, *Convivencia: Jews, Muslims and Christians in Medieval Spain* (New York, 1992).

Marshall, C., 'The Crusading Motivation of the Italian City Republics in the Latin East, c.1096–1104', *Rivista di Bizantinistica*, 1 (1991), 15 pp. (available electronically at http://www.deremilitari.org/RESOURCES/ARTICLES/marshall2.htm)

Marshall, C., *Warfare in the Latin East, 1192–1291* (Cambridge, 1992).

Marshall, C., 'The Crusading Motivation of the Italian City Republics in the Latin East c. 1096–1104', in Bull and Housley, eds, *Experience of Crusading*, 1 (2003), 60–79.

Mas Latrie, L: de, *Histoire de l'Ile de Chypre sous le règne de la maison de Lusignan* (3 vols, Paris, 1852–61).

Mayer, H., *Geschichte der Kreuzzüge* (Stuttgart, 1965, 9th edn, 2000; English translation, *The Crusades* [Oxford] 1972, 2nd edn, 1988).

Mayer, H., 'On the Beginning of the Communal Movement in the Holy Land: The Commune of Tyre', *Traditio*, 24 (1968), 443–57.**

Mayer, H., 'Studies in the History of Queen Melisende of Jerusalem', *Dumbarton Oaks Papers*, 26 (1972), 93–182.*

Mayer, H., 'Review of Ehrenkreutz, *Saladin*', in *Speculum*, 49 (1974), 724–7.

Mayer, H., *Bistümer, Klöster und Stifte im Königreich Jerusalem* (Stuttgart, 1977).

Mayer, H., 'Latins, Muslims and Greeks in the Latin Kingdom of Jerusalem', *History*, 63 (1978), 175–92.*

Mayer, H., 'Ibelin versus Ibelin: The Struggle for the Regency of Jerusalem, 1253–1258' *Proceedings of the American Philosophical Society*, 122 (1978), 25–57.*

Mayer, H., 'America and the Crusades', *Proceedings of the American Philosophical Society*, 125 (1981), 38–45.

Mayer, H., 'Carving Up Crusaders: The Early Ibelins and Ramlas', in Kedar *et al.*, eds, *Outremer* (1982), 101–18.***

Mayer, H., 'Henry II of England and the Holy Land', *English Historical Review*, 97 (1982), 721–39.***

Mayer, H., 'The Concordat of Nablus', *Journal of Ecclesiastical History*, 33 (1982) 531–43.***

Mayer, H., *Probleme des lateinischen Königreichs Jerusalem* (London, 1983), contains reprints of Mayer articles marked*.

Mayer, H., *Kruezzüge und lateinischer Osten* (London, 1983), contains reprints of Mayer articles marked**.

Mayer, H., 'John of Jaffa, His Opponents and His Fiefs', *Proceedings of the American Philosophical Society*, 128 (1984), 134–63.***

Mayer, H., 'The Double County of Jaffa and Ascalon: One Fief or Two?', in Edbury ed., *Crusade and Settlement* (1985), 181–90.***

Mayer, H., 'The Origins of the County of Jaffa', *Israel Exploration Journal*, 35 (1985), 35–45.***

Mayer, H., 'The Origins of the Lordships of Ramla and Lydda in the Latin Kingdom of Jerusalem', *Speculum*, 60 (1985), 537–52.***

Mayer, H., 'The Succession to Baldwin II of Jerusalem: English Impact on the East', *Dumbarton Oaks Papers*, 39 (1985), 139–47.***

Mayer, H., 'Die Hopfkapelle der Könige von Jerusalem', *Deutsches Archiv für Erforschung des Mittelalters*, 44 (1988), 489–509.***

Mayer, H., 'Manasses of Hierges in East and West', *Revue Belge de Philologie et d'Histoire*, 66 (1987), 757–66.***

Mayer H., 'Angevins versus Normans: The New Men of King Fulk of Jersualem', *Proceedings of the American Philosophical Society*, 133 (1989), 1–25.***

Mayer, H., 'The Wheel of Fortune: Seignorial Vicissitudes under King Fulk and Baldwin II of Jerusalem', *Speculum*, 65 (1990), 860–77.***

Mayer, H., 'The Beginnings of King Amalric of Jerusalem', in Kedar, B., ed, *Horns of Hattin* (1992), 121–35.

Mayer, H., *Kings and Lords in the Latin Kingdom of Jerusalem* (Aldershot, 1994), contains reprints of Mayer articles marked***.

Mayer, H., *Die Kanzlei der lateinischen Könige von Jerusalem* (Hanover, 1996).

Mazeika, R., 'Nowhere was the Fragility of their Sex Apparent: Women Warriors in the Baltic Crusade Chronicles', in A. Murray, ed., *From Clermont to Jerusalem* (Turnhout, 1998), 229–48.

Metcalf, D., *Coinage of the Crusades and the Latin East* (London, 1983).

Michau, F., 'Croisades et croises vus par les historiens arabes chrétiens d'Egypte', in R. Curiel and R. Gyselen, eds, *Itineraires d'Orient. Hommages a Claude Cahen* (Burges-Sur-Yvette, 1994), 169–87.

Michaud, J.F., *Histoire des Croisades* (3 vols, Paris, 1812–17, 6th edn, 6 vols, Paris, 1841; abridged in one vol. by Robert Delort and reprinted Paris, 1970).

Miller, T., *The Birth of the Hospital in the Byzantine Empire* (Baltimore, 1985).

Miller, W., *Latins in the Levant* (London, 1908; reprinted Cambridge, 1964).

Miller, W., *Essays on the Latin Orient* (Cambridge, 1921).

Mirot, L., 'Une Expedition française en Tunisie au XIVe siècle: Le siege de Mahdia (1390)', *Revue des études historiques*, 47 (1931), 357–406.

Mitchell, P., *Medicine in the Crusades: Warfare, Wounds and the Medieval Surgeon* (Cambridge, 2004).

Molin, K., *Unknown Crusader Castles* (London, 2001).

Mollat, M., 'Le passage de Saint Louis a Tunis. Sa place dans l'histoire des croisades', *Revue d'histoire economique et sociale*, 50 (1972).

Moore, R., *The Formation of a Persecuting Society* (Oxford, 1987).

Morgan, D., ed, *Medieval Historical Writing in the Christian and Islamic Worlds* (London, 1982).

Morgan, M., *The Chronicle of Ernoul and the Continuations of William of Tyre* (Oxford, 1973).

Morris, C., 'Geoffrey de Villehardouin and the Conquest of Constantinople', *History*, 43 (1968), 24–34.

Morris, C., 'Policy and Visions. The Case of the Holy Lance at Antioch', in J. Gillingham and J. Holt, eds, *War and Government in the Middle Ages* (Woodbridge, 1984), 33–45.

Morris, C., *The Papal Monarchy: The Western Church from 1050 to 1250* (Oxford, 1989).

Muldoon, J., *Popes, Lawyers and Infidels* (Liverpool, 1979).

Muller-Wiener, W., *Castles of the Crusaders* (London, 1966).

Mullett, M. and Smythe, D., eds, *Alexios I Komnenos. Papers of the Second Belfast International Colloqium of Byzantine Studies* (Belfast, 1996).

Munro, D., 'The Children's Crusade', *American Historical Review*, 19 (1913–14), 516–24.

Munro, D., 'The Western Attitude Toward Islam During the Period of the Crusades', *Speculum*, 6 (1931), 329–43.

Munz, P., *Frederick Barbarossa* (London, 1969).

Murphy, T.P., ed., *The Holy War* (Columbus, 1976).

Murray, A., 'The Origins of the Frankish Nobility of the Kingdom of Jerusalem', *Mediterranean Historical Review*, 4 (1989), 281–300.

Murray, A., 'The Army of Godfrey of Bouillon, 1096–1099: Structure and Dynamics of a Contingent on the First Crusade', *Revue Belge de Philologie et d'Histoire*, 70 (1992), 301–29.

Murray, A., 'Dynastic Continuity or Dynastic Change? The Accession of Baldwin II and the Nobility of the Kingdom of Jerusalem', *Medieval Prosopography*, 13 (1992), 1–28.

Murray, A., 'Baldwin II and His Nobles: Baronial Factionalism and Dissent in the Kingdom of Jerusalem, 1118–1134', *Nottingham Medieval Studies*, 38 (1994), 60–85.

Murray, A., 'Ethnic Identity in the Crusader States: The Frankish Race and the Settlement of Outremer', in S. Forde, L. Johnson and A. Murray, eds, *Concepts of National Identity in the Middle Ages* (Leeds, 1995), 59–74.

Murray, A., 'Galilee and Damascus in the Period of the Crusades', *Nottingham Medieval Studies*, 40 (1996), 190–3.

Murray, A., 'Mighty Against the Enemies of Christ: The Relic of the True Cross in the Armies of the Kingdom of Jerusalem', in France and Zajac, eds, *Crusades and Their Sources* (1998).

Murray, A., *The Crusader Kingdom of Jerusalem: A Dynastic History 1099–1125* (Oxford, 2000).

Murray, A., ed., *Crusade and Conversion on the Baltic Frontier 1150–1500* (Aldershot, 2001).

Nesbitt, J., 'The Rate of March of Crusading Armies in Europe: A Study and Computation', *Traditio*, 19 (1963), 167–82.

Nicholson, H., *Templars, Hospitallers and Teutonic Knights: Images of the Military Orders, 1128–1291* (Leicester, 1995).

Nicholson, H., 'Women on the Third Crusade', *Journal of Medieval History*, 23 (1997), 335–49.

Nicholson, H., *The Knights Templar: A New History* (Stroud, 2001).

Nicholson, H., *The Knights Hospitaller* (Woodbridge, 2001).

Nicholson, H., ed., *Palgrave Advances in the Crusades* (London, 2005).

Nicholson, H. and Nicolle, D., *God's Warriors: Crusaders, Saracens and the Battle for Jerusalem* (Oxford, 2005).

Nicholson, R., *Tancred: A Study of His Career and Work in Their Relation to the First Crusade and the Establishment of the Latin States in Syria and Palestine* (Chicago, 1940).

Nicholson, R., *Joscelyn III and the Fall of the Crusader States* (Leiden, 1973).

Nickerson, M., 'The Seigneurie of Beirut in the Twelfth Century and the Brisebarre Family of Beirut-Blanchegarde', *Byzantion*, 19 (1949), 141–85.

Nicol, D., *Byzantium and Venice: A Study in Diplomatic and Cultural Relations* (Cambridge, 1988).

Nicolle, D., *Arms and Armour of the Crusading Era, 1050–1350* (2 vols, London, 1986).

Nicolle, D., *Hattin 1187, Saladin's Greatest Victory* (Oxford, 1993).

Nicolle, D., *Essential Histories: The Crusades* (London, 2001).

Nicolle, D., *Crusader Castles in the Holy Land 1097–1192* (Oxford, 2004).

Nicolle, D., *Crusader Castles in the Holy Land 1192–1302* (Oxford, 2005).

Nirenberg, D., 'The Rhineland Massacres of the Jews in the First Crusade: Memories Medieval and Modern', in G. Althoff, J. Fried and P. Geary, eds, *Medieval Concepts of the Past* (Cambridge, 2002), 279–310.

Noble, P., 'Eyewitnesses of the Fourth Crusade – the War against Alexius III', *Reading Medieval Studies*, 25 (1999), 75–89.

Obolensky, D., *The Bogomils* (Cambridge, 1948).

Obolensky, D., 'The Principles and Methods of Byzantine Diplomacy', *Actes du XIIe congrès International d'Études Byzantines*, I (Belgrade, 1963), 45–61;.

Offler, H.S., 'Empire and Papacy: The Last Struggle', *Transactions of the Royal Historical Society*, Series 5, 6 (1956), 21–47.

Oikonomides, N., *Hommes D'Affaires Grecs et latines à Constantinople* (Paris, 1979).

Ostrogorsky, G., *History of the Byzantine State* (2nd edn, Oxford, 1968).

Panagopoulos, B., *Cistercian and Mendicant Monasteries in Medieval Greece* (Chicago, 1979).

Parry, V. and Yapp, M., eds, *War, Technology and Society in the Middle East* (London, 1975).

Partner, P., *The Knights Templar and Their Myth* (Oxford, 1981; revised 1990).

Patterson, L., *The World of the Troubadours* (Cambridge, 1993).

Pertusi, A., ed., *Venezia e il Levante Fino al Secolo XV* (2 vols, Florence, 1973).

Peters, R., *The Jihad in Medieval and Modern Islam* (Leiden, 1977).

Phillips, J., *Defenders of the Holy Land: Relations Between the Latin East and the West, 1119–1187* (Oxford, 1996).

Phillips, J., *The Crusades 1095–1197* (London, 2002).

Phillips, J., *The Fourth Crusade and the Sack of Constantinople* (London, 2004).

Phillips, J.R.S., *The Medieval Expansion of Europe* (Oxford, 1988).

Porges, W., 'The Clergy, the Poor and the Non-Combatants on the First Crusade', *Speculum*, 21 (1946), 1–23.

Postan, M.M., ed., *The Cambridge Economic History of Europe*, I (Cambridge, 1966).

Powell, J., *The Anatomy of a Crusade, 1213–1221* (Philadelphia, 1986).

Powell, J., 'The Role of Women in the Fifth Crusade', in B. Kedar, ed., *The Horns of Hattin* (Jerusalem, 1992), 294–301.

Powers, J., 'The Origins and Development of Municipal Military Service in the Leonese and Castilian Reconquest, 800–1250', *Traditio*, 26 (1970), 91–112.

Powicke, F.M., *King Henry III and the Lord Edward* (2 vols, Oxford, 1947).

Prawer, J., 'Colonisation Activities in the Latin Kingdom of Jerusalem', *Revue Belge de Philogie et d'Histoire*, 29 (1951), 1063–118.

Prawer, J., 'The *Assise de Teneure* and the *Assise de Vente*: A Study of Landed Property in the Latin Kingdom', *Economic History Review*, 41 (1951–2), 77–87.

Prawer, J., 'The Settlement of Latins in Jerusalem', *Speculum*, 27 (1952), 490–503.

Prawer, J., *Histoire du Royaume Latin de Jérusalem* (2 vols, Paris, 1970).

Prawer, J., *The World of the Crusaders* (London, 1972).

Prawer, J., *The Latin Kingdom of Jerusalem. European Colonialism in the Middle Ages* (London, 1972; reprinted as *The Crusaders' Kingdom*, London, 2001).

Prawer, J., 'Crusader Cities', in H. Miskimin, D. Herlihy and A. Udovitch, eds, *The Medieval City* (New Haven, 1977), 179–200.

Prawer, J., 'Military Orders and Crusader Politics in the Second Half of the XIIIth Century', in J. Fleckenstein and M. Hellmann, eds, *Die gestlichen Ritterorden Europas* (Sigmaringen, 1980), 217–29.

Prawer, J., *Crusader Institutions* (Oxford, 1988), contains revisions of earlier articles.

Prawer, J., *The History of the Jews in the Latin Kingdom of Jerusalem* (Oxford, 1988).

Prestwich, M., *Edward I* (London, 1988).

Pringle, D., 'Magna Mahumeria (al-Bira): The Archaeology of a Frankish New Town in Palestine', in Edbury, ed., *Crusade and Settlement* (1985).

Pringle, D., 'A Thirteenth-Century Hall at Montfort Castle in Western Galilee', *The Antiquaries Journal*, 76 (1986), 52–81.

Pringle, D., *The Red Tower (al-burj al-Ahmar)* (London, 1986).

Pringle, D., ed., *T.E. Lawrence, Crusader Castles* (Oxford, 1988).

Pringle, D., 'Cistercian Houses in the Kingdom of Jerusalem', in Gervers, ed., *The Second Crusade* (1992).

Pringle, D., *The Churches of the Crusader Kingdom of Jerusalem: A Corpus* (2 vols, Cambridge 1993, 1997, a third volume in press).

Pringle, D., *Secular Buildings in the Crusader Kingdom of Jerusalem: An Archaeological Gazetteer* (Cambridge, 1997).

Pringle, D., 'The Archaeology of the Crusader Kingdom of Jerusalem: A Review of Work 1947–97', *Journal of Medieval History*, 23 (1997), 388–408.

Pringle, D., ed., *C.N. Johns, Pilgrims' Castle ('Athlit), David's Tower (Jerusalem) and Qalat ar-Rabad (<Ajlun)* (Aldershot, 1997).

Pringle, D., *Fortification and Settlement in Crusader Palestine* (Aldershot, 2000).

Pringle, D., 'The Spring of the Cresson in Crusading History', in Balard *et al.*, eds, *Dei Gesta per Francos* (2001).

Purcell, M., *Papal Crusading Policy 1244–1291* (Leiden, 1975).

Purcell, M., 'Women Crusaders: A Temporary Canonical Aberration?', in L. Frappell, ed., *Principalities, Powers and Estates* (Adelaide, 1979), 57–67.

Queller, D. and Madden, T., *The Fourth Crusade: The Conquest of Constantinople* (2nd edn, Philadelphia, 1997).

Raedts, P., 'The Children's Crusade of 1212', *Journal of Medieval History*, 3 (1977), 279–323.

Reilley, B.F., *The Medieval Spains* (Cambridge, 1993).

Reuter, T., 'The Non-Crusade of 1149–50', in Phillips and Hoch, eds, *The Second Crusade: Scope and Consequences* (Manchester, 2001), 150–63.

Rey, E., ed., *Les familles d'Outremer de Du Cange* (Paris, 1869).

Rey, E., *Les colonies franques de Syrie aux XIIe et XIIIe siècles* (Paris, 1883).

Rey-Delqué, M., ed., *Les Croisades, L'Orient et L'Occident d'Urbain II à Saint Louis (1096–1270)* (Milan, 1997).

Richard, J., *Le comté de Tripoli sous la dynastie toulousaine (1102–1187)* (Paris, 1945; reprinted New York, 1980).

Richard, J., 'An Account of the Battle of Hattin Referring to the Frankish Mercenaries in Oriental Muslim States', *Speculum*, 27 (1952), 168–77.

Richard, J., 'The Mongols and the Franks', *Journal of Asian History*, 3 (1969), 45–57.

Richard, J., *The Latin Kingdom of Jerusalem* (2 vols, Amsterdam, 1969).

Richard, J., *La Papauté et les Missions d'Orient au Moyen Age (xiiie–xive siècles)* (Paris, 1977).

Richard, J., 'Frankish Power in the Eastern Mediterranean', *Mediterranean Historical Review*, 3 (1987), 168–87.

Richard, J., 'La croisade de 1270. premier "passage general" ', *Comptes rendus de l'Academie des Inscriptions* (1989).

Richard, J., *Saint Louis, Crusader King of France* (1983; English edn, Cambridge, 1992).

Richard, J., *The Crusades c.1071–c.1291* (Cambridge, 1999).

Richards, D., 'The Early History of Saladin', *Islamic Quarterly*, 17 (1973), 140–59.

Richardson, H., *The English Jewry Under Angevin Kings* (London, 1960).

Richardson, H. and Sayles, G., *The Governance of Medieval England* (Edinburgh, 1963).

Riley-Smith, J., *The Knights of St. John in Jerusalem and Cyprus, c.1050–1310* (London, 1967).

Riley-Smith, J., 'The Templars and the Castle of Tortosa in Syria', *English Historical Review*, 84 (1969), 278–88.

Riley-Smith, J., 'A Note on Confraternities in the Latin Kingdom of Jerusalem', *Bulletin of the Institute of Historical Research*, 45 (1971), 301–8.

Riley-Smith, J., 'The *Assise sur la Ligèce* and the Commune of Acre', *Traditio*, 27 (1971), 179–204.

Riley-Smith, J., 'Some Lesser Officials in Latin Syria', *English Historical Review*, 87 (1972), 1–26.

Riley-Smith, J., 'Government in Latin Syria and the Commercial Privileges of Foreign Merchants' in D. Baker, ed., *Relations Between East and West in the Middle Ages* (Edinburgh, 1973), 109–32.

Riley-Smith, J., *The Feudal Nobility and the Kingdom of Jerusalem, 1174–1277* (London, 1973).

Riley-Smith, J., *What Were the crusades?* (London, 1977; 2nd edn, 2000).

Riley-Smith, J., 'The Survival in Latin Palestine of the Muslim Administration', in Holt, ed., *The Eastern Mediterranean* (1977).

Riley-Smith, J., 'Peace Never Established: The Case of the Kingdom of Jerusalem', *Transactions of the Royal Historical Society*, Series 5, 28 (1978), 87–102.

Riley-Smith, J., 'Latin Titular Bishops in Palestine and Syria, 1137–1291', *Catholic Historical Review*, 54 (1978), 1–15.

Riley-Smith, J., 'The Templars and the Teutonic Knights in Cilician Armenia', in Boase, ed., *Cilician Armenia* (1978).

Riley-Smith, J., 'The Title of Godfrey of Bouillon', *Bulletin of the Institute of Historical Research*, 52 (1979), 83–7.

Riley-Smith, J., 'Crusading as an Act of Love', *History*, 65 (1980), 177–92; reprinted in Madden, *The Crusades* (2002).

Riley-Smith, J., 'An Approach to Crusading Ethics', *Reading Medieval Studies*, 6 (1980), 3–19.

Riley-Smith, J., 'The Motives of the Earliest Crusaders and the Settlement of Latin Palestine', *English Historical Review*, 98 (1983), 721–36.

Riley-Smith, J., 'The First Crusade and the Persecution of the Jews', in W. Shiels, ed., *Studies in Church History: Persecution and Toleration* 21 (Oxford, 1984), 51–72.

Riley-Smith, J., 'Death on the First Crusade', in D. Loades, ed., *The End of Strife* (Edinburgh, 1984), 14–31.

Riley-Smith, J., 'Further Thoughts on Baldwin II's *établissement* on the Confiscation of Fiefs' in Edbury, ed., *Crusade and Settlement* (1985).

Riley-Smith, J., 'The Venetian Crusade of 1122–24', in G. Airaldi and B. Kedar, eds, *I communi italiani nel regno crociato di Gerusalemme* (Genoa, 1986), 337–50.

Riley-Smith, J., *The First Crusade and the Idea of Crusading* (London, 1986).

Riley-Smith, J., *The Crusades: A Short History* (London, 1987).

Riley-Smith, J., 'The Latin Clergy and the Settlement of Palestine and Syria, 1098–1100', *The Catholic Historical Review*, 74 (1988), 539–57.

Riley-Smith, J., 'Family Traditions and Participation in the Second Crusade', in M. Gervers, ed., *The Second Crusade and the Cistercians* (New York, 1992), 101–8.

Riley-Smith, J., ed., *The Oxford Illustrated History of the Crusades* (Oxford, 1995; reprinted as *The Oxford History of the Crusades* [Oxford, 1999] with less photographs).

Riley-Smith, J., 'Early Crusaders to the East and the Cost of Crusading 1095–1130', in Goodich, ed., *Cross Cultural Convergences* (1995); reprinted in Madden, *The Crusades* (2002).

Riley-Smith, J., *The First Crusaders, 1095–1131* (Cambridge, 1997).

Riley-Smith, J., 'King Fulk of Jerusalem and the Sultan of Babylon', in Kedar, ed., *Montjoie* (1997).

Riley-Smith, J., 'Families, Crusades and Settlement in the Latin East, 1102–1131', in Mayer, ed., *Die Kreuzfahrerstaaten* (1997).

Riley-Smith, J., 'Raymond IV of St. Gilles, Achard of Arles and the Conquest of Lebanon', in J. France and W. Zajac, eds, *Crusades and their Sources* (Aldershot, 1998).

Riley-Smith, J., 'Government and the Indigenous in the Latin Kingdom of Jerusalem', in D. Abulafia and N. Berend, eds, *Medieval Frontiers* (2002).

Riley-Smith, J., 'Islam and the Crusades in History and Imagination, 8 November 1898–11 September 2002', *Crusades*, 2 (2003), 151–68.

Riley-Smith, L. and J., *The Crusades: Idea and Reality* (London, 1981).

Riquer, M. de, *L'Arnes del Cavalier* (Barcelona, 1968).

Robinson, C., *Islamic Historiography* (Cambridge, 2003).

Robinson, I., 'Gregory VII and the Soldiers of Christ', *History*, 58 (1973), 169–92.

Robinson, I., *The Papacy 1073–1198: Continuity and Change* (Cambridge, 1990).

Rodgers, M., *The Making of the Past: The Spread of Islam* (Oxford, 1976).

Rodgers, R., *Latin Siege Warfare in the Twelfth Century* (Oxford, 1992).

Rodinson, M., *Europe and the Mystique of Islam* (London, 1988).

Röhricht, R., *Die Kreuzfahrt Kaiser Friedrichs des Zweiten* (Innsbruck, 1872).

Röhricht, R., 'Der Kinderkreuzzug, 1212', *Historische Zeitschrift*, 36 (1876), 1–8.

Röhricht, R., 'Die Kreuzzüge des Grafen Theobald von Navarra und Richard von Cornwallis nach dem heiligen Lande', *Forschungen zur deutschen Geschichte*, 36 (1886), 67–81.

Röhricht, R., *Studien zur geschichte des fünften Kreuzzüges* (Innsbruck, 1891).

Röhricht, R., ed., *Regista Regni Hierosolomymitani 1097–1291* (2 vols, Innsbruck, 1893–1904; reprinted New York, 1960), contains all extant charters.

Röhricht, R., *Geschichte des Königsreichs Jerusalem (1100–1291)* (Innsbruck, 1898).

Röhricht, R., *Geschichte des ersten Kreuzzüges* (Innsbruck, 1901).

Roquebert, M., *L'Epopée Cathare 1198–1212: L'Invasion* (Paris, 1970).

Rosetti, R., 'The Battle of Nicopolis (1396)', *Slavonic Review*, 25 (1937), 629ff.

Rowe, J., 'Paschal II and the Relations between the Spiritual and Temporal Powers in the Kingdom of Jerusalem', *Speculum*, 32 (1957), 470–501.

Rowe, J., 'The Papacy and the Ecclesiastical Province of Tyre', *Bulletin of the John Rylands Library*, 43 (1960–1), 160–89.

Rowe, J., 'Paschal II, Bohemond of Antioch and the Byzantine Empire', *Bulletin of the John Rylands Library*, 49 (1966–7), 165–202.

Rozenberg, S., ed., *Knights of the Holy Land: The Crusader Kingdom of Jerusalem* (Jerusalem, 1999).

Rüdt-Collenberg, W.H., *The Rupenides, Hethumides and Lusignans. The Structure of the Armeno-Cilician Dynasties* (Lisbon, 1963).

Runciman, S., *The Medieval Manichee* (Cambridge, 1947).

Runciman, S., 'The Byzantine "Protectorate" in the Holy Land', *Byzantion*, 18 (1948), 207–15.

Runciman, S., *A History of the Crusades* (3 vols, Cambridge, 1951–4).

Runciman, S., *The Eastern Schism* (Oxford, 1955).

Runciman, S., 'The Decline of the Crusading Idea', in Giunta centrale per gli Studi Storici, ed., *X Congresso, Roma 4–11 Settembre 1955 Relazioni, III: Storia del Medioevo* (Florence, 1956), 637–52.

Runciman, S., 'The Greeks in Antioch at the Time of the Crusades', *Proceedings of the International Congress of Byzantine Studies, Thessalonica 1953*, II (Athens, 1956), 583–91.

Runciman, S., *The Sicilian Vespers* (Cambridge, 1958).

Runciman, S., 'The Visit of King Amalric I to Constantinople in 1171', in Kedar *et al.*, eds, *Outremer* (1982).

Runciman, S., 'Byzantium and the Crusades', in Goss and Bornstein, eds, *The Meeting of Two Worlds* (1986), reprinted in Madden, *The Crusades* (2002).

Russell, F., *The Just War in the Middle Ages* (Cambridge, 1975).

Salma Khadra Jayyusi, ed., *The Legacy of Muslim Spain* (Leiden, 1992).

Saunders, J., *Aspects of the Crusades* (Canterbury, 1962).

Saunders, J., *A History of Medieval Islam* (London, 1972; reprinted 1996).

Schacht, J. and Bosworth, C., eds, *The Legacy of Islam* (2nd edn, Oxford, 1974).

Schein, S., 'The Patriarchs of Jerusalem in the Late Thirteenth Century', in Kedar *et al.* eds, *Outremer* (1982).

Schein, S., 'Philip IV and the Crusade: A Reconsideration', in Edbury, ed., *Crusade and Settlement* (1985).

Schein, S., *Fideles Crucis: The Papacy, the West and the Recovery of the Holy Land 1274–1314* (Oxford, 1991).

Schlumberger, G., *Numismatique de L'Orient Latin* (Paris, 1878; reprinted Graz, 1954).

Schlumberger, G., Chalandon, F. and Blanchet, A., *Sigillographie de l'Orient Latin* (Paris, 1943).

Semaan, K., ed., *Islam and the Medieval West* (New York, 1980).

Setton, K., *Catalan Domination of Athens 1311–88* (New York, 1948; revised edn, London, 1975).

Setton, K., *The Papacy and the Levant* (4 vols, Philadelphia, 1976–84).

Setton, K., *Venice, Austria and the Turks in the Seventeenth Century* (Philadelphia, 1991).

Sevcenko, N. and Moss, C., eds, *Medieval Cyprus: Studies in Art, Architecture and History in Memory of Doula Mouriki* (Princeton, 1999).

Seward, D., *The Monks of War: The Military Religious Orders* (Harmondsworth, 1972; revised edn, 1995).

Shahar, S., *Childhood in the Middle Ages* (London, 1990).

Shahar, S., *Growing Old in the Middle Ages* (London, 1995).

Sharf, A., *Byzantine Jewry* (London, 1971).

Shatzmiller, M., ed., *Crusaders and Muslims in Twelfth Century Syria* (Leiden, 1993).

Shepard, J., 'The English and Byzantium: A Study of their Role in the Byzantine Army in the Eleventh Century', *Traditio*, 29 (1973), 52–93.

Shepard, J., 'When Greek Meets Greek: Alexius Comnenens and Bohemond in 1097–98', *Byzantine and Modern Greek Studies*, 12 (1988), 185–277.

Shepard, J., 'Cross-Purposes: Alexius Comneneus and the First Crusade', in J. Phillips, ed., *The First Crusade: Origins and Impact* (Manchester, 1997), 107–29.

Shepard, J. and Franklin, S., eds, *Byzantine Diplomacy* (Aldershot, 1992).

Siberry, E., 'Missionaries and Crusaders, 1095–1274: Opponents or Allies?', *Studies in Church History*, 20 (1983), 103–10.

Siberry, E., *Criticism of Crusading*, 1095–1274 (Oxford, 1985).

Smail, R., *Crusading Warfare* (Cambridge, 1956).

Smail, R., 'Latin Syria and the West 1149–1187', *Transactions of the Royal Historical Society*, Series 5, 19 (1969), 1–20.

Smail, R., *The Crusaders in Syria and the Holy Land* (London, 1971).

Smail, R., *The Crusaders* (London, 1973).

Smail, R., 'The International Status of the Latin Kingdom of Jerusalem 1150–1197', in Holt, ed., *The Eastern Mediterranean Lands*. (1977), 23–43.

Sola, J., Armistead, G. and Silverman, J., eds, *Hispania Judaica* (2 vols, Barcelona, 1985).

Southern, R., *Western Views of Islam in the Middle Ages* (Cambridge, Mass., 1962).

Southern, R., 'Peter of Blois and the Third Crusade', in H. Mayer-Harting and R. Moore, eds, *Studies in Medieval History Presented to R.H.C. Davis* (London, 1985), 207–18.

Spiteri, S., *Fortresses of the Cross: Hospitaller Military Architecture (1136–1798)* (Malta, 1994).

Spuler, B., *The Muslim World: A Historical Survey* (3 Parts, Leiden, 1960–9).

Stahl, A., *The Venetian Tornesello: A Medieval Colonial Coinage* (New York, 1985).

Stahl, A., 'Italian Sources for the Coinage of Cilician Armenia', *Armenian Numismatic Journa*, 15 (1989), 59–66.

Stahl, A., 'The Coinage of Venice in the Age of Enrico Dandolo', in E. Kittell and T. Madden, eds, *Medieval and Renaissance Venice* (Urbana, 1999), 124–40.

Steier, G., 'Bettelorden-Predigt als Massenmedium', in G. Heinzle, ed., *Litterarische Interessensbilddung im Mittelalter* (Stuttgart, 1993), 314–36.

Stephenson, P., 'Anna Comnena's *Alexiad* as a Source for the Second Crusade?', *Journal of Medieval History*, 29 (2003), 41–54.

Sternfeld, R., *Ludwigs des Heiligen Kreuzzug nach Tunis und die Politik Karls I von Sizilien* (Berlin, 1896).

Stevenson, W., *The Crusaders in the East* (Cambridge, 1907).

Stoyanov, Y., *The Other God* (New Haven, 2000).

Strayer, J., *The Albigensian Crusades* (Ann Arbor, 1971).

Strzygowski, J., 'Ruins of Tombs of the Latin Kings on the Haram in Jerusalem', *Speculum*, 11 (1936), 499–509.

Sturner, W., *Friedrich II. Der Kaiser 1220–1250* (Darmstadt, 2002).

Sumberg, L., 'The "Tafurs" and the First Crusade', *Medieval Studies*, 21 (1959), 224–46.

Sumption, J., *Pilgrimage* (London, 1975).

Sumption, J., *The Albigensian Crusade* (London, 1978).

Sybil, H. von, *Geschichte des ersten Kreuzzugs* (1841, 2nd edn, Leipzig, 1881; English translation as *The History and Literature of the Crusades*, London, 1905).

Tafel, G. and Thomas, F., eds, *Urkunden zur älteren Handels- und Staats geschichte der Republik Venedig* (3 vols, Vienna, 1856–7; reprinted Amsterdam, 1964).

Talmon-Heller, D., 'Arabic Sources on Muslim Villagers under Frankish Rule', in A. Murray, ed., *From Clermont to Jerusalem* (1998).

Thiriet, F., *La Romanie Vénitienne au Moyen Age* (Paris, 1975).

Thompson, J.W., 'The German Church and the Conversion of the Baltic Slavs', *American Journal of Theology*, 20 (1916), 205–30, 372–89.

Thomson, R., *Armenia and the Byzantine Empire* (Cambridge, Mass., 1947).

Thomson, R., *A Bibliography of Classical Armenian Literature to 1500AD* (Turnhout, 1995).

Thomson, R., 'William of Malmesbury, Historian of Crusade', *Reading Medieval Studies*, 23 (1997), 121–34.

Thomson, R., 'The Concept of "History" in Medieval Armenian Historians', in A. Eastmond, ed., *Eastern Approaches to Byzantium* (Aldershot, 2001), 89–100.

Thomson, R., 'The Crusaders through Armenian Eyes', in A. Laiou and R. Parviz Mottahedeh, eds, *The Crusades from the Perspective of Byzantium and the Muslim World* (Washington, 2001), 71–82.

Thorau, P., *The Lion of Egypt: Sultan Baybars I and the Near East in the Thirteenth Century* (London, 1974).

Throop, P., *Criticism of the Crusade: A Study of Public Opinion and Crusade Propaganda* (Amsterdam, 1940).

Tibble, S., *Monarchy and Lordships in the Latin Kingdom of Jerusalem 1099–1291* (Oxford, 1989).

Tillman, H., *Pope Innocent III* (Göttingen, 1954; English translation, Amsterdam, 1980).

Toumanoff, C., 'Armenia and Georgia', in J. Hussey, ed. *The Cambridge Medieval History*, IV (Cambridge, 1966), 593–637.

Triposkoufi, A. and Tsitouri, A., eds, *Venetians and Knights Hospitallers: Military Architecture Networks*: (Athens, 2002).

Trotter, D., *Medieval French Literature and the Crusades* (Geneva, 1988).

Tyerman, C., 'Marino Sanudo Torsello and the Lost Crusade: Lobbying in the Fourteenth Century', *Transactions of the Royal Historical Society*, Series 5, 32 (1982), 57–73.

Tyerman, C., 'Philip V of France, the Assemblies of 1319–20 and the Crusade', *Bulletin of the Institute of Historical Research*, 57 (1984), 15–34.

Tyerman, C., 'Sed Nihil Fecit? The Last Capetians and the Recovery of the Holy Land', in J. Gillingham and J.C. Holt, eds, *War and Government in the Middle Ages* (Woodbridge, 1984), 170–81.

Tyerman, C., 'The Holy Land and the Crusades of the Thirteenth and Fourteenth Centuries', in Edbury, ed., *Crusade and Settlement* (1985).

Tyerman, C., 'Philip VI and the Recovery of the Holy Land', *English Historical Review*, 100 (1985), 25–51.

Tyerman, C., *England and the Crusades 1095–1588* (Oxford, 1988).

Tyerman, C., 'Were There Any Crusades in the Twelfth Century?', *English Historical Review*, 110 (1995), 553–77; reprinted in Madden, *The Crusades* (2002).

Tyerman, C., *The Invention of the Crusades* (London, 1998).

Tyerman, C., *Fighting for Christendom, Holy War and the Crusades* (Oxford, 2004).

Ullmann, M., *Islamic Medicine* (Edinburgh 1978; reprinted 1997).

Ullmann, W., *The Origins of the Great Schism* (London, 1948).

Ullmann, W., *A Short History of the Papacy in the Middle Ages* (London, 1972).

Urban, W., 'The Organization of the Defence of the Livonian Frontier in the Thirteenth Century', *Speculum*, 58 (1973), 525–32.

Urban, W., *The Baltic Crusade* (1975; 2nd edn, chicago, 1994).

Urban, W., 'The Diplomacy of the Teutonic Knights at the Curia', *Journal of Balkan Studies* 9 (1978), 116–28.

Urban, W., 'The Wendish Princes and the *Drang nach dem Osten*', *Journal of Baltic Studies*, 9 (1978), 225–44.

Urban, W., *The Prussian Crusade* (1980; 2nd edn, Chicago, 2000).

Urban, W., *The Livonian Crusade* (Washington DC, 1981).

Urban, W., *The Samogitian Crusade* (Chicago, 1989).

Urban, W., *The Teutonic Knights: A Military History* (London, 2003).

Van Cleve, T., *Markward of Anweiler and the Sicilian Regency* (Princeton, 1937).

Van Cleve, T., *The Emperor Frederick II of Hohenstaufen* (Oxford, 1972).

Van der Werf, H., *The Chansons of the Troubadours and Trouvères* (Utrecht, 1972).

Vasiliev, A., 'Manuel Comnenus and Henry Plantagenet', *Byzantinische Zeitschrift*, 29 (1929–30), 233–44.

Vaughan, R., *Philip the Bold* (London, 1962).

Verlinden, C., *L'Esclavage dans L'Europe médiévale*, II (Ghent, 1977).

Vesey, D. 'William of Tyre and the Art of Historiography', *Medieval Studies*, 35 (1973), 433–55.

Vlasto, A.P., *The Entry of the Slavs into Christendom* (Cambridge, 1970).

Vryonis, S., 'Byzantium, the Social Basis for Decline in the Eleventh Century', *Greek, Roman and Byzantine Studies*, 2 (1959), 159–75.

Vryonis, S., *The Decline of Medieval Hellenism in Asia Minor and the Process of Islamization from the Eleventh Through the Fifteenth Century* (Berkeley, 1971).

Vryonis, S., 'Nomadization and Islamization in Asia Minor', *Dumbarton Oaks Papers*, 29 (1975), 41–72.

Wakefield, W., *Heresy, Crusade and Inquisition in Southern France 1100–1250* (London, 1974).

Walker, C., *Armenia: The Survival of a Nation* (2nd edn, London, 1990).

Warren, W.L., *Henry II* (London, 1973).

Watt, W., *The Influence of Islam on Medieval Europe* (Edinburgh, 1972).

Webb, D., *Medieval European Pilgrimage* (London, 2002), 44–77.

Weiler, B., 'The *Negotium Terrae Sanctae* in the Political Discourse of Latin Christendom, 1215–1311', *The International History Review*, 35 (2003), 1–36.

Weitzmann, K., 'Thirteenth-Century Crusader Icons on Mount Sinai', *Arts Bulletin*, 45 (1963), 179–203.

Weitzmann, K., 'Icon Painting in the Crusader Kingdom', *Dumbarton Oaks Papers*, 20 (1966), 49–84.

Wentlaff-Eggebert, F.-W., *Kreuzzugsdichtiung des Mittelalters* (Berlin, 1960).

Wieczorek, A. and Hinz, H.-M., eds, *Europas Mitte um 1000* (3 vols, Stuttgart, 2000).

Wilken, E., *Geschichte der Kreuzzüge nach morgentländischen und abendländischen Berichten* (8 vols, Leipzig, 1807–32).

Williams, J., 'The Making of a Crusade: The Genoese Anti-Muslim Attacks in Spain, 1146–8', *Journal of Medieval History*, 23 (1997), 29–53.

Wolf, K., 'Crusade and Narrative: Bohemond and the *Gesta Francorum*', *Journal of Medieval History*, 17 (1991), 207–16.

Wright, J., *The Geographical Lore in the Time of the Crusades* (New York, 1925).

Yewdale, R.W., *Bohemond I, Prince of Antioch* (Princeton, 1924; reprinted Amsterdam, 1970).

Zachariadou, E., *Trade and Crusade: Venetian Crete and the Emirates of Menteshe and Aydin (1300–1415)* (Venice, 1983).

5 The Crusades on the Internet

At the time of writing, if you type 'First Crusade' into a search engine you are presented with 481,000 sites and 316,000 sites for 'Crusades'. Most of these will prove too simple for your needs or will be unreliable, unhelpful or misleading.

Using the web can be a very blunt instrument for research, so beware. There are often copyright reasons why only partial texts or somewhat old-fashioned translations are given. This is one of the weaknesses of the web for medievalists.

The following sites may be used to your advantage:

(1) http://www.fordham.edu/halsall/sbook1.html

This site is also known as the Medieval History Sourcebook and contains many texts in translation from medieval Europe, not all of them complete for copyright reasons. Anna Komnene may be consulted here, with the bulk of her material (*Alexiad*, books 10–11) on the First Crusade. It also contains useful maps, but see (4) below. You will also find extracts from previously published collections of crusader texts by D.C. Munro (1896), A.C. Krey (1921) and J. Brundage (1962).

(2) http://libtext.library.wisc.edu/Hist Crusades/About.html

Provides the full text of all six volumes of K. Setton, ed., *A History of the Crusades* (6 vols, Madison, 1969–89). This is a fundamental reference work with excellent chronological tables and maps. Volume VI, pages 511–664, has a very full select bibliography of primary and secondary sources (up to 1986).

(3) http://www.unf.edu/classes/crusades/crusadebibliography.htm
An excellent practical bibliography created by Paul Halsall, not exhaustive but regularly updated.

(4) http://www.deremilitari.org/
A site devoted to the history of warfare. It is a fascinating site in its range – and not just for war buffs. Reprints of important articles by Cowdrey, France and Magdalino may be found here, as well as links to other sites.

(5) http://www.allcrusades.com/MAPS
This site is useful for maps. Most of the information here is reliable, but very elementary for undergraduate students.

(6) http://freespace.virgin.net/nigel.nicholson/SSCLE/SSCLEhome.html
This is the homepage of the Society for the Study of the Crusades and the Latin East (SSCLE). It contains information on events and archaeological work in progress, as well as links to other crusader websites.

(7) http://the-orb.net/encyclop/religion/crusades/crusade/html
ORB, or The Online Reference Book for Medieval Studies, is useful for sources in translation and for electronically available articles.

(8) http://www.dmgh.de/
Gives free access to the whole corpus of the primary sources edited under the auspices of the Monumenta Germaniae Historica, many of which bear directly on the crusades.

VIII
GENEALOGICAL TABLES

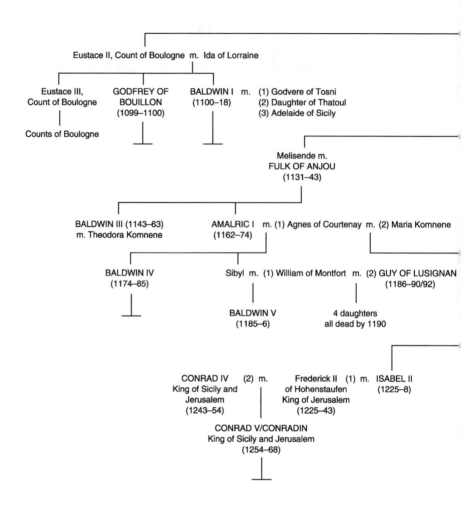

Table 1 Family tree of the Kings of Jerusalem, 1099–1291

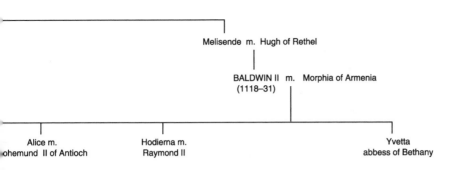

Melisende m. Hugh of Rethel

BALDWIN II m. Morphia of Armenia
(1118–31)

Alice m.
.ohemund II of Antioch

Hodierna m.
Raymond II

Yvetta
abbess of Bethany

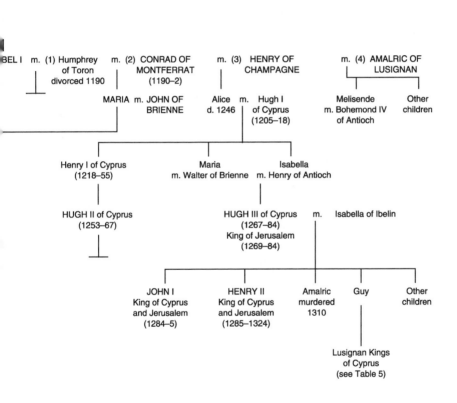

BEL I m. (1) Humphrey   m. (2) CONRAD OF   m. (3) HENRY OF   m. (4) AMALRIC OF
          of Toron   MONTFERRAT   CHAMPAGNE   LUSIGNAN
          divorced 1190   (1190–2)

MARIA m. JOHN OF
          BRIENNE

Alice   m.   Hugh I
d. 1246   of Cyprus
               (1205–18)

Melisende
m. Bohemond IV
of Antioch

Other
children

Henry I of Cyprus
(1218–55)

Maria
m. Walter of Brienne

Isabella
m. Henry of Antioch

HUGH II of Cyprus
(1253–67)

HUGH III of Cyprus   m.   Isabella of Ibelin
(1267–84)
King of Jerusalem
(1269–84)

JOHN I
King of Cyprus
and Jerusalem
(1284–5)

HENRY II
King of Cyprus
and Jerusalem
(1285–1324)

Amalric
murdered
1310

Guy

Other
children

Lusignan Kings
of Cyprus
(see Table 5)

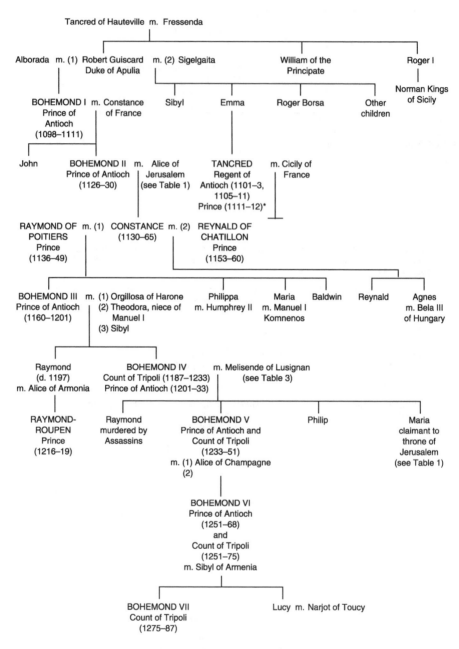

Tancred of Hauteville m. Fressenda

Alborada m. (1) Robert Guiscard m. (2) Sigelgaita   William of the   Roger I
           Duke of Apulia   Principate

BOHEMOND I m. Constance   Sibyl   Emma   Roger Borsa   Other   Norman Kings
Prince of   of France   children   of Sicily
Antioch
(1098–1111)

John   BOHEMOND II m. Alice of   TANCRED   m. Cicily of
        Prince of Antioch   Jerusalem   Regent of   France
        (1126–30)   (see Table 1)   Antioch (1101–3,
                                      1105–11)
                                      Prince (1111–12)*

RAYMOND OF m. (1) CONSTANCE m. (2) REYNALD OF
POITIERS   (1130–65)   CHATILLON
Prince   Prince
(1136–49)   (1153–60)

BOHEMOND III m. (1) Orgillosa of Harone   Philippa   Maria   Baldwin   Reynald   Agnes
Prince of Antioch   (2) Theodora, niece of   m. Humphrey II   m. Manuel I   m. Bela III
(1160–1201)   Manuel I   Komnenos   of Hungary
           (3) Sibyl

Raymond   BOHEMOND IV   m. Melisende of Lusignan
(d. 1197)   Count of Tripoli (1187–1233)   (see Table 3)
m. Alice of Armonia   Prince of Antioch (1201–33)

RAYMOND-   Raymond   BOHEMOND V   Philip   Maria
ROUPEN   murdered by   Prince of Antioch and   claimant to
Prince   Assassins   Count of Tripoli   throne of
(1216–19)   (1233–51)   Jerusalem
                   m. (1) Alice of Champagne   (see Table 1)
                   (2)

BOHEMOND VI
Prince of Antioch
(1251–68)
and
Count of Tripoli
(1251–75)
m. Sibyl of Armenia

BOHEMOND VII   Lucy m. Narjot of Toucy
Count of Tripoli
(1275–87)

* Tancred was succeeded by his nephew Roger of Salerno (1112–19).
   Baldwin II of Jerusalem was regent for Bohemond II (1119–26)

Table 2 Family tree of the Princes of Antioch (simplified)

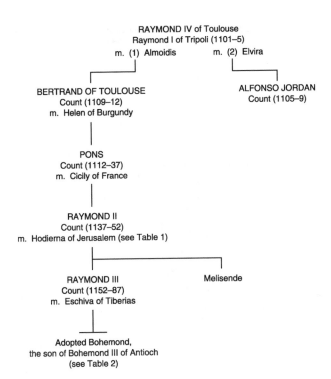

Table 3 Family tree of the counts of Tripoli

On becoming ruler of Jerusalem, Baldwin of Boulogne conferred the County of Edessa on his cousin Baldwin Le Bourg/Rethel, who in turn conferred it on his kinsman Joscelin of Courtenay in 1118 (see Table 1).

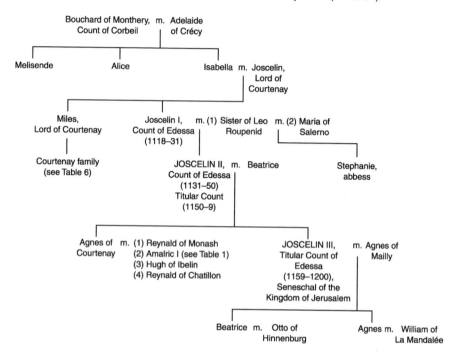

Table 4 Family tree of the counts of Edessa

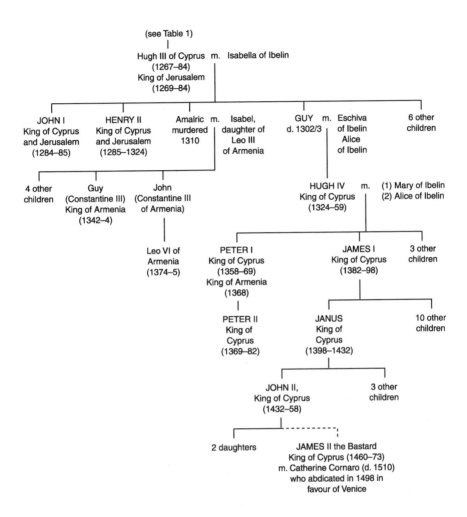

Table 5 Family tree of the Lusignans of Cyprus (simplified)

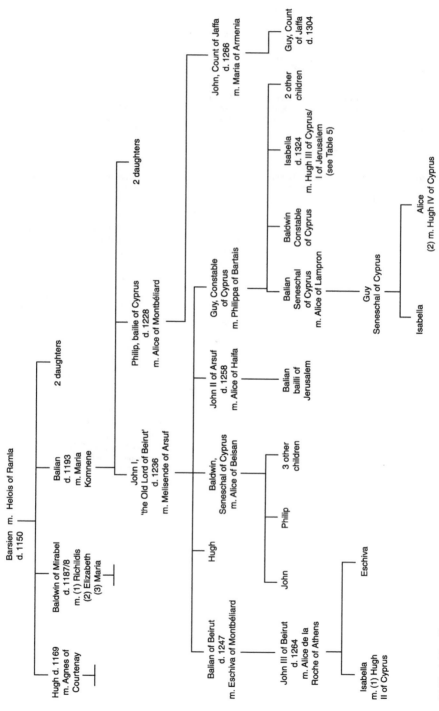

Table 6 Family tree of the Ibelins of Jerusalem and Cyprus

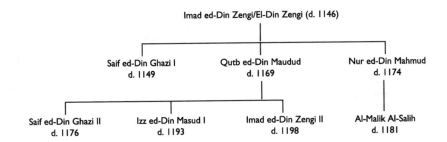

Table 7 The Zengids (simplified)

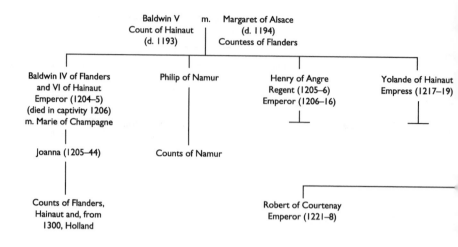

Table 8 The Latin Emperors of Constantinople

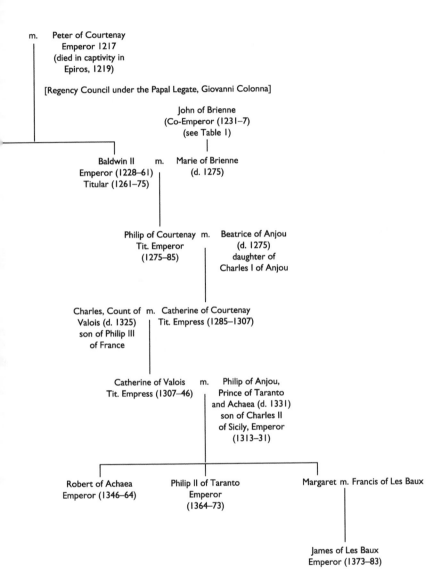

m.   Peter of Courtenay
Emperor 1217
(died in captivity in
Epiros, 1219)

[Regency Council under the Papal Legate, Giovanni Colonna]

John of Brienne
(Co-Emperor (1231–7)
(see Table 1)

Baldwin II   m.   Marie of Brienne
Emperor (1228–61)   (d. 1275)
Titular (1261–75)

Philip of Courtenay m. Beatrice of Anjou
Tit. Emperor   (d. 1275)
(1275–85)   daughter of
Charles I of Anjou

Charles, Count of m. Catherine of Courtenay
Valois (d. 1325)   Tit. Empress (1285–1307)
son of Philip III
of France

Catherine of Valois   m.   Philip of Anjou,
Tit. Empress (1307–46)   Prince of Taranto
and Achaea (d. 1331)
son of Charles II
of Sicily, Emperor
(1313–31)

Robert of Achaea   Philip II of Taranto   Margaret m. Francis of Les Baux
Emperor (1346–64)   Emperor
(1364–73)

James of Les Baux
Emperor (1373–83)

493

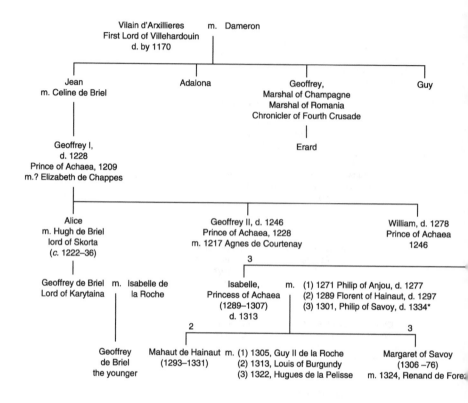

Vilain d'Arxillieres   m.   Dameron
First Lord of Villehardouin
d. by 1170

Jean   Adalona   Geoffrey,   Guy
m. Celine de Briel   Marshal of Champagne
                                          Marshal of Romania
                                          Chronicler of Fourth Crusade

Geoffrey I,   Erard
d. 1228
Prince of Achaea, 1209
m.? Elizabeth de Chappes

Alice   Geoffrey II, d. 1246   William, d. 1278
m. Hugh de Briel   Prince of Achaea, 1228   Prince of Achaea
lord of Skorta   m. 1217 Agnes de Courtenay   1246
(c. 1222–36)
                                    3

Geoffrey de Briel   m. Isabelle de   Isabelle,   m.   (1) 1271 Philip of Anjou, d. 1277
Lord of Karytaina   la Roche   Princess of Achaea   (2) 1289 Florent of Hainaut, d. 1297
                                         (1289–1307)   (3) 1301, Philip of Savoy, d. 1334*
                                         d. 1313

                                    2   3

Geoffrey   Mahaut de Hainaut m. (1) 1305, Guy II de la Roche   Margaret of Savoy
de Briel   (1293–1331)   (2) 1313, Louis of Burgundy   (1306 –76)
the younger   (3) 1322, Hugues de la Pelisse   m. 1324, Renand de Fore:

Table 9 The princes of Achaea

494

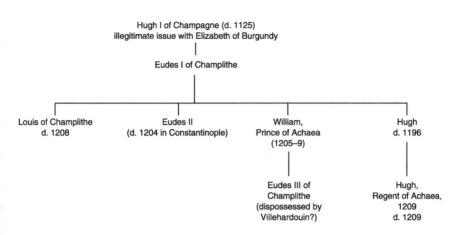

Hugh I of Champagne (d. 1125)
illegitimate issue with Elizabeth of Burgundy

Eudes I of Champlithe

| Louis of Champlithe d. 1208 | Eudes II (d. 1204 in Constantinople) | William, Prince of Achaea (1205–9) | Hugh d. 1196 |

Eudes III of Champlithe (dispossessed by Villehardouin?)

Hugh, Regent of Achaea, 1209 d. 1209

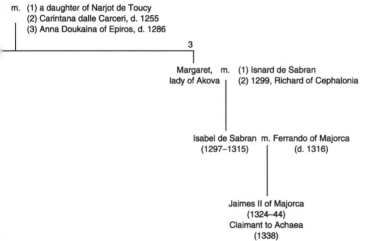

m. (1) a daughter of Narjot de Toucy
(2) Carintana dalle Carceri, d. 1255
(3) Anna Doukaina of Epiros, d. 1286

3

Margaret, m. (1) Isnard de Sabran
lady of Akova (2) 1299, Richard of Cephalonia

Isabel de Sabran m. Ferrando of Majorca
(1297–1315)   (d. 1316)

Jaimes II of Majorca
(1324–44)
Claimant to Achaea
(1338)

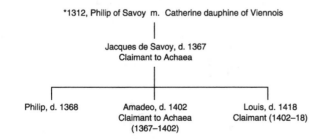

*1312, Philip of Savoy m. Catherine dauphine of Viennois

Jacques de Savoy, d. 1367
Claimant to Achaea

| Philip, d. 1368 | Amadeo, d. 1402 Claimant to Achaea (1367–1402) | Louis, d. 1418 Claimant (1402–18) |

495

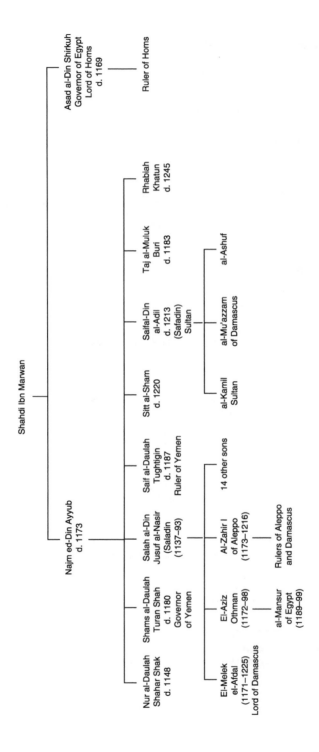

Table 10 The Ayyubids (simplified)

IX
MAPS

Map 1 Byzantium and the Near East at the time of the First Crusade
Source: After BBC, *Background to the Crusades* (London, 1963), 20–1

CUMANS

SEA OF AZOV

Caffa

Cherson

BLACK SEA

NOPLE (Byzantium)
is (Scutari)

Amastris
Heraclia
hedia
a (Isnik)
se
HYNIA
Dorylaeum
Amorion
TANATE OF RUM
tus

Castra Comnenon (Kastamuni)

Sinope

Samsun

Amasea

Trebizond

ARMENIA

Ani

PAPHLAGONIA

Neocaesarea

Ankara

Myriokephalon

Nyssa

DANISH MENDS

Caesarea

CAPPADOCIA

Sebastea

PONTUS

Erzerum

Manzikert

Lake Van

GEORGIA

Melitene

Coxon

Nazianzus

Antioch-in-
Pisidia

Iconium
(Konya)

Tyana

Heraclea

Sis

Cicilian
Gates

Marash
(Germanicea)

ARMENIA
MINOR

Edessa

Daras

Nisibis

Mamistra

Mosul

SELJUK
ATABEG
OF MOSUL

ISAURIA

PISIDIA
PAMPHYLIA

lia

CILICIA

Adana

Tarsus

Seleucia

St. Symeon

CYPRUS

Limassol

Harran

OQALID
EMIRS

SELJUK KINGDOM
OF ALEPPO

ANTIOCH

Aleppo

Lattakieh

Tortosa

Shaizar

Hama

BANU MUNKIDH

Homs

BANU AMMAR

Tripoli

Beirut

Sidon

Tyre

Acre

Caesarea

Jaffa

Ascalon
Gaza

Damietta

exandria

Baalbek

DAMASCUS

Hattin

Nazareth

Bothra
(Bosra)

JERUSALEM

Bethlehem

Petra

Palmyra

S
Y
R
I
A

SELJUK
KINGDOM OF
DAMASCUS

Approximate boundary of the
Eastern Empire shortly after
the death of Basil II (1025)

Routes taken by the First Crusade

0   200 miles

499

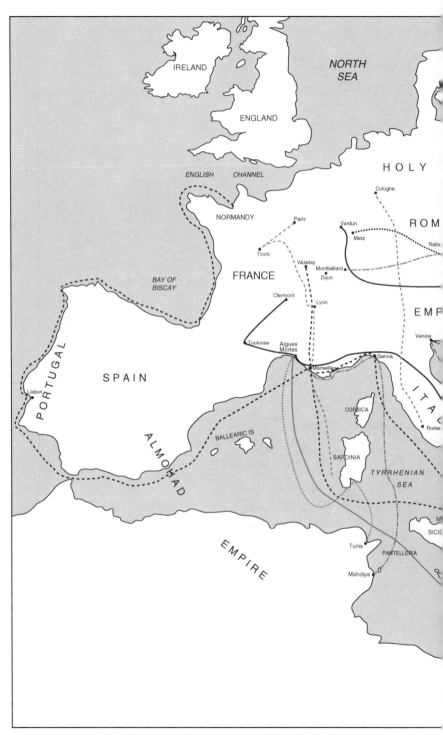

Map 2 Routes of the crusades to the East

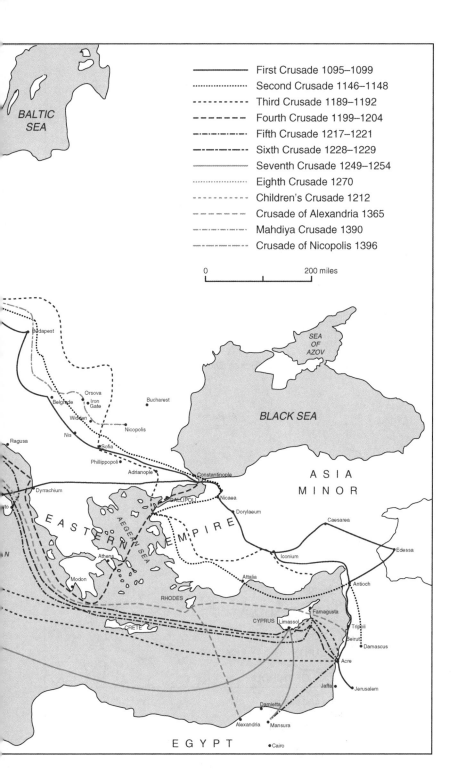

First Crusade 1095–1099
Second Crusade 1146–1148
Third Crusade 1189–1192
Fourth Crusade 1199–1204
Fifth Crusade 1217–1221
Sixth Crusade 1228–1229
Seventh Crusade 1249–1254
Eighth Crusade 1270
Children's Crusade 1212
Crusade of Alexandria 1365
Mahdiya Crusade 1390
Crusade of Nicopolis 1396

0   200 miles

BALTIC
SEA

SEA
OF
AZOV

BLACK SEA

Budapest

Orsova
Belgrade Iron
Gate
Widden
Nis   Nicopolis
Ragusa   Sofia
Phillippopoli
Adrianople   Constantinople

Bucharest

ASIA
MINOR

Dyrrachium   GALLIPOLI Nicaea
EASTERN   Dorylaeum
AEGEAN EMPIRE
N SEA   Caesarea
Athens   Iconium   Edessa
Modon   Attalia
                              Antioch
RHODES
                    Famagusta
CYPRUS Limassol   Tripoli
CRETE   Beirut
                         Damascus
                    Acre
                Jaffa Jerusalem
Damietta
Alexandria Mansura
EGYPT   Cairo

501

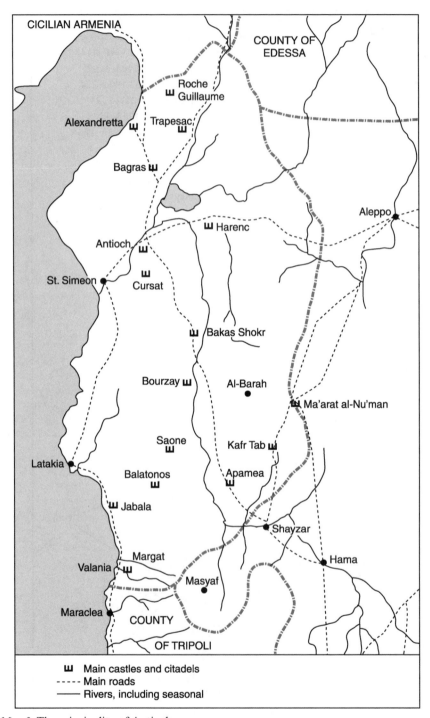

Map 3 The principality of Antioch
Source: After M. Balard, *Croisade et Orient latin* (Paris, 2001), 72.

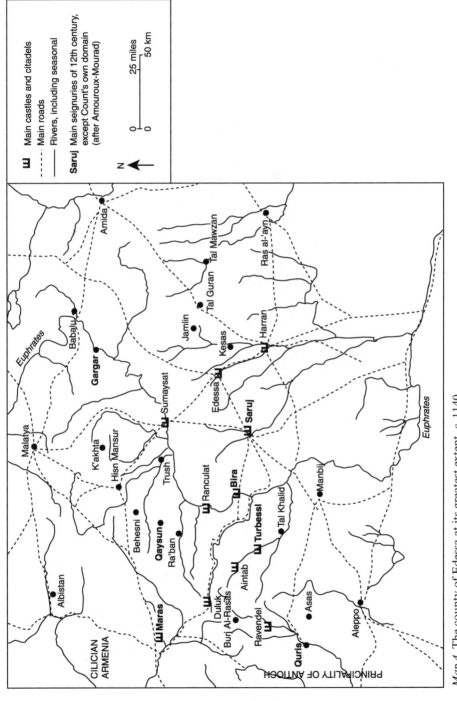

Map 4 The county of Edessa at its greatest extent, c. 1140

Source: After J. Richard, *The Crusades c.1071–c.1291* (Cambridge, 1999), 84.

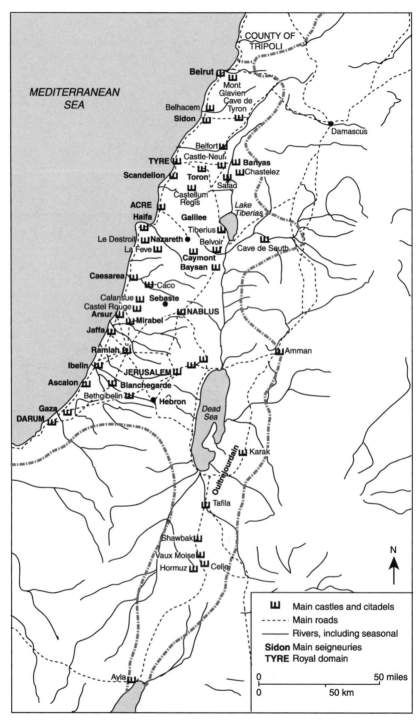

Map 5 The Kingdom of Jerusalem, *c.* 1160
Source: After S. Rozenberg, ed., *Knights of the Holy Land* (Jerusalem, 1999), 13.

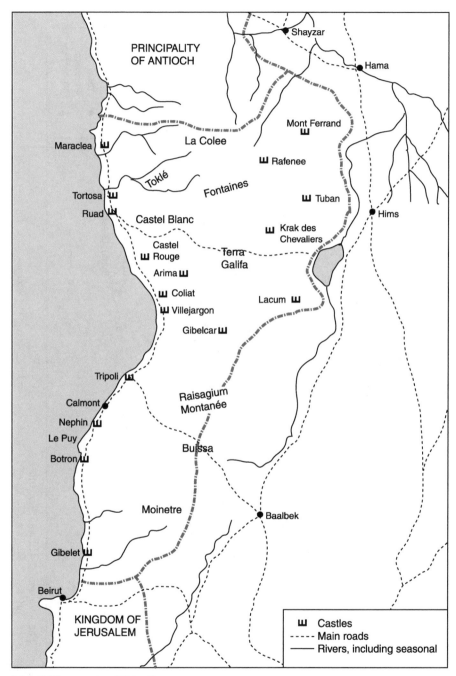

Map 6 The county of Tripoli
Source: After J. Richard, *The Crusades, c.1071–c.1291* (Cambridge, 1999), 85.

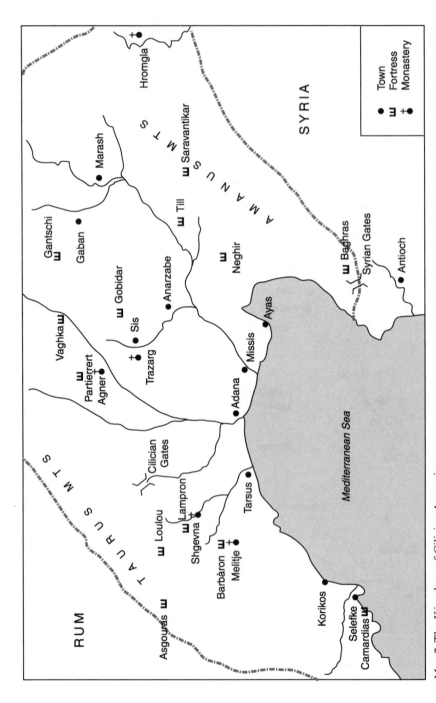

Map 7 The Kingdom of Cilician Armenia
Source: After W.H. Rüt-Collenberg, *The Rupenides, Hethumides and Lusignans . The Structure of the Armeno-Cilician Dynasties* (Lisbon, 1963), 30.

Legend:
- ● Town
- Ш Fortress
- † Monastery

Labels on map:

SYRIA

RUM

Mediterranean Sea

TAURUS MTS

AMANUS MTS

Hromgla †

Marash ●

Saravantikar Ш

Gantschi Ш
Gaban ●

Till Ш

Gobidar Ш
Anarzabe ●
Sis ●

Neghir Ш

Vaghka Ш

Trazarg †

Partierrert Ш
Agner †

Ayas ●

Missis ●

Adana ●

Baghras Ш
Syrian Gates

Antioch ●

Cilician Gates

Lampron Ш
Loulou Ш
Shgevna Ш

Tarsus ●

Barbaron Ш
Melitje †●

Asgouras Ш

Korikos ●

Selefke ●
Camardias Ш

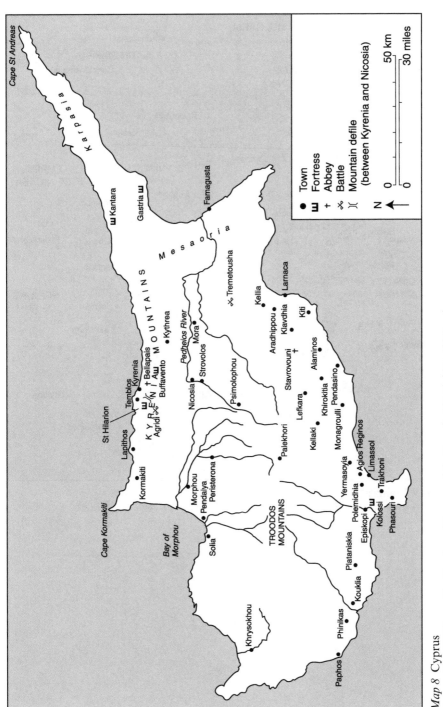

Map 8 Cyprus
Source: After P. Edbury, *The Kingdom of Cyprus and the Crusades* (Cambridge, 1991), xvi.

Cape St Andreas

Karpasia

Kantara
Gastria

Famagusta

Mesaoria

Tremetousha

Larnaca

Kellia

Aradhippou
Klavdhia
Kiti

K Y R E N I A   M O U N T A I N S

Temblos
Kyrenia
Bellapais
Buffavento
Agridi
St Hilarion
Lapithos

Kormakiti

Cape Kormakiti

Pedheios River
Mora
Strovolos
Nicosia
Psimolophou

Stavrovouni
Alaminos
Lefkara
Khirokitia
Pendasino

Kellaki
Monagroulli

Palekhori

Agios Reginos
Yermasoyia
Limassol
Trakhoni
Polemidhia
Kolossi
Episkopi
Phasouri

Morphou
Pendaiya
Peristerona

Bay of
Morphou

Solia

TROODOS
MOUNTAINS

Plataniskia

Kouklia

Khrysokhou

Phinikas

Paphos

Town
Fortress
Abbey
Battle
Mountain defile
(between Kyrenia and Nicosia)

N

50 km
30 miles

0
0

Map 9 Frankish Greece
Source: After P. Lock, *The Franks in the Aegean* (London, 1995), 380.

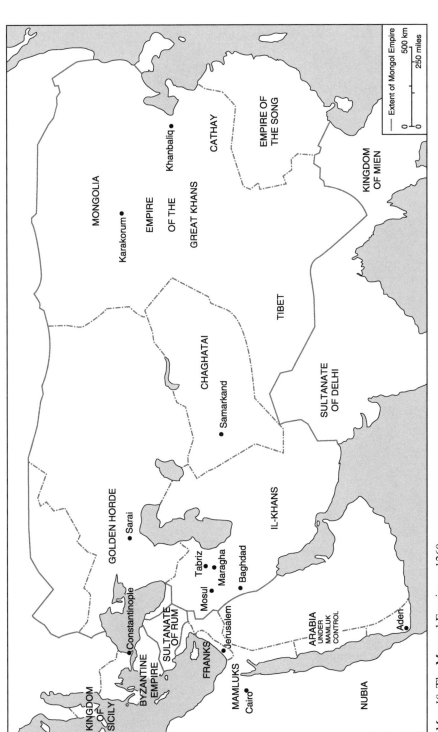

Map 10 The Mongol Empire, c. 1260
Source: After J. Richard, The Crusades c.1071-c.1291 (Cambridge, 1999), 412.

INDEX

Page references in *italics* denote chronological entries
Page references in **bold** denote major section entries

INDEX

Guiscard, Robert *14*, *15*, *17*, *18*, 232, 307, 383
Guntersblum, church at 419
Gunther of Bamberg, Bishop *15*, 412
Guy, abbot of Vaux-Cernay 159
Guy II 191
Guy of Lusignan *69*, *70*, *73–4*, *76*, *79*, 153, 154, 231, 234, **238**, 239, 251, 348

Haddad, Z. 420
Hagenmeyer, Heinrich **279**
al-Hakim *11*, *12*
Halmyros, battle of (1311) *125*, 191
Hamburg: destruction of by Wends (983) *10*, 216
Hamilton, Bernard 431
Harim *50*, *54*
al-Hasan ibn-al-Sabah *19*, *37* (Sabbah on p. 19)
Hattin, battle of (1187) *71*, 151, 237, 238, 249, 250, 348, 352
Hedwig glasses 419
Hekataeos of Miletos 376
Helion of Villeneuve 192
Helmold of Bossau *60*, 149, 217, 218
Henry of Albano 152, 314
Henry of Almain *117*, 184
Henry of Asti 193
Henry of Champagne *75*, *78*, *79*, *81*, 173, **238**, 242
Henry, duke of Burgundy 321
Henry of Flanders *88*, *89*, *91*, **238–9**, 379
Henry I of Cyprus *109*
Henry II of Cyprus *123*, 196, 426
Henry II of England *73*, *74*, 152, 153, 239, 332, 334, 344
Henry III of England *115*, 167, 184
Henry IV, Emperor *16*, 304
Henry of Limburg, Duke 169–70
Henry the Lion *55*, 149, 217, 218–19, 233; crusade of (1172) **151**
Henry of Malta 169
Henry of Trastamara 198
Henry VI, German emperor *80*, *81*, 155, 156, 366
Henry VII, German emperor 190
Heraclius, patriarch of Jerusalem *69–70*, 227, **239**, 340
Heraklea *22*, 143
Heraklios *4*, 293, 299
Herluin 339, 433
Hermann of Carinthia 213, 247

Hermann of Salza *103*, 221
Hethoum I of Armenia 180, 189, 378, 380, 381
Hethoumids 378, 380
Hillenbrand, Carole 272, 349, 415
Himerios *8*
Hisham III 208
historiography 257–72
Holocaust 289, 402
Holy Lance *23*, 141, 248
Holy League (1343) *127*, **192–3**, 194, 355, 391
holy wars 292, 293–4
Holy Years (1300) 187
Homs *40*, *43*; defeat of Armenians at (1281) 381
Honorius III, Pope *91*, *92*, *95–6*, *97*, 165, 167, 169, 172, 220, 247, 266
Horns of Hammah, Battle of (1175) *62*
horses 329
Hospitallers *105*, *113*, *117*, *124–6*, *128*, *130*, 174, 193, 198, 211, 276, 340, 352, 353, 354–5, 381, 423
Hubert (Albert) of St Everard 431
Hugh, bishop of Jabala 148, 340
Hugh of Burgundy *77*, 153, 173, 174
Hugh of Die 313
Hugh I of Cyprus *89*, *92*
Hugh II of Cyprus *109*, *115*
Hugh III, of Cyprus *115*, *116*, *120*
Hugh IV of Cyprus 184, 192, 195
Hugh of Ibelin 227
Hugh of Le Puiset *30*, *41*, *42*, 246
Hugh of Payns *34*, *40*, 146, **239**, 340, 355
Hugh of Vermondois *20–1*, *23*, 140, 143, **239–40**, 240, 339
Humbert of Beajeau 165
Humbert II of Viennois: crusade of (1345–7) **193–5**
Humphrey of Tibnine 153
Humphrey of Toron *70*
Hundred Years War 198
Hunyadi, John 202, 203
Hus, John 201
Hussites: crusades against (1420–31) *132*, **201–2**, 204

Ibelin family **240**, 380
Iberian Peninsula 149; crusades in **205–13**; expulsion of Muslim and Jews (1492) 213; military orders founded in 211; Muslim conquest of 207; *see also* Spain
Ibn abd al-Zahir 415

518

Routledge History

The Crusades and the Expansion of Catholic Christendom, 1000–1714

John France

The Crusades and the Expansion of Catholic Christendom is a fascinating and accessible survey that places the medieval Crusades in their European context, and examines, for the first time, their impact on European expansion.

Taking a unique approach that focuses on the motivation behind the crusades, John France chronologically examines the whole crusading movement, from the development of a 'crusading impulse' in the eleventh century through to an examination of the relationship between the Crusades and the imperialist imperatives of the early modern period.

France provides a detailed examination of the first Crusade, the expansion and climax of crusading during the twelfth and thirteenth centuries and the failure and fragmentation of such practices in the fourteenth and fifteenth centuries.

Concluding with an assessment of the influence of the Crusades across history and replete with illustrations, maps, timelines, guides for further reading, and a detailed list of rulers across Europe and the Muslim world, this study provides students with an essential guide to a central aspect of medieval history.

Hb 0–415–37127–9
Pb 0–415–37128–7

Routledge History

The Medieval World
Edited by Peter Linehan
and Janet L. Nelson

'The editors should be toasted for having distilled something of the lively spirit and substance of their subject into a single, concentrated product. Those with a taste, whether refined or modest, for the Middle Ages are urged to partake.' *History Today*

This groundbreaking collection brings the Middle Ages to life and conveys the distinctiveness of this diverse, constantly changing period. From the contributions of 38 scholars, one medieval world, from Connacht to Constantinople and from Tynemouth to Timbuktu, emerges from many disparate worlds. This extraordinary set of reconstructions presents the reader with the future of the medieval past, offering fresh appraisals of the evidence and modern historical writing.

Hb 0–415–18151–8
Pb 0–415–30234–X

Available at all good bookshops
For ordering and further information please visit:
www.routledge.com

Routledge History

The Two Cities: Medieval Europe, 1050-1320

Malcolm Barber

'Meets every conceivable need and effectively renders redundant all earlier textbooks on the high Middle Ages ... in short, the book is excellent in every respect.' *History Today*

First published to wide critical acclaim in 1992, *The Two Cities* has become an essential text for students of medieval history. For the second edition, the author has thoroughly revised each chapter, bringing the material up to date and taking the historiography of the past decade into account.

The Two Cities covers a colourful period from the schism between the eastern and western churches to the death of Dante. It encompasses the Crusades, the expansionist force of the Normans, major developments in the way kings, emperors and Popes exercised their powers, a great flourishing of art and architecture and the foundation of the very first universities. Running through it is the defining characteristic of the high Middle Ages – the delicate relationship between the spiritual and secular worlds, the two 'cities' of the title.

This survey provides all the facts and background information that students need, and is defined into straightforward thematic chapters. It makes extensive use of primary sources, and makes new trends in research accessible to students. Its fresh approach gives students the most rounded, lively and integrated view of the high Middle Ages available.

Hb 0–415–17414–7
Pb 0–415–17415–5

Available at all good bookshops
For ordering and further information please visit:
www.routledge.com

Routledge History

The Routledge Companion
to Medieval Warfare
Jim Bradbury

'This work of reference is useful ... [it] has some very useful and well-set-out material ... [a] very good handbook.' *History*

This comprehensive volume provides easily-accessible factual material on all major areas of warfare in the medieval west. The whole geographical area of medieval Europe, including eastern Europe, is covered, including essential elements from outside Europe such as Byzantine warfare, nomadic horde invasions and the Crusades.

Progressing chronologically, the work is presented in themed, illustrated sections, with a narrative outline offering a brief introduction to the area. Within each chronological section, Jim Bradbury presents clear and informative pieces on battles, sieges, and generals.

Hb 0–415–22126–9

Available at all good bookshops
For ordering and further information please visit:
www.routledge.com

Routledge History

Medieval Religion: New Approaches
Edited by Constance Hoffman Berman

Constance Hoffman Berman presents an indispensable new collection of the most influential and revisionist work to be done on religion in the Middle Ages in the last couple of decades. Bringing together an authoritative list of scholars from around the world, the book provides a valuable service to students of religious history in providing a compilation of the most important new work. The collection includes considerations of gender, 'otherness', the body, and diversity of beliefs between the eleventh and fifteenth centuries. *Medieval Religion: New Approaches* is essential reading for all those who study the Middle Ages, church history or religion.

Hb 0–415–31686–3
Pb 0–415–31687–1

Available at all good bookshops
For ordering and further information please visit:
www.routledge.com

Routledge History

Western Warfare in the
Age of the Crusades,
1000–1300
John France

'I am full of admiration for this excellent story of the practice of warfare in the Central Middle Ages. It is a work of both scholarship and synthesis, full of insight and communicated in an accessible and professional way' – *Norman Housley, University of Leicester*

In 1095 the First Crusades was launches, establishing a great military endeavour which was a central preoccupation of Europeans until the end of the thirteenth century. In *Western Warfare in the Age of the Crusades, 1000–1300* John France offers a wide-ranging and challenging survey of war and warfare and its place in the development of European society, culture and economy in the period of the Crusades. Placing the crusades in a wider context, this book brings together the wealth of recent scholarly research on such issues as knighthood, siege warfare, chivalry and fortifications into an accessible form.

Western Warfare in the Age of the Crusades, 1000–1300 examines war in the three hundred years between 1000 and 1300 and argues that it was primarily shaped by the people who conducted war – the landowners. John France illuminates the role of property concerns in producing the characteristic instruments of war: the castle and the knight. This authoritative study details the way in which war was fought and the reasons for it as well as reflecting on the society which produced the crusades.

Hb 1–85728–466–6
Pb 1–85728–467–4

Available at all good bookshops
For ordering and further information please visit:
www.routledge.com

Routledge History

The Mystic Mind: The Psychology of Medieval Mystics and Ascetics
Jerome Kroll and Bernard Bachrach

'A truly pioneering, unique study that should attract considerable attention among specialists and a wide range of general readers' – *Ursula King, University of Bristol and SOAS, University of London*

'This study presents an original and stimulating analysis of the nature and experience of medieval mysticism' – *Katherine Lewis, University of Huddersfield*

The Mystic Mind is the result of a fascinating collaboration between a medieval historian and a professor of psychiatry, applying moder biological and psychological research findings to the lives of medieval mystics and ascetics. This illuminating study examines the relationship between medieval mystical experiences, and the religious practices of mortification of the body. Laceration of the flesh, sleep deprivation and extreme starvation, while undoubtedly related to cultural and religious motivations, directly produced dramatic effects upon the body and brain functioning of the heroic ascetics, that in turn brought about altered states of consciousness. Applying modern understandings of physiology, the authors demonstrate how heroic asceticism could be used to obtain a desired mystical state, as well as examining and disputing much contemporary writing about the political and gender motivation in the medieval quest for closeness with God.

Drawing upon a database of 1,462 medieval holy persons as well as in-depth studies of individual saints, *The Mystic Mind* is essential reading for all those with an interest in medieval religion or the effects of self-injurous behaviour on the mind.

Hb 0–415–34050–0
Pb 0–415–34051–9

Available at all good bookshops
For ordering and further information please visit:
www.routledge.com